The Proof of the Gospel

The
Proof
of the
Gospel

EUSEBIUS

Edited and translated by
W. J. Ferrar

VOLUME I

BAKER BOOK HOUSE
Grand Rapids, Michigan 49506

Reprinted 1981 by Baker Book House Company
from the 2-volume edition published in 1920 by
S.P.C.K. (London) and The Macmillan Company (New York)

ISBN: 0-8010-3366-7

PREFACE

It is a high privilege to have been allowed to provide a translation of the *Demonstratio ;* for in default of a better it must for some time fill the vacant place in English book-shelves beside the noble edition of the *Praeparatio,* which was the work of Archdeacon Gifford's declining years.

Yet it is an appalling thought that this translation, continuing as it does the work of Gifford, should in any sense be thought to seek comparison with it. The writer has but endeavoured according to his powers, and amid other absorbing duties, to fill a recognized gap, by giving a faithful rendering of the words of Eusebius, so that it may be possible for the English student to become acquainted with all that remains of the work to which the *Praeparatio* was the Introduction.

He has erred perhaps rather in the direction of literal exactness than of free paraphrase, especially in doctrinal sections, thinking it primarily necessary to make it clear what Eusebius actually said.

Limitations of space have made it impossible to repro-duce the long passages from the Old Testament upon which Eusebius based his arguments. To have retained them in full would have been interesting because of their variations from the text of the LXX : but this consideration was hardly important enough to make their inclusion essential.

The translator would gratefully record his indebtedness to the Rev. W. K. Lowther Clarke, the Secretary of S.P.C.K., for his constant interest, scholarly guidance, and invaluable suggestions during the progress of the work : but for his help it would be far more imperfect than it is.

W. J. Ferrar.

East Finchley.
Easter, 1920.

CONTENTS

ABBREVIATIONS

D.C.B. Smith and Wace, *Dictionary of Christian Biography*, 1877–1887.

D.C.A. Smith and Cheetham, *Dictionary of Christian Antiquities*, 1875–1880.

D.A.C. Hastings' *Dictionary of the Apostolic Church*, 1915–1918.

H.D.B. Hastings' *Dictionary of the Bible*, 1898–1906.

E.R.E. *Encyclopædia of Religion and Ethics.*

Enc. Bib. *Encyclopædia Biblica.*

S. Swete's *Old Testament in Greek according to the Septuagint*, vols. i., ii., and iii. 4th edn. 1912.

W.H. Westcott and Hort's *New Testament in Greek*, 1882.

G.P.E. E. H. Gifford's edition of the *Praeparatio Evangelica.* Text, Translation, and Notes. (Oxford, 1903.)

Eus., H.E. The *Ecclesiastical History* of Eusebius.

INTRODUCTION

§ 1. Object and Occasion

THE *Demonstratio Evangelica* (Εὐαγγελικῆς Ἀποδείξεως
δέκα λόγοι) originally consisted of twenty books, of which
only ten remain. It was the concluding portion of the
complete work, which included the *Praeparatio*. At the
beginning of the latter Eusebius stated his object to be "to
shew the nature of Christianity to those who know not what
it means";[1] the purpose of its pages was to give an answer
to all reasonable questions both from Jewish or Greek
inquirers about Christianity, and its relation to other
religions. Thus the *Praeparatio* was intended to be "a
guide, by occupying the place of elementary instruction and
introduction, and suiting itself to our recent converts from
among the heathen."[2]

The *Demonstratio*, Eusebius promises in the same passage,
will go further. It will adapt itself "to those who have
passed beyond this, and are already in a state prepared for
the reception of the higher truths." It will "convey the
exact knowledge of the most stringent proofs of God's
mysterious dispensation in regard to our Lord and Saviour
Jesus Christ."[3] All apologetics, no doubt, have a double
object, to convince the unbeliever and to strengthen the
faithful. And it would certainly be an error to discriminate
the stress on either of these objects too sharply in the case
of any particular work. It is true from Justin to Butler that
evidential works circulate as widely (or indeed more widely)
in the Church as manuals of teaching than in the world as
weapons of defence. But we can recognize a difference of

---

[1] Gifford, *Praeparatio Evangelica*, p. i. a, hereafter often cited as
G.P.E.
[2] G.P.E. p. 3 b.
[3] G.P.E. p. 3 c.

ix

emphasis in the tone and scope of apologetic works, dependent on the circumstances and environment of the age of their production, which inclines the balance perceptibly either in the direction of apology proper, or in that of dogmatic instruction. The *Demonstratio* then would seem to be of the latter class, rather than of the former. It is a manual of instruction for the faithful, rather than a challenge to the unbelieving.

This impression, however, must be balanced by the fact that certain sections of the argument seem to be deliberately planned to convince the unbeliever, notably where Eusebius restricts himself to unfolding the unique beauty of our Lord's Humanity in His Life and Work; and while reserving his "prophetic" arguments for the edification of the faithful, speaks of Him from the human and historic level, ὡς περὶ ἀνδρὸς κοινοῦ, καὶ τοῖς λοιποῖς παραπλησίου (102 b). Or when in the same book he constructs his powerful *reductio ad absurdum* of the suggestion that Christ was a wizard or a charlatan.

The studied statements at the opening of the whole work give then the impression that the central object of Eusebius, in relation to the circumstances of his time, differed materially from that of the earlier Apologists like Justin and Aristides. They provided a reasoned defence of Christianity for the consideration of the rulers of the heathen world, and endeavoured to meet the subtle criticism of pagan philosophers with convincing force. He aims primarily at strengthening the convictions of those already convinced. He desires to provide a completer enlightenment for those who are already members of the Church of Christ.

Though certain passages both in the *Praeparatio* and the *Demonstratio* speak of pagan persecution in the present tense (*Praep. Ev.* 584 a, b, *Dem.* 82 c), and if the tense is pressed must have been written before the close of the Diocletian and Galerian Terror by the Edict of Milan, A.D. 312 (Eus., *H.E.* x. 5), other passages present the picture, frequent in the earlier apologies, of a Church at peace and developing in all parts of the Empire (*Praep. Ev.* 9 d, *Dem.* 103 c, 138 b). This discrepancy we will examine below. But assuming that the work appeared after the persecution it will be recognized that the moment was opportune for the publication of a book, "shewing what Christianity is to them that do not know," and for offering a deep and sound foundation for the faith of the half-convinced. For years the martyrs had been prominent in the world's eyes. The Church as a whole had been supernaturally loyal. The future seemed to be with the no longer despised Christians. There must have been many thoughtful people ready to examine their claims, and to inquire into the secret of their constancy. Many again, conquered by the bright spectacle of their endurance, had already entered the Church's gate led chiefly by faith and hope, and were now ripe to sit at the feet of teachers who could philosophically unveil her heavenly knowledge.

Nor should we suppose that, though the Imperial Government had decided that the coercion of so powerful a mass of conviction was impossible, the prejudice of pagan priesthoods and of the leaders of philosophy was inclined to yield without every effort that criticism, ridicule, and conservative tradition could exert. Celsus had been followed as protagonist against Christianity by Porphyry, and it was against him that the polemical weapons of the *Demonstratio* were forged. Porphyry had a very intimate knowledge of the Christian faith. He had possibly been a convert (Soc., *H.E.* iii. 23) and a pupil of Origen (Eus., *H.E.* vi. 19). He had written a book, *Contra Christianos*, full of acute criticisms, some of which the mind of the later Church has justified and accepted. There are quotations from this work in *Praep. Ev.* 28 c, 29 b, 179 d, 237 a to 241 b; and allusions to Porphyry in *Praep. Ev.* 143 c, 144 b, 190 a; *Dem. Ev.* 134. The high level of the attack would account for the comprehensiveness, the massive learning, and the dignity of the rejoinder, which gathers together and sums up the labours of previous Apologists. But, as we shall see, Eusebius did not set out to refute the arguments of Porphyry point by point, as Origen dealt with Celsus, or Justin with the Jew Trypho. He preferred to confront followers of the acute critic with the fact of Christianity as a blessed and growing power. He aimed at showing the supernatural agreement of its Founder's life and death with the prophecies. He felt that on the flowing tide of divine power he could afford to disregard the eddying currents that ran impotently across it. Eusebius indeed wrote a definite rejoinder to Porphyry, the κατὰ Πορφορίου, a work in twenty-five books; this in all probability was later in his life.[1] In this book it is quite likely that he attempted to meet the objections of Porphyry *seriatim*. His aim in the *Demonstratio* was of a more general character.

To sum up, it was the cessation of persecution, the profound impression made on the educated and uneducated alike by the imperial change of front, the proud sense within the Church itself that its patience had triumphed, combined with the presence of the opposing criticism of the cultured, which may be said to have been the occasion for the great literary effort, which is called by Lightfoot "probably the most important apologetic work of the Early Church."[2]

§ 2. THE DATE

This question is involved in conflicting internal evidence. Is the *Demonstratio* earlier or later than the *History*, which is generally dated A.D. 325? The passage εἰ γοῦν τι δύναται ἡ ἡμετέρα ἱστορία (*Dem.* 273 d) proves nothing, for we must translate with Lightfoot, not "my history," but "my personal observation." Neither can the passage in the *History* (*H.E.* i. 2 *ad fin.*) be safely regarded as referring to the *Demonstratio*. There is a direct reference to the *Quaestiones ad Stephanum* in *Dem.* 353 c, but this does not prove that the whole of the latter work was anterior to the *Demonstratio*, for the *Quaestiones* have a cross-reference to the *Demonstratio* in col. 912—ὥσπερ οὖν συνεστήσαμεν ἐν ταῖς εὐαγγελικαῖς ἀποδείξεσιν. It is suggested by Lightfoot that this part of the *Quaestiones*, the epitome or ἐκλογὴ ἐν συντόμῳ, was added at a later date, in which case the *Demonstratio* would come between the *Quaestiones* and the *Epitome*.

Evidence from the mention of contemporary events is again conflicting, if we are seeking the date of the work as a whole. There is an obvious contrast between passages that speak of the Church as still undergoing persecution, e. g. *Dem.* 119 b, ὃ καί ἐστιν εἰς δεῦρο θεωροῦντας ἐνεργούμενον, cf. 182 d (εἰσέτι καὶ νῦν) and 82 c, and those which in the manner of the earlier Apologists represent it as progressing and flourishing—e. g. *Dem.* 103 c and *Praep. Ev.* 9 d. The

---

[1] Lightfoot, *D.C.B.* ii. 329.　　[2] *Ibid.* 331.

usual explanation of these discrepancies is to suppose that different sections of the work took shape at different times, the former towards the end of the Terror, the latter after its conclusion. (Gifford, *Praeparatio*, Tom. iii. pars. i. p. xii.)

But there seems nothing unreasonable in supposing that an historical writer, engaged in defending Christianity on the ground of its endurance and success, while surveying in one *coup d'œil* the three centuries of its past struggle, might very naturally refer to a persecution, that had but recently relaxed its pressure, as present. If this be thought probable we may consider the whole work to have been written between A.D. 314 and A.D. 318. For the more than probable allusion in *Praep. Ev.* 135 c to the punishment by Licinius of the Antiochene theosophical impostors, described in *H. E.* ix. 11, would place the date after A.D. 314, whereas the theological language would seem to be too unguarded to allow it to be likely that it was penned near the time when the decision of the Arian controversy was imminent. And Arius was already attracting attention in A.D. 319. (Bright: *Church of the Fathers*, i. 56.)

§ 3. Contents

Books I and II form an Introduction, for the opening of Book III regards them as " prolegomena." They describe the simplicity of Christian teaching, challenge the assumption that Christianity rests not on reason but on faith, and in claiming to use the Jewish scriptures, while rejecting the Jewish religion, establish the thesis that Christianity is a republication of the primitive religion of the patriarchs, from which the Mosaic religion was a declension, allowed by God because of the deterioration of the Jews under the assaults of the dæmons during their exile in Egypt. Abundant prophetic evidence is given in Book II, that the coming of Messiah would synchronize with the downfall of the Jewish state, and the preaching of the Gospel to the Gentiles.

Book III treats of Christ's Humanity, and is perhaps the most modern part of the argument. By an elaborate *reductio ad absurdum* the impossibility of Jesus Christ being aught but Perfect Man and Divine also is dramatically and cogently shown.

Books IV and V deal with the Divinity of Christ as Son and Logos, and it is in them that passages of an Arian ring have roused the anger of orthodox commentators.

Book VI and the following books deal with our Lord's Incarnate life as the fulfilment of prophecy. Book X reaches the Passion and is especially occupied with Judas and the Betrayal.

We may suppose with Lightfoot that the remainder of the work shewed the agreement of the Resurrection and Ascension of our Lord, the gift of the Holy Spirit, and the foundation and growth of the Church with the predictions of the Jewish prophets.

A fragment of Book XV relates to the four kingdoms of the Book of Daniel, and suggests that that section of the work dealt with the doctrine of the Holy Catholic Church.

§ 4. RELATION TO EARLIER APOLOGIES

The *Demonstratio* comes at the end of a long series of apologetical works, and embodies and codifies their results. It is the work of a man of extraordinarily wide scholarship, which marshals and buttresses with additional support the "loci communes" of his predecessors. Eusebius is no adventurer breaking fresh ground.

A comparison of the *Demonstratio* with the *Trypho* or the *contra Celsum* reveals only a more systematic application of the argument from prophecy used by Justin and Origen. In some cases the prophecies are explained in almost identical language. We may instance the exegesis of Psalm xxii. in Book X with that of Justin, in *Trypho*, cc. 98–106, the references to Isaiah vii. 14, where he uses the language of Origen, *contra Celsum*, i. 35, points out that Jesus Christ alone suits the passage, and quotes Deut. xxii. 23, 24 in support of the translation of νεᾶνις. The question of the Christian's rejection of the Jewish Law and his acceptance of the Jewish scriptures had been handled by Justin, and the most striking portion of the *Demonstratio*, the argument in Book III, that Christ was no sorcerer, may be said to have been suggested by Origen, *contra Celsum*, ii. 48, and Justin, *1st Apol.* c. 30. His explanation of the Old Testament Theophanies is that of the earlier Apologists, his insistence that Christianity rests on reason as well as faith, and his allegorical method, are plainly those of Origen and the Alexandrian school. It could hardly have been otherwise. After two centuries of defensive warfare against Jews and Greeks, the lines of controversy were clearly defined, and the apologetic writer but reiterated in a new form against the critics of his own day, what his predecessors had said against a previous generation of critics. His "loci communes" were well known to the Catechist, just as the ordinary course of instruction to candidates for Confirmation follows a definite line to-day. The most he could achieve was to present in a systematic form such a codification of existing arguments as the circle around him required.

Yet the *Praeparatio* opens with a remarkable claim to originality of method. Eusebius contrasts the "more logical" nature of his proofs with "refutations and con-tradictions of opposing arguments, exegesis of scripture, and controversial advocacy" (*Praep. Ev.* i. 3). Here alluding to a mass of evidential literature he proposes to reject "all deceitful and sophistical plausibilities" in favour of the evidence of the fulfilment of the Jewish prophecies in Christ, and the developing life of His Church. But this is very much what the earlier Apologists set out to do. In what sense can Eusebius say: "The purpose, however, which we have in hand is to be worked out in a way of our own" (*Praep. Ev.* 7 a)?

Lightfoot argues that Eusebius is referring to the use of lengthy quotations, by means of which religious ideals, that clash with Christianity, may be allowed to speak for them-selves, as is stated in *Praep. Ev.* 16 d. "I shall not set down my own words, but those of the very persons who have taken the deepest interest in the worship of them whom they call Gods." But he admits that there was little originality in this method of controversy. It had been employed by the earlier Apologists.

The real claim of Eusebius seems to be made clear by the context. He quotes 1 Cor. ii. 14; iii. 6; and 2 Cor. iii. 5 as guides for avoiding "deceitful and sophistical plausibilities" and for the use of proofs free from ambiguity. And he contrasts the value of "words" with that of the evidence of "works" on which he prefers to rely. By "works" he means the power of Christ as a living, moving

energy in human life. The exact fulfilment of Christ's
anticipations, the triumph of His Church as foretold in
Matt. xvi. 18, the fate of the Jews, and the wonderful
fulfilment of the predictions of the Hebrew prophets are
the "works" upon which Eusebius proposes to base his
"demonstration."

But even so it can hardly be said that there was anything
novel in such an intention, looking back to the apologies
of Justin, Athenagoras, Aristides and Tatian. There is
a series of chapters in Justin which reads almost like an
outline sketch of the *Demonstratio*. Eusebius, therefore,
can hardly have meant that the method which he adopted
was new in the sense that it had not been used before.
What then did he mean? Surely he must have had in his
mind the methods of evidential writers of his own day.
He must have been thinking of dialectical encounters with
literary opponents. He may only have intended to stress
his determination to abstain in the *Demonstratio* from
meeting the objections of Porphyry and his followers point
by point, as Origen had dealt with Celsus. If the method
of Origen had made a deep impression on the educated
world, and if Eusebius was regarded in any sense as belonging to the school of Origen, it was natural for him to state
definitely that he proposed in his new work to follow a
different course from Origen's. Origen's method was to
follow every turn of the trail of a slippery foe: his opponent,
so to say, made the game. Eusebius wished it to be
understood that he started with a well-ordered programme
of Scriptural exposition, and did not intend to be drawn
aside into detailed controversy on points that had been
raised by individual controversialists.

This intention, however fitfully and diffusely it is carried
through, can never be said to be lost sight of in the *Demonstratio*. We have a constant recurrence to the massive
evidence of a growing and flourishing Church, a changed
society, a converted character. The heart of the argument
is the connection of this external evidence with the Divine
and Human Person of Christ.

The lever that is intended to move the mind to realize
the uniqueness of Christ is the exposition of a series of
prophecies, whose selection, systematic arrangement and
treatment confers on Eusebius, if not the crown of origin-

ality, at least the praise of having carefully codified the work of his predecessors.

The *Demonstratio* then, like all the best apologetic work of the early Church, is based on the continuous living evidence of the action of a Divine Power. "The help," says Eusebius, "which comes down from the God of the Universe supplies to the teaching and Name of our Saviour its irresistible and invincible force, and its victorious power against its enemies" (*Praep. Ev.* 9 d).

Compared with the *Octavius*, the *Trypho*, or the *contra Celsum* the *Demonstratio* may seem cold and academic, for it lacks the charm and interest of the dialogue-form. Where they are redolent of the open air, and the market-place, it suggests the lecture-hall and the pulpit. Much of the warmth, directness, and reality has evaporated from the appeal of Eusebius. These are obvious criticisms. But it must be remembered that Eusebius wrote for the cultured people of his own age. His method and manner are less perhaps the result of his own temperament than the production of a stately and courtly entourage. As the heir of the apologetic of the market-place, and of a struggling sect of believers, he was called by the genius of his own time to reproduce in a polished and rhetorical style, for an educated circle, the old arguments which had welled forth from the lips of the infant Church in spontaneous freedom and life. There can be no doubt that the world for which they were intended received in the *Praeparatio* and the *Demonstratio* what was for it the most unanswerable defence of the Christian Religion.

§ 5. THE ARGUMENT OF THE THIRD BOOK

The Third Book of the *Demonstratio* seems to claim special consideration. As a piece of apologetic it is extraordinarily full and to the point. It seizes the real salients in the evidential controversy, and is occupied with topics which must always come foremost in the defence of Christianity. It is no argument in the air, it comes down to meet the ordinary unbeliever in the crowd, and begins by speaking to him of Christ as "one bearing ordinary humanity and like the rest." Upon the acknowledged basis of the beauty of His human life, and the perfection of His ethical teaching

better understood and more universally acknowledged
by non-Christians in the modern world than they were then
except by a few thinkers like Porphyry, the argument passes
to the Miracles, which are the evidence that Christ is something more than human, to hypotheses which professed to
account for them, viz. invention and sorcery, and to the
question of the credibility of the witnesses to our Lord's
abnormal acts. It is remarkable that one who could be
so diffuse should, in so short a space, have combined so
many arguments in one connected scheme; and still more
that he should have made central the points that *are* central,
viz. the historical Person of Christ, His Ethics, His miraculous Power, and the credibility of the Gospel-writers, treated
as involving generally all belief in witness to historical
facts.

The great mass of the *Demonstratio* is an elaborate
réchauffée of past apologetics, but in this book we feel the
touch of something fresh, free, original, something that
springs from keen, personal interest, warm perception, and
ardent conviction. It is not sword-play, but actual warfare,
and there are rapier-strokes of satire, which the hand of
Swift might have dealt. In literary quality, as well as in
appositeness to the subject discussed, the book is remarkable. Its finish, completeness in itself, and contrast with
the *Demonstratio* as a whole might suggest that it was a
separate essay, written in actual controversy with an opponent
who drew out Eusebius' keenest logic and dialectical skill,
and that this essay was eventually incorporated in the greater
but more academic work.

Its argument may be summarized as follows:

(87-102)   Jesus claimed in the synagogue at Nazareth (Luke iv. 21)
to be the fulfilment of the prophecy of a Saviour (Isa. lxi. 1).
Moses' prophecy of a successor "like himself" (Deut.
xviii. 15), who should come at the fall of the Jewish kingdom
(Gen. xlix. 10), Isaiah's "Root of Jesse" (Isa. xi. 1),
Micah's prediction of Bethlehem (Micah v. 2), Isaiah's
"suffering servant" (Isa. liii. 3-8), who died that He might
rise to rule over the world through His Church, are only
fulfilled in Christ.

Reply to attacks upon Christ as (i) *deceiver;* (ii) *wizard.*—
First on the basis of mere humanity (ὡς περὶ κοινοῦ καὶ τοῖς
(102-107c) λοιποῖς παραπλησίου) Christ must be realized as the best

man who ever lived. Consider the ethical outcome of His teaching, in purity, meekness, sanity of mind, benevolence, love of truth. He called back the lost ideals of Abraham, and gave them to the whole world; their value is admitted, for even the Greek oracles praise Abraham's monotheism. He abjured a sacrificial worship, but so did Porphyry (*de Abst.* ii. 34) and Apollonius of Tyana. He taught that the world was created and would one day be destroyed, even as Plato did, and also the doctrine of the Immortality of the Soul, and thus made His poor disciples wiser than supercilious philosophers, who seem proud to claim identity with the flea, the worm, and the fly. He stressed a divine judgment, punishment, and an eternal life with God. He recognized angels and dæmons, helpers and foes of the soul just as the Hebrews did. All this is ethically sound.

But there was a divine side to Christ, as is shown by His Miracles of mercy and love; He died voluntarily, rose again, and ascended to heaven. The miraculous in the life of Christ is in line with the miraculous in Christianity. Those who deny it must either prove that it was invented, or the result of sorcery. Now the type of teaching Christ gave His disciples is utterly opposed to their inventing falsehoods. It was ascetic, and made truth and purity the first essentials of conduct. If you admit the fanciful hypothesis that He really taught them fraud and specious lying you are landed in absurdities. Deceit could afford no corporate cohesion, κακῷ κακὸς οὐ φίλος, οὐδὲ ἀγαθῷ: and again, what had they to expect but a death like His? After His death, too, they only honoured Him the more! They were even ready to die for Him. It is inconceivable that they knew Him to be really vicious. And equally impossible that, if they were, they should propose to convert the whole world, and actually do so, poor and uneducated as they were. You must imagine them meeting secretly after the Crucifixion, admitting Christ's deceit, and yet conspiring to propagate the Gospel-story: "Let us see," they say, "that our freak lasts even to death. There is nothing ridiculous in dying for nothing at all." "What could be finer than to make both gods and men our enemies for no possible reason? . . . And suppose we convince no one, we shall have the satisfaction of drawing

(107d–125b)

down upon ourselves in return for our inventions the retribution for our deceit." Such theories are ridiculous, for there is no doubt that persecution and death faced the Apostles. Yet there was no traitor among them after the Ascension. And they actually succeeded in their adventure. Now this hypothesis of a conspiracy to deceive might be used with equal force with regard to Moses, or the Greek philosophers, and indeed all those whose lives history records.

The simplicity, devotion, and ascetic lives of the Apostles guarantee their honesty. They faced all for truth and the Name of Christ. The Gospels reveal their modesty and straightforwardness in unexpected ways. It has been well said : " We must put complete confidence in the disciples of Jesus, or none at all "; distrust of them logically means distrust of all writers. Why allow invidious distinctions ? The Passion is the crowning *crux*, how could they have invented a story which would handicap all their efforts ? That they gave a true account of it really authenticates their accounts of the Miracles, and glorious manifestations of Christ.

The evidence of Josephus, too, may be called in with good effect. (See note on this passage.)

(125b-
141a)

Against the alternative view that Christ was a sorcerer.— The suggestion is opposed to the whole trend of His teaching and manner of life. He was unworldly, pure, and retiring ; sorcerers are the reverse. If He had been one His followers would have resembled Him, but the great mark of the whole Christian Church is its abhorrence of magic. No Christian has ever admitted himself to be a sorcerer even to escape death. And this argument may be extended—in all ways the virtues of Christians vouch for the character of their Master. They afford " clear evidence of the nurture of His words." The Greeks boast of the self-sacrifice of Democritus and Krates, but Christian zealots can be counted by the myriad. They know what Plato alone knew about God, but he was confessedly unable to make God known, whereas it is the common task of the Christians.

But was Christ's sorcery self-taught, or learned from others ? If the former then it showed something of the nature of supernatural power, if the latter, meaning that He was taught it in Egypt, what a strange thing that Christ should so utterly outstrip His teachers, and institute a new nation and new laws, as He has done. Once more note that He paid no court to the dæmons, and that they even now shudder at His Name. Think of His union with the Father, His purity, justice and truth, His perfect character, and you will laugh at the suggestion. The very dæmons bear witness to him in the Oracles quoted by Porphyry as "a man signal in holiness." His grandeur is shown by His choice of poor men for apostles, "because maybe he had in mind to do the most unlikely things." And what a design it was—to rule the whole world! And His followers were to do the work simply "in His Name." That alone explains their success. They had to preach the paradox, that God came on an embassy in a human body, and died on a Cross! The only explanation of their success is His co-operation with them, for the Gospel in itself is not plausible. The Power He gave them to work miracles amazed their hearers, and induced them to yield to the message: without His Power they could never have succeeded.

And you may add to this the providential preparation of the world for the preaching of the Gospel through the establishment of the Roman Empire, whose Heads both by their leniency and severity have assisted the divine purpose of spreading the Gospel. (141a)

. . . .

Such a summary as the above is but a sorry skeleton. It is void of all the life and vividness, the subtle turns, the satirical touches of the argument. But it reveals on what ground the writer really rested in his defence of Christianity. His apology is seen to be not abstract and *a priori*, but almost modern in its hold on historical fact. Let us consider the points that stand out.

(i) There is the argument from Prophecy. It is fashionable to say that the Apologists were deluded in their persistent efforts to link the Gospel facts with prophetic predictions. No doubt they were in a sense deluded, and the greater part of the *Demonstratio* is a monument to the delusion. But yet, though the method is changed, there is still an argument from prophecy. The lines of optimistic hope for mankind that run through the Hebrew prophets *do* meet at the feet of Christ. He alone satisfies their majestic anticipations.

"We may say," writes Prof. W. E. Barnes, in his essay *On the Permanent Value of the Old Testament,*[1] "that the prophets saw, each under a form suited to his own age, a vision of God's presence with men, realised to a new degree, and 'specialised' (if the word may be used) in Israel through the instrumentality of a visible leader of Israel. The ideas of a chosen people and of a chosen leader upon whom the Spirit of God rests are found in those prophetic passages." The prophecies to which he alludes are Micah iv. 8 to v. 6; Isa. ix. 1–7, xi. 1–10, lii. 13 to liii. 12; Jer. xxiii. 15, 16. It is worthy of remark that in selecting five passages of typical Messianic prophecy, the fourth-century and the twentieth-century scholar choose three out of the five the same.

(ii) The historical Personality of Jesus as perfect Man stands out in a very modern way. The ἐν ἀνθρώποις πολιτευσάμενον καὶ παθόντα of the Creed of Cæsarea, upon which Eusebius had been brought up, had not failed of its effect; neither had his patient study of the Gospels. Whatever his theory of the union of the Divinity with the Humanity, he had a very clear and a very true conception of the Humanity of our Lord. He speaks of the Man Christ Jesus almost as One Whom he has known. He follows Him on His works of mercy. He catches the spirit of His words. He feels their supreme truth, their unexampled beauty, their divine audacity, their kingly authority. He imagines correctly Christ's effect upon His followers, he argues back from the ideals of the followers to the uniqueness of the Master.

It is quite remarkable that Eusebius should start with the human Christ, and describe him as the best man that ever lived, before introducing the conception forced upon him by the Miracles that He was divine as well. It was the method of the Master Himself, and therefore the right one.

(iii) Eusebius' view of the value of the witness of the writers of the Gospels, and of the first teachers of Christianity, has been a feature of many volumes of evidences to

---

[1] *Cambridge Theological Essays* (London 1906), p. 350.

the days of Butler and Paley and our own time. But it may be doubted whether the argument from the simplicity and transparent honesty of these "unlearned and ignorant men" has ever been more cogently put, their bravery, their persistence, their devotion, their facing the certainty of "labours, dangers and sufferings," the magnificence of the design with which they set out, the paradox they were called to preach, the divine power that made them triumph.

In the last fifty years of New Testament criticism how often has it been evident that these books and their writers were being put to tests, from which all other records were exempt. This, too, Eusebius deprecated. Criticism should treat all alike, and to treat all as the Gospels have been treated would leave history a mass of questionable documents and disputed statements.

(iv) There is an ethical stress of deep significance in the whole book. The Humanity of Christ and His teaching are made to challenge the unbeliever first of all by *their moral value;* it is claimed for them that they satisfy, and more than satisfy, human aspirations after goodness. The Miracles are presented as worked for moral ends. It is the ethical interest that gives the fire of indignation and the sting of satire to the arguments that Christ is neither charlatan nor sorcerer. Again and again the purity and self-control, the justice and love of truth, the unselfishness and benevolence of the Christian teaching, and of its result in countless lives that philosophy would have been powerless to affect, are dwelt upon. As we have seen, Eusebius reads back from the lives of Christians the character of Christ—that is to say, he finds in actual life around him something of the moral ideal that he knows to be summed up in Christ from Whom the life of men around receives it. He shews throughout a very real appreciation of the bearing of faith on conduct. The life of the Christian is the ultimate Court of Appeal for the reality of Christ. Ethical value demonstrates a divine power as its spring and source. They that overcome the world prove the truth of the Gospel. Eusebius is defending the Gospel of a divine Christ; the merely human Christ is One Whose character implies the divine as well; and He is the source and stay of moral progress. Eusebius realized this; the

world of our day doubts it. But as has been well said :
" There is no proof that the ethical principles have existed
effectively in the past except in connection with Christian
doctrine, so there is little probability that they can ever
exist in the future, for the mass of men at least, except in
dependence on a living Christ." [1]

§ 6. THE CHRISTOLOGY OF EUSEBIUS

Eusebius was in his day the leading representative of
ecclesiastical conservatism. That is to say, his theology
was, allowing for the difference of period, almost precisely
that of Origen. For as Dr. Bigg [2] has remarked : " What
struck later ages as the novelty and audacity of Origen's
doctrine was in truth its archaism and conservatism."
This system of doctrine had captured the Eastern Church,
and men like Eusebius had absorbed it from the lips of
those who had sat at the feet of Origen himself. It
was in accord with the general outlook of cultured men.
It appeared to be the logical development of orthodox
thought. It is true that elements that had been prominent
in heretical teaching were included in it, but they were the
good elements, and their carefully limited position in the
system made them innocuous. It was the unfolding of
the Logos-doctrine on a basis loyal to Scripture and the
Rule of Faith. The Logos-theology was the natural way
then to think about the immanence of God. It had been
appropriated for the Christian Religion long ago by the
Apologists. The theology based upon it stood not only
for a fascinating idealistic faith, but also for the strongest
bulwark against what orthodoxy dreaded most—the heresies
which tended to make the divine Persons but temporary
manifestations of one Godhead, viz. Modalism or Sabellianism. The Logos-theology stressed the unchangeable-
ness of the Father, and His distinction from the Son, one in
essence though They might be. For the moment the distinction of the Son from the Father was more important
to the Church than the question how far such a distinction
implied subordination and inferiority. Justin had not

[1] J. F. Bethune-Baker, " Christian Doctrines and their Ethical
Significance," in *Cambridge Theological Essays* (London 1906), p. 571.
[2] C. Bigg, *The Christian Platonists of Alexandra*, p. 182.

shirked the phrase δεύτερος θεός, neither did Origen.   As Dr. Sanday has said: "The reaction against Sabellianism (which became a general term including all forms of Monarchianism) had not a little to do with the exaggerations on the other side; and in particular the dread of this form of error contributed to the rapid rise and spread of Arianism." [1] The point where Arianism touched this established and somewhat quiescent theology was exactly where Origen had discouraged speculation.   He had given to the Church the doctrine of the eternal generation, but pronounced its comprehension beyond human reason.   Arians claimed the right to open a door that was shut.   But the disciples of Origen were not perhaps so much disposed to quarrel with adventurers into the uncharted realms "of the ineffable relations of the Godhead before the remotest beginnings of time," [2] provided they held some form of the Logos-doctrine, as they were to withstand those who rejected it altogether.   And their own language is to a later age sometimes indistinguishable from Arianism.   Of such a theology the doctrinal parts of the *Demonstratio* may be considered representative.   Let us briefly examine it.

As Harnack says: "Eusebius was more convinced than Origen that the idea of deity was completely exhausted in that of the strictly one and unchangeable ὄν the πρώτη οὐσία; he separated the δεύτερος θεός much further from God than the Apologists." [3]   We therefore find the utmost emphasis laid on the Absolute Character of God the Unbegotten.   He is "the One ἀρχή born before the first, earlier than the Monad" (145 b).   He precedes the Son in existence (147), is "the greater God, and as such alone holds the name in His own right" (κυρίως) (226).   He is as the Sun to the world, too mighty to mingle with created things directly, requiring a Mediator, through whom to create and govern the created world (154).

Therefore by His own will He begets the Logos, "the first-born Wisdom altogether formed of Wisdom, and Reason and Mind, or rather Wisdom itself, Reason itself, and Mind itself" (146 a).   He "alone bears the inconceivable image in Himself through which He is God, and also because of

---

[1] *Christologies, Ancient and Modern*, p. 40.
[2] Stanley, *Eastern Church*, iii. 80.
[3] *History of Dogma*, iii. 136 (note).

His appointment to guide the Universe " (146 c) ; *i. e.* He is divine by essence as well as by office.

Eusebius uses the well-worn similes of the Apologists : the relation of the Father to the Son is as light to its ray, as myrrh to its scent, as a king to his portrait. But there is the important difference sufficiently stressed, that having been begotten the Son exists apart from the Father in His own essence (147). Yet worship is due to Him as δεύτερος θεός because the greater God dwells in Him (226 d), as the image of a king is honoured not for its own sake, but for the sake of the king. So the words, "They shall know Thee the only true God " cannot be referred to the Logos or Holy Spirit, but only to the Unbegotten (231).

In the work of creation He stands "midway between the begotten and the Unbegotten." As with Origen and the Neoplatonists He is the "idea of the world," the basis (θεμέλιος) for all created things (213). And it is because of His connection with the world that lower predicates are attached to Him—He is now God's δημιούργημα (146 b) and ὑπουργός (257 b); the "second cause " (216 b); "a second Lord " (227 d), and is said "to have attained secondary honours " (δευτερείων ἠξιῶσθαι) (227 d). So the Father is " Lord and God " of the Son (233 a).

In the Incarnation Eusebius teaches the distinctive doctrine of Origen that the Logos associates Himself with a pure, unfallen human soul. "He remains Himself immaterial and unembodied as He was before with the Father" (169 b). "No evil deed can harm Him, because He is not really embodied" (168). "He shared His own gifts with men, and received nothing in return " (*ib.*).

His Body is but the earthen lamp through which His light shines (188). He comes to republish the true doctrine, from which man has fallen away through the deceptions of the dæmons, to establish a Church to preach it, and to bring man back to God. Once Eusebius uses the word συναποθεόω, "to deify men with Himself" as the object of the Incarnation (170). Five reasons are given for the Death on the Cross (167). It is chiefly the decisive triumph over the dæmons, but it is also an expiatory sacrifice for the sins of men. "He offered Himself and the Humanity He assumed to the higher and greater God." In His earthly life Christ now revealed the Humanity and now the Divinity (165); and it is possible for Eusebius, leaving the Logos in the background, to devote part of a Book to meeting the common man on his own ground, and to treat of the perfection of Christ's life and teaching as merely human.

The missing Books no doubt dealt with the Risen and Ascended Christ, and the Holy Spirit. There are only hints on these topics in the Books before us. He is "Priest of the obedient to the Father" (164 d). There is a passage (220 a) which especially rouses the anger of de Billy, a famous student of the Greek Fathers in the sixteenth century. It is the interpretation of Ps. cix.: "The Lord said unto My Lord," where the first Lord is said to mean the Father, and the second the Son, Who is thus confessed by the Holy Spirit in David, to be his Lord: "Quod quidem credere quid aliud est quam horrendae impietatis crimine se astringere!" (Billius, *Obs. Sac.* I. 29, p. 48).

It is clear that the theology of Origen is presented here either directly or by implication: Origen taught that God is the only real essence, that by the necessity of His Nature He reveals Himself; that by an act of will He eternally begets the Logos, which is His Consciousness, and also the Idea of the World; that the Logos being the Image of God is essentially God, not begotten in time nor out of the non-existent; that He is no impersonal Force, but a Second Person in the Godhead. That as the Idea of the World He is subordinate, and in His office to creation both $\kappa\tau\acute{\iota}\sigma\mu\alpha$ and $\delta\eta\mu\iota\upsilon\acute{\nu}\rho\gamma\eta\mu\alpha$; that His Incarnation is a Union (almost docetic) with an unfallen soul, with which He lives and which He draws up to Himself by bonds of mutual love; that His work on earth is chiefly the republication of truth to enlighten men blinded by dæmons; that His Death was complete Victory over them, and also sacrificial; that the Humanity was gradually deified until at last the man Jesus passed into the Logos, and that this deification is the destiny of all who share the Logos now.

Such is a bald summary of perhaps the greatest theological system of antiquity, and it is obvious how it lies behind and beneath all that Eusebius says. Like Origen, he rests on Biblical exegesis and is dominated by the Rule of Faith; like Origen, he refrains from speculation on the mystery of the coming-into-being ($\upsilon\dot{\upsilon}\sigma\acute{\iota}\omega\sigma\iota\varsigma$) of the Logos. He expresses

the point-of-view of a dominant theology in an assured
tone. He speaks as one who voices the opinion of the
great mass of cultured believers; for Origen was in possession, and Arius and the Homoousians were alike
innovators.

The Creed of the Church of Cæsarea, which Eusebius
presented at Nicæa as an eirenicon to be accepted by both
parties, embodied this theology. "It bears," says Dr.
Bright, "a considerable resemblance to that which the
Council ultimately framed : it was emphatic on the personal
distinctions in the Holy Trinity, asserting each Person to
be and to exist as truly Father, Son, and Holy .Spirit; it
recognizes "One Lord Jesus Christ as 'the Word of God,
God from God, Light from Light, Life from Life, Only-
begotten Son, First-born of all Creation, Begotten before
all ages, and through Whom all things come into being,'
and it mentioned also His becoming 'incarnate for our
salvation, His Life among men, His Passion, Resurrection
on the third day, Ascension to the Father, and future
Coming in glory to judge (the) quick and dead,' and concluded as then quoted, with 'We believe also in one Holy
Spirit'; yet it was not sufficiently explicit as to the main
point at stake, His eternal relation to the Father." [1]

This deficiency was to be supplied by the inclusion of
the Homoousion. The Son must be defined as "of the
same essence" as the Father. No statement that He was
begotten before time was adequate. The Logos must be
distinctly separated from the created Universe. And this
the Homoousion alone would effect for minds of that day.
But it was unfortunately a suspected term. It had been
anathematized at the Council of Antioch (A.D. 269) when
employed by Paul of Samosata. Athanasius used it sparingly
in its hour of victory. Later on the Semi-Arians rejected
it as savouring of Sabellianism. No wonder it seemed to
steady conservatives like Eusebius, who did not wish to
define the ineffable, to head straight for Modalistic views.
How could two "of the same essence" be aught but one
under different aspects? The doctrinal trend of Eusebius,
as Harnack recognizes, was to widen the gulf between the
πρώτη αἰτία and the Logos, rather than to lessen it. The

---

[1] W. Bright, *Church of the Fathers*, i. vi. 88. The creed is given.
Theodoret, *H.E.* i. 1.

Homoousion seemed perilously like filling it up. But with the necessary limitations he could conscientiously sign it. Safe-guarded from Sabellian implications it was harmless. The theology of the *Demonstratio* shows quite clearly how and in what sense the word could be used credally by an exponent of the Origenic theology without any violence to conscience. It makes his attitude throughout the momentous days at Nicæa intelligible and creditable to him as a peace-maker. The letter[1] he wrote to his diocese becomes no mere shuffling apology, but an honest statement. He makes it perfectly clear in what sense he understands the Homoousion. He explains that he has signed on the representation of the Emperor that "consubstantial" implied nothing physical, but must be regarded as having "a divine and mysterious signification." Thus, he says that it does not imply that the Son is "a part of the Father," nor does "Begotten, not made," mean more than that the Son does not form part of the created Universe, and "does not resemble in any respect the creatures which He has made, but that to the Father alone, Who begat Him, He is in all points perfectly like; for He is of the essence and of the substance of none save the Father."

He also said that he agreed to the anathemas on those who said that the Son "came out of the non-existent," or that "there was a time when He was not," because of the un-Scriptural nature of such expressions. Finally, he definitely asserted that the new formula was in agreement with the Creed that he had originally proposed.

Acquaintance with the *Demonstratio* guarantees the sincerity of the statement. If the Homoousion was to be understood as explained by Constantine, signing it involved no violent wrench with the past. It was capable of being transplanted into the creed of Eusebius. Even Origen had used the word in the sense now applied to it. If Eusebius signed with reluctance, he signed with sincerity.

There is a statement of Harnack's that the Logos-doctrine as held by Eusebius "effaced the historical Christ." It would give the impression that theologians of the school of Origen necessarily followed the Gnostics

---

[1] Theodoret, *H.E.* i. 12.

in all their flights.   If Hellenic speculation had been the
only wing of their theology, they might logically have held
a faith of mere abstractions.   But the school, like its
master, was marked by its devotion to Scriptural exegesis.
It was Biblical to the core.   Hence such a statement as
Harnack's in the face of the earlier part of the *Demonstratio*
appears grotesque and exaggerated.   At any rate Eusebius'
hold on the Gospel history was firm and sure.   No one
can read the third Book without realizing that Eusebius
had an interest in the earthly life of our Lord that effectu-
ally neutralized the dangers of Gnostic abstract speculation.
He had an evangelical sense of the value of all the words
and deeds of the Incarnate Christ.   His picture of Jesus
Christ is not a mass of high-sounding phrases and Biblical
images, it is the work of a pastor of souls, who, however
abstract his formal theology may be, understands quite
well, that it is the concrete historical facts that move men,
not the philosophical theories that underlie them, and that
the Word took flesh and wrought the Creed of Creeds,
that He might enter in at the doors, not only of the lowly,
but of all who are formed of human elements.

§ 7. The References to the Eucharist in the *Demonstratio*

It will be useful, perhaps, to bring together here the
passages in the *Demonstratio* which allude to the Eucharist.
They are all incidental to the argument, and therefore
doctrinally all the more interesting.   They express the
common sense of the Eastern Church on the subject in
a spontaneous way.

(i) 37 *b. sqq.*—Jesus the Lamb of God by His sacrifice
frees us from the Mosaic Law.   "We are therefore right in
celebrating daily His memory, and the Memorial of His
Body and Blood (τὴν τούτου μνήμην τοῦ τε σώματος αὐτοῦ καὶ
τοῦ αἵματος τὴν ὑπόμνησιν ὁσημέραι ἐπιτελοῦντες)."   "Thus we
enter on a greater sacrifice and priestly act (θυσία and
ἱερουργία) than that of the ancients."   The earlier sacrifices
were "weak and beggarly elements," mere symbols and
images (σύμβολα καὶ εἰκόνες), not embracing truth itself.
We notice here the use of the words μνήμη, ὑπόμνησις,
θυσία and ἱερουργία, and the application of σύμβολα καὶ

εἰκόνες in a depreciatory sense to the Jewish sacrifices, as not "embracing the truth." The words are later on applied to the Sacraments, in the sense that they do embrace truth. (See Note on passage.)

A little lower it proceeds—

"We have received through Christ's mystic dispensation the symbols that are true, and archetypal of the images that preceded them " (τὰ ἀληθῆ καὶ τῶν εἰκόνων τὰ ἀρχέτυπα). For Christ offered to the Father "a wonderful sacrifice and unique victim" (θῦμα καὶ σφάγιον), and "delivered us a memory (μνήμη) to offer continually to God in place of a sacrifice (προσφέρειν ἀντὶ θυσίας)."

This μνήμη is "celebrated on a table by means of the symbols of His Body and His saving Blood (ἐπὶ τραπέζης διὰ συμβόλων τοῦ τε σώματος αὐτοῦ καὶ τοῦ σωτηρίου αἵματος)." It fulfils Ps. xxiii. 5. "Thus in our rites we have been taught to offer through our whole lives bloodless and reasonable and acceptable sacrifices through His Supreme High Priest." (Cf. Pss. l. 14, 15; cxli. 2; li. 17; Mal. i. 11.) It is our sacrifice of praise : "we sacrifice in a new way according to the new covenant, the pure sacrifice." "A contrite heart" has been called a sacrifice to God (Ps. li. 17). And we burn the incense, "the sweet-smelling fruit of excellent theology, offering it by means of our prayers." "So we sacrifice and burn incense, celebrating the memory of the great sacrifice in the mysteries which He has delivered to us, and bringing to God our Thanksgiving for our Salvation (τὴν ὑπὲρ σωτηρίας ἡμῶν εὐχαριστίαν) by means of pious hymns and prayers, dedicating ourselves wholly to Him and His High Priest, the Word Himself, making our offering in body and soul (ἀνακείμενοι)."

Here we have σύμβολον used in the sacramental sense ; and the inner nature of the sacrifice is stressed ; the real sacrifice is the contrite heart offered through the Great High Priest, and the incense (non-existent materially in the service then) is the θεολογία of the worshipper. It is a choral, prayerful self-dedication and Eucharist.

(ii) 223 b.—Christ fulfilled the priesthood of Melchizedek, not Aaron. "And our Saviour Jesus, the Christ of God, after the manner of Melchizedek still even now accomplishes by means of His ministers the rites of His priestly work amongst men." Like Melchizedek, Christ first and His priests after Him "accomplishing their spiritual sacrificial work according to the laws of the Church, represent with wine and bread the mysteries of His Body and saving Blood" (οἴνῳ καὶ ἄρτῳ τοῦ τε σώματος αὐτοῦ καὶ τοῦ σωτηρίου αἵματος αἰνίττονται τὰ μυστήρια).

(iii) 380 d.—The expressions in Zech. ix. 9 and 15, are allusions to the Eucharist, and point to the joy given by the mystic wine, and the glory and purity of the mystic food. "For He delivered the symbols (σύμβολα) of His divine dispensation to His disciples, bidding them make the image of His own Body (τὴν εἰκόνα τοῦ ἰδίου σώματος ποιεῖσθαι)." Rejecting the Mosaic sacrifices, He delivered them bread to use as a symbol of His Body (ἄρτῳ χρῆσθαι συμβόλῳ τοῦ ἰδίου σώματος).

This further illustrates the use of σύμβολον.

We gather from these passages :—(i) That the Mosaic Sacrifice, the Sacrifice on the Cross, and the Eucharistic Sacrifice are intimately related. The latter is a Memorial of the Sacrifice of the Cross in a far higher sense than the Jewish sacrifices were foreshadowings of it. They were but symbols that were unreal, the Eucharist is a symbol but it "embraces reality," *i.e.* it includes what it represents. It is the archetype of which they were symbols.

(ii) The Eucharist is nothing, if it is not inward. It is a means for the offering of a contrite heart, and the incense of true knowledge of God. It is no mere outward act ; in and through the outward act is the inner oblation.

(iii) Though in line with the Mosaic system the Eucharist is far more in line with the primeval offering of blessing made by Melchizedek with bread and wine, not with animal victims.

(iv) The Eucharist we gather was celebrated daily, and with music.

[Cf. Darwell Stone, *A History of the Doctrine of the Eucharist*, London, 1909, vol. i. 109–11. A. Harnack, *History of Dogma*, iv. 291.]

§ 8. MSS., ETC.

The earliest MS. of the *Demonstratio* is the Codex known as the Medicean or "Parisinus 469," of the twelfth century, registered in the Catalogue of the Library of Paris, vol. ii. p. 65. It is deficient at the beginning and end, beginning with the words ἡ παιδίσκη σοι, p. 17, and ending at τῆς σωτῆρος ἡμῶν παρακελεύσεως, p. 688. These deficiencies were supplied by J. A. Fabricius in his *Delectus argumentorum et syllabus scriptorum, qui veritatem religionis Christianæ adversos atheos . . . asseruerunt*, who used a copy that had been made by Stephen Bergler, at Hamburg, in 1725, from a MS. in the possession of Nicholas Mavrocordato, Prince of Wallachia, who collected many Greek MSS. from Mount Athos and other monasteries. The MS. was unfortunately lost at the death of the Prince. Bergler gave no information about its age or condition. It was almost certain that it was either derived from Parisinus 469 before its mutilation, or from a MS. of the same family.

There are four other MSS. of the *Demonstratio* at Paris, parchments of the sixteenth century numbered 470, 471, 472 and 473 in the Catalogue, vol. ii. pp. 65, 66. And there is at St. John's College, Oxford, a parchment MS. of the fifteenth century (No. 41 in the Catalogue of O. Coxius, p. 12). As all these have the same deficiencies, there is little doubt that they come from the common source, Parisinus 469.

There is a sixth MS. in the Ambrosian Library, at Milan, of the fifteenth century, of the same family (Montfaucon in *Bibliotheca Bibliothecarum*, vol. i. p. 527). And a seventh was possessed by T. F. Mirandola, and was used by Donatus of Verona for his Latin version, first published at Rome in 1498.

Of the four later Paris MSS., 473 bears the date 1543, and was written at Venice (or 1533 according to Montfaucon, *Diario Italico*, p. 408) by Valeriano of Forli. One of the four was no doubt the foundation of Stephen's Paris edition of 1548.

The Oxford MS. was collated by Gaisford with this edition of Robert Stephen in 1548 with the minutest care. But in the opinion of Dindorf his work added little to the elucidation of the text, beyond the correction of a few slight mistakes of copying, the divergencies in the quotations from the LXX being probably changes made by later scribes in order to bring the quotations into agreement with the accepted text.

Dindorf's conclusion is that a satisfactory text is secured by the use of the Parisinus 469, on which his own edition (Teubner series) is based. It is, he says, comparatively free from the errors of transcribers, with the exception of some lacunæ (pp. 195 d, 210 a, 217 b), and from the frequent interpolations of the *Praeparatio* and the *History*, because the *Demonstratio*, having fewer readers, was seldom copied. There is, therefore, little room in the study of the text for conjectural emendation.

The first Edition of the Greek was that of Robert Stephen, 1548.

Viguier's *Praeparatio* was published at Paris in 1628, with the *Demonstratio* and other works of Eusebius, and the Latin translation of Donatus.

Gaisford's edition (2 vols., Oxford) appeared in 1852 with critical apparatus and the same Latin translation.

The *Demonstratio* forms vol. xxii. of the *Greek Patrology* of Migne (1857), who uses the Paris edition of 1628 with the same translation.

The most recent text is W. Dindorf's in the Teubner Series (Leipzig, 1867), from whose Preface the data of the above are drawn.

The Latin version of Donatus (Rome, 1498) was reprinted at Basle in 1542, 1549, 1559 and 1570, and with the Scholia of J. J. Grynaeus at Paris in 1587. It is remarkable for its omissions and alterations of passages doctrinally suspected.

The present translation is made from the text of Gaisford (Oxford, 1852), with reference to Migne.

LIST OF CHAPTERS

The Contents of the First Book of the Proof of the Gospel of Our Saviour

1. The Object and Contents of the Work.

2. The Character of the Christian Religion.

3. That the System of Moses was not Suitable for All Nations.

4. Why is it we reject the Jews' Way of Life, though we accept their Writings?

5. The Character of the New Covenant of Christ.

6. The Nature of the Life according to the New Covenant proclaimed by Christ.

7. How Christ having first fulfilled the Law of Moses became the Introducer of a New and Fresh System.

8. That the Christian Life is of Two Distinct Characters.

9. Why a Numerous Offspring is not as Great a Concern to us as it was to them of Old Time.

10. Why we are not bidden to burn Incense and to sacrifice the Fruits of the Earth to God, as were the Men of Old Time.

The Contents of Book II

1. That we have not embraced the Prophetic Books of the Hebrews without Aim and Object.

2. That their Prophets gave their Best Predictions for us of the Foreign Nations.

    1, 2, 3. From Genesis.
    4. From Deuteronomy.
    5. From Psalm xxi.
    6. From Psalm xlvi.
    7. From Psalm lxxxv.
    8. From Psalm xcv.
    9. From Zechariah.
    10, 11. From Isaiah.

3. That the same Prophets foretold that at the Coming of Christ All Nations would learn the Knowledge and Holiness of the God, Who formerly was only known to the Hebrews.

    12. From Psalm ii.
    13. From Psalm lxxi.
    14. From Psalm xcvii.
    15. From Genesis.
    16, 17. From Zephaniah.
    18. From Zechariah.
    19, 20, 21, 22, 23. From Isaiah.

4. That the Call of the Gentiles coming to pass through Christ, there would be a Decline in the Jewish Nation from its Godly Holiness.

    24, 25. From Jeremiah.
    26. From Amos.
    27. From Micah.
    28. From Zechariah.

The Contents of Book III

The Contents of Book IV

The Contents of Book V

How the Hebrew Prophets predicted the Future, and shed the Light of True Theology. And how many Prophetic Voices made Mention of the Divine Pre-existence of the Saviour.

1. From the Proverbs.
2. From Psalm xlv.
3. Psalm cix.
4. Isaiah.
5. Psalm xxxii.
6. Isaiah.
7, 8, 9, 10, 11, 12. Genesis.
13, 14, 15, 16, 17. Exodus.
18. From Numbers.
19. Joshua, son of Nave.
20. Job.
21. Psalm xc.
22. Hosea.
23. Amos.
24. Obadiah.
25, 26, 27. Zechariah.
28, 29. Malachi.
30. Jeremiah.

The Contents of Book VI

Of His Sojourn among Men from the following Scriptures.

1. From Psalm xvii.
2. From Psalm xlvi.
3. From Psalm xlix.
4. From Psalm lxxxiii.
5. From Psalm xcv.
6. From Psalm xcvii.
7. From Psalm cvi.
8. From Psalms cxvi. and cxvii.
9. From Psalm cxliii.
10. From Psalm cxlvii.
11. From the Second Book of Kings.
12. From the Third Book of Kings.
13. From Micah.
14. From Habakkuk.

9. From Psalm lxvii.
10. From Isaiah.
11. From Deuteronomy.
12. From Job.
13, 14, 15, 16. From Isaiah.
17. From Zechariah.
18. From Psalm cxvii.

The Contents of Book X

Of the Conspiracy of Judas the Traitor and those with Him, to be formed against Christ, from the following Scriptures.

1. From Psalm xl.
2. From Psalm liv.
3. From Psalm cviii.
4. From Zechariah.
5. From Jeremiah.

Of the Events at the Time of His Passion.

6. From Amos.
7. From Zechariah.
8. From Psalm xxi.

. . . .

The above list of chapters was given at the beginning of each book. It was lost from the Paris Codex for Book I together with the first pages of that book, and from the copies, one of which Robert Stephen used in his edition of 1545. In the Paris edition of 1628, the editor composed the headings of the first three chapters, and supplied the others from a second catalogue, which is given at the head of each chapter throughout the work. Though no doubt the catalogue was complete in the Mavrocordato Codex, Stephen Bergler omitted to give it in the portion of the work which he supplied for the edition of Fabricius.

The headings of the separate chapters, which are in our translation given in their places and form a second catalogue, are much fuller than the introductory list, being enriched by outlines of the prophetic passages that are used.

EUSEBIUS: SON OF PAMPHILUS[1]

THE PROOF OF THE GOSPEL

BOOK I

INTRODUCTION[2]

SEE now, Theodotus,[3] miracle of bishops, holy man of
God, I am carrying through[4] this great work with the help
of God and our Saviour the Word of God, after completing
at the cost of great labour my *Preparation for the Gospel* in (2)
fifteen books.

Grant then, dear friend, my request, and labour with me
henceforward in your prayers in my effort to present the
Proof of the Gospel from the prophecies extant among
the Hebrews from the earliest times. I propose to adopt
this method. I propose to use as witnesses those men,
beloved by God, whose fame you know to be far-spread
in the world: Moses, I mean, and his successors, who (2)
shone forth with resplendent godliness, and the blessed
prophets and sacred writers. I propose to shew, by
quotations from them, how they forestalled events that
came to the light long ages after their time, the actual

---

[1] The Title: "*son* of Pamphilus" either by adoption, or E. assumed
the name from affection (G.P.E. vol. iii. p. 2). Genitive of kinship
cannot mean "friend of P."

[2] The paging in the margin is that of J. A. Fabricius, who first
edited the opening of the work (pp. 1, 4–17, 18) from the Mavrocordato
Codex; R. Stephen (1545) and the Paris edition (1628) derive from
the Paris Codex (469) which had lost the beginning of the work up to
ἡ παιδίσκη καὶ ὁ προσήλυτος (page 14 of this translation).

[3] Theodotus, Bishop of Laodicea in Syria, about A.D. 310–340: the
Praeparatio is dedicated to him. See also *H.E.* vii. 32, 23 for a
panegyric of him.

[4] ἐξανύεται. Lit., is being brought to a conclusion. The introduction was written last.

circumstances of the Saviour's own presentment of the Gospel, and the things which in our own day are being fulfilled by the Holy Spirit before our very eyes.   It shall be my task to prove that they saw that which was not

(d) present as present, and that which as yet was not in exist- ence as actually existing; and not only this, but that they foretold in writing the events of the future for posterity, so that by their help others can even now know what is coming, and look forward daily to the fulfilment of their oracles.   What sort of fulfilment, do you ask?   They are

(3) fulfilled in countless and all kinds of ways, and amid all circumstances, both generally and in minute detail, in the lives of individual men, and in their corporate life, now nationally in the course of Hebrew history, and now in that of foreign nations.   Such things as civic revolutions, changes of times, national vicissitudes, the coming of fore- told prosperity, the assaults of adversity, the enslaving of races, the besieging of cities, the downfall and restoration of whole states, and countless other things that were to take place a long time after, were foretold by these writers.

But it is not now the time for me to provide full proof of this.   I will postpone most of it for the present, and per- haps, from the truth of what I shall put before you, there will be some guarantee of the possibility of proving what is passed over in silence.

CHAPTER 1

The Object and Contents of the Work.

IT seems now time to say what I consider to be desirable at present to draw from the prophetic writings for the proof

(4) of the Gospel.   They said that Christ, (Whom they named) the Word of God, and Himself both God and Lord, and Angel of Great Counsel, would one day dwell among men, and would become for all the nations of the world, both Greek and Barbarian, a teacher of true knowledge of God, and of such duty to God the Maker of the Universe, as the preaching of the Gospel includes.   They said that He would become a little child, and would be called the Son of Man, as born of the race of Mankind.   They foretold the

wondrous fashion of His birth from a Virgin, and—strangest
of all—they did not omit to name Bethlehem [1] the place of
His birth, which is to-day so famous that men still hasten
from the ends of the earth to see it, but shouted it out
with the greatest clearness.   As if they stole a march on
history these same writers proclaimed the very time of His
appearance, the precise period of His sojourn on earth.

It is possible for you, if you care to take the trouble, to
see with your eyes, comprehended in the prophetic writings,
all the wonderful miracles of our Saviour Jesus Christ
Himself, that are witnessed to by the heavenly Gospels,
and to hear His divine and perfect teaching about true
holiness.   How it must move our wonder, when they unmis-
takably proclaim the new ideal of religion preached by
Him to all men, the call of His disciples, and the teaching
of the new Covenant.   Yes, and in addition to all this they (5)
foretell the Jews' disbelief in Him, and disputing, the plots
of the rulers, the envy of the Scribes, the treachery of one
of His disciples, the schemes of enemies, the accusations of
false witnesses, the condemnations of His judges, the shameful violence, unspeakable scourging, ill-omened abuse, and,
crowning all, the death of shame.   They portray Christ's
wonderful silence, His gentleness and fortitude, and the
unimaginable depths of His forbearance and forgiveness.

The most ancient Hebrew oracles present all these things
definitely about One Who would come in the last times, and
Who would undergo such sufferings among men, and they
clearly tell the source of their foreknowledge.   They bear
witness to the Resurrection from the dead of the Being
Whom they revealed, His appearance to His disciples, His
gift of the Holy Spirit to them, His return to heaven,
His establishment as King on His Father's throne and His
glorious second Advent yet to be at the consummation of
the age.   In addition to all this you can hear the wailings
and lamentations of each of the prophets, wailing and
lamenting characteristically over the calamities which will
overtake the Jewish people because of their impiety to
Him Who had been foretold.   How their kingdom, that (6)
had continued from the days of a remote ancestry to
their own, would be utterly destroyed after their sin against

[1] For Bethlehem as a place of pilgrimage see also 97 c (and note)
and 341 b, and Origen, *c. Cels.* i. 51.

Christ; how their fathers' Laws would be abrogated, they themselves deprived of their ancient worship, robbed of the independence of their forefathers, and made slaves of their enemies, instead of free men; how their royal metropolis would be burned with fire, their venerable and holy altar undergo the flames and extreme desolation, their city be inhabited no longer by its old possessors but by races of other stock,[1] while they would be dispersed among the Gentiles through the whole world, with never a hope of any cessation of evil, or breathing-space from troubles. And it is plain even to the blind, that what they saw and foretold is fulfilled in actual facts from the very day the Jews laid godless hands on Christ, and drew down on themselves the beginning of the train of sorrows.

But the prophecies of these inspired men did not begin and end in gloom, nor did their prescience extend no further than the reign of sorrow. They could change their note to joy, and proclaim a universal message of good tidings to all men in the coming of Christ: they could preach the good news that though one race were lost every nation and race of men would know God, escape from the dæmons,[2] (7) cease from ignorance and deceit and enjoy the light of holiness: they could picture the disciples of Christ filling the whole world with their teaching, and the preaching of their gospel introducing among all men a fresh and unknown ideal of holiness: they could see churches of Christ established by their means among all nations, and Christian people throughout the whole world bearing one common name: they could give assurance that the attacks of rulers and kings from time to time against the Church of Christ will avail nothing to cast it down, strengthened as it is by God. If so many things were proclaimed by the Hebrew divines, and if their fulfilment is so clear to us all to-day, who would not marvel at their inspiration? Who will not agree that their religious and philosophic teaching and beliefs must be sure and true, since their proof is to be found not

---

[1] ἀλλοφύλων: so Fabricius.

[2] δαιμόνων ἀποφυγήν. See Harnack: *Expansion of Christianity*. Excursus on "The Conflict with Demons." E. T. i. 152–180. For dæmons as fallen angels, heathen gods, and oracles, cf. P.E. 329. See Jewish legends, Book of Jubilees, 10 3. 6. 8; 15; 22 17; 1 Enoch 6; 15 8. 9. 11; 167; 69 2. 3; 86, 106 13. 14. e'c.

in artificial arguments, not in clever words, or deceptive syllogistic reasoning, but in simple and straightforward teaching, whose genuine and sincere character is attested by the virtue and knowledge of God evident in these inspired men? Men who were enabled not by human but by divine inspiration to see from a myriad ages back what was to (8) happen long years after, may surely claim our confidence for the belief which they taught their pupils.

Now I am quite well aware, that it is usual in the case of all who have been properly taught that our Lord and Saviour Jesus is truly the Christ of God to persuade themselves in the first place that their belief is strictly in agreement with what the prophets witness about Him. And secondly, to forewarn all those, with whom they may enter on an argument, that it is by no means easy to establish their position by definite proofs. And this is why in attacking this subject myself I must of course endeavour, with God's help, to supply a complete treatment of the Proof of the Gospel from these Hebrew theologians.[1] And the importance of my writing does not lie in the fact that it is, as might be suggested, a polemic against the Jews. Perish the thought, far from that! For if they would fairly consider it,[2] it is really on their side. For as it establishes Christianity on the basis of the antecedent prophecies, so it establishes Judaism from the complete fulfilment of its prophecies. To the Gentiles too it should appeal, if they would fairly consider it, because of the extraordinary foreknowledge shown in the prophetic (9) writers, and of the actual events that occurred in agreement with their prophecies. It should convince them of the inspired and certain nature of the truth we hold: it should silence the tongues of false accusers by a more logical method of proof, which slanderers contend that we never offer, who in their daily arguments with us keep pounding away [3] with all their might with the implication forsooth that we are unable to give a logical demonstration of our case, but require those who come to us to rest on faith alone.[4]

---

[1] πραγματείαν: so P.E., 6 d, τὴν καθόλου πραγματείαν τῆς Εὐαγγελικῆς Ἀποδείξεως, "general treatment of the Demonstration of the Gospel" : (G).

[2] εἰ εὐγνωμονοῖεν, "if they would learn wisdom." (Lightfoot.) D.C.B., art. "Eusebius," ii. 330.

[3] ἐπεντριβόμενοι.

[4] The Introduction to the *Praeparatio* deals luminously in the manner

My present work ought to have something to say to a
calumny like this, as it will assuredly rebut the empty lies
and blasphemy of godless heretics against the holy prophets
by its exposition of the agreement of the new with the old.
My argument will dispense with a longer systematic interpretation [1] of the prophecies, and will leave such a task to
any who wish to make the study, and are able to expound
such works.[2]   And I shall take as my teacher the sacred
command which says "sum up many things in few words,"
and aspire to follow it.   I shall only offer such help in
regard to the texts, and to the points which bear on the
subject under consideration, as is absolutely necessary for
their clear interpretation.

Sir. xxxii. 9.

(10)   But I will now cease my Introduction and begin my
Proof.   As we have such a mob of slanderers flooding
us with the accusation that we are unable logically to
present a clear demonstration of the truth we hold, and
think it enough to retain those who come to us by faith
alone, and as they say that we only teach our followers like
irrational animals to shut their eyes and staunchly obey what
we say without examining it at all, and call them therefore
"the faithful" because of their faith as distinct from reason,
I made a natural division of the calumnies of our position
in my "Preparation" of the subject as a whole.   On the one
side I placed the attacks of the polytheistic Gentiles, who
accuse us of apostasy from our ancestral gods, and make
a great point of the implication, that in recognizing the
Hebrew oracles we honour the work of Barbarians more

---

of Origen with the spheres of Reason and Faith (pp. 14–16).   The
charge that Christians said: "Do not examine, but only believe," and
"Thy faith shall save thee" was always advanced by the educated
heathen: e.g. *c. Cels.* i. 9; iii. 44.   Origen and Eusebius repudiated it.
Clement of Alexandria, as T. R. Glover notes, saw both sides of the
question; he could rebuke those who decried Reason (*Strom.* i. 43),
and insist on the co-operation of Faith with rational inquiry, and yet
say τὸ πιστεῦσαι μόνον καὶ ἀναγεννηθῆναι τελείωσίς ἐστιν ἐν ζωῇ (*Paed.* i.
27).   *Conflict of Religions in the Early Roman Empire*, p. 242.
Modern apologetics, while rejecting a "Credo quia impossibile," are
supported by the psychology of William James in holding that Faith in
a sense must precede Reason. (Cf. W. James, *The Will to believe*,
pp. 1–31 and 63–110: 1915.   First published 1896.)

[1] διεξοδικὴν ἑρμηνείαν, cf. P.E. 537 c, 706 d.
[2] οἷοι τ' ἂν εἶεν εἰπεῖν τὸν τρόπον.

than those of the Greeks.   And on the other side I set the
accusation of the Jews, in which they claim to be justly
incensed against us, because we do not embrace their
manner of life, though we make use of their sacred writings.
Such being the division, I met the first so far as I could in
my *Preparation for the Gospel* by allowing that we were
originally Greeks, or men of other nations who had absorbed
Greek ideas,[1] and enslaved by ancestral ties in the deceits
of polytheism.   But I went on to say that our conversion
was due not to emotional and unexamined impulse, but (11)
to judgment and sober reasoning, and that our devotion
to the oracles of the Hebrews thus had the support of
judgment and sound reason.

And now I have to defend myself against the second
class of opponents, and to embark on the investigation it
requires.   It has to do with those of the Circumcision, it
has not yet been investigated,[2] but I hope in time to dispose
of it in the present work on the Proof of the Gospel.   And
so now with an invocation of the God of Jews and Greeks
alike in our Saviour's Name we will take as our first object
of inquiry, what is the character of the religion set before
Christians.   And in this same inquiry we shall record the
solutions of all the points investigated.

CHAPTER 2

The Character of the Christian Religion.

I HAVE already laid down in my *Preparation* that Christianity is neither a form of Hellenism, nor of Judaism,
but that it is a religion with its own characteristic stamp,
and that this is not anything novel or original,[3] but something of the greatest antiquity, something natural and
familiar to the godly men before the times of Moses who (12)

---

[1] τὰ Ἑλλήνων πεφρονηκότες.

[2] *i. e.* Not in P.E., for many Apologies had already addressed the
Jews.

[3] ἐκτετοπισμένον, cf. P.E. 60 a, "to be carried out of the course."
Christianity is in the main stream of man's spiritual purpose, and is
identical with his earliest true religion.

are remembered for their holiness and justice. But now let us consider the nature of Hellenism and Judaism, and inquire under which banner we should find these pre Mosaic saints, whose godliness and holiness is attested by Moses himself. Judaism would be correctly defined as the polity constituted according to the Law of Moses, dependent on the one, omnipotent God. Hellenism you might summarily describe as the worship of many Gods according to the ancestral religions of all nations. What then would you say about the pre-Mosaic and pre-Judaic saints,[1] whose lives are recorded by Moses, Enoch for instance, of whom he says :

Gen. v. 22.　　"And Enoch pleased God."

Or Noah, of whom he says again :

Gen. vi. 9.　　"And Noah was a man righteous in his generation '

Or Seth, and Japheth, of whom he writes :

Gen. ix. 26, 27.　　"Blessed be the Lord God of Seth[2] (Shem), . . . and may God make room for Japheth."

Add to these Abraham, Isaac, and Jacob, include as is right the patriarch Job, and all the rest who lived according to the ideals of these men ; they must, you may think, have been either Jews or Greeks. But yet they could not properly be called Jews, inasmuch as the system of Moses' Law had not yet been brought into being. For if (as we have (13) admitted) Judaism is only the observance of Moses' Law, and Moses did not appear until long after the date of the men named, it is obvious that those whose holiness he records who lived before him, were not Jews. Neither can we regard them as Greeks,[3] inasmuch as they were not under the dominion of polytheistic superstition. For it is recorded of Abraham that he left his father's house and his

---

[1] This seems the best equivalent for θεοφιλής in the fathers.

[2] S. Shem, followed by " And Canaan shall be his servant." S. throughout these notes refers to Dr. Swete's edition of the Septuagint.

[3] The religious use of " Greek " for " heathen " runs back to St. Paul ; " like a born Jew and Pharisee he usually bisects humanity into circumcized and uncircumcized—the latter being described for the sake of brevity as Greeks." (Harnack, *Expansion of Christianity*, i. 304), *e. g.* 1 Cor. x. 32, Gal. iii. 28, Ephes. ii. 11. Cf. *Preaching of Peter*, ap. Clem. *Strom.* vi. 5, 41, " Worship not as the Greeks nor as the Jews." *Epistle to Diognetus*, c. 1 and c. 5. *Apology of Aristides*, c. ii. Clement of Alexandria, *Strom.* iii. 10, 70 ; v. 14, 98 ; vi. 5, 42, and Fathers generally when dealing with the Church as the " third race."

kindred altogether, and cleaved to the One God alone,
Whom he confesses when he says:

> " I will stretch out [1] (my hand) to the most-high God,
> who created the heaven and the earth."

Gen. xiv. 22.

And Jacob is recorded by Moses as saying to his house and
all his people:

> " 2. Remove the strange gods from your midst,[2] 3. and
> let us arise and go to Bethel, and make there an altar
> to the Lord that heard me in the day of affliction, who
> was with me, and preserved me in the way wherein I
> went.   4. And they gave to Jacob the strange gods, which
> were in their hands, and the ear-rings in their ears, and
> Jacob hid them under the terebinth that is in Shechem,
> and destroyed [3] them to this day."

Gen. xxxv. 2.

These men, then, were not involved in the errors of idolatry, moreover they were outside the pale of Judaism; yet,
though they were neither Jew nor Greek by birth, we know
them to have been conspicuously pious, holy, and just.
This compels us to conceive some other ideal of religion, by (14)
which they must have guided their lives.   Would not this
be exactly that third form of religion midway between
Judaism and Hellenism, which I have already deduced,
as the most ancient and most venerable of all religions,
and which has been preached of late to all nations through
our Saviour.   Christianity would therefore be not a form
of Hellenism nor of Judaism, but something between the
two, the most ancient organization for holiness, and the
most venerable philosophy, only lately codified as the law [4]
for all mankind in the whole world.   The convert from
Hellenism to Christianity does not land in Judaism, nor
does one who rejects the Jewish worship [5] become *ipso facto*
a Greek.   From whichever side they come, whether it be
Hellenism or Judaism, they find their place in that intermediate law of life preached by the godly and holy men of
old time, which our Lord and Saviour has raised up anew
after its long sleep, in accordance with Moses' own
prophecies, and those of the other prophets on the point.
Yes, Moses himself writes prophetically in the oracles

---

[1] S. adds " my hand."
[2] S. adds " be purified and change your garments."
[3] ἀπώλεσεν.   [4] νενομοθετημένη.
[5] ἐθελοθρησκείας, self-chosen worship, cf. Col. ii. 23.

addressed to Abraham, that in days to come not only
(15) Abraham's descendants, his Jewish seed, but all the tribes
and nations of the earth will be counted worthy of God's
blessing on the common basis of a piety like Abraham's.

"1. And the Lord said to Abram, Go forth out of thy
land, and from thy kindred, and from the house of thy
father, and come hither into the land which I shall
shew thee. 2. And I will make of thee a great nation,
and I will bless thee and magnify thy name, and thou
shalt be blessed, 3. and I will bless those that bless thee,
and I will curse those that curse thee, and in thee all
the tribes of the earth shall be blessed."

Gen. xii. 1.

And again God said :

"Shall I hide from Abraham my servant that I shall
do? For Abraham shall become a great and numerous
nation, and in him all the nations of the earth shall be
blessed."

Gen. xviii.
17.

How could all the nations and families of the earth be
blessed in Abraham, if there was no connection between
him and them, either of spiritual character [1] or physical
kinship? There was assuredly no physical kinship between
Abraham and the Scythians, or the Egyptians, or the
Æthiopians, or the Indians, or the Britons, or the
Spaniards: such nations and others more distant than
they could not surely hope to receive any blessing because
of any physical kinship to Abraham. It was quite as unlikely that all the nations would have any common claim to
(16) share the spiritual blessings of Abraham. For some of them [2]
practised marriage with mothers and incest with daughters,
some of them unmentionable vice. The religion of others lay
in slaughter, and the deification of animals, idols of lifeless
wood, and superstitions of deceiving spirits. Others burned
their old men alive, and commended as holy and good the
customs of delivering their dearest to the flames, or feasting
on dead bodies. Men brought up in such savage ways

---

[1] κατὰ ψυχῆς τρόπον.
[2] For a similar catalogue see P.E. 301 a, also 11 b, where G. quotes
Herodotus (i. 216) of customs of Massagetae, Strabo (513 and 520) of
the Derbices. See also Herod. iii. 38, 39. Sext. Emp. *c. Math.* xi.
192. Clem. Alex. *Paed.* i. 7. (Persian Princes.) Diog. Laert. *Proem.* 7
and ix. ii. Sext. Emp. *Hyp.* iii. 205. Cf. Zeller: *Stoics* (E.T.) 308. For
devouring parents see Origen, *c. Cels.* 2. 307 (of the Callatians).

could not surely share in the blessing of the godly, unless they escaped from their savagery; and embraced a way of life similar to the piety of Abraham. For even he, a foreigner and a stranger to the religion which he afterwards embraced, is said to have changed his life, to have cast away his ancestral superstition, to have left his home and kindred and fathers' customs, and the manner of life in which he was born and reared, and to have followed God, Who gave him the oracles which are preserved in the Scriptures.

If Moses then, who came after Abraham and established a polity for the Jewish race on the basis of the law which he gave them, had laid down the kind of laws which were the guide of godly men before his own time, and such as it was possible for all nations to adopt, so that it should be possible for all the tribes and nations of the world to worship according to Moses' enactments ; which is the (17) same as saying that the oracles foretold that through Moses' lawgiving men of all nations would worship God and follow Judaism, being brought to it by the law, and would be blessed with the blessing of Abraham—then it would have been right for us to be keeping the enactments of Moses. But if the polity of Moses was not applicable to the other nations, but only to the Jews and not to all of them, but only to the inhabitants of Judæa, then it was altogether necessary to set up another kind of religion different from the law of Moses, that all the nations of the world might take it as their guide with Abraham, and receive an equal share of blessing with him.

CHAPTER 3

That the System of Moses was not Suitable for All Nations.

THAT the enactments of Moses, as I said, were only applic- able to the Jews, but not to all of them, and certainly not to the dispersed (among the Gentiles), only in fact to the inhabitants of Palestine, will be plain to you if you reflect thus. For the law of Moses says :

(18)   " Thrice in the year shall all thy males appear before

Ex. xxiii.   the Lord thy God."

17.

And it defines more exactly at what place they should all
meet, when it says :

" Three times in the year shall thy males appear before

Ex. xxxiv.   the Lord, thy God, in the place which the Lord shall

23.   choose."

Deut. xvi.   You see that it does not bid them meet in each city, or in

16.   any indefinite place, but " in the place which the Lord thy
God shall choose." There thrice a year it enacts that they
must assemble together, and it determines the times, when
they must meet at the place where the rites of the worship
there are to be celebrated. One season is that of the
Passover, the second, fifty days later, is called the Feast of
Pentecost, and the third is in the seventh month after the
Passover, on the Day of Atonement, when all the Jews still
perform their fast. And a curse is laid on all who do not
obey what is enacted. It is plain that all who were to meet
at Jerusalem thrice in the year and perform their rites would
not be able to live far from Judæa : but they live all round
its boundaries. If then it would be impossible even for the
Jews whose home is the farthest from Palestine to obey their

(19) law, it would be absurd to hold that it could be applicable
to all nations and to men in the uttermost parts of the
earth.

Hear now in what way women after childbirth are bidden
by the same Lawgiver to go and present their offerings to
God, as follows :

" And the Lord spake to Moses, saying, Speak to the
children of Israel, and thou shalt say to them, Whatsoever
woman shall have conceived and borne a male-child shall

Lev. xii. 1.   be unclean seven days."

And he adds after saying something else :

" 6. And when the days of her purification shall have
been fulfilled for a son or a daughter, she shall bring a
lamb of a year old without blemish for a whole burnt-
offering, and a young pigeon or a turtle-dove for a
sin-offering to the door of the tabernacle of witness to
the priest, 7. she shall present [them] before the Lord.
And the priest shall make atonement for her, and shall

Lev. xii. 6.   purify her from the issue of her blood ; this is the law
of her who bears a male or a female."

Again, in addition to this the same law bids those who have contracted defilement by mourning or touching a corpse only to be purified by the ashes of an heifer, and to abstain from their accustomed work for seven days. This is what it says :

" 10. And it shall be a perpetual statute to the children of Israel and to the proselytes in the midst of them. 11. He that touches the dead body of any soul of man shall be unclean seven days, 12. shall be purified on the third day and shall be made clean on the seventh day. (20) And if he be not purified on the third day, and on the seventh day, he shall not be clean.   13. Every one who touches the dead body of a soul of a man, if he shall have died, and he be not purified, he has defiled the tabernacle of the witness of the Lord. That soul shall be cut off from Israel, because the water of cleansing has not been sprinkled on him.   He is unclean, uncleanness is on him.   14. And this is the law : if a man die in a house, everyone that goeth into that house, and all the things that are in the house, are unclean seven days.   15. And every open vessel [1] which is not bound with a fastening, shall be unclean ; 16. and every one who shall touch on the face any man slain by the sword, or a corpse, or a human bone, or a sepulchre, shall be unclean seven days. 17. And they shall take for the unclean of the burnt ashes of purification, and shall pour it into a vessel, 18, and [2] shall take hyssop.   And a clean man shall dip it, and sprinkle it on the house and the furniture and the souls that are therein, and on him that has touched the human bone, or the slain man, or the dead, or the sepulchre.   19. And the clean man shall sprinkle it on the unclean on the third day, and [3] on the seventh day, and he shall wash (21) his garments, and shall wash [his body] with water, and shall be unclean until the evening.   20. And a man, if he be defiled, and not purified, that soul shall be cast out of the congregation,[4] because the water of purification has not been sprinkled on him ; and this shall be a perpetual law to you."

Num. xix. 10.

---

[1] S. ὅσα οὐχὶ δεσμὸν καταδέδεται ἐν αὐτῷ for ὅσα οὐχὶ δεσμῷ κατα-δέδεται.

[2] S. " he shall take."   [3] S. adds " he shall be purified."

[4] S. adds " because he defiled the holy things of the Lord."

When Moses made this law he even determined the ritual of the sprinkling with water. He said that a red heifer without spot must be completely burnt, and that a portion of its ashes must be cast into the water, with which those who had been defiled by a corpse were to be purified. Where the heifer is to be burnt, where the woman is to bring her offerings after childbirth, where she is to celebrate the other rites, is not in doubt. It is not to be done indifferently in every place, but only in that place which he defines. This is plain from his enactment, when he says :

Deut. xii.
11.

"And there shall be a place, which the Lord your God shall choose, in which his name shall be called upon, there shall ye bear whatsoever I bid you to-day."

And he explains in accurate order, adding :

"13. Take heed to thyself that thou offer not thy whole burnt-offerings in any place, which thou mayst see, 14. but in the place which the Lord thy God shall choose, in one of thy cities ; there shalt thou offer thy whole burnt-offerings, and there shalt thou do whatsoever I bid you to-day."

Deut. xii.
13, 14.

And he makes this addition :

(22)

"17. Thou shalt not be able to eat in all thy cities the tenth of thy corn and wine and oil, the firstborn of thy herd and thy flock, and all thy vows whatsoever thou hast vowed, and thy thank-offerings, and the firstfruits of thine hands. 18. But before the Lord shalt thou eat it in the place which the Lord thy God shall choose for. himself, thou and thy sons and thy daughter, and thy servant, and thy maid, and the stranger [1] that is in thy cities."

(1)
Deut. xii.
17.

And proceeding he confirms the statement, where he says :

"But thou shalt take thy holy things, if thou hast any, and thy vows, and shalt come to the place, which the Lord thy God shall choose for himself."

Deut. xii.
26.

And again :

"Thou shalt tithe a tenth of all the produce of thy seed, the produce of thy field year by year. And thou

---

[1] It is at this point that the Paris Codex 469, the basis of the edition of Stephen, and the Paris edition of 1628, begins. Up to this point we are dependent on the edition of the lost Mavrocordato Codex by Fabricius and on his paging. The paging is now that of Stephen and starts here as page 1.

shalt eat it in the place which the Lord thy God shall (2)
choose to have his name called on there."

Deut. **xiv.** 22.

And then in considering what ought to be done if the
place designated by him were far off, and the yield of fruit
large, how the year's fruits for the whole burnt-offering
could be carried to the place of God, he lays down the
following law :

" 23. And if the journey be too far for thee, and thou
art not able to bring them, because the place is far from
thee, which the Lord your God shall choose to have
his name called on there, because the Lord thy God
shall bless thee ; 24. and thou shalt sell them for money,
and shalt take the money in thy hands, and shalt go to (b)
the place which the Lord thy God shall choose.
25. And thou shalt give the money for whatsoever thy
soul desireth for oxen or sheep, or wine, or strong drink,
or for whatsoever thy soul desireth and thou shalt consume it there before the Lord."

Deut. **xiv.** 23.

And he again sets his seal on the actual place, when he
says :

" 19. Every firstborn that shall be born of thy kine and
sheep, thou shalt offer the males to the Lord thy God ;
thou shalt not work with thy firstborn calf, and thou
shalt not shear thy firstborn sheep : 20. thou shalt eat it
before the Lord year by year, in the place which the (c)
Lord thy God shall choose, thou and thy house."

Deut. **xv.** 19.

Next notice how he arranges the celebration of the feasts,
not anywhere in the land, but only in the appointed place.
For he says :

"Observe the month of new corn, and thou shalt
keep the Passover to the Lord thy God,[1] sheep and
bulls, in the place which the Lord thy God shall
choose."

Deut. **xvi.** 1.

And he again reminds them, saying :

" 5. Thou shalt not be able to sacrifice the passover (d)
in any of the cities which the Lord thy God gives thee ;
6. But in the place which the Lord thy God shall
choose, to have his name called on there, thou shalt
sacrifice the passover at even at the setting of the sun

---

[1] S. adds : "Because in the month of the new corn thou camest out
of Egypt by night, and thou shalt sacrifice the Passover to the Lord
thy God."

at the time when thou camest out of Egypt. 7. And
thou shalt boil and eat [1] it in the place which the Lord
thy God shall choose."

Such, then, is the law of the Feast of the Passover.
Hear that of Pentecost:

"9. Seven weeks in full shalt thou number to thyself,
from when thou beginnest to put the sickle in the corn,[2]
10. and thou shalt keep a feast of weeks to the Lord
thy God, according as thy hand has power in whatsoever things the Lord thy God gives thee to bless
thee. 11. And thou shalt rejoice before the Lord thy
God, thou and thy son, and thy daughter, thy servant,
and thy maid, and the Levite that is in thy cities, and
the proselyte, and the orphan, and the widow that is
among you, in the place which the Lord thy God shall
choose for himself, to have his name called on there."

And hear where he commands the third feast to be
celebrated:

"13. And thou shalt keep the feast of tabernacles
when thou gatherest in from thy corn-floor and from thy
wine-press, 14. and shalt rejoice in thy feast, thou and
thy son, and thy daughter, and thy servant, and thy
maid, and the widow,[3] in the place which the Lord thy
God shall choose for himself."

As he is so insistent on the selected place, and says so
many times that they are to meet there in all their tribes
and in all their families, the law could hardly apply to
those living even a little way from Judæa, and still less
to the nations of the whole world, especially as he allows
no pardon to those who transgress his ordinances, and
invokes a curse on those who do not carry them all out to
the minutest detail, in the following words:

"Cursed is he who continueth not in all things
written in this law to do them."[4]

Consider, again, other instances of the impossibility of
all men following the law of Moses. He makes a distinction between voluntary transgressions and those hard to
evade, and after assigning penalties to sins which deserve

Deut. xvi. 5.

(3)

Deut. xvi. 9.

(b)

Deut. xvi. 13.

(c)

Deut. xxvii. 26.

---

[1] S. adds: "and roast."
[2] S. adds: "thou shalt begin to number the weeks."
[3] S. adds: "and the Levite, and the proselyte, and the orphan."
[4] S. adds: "every man" and "in all the words of this law."

the severest punishment, he provides laws by which those who sin unwittingly are to receive different treatment. One of these runs as follows:

" 27. And if a soul of the people of the land shall sin unwittingly by doing anything contrary to the commandments of the Lord that ought not to be done, and shall transgress, 28. and his sin shall be known to him, wherein he hath sinned [in it], then shall he bring [his gift] a kid of the goats, a female without blemish, he shall (d) bring it for his sin that he hath sinned [1] 29. in the place where they slay the whole burnt-offerings, 30. and the priest shall take of the blood." Lev. iv 27.

You see here how one who has sinned unintentionally is required to present himself at the place where the whole burnt-offerings are sacrificed. And this is the place the law has already so often mentioned, when it says:

"The place which the Lord thy God shall choose."

But, indeed, the Lawgiver himself perceived the impossibility for all mankind to carry out the law, and clearly noted it by not promulgating his law universally for all, but with this limitation:

"If a soul sin unwittingly of the people of the land."

And he lays down a second law which says: (4)

" And if a soul [2] hear the voice of the swearing of an oath, and he is a witness or has seen or been conscious of it, if he do not report it, he shall bear the iniquity." Lev. v. 1.

What is he to do? He is to take the victim in his hands and go with all speed to the purification. And of course that must take place where the whole-burnt-offerings are sacrificed.

And once more a third law:

" 2. The soul, it says, which shall touch any unclean thing,[3] or carcases of unclean cattle, and should take from it, he also himself is defiled and transgresses, 3. or if he touch the uncleanness of a man, and by all the uncleanness that he touches be defiled, and know it (b) not, and afterwards should know it and transgress." Lev. v. 2.

---

[1] S. adds: "and he shall lay his hand upon the head of the sin-offering (ἁμαρτήματος) and they shall slay the kid of his sin-offering."
[2] S. adds: "sin, and."
[3] S. adds: "either of a beast that has died, or one caught by wild beasts, or carcases, or unclean abominations,"

Here the only thing necessary for the polluted person is for him to go once more to the sacred place, and offer for the sin which he has sinned a female animal from his flock, a lamb or a kid of the goats, for his sin. And the law was the same in the case of a soul, which shall "swear pronouncing with his lips to do evil or to do good, whatsoever it be that a man shall pronounce with an oath, and it be hid from him ; and when he knoweth of it and is guilty in one of those things, and shall confess the sin that he hath sinned :" he too, the law says, taking the same offering, is to go with all speed to the sacred place, and the priest is to pray on his behalf for the sin, and his sin shall be forgiven. And another law besides those I have quoted makes this provision :

Lev. v. 4, 5, 6.

"The soul which shall be really unconscious, and shall sin unwittingly in any of the holy things of the Lord, even he shall bear a ram for his transgression to the Lord. [And he shall bear it again to the high-priest to the place, that is to say the chosen place."[1]

Lev. v. 15.

And he adds a sixth law in these words :

(d)

"And the soul which shall sin and do one thing against the commandments of the Lord, which it is not right to do, and hath not known it, and shall have transgressed and contracted guilt, he shall even bring a ram[2] to the High Priest, and the priest shall make atonement for his trespass of ignorance, and he knew it not, and it shall be forgiven him."

Lev. v. 17.

The following is a seventh law :

" 2. The soul which shall have sinned and surely over-looked the commandments of the Lord, and shall deal falsely in the affairs of his neighbour in the matter of a deposit, or concerning association (in business), or plunder, or has in any way wronged his neighbour, 3. or has found that which was lost, and has lied concerning it, and shall have sworn unjustly concerning any one of all the things, whatsoever a man may do, so as to sin thereby ; 4. it shall come to pass, whenever he so hath sinned and transgressed, that he shall restore the plunder he has seized, or redress the injustice he has

---

[1] A paraphrase of S. text.

[2] S. adds : "without blemish from the sheep of the price of the money for his trespass," and has "priest" for "high-priest,"

committed, or restore the deposit which was entrusted
to him, 5. or the lost article he has found of any kind, (5)
about which he swore unjustly, he shall even restore it
in full, and shall add to it the fifth part." Lev. vi. 2.

Here, again, after confession and reparation the transgressor had to go with all speed, putting everything else on
one side, to the place, which the Lord our God should
choose, and offer for his sin an unblemished ram, and the
priest was to pray for him before the Lord, and he would
be forgiven. (b)

In this careful way our wonderful Moses distinguished
sins done unwittingly and ignorantly from intentional
offences, on which in the government of his people he set
rigorous penalties. For he that would not pardon the
unwitting offender before he had confessed his offence,
exacted a small penalty from him in the sacrifice ordained,
by requiring him to repair with all speed to the sacred (c)
place fostered both the religious spirit and watchfulness of
those who worshipped God by his rule, and of course restrained even more the desires of willing offenders. What,
then, must be our conclusion from all this, when, as we have
said, we find Moses summing up his whole system with a
curse, where he says:

[1] " Cursed is everyone, who shall not remain in all the Deut.
things written in this law, to do them "? xxvii. 26.

Was it, then, meant that Moses' future disciples from the
ends of the earth must do all these things, if they were to
escape the curse and receive the blessing promised to
Abraham? Were they to go thrice a year to Jerusalem, (d)
and were the female worshippers of all nations, fresh from
the pangs of childbirth, to undertake so long a journey, to
offer the sacrifice ordained by Moses for each one of their
children? Were those who had touched a dead body, or
had forsworn themselves, or had sinned against their will,
to come from the ends of the earth, to run and hasten
to the purification that was required by the law, in order
to escape the visitation of the curse? Of course it is clear
to you that it was hard enough to follow Moses' rule of
life for those who lived round Jerusalem, or only inhabited
Judæa, and that it was quite out of the question for the

[1] R.V. "confirmeth not the words of this law to do them."
Cf. Gal. iii. 10.

other nations to fulfil it.   Hence, of course, our Lord and
Saviour, Jesus the Son of God, said to His disciples after
His Resurrection :

(6)   "Go and make disciples of all the nations," and
added :
        " Teaching them to observe all things, whatsoever I
have commanded you." [1]

For He did not bid them to teach the laws of Moses to
all nations, but whatsoever He Himself had commanded :
that is to say, the contents of the Gospels.   And agreeably
to this His disciples and apostles in considering the requirements of the Gentiles decided that Moses' enactments were
unsuitable to their needs, since neither they themselves nor
their fathers had found them easy to be kept.   As St. Peter
(b) says in the Acts :
        "Now therefore why do ye attempt to lay a yoke

Acts xv.   upon the necks of the disciples, which neither our
10.   fathers nor we were able to bear ? "

And agreeably to this Moses himself for this very reason
said that another prophet would be raised up "like unto
him"; and publishes the good news that he should be a
lawgiver for all the nations.   He speaks of Christ in a
riddle.   He orders his followers to obey him in these
prophetic words.

(c)   "15. A prophet shall the Lord your God raise up to
you from your brethren, like unto me, ye shall hear
him [whatsoever he saith unto you].   19. And it shall

---

[1] Matt. xxviii. 19.   The verse is quoted thus seven times in the
Demonstratio with the omission of the reference to Baptism and the
Trinity.   Conybeare (*Hibbert Journal*, i. (1902–3) p. 102), who holds
that the reference was interpolated for dogmatic reasons, and was not
fully assured in the text till after the Council of Nicæa, supports his
view from the practice of Eusebius.   This is the view of Kirsopp
Lake, *E.R.E.* ii. 380 and Moffatt, *The Historical New Test.* 1901,
p. 647.   The historicity of the words as *ipsissima verba* is denied by
Harnack, Clemen, and J. A. Robinson, *Enc. Bibl.*, art. "Baptism."
From the Acts taken literally it would be gathered that apostolic
Baptism was simply in the Name of Jesus.—(Acts viii. 12–16 ; ix. 18 ;
xxii. 16, etc.)
  But the threefold formula occurs in the *Didache*, ch. vii., and is
supported by Justin Martyr, *Apol.* i. 61 and Irenæus, who, however,
bases it not on Matt. xxviii. 19, but on tradition. (A. Harnack, *History
of Dogma*, ii. 22.)   The textual authority of the text as it stands is
unassailable, and the problem is to reconcile it with the statements
in Acts.

be that every soul who will not hear that prophet shall Deut.
be cast out of its race." [1]   xviii. 15,

And that this prophet, who is clearly the Christ, should [19.]
come forth from the Jews and rule all nations, he proclaims
again when he says :

" 5. How fair are thy dwellings, O Jacob, and thy (d)
tents, O Israel, 6. as shady groves, and as a garden by
a river, and as tents which God pitched.[2] 7. There
shall come a man out of his seed, and he shall rule Num.
over many nations,[3] and his kingdom shall be exalted." xxiv. 5.

He makes it clear from which tribe of all the twelve
that comprised the Hebrew race, namely the tribe of
Judah, Christ the Lawgiver of the Gentiles according to
the prophecy should arise. He is clear as to the date, for
it would be after the cessation of the Jewish monarchy
which had been handed down from their forefathers.

"A ruler shall not fail from Juda, nor a prince from
his loins, until there come the things stored up for
him ; and he is the expectation of the nations." [4]

What "expectation" could this be, but that expressed in
the promise to Abraham that in him all the families of
the earth should be blessed? Moses has, therefore, made

---

[1] S. : "And the man who will not hear whatsoever that prophet
speaks in my name, I will judge him" (19). Verse 18 is "I will raise
up a prophet to them of their brethren like unto thee, and I will give
my words into his mouth, and he shall speak to them as I command
him."

[2] S. adds : "as cedars by the waters."

[3] S. adds : καὶ ὑψωθήσεται ἢ Γὼγ βασιλεία—R.V. "His king shall
be higher than Agag."

[4] Here E. quotes τὰ ἀποκείμενα αὐτῷ, the text accepted by Swete, but
pp. 50 c, 95 c, and 332 d, he quotes from another text ᾧ ἀπόκειται,
which he says (332 d) in Hebrew is Σιλωάμ or "sent." τὰ ἀποκειμένα
αὐτῷ, the reading of G. and Theodotion = "that which is his," and is
adopted with hesitation by Driver, as the meaning of the Hebrew.
ᾧ ἀπόκειται = "whose it is" was adopted by Justin, Ap. i. 32, supplying τὸ βασίλειον, and Trypho, cxx., Iren. iv. x. 2, and by Origen(often) :
also by Onkelos, and the Peshitta. This rendering is adopted by Gunkel.
    A.V. translates, "Until Shiloh come," R.V. (margin), "Till he
come to Shiloh," noticing the two LXX renderings ; and this rendering
is accepted in default of a better, by Delitzsch, Dillman, and S.
Davidson. There are many other suggestions, including Wellhausen's
"that the verse denotes an ideal limit of time, the coming of the
Messiah, and presupposes the Davidic monarchy."
    (H.D.B. iv. 501, A. S. Aglen. See also S. Davidson, Introd. to
O.T., vol. i.)

it quite plain from his own words that he was quite well
(7) aware of the failure of the law he had laid down to apply
to all nations, and that another prophet would be necessary
for the fulfilment of the oracles given to Abraham.   And
this was He, of Whom his prophecy proclaimed the good
news that one should arise from the tribe of Judah and
rule all nations.

CHAPTER 4

*Why it is we reject the Jews' Way of Life, though we
accept their Writings.*

THESE, then, are the reasons why we have accepted and
loved as belonging to ourselves the sacred books of the
Hebrews, including as they do prophecies relating to us
Gentiles.   And the more so, since it was not Moses only
who foretold the coming of the Lawgiver of the Gentiles
(c) after him, but really the whole succession of the prophets,
who proclaimed the same truth with one voice, as David,
when he said :
     " Appoint, O Lord, a Lawgiver over them : let the
Ps. ix. 20.   nations know that they are but men."
See how he too speaks of a second Lawgiver of the nations.
And in the same spirit in another [1] (psalm) he calls on the
Gentiles to sing, not the ancient song of Moses, but a new
song, when he says :
     " 1. Sing to the Lord a new song ; | sing to the
Lord all the whole earth : | 3. proclaim among the
nations his glory, | among all peoples his wonders : |
4. For great is the Lord, and very worthy to be
(d)   praised, | he is terrible above all gods. | 5. For all
the gods of the nations are demons, | but it is the
Lord that made the heavens. | 7. Bring to the Lord
ye families of the nations ; | 8. bring to the Lord glory
Ps. xcv. 1.   to his name."
  And again :
     " 10. Say among the nations, The Lord is King. |

---

[1] ἐν ἑτέρῳ ψαλμῷ.   Paris Codex.

For he has established the world, that it shall not be shaken."

And again :

Ps. xcv. 10.

" 1. Sing to the Lord a new song, | for he hath done marvellous things, | 2. The Lord hath made known his salvation; | Before the nations he hath revealed righteousness. | 3. All the ends of the earth have seen the salvation of our God."[1]

Ps. xcviii. 1.

And notice how he ordains the new song not for the Jewish race only; the ancient song of Moses suited them, but for all the nations. This new song is called by Jeremiah, another Hebrew prophet, "a new covenant" where he says :

(8)

" 31. Behold the days come, saith the Lord, when I will make a new covenant with the house of Israel, and with the house of Juda : 32. not according to the covenant that I made with their fathers, in the day that I took them by the hand to lead them out of the land of Egypt: for they abode not in my covenant, and I disregarded them, saith the Lord. 33. For this is my, covenant which I will make with the house of Israel,[2] saith the Lord, I will put my laws[3] in their minds, and on their hearts I will write (them), and I will be their God, and they shall be my people."

(b)

Jer. xxxi. 31.

You see here that he distinguishes two covenants, the old and the new, and says that the new would not be like the old which was given to the fathers. For the old covenant was given as a law to the Jews, when they had fallen from the religion of their forefathers, and had embraced the manners and life of the Egyptians, and had declined to the errors of polytheism, and the idolatrous superstitions of the Gentiles. It was intended to raise up the fallen, and to set on their feet those who were lying on their faces, by suitable teaching.

(c)

"For the law, it is said, is not for the righteous, but for the unjust[4] and disorderly, for the unrighteous and for sinners, and for those like them."

I Tim. i. 9.

But the new covenant leads those who, through our Saviour

---

[1] E. shortens the passage considerably.
[2] E. omits "after these days."　　　[3] E. omits "I will give."
[4] W.H.: δικαίῳ νόμος οὐ κεῖται.　E.: δικαίοις γὰρ, φησὶ, νόμος οὐ κεῖται . . . καὶ τοῖς παραπλησίοις.

by the grace and gift of God are raised up, to a rapid
march into the kingdom promised by God.   It summons
all men equally to share together the same good things.
This "new covenant" Isaiah, another of the Hebrew
prophets, calls the "new law," when he says:

(d)   "3. For out of Sion shall go forth a law, and the
word of the Lord from Jerusalem.   And all the nations
shall go, and all the peoples shall be gathered together,
and [1] shall say, Let us go up to the Mount of the Lord,
Isa. ii. 3.   and to the house of the God of Jacob."

This law going forth from Sion, different from the law
enacted in the desert by Moses on Mount Sinai, what can
it be but the word of the Gospel, "going forth from Sion"
through our Saviour Jesus Christ, and going through all
the nations?   For it is plain that it was in Jerusalem and

(9) Mount Sion adjacent thereto, where our Lord and Saviour
for the most part lived and taught, that the law of the
new covenant began and from thence went forth and shone
upon all, according to the commands which He gave his
disciples when He said:

"Go ye, and make disciples of all the nations,
teaching them to observe all things, whatsoever I have
commanded you."

What could He mean but the teaching and discipline of
the new covenant?   Since, then, I have proved my facts,
let us proceed to investigate together the character of the
new covenant, and the new song and the new law that
were foretold.

(b)   CHAPTER 5

The Character of the New Covenant of Christ.

I HAVE now proved that the old covenant and the law
given by Moses was only applicable to the Jewish race, and
only to such of them as lived in their own land.   It did
(c) not apply to other nations of the world nor to Jews

---

[1] E. gives latter half, ἐκ γὰρ Σιὼν . . . ʼΙερουσαλήμ first, and first
half last, καὶ ἥξουσι . . . . . . ʼΙακώβ.

inhabiting foreign soil. And I have shown that the ideal of the new covenant must be helpful to the life of all nations : the members of its kingdom are to be restricted in no way whatever. Considerations of country, race or locality, or anything else are not to affect them in any way at all. The law and life of our Saviour Jesus Christ shows itself to be such, being a renewal of the ancient pre-Mosaic religion, in which Abraham, the friend of God, and (d) his forefathers are shown to have lived. And if you cared to compare the life of Christians and the worship introduced among all nations by Christ with the lives of the men who with Abraham are witnessed to by Scripture as holy and righteous, you would find cne and the same ideal. For they too turned their backs on the errors of polytheism, they relinquished idolatrous superstition, they looked beyond [1] the whole of the visible creation and deified neither sun nor moon, nor any part of the whole. They raised themselves to the Supreme God, Himself the Highest, the Creator of heaven and earth. And Moses himself bears (10) this out in his history of ancient times when he records Abraham's saying :

"I will stretch forth my hand unto God most high, who hath created the heaven and the earth." Gen. xiv. 22.

And when, before this, he introduces Melchizedek, whom he calls the priest of the Most High God, blessing Abraham as follows :

"Blessed be Abraham by God most high, who hath created the heaven and the earth." Gen. xiv. 19.

And you would find that Enoch and Noah were reckoned (b) just and well-pleasing to God in the same way as Abraham. Job, too, a just, true, blameless, devout man, averse from everything evil, is recorded as pre-Mosaic.[2] He underwent a

[1] ὑπερκύψαντες : " to bend, stretch and peep over " : cf. P.E. 17 A., περκύψαντες τὸ ὁρώμενον.

[2] The postscript to 𝕲. text confounds Job with Jobab, king of Edom (Gen. xxxvi. 33). The statement, which is not found in Aquila or Symmachus, and only partly in Theodotion, runs as follows : " This man is described in the Syriac book as living in the land of Ausis, on the borders of Idumæa and Arabia ; and his name before was Jobab, and having taken a wife from Arabia, he begat a son whose name was Ennom." (H.D.B., art. " Job," cf. Enc. Bib., Book of Job). Jobab is the second in the list of eight Edomite kings who reigned " before there reigned any king over the children of Israel " (lcc. cit. v. 30), i.e. up to date of Saul.

trial of his utter devotion to the God of the Universe when he lost everything he had, and left the greatest example of holiness to posterity, when he spoke these philosophic words:

(c)   " 21. I myself came forth naked from my mother's womb, and naked shall I depart. The Lord gave, the Lord hath taken away. As the Lord pleased, so it came

Job i. 21.   to pass. Blessed be the name of the Lord."

That he said this as a worshipper of the God of the universe is made quite clear when he goes on to say:

" 4. For he is wise in mind and mighty and great;[1] 6. Who shakes the (earth) under heaven from its foundation and its pillars totter. 7. Who commands the sun and it rises not, and he seals up the stars;[2]

Job ix. 4.   8. Who alone has stretched out the heaven."

If then the teaching of Christ has bidden all nations now to worship no other God but Him whom the men of

(d) old and the pre-Mosaic saints believed in, we are clearly partakers of the religion of these men of old time. And if we partake of their religion we shall surely share their blessing. Yes, and equally with us they knew and bore witness to the Word of God, Whom we love to call Christ. They were thought worthy in very remarkable ways of beholding His actual presence and theophany.

Remember how Moses calls the Being, Who appeared to the patriarchs, and often delivered to them the oracles afterwards written down in Scripture[3] sometimes God and Lord, and sometimes the Angel of the Lord. He clearly implies that this was not the Omnipotent God, but a secondary

(b) Being,[4] rightly called the God and Lord of holy men, but

(11) the Angel of the Most High His Father. Thus he says:

" 10. And Jacob went forth[5] . . . to Charran, 11. and came to a certain place, and he slept there. . . . And he

---

[1] S. adds: τίς σχληρὸς γενόμενος ἐναντίον αὐτοῦ ὑπέμεινεν; ὁ παλαιῶν ὄρη, οὐκ οἴδασιν, ὁ καταστρέφων αὐτὰ ὀργῇ.

[2] S. adds: κατὰ δὲ ἀγγέλων αὐτοῦ σκόλιόν τι ἐπενόησεν.

[3] χρηματίσματα τὰ ἀναγεγραμμένα. The Greek means that the oracle was given verbally and written down afterwards. It need not imply a transcription before that of Moses.

[4] ἀλλά τις δεύτερος, θεός μὲν καὶ κύριος τῶν θεοφιλῶν ἀνδρῶν ἀνηγορευμένος: one of the "Arian" passages: cf. 227 d and δευτέρα μετὰ τὸν Πατέρα οὐσία, 257 a. See Introduction, p. xxvi.

[5] S. adds: "from the well of the oath."

took of the stones of the place, and put it at his head, and
lay down to sleep in that place, 12. and he dreamed : and
behold, a ladder fixed on the earth whose top reached
to heaven, and the angels of God ascended and
descended on it.   13. And the Lord stood upon it, and
said, I [1] am the God of Abraham thy father, and the God
of Isaac : fear not, the earth, the land on which thou (b)
liest, to thee will I give it, and to thy seed : 14 and Gen.
thy seed shall be as the sand of the earth."   xxviii. 10.
To which he adds :

"16. And Jacob arose in the morning, and took the
stone, which he had put under his head, and set it up Gen.
as a pillar."   xxviii. 16
Then further on he calls this God and Lord Who
appeared to him the Angel of God.   For Jacob says :

"11. For the Angel of God said to me in a dream, Gen.
Jacob.[2]   And I said, What is it ? "   xxxi. 11.
And then :

"12. I have seen, he says, all that Laban does to thee.
I am the God that was seen by thee in the place of (c)
God, where thou anointedst for me there a pillar, and Gen. xxxi.
thou vowedst to me there a vow."   12.
This same being who appeared to Abraham is called
Lord and God.   He teaches the saint mysteriously of His
Father's rule,[3] and speaks some things, as it were, of
another God, which I will examine in their place.   Then,
again, it is impious [4] to suppose that the Being who
answered Job after his severe trial [5] was the same.   For
when He shows Himself first in the whirlwind and the
clouds He reveals Himself as the God of the Universe, but
He goes on to reveal Himself in a way which makes Job
say :

"4. Hear me, O Lord, and I will speak.[6]   5. I heard (d)
of thee before by the hearing of the ears, but now mine
eye hath seen thee.'   Job xlii. 4.
And if it is not possible for the Most High God,[7] the

---

[1] S. adds : "the Lord."   [2] S. repeats "Jacob."
[3] αὐθεντίας, cf. P.E. 314 A., ἀνθρώποις αὐθέντην νόμων εἶναι καὶ κύριον.
[4] Paris Codex omits οὐ.
[5] μετὰ τὴν αὐτάρκη διαγυμνασίαν : so of *virtue*, Ar., *Eth.* i. 7. 6.
[6] S. adds : "I will ask Thee, and do Thou tell me."
[7] τὸν ἐπέκεινα Θεοῦ.

Job xlii. 4. Invisible, the Uncreated, and the Omnipotent to be said to be seen in mortal form, the Being Who was seen must have been the Word of God, Whom we call Lord as we do the Father. But it is needless for me to labour the point, since it is possible to find instances in Holy Scripture. These I will collect at leisure in connection with my present work [1] to prove that He Who was seen by the patriarchal saints was none other than the Word of God.

(12)   Therefore besides the conception of the Creator of the Universe, we and they have inherited also the conception of Christ in common. Hence you can find instances of the pre-Mosaic saints being called " Christs," just as we are called Christians. Hear what the oracle in the Psalms says about them :

" 12. When they were few in numbers, very few, and strangers in the land, 13. and they went from nation to nation, from (one) kingdom to another people : 14. He suffered no man to wrong them, and he reproved kings for their sakes, saying : 15. ' Touch not my Christs, and do no evil to my prophets.' "

Ps. cv. 12.

(b) The whole context shows that this must be referred to Abraham, Isaac, and Jacob : they therefore shared the name of Christ with us.

CHAPTER 6

The Nature of the Life according to the New Covenant proclaimed to All Men by Christ.

(c) JUST as a life of virtue and a system of holiness is through the teaching of Christ preached to all nations without any reference to the Mosaic legislation, so by these men of old time the same independent ideal of holiness was upheld. They cared nothing for circumcision, nor do we. They did not abstain from eating certain beasts, neither do we. For instance, Moses introduces Melchizedek, priest of the Most High God, uncircumcised, not anointed with prepared

[1] ὑπόθ:σιν.

ointment according to Moses, knowing naught of the Sabbath, paying no heed whatever to the commandments afterwards given by Moses to the whole Jewish race, but living exactly according to the Gospel of Christ. And yet Moses says he was the priest of the Most High God, and the superior of Abraham. For he is introduced as blessing Abraham. Such too was Noah, a just man in his (13) generation, whom as a kindling seed [1] of the human race Almighty God preserved in the destruction by the flood when all men on earth were destroyed. He again was quite ignorant of Jewish customs, he was uncircumcised, he did not follow the Mosaic law in any point, yet he is recognized as conspicuously just. And Enoch before him, who is said to have pleased God, and to have been translated, so that his death was not seen, was another like person, uncircumcised, with no part or lot in the law of Moses, living a distinctly Christian rather than a Jewish life.   (b)

And Abraham himself, coming later than those already named, being younger than they according to the age men reached in those times, though an old man in reality, was the first to receive circumcision as a seal, for the sake of his descendants, and he left it to those who should be born of him according to the flesh as a sign of their descent from him. He too before he had a son, and before he was circumcised, by his rejection of idolatry, and his confession of the one omnipotent God, yea, by his virtuous life alone is shown to be one who lived as a Christian, not as a Jew. For he is represented as having kept the commandments (c) and the precepts and the ordinances of God before the enactments of Moses. That is why God giving the oracle to Isaac says :

"And I will give to thy seed all this land, and in thy seed shall all the nations of the earth be blessed. Because Abraham thy father heard my voice, and kept (d) my commandments, and my laws, and my judgments, Gen. xxvi. and my statutes."   4.

So there were before the Mosaic law other commandments of God, and ordinances not like those of Moses, other laws and precepts of Christ, by which they were justified. Moses

---

[1] ζώπυρον σπέρμα, "kindling." Cf. Philostratus, 42. So Plato, Legg. 677 B. speaks of survivors of the Flood as σμικρὰ ζώπυρα τοῦ τῶν ἀνθρώπων γένους.

clearly shews that these were not the same as his own enactments, when he says to the people:

> "Hear, Israel, the ordinances and the judgments, all that I speak in your ears this day, and ye shall learn them, and observe to do them. The Lord your God made a covenant with you in Choreb; the Lord did not make this covenant with your fathers, but with you."

(14)
Deut. v. 1.

See how distinctly he alludes to this covenant, when he says God did not give the same covenant to their fathers. For if he had said that absolutely no covenant was given to their fathers it would have been a false statement. For Holy Scripture testifies that a covenant of some kind was given both to Abraham and Noah. And so Moses adds that one "not the same" was given to their fathers, implying that other greater and glorious covenant, by which they (b) were shown forth as friends of God. So Moses records that Abraham by his faith in Almighty God attained righteousness when he says:

> "Abraham believed in God, and it was counted unto him for righteousness."

Gen. xv. 6.

This text shews clearly that he received the sign of circumcision after his attainment of righteousness, and after the witness to his holiness, and that this added nothing at all to his justification.

Again, you would find Joseph in pre-Mosaic times in the palaces of the Egyptians living in freedom not burdened (c) by Judaism. Moses himself, the leader and lawgiver of the Jews, lived from his babyhood with the daughter of the King of Egypt, and partook of the Egyptian food without question. What is to be said of Job the thrice-blessed, the true, the blameless, the just, the holy, what was the cause of his holiness and justice, was it Moses' commandments? Certainly not. Was it the keeping of the Sabbath, (d) or any other Jewish observance? How could that be, if Job was earlier than the time of Moses and his legislation? For Moses was seventh from Abraham, and Job fifth, preceding him by two generations.[1] And if you regard his life, you will see it was untouched by the Mosaic legislation, but not foreign to the teaching of our Saviour. Thus in reviewing his life in his apology to his friends he says:

[1] See note p. 25.

" 12. For I saved the poor from the hand of the powerful, and I helped the orphan who had no helper.[1] The mouth of the widow blessed me, 14. and I was clad in righteousness. I put on judgment as a cloak, 15. an eye was I to the blind, a foot to the lame, 16. I was a father of the weak." Job xxix. 12. (15)

This surely is exactly the same teaching which is preached to us all in the Gospel. Then again as one well acquainted with the words, "Weep with those that weep,"[2] and "Blessed are they that weep, for they shall laugh"; and "If one member suffer, all the members suffer with it," which are included in the Gospel teaching, he shews his sympathy for the miserable by saying: Rom. xii. 15; Luke vi. 21; 1 Cor. xii. 26 (b)

" 25. And I wept for every weak one—I groaned when I saw a man in difficulties." Job xxx. 25.

Then, again, this holy man forestalls the Gospel teaching, which forbids unseemly laughter, when he says:

" 5. But if I had gone with scorners, and if my foot has hasted to deceit. 6. For I am weighed in a just balance, and the Lord knows my innocence." Job xxxi. 5.

And where the Mosaic law says "Thou shalt not commit adultery," and assigns death as the punishment of adulterers, He who draws out the law of the Gospel teaching, says: "It was said to them of old time, Thou shalt not commit adultery; but I say unto you,[3] thou shalt not desire at all." Matt. v. 27. (c)

Look well at the man of whom we are speaking; he was so good a Christian in his life that he restrained even his looks when they were wayward, and made it his boast so to do— for he says:

" 9. And if my heart has followed my eye for the wife of another man."[4] Job xxxi. 9.

And he gives the reason, as he continues:

" 11. For the spirit[5] of a man is not to be stayed, in the case of defiling another man's wife. 12. For it is a fire burning on every side, and where it enters, it utterly destroys." Job xxxi 11.

---

[1] S. adds: εὐλογία ἀπολλυμένου ἐπ᾽ ἐμὲ ἔλθοι.

[2] E. ὅτι γελάσονται ; W.H. ὅτι γελάσετε.

[3] E. has μηδὲ τὴν ἀρχὴν ἐπιθυμεῖν for ὅτι πᾶς ὁ βλέπων γυναῖκα πρὸς τὸ ἐπιθυμῆσαι [αὐτήν].—W.H.

[4] S. has εἰ ἐξηκολούθησεν ἡ καρδία μου. . . E. εἰ δὲ καὶ τῷ ὀφθαλμῷ ἐπηκολούθησεν ἡ καρδία. . .

[5] S.: ὀργῆς. E.: ἀνδρὸς.

Here he shows his incorruptibility :

> "7. If, too, I have touched gifts with my hands;
> 8. then let me sow, and others eat, and let me be
> uprooted from the earth."

Job xxxi.
7.

(d) How he treated his servants we may learn from his teaching here :

> "13. And if I have trifled with the cause of my
> servant, or handmaiden, when they pleaded with me."

Job xxxi.
13.

And again he gives the reason :

> "14. What, then, should I do, if the Lord should try
> me? . . . 15. Were not they also formed as I was in
> the womb? Yea, we were formed in the same womb."

Job xxxi.
14.

He adds :

> "16. I did not cause the eye of the widow to fail.
> 17. And if I did eat my morsel alone, and did not share
> it with the orphan,[1] . . . 19. and if I saw the naked
> perishing, and did not clothe him."

Job xxxi.
16.

And again he proceeds :

> "24. And if I trusted in a precious stone, 25. and if
> I rejoiced when my wealth was great, and if I laid my
> hand on unnumbered (treasures)."

Job xxxi.
24.

And again he gives the reason :

(16)
Job xxxi.
26.

> "26. Do we not see the sun waxing and waning, and
> the moon eclipsed?"

So, again, whereas the teaching of the Gospel says :

> "43. It was said to them of old time,[2] Thou shalt
> love thy neighbour and hate thine enemy. But I say
> unto you, Love your enemies": Job wonderfully antici-
> pating the command by his own original teaching
> actually carried it out, for he says :

Matt. v.
43.

> "29. And if I, too, was glad at the fall of my enemies,
> and said in my· heart, It is well—30. then let my ear
> hear my curse."

(b)
Job xxxi.
29.

And he adds :

> "But the stranger did not remain outside, and my
> door was opened to all that came,"

Job xxxi.
32.

showing himself no stranger in spirit to Him, who said,
"I was a stranger, and ye took me in." Then hear what
he says about offences done unintentionally :

Matt. xxv.
35.

---

[1] E. omits v. 18. S. has ὑπερεῖδον for εἶδον.
[2] W.H.: ἠκούσατε ὅτι ἐρρέθη. E.: ἐρρέθη τοῖς ἀρχαίοις.

"33. Or if, too, having sinned unintentionally, I hid Job xxxi.
my sin.   34. For I did not stand in awe of a great 33.
multitude, so as not to speak boldly before them.   And
if I did not let the poor depart (from my door) with an
empty bosom . . .   35. And if I had not feared the
hand of the Lord.   And as to the written charge which
I had against any . . .   37. I did not rend it and (c)
return it, taking nothing from the debtor."

So and in such ways the pre-Mosaic saints (for from
the record of one we may imagine the life of all), waged
their renowned contests for good, and were reckoned friends
of God, and prophets.   What need had they of the commandments of Moses, which were given to weak and sinful
men?   From all this it is abundantly proved that the Word (d)
of God announced to all nations the ancient form of their
ancestors' religion, as the new covenant does not differ
from the form of holiness, which was very ancient even in
the time of Moses, so that it is at the same time both old
and new.   It is, as I have shown, very, very old; and, on
the other hand, it is new through having been as it were
hidden away from men through a long period between, and
now come to life again by the Saviour's teaching.

And it was in this intermediate period, while the ideal of
the new covenant was hidden from men, and as it were
asleep, that the law of Moses was interposed[1] in the interval.
It was like a nurse[2] and governess of childish and imperfect
souls.   It was like a doctor to heal the whole Jewish race, (17)
worn away by the terrible disease of Egypt.   As such it
offered a lower and less perfect way of life to the children
of Abraham, who were too weak to follow in the steps of
their forefathers.   For through their long sojourn in Egypt,
after the death of their godly forefathers, they adopted
Egyptian customs,[3] and, as I said, fell into idolatrous superstition.   They aimed no higher than the Egyptians, they
became in all respects like them, both in worshipping idols,

---

[1] παρεισελθών, "coming in beside" with idea of stealth. Cf. Rom.
v. 20, "came into the side of a state of things already existing."
San lay and Headlam, ad loc.

[2] Cf. Gal. iii. 24.

[3] ταῖς Αἰγυπτιακαῖς ὁμοιοτροπία,s. Cf. P.E. 305 B. ἀποφύγην τε
τῶν φαυλῶν ὁμοτροπίας, and ib. 312, c. 6; also Strabo 21, Herod
(ὁμότροπος) ii. 49, viii. 144.   Gaisford, "Hoc est idolatria." Cf. p. 8 b,
βίον Αἰγυπτιακόν, and above, Αἰγυπτιακὴ νόσος.

(b) and in other matters. Moses tore them from their godless
polytheism, he led them back to God, the Creator of all
things ; he drew them up as it were from an abyss of evil,
but it was natural for him to build first this step of holiness
at the threshold and entrance of the Temple of the more
Perfect.   Therefore he forbade them to murder, to commit
adultery, to steal, to swear falsely, to work uncleanness, to
lie with mother, sister or daughter, to do many actions
(c) which till then they had done without restraint.   He rescued
them from their wild and savage life, and gave them a
polity based on better reason and good law as the times
went, and was the first lawgiver to codify his enactments in
writing,[1] a practice which was not yet known to all men.   He
dealt with them as imperfect, and when he forbade idolatry,
he commanded them to worship the One Omnipotent God
by sacrifices and bodily ceremonies.   He enacted that they
should conduct by certain mystic symbols the ritual that he
ordained, which the Holy Spirit taught him in a wonderful
(d) way was only to be temporary : he drew a circle round one
place and forbade them to celebrate his ordinances anywhere, except in one place alone, namely at the Temple in
Jerusalem, and never outside it.   And to this day it is
forbidden for the children of the Hebrews outside the
boundaries of their ruined mother-city to sacrifice according
to the law, to build a temple or an altar, to anoint kings or
priests, to celebrate the Mosaic gatherings and feasts,[2] to be
cleansed from pollution, to be loosed from offences, to bear
gifts to God, or to propitiate Him according to the legal
requirements.

     And therefore, of course, they have fallen under Moses'
(18) curse, attempting to keep it in part, but breaking it in the
whole, as Moses makes absolutely clear :

Deut.   " Accursed is he, who does not continue in all the
xxvii. 26.   things written in this law, to do them."

And they have come to this *impasse*, although Moses himself foresaw by the Holy Spirit, that, when the new covenant
was revived by Christ and preached to all nations, his own
legislation would become superfluous, he rightly confined
its influence to one place, so that if they were ever deprived

---

[1] Cf. P. E. 305, where similar stress is laid on Moses committing
laws to writing.
[2] πανηγύρεις καὶ ἑορτὰς.

of it, and shut out of their national freedom, it might not (b) be possible for them to carry out the ordinances of his law in a foreign country, and as of necessity they would have to receive the new covenant announced by Christ. Moses had foretold this very thing, and in due course Christ sojourned in this life, and the teaching of the new covenant was borne to all nations, and at once[1] the Romans besieged Jerusalem, and destroyed it and the Temple there. At once the whole of the Mosaic law was abolished, with all (c) that remained of the old covenant, and the curse passed over to those who became lawbreakers, because they obeyed Moses' law, when its time had gone by, and still clung ardently to it, for at that very moment the perfect teaching of the new Law was introduced in its place. And, therefore, our Lord and Saviour rightly says to those who suppose that God ought only to be worshipped in Jerusalem, or in certain mountains, or some definite places :

"1. The hour cometh and now is, when the true (d) worshippers shall neither in this mountain nor in Jerusalem worship the Father. For God is a Spirit, and they that worship him must worship him in John iv. spirit and in truth."   23.

So He said, and presently, not long after, Jerusalem was besieged, the holy place and the altar by it and the worship conducted according to Moses' ordinances were destroyed, and the archetypal holiness of the pre-Mosaic men of God reappeared. And the blessing assured thereby to all nations came, to lead those who came to it from the first step and (19) from the first elements of the Mosaic worship to a better and more perfect life.[2] Yes, the religion of those blessed and godly men, who did not worship in any one place exclusively, neither by symbols nor types, but as our Lord and Saviour requires "in spirit and in truth," by our Saviour's appearance became the possession of all the nations, as the prophets of old foresaw. For Zephaniah says the very same thing :

"The Lord shall appear against them, and shall (b) utterly destroy all the gods of the nations of the earth.

---

[1] παραχρῆμα "immediately," and αὐτίκα below. Eusebius passes lightly over the space till A.D. 70.

[2] τῆς πρώτης στοιχειώσεως. Cf. P.E. 4 b and 761 b. στοιχείωσις is used for "the alphabet" in Epiphanius.

And they shall worship him each one from his own place."

Malachi as well contends against those of the circumcision, and speaks on behalf of the Gentiles, when he says :

"10. I have no pleasure (in you),[1] saith the Lord Almighty, and I will not accept a sacrifice at your hands. 11. For from the rising of the sun even to the setting [2] my name has been glorified among the Gentiles ; and in every place incense is offered to my
name, and a pure offering." [3]

(c) By "the incense and offering to be offered to God in every place," what else can he mean, but that no longer in Jerusalem nor exclusively in that (sacred) place, but in every land and among all nations they will offer to the Supreme God the incense of prayer and the sacrifice called
(d) "pure," because it is not a sacrifice of blood but of good works? And Isaiah literally shouts and cries his prophecy to the same effect :

"19. There shall be an altar to the Lord in the land of Egypt.[4] . . . And the Lord shall be known to the Egyptians . . . 20. And he shall send to them a man who shall save them, . . . 21, and the Egyptians shall know the Lord in that day, and shall offer sacrifice, and vow vows to the Lord and pay (them).[5] And they
shall be turned to the Lord, and he shall hear them and heal them."

Do we not say truly then that the prophets were inspired to foretell a change of the Mosaic Law, nay its end and conclusion? Moses lays down that the altar and the

---

[1] E. omits ἐν ὑμῖν (S.).   [2] E. omits ἡλίου (S.).
[3] The "incense" of the prophecy is referred to prayer and the "sacrifice" to good works ; Eusebius does not regard it directly as a prophecy of the Eucharist. But see I. 6 c. " θυσιαστήριον ἀναίμων καὶ λογικῶν θυσιῶν κατὰ τὰ καινὰ μυστήρια." "An altar of unbloody and reasonable sacrifices according to the new mysteries," I. 10 b. τὴν τούτου μνήμην τοῦ τε σώματος αὐτοῦ καὶ τοῦ αἵματος τὴν ὑπόμνησιν ὁσημέραι ἐπιτελοῦντες (in contrast with Jewish sacrifices) : we are "admitted to a greater sacrifice of the Ancient Law " (ibid.).
[4] E. omits καὶ στήλη πρὸς τὸ ὅριον αὐτῆς τῷ κυρίῳ. καὶ ἔσται εἰς σημεῖον εἰς τὸν αἰῶνα κυρίῳ ἐν χώρᾳ Αἰγύπτου ὅτι κεκράξονται πρὸς κύριον διὰ τοὺς θλίβοντας αὐτούς, and inverts the two following clauses, omitting κρίνων σώσει αὐτούς.
[5] E. omits καὶ πατάξει κύριος τοὺς Αἰγυπτίους πληγῇ, καὶ ἰάσεται αὐτούς.

sacrifices should be nowhere else on earth but in Judæa, and there only in one city.   But this prophecy says that an altar to the Lord shall be set up in Egypt,[1] and that Egyptians shall celebrate[2] their sacrifices to the Lord of the prophets and no longer to their ancestral gods.   It foretells that Moses shall not be the medium of their knowledge of God, nor any other of the prophets, but a man fresh and new sent from God.   Now if the altar is changed contrary to the commandment of Moses, it is (20) beyond doubt necessary that the Law of Moses should be changed also.   Then, too, the Egyptians, if they "sacrifice to the Supreme God," must be admittedly worthy of the priesthood.   And if the Egyptians are priests Moses' enactments about the Levites and the Aaronic succession would be useless to the Egyptians.   The time, therefore, will have come when a new legislation will be needed for their support.   What follows?   Have I spoken at random?   Or have I proved my contention?   Behold how to day, yes (b) in our own times, our eyes see not only Egyptians, but every race of men who used to be idolaters, whom the prophet meant when he said "Egyptians," released from the errors of polytheism and the dæmons, and calling on

[1] The altar in Egypt (cf. Jer. xliv. 1, 15, 24).   Remarkable discoveries of papyri in Egypt were made at Assouan, the ancient Syene, and Elephantine, 400 miles south of Cairo, in 1904, and edited by Prof. Sayce and Dr. Cowley in 1906.   They date from 471 B.C. to 411 B.C., and are legal documents of a Jewish family.   A house mentioned adjoins a "temple of the God Yahu" (Jehovah).   Further papyri came to light in 1907, including a petition dated 408 B.C. to Bagoas (Jos. *Ant. Jud.* xvii. 2, 4), the Persian Governor of Judah, to rebuild this temple, which had been destroyed by the priests of the Egyptian God Chnut.   We are told it had been built for 120 years, had seven gates, and the same apparatus for sacrifice as the temple on Mount Zion.   Another document is a memorandum of the reply of Bagoas that the request is granted.   The point is that this Jewish Colony did not consider itself bound by the law of the "single sanctuary."

[See J. R. Driver, *Schweich Lectures*, 1908, p. 30.   A. Deissman, *Light from the Ancient East*, p. 30, giving German editions of and monographs on the papyri, including Lietzmann's *Kleine Texte*, Nos. 22, 23 (1907), and 32 (1908).   H. Sayce and A. E. Cowley, *Aramaic Papyri*, Oxford 1906, and *Jewish Documents of the Time of Ezra*, 1919.]

[2] καλλιερήσειν τὰς θυσίας : cf. P. E. 157 c., a quotation from Clement, *Protrepticus*, c. iii. p. 12, Sylb. where καλλιερεῖν means "to yield good omens."

the God of the prophets! They pray no longer to lords many, but to one Lord according to the sacred oracle; they have raised to Him an altar of unbloody and reason-
(c) able sacrifices according to the new mysteries of the fresh and new covenant throughout the whole of the inhabited world, and in Egypt itself and among the other nations, Egyptian[1] in their superstitious errors. Yes, in our own time the knowledge of the Omnipotent God shines forth, and sets a seal of certainty on the forecasts of the prophets. You see this actually going on, you no longer only expect to hear of it, and if you ask the moment when the change began, for all your inquiry you will receive no other answer
(d) but the moment of the appearance of the Saviour. For He it was, of Whom the prophet spoke, when he said that the Supreme God and Lord would send a man to the Egyptians, to save them, as also the Mosaic oracles taught in these words: "A man shall come forth from his seed, and shall rule over many nations"; among which nations the Egyptians would certainly be numbered. But a great deal could be said on these points, and with sufficient leisure one could deal with them more exhaustively. Suffice it to say now, that we must hold to the truth, that the prophecies have only been fulfilled after the coming of Jesus our Saviour. For it is through Him that in our day that old system of Abraham, the most ancient and venerable form of religion, is followed by the Egyptians, the Persians, the Syrians and the Armenians. The Barbarians from the
(21) end of the earth, those of them who were of old the most uncivilized and wild, yea, they that inhabit the isles, for prophecy thought well even to mention them, follow it as well.[2] And who would not be struck by the extraordinary change—that men who for ages have paid divine honour to wood and stone and dæmons, wild beasts that feed on human flesh, poisonous[3] reptiles, animals of every kind, repulsive monsters,[4] fire and earth, and the lifeless elements of the universe should after our Saviour's coming pray to the

Num.
xxiv. 7.

---

[1] αἰγυπτιάζουσι "acting as Egyptians," analogous to Ἑλληνίζω, and Ἰουδαΐζω.

[2] See note, p. 130. For "the isles," *i.e.* Britain; cf. Tertullian, *adv. Jud.* vii.

[3] ἰοβόλοις, cf. P. E. 40 d. "of wild beasts."

[4] εἰδεχθέσι κνωδάλοις, cf. P.E. 370 c. ("animals") in *Letter of Aristeas*, there quoted, also 375 b.

Most High God, Creator of Heaven and earth, the actual Lord of the prophets, and the God of Abraham and his (b) forefathers? That men a little while before involved in marriage with mothers and daughters, in unspeakable vice and all sorts of vileness, men who lived like wild beasts, now converted by the divine power of our Saviour, and become like different beings, should crowd the public (c) schools[1] and learn lessons of virtue and purity. That not men only, but women, poor and rich, learned and simple, children even and slaves, should be taught in their daily occupation in town or country the loftiest ethics, which forbids to look with eyes unbridled, to be careless even in words, or to follow the path of custom and fashion. That they should learn the true ideal of worshipping the Supreme God, and serving Him in every place, according to the prophecy, which says: "And they shall worship Him each (d) from his own place." Every one, then, whether Greek or Zeph. ii. Barbarian, is worshipping the Supreme God, not running 11. to Jerusalem, nor made holy with bloody sacrifices, but staying at home in his own land, and offering in spirit and in truth his pure and bloodless offering. And theirs is the new covenant, not according to the old. Do not allow the covenant of the pre-Mosaic Saints to be called "the old covenant," but that which was given to the Jews by the Law of Moses. For the text which says that the new will be quite unlike the old clearly implies which one was the old:

"I will make[2] a new covenant, not according to (22) the covenant I made with their fathers, in the day that I took them by the hand to lead them out of Jer. xxxi. Egypt." 31.

"Not according to the covenant of the Mosaic Law," he says. For that was introduced to the Jews at the exodus from Egypt. It might have seemed that he was introducing a new covenant opposed to the religious ideals of the Abrahamic Saints, if he had not distinctly said: (b)

"Not according to the covenant, which I made with their fathers, in the day that I took them by the hand to lead them out of Egypt."

---

[1] συνιόντες εἰς τὰ κοινὰ διδασκαλεῖα. Cf. Thuc. vii. 29. Antipho, 142, 33, and Hyperid. *Euxen*—τὰ παιδία τὰ ἐκ τῶν διδασκαλειῶν.
[2] S.: διαθήσομαι τῷ οἴκῳ Ἰσραὴλ κὰι τῷ οἴκῳ Ἰούδα.

He prophesied that the new covenant would not be
according to the one enacted at the time of the Exodus
and the wanderings in the wilderness, but according to the
ancient one under which the pre-Mosaic saints flourished.
And, therefore, for the future you may confidently classify
(c) the ideals [1] of religious worshippers under three heads,
not two : the completely idolatrous, who have fallen into
the errors of polytheism ; those of the circumcision, who
by the aid of Moses have reached the first step of
holiness ; and thirdly, those who have ascended by the
stair of Gospel teaching. If you regard this as a mean
between the other two, you will no longer suppose that
perverts from Judaism necessarily fall into Hellenism, nor
that those that forsake Hellenism are, therefore, Jews.
Recognizing the third division in the middle, you will see
(d) it standing up on high, as if it were set on a very lofty
mountain ridge, with the others left below on each side
of the height. For as it has escaped Greek godlessness,
error, superstition, unbridled lust and disorder, so it has
left behind Jewish unprofitable observances, designed by
Moses to meet the needs of those who were like infants
and invalids. And as it stands on high, hear what it says
as it proclaims the law, which suits not Jews alone, but
(23) Greeks and barbarians, and all nations under the sun :
    "O man ! and all the human race ! the Law of
Moses, beginning from one race of men, first called the
whole race of the Jews, because of the promise given
to their holy forefathers, to the knowledge of the one
God, and released its servants from bitter slavery to the
dæmons. But I am the herald to all men and to the
nations of the whole world of a loftier knowledge of
God and holiness ; I call them to live according to the
ideals of those of Abraham's day, and men still more
(b)   ancient of pre-Mosaic date, with whom many of all races
are recorded to have shone in holiness as lights in the
world.
And again :
    The Law of Moses required all who desired to be
holy to speed from all directions to one definite place ;
but I, giving freedom to all, teach men not to look for

---

[1] τὰς προαιρέσεις.

God in a corner of the earth, nor in mountains, nor in temples made with hands, but that each should worship and adore Him at home.

And again :

The old law commanded that God should be (c worshipped by the sacrifice of slain beasts, of incense and fire and divers other similar external purifications. But I, introducing the rites of the soul,[1] command that God should be glorified with a clean heart and a pure mind, in purity and a life of virtue, and by true and holy teaching.

And again :

Moses forbade the men of his time who were defiled (d) with blood to kill; but I lay down a more perfect law for those who have him for a schoolmaster and have kept the earlier commandment—when I ordain that men must not be slaves to anger.   Matt. v.

And once more :   22.

The Law of Moses enacted to adulterers and the impure that they must not commit adultery, or indulge in vice, or pursue unnatural pleasures, and made death the penalty of transgression; but I do not wish my disciples even to look upon a woman with lustful desire.   Matt. v.

And again, it said :   28.

Thou shalt not forswear thyself, but shalt perform unto the Lord[2] thine oaths; but I say unto you, Swear Matt. v. not at all,[3] but let your communication be Yea, yea ; Nay, 33. nay : for whatsoever is more than these cometh of evil.

And again, it commanded resistance against the unjust, and reprisal, when it said :

An eye for an eye, and a tooth for a tooth; but (24) I say unto you, That ye resist not evil; but whosoever shall smite thee on thy right cheek, turn to him the other also.   And he who will sue thee at the law, and take away thy coat, let him have thy cloak also.   Matt. v.

And again, it exhorts to love your friend, and to hate your 38-40. enemies; but I in my excess of goodwill and forbearance lay down the law :

Pray for[4] persecutors, that you may be children

---

[1] τὰ ψυχῆs ὄργια παραδιδούs.   [2] E. omits vv. 35, 36.
[3] W.H.: θεῷ κυρίῳ.   [4] W.H. adds ὑμᾶs.

of your Father in heaven, who [1] letteth his sun rise on
the evil and on the good, and sendeth rain on the just
and the unjust.

Matt. v. 44.

(b)   And, moreover, the Mosaic Law was suited to the hardness of heart of the vulgar, gave ordinances corresponding
to those under the rule of sense, [2] and provided a form of
religion, reduced and inferior to the old. But I summon
all to the holy and godly life of the holy men of the earlier
days. And in fine, it promises, as to children, a land flowing with milk and honey, while I make citizens [3] of the
Kingdom of Heaven those who are worthy to enter therein.

(c)   Such was the message to all nations given by the word
of the new covenant by the teaching of Christ. And the
Christ of God bade His disciples teach them to all nations,
saying :

"Go ye into all the world, and make disciples of all
the nations . . . teaching them to observe whatsoever
I have commanded you."

Matt. xxviii. 19.

And in giving them to all men both Greeks and barbarians
to keep He clearly revealed the nature of Christianity, the
nature of Christians, and the nature of the Teacher of the
words and instruction, our Lord and Saviour the Christ of
God Himself. He set up this new and perfect system
throughout the whole world, that such teaching and such
wisdom might be the food, not only of men but of women,
of rich and poor alike, and of slaves with their masters.
And yet the introducer of this new law is represented as
having lived in all ways according to the Law of Moses.
And this is a wonderful fact, that though He was going to
come forward as the legislator of a new polity, according
to the Gospel of His new covenant, He did not revolt from
(25) Moses as opposed to him and contrary. If He had thought
good to command things opposed to Moses, He would
have afforded to godless sectaries [4] against Moses and
the prophets material for much scandal, and to those of
the circumcision a specious handle for attacking Him,
particularly in view of the fact that they actually contrived
their plot against His life as a transgressor and breaker of
the law.

[1] W.H.: ὅτι. E.: ὅστις.   [2] κατάλληλα ἐμπαθέσι.
[3] προξενῶ. Cf. P.E. 2 a, 69 a and 169 d.   [4] αἱρεσιώταις.

CHAPTER 7

How Christ, having first fulfilled the Law of Moses, became the Introducer of a New and Fresh System.

AND now having lived in all ways according to the Law (b) of Moses, He made use of His Apostles as ministers of the new legislation, on the one hand teaching them that they must not consider the Law of Moses either foreign or unfriendly to their own religion, on the other as being the author and introducer of a legislation new and salutary for all men, so that He did not in any way break Moses' enactments, but rather crowned them, and was their fulfilment, (c) and then passed on to the institution of the Gospel Law. Hear Him speaking in this strain : [1]

3. "I have not come to destroy the law but to fulfil it." For if He had been a transgressor of the Law of Moses, He would reasonably have been considered to have rescinded it and given a contrary law : and if He had been wicked and a law-breaker He could not have been believed to be the Christ. And if He had rescinded Moses' Law, He could (d) never have been considered to be One foretold by Moses and the prophets. Nor would His new Law have had any authority. For He would have had to embark on a new Law,[2] in order to escape the penalty of breaking the old. But as a matter of fact He has rescinded nothing

---

[1] The doctrine that Christianity is a "republication" of primitive truth seems implicit in the Pauline teaching that the law is but an episode in the evolution of history (Gal. iii. 17–19). For the unity of the Christians with the patriarchs and Melchizedek, cf. Just. *Trypho*, c. xix., xxiii., xxv. ; Tertullian, *adv. Jud.* c. ii. Origen does not use the argument against Celsus, as he might have done, *c. Cels.* ii. c. 7. In the English theology of the eighteenth century the doctrine that Christianity was a republication of natural religion played a great part. But the Law of Moses was in the same position, supported like Christianity by miracles. "The Law of Moses and the Gospel of Christ are authoritative publications of the religion of nature ; they afford a proof of God's general providence as moral governor of the world, as well as of His particular dispensations of providence towards sinful creatures revealed in the law and the Gospel."—*Analogy of Religion*, Bp. Butler, Part II. c. i. Cf. Mark Pattison, *Essays*, vol. ii. Essay 13.

[2] ἐπὶ τὴν καινοτομίαν ἐληλυθέναι. For καινοτομία cf. P.E. 16 d, 130 d.

whatever in the Law, but fulfilled it. It is, as one might say, Mosaically perfect. Yet since it was no longer possible for the causes I have stated already to accommodate the Law of Moses to the needs of the other nations, and it was necessary, thanks to the love of God the All-good, "that all men should be saved and come to a knowledge of the truth," [1]

(26) He laid down a law suitable and possible for all. Nor did He forbid His Apostles to preach Moses' Law to all men, except when it was likely to be a stumbling-block to them, as the apostle says :

"For that which was impossible by the law, in that it was weak, God sending his own son in the likeness of sinful flesh," [2] etc.

Rom. viii. 3.

And it was "impossible" for all the nations to go up thrice a year to Jerusalem as the Law of Moses required, for a woman after childbirth to hasten there from the ends of the earth to pay the fees of her purification, and in many other ways, which you can arrive at for yourselves at your

(b) leisure. Since then it was not possible for the nations living outside Judæa to keep these things even if they wished, our Lord and Saviour could hardly be said to have rescinded them, but was the fulfilment of the Law, and gave a proof to those who could see, that He was indeed the Christ of God foretold by the old Jewish prophets. This He did, when He gave to all nations through His own disciples enactments that suited them. And, therefore, we reject Jewish customs, on the ground that they were not laid down for us, and that it is impossible to accommodate them to the needs of the Gentiles,

(c) while we gladly accept the Jewish prophecies as containing predictions about ourselves. Thus the Saviour on the one side is our teacher, and on the other the fulfilment of the Law of Moses, and of the prophets who followed him.

For since as yet the prophecies lacked the fulfilment of their conclusions and of their words, He must necessarily fulfil them. As for example the prophecy in Moses says :

"A prophet shall the Lord your God raise up to you like unto me, him shall ye hear in all things, whatsoever that prophet shall speak to you."

Deut. xviii. 15.

(d) He fulfilled what remained to be fulfilled in this prophecy,

---

[1] i Tim. ii. 4.　　　　[2] W.H. adds διὰ τῆς σαρκός.

appearing as the second Lawgiver after Moses, giving to
men the Law of the Supreme God's true holiness.   For
Moses does not say simply "a prophet," but adds "like
unto me": ("For a prophet," he says, "shall the Lord your
God raise up unto you, like unto me.   Him shall ye hear"),
and this can only mean that He who was foretold would
be equal to Moses.   And Moses was the giver of the Law
of holiness of the Supreme God.   So He that was foretold,
to be like Moses, would probably be like him in being a
Lawgiver.   And though there were many prophets in later
days, none of them is recorded to have been "like Moses."
For they all referred their hearers to him.   Even Scripture (27)
bears witness that "a prophet has not arisen like Moses":
neither Jeremiah, nor Isaiah, nor any other of the prophets
was like him, because not one of them was a Lawgiver.
When the expectation was that a prophet who was also
a Lawgiver like Moses should arise, Jesus Christ came
giving a Law to all nations, and accomplishing what the
Law could not.   As He said: (b)
 "It was said to them of old time, Thou shalt not
commit adultery: but I say unto you, Thou shalt not Matt. v.
desire to."   And, "It was said to them of old time, 28.
Thou shalt not kill, but I say unto you, Thou shalt not Matt. v.
be angry."   And, "No more in Jerusalem, but in every John iv.
place must you worship."   And, "Worship not with in- 21.
cense and sacrifices, but in spirit and in truth."[1]   And all John iv.
such things that are recorded of His teaching are surely 24.
the laws of a Lawgiver very wise and very perfect.
Wherefore Holy Scripture says His hearers were "astounded," because He taught them "as one having authority, and not as the Scribes and the Pharisees"[2]—an (c)
oracle which supplied what was lacking to the fulfilment
of the prophecy of Moses.   And the same can be said of
the other prophecies about Him, and the calling of the
Gentiles.   He was, therefore, the fulfiller of the Law and
the prophets since He brought the predictions referring
to Himself to a conclusion.
 He ordained that the former Law should stand till He
came, and He was revealed as the originator of the second
Law of the new covenant preached to all nations, as being

---

[1] This is of course a paraphrase.
[2] Matt. v. 29.   E. adds καὶ οἱ Φαρασαῖοι,

responsible for the Law and influence of the two religions,
(d) I mean Judaism and Christianity. And it is wonderful
that divine prophecy should accord :

"Behold, I lay in [1] Zion a stone, choice, a corner-
stone ; precious, and he that believes on him shall
not be ashamed."

Isa. xxviii.
16.

Who could be the corner-stone but He, the living and
precious stone Who supports by His teaching two buildings
and makes them one? For He set up the Mosaic building, which was to last till His day, and then fitted on to
one side of it our building of the Gospel.[2] Hence He
is called the corner-stone. And it is said in the Psalms :

"22. The stone which the builders refused, the
same is become the head of the corner. 23. This
is of the Lord, and it is marvellous in our eyes."[3]

Ps. cxviii.
22.

(28) This oracle too indubitably indicates the Jewish conspiracy
against the subject of the prophecy, how He has been set
at naught by the builders of the old wall, meaning the
Scribes and Pharisees, the High-Priests and all the rulers
of the Jews. And it prophesied that though He should
be despised and cast out He would become the head of
the corner, regarding Him as the originator of the new
covenant, according to the above proofs.

(b) So then we are not apostates from Hellenism who have
embraced Judaism, nor are we at fault in accepting the
law of Moses and the Hebrew Prophets, and we do not
live as Jews, but according to the system of the men of
God who lived before Moses. Nay, we claim that in this

---

[1] E. omits εἰς τὰ θεμέλια . . . πολυτελῆ . . . εἰς τὰ θεμέλια αὐτῆς.

[2] ἐπισυνῆψεν ἐκ θατέρου. Cf. P.E. 232 d of "appending" a
quotation.

[3] ἀρχηγὸς δευτέρου τοῦ . . . νόμου. For Christ as initiator of a
new Law, cf. p. 444 a. νομοθέτης ὁμοῦ καὶ προφήτης, where He is
Lawgiver for all nations. Cf. T. B. Strong, *Christian Ethics*, on the
relation of the Sermon on the Mount to the Jewish Law. "It takes
its place rather with the old dispensation than the new. It is still a
Law," p. 21. It is by means of the Life and Death of Christ and the
gift of the Spirit, that the Christian Law changes from an external to an
inward Law. The Law and the powers by which it is fulfilled are distinct, therefore the earliest writings, *e.g.* "the two ways" of the *Didache*,
the *Mandates* of Hermas present detailed codes of conduct, as the
Law of the Christian Society, and Christ as here tends to be regarded
not so much as inner Life, but as a new and greater Moses. Cf. Justin,
Trypho, c. 11 ; Tertullian, *adv. Jud.* c. vi., "a giver of the new law,"

we authenticate Moses and the succeeding prophets, in that
we accept the Christ foretold by them, and obey His laws,
and endeavour prayerfully to tread in the steps of His
teaching, for so we do what Moses himself would approve.
For he says, in foretelling that God will raise up a prophet (c)
like himself, "and every soul which doth not hear that
prophet shall be cast out from its race." Therefore the Deut.
Jews, because they rejected the prophet, and did not hearken xviii. 19.
to His holy words, have suffered extreme ruin according to
the prediction. For they neither received the law of Christ
of the new covenant, nor were they able to keep the commands of Moses without some breach of his law ; and so (d)
they fell under the curse of Moses, in not being able to
carry out what was ordained by him, being exiled as they
were from their mother-city, which was destroyed, where
alone it was allowed to celebrate the Mosaic worship.
Whereas we, who accept Him that was foretold by Moses
and the prophets, and endeavour to obey Him prayerfully,
must surely be fulfilling the prophecy of Moses, where he
said : "And every soul, which doth not hear that prophet,
shall be cast out from its race." And we heard just now
what the ordinances of the prophet were, which we must
obey, their wisdom, perfection and heavenliness, which he
thought fit to inscribe, not on tables of stone like Moses,
nor yet with ink and parchment, but on the hearts of his (29)
pupils, purified and open to reason.[1] On them he wrote
the laws of the new covenant, and actually fulfilled the
prophecy of Jeremiah.

"I will make a new covenant, not according to the
covenant which I made with their fathers. For this is Jer. xxxi.
the covenant which I will make with the house of 38-39.
Israel, I will give my laws into their mind, and upon
their heart I will write them, and I will be their God,
and they shall be my people.[2]

---

[1] νοερὰν οὐσίαν κεκτημέναις.

[2] E. omits τῷ οἴκῳ . . . Ἰούδα, and verse 32 : ἐν ἡμέρᾳ . . . Κύριος,
and verse 33 : μετὰ . . . Κύριος. He has Θεὸς and λαὸς for εἰς θ όν
and εἰς λαόν.

CHAPTER 8

That the Christian Life is of Two Distinct Characters.

(b) THE one wrote on lifeless tables, the Other wrote the
perfect commandments of the new covenant on living
minds. And His disciples, accommodating their teaching
to the minds of the people, according to the Master's will,
delivered on the one hand to those who were able to
receive it, the teaching given by the perfect master to
those who rose above human nature.[1] While on the other
the side of the teaching which they considered was suitable
to men still in the world of passion and needing treatment,
they accommodated to the weakness of the majority, and
handed over to them to keep sometimes in writing, and sometimes by unwritten ordinances to be observed by them. Two
ways of life were thus given by the law of Christ to His
Church. The one is above nature, and beyond common
(d) human living; it admits not marriage, child-bearing, property nor the possession of wealth, but wholly and per-
manently separate from the common customary life of
mankind, it devotes itself to the service of God alone in
its wealth of heavenly love![2] And they who enter on this
course, appear to die to the life of mortals, to bear with
them nothing earthly but their body, and in mind and
spirit to have passed to heaven. Like some celestial beings
they gaze upon human life, performing the duty of a
priesthood[3] to Almighty God for the whole race, not with

[1] τὴν ἕξιν διαβεβηκόσι: ἕξις is the settled permanent condition
either of mind or body of an adult human being: this is transcended
by the Christian Saint, as he escapes from the tyranny of the lower
nature. Cf. P.E. 528 B. κατὰ ἕξιν, "in a permanent state."

[2] For ἔρως of sacred love, cf. ὁ ἐμὸς ἔρως ἐσταύρωται, Ignatius, *Romans*
vii. (which however Lightfoot translates "my lust," not "the one I
love.") ; ἐραστὴς φιλοσοφίας of Justin, Eus., *H.E.* iv. 8. St. Dionysius,
placed by Harnack after A.D. 350, uses much erotic language, quoting
the words of Ignatius (W. R. Inge. *Christian Mysticism*, p. 110).
Inge agrees with Bigg (*Bampton Lectures*, Intr. pp. viii., ix.) that
Ignatius refers to our Lord.

[3] This interesting passage is a strong proof of the firm establishment
of the ascetic ideal in the Church before the recognition of monasticism.
The doctrine of "the two vocations" is plainly stated as part of the
law of Christ: one implying a renunciation of property and marriage,
a priesthood for the whole race ; the other, a life involved in all
secular interests. Asceticism had its roots in our Lord's teaching and

sacrifices of bulls and blood, nor with libations and
unguents, nor with smoke and consuming fire and destruction of bodily things, but with right principles of true
holiness, and of a soul purified in disposition, and above
all with virtuous deeds and words ; with such they propitiate the Divinity, and celebrate their priestly rites for
themselves and their race.   Such then is the perfect form (30)
of the Christian life.   And the other more humble, more
human, permits men to join in pure nuptials and to produce children, to undertake government, to give orders to
soldiers fighting for right ;[1] it allows them to have minds
for farming, for trade, and the other more secular interests

in that of the Apostles.   There were devotees in the sub-apostolic age.
(*Didache* 6 ; cf. I Clem. 38, Ign. *ad Polyc.* 5, and Eusebius' description
of Justin, *H.E.* iv. 38.).   Traces of a semi-separation from the world
are found after A.D. 150 (Athenagoras, *Apol. pro Chr.* xxviii. 129 ;
Irenæus, ap. Eus., *H.E.* v. 241 ; Clem. Alex., "*Quis dives ?*" 36 ;
Clem. *Strom.* viii. 15.)   The incident of Dionysius of Corinth and
Pinytus, Bishop of the Cnossians, shews the growing tendency to
rigour.   (Euseb., *H.E.* iv. 21.)   The Gnostic sects were rigorously
ascetic.   Consecration to virginity by a solemn vow was customary for
women in Cyprian's time.   Egyptian retirement to solitude was organized by St. Anthony about 305, and was probably due to the pressure
of the Decian persecution, and the ideas of the Alexandrian School.
Pachomius began a "Coenobium," or common monastic life under
rule about 320.   Hilarion, a little later, introduced monasticism into
Palestine.   Thus the movement was, as E.'s words suggest, new and
captivating from its novelty and apparent harmony with Gospel
precept, at a time when the Church was conscious of a great victory
and escape from danger.   Cf. Clarke, *St. Basil the Great*, pp. 26–42 ;
Lausiac History of Palladius, pp. 20–24 ; Butler, chapter on "Monasticism," *Cambridge Medieval History*, I. 521 ff. ; Duchesne, *Histoire
Ancienne de l'Eglise*, ii. 485 f. ; *E.R.E.*, art. "Monasticism."

[1] This seems to recognize Christians serving in magistracies and as
officers in the army, though the expression is peculiar.   Though in the
second century Tertullian (*de Idol.* c. 19, *de Coron. Mil.* c. 11), and
Origen (*c. Cels.* viii. 73), and later Lactantius (*Institutiones*, vi. c. 20),
consider that Christians should not bear arms, yet there is no doubt
they did.   Cf. Tertullian, *Apologet.* c. 37, 42, and Euseb., *H.E.* v. 5
("The Thundering Legion").

By this time the duties of holding magistracies, and serving in the
army were freely admitted, and the doctrine of "the two vocations," as
expressed here, no doubt witnessed to the change of Christian opinion
on this as on other matters.

For the relation of the Curia to the Church cf. C. Bigg, *The Church's
Task under the Roman Empire*, pp. 128 ff., and for an historical
survey of the Christian attitude to war up to Augustine, Moffatt,
D.A.C. vol. ii. pp. 646–673.

as well as for religion : and it is for them that times of
(b) retreat and instruction, and days for hearing sacred things
are set apart.[1]   And a kind of secondary grade of piety is
attributed to them, giving just such help as such lives
require, so that all men, whether Greeks or barbarians, have
their part in the coming of salvation, and profit by the
teaching of the Gospel.

CHAPTER 9

*Why a Numerous Offspring is not as Great a Concern to us
as it was to them of Old Time.*

(c) THIS being so, the question naturally arises, if we claim
that the Gospel teaching of our Saviour Christ bids us
worship God as did the men of old, and the pre-Mosaic
men of God, and that our religion is the same as theirs,
and our knowledge of God the same, why were they keenly
concerned with marriage and reproduction, while we to
(d) some extent disregard it?   And again, why are they
recorded as propitiating God with animal sacrifices, while
we are forbidden to do so, and are told to regard it as
impious.   For those two things alone, which are by no
means unimportant, would seem to conflict with what I
have said ; they would imply that in these matters we have
not preserved the ancient ideal of religion.   But it is possible for us to refute this charge by a study of the Hebrew
writings.   The men renowned for piety before Moses are
recorded as having lived when human life was first beginning and organizing itself, while we live when it is nearing
its end.   And so they were anxious for the increase of
their descendants, that men might multiply, that the human
race might grow and flourish at that time, and reach its
(31) height ; but these things are of little moment to us, who
believe the world to be perishing and running down [2] and
reaching its last end, since it is expressly said that the
gospel teaching will be at the door before the consumma-

---

[1] Common Christianity admits marriage, family-life, war, agriculture,
trade, politics : and is sustained by periods of retreat for spiritual
instruction.
[2] ἀπολληγόντων.

tion of life, while a new creation and the birth of another
age at no distant time is foretold. Such is one reply, and
this is a second. The men of old days lived an easier and (b)
a freer life, and their care of home and family did not
compete with their leisure for religion ; they were able to
worship God without distraction from their wives and
children and domestic cares, and were in no way drawn
by external things from the things that mattered most.[1]
But in our days there are many external interests that
draw us away, and involve us in uncongenial thoughts, and
seduce us from our zeal for the things which please God.
The word of the Gospel teaching certainly gives this as
the cause of the limitation of marriage,[2] when it says :   (c)

29. But this I say, brethren, the time is short: it
remaineth that they who have wives be as though they
had none.   30. And those that wept as though they
wept not, and they that rejoice as though they rejoiced
not ; and they that buy as though they possessed not ;
31. and they that use this world as not abusing it, for
the fashion of this world passeth away.   32. But I
would have you without carefulness. He that is unmarried careth for the things of the Lord, how he may
please the Lord ; but he that is married careth for the
things of the world, how he may please his wife, and is
divided.   34. And the unmarried woman and the virgin
careth for the things of the Lord (how she may please (d)
the Lord),[3] that she may be holy both in body and in
spirit ; but she that is married careth for the things of
the world, how she may please her husband.   35. And
this I speak for your profit ; not that I may cast a
cord upon you, but for that which is comely, and that 1 Cor. vii.
ye may attend upon the Lord without distraction.   29-35.

---

[1] τῆς περὶ τὰ κρείττω προθέσεως.

[2] τῆς τῶν γάμων συστολῆς. Cf. P.E. 337 c. of a "limitation" of
God in creation. It is interesting to find the eschatological motive of
1 Cor. vii. 29 adduced as the justification for celibacy in the fourth
century. It was no doubt a more potent factor in the rise of Egyptian
monasticism than has been recognized. Joined with the terror of the
Decian Persecution, c. 250, and the pressure of taxation which drove
men into the desert, were the spiritual causes, among which were the
sense of the small value of earthly things in face of the speedy coming
of the end.

[3] W.H. omit ἵνα ἀρέσῃ τῷ Κυρίῳ.

This expressly attributes the decrease of marriage to the evils of the time and of external circumstances, such as did not affect the ancients.

And I might give this third reason why the godly men of old were so devoted to the procreation of children. The rest of mankind were increasing in evil, they had fallen into an uncivilized, inhuman, and savage mode of life, they had (32) given themselves up completely to godlessness and impiety, while they themselves, a very scanty remnant, had divorced themselves from the life of the many, and from common association with other men. They were living apart from other nations and in isolation, and were organizing a new kind of polity ; they were evolving a life of true wisdom and (b) religion, unmingled with other men. They wished to hand on to posterity the fiery seed of their own religion ; they did not intend that their piety should fail and perish when they themselves died, and so they had foresight for producing and rearing children. They knew they could be the teachers and guides of their families, and considered it their object to hand on to posterity the inheritance of their own good qualities. Hence many prophets and righteous men, (c) yea, even our Lord and Saviour Himself, with His apostles and disciples, have come from their line.[1]

And if some of them turned out wicked, like straw growing up with the corn, we must not blame the sowers, nor those who tended the crop, just as we should admit that even some of our Saviour's disciples have erred from the right way through self-will. And this explanation of the ancient men of God begetting children cannot be said to (d) apply to the Christians to-day, when by God's help through our Saviour's Gospel teaching we can see with our own eyes many peoples and nations in city and country and field all hastening together, and united in running to learn the godly course of the teaching of the Gospel,[2] for whom I am glad to say we are able to provide teachers and preachers of the word of holiness, free from all ties of life and anxious thoughts. And in our day these men are necessarily devoted to

---

[1] Oxford codex, διαδοχῆς. Gaisford reads with P. διδαχῆς, "from their teaching."

[2] One of several passages emphasizing the flourishing state of the Church generally ; important as evidence for the date of the *Demonstratio.* Cf. : 138 b.

celibacy[1] that they may have leisure for higher things; they have undertaken to bring up not one or two children but a prodigious number, and to educate them in godliness, and to care for their life generally.[2] On the top of all this, if we care- (33) fully examine the lives of the ancient men of whom I am speaking, we shall find that they had children in early life, but later on abstained and ceased from having them. For it is written that "Enoch pleased God after Methusaleh was Gen. v. 22. born." Scripture expressly records that he pleased God *after* the birth of his son, and tells nothing of his having children afterwards. And Noah, that just man, who was saved alone with his family when the whole world was destroyed, after the birth of his children, though he lived many years more, is not related to have begotten more children. And Isaac is said, after becoming the father (b) of twins by one wife, to have ceased cohabitation with her. Joseph again (and this was when he lived among the Egyptians) was only the father of two sons, and married to their mother only, while Moses himself and Aaron his (c) brother are recorded as having had children before the appearance of God, but after the giving of the divine oracles as having begotten no more children. What must I say of Melchisedek? He had no son at all, no family, no descendants. And the same is true of Joshua, the successor of Moses, and many other prophets.

If there is any question about the families of Abraham and Jacob, a longer discussion will be found in the book I wrote about the polygamy and large families of the ancient men of God.[3] To this I must refer the student, only warning him that according to the laws of the new (d) covenant the producing of children is certainly not forbidden, but the provisions are similar to those followed by the ancient men of God. "For a bishop," says the Scripture, "must be the husband of one wife." Yet it is fitting that 1 Tim. iii. 2.

---

[1] ἡ τῶν γάμων ἀναχώρησις.

[2] A further justification of celibacy on grounds familiar to-day.

[3] The title of this lost work was περὶ τῆς τῶν παλαιῶν ἀνδρῶν πολυπαιδίας. See P. E. vii. 8, 29. It is referred to by Basil (*de Sp. Sanct.* 29), as "Difficulties respecting the Polygamy of the Ancients." The justification of the marriage customs of antiquity is a frequent topic in Eusebius: the growing asceticism of the Church and the criticism of opponents called for a statement accounting for the primitive freedom shewn in Genesis.

those in the priesthood and occupied in the service of God,
should abstain after ordination from the intercourse of
marriage   To all who have not undertaken this wondrous
priesthood, Scripture almost completely gives way, when it
says : " Marriage is honourable, and the bed undefiled, but
whoremongers and adulterers God will judge." This, then, is
my answer to the first question.

Heb.
xiii. 4.

CHAPTER 10

Why we are not bidden to burn Incense and to sacrifice the
Fruits of the Earth to God as were the Men of Old Time.

(34) I SHOULD give the following reply to those who ask why
we do not sacrifice animals to Almighty God, as the men of
God of old did, whom we claim to imitate.   Greek ideas,
and what is actually found in the sacred books of the
(b) Hebrews, do not agree about the *cultus* of the ancient
primitive men.   The Greeks say that early men did not
ever sacrifice animals, nor burn incense to the gods, but
" herbage, which they lifted up in their hands as the bloom
of the productive power of nature," [1] and burnt grass and
leaves and roots in the fire to the sun and the stars of heaven.
And that in the next stage men launching far into wickedness stained the altars with the sacrifice of animals, and that
(c) this was a sacrifice sinful, unrighteous, and quite displeasing
to God.   For man and beast in no way differ in their
reasonable soul.   So they said that those who offer animals
are open to the charge of murder, the soul being one and
the same in man and brute.   This was the view of the
ancient Greeks, but it does not agree with the Hebrew
Scriptures.   They record that the first men, as soon as they

---

[1] Eusebius is representing the views of Porphyry, and he reproduces
the phrases of the passage quoted in P.E. from *de Abst.* ii. 5 and ii. 7
(Nauck) :   " Of those they made no offerings formerly, but of herbage,
which they lifted up in their hands as the bloom (χνούς) of the productive power of nature " (τῆς γονίμου φύσεως) : for Porphyry see notes
pp. 120 and 155.   He was probably the opponent that the *Demonstratio*
chiefly had in view.

were created, honoured God with animal sacrifices at the
very creation of their life. For they say: (d)
    "And it came to pass after some days that Cain
brought of the fruits of the earth a sacrifice to the Lord.
And Abel also brought of the first-born of his sheep.
. . . And God looked upon Abel and his gifts. But
Cain and his sacrifices he regarded not." Gen. iv. 3.
Here you will understand that he who sacrificed an animal
is said to have been more accepted by God than he who
brought an offering of the fruits of the earth. Noah again
brought to the altar his first-fruits of all clean cattle, and of
all clean fowls ; Abraham also is described as sacrificing :
so that if we accept the evidence of Holy Scripture, the first (35)
sacrifices thought of by the ancient men of God were those
of animals.

    And this thought, I hold, was not due to accident, nor
was its source in man, but it was divinely suggested. For
when they saw since they were holy, brought nigh to God,
and enlightened by the Divine Spirit in their souls that
there was need of great stress on the cleansing of the sons
of men, they thought that a ransom was due to the source [1]
of life and soul in return for their own salvation. And then
as they had nothing better or more valuable than their own
life [2] to sacrifice, in place of it they brought a sacrifice (b)
through that of the unreasoning beasts, providing a life
instead of their own life. They did not consider this was
sinful or unrighteous. They had not been taught that the
soul of the brutes was like man's, which has discourse of
reason : they had only learned that it was the animal's
blood, and that in the blood is the principle of life, which
they offered themselves, sacrificing as it were to God one
life instead of another.

---

[1] χορηγῷ.
[2] For the vicarious nature of sacrifice see J. G. Fraser, *Folklore in
the O. T.* i. 426, *e.g.* of practice of Arabs of Moab : "It is a substitute
which the deity deigns to accept instead of human and animal life."
Prof. S. I. Curtiss' researches into Syrian customs to-day show that the
essence of their domestic sacrifices is vicarious, see S. I. Curtiss,
Primitive Semitic Religion To-day (Chicago, 1902), pp. 195 *sq.* But
if sacrifice is vicarious, there is also, notably in the Blood Covenant, a
process of identification of the worshipper with the thing offered, as is
shown by W. Robertson Smith, *Religion of the Semites*, pp. 480 *sq.*
and C. H. Trumbull, *The Blood Covenant*.

Moses makes this abundantly clear, when he says:

(c) "For the life of all flesh is the blood, and I have given it to you upon the altar to make atonement for your sins: for the blood shall make atonement for the soul. Therefore I said to the children of Israel, No soul of you shall eat blood."

Levit. xvii. 11.

Note carefully in the above the words, "I gave to you upon the altar to make atonement for your souls; for the blood shall make atonement for the soul."

(d) He says clearly that the blood of the victims slain is a propitiation in the place of human life. And the law about sacrifices suggests that it should be so regarded, if it is carefully considered. For it requires him who is sacrificing always to lay his hands on the head of the victim, and to bear the animal to the priest held by its head, as one offering a sacrifice on behalf of himself. Thus he says in each case:

Levit. iii. 1.

"He shall bring it before the Lord. And he shall lay his hands on the head of the gift."

Such is the ritual in every case, no sacrifice is ever brought up otherwise. And so the argument holds that the victims are brought in place of the lives of them who bring them. In teaching that the blood of the brutes is their life, it in no way implies that they share in the essence of (36) thought and reason, for they are composed of matter and body, in the same way as the vegetation of the earth and plants. Thus Moses tells that God said in one creative word:

Gen. i. 11.

"Let the earth bring forth herb of grass and the fruit tree."

And again in like manner:

"Let the earth bring forth four-footed things, and creeping things, and wild beasts of the earth after their kind."

We must, therefore, regard the brutes as akin in kind and (b) nature and essence to the vegetation of the earth and the plants, and conclude that those who sacrifice them commit no sin. Noah indeed was told to eat flesh, as the herb of the field.

While then the better, the great and worthy and divine sacrifice was not yet available for men, it was necessary for them by the offering of animals to pay a ransom for their own life, and this was fitly a life that represented their own nature. Thus did the holy men of old, anticipating by the Holy Spirit that a holy victim, dear to God and great, would one day come for men, as the offering for the sins of the world, believing that as prophets they must perform in symbol his sacrifice, and shew forth in type what was yet (c) to be. But when that which was perfect was come, in accordance with the predictions of the prophets, the former sacrifices ceased at once because of the better and true Sacrifice.

This Sacrifice was the Christ of God, from far distant times foretold as coming to men, to be sacrificed like a sheep for the whole human race. As Isaiah the prophet says of him :

"As a sheep he was led to slaughter, and as a lamb dumb before her shearers."

Is. liii. 7

And he adds :

"4. He bears our sins and is pained for us ; yet we (d) accounted him to be in trouble, and in suffering and in affliction. 5. But he was wounded on account of our sins, and he was made sick on account of our iniquities, the chastisement of our peace was upon him, and with his stripe we are healed. . . . 6. And the Lord hath given him up for our iniquities . . . .9 for he did no sin himself, nor was guile found in his Is. liii. 4– mouth."

9.

Jeremiah, another Hebrew prophet, speaks similarly in the person of Christ : "I was led as a lamb to the slaughter." Jer. xi. 19.

John Baptist sets the seal on their predictions at the appearance of our Saviour. For beholding Him, and point- (37) ing Him out to those present as the one foretold by the prophets, he cried : "Behold the Lamb of God, which·taketh away the sin of the world."

John i. 29.

Since then according to the witness of the prophets the great and precious ransom has been found for Jews and Greeks alike, the propitiation for the whole world, the life given for the life of all men, the pure offering for every stain and sin, the Lamb of God, the holy sheep dear to God, the Lamb that was foretold, by Whose inspired and (b) mystic teaching all we Gentiles have procured the forgive·ness of our former sins, and such Jews as hope in Him

are freed from the curse of Moses, daily celebrating[1] His memorial, the remembrance of His Body and Blood, and are admitted to a greater sacrifice than that of the ancient law,[2] we do not reckon it right to fall back upon the first
(c) beggarly elements, which are symbols and likenesses but do not contain the truth itself.   And any Jews, of course, who have taken refuge in Christ, even if they attend no longer to the ordinances of Moses, but live according to the new covenant, are free from the curse ordained by Moses, for the Lamb of God has surely not only taken on Himself the sin of the world, but also the curse involved in the breach of the commandments of Moses as well.   The
(d) Lamb of God is made thus both sin and curse—sin for the sinners in the world, and curse for those remaining in all the things written in Moses' law.   And so the Apostle

Gal. iii. 13.   says : "Christ has redeemed us from the curse of the law,
2 Cor. v.   being made a curse for us"; and "Him that knew no sin,
21.   for our sakes he made sin."   For what is there that the Offering for the whole world could not effect, the Life given for the life of sinners, Who was led as a lamb to the slaughter, and as a lamb to the sacrifice, and all this for us and on our behalf?   And this was why those ancient men of God, as they had not yet the reality, held fast to their symbols.
(38) This is exactly what our Saviour teaches, saying :

"Many prophets and righteous men have desired to see those things which ye see, and have not seen them ;

Matt. xiii.   and to hear those things which ye hear, and have not
17.   heard them."

And we, who have received both the truth, and the archetypes of the early copies through the mysterious dispensation of Christ, can have no further need for the things of old.

---

[1] Acts ii. 46 seems to imply a daily Communion.   In Acts xx. 7, the day is the Lord's Day.   In Bithynia the Christians meet "stato die" (Pliny, *Ep.* x. 97), i. e. *not* daily.   Justin, *Apol.* i. 67, mentions Sunday as the day for the Eucharist.   Wednesday and Friday are added later (Tertullian, *De Oratione*, c. 14), and Saturday (Basil, *Ep.* 289, but cf. Epiphanius, *Expositio Fidei*, c. 22, p. 1104).   In Chrysostom's time, the celebration was daily in the Church of Constantinople (*in Ephes. Hom.* iii. p. 23).   S. Augustine (*Ep.* 118) states for African Church, "in some places no day passes without an offering ; in others offering is made on the Sabbath only and the Lord's Day ; in others on the Lord's Day only."   Jerome (*Ep.* 71) seems to imply that the celebration was daily in the Churches of Rome and Spain.
[2] Cf. I. 6 c.

He then that was alone of those who ever existed, the Word of God,[1] before all worlds, and High Priest of every creature that has mind and reason, separated One of like passions with us, as a sheep or lamb from the human flock, branded on Him all our sins, and fastened on Him as well the curse that was adjudged by Moses' law, as Moses foretells : "Cursed is every one that hangeth on a tree." (b) Gal. iii. This He suffered "being made a curse for us ; and making 13. himself sin for our sakes." And then "He made him sin for our sakes who knew no sin," and laid on Him all the (c) 2 Cor. punishments due to us for our sins, bonds, insults, con- v. 21. tumelies, scourging, and shameful blows, and the crowning trophy of the Cross. And after all this when He had offered such a wondrous offering and choice victim to the Father, and sacrificed for the salvation of us all, He delivered a memorial to us to offer to God continually instead of a sacrifice.

This also the wondrous David inspired by the Holy Spirit to foresee the future, foretold in these words :

"I waited patiently for the Lord, and he inclined unto me |, and heard my calling |.   2. And he brought (d) me up out of a pit of misery |, and from miry clay |. And he set my feet on a rock | and ordered my steps aright |.   3. And he hath put a new song in my mouth |, Ps. xl. 1-3. a hymn to our God. | "

And he shews clearly what "the new song" is when he goes on to say :

"7. Sacrifice and offering thou wouldest not | ; but

---

[1] The Logos as High Priest of Humanity sets aside for sacrifice the human Jesus, laying on Him our sins and Moses' curse. For this view of the Logos, cf. Origen, *de Prin.* ii. 6 ; iv. 31 ; *c. Cels.* II. 9, 20-25.

It is Origen's solution of the problem of the Incarnation, and, according to Harnack, aims at guarding the truth from Docetism and Ebionitism. "The Logos could unite itself with the body only through the medium of a human soul. This soul was a pure, unfallen spirit, which had destined itself for the soul in order to serve the purposes of redemption. It was a pure spirit fundamentally united with the Logos, and became then by reason of its moral worthiness, a medium for the incarnation of the Logos (closest inner union, but really perfect only through incessant exercise of will from both sides ; therefore no mingling). The Logos remains unchangeable ; only the soul hungers and suffers, inasmuch as it, like the body, is truly human."— *Outlines of the History of Dogma* (E.T. 1893), p. 163. Cf. *History of Dogma* (E.T.), vol. ii. 371.

a body hast thou prepared me | ; whole burnt-offering,
and sin offering thou didst take no pleasure in |. 8. Then
said I, Lo, I come : | in the volume of the book it is
written of me |, to do thy will, O God, I desired. | "

Ps. xl. 6.

And he adds : " I have preached righteousness in the great
congregation." He plainly teaches that in place of the
ancient sacrifices and whole burnt-offerings the incarnate
presence of Christ that was prepared was offered. And
this very thing He proclaims to his Church as a great mystery
expressed with prophetic voice in the volume of the book.
As we have received a memorial of this offering which we
celebrate on a table [1] by means of symbols of His Body and
saving Blood according to the laws of the new covenant,
we are taught again by the prophet David to say :

Ps. xl. 9.
(39)

" 5. Thou hast prepared a table before me in the
face of my persecutors |. Thou hast anointed my head
with oil |, and thy cup cheers me as the strongest
(wine). | "

(b)

Ps. xxii. 5.

Here it is plainly the mystic Chrism [2] and the holy Sacrifices

---

[1] Psalm xxii. is referred to the Memorial ($\mu\nu\eta\mu\eta$) of Christ's Sacrifice
which is performed, " ἐπὶ τραπέζης διὰ συμβόλων τοῦ τε σώματος αὐτοῦ
καὶ τοῦ σωτηρίου αἵματος." διὰ συμβόλων is emphatic. E. has indeed
said (37 c) that the Jewish sacrifices are σύμβολα καὶ εἰκόνες, but that
they do not embrace truth (περιέχουσι ἀλήθειαν). The Eucharistic
"symbols" *do* embrace truth, *i. e.* they give what they represent. So,
355 d, the elements are τὰ σύμβολα τῆς ἐνθέου οἰκονομίας . . . τὴν
εἰκόνα τοῦ ἰδίου σώματος. So Harnack says, " What we nowadays
understand by a symbol is a thing which is not that which it represents ;
at that time (in the second century) symbol denoted a thing which, in
some kind of way, is what it represents" (*History of Dogma*, vol. ii.
p. 144). The thing was behind the symbol, but not identical with it.
Cf. W. R. Inge, *Christian Mysticism*, pp. 252-261. For sacramental
symbolism as an integral part of all early Gentile Christianity, see
Harnack, *Expansion of Christianity*, vol. i. pp. 285-299, *e. g.* " The
Christian religion was intelligible and impressive owing to the fact that
it offered men sacraments."

[2] τὸ μυστικὸν χρῖσμα. For the unction of the whole body with
exorcized oil *before* Baptism, which was very early in the East and is
continued in the Greek Church, cf. Cyril, *Catech. Myst.* ii, 3, 4 ; *Apost.
Const.* vii. 22 ; Chrys. *Hom. VI in Ep. ad Coloss. c.* 4. It was much
later in the West.

For unction after Baptism, there is evidence from the early Coptic
Church, cf. Tatham's *Apost. Const. Copt.* 59, and abundant references
in Western Fathers from Tertullian (*De Bapt.* 7, A.D. 192) onwards.
This was on the head.

We do not hear of Unction at Confirmation till the fifth century.

of Christ's Table that are meant, by which we are taught
to offer to Almighty God through our great High Priest all
through our life the celebration of our sacrifices, bloodless,
reasonable, and well-pleasing to Him.   And this very thing
the great prophet Isaiah wonderfully foreknew by the Holy
Spirit, and foretold.   And he therefore says thus :   (c)

> "O Lord, my God, I will glorify thee, I will hymn
> thy name, for thou hast done marvellous things."   Isa. xxv. 1.

And he goes on to explain what these things so truly
"wonderful" are :

> "And the Lord of Sabaoth shall make a feast for all
> the nations.   They shall drink joy, they shall drink
> wine, they shall be anointed with myrrh (on this
> mountain).   Impart thou all these things to the nations.
> For this is God's counsel upon all the nations."   Isa xxv. 6.

These were Isaiah's "wonders," the promise of the anointing with ointment of a good smell, and with myrrh made
not to Israel but to all nations.   Whence not unnaturally (d)
through the chrism of myrrh they gained the name of
Christians.   But he also prophesies the "wine of joy" to
the nations, darkly alluding to the sacrament of the new
covenant of Christ, which is now openly celebrated among
the nations.   And these unembodied and spiritual sacrifices
the oracle of the prophet also proclaims, in a certain
place :

> "Offer to God the sacrifice of praise, and give the
> Highest thy vows : And call upon me in the day of
> thy affliction, and I will deliver thee, and thou shalt
> glorify me."   Ps. l. 14.

And again : "The lifting up of my hands is an evening Ps. cxli. 2.
sacrifice."   And once more : "The sacrifice of God is a
contrite spirit."   Ps. li. 17.

And so all these predictions of immemorial prophecy (40)
are being fulfilled at this present time through the teaching
of our Saviour among all nations.   Truth bears witness
with the prophetic voice with which God, rejecting the
Mosaic sacrifices, foretells that the future lies with us :

The compound μύρον, which came to be used instead of pure oil, was
similar to the "Unguentum regale" of the Parthians, the recipe for
which is given by Pliny, *Nat. Hist.* xiii. 1. (See *D.C.A.*, art.
"Unction.")

"Wherefore from the rising of the sun unto the setting my name shall be glorified among the nations. And in every place incense shall be offered to my name, and a pure offering."

Mal. i. 11.

We sacrifice, therefore, to Almighty God a sacrifice of praise. We sacrifice the divine and holy and sacred (b) offering. We sacrifice anew according to the new covenant the pure sacrifice. But the sacrifice to God is called "a contrite heart." "A humble and a contrite heart thou wilt not despise." Yes, and we offer the incense of the prophet, in every place bringing to Him the sweet-smelling fruit of the sincere Word of God, offering it in our prayers to Him. This yet another prophet teaches, who says:

Ps. l. 17.

Ps. cxl. 2. "Let my prayer be as incense in thy sight."

So, then, we sacrifice and offer incense:[1] On the one (c) hand when we celebrate the Memorial of His great Sacrifice according to the Mysteries He delivered to us, and bring to God the Eucharist for our salvation with holy hymns and prayers; while on the other we consecrate ourselves to Him alone and to the Word His High Priest, devoted to Him in body and soul. Therefore we are careful to keep our bodies pure and undefiled from all evil, and we bring our hearts purified from every passion and stain of sin, and worship Him with sincere thoughts, real intention, and true beliefs. For these are more acceptable to Him, so we are taught, than a multitude of sacrifices offered with blood and smoke and fat.

---

[1] There is no trace of incense in Christian worship during the first four centuries. In the *Pilgrimage of Etheria* (see edition in this series, p. 49) it seems to be used as a fumigatory before the service, cf. Tertullian, *de Cor.* c. 10. See Clem. Alex. (A.D. 192), *Strom.* VII. c. vi. § 32. Lactantius (A.D. 320), *Divin. Inst.* Epit. 2. St. Augustine (A.D. 396), *Enarr. in Ps.* xlix. § 21.

BOOK II

PREFACE

That we have not embraced the Prophetic Books of the (43)
Hebrews with so much Zeal without Aim or Object.

IN my survey of the ideal of true religion brought
before all men by the Gospel teaching and of the Life
in Christ in the previous book, I have argued and I (b)
believe demonstrated the impossibility of all the nations
living by the Jewish law, even if they wished. My
present object is to resume the argument at a point
further back,[1] to return to the evidence of the prophetic
books, and to give a more complete answer to the charges
of those of the Circumcision, who say that we have no (c)
share whatever in the promises of their Scriptures. They
hold that the prophets were theirs, that the Christ, Whom
they love to call Saviour and Redeemer, was foretold to
them, and that it is to be expected that the written promises
will be fulfilled for them. They despise us as being of
alien races, about which the prophets are unanimous in
foretelling evil. I propose to meet these attacks by evidence derived straight from their own prophetic books. (d)
With regard to the Christ of God having been promised
in their land, and His advent preaching salvation to Israel,
we should be the last to deny it; all would agree that this
is the plain teaching of all their writings. But with regard
to the Gentiles being debarred from the expected benefits
in Christ, on the ground that the promise was limited to
Israel, it is quite impossible to yield to what they advance
against the evidence of Holy Scripture.

---

[1] ἄνωθεν ἐπαναλαβών τὸν λόγον, ἐπάνειμι ἐπί. Cf. ἐπαναβεβηκός,
P.E. 130 b.

63

CHAPTER 1

(44) *That their Prophets gave their Best Predictions for Us of the Foreign Nations.*

(b) In the first place, as it is their constant habit to pick out the prophecies which are more favourable to themselves, and to have them ever on their lips, I must array against them my proofs from the prophecies about the Gentiles, making it clear how full they are of predictions of good and salvation for all nations, and how strongly they asserted that their promises to the Gentile world could only be fulfilled by the coming of the Christ. When we shall have reached that point of the argument, I think I shall have proved that it is untrue to say that the hope of the Messiah was more proper for them than for us.

(c) Then having demonstrated that for Jews and Greeks the hope of the promise was on an equality, so that those of the Gentiles would be saved through Christ would be in exactly the same position as the Jews, I shall proceed to show with super-abundance of evidence,[1] that the divine oracles foretold that the Advent of Christ and the call of the Gentiles would be accompanied by the total collapse and ruin of the whole Jewish race, and prophesied good fortune only for a scanty few easy to number, while their city

(d) with its temple would be captured, and all its holy things taken away—prophecies which have all been exactly fulfilled. How under one head and at the same time holy Scripture can foretell for Israel at Christ's coming both a ransom from evil and the enjoyment of prosperity, and also adversity and the overturning of the worship of God, I will make clear when the proper time comes. For the present let us go on with our first task ; viz., to select a few statements to prove my contentions from a great number of prophecies.

Inasmuch, then, as they always use in argument with us the prophecies about themselves, which are most favourable, as if the privileges of the old dispensation were limited to them, it is time for us to array against them the

---

[1] ἐκ περιουσίας : generally a rhetorical figure—"from superabundant evidence." Gifford [P.E. 64 a, 2] quotes Plato, *Theat.* : "sparring for mere amusement."

promises about the Gentiles, as contained in their own prophets.

1. From Genesis.   (45)

How the Nations of the World will be blessed in the same Way as those named after Abraham.

[Passage quoted, Gen. xviii. 27.]

The oracle says that God will not hide from the' man dear to Him a mystery that is hidden and secret to many, but will reveal it to him. And this was the promise that (b) all the nations should be blessed, which had of old been hidden through all the nations in Abraham's day being given over to unspeakably false superstition, but is now unveiled in our time, through the Gospel teaching of our Saviour that he who worships God in the manner of Abraham will share His blessing. We must not suppose (c) that this oracle referred to Jewish proselytes, since we have very fully shown in the preceding book the impossibility of all nations following the law of Moses. And as I have proved in the same book that the blessing on all nations given to Abraham could only apply to the Christians of all nations, I will refer those interested to the former passage.

2. From the same.

That all the Nations of the Earth will be blessed in the Seed that is to come from the Line of Isaac.

The Lord conferring with Isaac, after saying other things, (d) proceeds—

[Passage quoted, Gen. xxvi. 3.]

Our Lord and Saviour Jesus Christ was born of the seed of Isaac, according to the flesh, in Whom all the nations of the earth are blessed, in learning through Him of Almighty God, and in being taught through Him to bless men dear to God. So there is reciprocal blessing, they enjoying the same blessing as the men they bless, according to God's saying to Abraham : "Blessed be they Num. that bless thee."[1]   xxiv. 9

---

[1] The words of Balaam. Cf. Gen. xii. 3.

(46)   3. From the same.

*Of many Nations, and Multitudes of Nations, arising out of
Jacob, although only the Nation of the Jews has come forth
from him.*

[Passage quoted, Gen. xxxv. 11.]

As it is quite certain that only one nation, that of the
Jews, arose from Jacob, how can this oracle speak truly
of a multitude of nations? Since the Christ of God being
born of the seed of Jacob brought together many multitudes of nations by His Gospel teaching, in Him and
(b) through Him the prophecy has attained its natural fulfilment already, and will attain it still more.

4. From Deuteronomy.

The Joy in God of the Nations.

[Passage quoted, Deut. xxxii. 43.]

(c)   Instead of "Rejoice ye Gentiles with his people,"
Aquila[1] reads, "Cry out, nations of his people." And
Theodotion,[2] "Exult, ye nations of his people."

5. From Psalm xxi.

*How from the ends of the Earth, and from all Nations there
shall be a Turning to God, and how the Generation to
come and the People that shall be begotten shall learn
Righteousness.*

[Passage quoted, Ps. xxi. 28-32.]

This is clear enough to need no interpretation.

---

[1] Aquila, a Jewish proselyte, probably of Hadrian's time (A.D.
117-138), who produced a Greek version of O.T. which occupies
the third column of Origen's *Hexapla*. His version is slavishly
literal, and attempts to give a word for word translation, thus throwing
great light on the then state of the Hebrew text. The Fathers on the
whole regard the version as having an anti-Christian bias. Deutsch
(*Dict. Bib.* III. 1642) would identify A. with Onkelos.

[2] Theodotion, like A. first mentioned by Irenæus (iii. xxi. 1, p. 215),
probably an Ephesian Jewish proselyte. He wrote his version probably about A.D. 180 (it is a very vexed question) or earlier. It
occupies the sixth column of the *Hexapla*.

6. From Psalm xlvi.   (47)

An Announcement of Holiness and Purity to the Nations,
and the Kingdom of God over the Nations.

[Passages quoted, Ps. xlvi. 1, 2 and 8]

This is clear, and needs no interpretation.

7. From Psalm lxxxv.

The holiness of the nations.

[Passage quoted, Ps. lxxxv. 8–10.]

8. From Psalm xcv.

Of the Holiness of all the Heathen, and of the new Song,
and of the Kingdom of God, and of the Happiness of the
World.

[Passages quoted, Ps. xcv. 1–4, 7, and 10.]

This is clear.

9. From Zechariah.

Of all the Nations, and of the Egyptians the most superstitious
of them all, of the Knowledge of the only true God, and
of the spiritual Worship and Festival according to the
divine Law.

[Passage quoted, Zech. xiv. 16–19.]   (48)

This passage clearly implies the calling of all the
Gentiles, if we only regard the sense of what is said about
Jerusalem and the tabernacle, to which I will give the
proper interpretation in its right place.

10. From Isaiah.

Of the Choice of the Apostles, and the Calling of the Gentiles.

[Passage quoted, Isa. ix. 1–2.]

11. From the same.

Of the Calling of the Gentiles.

[Passage quoted, Isa. xlix. 1.]

In which he adds more about the Gentiles and about (c)
Christ.

[Passage quoted, Isa. xlix. 6.]

And you could yourself find many such passages, dispersed through the prophets in the promises to the nations, which there is no time now to select or interpret. Those that I have chosen are sufficient to prove my point. And this was simply to demonstrate to the Circumcision, who proudly and boastfully claim, that God has preferred them (d) before all other nations, and given them a peculiar privilege in His divine promises, that nothing of the kind is to be found in the divine promises themselves.

And now that I have proved the inclusion of the Gentiles in the divine promises, I would ask you to consider the reason of their being called and admitted to the promises. For it will be good for us to realize the reason why they can be said to be associated in their benefits. This can only be the coming of Christ, through Whom those of the Circumcision also agree that they look for their own redemption. I have then only to prove that the hope (49) of the call of the Gentiles was nothing else but the Christ of God, looked for as the Saviour, not only of the Jews, but of the whole Gentile world. And for the present I will give the mere texts of the prophets without interpretation, as I shall be able to interpret them individually at leisure more broadly[1] altogether, when with God's help I have collected the predictions about the nations.

CHAPTER 2

12. From Psalm ii.

(c) *Of the Plotting against Christ, and He*[2] *that is called the Son of God, receiving His Portion and the Gentiles from the Father.*

[Passages quoted, Ps. ii. 1, 2, and 7, 8.]

---

[1] εἰς πλάτος.   [2] Nominative.

13. From Psalm lxxi.

Of Christ's Kingdom, and the Call of the Gentiles, and the (50)
Blessing of all the Tribes of the Earth.

[Passages quoted, Ps. lxxi. 1, 2, 8, 11, 17, 19.]

14. From Psalm xcvii.

Of the new Song, and of the Arm of the Lord, and of the
Shewing of His Salvation to all Nations ; the Salvation
of the Son is shewn by the Name in the Hebrew.

15. From Genesis.

How after the Cessation of the Kingdom of the Jews, the (c)
Christ Himself coming will be the Expectation of the
Gentiles.

"There shall not fail a prince from Juda, nor a
governor from his loins, until he come in whom it is
laid up,[1] and he is the expectation of the Gentiles." Gen. xlix.
10.

16. From Zephaniah.

A Shewing forth of the Appearing of Christ, and of the (d)
Destruction of Idolatry, and of the Piety of the Nations
towards God.

[Passage quoted, Zeph. ii. 11.]

17. From the same.

A Shewing forth of the Day of Christ's Resurrection, and (51)
the Gathering of Nations, and of all Men knowing God,
and Turning to Holiness, and how the Ethiopians will
bring Sacrifices to him.

[Passage quoted, Zeph. iii. 8.]

18. From Zechariah.

A Shewing forth of the Appearing of Christ, and of the (h)
Fleeing of many Nations to Him, and how the Peoples
of the Nations shall be established in the Lord.

[Passage quoted, Zech. ii. 10.]

[1] See note, p. 21.

19. From Isaiah.

(c) *A Shewing forth of the Birth of Christ coming from the Root of David, and the Call by Him of all the Nations.*

[Passages quoted, Isa. xi. 1, 10.]

20. From the same.

(52) *A Shewing forth of the Appearing of Christ, and of the*
(d) *Benefits brought by him to all the Nations.*

[Passages quoted, Isa. xlii. 1–4 and 6–9.]

21. From the same.

(b) *A Shewing forth of Christ and his Birth, and the Call of the Gentiles.*

[Passage quoted, Isa. xlix. 1.]

22. From the same.

(c) *The Shewing forth of the Coming of Christ and of the Call of the Gentiles.*

[Passage quoted, Isa. xlix, 7.]

23. From the same.

(53) *À Shewing forth of Christ, and the Call of the Gentiles.*

[Passage quoted, Isa. lv. 3–5.]

And now that we have learned from these passages that the presence of Christ was intended to be the salvation not only of the Jews, but of all nations as well, let me prove my third point, that prophecies not only foretold that good things for the nations would be associated with the date of His appearance, but also the reverse for the Jews. Yes, the Hebrew oracles foretell distinctly the fall and ruin of the Jewish race through their disbelief in Christ, so that we should no longer appear equal to them, but better than they. And I will now present the bare quotations from the prophets without any comment on them, because they are quite clear, and because I intend at my leisure to examine them thoroughly.

CHAPTER 3

24. From Jeremiah.   (d)

Shewing forth the Refusal of the Jewish Race, and the (54)
Substitution of the Gentiles in their Place.

[Passage quoted, Jer. vi. 16.]

25. From the same.

*Shewing forth of the Piety of the Nations, and Accusation
of the Impiety of the Jewish Race. Prediction of the
Evils to overtake them after the Coming of Christ.*

[Passage quoted, Jer. xvi. 19–xvii. 4.] [1]

26. From Amos.   (d)

*Concerning the Dispersion of the Jewish Race among all the
Nations, and the Renewing of Christ's Coming and Kingdom, and the Call of all the Nations consequent upon it.*

[Passage quoted, Amos ix. 9.]

27. From Micah.   (55)

*Accusation of the Rulers of the Jewish People, and a Shewing
forth of the Desolation of their Mother-city, and the Appearance of Christ and of the House of God His Church,
the Entrance of His Word and His Law, and its Shewing
to all Nations.* [2]

[Passages quoted, Mic. iii. 9–iv. 2.]

28. From Zechariah.

*Shewing forth of Christ's Appearing, and the Destruction of
the warlike Preparation of the Jews, and the Peace of the
Nations, and the Kingdom of the Lord unto the Ends of
the World.*

[Passage quoted, Zech. ix. 9–10.]

29. From Malachi.   (56)

*Rebuke of the Jewish Race, and Refusal of the Mosaic out-
ward Worship, and of the spiritual Worship delivered
by Christ to all Nations.*

[Passage quoted, Mal. i. 10–12.]

---

[1] Jer. xvii. 1–4 is wanting from LX , but given in some codices
with asterisks.   See also 484 c.

[2] τῶν ἐθνῶν ἁπάντων.

30. From Isaiah.

(b) *The Apostasy of the Jewish Race and the Revelation of the Word of God, and of the new Law, and of His House, and the Shewing forth of the Piety of all the Nations.*

[Passages quoted, Isa. i. 8, 21, 30 ; ii. 2–4.]

31. From the same.

(57)

The Destruction of the Glory of the People of the Jews, and the Turning of the Nations from Idolatry to the God of the Universe, and the Prophecy of the Desolation of the Jewish Cities, and of their Unfaithfulness to their God.

[Passage quoted, Isa. xvii. 5–11.]

32. From the same.

Shewing forth of the destruction of the Jewish cities, and of the joy of the Gentiles in God.

[Passage quoted, Isa. xxv. 1–8.]

33. From the same.

(d)

The Message of good News to the Church of the Nations desolate of old, and the Rejection of the Jewish Nation, and Accusation of their Sins, and the Call of all the Gentiles.

[Passages quoted, Isa. xliii. 18–25 ; xlv. 22–25.]

34. From the same.

Shewing forth of the Coming of Christ to Men. And Reproof of the Jewish Race, and Promise of good Things to all Nations.

[Passages quoted, Isa. l. 1, 2, 10 ; li. 4, 5.]

(59)   ### 35. From the same.

Reproof of the Sins of the Jewish People, and their Fall from Piety, and the Shewing forth of the Cail of all the Gentiles.

[Passages quoted, Isa. lix. 1–11, 19.]

(d)   But although there are a number of prophecies on this subject, I will be content with the evidence I have pro-

duced, and I will return to them again and explain [1] them
at the proper time, as I consider that by the use of these
numerous texts and of their evidence I have given adequate
proof that the Jews hold no privilege beyond other nations.
For if they say that they alone partake of the blessing of
Abraham, the friend of God, by reason of their descent
from him, it can be answered that God promised to the
Gentiles that He would give them an equal share of the
blessing not only of Abraham but of Isaac and Jacob
also, since He expressly predicted that all nations would
be blessed like them, and summoned the rest of the
nations under one and the same (rule of) joy as the
blessed and the godly, in saying: "Rejoice ye Gentiles   Deut.
with his people," and: "The princes of the peoples were   xxxii. 43 ;
gathered together with the God of Abraham."   Ps. xlvii.
                                                             9.
    And if it is on the kingdom of God they plume them-   (60)
selves, as being His portion, it can be answered that God
prophesies that He will reign over all other nations. For
he says: "Tell it out among the heathen that the Lord is   Ps. xcvi.
King." And again: "God reigneth over all the nations."   10.
    And if they say that they were chosen out to act as   Ps. xlvii.
priests and to offer worship to God, it can be shewn that   8.
the Word promised that He would give to the Gentiles
an equal share in His service, when He said: "Render
to the Lord, O ye kindreds of the nations, render to the
Lord glory and honour: bring sacrifices and come into   Ps. xcvi. 7.
his courts." To which the oracle in Isaiah may be con-   (b)
joined, which says: "There shall be an altar to the Lord
in the land of Egypt . . . and the Egyptians will know
the Lord. And they shall do sacrifice, and say prayers to
the Lord, and offer." And in this you will understand   Isa. xix.19
that it is prophesied that an altar will be built to the Lord
away from Jerusalem in Egypt, and that the Egyptians will
there offer sacrifice, say prayers and give gifts to the Lord.
Yes, and not only in Egypt, but in the true Jerusalem
itself, whatever it is thought to be, all the nations, and the (c)
Egyptians forsooth, the most superstitious of them all, are
invited to keep the Feast of Tabernacles, as a feast of the
heart.[2]

---

[1] ἐξομαλίσομεν.

[2] τὴν κατὰ διάνοιαν θεωρουμένην σκηνοπηγίαν. Or, "the Feast of
Tabernacles in a spiritual sense."

Deut.
xxxii. 9. And if it was true long ago: "Jacob is become the portion of the Lord, and Israel the rope of his inheritance."

Yet afterwards it was also said that all the nations would be given to the Lord for His inheritance, the Father saying Ps. ii. 8. to him: "Desire of me, and I shall give thee the heathen for thine inheritance." And it is also prophesied that He shall rule from sea to sea and to the ends of the world: Ps. lxxii.
11, 17. "All the Gentiles shall serve him, and in him shall the tribes of the earth be blessed." And the reason of this (d) was that the Supreme God should make known His salvation before all nations. And I have already noted before that the name of Jesus translated from Hebrew into Greek would give "salvation," so that "the salvation of God" is simply the appellation of our Saviour Jesus Christ.

And Simeon bears witness to this in the Gospel, when he takes the infant in his hands, I mean of course Jesus, and prays:

(61)   "Now, Lord, lettest thou thy servant depart in peace, according to thy word:

For mine eyes have seen thy salvation,

Which thou hast prepared before the face of all people;

Luke ii. 29.   A light to lighten the Gentiles."

And this same salvation the Psalmist meant, when he said:

Ps. xcvii. 2.   "The Lord declared his salvation, in the sight of the heathen he openly shewed his righteousness."

And, according to Isaiah, it will be when they behold this very salvation that all men will worship the supreme God, (b) Who has bestowed His salvation on all ungrudgingly. And they will worship Him not in Jerusalem below, which is in Palestine, but each from his own place, and all who are in the isles of the Gentiles; and then, too, the oracle shall be fulfilled which said that all men should call no longer on their ancestral gods, nor on idols, nor on dæmons, but on the Name of the Lord, and shall serve Him under one yoke, and shall offer to Him from the furthest rivers of Ethiopia the reasonable and bloodless sacrifices of the new Covenant of Christ, to be sacrificed not in Jerusalem below, nor on the altar there, but in the aforesaid borders of Ethiopia.

(c)   And if it be admitted to be a noble privilege to be and

to be reckoned the people of God, and if this one thing is
the noblest of the divine promises, that God should say of
those who are worthy of Him, "I will be their God, and Jer. xxxi.
they shall be my people," Israel was naturally proud in 33.
days of old of being the only people of God, but now the
Lord has come to sojourn with us and promises graciously
to extend this privilege to the Gentiles, saying :

"Lo, I come, and I will dwell in the midst of you, Zech. ii.
and many nations shall flee unto the Lord, and they 10.
shall be to him a people."

On which I may aptly quote : "And I will say to a people (d)
that were not my people, Ye are my people. And they Hos. ii. 23.
shall say, Thou art the Lord our God." And if it is the
Christ and no one else Who is prophesied as springing from
the root of Jesse, and this at least is so strongly held by
the Hebrews themselves, that not one of them questions
its truth at all, consider how He is proclaimed as about to
arise to reign not over Israel but over the Gentiles, and
how the Gentiles are said to be about to hope in Him,
and not Israel, inasmuch as He is the expectation of the
Gentiles. Wherefore He is said "to be about to bring Isa. xlii.
judgment to the Gentiles," and "to be for a light to the 1, 6.
Gentiles." And again it is said : "In his name shall the
Gentiles trust," and that He shall be given for salvation
not only to the Jews but to all men, even to those at the
ends of the earth. Wherefore it was said to Him by the
Father that sent Him down :   (62)

"I gave thee for a covenant of the race, for a light of Isa. xlix. 8.
the Gentiles, to establish the earth, and to inherit the waste
heritages." He says He is "a witness to the Gentiles,"
meaning that nations which have never before learned
anything about Christ, when they knew His dispensation,
and the might that was in Him, have called on Him, and
that the peoples who did not before of old know Him, have
taken refuge in Him.

But why need I say more, since it is possible from these
prophetic sayings which I have laid before you, and from
others to be found in Holy Scripture which I will record at
leisure, for any one who wishes, to collect the words of the (b)
prophets, and by their aid to put to silence those of the
Circumcision, who say the promises of God were given to
them alone, and that we who are of the Gentiles are super-

numerary[1] and alien to the divine promises? For I have
proved, on the contrary, that it was prophesied that all the
Gentiles would benefit by the coming of Christ, while the
multitudes of the Jews would lose the promises given to
their forefathers through their unbelief in Christ, few of
(c) them believing in our Lord and Saviour, and therefore
attaining the promised spiritual redemption through Him.

About which the wonderful Apostle teaches something
when he says:

" 27. Isaiah also crieth concerning Israel, Though
the number of the children of Israel be as the sand of
the sea, the remnant[2] shall be saved: 28. For finishing the word and cutting it short in righteousness,
because a word cut short[3] will the Lord do upon the
earth. 29. And as Isaiah said before, If the Lord of
Sabaoth had not left to us a seed, we should have

Rom. ix.   been as Sodom, and we should have been like to
27-29.   Gomorrah."

(d) To which he adds after other things:

" 1. Hath God cast away his people? God forbid.
For I also am an Israelite, of the seed of Abraham, of
the tribe of Benjamin. 2. God hath not cast away his
people, which he foreknew. Know ye not what the
Scripture saith of Elias? how he intercedes with God,
speaking of Israel,[4] 3. Lord, they have killed thy
prophets, and digged down thine altars; and I only
am left, and they seek my life to take it away.[5] 4. But
what saith the answer of God to him? I have reserved to myself 7000 men, who have not bowed the
knee to Baal. 5. Even so then at this present time

Rom. xi.   also there is a remnant according to the election of
1-5.   grace."

(63) In these words the Apostle clearly separates, in the falling
away of the whole Jewish people, himself and the Apostles
and the Evangelists of our Saviour like Himself and all the

---

[1] περιττοὺς εἶναι.
[2] κατάλειμμα. LXX : D.F.K.L.P.—ὑπόλειμμα—‎א A.B.
[3] R.V. "For the Lord will execute his word upon the earth,
finishing it and cutting it short." ἐν . . . συντετμημένον. Omitted
by ‎א A.B. 47. W.H. retain with Western and Syrian.
[4] W.H.: κατὰ τοῦ Ἰσραήλ. E. λέγων περὶ τοῦ Ἰσραήλ.
[5] W.H.: omit τοῦ λαβεῖν αὐτήν.

Jews now who believe in Christ, as the seed named by
the prophet in the words : " Unless the Lord of Sabaoth
had left unto us a seed." And he implies that they also
are that which is styled in the other prophecies " the
remnant," which he says was preserved by the election of
grace. And with reference to this remnant I will now
return to the prophets and explain what they say, so that
the argument may be based on more evidence, that God
did not promise to the whole Jewish nation absolutely that (b)
the coming of Christ would be their salvation, but only
to a small and quite scanty number who should believe
in our Lord and Saviour, as has actually taken place in
agreement with the predictions.

36. From Isaiah.

That the Divine Promises did not extend to the whole (c)
Jewish Nation, but only to a few of them.

[Passage quoted Isa. i. 7–9.]

This great and wonderful prophet at the opening of his
own book here tells us that the whole scheme of his
prophecy includes a vision and a revelation against Judæa
and Jerusalem, then he attacks the whole race of the Jews, (d)
first saying :

" 3. The ox knoweth his owner, and the ass his
master's manger, but Israel doth not know, my people
doth not understand." Isa. i. 3

And then he laments the whole race, and adds :

" 4. Woe, race of sinners, a people full of iniquity,
an evil seed, unrighteous children."

Having brought these charges against them in the beginning
of his book, and shewn beforehand the reasons for the later
predictions that he is to bring against them, he goes on to
say, " Your land is desolate," though it was not desolate at
the time when he prophesied : " Your cities are burnt with
fire." Nor had this yet taken place, and strangers had
not devoured their land. And yet he says, " Your land, (64)
strangers devour it before your eyes," and that which follows.
But if you came down to the coming of our Saviour Jesus
Christ, and of those He sent, and to the present time, you
would find all the sayings fulfilled. For the daughter of

Zion (by whom was meant the worship celebrated on Mount
Zion) from the time of the coming of our Saviour has
(b) been left as a tent in a vineyard, as a hut in a garden of
cucumbers, or as anything that is more desolate than these.
And strangers devour the land before their eyes, now
exacting tax and tribute,[1] and now appropriating for themselves the land which belonged of old to Jews. Yea, and
the beauteous Temple of their mother-city was laid low,
being cast down by alien peoples, and their cities were burnt
with fire, and Jerusalem became truly a besieged city. But
(c) since, when all this happened, the choir of the Apostles,
and those of the Hebrews who believed in Christ, were
preserved from among them as a fruitful seed, and going
through every race of men in the whole world, filled every
city and place and country with the seed of Christianity
and Israel, so that like corn springing from it, the churches
which are founded in our Saviour's name have come into
being, the divine prophet naturally adds to his previous
threats against them : "We should have been as Sodom,
(d) and we should have been like unto Gomorrah." Which
the holy Apostle in the Epistle to the Romans more clearly
defines and interprets.

[The passages Rom. ix. 17–29 and xi. 1–5, already
quoted 62 c, d, are repeated.]

And to shew that the prophecy can only refer to the
(b) time of our Saviour's coming, the words that follow the
text—"unless the Lord of Sabaoth had left unto us a very
small remnant, we should have been as Sodom, and we
should have been like unto Gomorrah," naming the whole
people of the Jews as the people of Gomorrah, and their
rulers as the princes of Sodom—imply a rejection of the
Mosaic worship, and introduce in the prediction about them
the characteristics of the covenant announced to all men by
our Saviour, I mean regeneration by water,[2] and the word
and law completely new. For it says :

(c)   "Hear the word of the Lord, ye rulers of Sodom,
        give heed to the law of God, ye people of Gomorrah,
Isa. i. 10.   What is the multitude of your sacrifices to me?"
and that which follows. Thus it takes away what belongs

---

[1] δασμοὺς καὶ φόρους
[2] τὸν διὰ λουτροῦ παλιγγενεσίας.

to the Mosaic law, and introduces in its place another
mode of the forgiveness of sins, through the washing of
salvation and the life preached in accordance with it,
saying: "Wash you, be ye clean; take away the evils from   Isa. i. 16.
your souls."

And the prophet himself at once supplies the reason,
why he called them rulers of Sodom, and people of
Gomorrah: "For your hands are full of blood."

And again a little further on:

"They have proclaimed their sin as Sodom and (d)
made it manifest. Woe to their soul, because they
have taken evil counsel with themselves, saying,[1] We
will bind the just, for he is burdensome to us."   Isa. iii. 9.
Since he so very clearly mentions some one's blood, and
a plot against some one just man, what could this be but
the plot against our Saviour Jesus Christ, through which [2]
and after which all the things aforesaid overtook them?

37. From the same Isaiah.

[Passage quoted Isa. iv. 2.]

And the meaning of "the remnant of Israel" the prophet (66)
himself clearly explains by the words, "All who are
registered in Jerusalem, and called holy." It will be clear
to you, if you run through the whole course of this section,
what that day is, in which it is said God will glorify and
exalt the remnant of Israel and those who are called holy
and to be written in (the book of) life. For in the begin- (b)
ning of his complete book the prophet having seen the
vision against Judah and Jerusalem, and numbered in
many words the sins of the whole people of the Jews, and
uttered threats and spoken about their ruin and the complete desolation of Jerusalem, brings his vision about them
to an end with the words:

"30. For they shall be as a terebinth that has cast
her leaves, and as a garden without water. 31. And
their strength shall be as a thread of tow, and their
works as sparks of fire, and the transgressors and the   Isa. i. 30
sinners shall be burnt together, and there shall be none (c)
to quench them."

---

[1] LXX takes $\kappa\alpha\theta'$ $\dot{\epsilon}\alpha\upsilon\tau\hat{\omega}\nu$ with $\epsilon\dot{\iota}\pi\acute{o}\nu\tau\epsilon\varsigma$,
[2] Paris text has $\delta\iota'$ $\ddot{o}\nu$—$\ddot{o}\nu$—$\alpha\dot{\upsilon}\tauo\dot{\upsilon}\varsigma$.

And having inscribed here the prediction against them, he
"lowers his tone "[1]: and making another start he enters on
a second subject, and as a preface, so to say, employs
such words as these, " The word which came to Isaiah the
(d) son of Amos concerning Judah and Jerusalem"; or, as
Symmachus [2] interpreted it, "on behalf of Judah and
Jerusalem." From which one would perhaps expect that
he was about to change to more favourable prophecies
about the same peoples on whom his former predictions
had showered sadness. But the succeeding passages would
certainly not confirm the expectation, since they contain
nothing at all that is good with regard to the race of the
Jews, or that which is called Israel, neither for Judah nor
Jerusalem. On the contrary, they bring many charges and
accusations against Israel, and gloomy threats against Jerusalem, and prophesy for all the Gentiles salvation in their
call and in the knowledge of the Supreme God. While in
addition to this they tell of the coming of a new Mount,
and the manifesting of another House of God, besides the
one in Jerusalem. For he says after speaking about Judæa
and Jerusalem :

(67)   " 2. In the last days the Mount of the Lord shall be
manifest, and the house of the Lord upon the tops of
the mountains, and it shall be exalted above the hills,
3. and all nations shall come to it, and shall say, Come
and let us go up to the Mount of the Lord, and to the
Isa. ii. 2.   house of the God of Jacob."

Such are his prophecies about all the Gentiles. Hear
what he proceeds to add about the Jews :

" 6. For he has rejected his people, the house of the
God of Jacob,[3] for the land is filled as at the beginning
with auguries, as the land of strangers, and many

---

[1] ὑποστολῇ χρῆται, "a lowering of diet," Plut. 2, 129 c. ; "an
evasion," Hesych. cf. Heb. x. 39.
[2] Symmachus, author of the third great Jewish version of the O.T.,
which comes in Origen's *Hexapla* after that of Aquila. Eusebius
(*H.E.* vi. 17, *Dem. Ev.* 316 c) makes him an Ebionite Christian, and
is followed by Jerome. Epiphanius' statement that he was a Samaritan
Jew is to be rejected (see Gwynne's art. in *D.C.B.* iv. p. 749). He
probably lived in the reign of Marcus Aurelius, and wrote his version
aiming at the same literal accuracy as Aquila, but at more refinement
of expression.
[3] LXX : οἶκον τοῦ Ἰσραήλ.

children of strangers are born to them.　7. For the
land was filled with silver and gold, and there was (b)
no end of their treasures."

And that which follows after this, to which he adds:

"9. And they worshipped that which their own
fingers had made, and a man bowed down, and was
humbled, and I will not reject them.　10. And now
enter ye into the rocks, and hide yourselves in the
earth from the face of the fear of the Lord, and from
the face of his glory, when he arises to shake the
earth."

And in this he teaches that there will be a Resurrection
of the Lord, at which all the land of the Jewish people (c)
will be shattered.　For the whole portion refers to them,
in the following sections as well, saying: "For the day of
the Lord of Sabaoth shall be upon every one that is proud
and insolent, and upon every one that is lofty and exalted."
And that which follows.　Wherefore it is on the day of
the Lord's Resurrection, that the prophet having first
addressed those who lift themselves up against the knowledge of God, says: "On this very day"; "the Lord
shall be exalted in that very day, and they shall hide all
the work of their hands, bearing them into the caves," (d)
clearly showing the destruction of the idols, which the
Jews themselves and all other men cast away after the
appearance of the Saviour, despising all superstitions:

"20. On that day, he says, a man shall cast away his
abominations of gold and silver which they made to
worship vanities."

Thus speaking, it would seem, generally about all men,
because of the coming call of the Gentiles.　But he alludes
particularly again to the Jewish race under one head as
follows:

"Behold now, the Lord, the Lord of Sabaoth, will take
away from Judæa and from Jerusalem the strong man and
strong woman, the strength of bread, and the strength
of water, 2. The giant and the strong man, and the
man of war, and the judge, and the prophet, and (68)
the counsellor, and elder, and captain of fifty, 3. And
the wonderful counsellor, and the clever artificer,
and the wise hearer."

And that which follows.　Stop at this point, and set

Isa.iii.1-3.

beside the above the introduction to the prophecy, in which it was said: "The word that came from the Lord to Isaiah the son of Amoz on behalf of Judah and Jerusalem," and see how much more in accordance with what follows "against" is than "for," unless indeed some hidden meaning is contained in the words. For how could one about to take away from Judah and Jerusalem strong

(b) man and strong woman, the strength of bread and the strength of water, and all things that of old were beautiful among them, introduce his prophecy by saying it was "for" Judah and Jerusalem? And how could that which follows again be "for" them :

"Jerusalem is forsaken, and Judæa hath fallen, and their tongues [have spoken] with iniquity, disbelieving the things of the Lord"?

Isa. iii. 8.

Nay, rather, at a time when it should be necessary for the Mountain of the Lord to be proclaimed to all the Gentiles, and the House of God on the Mount, when all

(c) the Gentiles meet and say: "Come and let us go up to the Mount of the Lord, and to the House of the God of Jacob": the Scripture using such accusations of the Jewish race, and threatening them so sorely, adds thereto all the sayings I have quoted, and teaches that of the whole Jewish race which will fall away from the holiness of God, there will be left over some of them not immersed in their common evils ; and further, that being saved as it were from the sinful and lawless, and embracing piety in sincerity and truth, they will be reckoned worthy of

(d) God's Scripture, and will be called holy servants of God. And it means by these, the apostles, disciples, and evangelists of our Saviour, and all the others of the Circumcision, who believed on Him, at the time of the falling away of their whole race. Scripture darkly implies this, when it says: "In that day"—*i.e.* the day in which plainly all the aforesaid things shall take place connected with the calling of the Gentiles, and the falling away of the Jews—"God shall shine gloriously in counsel on the earth, to uplift and to glorify the remnant of Israel, and there shall be a remnant in Sion, and a remnant in Jerusalem, and all who are written for life in Jerusalem

Isa. iv. 2.
(69) shall be called holy."

And it was these, who came forth from Judæa and

Jerusalem that the preface meant the prophecy to allude
to, when it said: "For Judæa and Jerusalem," yea, both
the actual Jerusalem, and the figurative Jerusalem thought
of as analogous to it.   And which of the apostles of our
Saviour or of His evangelists, beholding the inspired power (b)
by which "their sound is gone out into all lands, and their
words to the ends of the earth," and by which all the
Churches of Christ from that day to this have their words
and teaching on their lips, and the laws of Christ of the
new covenant preached by them, would not bear witness
to the truth of the prophecy, which says that God openly
will exalt and glorify in counsel and with glory the
remnant of Israel through all the world, and that the
remnant in Sion and the remnant in Jerusalem shall be (c)
called holy, all they who are written in the book of life?

Instead of the reading of the LXX, "in counsel with
glory," Aquila and Theodotion agree in interpreting "for
power and glory" indicating the power given to the
apostles by God, and their consequent glory with God—
according to the words: "The Lord will give a word to Ps. lxviii.
the preachers with much power."   11.

And this which has really come to pass :

"9. Ye shall hear indeed, and shall not understand :
and seeing ye shall see and not perceive.   10. For
the heart of this people is waxed gross, and they hear (d)
with heavy ears, and they have closed their eyes, lest
they should ever see with their eyes, and hear with their
ears,[1] and turn, and I should heal them.[2]   11. And I
said, Until when, O Lord?   And he said, Until the
cities be desolated that none dwell in them, and houses
that no men be in them, and the earth be left desolate.
12. And afterwards God will increase men, and they
that are left on the earth shall be increased."   Isa. vi. 9.

And notice here how they that are left again on the earth,
all the rest of the earth being desolate, alone are said to
multiply.   These must surely be our Saviour's Hebrew
disciples, going forth to all men, who being left behind (70)
like a seed have brought forth much fruit, namely, the
Churches of the Gentiles throughout the whole world.
And see, too, how at the same time he says that only those
will multiply who are left behind from the falling away of

---

[1] S.: καὶ τῇ καρδίᾳ συνῶσιν.   [2] S.: ἰάσομαι.   E.: ἰάσωμαι.

the Jews, while the Jews themselves are utterly desolate:
"Their land," he says, "shall be left unto them desolate."
And this was also said to them before by the same prophet:
"Your land is desolate, your cities are burnt with fire, your
country strangers devour it before your eyes."

(b)   And when was this fulfilled, except from the times of
our Saviour? For up to the time they had not yet dared to
do impiety to Him, their land was not desolate, their cities
were not burned with fire, nor did strangers devour their
land. But from that inspired word, by which our Lord
and Saviour Himself predicted what was about to fall
on them, saying: "Your house is left unto you desolate,"
from that moment and not long after the prediction they
were besieged by the Romans and brought to desolation.

(c) And the word of prophecy gives the cause of the desolation, making the interpretation almost certain, and showing
the cause of their falling away. For when they heard our
Saviour teaching among them, and would not listen with
their mind's ear, nor understood Who He was, seeing Him
with their eyes, but not beholding Him with the eyes of
their spirit, "they hardened their heart, and all but closed
Isa. vi. 10. the eyes of their mind, and made their ears heavy."

As the prophecy says, because of this He says that their
cities would be made desolate so that none should dwell
in them, and their land should become desolate, and only

(d) a few of them be left behind, kept like fruitful and spark-
like seed, who it is said, should go forth to all men, and
multiply on the earth.

But also even after the departure of those who are
clearly the apostles of our Saviour, he says that "a tenth"
will still remain on Jewish soil:

"And again it shall be for a spoil, as a terebinth, and
Isa. vi. 13.   as an acorn, when it falls out of its husk."

The Scripture, as I suppose, means by this, that after
the first siege, which they are recorded to have undergone

(71) in the time of the apostles, and of Vespasian, Emperor
of the Romans, being a second time besieged again
under Hadrian they were completely debarred from entering the place, so that they were not even allowed to tread
the soil of Jerusalem.[1] And this he darkly suggests in the

[1] Cf. *H.E.* iv. c. 6; Tertullian, *Apol.* c. 16. Origen, *c. Celsum*
viii. *ad fin.*; Gregory Naz., *Orat.* xii. After the founding of Ælia

words: "And again it shall be for a spoil, as a terebinth, and as an acorn when it falls out of its husk": Isa. vii 21.

21. "And it shall come to pass in that day, a man will nourish a heifer and two sheep. 22. And it shall come to pass from their drinking much milk, every one left on the land shall eat butter and honey."

Here if you inquire to what day the prophet looks forward, (b) you will find it to be the very time of the appearance of our Saviour. For when the prophet says: "Behold a virgin shall be with child, and shall bring forth a son,"[1] though he interposes many things, yet he prophesies of the things that will come to pass on that very day, that is to say about the time of our Saviour's appearance.

For he says that unseen powers, and foes and enemies, (c) allegorically designated flies and bees, will attack the land of the Jews, and that the Lord with the razor of its foes will shave the head of the Jewish race, as if it were one great body, and the hairs from its feet, and its beard—in a word its whole glory. And this being done in the day prophesied when He shall be born of a virgin, he foretells that a man who is left from the destruction of the whole race, that is to say all of them who believe in the Christ of God, shall nourish a heifer of the bulls and two sheep, and from their producing very much milk shall eat butter and honey: and you will understand that this is mystically fulfilled in our Saviour's apostles. For each one of them (d) in the churches which he established by Christ's help, nourished two sheep, that is to say two orders of disciples coming like sheep into the sheepfold of Christ, the one as yet probationary, the other already enlightened by baptism,[2] and in addition to these one heifer, the ecclesiastical rule of those who preside with their inspired food of the word, and produced from them a fruitful increase of milk and honey from the food they have laboured to provide.

Capitolina, Milman says, "An edict was issued prohibiting any Jew from entering the new city on pain of death, or approaching its environs so as to contemplate even at a distance its sacred height."— *History of the Jews*, Book XVIII. *ad fin.*

[1] Isa. vii. 14.   Cf. 98 a, and Origen, *c. Celsum*, i. 35.

[2] τὸ μὲν εἰσέτι στοιχειούμενον, τὸ δὲ ἤδη διὰ τοῦ λουτροῦ πεφω-τισμένον.

(72)   That holy Scripture often likens the multitudes of less perfect disciples to sheep I need not say; every scripture teaches it.   And its comparison of the perfect man, who being the leader works the body of the Church as a farmer, to the work of bulls on the soil, the holy apostle uses, when he says:

> "Doth God take care for oxen?   Or saith he it altogether for our sakes?[1]   That he that ploweth should plow in hope, and that he that thresheth, should thresh in hope of partaking."

I Cor ix. 9.

And if any one is disgusted with such metaphorical interpretation, let him beware lest refusing to regard figuratively what are called flies, or bees, or a razor, or a beard, (b) or hairs on the feet, he falls into absurd and inconsistent mythology.   But if these things can only be figuratively understood, the same may certainly be said of the following:

> "18. In that day the mountains shall be consumed, and the hills, and forests, and shall be devoured from soul to body.   And he that flees shall be as one that fleeth from burning flame, 19. and they that are left of them shall be a number, and a little child[2] shall write them.   20. And it shall come to pass in that (c) day, the remnant of Israel shall no more be added, and they that are saved of Jacob shall no more trust in those that wronged them, and they shall trust in the God the holy one of Israel in truth, 21. and the remnant of Israel shall turn[3] to the mighty God. 22. And though the people of Israel be as the sand of the sea, the remnant of them shall be saved. 23. For he will finish the account, and cut it short in righteousness, for God will make a short account in the whole world."

Isa. x. 18.

And notice here, that in his denunciations of gloom, he says:

> "He that fleeth shall be as one that fleeth from a burning flame; and their remnant shall be a number, (d)   and a little child shall write them"—

by which he emphasizes the scanty number of those of the Circumcision who will escape destruction, and the

---

[1] W.H. add : δι' ἡμᾶς γὰρ ἐγράφη.   [2] E. adds μικρόν.
[3] S.: ἔσται.   E.: ἀναστρέψει.

burning of Jerusalem. "And they who are left," he says, "will be a number": that is they will be amenable to number, or few and easily numbered. As many, then, as those who believed in our Lord and Saviour were in comparison of the whole Jewish race, who also were thought worthy of being enrolled by Him, as the verse shews, which says: "And a little child shall write them." Having told us before Who the little child was, where he said: "Behold, the virgin shall be with child, and shall bring forth a son." And: "Before the child shall (73) know to call on its father or mother."

And since in this place he says: "A little child shall write them," it can be seen why he said in the previous one: "And these shall be a remnant in Sion, and a remnant in Jerusalem, all shall be called holy, and shall be written in [the book of] life." As therefore among them a remnant is named, and it is they who were written in [the book of] life, so also here "the remnant from them shall be a number, and a little child shall write them." And this "remnant from Israel, and they that are saved from Jacob no more" he says "shall be with those that do them wrong, but shall (b) trust in the Lord, the Holy One of Israel." So note if it is not with this very trust that they who went forth from the Jewish race, those who were left behind in the falling away of Israel, the disciples and apostles of our Saviour, taking no notice of the rulers of this world, or of the rulers of the people of the Circumcision who did them wrong of old, went forth to all the nations, preaching the word of Christ, and by their trust in God (for according to the prophecy " they were trusting in God, the holy one of Israel, in truth," for they (c) gave up their whole selves in hope, without deceit or hypocrisy, but with truth) not only went forth from their own land, but prospered in that whereto they were sent. And this same remnant was like the seed of the falling away of Jacob that trusted in the strength of God, and this remnant of the whole race that once was as the sand of the sea, but not as the stars of the heaven, was thought worthy of salvation by God, as the Apostle bore witness saying:

"Isaiah cries concerning Israel, If the number of the (d) children of Israel shall be as the sand of the sea, a remnant shall be saved."

For of the promises gives by the oracle to Abraham

concerning those who were to come after him that "they shall
be as the stars of the heaven, and as the sand of the sea,"
the friends of God are meant, on the one hand shining like
the heavenly lights, such as were those of old, the prophets
and our Saviour's apostles, to whom He bore witness saying :
"Ye are the light of the world"; but, on the other, the earth-
born who lie upon the ground are compared to the sand of
the shore.   The prophetic word speaks rightly in the above,
first where the whole multitude of Israel's sons, fallen from
(74) their true and magnificent virtue to the ground, is compared
to the sand of the sea, and then when it says only the
remnant shall be saved.   But I have now dealt sufficiently
with the question of the remnant.   And he says that this
will come to pass, when "the Lord cutting short and completing his word shall accomplish it through the whole world" :
clearly pointing to the Gospel preaching, by which, the
whole Mosaic circle of symbols and signs and bodily
(b) ordinances being taken away, the complete word of the
Gospel given to all men has confirmed the truth of the
prophecy.

  " 10. And in that day there shall be a root of Jesse,
and one arising to rule the Gentiles.   In him shall the
Gentiles hope, and his rest shall be glory.   11. And it
shall be in that day, the Lord shall again shew his hand,
to be jealous and to seek [1] the remnant remaining from his
people, which is left by the Assyrians, and from Egypt,
(c)   and Babylon, and Ethiopia, and from the Elamites, and
from the East, and from the isles of the sea.[2]   12. And
he will raise a standard to the nations, and will gather
together [3] the dispersed of Judah, from the four corners
Isa. xi. 10.   of the earth."

  As certain events were many times foretold as about to
take place on a definite day, that is to say, when a certain
time had come, I have by the use of reasoning proved that
the said events must follow the appearance of God, for when
He appears, the whole Jewish race falling away, holy Scripture
makes it clear that a scanty few of them will be left behind,
(d) while the passage now in our hands shews in the clearest
way both the day, and the time meant by it, and the events

---

[1] E. adds καὶ ζητῆσαι.
[2] LXX : καὶ ἐξ ᾿Αραβίας.   E.: καὶ ἀπὸ τῶν νήσων τῆς θαλάσσης.
[3] E. omits τοὺς ἀπολομένους ᾿Ισραήλ, καὶ.   (S.)

that were to follow it.   For it prophesies the birth of the
Christ of the seed of David, and at the same time foretells
the falling away of the Jews.   For it says thus :

   "Behold, the Lord, the Lord of Sabaoth, will mightily
   confound the glorious ones, and the lofty men shall be
   humbled, and the lofty shall fall by the sword, and Isa. x. 33.
   Libanus shall fall with the lofty."

By Libanus here Jerusalem is meant, as I have shewn
elsewhere, which Scripture threatens shall fall with all its
venerable and glorious men within it.   And having thus
begun, it says afterwards : "And a rod shall come out of (75)
the stem of Jesse, and a flower shall spring up from his Isa. xi. 1
root."

By showing very clearly that the birth of Christ should be
from the root of Jesse, who was the father of David, it
explains upon what birth the call of the Gentiles should
follow, which it had previously only given obscurely in the
prophetic manner.   For "the wolf shall feed with the lamb,
and the leopard shall lie down with the kid," and such
passages, are only intended to shew the change of savage
and uncivilized nations in no way differing from wild beasts
to a holy, mild, and social way of life.   And this is what it (b)
teaches afterwards without disguise, in the words : "The
whole [earth] shall be filled with the knowledge of the Lord,
as the waters cover the sea."   And moreover the prophetic
word proceeds to interpret itself :

   "And there shall be in that day a root of Jesse, and
   one arising to rule the Gentiles.   In him shall the
   Gentiles trust, and his rest shall be glory."

Since, then, it had predicted the falling away of the Jewish
race in a veiled way, and then the calling of the Gentiles,
first in a veiled way and then openly, it is natural for it (c)
in returning to the same topic to mention those of the
Circumcision who should believe in Christ, that it may not
seem to shut them altogether from hope in Christ.

   "For there shall be," it says, "one to arise to rule
   over the Gentiles."

Who could this be Who is to arise, but the root of Jesse,
whom it so clearly says is to reign over the Gentiles,
but not over Israel?   Since then it had taught in various
ways of the conversion of the Gentiles consequent upon
the birth and growth of Him Who came from the root of

Jesse, and had then nothing bright to say of those of the
Circumcision, it naturally here supplies the gap in the prediction, saying, "And it shall come to pass in that day,"
(d) *i.e.* in the time of him that is born of the root of Jesse,
the Lord moreover shall put forth His power,[1] to be jealous
for and to seek the remnant remaining of His people that
were left of such and such enemies.

In place of which Aquila has read :

"And it shall be in that day, the Lord will shew his
hand a second time, to possess the remnant of his
people, which shall be left by the Assyrians," etc.

And you will understand this, if you consider that the
enemies of the people of God are certain intelligent and
spiritual beings, either evil dæmons, or powers opposed
to the word of holiness, who in invisible leadership of the
(76) nations named, in days of old laid siege to the souls of
Israel, involved them in various passions, seducing them [2]
and enslaving them to a life like that of the other nations.
When, then, you may almost say that the whole people was
taken captive in soul by these powers, they who were kept
safe and intact, unwounded and undespoiled according to
(b) the prophecy received the message, that they should see
the hand of the Lord, and become His possession, according to the words of the oracle, "the Lord will add to shew
his hand, to be jealous for the remnant remaining of his
people."

But what will the Lord add? Surely to those to whom
once long before He had proclaimed by the prophets "the
hand of the Lord has been added," yea, to those who are,
as it were, preserved in the fall of the whole people He
proclaims that He will add what was lacking to the former.
And these are the mysteries of the new covenant, shewn
by the hand of the Lord to the remnant of the people.
(c) But He also says that "He will be jealous of the remnant
that is left of the people." Instead of which Aquila and
Theodotion agree in reading : "that He must acquire the
remnant of His people, whatever is left from the Assyrians,
and the other nations that were their enemies."

And this remnant which is left of His people "shall lift

Lit. "moreover shall add to shew his hand."
ὑποσύροντες. Cf. P.E. 317 a, Of the Serpent.

up" he says "a standard to the Gentiles." Through them clearly the Lord will shew His sign among all the Gentiles, and through them will gather together the lost (d) of Israel and the scattered abroad of Judah from the four corners [1] of the earth to the Christ of God, who take refuge in Him through the preaching of His apostles, saying that those gathered together come from them who of old were exiled and cut off from the figurative Israel and Judah. The ideals of such souls shew them to be the true Israel of God, for in contrast to them the weak and sinful nature of Israel according to the flesh makes Him prophetically call them : "Rulers of Sodom and people of Gomorrah."   Rom. xi 5.

Thus the "remnant according to the election of grace," and that which is called in the prophecy, "the remnant that is left of the people," has proclaimed the sign of the Lord to all the Gentiles, and has joined to God as one people, that is drawn to Him, the souls of the Gentiles that are brought out of destruction to the knowledge of the Lord, a people which from the four corners of the earth even now is welded together by the power of Christ.[2] And these same refugees from the lost race of the Jews, (77) the disciples and apostles of our Saviour belonging to different tribes, thought worthy of one calling, and one grace and one Holy Spirit, will cast away all the love, which the tribes of the Hebrew race had to them, as the prophecy says. Bound together, then, by the same mind and will, they have not only traversed the continent, but the isles of the Gentiles also, making plunder of all the (b) souls of men everywhere, and bringing them into captivity to the obedience of Christ, according to the oracle, which said :

> "And they shall fly in the ships of strangers ; they shall at the same time spoil the sea, and them from the sun-rising."   Isa. xi. 14.

And the remainder of this prophecy you will examine as I have done, testing each passage by yourself, and while you reject everything inconsistent and unworthy in it, yet you will recognize the mind of the Spirit, as the Spirit of (c) God itself suggests your meditation. For time does not

---

[1] Lit. wings.
[2] ἐφελκυσάμενον ἕνα λαὸν συνῆξε τῷ θεῷ . . . . συγκροτούμενον.

allow me to linger on these subjects, as I must press on
to complete the task before me.

"13. And I will command evils for the whole world,
and their sins for the unholy, and I will destroy the
pride of the lawless, and will humble the pride of the
insolent, 14. and they that are left shall be more
precious than gold unsmelted, and a man shall be more
precious than the stone of Suphir." And afterwards
(d) it adds: "And they that are left shall be as a fleeing
Isa.xiii. 11. fawn, or as a straying sheep."

In this too the Scripture shews most plainly the small
number of the saved in the time of the ruin of the wicked,
so that it is not possible to expect that absolutely all the
circumcised without exception and the whole Jewish race
will attain to the promises of God.

"4. And there shall be in that day a failing of the
glory of Jacob, and the riches of his glory shall be
(78) shaken. 5. And it shall be as when one gathers standing corn, and reaps the grain of the ears; 6. And it
shall be as when one gathers ears in a rich valley, and
stubble is left. Or as the berries of an olive tree are
left, two or three on the topmost bough, or four or five
on its branches, thus saith the Lord God of Israel.
7. In that day a man shall trust in him that made him,
and his eyes shall look on the Holy One of Israel,
8. and they shall not trust in the altars, nor in the work
Isa.xvii. 4. of their hands, which their own fingers have made."

And in this it is clearly prophesied how Israel's glory
(b) and all her riches will be taken away, and how but a few,
easily numbered, like the few berries on the branch of an
olive tree, are said to be left; and these would be those
of them who are believers in our Lord. And immediately
after what is said about these, there is a prophecy of the
whole race of mankind turning away from the error of
idolatry, and coming to know the God of Israel.

"Hear ye isles,[1] which are forsaken and tortured,
(c) hear, what I heard from the Lord of Sabaoth: the God
Isa. xxi.10. of Israel has announced (it) to us.

Note the way in this passage also in which he does not
call those of the Circumcision to hear the unspeakable

---

[1] S. omits νῆσοι.

words, but those only, whom he calls "forsaken and tortured," as were those in the apostolic age who bewailed and lamented the evil of the life of men.

"4 *b*. The lofty men of the earth mourned, 5. and the earth waxed lawless through her inhabitants.[1] 6*b*. Therefore, the inhabitants of the earth shall be poor, (d) and few men shall be left."   Isa.xxiv.4.

Here again having rebuked the transgressors of the law of the covenant of God who belong to the people of the circumcision, and threatened them with what was written, he prophesies that some few men of them will be left. And these would be those named of the apostle "the remnant according to the election of grace."

"12. Cities shall be left desolate, and houses deserted shall fall to ruin. 13. All these things shall come to pass in the earth in the midst of the nations, as if one should strip an olive tree, so shall they be stripped. (79) 14. But when the vintage is stopped, then shall they cry aloud, and the remnant on the earth shall rejoice Isa. xxiv. with the glory of God."   12.

And here they who are left alone are said to rejoice, all the others being delivered to the woes prophesied.

"3. The crown of pride, the hirelings of Ephraim shall be beaten down. 4. And the fading flower of glorious hope on the top of the high mountain shall be as the early fig : he that sees it will desire to swallow (b) it, before he takes it into his hand. 5. In that day the Lord shall be the crown of hope, the garland of glory to the remnant of his people ; for they shall be left in Is. xxviii. the spirit of judgment."   3.

And here he prophesies that the Lord will be "a crown of hope and glory" to the remnant of his people, not to all their nation, but to those only signified by the remnant, and names the others in contrast to the remnant of his people "a crown of shame and hirelings of Ephraim."

"And they that are left in Judæa, shall take root (c) downwards, and bear fruit upwards, because there shall be a remnant from Jerusalem, and the preserved from Mount Sion. The zeal of the Lord of Sabaoth will Isa.xxxvii. do this."   31.

---

[1] Omission in E of 5 b, 6 a, owing to error of scribe because of τοὺς κατοικοῦντας αὐτήν (5 a) and οἱ κατοικοῦντες αὐτήν (6 a).

He prophesies that those of the Jewish race that are left according to the election of grace, will cast root downwards and bear fruit upwards, shewing very clearly the (d) election of the apostles and disciples of our Saviour. For they, being left from those of the Circumcision, thrust down into the earth the roots of their teaching, so that they have fixed and rooted their teaching throughout the whole world : and they have exhorted men to bear both seed and fruit upwards towards the heavenly promises.

Thus those men themselves, who were left of the Jewish race, when the rest were destroyed, alone are said to be saved. The zeal of the Lord has accomplished this. The zeal of the Lord elected them, in order to provoke the wicked of the Circumcision to jealousy, and He provoked them to jealousy, according to the saying of Moses:

"They have provoked me to jealousy by that which is not God,[1] and I will provoke them to jealousy by that which is not a people. By a foolish people I will anger them."

Deut. xxxii. 8.

(80)

"8. Thus saith the Lord, as a grape-stone shall be found in the cluster, and they shall say, Destroy it not, for a blessing is in it: so will I for the sake of him that serves me, for his sake I will not destroy all. 9. And I will lead out the seed of Jacob and Juda, and they shall inherit my holy mountain : and my chosen and my servants shall inherit it and dwell there. 10. And there shall be in the forest a fold[2] of sheep, and the valley of Achor shall be a resting-place for the herds of my people, who have sought me.

(b)

"11. But ye are they that have left me, and forget my holy mountain and prepare a table for chance, 12. and fill up the drink-offering to the Demon.[3] I will deliver you up to the sword, ye shall all fall by slaughter, because I called you and ye did not hear, and did evil before me, and chose that which I willed not."

Isa. lxv. 8.

In this passage the Scripture distinguishes, and says that but a small seed from Jacob will attain the promises, and that the elect are those that dwell in the wood. It points here to the calling of the Gentiles, in which the elect of

---

[1] S. adds : Παρώξυνάν με ἐν τοῖς εἰδώλοις αὐτῶν—"They have provoked me with their idols."

[2] LXX: pl.   [3] LXX ; τῷ δαίμονι . . . τῇ τυχῇ.

the Lord and the seed of Jacob are [included], and these (c)
would be the apostles and disciples of our Saviour, and
the rest beyond them are subject to the before-mentioned
threats, Scripture stating as clearly as possible, that the
whole Jewish nation could not attain the promises of God,
but only the seed which is named, and those called "the
elect of God."   For many are called, but few are chosen. Matt. xx.
On them Scripture now proceeds to prophesy that a new 16.
name shall be conferred, saying to the wicked :

"For your name shall be left,[1] as a loathing for my (d)
chosen, and the Lord shall destroy you : but my servants
shall be called by a new name."   Is. lxv. 15.

And this new name, which was not known to them of
old time, what could it be but the name of "Christians,"
blessed through all the world, formed from the name of
our Saviour Jesus Christ?

50. From Micah.
[Passage quoted, Micah ii. 11.]

Micah, too, agrees with the passages from Isaiah in stating (81)
that God will not receive all without qualification, but only
those who are left.   And as in Isaiah "their remnant"
was called "a seed," so now those of them that are to be
saved are called "a drop."   And the choir of the apostles
is shewn forth by those figures, as being a drop and a seed
from the Jewish race, a drop from which all they that have
known the Christ of God through the whole world and
received His teaching, have been made worthy of the
congregation foretold, having obtained redemption from
their enemies.

"2. And thou Bethlehem, house of Ephratha, art the (b)
least among the thousands of Juda.   Out of thee shall
come forth my leader, to be for a prince to Israel, and
his goings forth from the beginning are from the days of
eternity.   3. Therefore shall he give them until the time
of her that brings forth.   She shall bring forth, and the Micah v.
remainder of their brethren shall turn."   2, 3.

And after a little he adds :

"7. And the remnant of Jacob shall be among the
nations, in the midst of many peoples, as dew falling

---

[1] S. : καταλείψετε.

(c)

from the Lord, and as lambs on the pasture ; that none may assemble or resist among the sons of men. 8. And the remnant of Jacob shall be among the nations in the midst of many peoples, as a lion among cattle [1] in the forest, and as a lion's whelp in the pastures of sheep : as when he goes through and chooses and carries off, and there is none to deliver. 9. Thine hand shall be exalted against them that afflict thee, and all thine enemies shall be utterly destroyed."

Micah v. 7.

Nothing surely could be more clear than this ; at one and the same time it proclaims the birth of the Saviour at Bethlehem,[2] and His existence before eternity,[3] His Birth of the Virgin, the call of His apostles and disciples, and their preaching of the Christ carried throughout all the world. For when this Ruler, Whose goings forth the Scripture says are from eternity, shall have gone forth from Bethlehem, and when the holy maiden who was to bear Him shall have brought Him forth, it does not say that all they of the Circumcision will be saved, but only they that are left, who will be also a remnant of Jacob, and will be given as dew to all the Gentiles. For the remnant of Jacob, he says, shall be among the nations, as dew falling from the Lord, and as lambs in a pasture. Instead of which Aquila translates, "as drops on the grass," and Theodotion, "as snow on grass." And again, instead of "so that none may assemble or resist among the sons of men, and no son of men attack," Theodotion reads "who shall not wait for man, and shall not hope in the son of man." And Aquila " who shall not await a man, and shall not be concerned with the sons of men." [4]

(82)

Through which the whole hope of the apostles of our Saviour is [shown to be] not in man, but in their Lord and Saviour, and He was the Word of God. And it says lower down :

(b)

" And the remnant of Jacob shall be among the nations in the midst of many peoples, as a lion among the cattle of the forest, and as a lion's whelp in the

---

[1] LXX : ὡς λέων ἐν κτήνεσιν ἐν τῷ δρυμῷ.

[2] Cf. 97 c, 275 a, 340 d, and Origen c. Celsum 453.

[3] τὴν πρὸ· αἰῶνος οὐσίωσιν—cf. P.E. 314 b, 554 c and 541 a : " It is literally the act which gives τὸ εἶναί τε καὶ τὴν οὐσίαν." [G.]

[4] οὐ περὶ υἱοὺς ἀνθρώπων.

pastures of sheep ; as when he goes through, and
chooses, and spoils, and there is none to save."
By which I think is meant the bravery and intrepidity of
the apostles' preaching.   They threw themselves like a lion
and a lion's whelp on the thicket of the Gentiles and on the
flocks of human sheep, they parted the worthy from the (c)
unworthy, and subjected them to the word of Christ.

And then His victories are proclaimed to Him :   " Thy
hand shall be exalted against them that trouble thee, and all
thy enemies shall be destroyed."

And we can see this with our own eyes.[1]   For though
many have afflicted the word of Christ, and are even now
contending with it, yet it is lifted above them and become
stronger than them all.   Yes, verily, the hand of Christ
is raised against all that afflicted Him, and all His enemies
who from time to time rise up against His Church are said
to be " utterly destroyed."

52. From Zephaniah.

[Passage quoted, Zeph. iii. 9.]

And in this passage the Lord promised that there will be (83)
left for Him a people meek and lowly, meaning none others
but they of the Circumcision who believed in His Christ.
And He again proclaimed that only the remnant of Israel
should be saved, with those called from the other nations, as
He shewed in the beginning of the prophecy.

53. From Zechariah.

[Passage quoted, Zech. xiv. 1, 2.][2]

The fulfilment of this also agrees with the passages
quoted on the destruction of the whole Jewish race, which
came upon them after the coming of Christ.   For Zechariah (c)
writes this prophecy after the return from Babylon, foretelling the final siege of the people by the Romans, through
which the whole Jewish race was to become subject to their

---

[1] Interesting as an echo of recent persecution.

[2] Zech. xiv.   This is a post-exilic prophecy of an eschatological
nature, being one of the fragments appended to Zechariah.   It is
dependent on Ezekiel xxxviii.   Zechariah's prophecies are confined to
cc. i.–viii., and his activity, according to Zech. i. 1 and vii. 1, was from
the second to the fourth year of Darius.   [See Hastings, *D.B.* iv. 967.]

enemies : he says that only the remnant of the people shall
be saved, exactly describing the apostles of our Saviour.

54. From Jeremiah.
[Passage quoted Jer. iii. 14–16.]

Here again he prophesies that the conversion of Israel
will be at the coming of our Saviour Jesus Christ, in which
He will choose one from a city, and two from a family, very
few and small in number, to be shepherds of the nations
that have believed on Him and of the nations that have
been increased upon the earth through their destined call by
them. No more, he says, will they say " the ark of the
covenant of the Lord "—for they will no longer run after the
more external worship, having received a new covenant.

(84)   ### 55. From the same.
[Passage quoted, Jer. v. 6–10.]

Here once more the charge against their whole race is
shewn, and the siege that came on them, and the remnant
again, which he names " the foundation " as belonging to the
Lord. Because being inspired and strengthened by their
faith in the Christ of God, they did not undergo such
sufferings as the rest of their race.

56. From Ezekiel.
[Passage quoted, Ezek. vi. 7.]

This also seems to me to agree with the passages from
the other prophets. For whom could you call the " saved "
but those called by the others " a remnant, and the drop,
and the dew of that people," by which was signified the
band of the Apostles of our Saviour? They truly being
saved from the destruction of all their race, even in their
(d) scattering remembered God, so that it must be agreed that
what was written referred to them.

57. From the same.
[Passage quoted, Ezek. xi. 16.]

And here he has called the same men by another name,
meaning by " a little sanctuary," those of them who shall be
saved and survive.

58. From the same.   (85)

[Passage quoted, Ezek. xii. 14–16.]

In the dispersion of the whole people He says that even now few in number will be left for Himself, meaning the same men as in the preceding prophecy.   (b)

59. From the same.

[Passage quoted, Ezek. xiv. 21.]

This in no way differs from the preceding.

60. From the same.

[Passage quoted, Ezek. xx. 36.]

Here, again, is a clear witness that but few will come under God's staff, and that this will be when the rest of Israel has fallen away from the promises.

But now that I have proved that the divine prophecies did not foretell good things to all the members of the Jewish race universally and indiscriminately whatever happened, to the evil and unholy and those who were the reverse, but to few of them and those easily numbered, in fact to those of them who believed in our Lord and Saviour, or those justified before His coming, I consider that I have shewn sufficiently, that the divine promises were fulfilled (d) not indiscriminately to all the Jews, and that the oracles of the prophets are not more applicable to them than to those of the Gentiles who have received the Christ of God. And the full meaning of the divine promises I will unfold in the fitting place.

I have but collected these passages, as I was bound to do, in order to refute the impudent assertions of those of the Circumcision, who, in their brainless boasting, say that the Christ will come for them only, and not for all mankind. I wished also to prove that my study of their sacred books (86) had been to good purpose. In the previous book I have already accounted for our not becoming Jews, although we have this delight in their prophetic writings. And I explained there also, as far as was possible, what kind of a life the Christian life is which is preached to all nations, and the ancient character of the ideal of the system of the

(b) Gospel. So now that this preliminary work is done, it is high time to attack more mysterious subjects, those which are concerned with the mystical dispensation relating to our Lord and Saviour, Jesus the Christ of God : so that we may learn why He made His appearance to all men now, and not before, and the reason why He began the call of the Gentiles, not in days long past, but now after the length of ages ; and many other things which are germane to the mysterious theology of His Person.

(c)   Now, therefore, let us discuss the subject of His Incarnation, which is my first topic at this second beginning of my work, which is addressed to unbelievers, calling on Him Who is, indeed, the Word of God to aid us.

BOOK III

I HAVE now adequately completed the prolegomena [1] to (87) my *Proof of the Gospel:* I have shewn the nature of our Saviour's Gospel teaching, and given the reason of our regard for the oracles of the Jews, while we reject their rule of life. And I have also made it clear that their (88 prophetic writings in their foresight of the future recorded our own calling through Christ, so that we make use of them not as books alien to us, but as our own property. And now it is time for me to embark on my actual work, and to begin to treat of the promises. How these were actually concerned with the human dispensation of Jesus the Christ of God, and the teaching of the Hebrew prophets on the theology based on His Person, and predictions of His appearance among men, which I shall (b) shew immediately from their clear fulfilment can only apply to Him alone. But I must first of necessity consider the fact that the prophets definitely made mention [2] of the Gospel of the Christ.

CHAPTER 1

That the Prophets made Mention of the Gospel of the Christ.

MY witness of this shall be from the words of Isaiah, who cries in the Person of Christ:

[1] Books I. and II. are the "prolegomena." The *Demonstratio* itself begins here. Eusebius claims by his arguments to have established the Christian use of the O.T., since Christianity is its real fulfilment. The way is now clear for the work itself, ἡ αὐτὴ ὑπόθεσις, which is an examination of the prophetic witness to Christ, and of the correspondence of Jesus Christ with that witness, as described in the Gospels, and as evident in the effects of His coming on the world of heathenism.

[2] παρέλαβον = state concisely.

"The Spirit of the Lord is upon me, because he has
sent me to preach good news to the poor, to proclaim
deliverance to the captives, and recovery of sight to the
blind."

(c)

Isa. lxi. 1.

Our Saviour, after reading this prophecy through in the
Synagogue one day to a multitude of Jews, shut the book
and said : "This day is this Scripture fulfilled in your ears."
And beginning His own teaching from that point He began
to preach the Gospel to the poor, putting in the forefront
of His blessings : "Blessed are the poor in spirit, for theirs
is the kingdom of heaven." Yea, and to those who were
hampered by evil spirits, and bound for a long time like
slaves by dæmons, He proclaimed forgiveness, inviting all
to be free and to escape from the bonds of sin, when He
said : "Come unto me, all ye that labour, and are heavy
laden, and I will refresh you."

Luke iv.
21.

Matt. v. 3.

(d)

Matt. xi.
28.

And to the blind He gave sight, giving the power of
seeing to those whose bodily vision was destroyed, and
dowering with the vision of the light of true religion those
who of old in their minds were blind[1] to the truth. The
prophecy before us shews it to be essential that Christ
Himself should be the originator and leader of the Gospel
activity, and the same prophet foretells that after Him His
own disciples should be ministers of the same system :

(89)

Isa. lii. 7;
Rom. x.
15.

"How beautiful are the feet of them that bring good
tidings of good things, and of those that bring good
tidings of peace."

Here he says very particularly that it is *the feet* of those
who publish the good news of Christ that are beautiful.
For how could they not be beautiful, which in so small,
so short a time have run over the whole earth, and filled
every place with the holy teaching about the Saviour of the
world?

(b)

And that they did not use human words to persuade their
hearers, but that it was the power of God that worked
with them in the Gospel preaching, again another prophet
says :

Ps. lxviii.
11.

"The Lord will give a word to those that bring good
tidings with much power."

---

[1] Following Gaisford, who for ἀναβλέπουσι suggests ἀμβλυώττουσι.
Diodatus had evidently read—ἀναπήροις οὖσι.

And again Isaiah :

> "9. Go up to the high mountain, thou that bringest
> good tidings in Zion, lift up thy voice with strength
> thou that bringest good tidings to Jerusalem ; lift it up,
> be not afraid, Say to the cities of Juda, Behold your
> God, 10. Behold the Lord comes with strength,[1] and
> his arm with power. Behold his reward is with him, (c)
> and his work before him. 11. As a shepherd feeds
> his flock, and gathers the lambs in his arms, and
> comforts those that are great with young."   Isa. xl. 9.

We shall know in what sense this is to be taken, when we
have reached a further point on the road of Gospel teaching.   But at least it is established that the voices of the
prophets witnessed to the Gospel, and even to the name
of the Gospel, and you have clear and definite proofs from
whom the Gospel will take its origin, that is to say from
Christ Himself, and by whom it will be preached, that it
will be through His Apostles.   At least (we are told) by
what power it will gain the mastery, that it will not be (d)
human : since this is established by the words : "The
Lord will give a word to those that bring good tidings
with much power."   So then it only remains to quote a
few out of the many other ancient Hebrew prophecies
concerning Christ, that you may know what the good
tidings were that would be preached in after days, and may
realize the wonderful foreknowledge of future events in the
prophets, and the fulfilments of their predictions, how they
stand fulfilled in our Lord and Saviour, Jesus the Christ
of God.

CHAPTER 2

That the Hebrew Prophets prophesied of Christ.

MOSES was the first of the prophets to tell the good news (90)
that another prophet like unto himself would arise.   For
since his legislation was only applicable to the Jewish race,
and only to that part of it resident in the land of Judæa or
its neighbourhood, and not to those living far away abroad

---

[1] LXX : ἰδοὺ κύριος· κύριος μετὰ ἰσχύος ἔρχεται.

(as has been seen in my previous book); and as it was surely necessary that He Who was not only the God of the Jews, but also of the Gentiles, should provide helpful means for all the Gentiles to know Him and to become holy in their lives, He makes known by the oracle accordingly (b) that another prophet will arise from the Jewish race, no whit inferior to His own dispensation. And God Himself names him in this manner:

"A prophet will I raise up to them from their brethren like unto thee, and I will put my word in his mouth, and he shall speak to them according to what I command him. And whatsoever man shall not hear that prophet['s words], whatsoever he shall speak in my name, I will take vengeance on him."

Deut. xviii. 18.

And Moses speaks similar words when interpreting the oracle of God to the people:

(c)   "A prophet shall the Lord thy God raise up of your brethren like unto me. Him shall ye hear according to all things that ye asked of the Lord God in Horeb in the day of the assembly."

Deut. xviii. 15.

Was then any of the prophets after Moses, Isaiah, say, or Jeremiah, or Ezekiel, or Daniel, or any of the twelve, like Moses in being a lawgiver? Not one. Did any of them behave like Moses? One cannot affirm it. For each of (d) them from the first to the last referred their hearers to Moses, and based their rebukes of the people on their breaches of the Mosaic law, and did nothing but exhort them to hold fast to the Mosaic enactments. You could not say that any of them was like him: and yet Moses speaks definitely of one who should be. Whom then does the oracle prophesy will be a prophet like unto Moses, but our Lord and Saviour Jesus Christ, and none other?

We must consider thoroughly why this was said. Moses was the first leader of the Jewish race. He found them attached to the deceitful polytheism of Egypt, and was the first to turn them from it, by enacting the severest punish-(91) ment for idolatry. He was the first also to publish the theology of the one God, bidding them worship only the Creator and Maker of all things. He was the first to draw up for the same hearers a scheme of religious life, and is acknowledged to have been the first and only lawgiver of their religious polity. But Jesus Christ too, like Moses,

only on a grander stage, was the first to originate the
teaching according to holiness for the other nations, and
first accomplished the rout of the idolatry that embraced (b)
the whole world.   He was the first to introduce to all men
the knowledge and religion of the one Almighty God. And
He is proved to be the first Author and Lawgiver of a new
life and of a system adapted to the holy.

And with regard to the other teaching on the genesis
of the world, and the immortality of the soul, and other
doctrines of philosophy which Moses was the first to teach (c)
the Jewish race, Jesus Christ has been the first to publish
them to the other nations by His disciples in a far diviner
form.   So that Moses may properly be called the first and
only lawgiver of religion to the Jews, and Jesus Christ the
same to all nations, according to the prophecy which says
of Him :

"Set, O Lord, a lawgiver over them : that the Gentiles
may know themselves to be but men." [1]

Ps. ix. 20.

Moses again by wonderful works and miracles authenticated (d)
the religion that he proclaimed : Christ likewise, using His
recorded miracles to inspire faith in those who saw them,
established the new discipline of the Gospel teaching.
Moses again transferred the Jewish race from the bitterness
of Egyptian slavery to freedom : while Jesus Christ summoned the whole human race to freedom from their impious
Egyptian idolatry under evil dæmons. Moses, too, promised
a holy land and a holy life therein under a blessing to
those who kept his laws : while Jesus Christ says likewise :
"Blessed are the meek, for they shall inherit the earth,"
promising a far better land in truth, and a holy and godly,
not the land of Judæa, which in no way excels the rest (of
the earth), but the heavenly country which suits souls that (92)
love God, to those who follow out the life proclaimed by
Him.   And that He might make it plainer still, He proclaimed the kingdom of heaven to those blessed by Him.
And you will find other works done by our Saviour with
greater power than those of Moses, and yet resembling the
works which Moses did. As, for example, Moses fasted
forty days continuously, as Scripture witnesses, saying :
"And (Moses) was there with the Lord forty days and (b)

[1] S. : οἱ ἄνθρωποι.   Prayer Book Version : "Put them in fear."

Exod.
xxxiv. 28.

Luke iv. 1.

Exod. xvi.
4.

(c)
Exod. xvi.
14.

Matt. xvi.
8.

(d)

Exod. xiv.
21-22.

Matt. xiv.
25.

(93)

forty nights; he did neither eat bread nor drink water."
And Christ likewise: For it is written: "And he was led by
the Spirit into the wilderness, being forty days tempted
of the devil; and in those days he did eat nothing."

Moses again fed the people in the wilderness: for
Scripture says: Behold, I give[1] you bread from heaven."
And after a little:

"It came to pass as the dew ceased round about the
camp, and behold on the face of the wilderness a small
thing, like white coriander seed, as frost upon the
ground."

And our Lord and Saviour likewise says to His disciples:

"8. O ye of little faith, why reason ye among yourselves, because ye have brought no bread? 9. Do ye
not yet understand, neither remember the five loaves of
the five thousand, and how many baskets ye took up?
10. Neither the seven loaves of the four thousand, and
how many baskets ye took up?"

Moses again went through the midst of the sea, and led
the people; for Scripture says:

"And Moses stretched forth his hand over the sea,
and the Lord carried back the sea with a strong south
wind all the night, and the water was divided. And
the children of Israel passed through the midst of the
sea on the dry land, and the water was a wall to them
on the right and a wall on the left."

In the same way, only more divinely, Jesus the Christ of
God walked on the sea, and caused Peter to walk on it.
For it is written:

"25. And in the fourth watch of the night he *went*
unto them, walking on the sea. 26. And when they
saw him walking on the sea, they were troubled."

And shortly after:

"28. And Peter answered him and said, Lord, if it
be thou, bid me come unto thee on the water. 29. And
he said, Come. And when Peter was come down out
of the ship, he walked on the water."

Moses again made the sea dry with a strong south wind.
For Scripture says: "Moses stretched forth his hand over
the sea, and the Lord drave back the sea with a strong

[1] S. reads for δίδωμι ("give"), ὕω—"rain down."

south wind," and he adds : " The waves were congealed in
the midst of the sea." In like manner, only much more
grandly, our Saviour " rebuked the winds and the sea, and
there was a great calm." Again when Moses descended
from the Mount, his face was seen full of glory : for it is
written :

> "And Moses descending from the Mount did not
> know that the appearance of the skin of his face was (b)
> glorified while He spake to him. And Aaron and all
> the elders [of the children] of Israel saw Moses, and Exod.
> the appearance of the skin of his face was glorified." xxxiv. 29.

In the same way only more grandly our Saviour led
His disciples " to a very high mountain,[1] and he was trans-
figured before them, and his face did shine as the sun, and Matt. xvii.
his garments were white like the light." 2.

Again Moses cleansed a leper : for it is written : " And Num. xii.
behold Miriam (was) leprous (as white) as snow." 10.

And a little further on : " And Moses cried to the Lord :
O God, I pray thee to heal her."

And in the same way, but with more superb power, the (c)
Christ of God, when a leper came to him, saying : " If
thou wilt, thou canst make me clean ; answered : I will ; be Matt. viii.
thou clean. And his leprosy was cleansed." 2.

Moses, again, said that the law was written with the
finger of God : for it is written :

> "And he gave to Moses, when he ceased speaking
> to him in Mount Sinai, the two tables of witness, stone Exod.xxxi.
> tables written with the finger of God." 18.

And in Exodus : " The magicians therefore said to Pharaoh, (d)
It is the finger of God." Exod. viii.

In like manner Jesus, the Christ of God, said to the 19.
Pharisees : " If I by the finger of God[2] cast out devils." Matt. xii.
Moreover, Moses changed the name of Nave to Jesus, and 27.
likewise the Saviour changed that of Simon to Peter. And
Moses set up seventy men as leaders to the people. For
Scripture says :

> " 16. Bring together to me seventy men of the elders
> of Israel,[3] 17. and I will take of the spirit that is upon

---

[1] W.H. add κατ' ἰδίαν.

[2] E. : ἐν δακτύλῳ Θεοῦ. W.H. : ἐν πνεύματι Θεοῦ.

[3] S. adds : " whom you yourself know to be elders of the people
and their scribes, and thou shalt bring them to the tabernacle of

Num. xi.
16.

thee, and I will put it upon them. . . . 24. And he brought together seventy men." [1]

Likewise our Saviour "chose out His seventy disciples,[2]

Luke x. 1.
(94)

and sent them[3] two and two before his face." Moses again sent out twelve men to spy out the land, and likewise, only with far higher aims, our Saviour sent out twelve Apostles to visit all the Gentiles. Moses again legislates saying :

Deut. v.
17.

"Thou shalt not kill, Thou shalt not commit adultery, Thou shalt not steal, Thou shalt not forswear thyself." [4] But our Saviour, extending the law, not only forbids to kill, but also to be angry : instead of "Thou shalt not commit adultery," He forbids to look on a woman with unbridled lust. Instead of "Thou shalt not steal," He enjoins that we should give what is our own to the needy. And transcending the law against false swearing, He lays down the rule of not swearing at all. But why need I seek further

(b) for proof that Moses and Jesus our Lord and Saviour acted in closely similar ways, since it is possible for any one who likes to gather instances at his leisure? Even when they say that no man knew the death of Moses, or his sepulchre, so (none saw) our Saviour's change after His Resurrection into the divine. If then no one but our Saviour can be shewn to have resembled Moses in so many ways, surely it only remains for us to apply to Him, and to none other, the prophecy of Moses, in which he foretold that God

(c) would raise up one like unto himself, saying :

"18. I will raise a prophet to them of their brethren like thee ; and I will put my words in his mouth, and he shall speak to them, as I shall bid him. 19. And

Deut. xviii.
18.

whatever man will not hear whatsoever words that prophet saith, I will take vengeance on him."

And Moses himself, interpreting the words to the people, said :

(d)

"15. A prophet shall the Lord thy God raise up to

---

witness, and they shall stand there with thee. And I will descend and speak there with thee."

[1] S. "He brought the seventy men" follows in verse 24.

[2] E. : μαθητάς. W.H. : ἑτέρους.   [3] E. omits αὐτούς.

[4] S. reads: "Thou shalt not commit adultery. Thou shalt not kill. Thou shalt not steal. Thou shalt not bear false witness (ψευδομαρτυρύσεις for ἐπιορκήσεις) against thy neighbour."

thee of thy brethren, like me; him ye shall hear;
16. according to all things which you desired of the Deut.xviii
Lord your God in Horeb in the day of the assembly."   15.

But the Old Testament [1] clearly teaches that, of the
prophets after Moses, no one before our Saviour was
raised up like unto Moses, when it says :

"And there has not arisen yet a prophet like Moses
whom the Lord knew face to face in all his signs and Deut.
wonders."   xxxiv. 10.

I have then proved that the Divine Spirit prophesied
through Moses of our Saviour, if He alone and none other
has been shewn to fulfil the requirements of Moses' words.
But note another recorded prophecy. We know that many (95)
multitudes among all the nations call our Lord and Saviour
Lord, though He was born according to the flesh of the
seed of Israel, confessing Him as Lord because of His
divine power. And this also Moses knew by the Divine
Spirit, and proclaimed in this manner in writing :

"There shall come a man from his seed" (He means
Israel's), "and he shall be Lord over the Gentiles, and Num.xxiv.
his kingdom shall be exalted."   7.

Now if none other of the kings and rulers of those of
the Circumcision has ever at any period been Lord of many
Gentiles (and no record suggests it) while truth cries and (b)
shouts of our Saviour's unique rule, that many multitudes
from all nations confess Him to be Lord not only with
their lips but with the most genuine affection,[2] what can
hinder us from saying that He is the one foretold by the
prophet? That Moses' prediction was not indefinite, and
that he did not see his prophecy in the shadows of illimi-
table and unmeasured time, but circumscribed the fulfilment
of his predictions with the greatest accuracy by temporal
limits, hear how he speaks prophetically about Him :   (c)

"There shall not fail a prince from Juda, and a
leader from his loins until he come in whom it is laid Gen. xlix.
up,[3] and he is the expectation of the Gentiles"—   10.

which means that the order and succession of rulers and
leaders of the Jewish race will not fail until the coming
of the Prophesied, but that when there is a failure of their

---

[1] ἡ παλαιὰ γραφή, or " ancient records."
[2] διαθέσει γνησιωτάτῃ.   [3] See note, page 21.

(d) rulers the Prophesied will come. By Judah here he does not mean the tribe of Judah, but since in later days the whole race of the Jews came to be called after the kingly tribe, as even now we call them Jews, in a very wonderful and prophetic way he named the whole Jewish race, just as we do when we call them Jews.

Next he says that the rulers and heads of their race will not fail, before the Prophesied appear: and that on his arrival the Jewish state will be at once dissolved, and that he will be no longer the expectation of the Jews, but of the Gentiles. Now you could not apply this prophecy (96) to any of the prophets, but only to our Lord and Saviour. For immediately on his appearance the kingdom of the Jews was taken away. For at once their king in the direct line failed, who ruled them according to their own laws, Augustus then being the first Roman Emperor, and Herod, who was of an alien race, becoming their king.[1] And while they failed, the expectation of the Gentiles throughout the whole world appeared according to the divine prophecy, (b) so that even now all men of all nations who believe in Him place the hope of godly expectation in Him.

All these good tidings, and many others besides these, does Moses give us concerning the Christ. And Isaiah definitely foretells in words akin to his of one who shall rise from the seed and line of King David:

"A rod shall come forth from the root of Jesse, and a flower shall spring forth from his root, and the spirit of God shall rest on him, the spirit of wisdom and Isa. xi. 1.   understanding."

And then he proceeds in prophetic style to paint the (c) change that will transform all races of men, both Greek and barbarian, from savagery and barbarism to gentleness and mildness. For he says:

"And the wolf shall feed with the lamb, and the

---

[1] The ancestor of the Herods was Antipater, governor of Judæa under Alexander Jannæus (104–78 B.C.). Nicolaus of Damascus, Herod's minister, represented him as a Jew, but Josephus states that he was an Idumæan of high birth. (Jos., *B.J.* i. 6. 2; *Ant.* xiv. 8. 1.) The stories of his servile and Philistine origin, common among Jews and Christians, have no foundation: *e. g.* Just. Mart., *Tryph.* 52: Ἡρώδην Ἀσκαλωίττην: Julius Africannus ap Eus., *H. E.* i. 7. 11. See Schürer, *History of the Jewish People*, i. 314 n.

leopard shall lie down with the goat, and the calf and Isa. xi. 6.
the bull and lion shall feed together."

And similar things, which he at once makes clear by
interpretation, saying :

"And he that arises to rule the Gentiles, on him
shall the Gentiles trust."

Thus he has made it clear that the unreasoning animals, (d)
and the wild beasts mentioned in the passage, represent
the Gentiles, by reason of their being by nature like wild
beasts ; and he says that one arising from the seed of Jesse,
from whom the genealogy of our Lord and Saviour runs,
will rule over the Gentiles ; on Him the nations that now
believe in Him fix their hope, agreeably to the prediction,
"And it shall be that he who shall rise to reign over the
Gentiles, in him shall the Gentiles trust."   And the words
"In him shall the Gentiles trust" are the same as "And
he will be the expectation of the Gentiles."   For there is (97)
no difference between saying "In him shall the Gentiles
trust" and "He shall be the expectation of the Gentiles."
And the same Isaiah, continuing, prophesies these things
about Christ :

"Behold my servant, whom I have chosen, my
beloved in whom my soul is well pleased, he shall
bring judgment to the nations."   Isa. xlii. 1.

And he adds : "Till he place judgment upon the earth,
and in his name shall the Gentiles trust."

Here, then, the second time the prophet states that the
Gentiles will hope in Christ, having said above "In Him
shall the Gentiles trust."   Though here it is "In His
name shall the Gentiles trust."   And it was said also to
David, that "of the fruit of thy body shall one be raised (b)
up," about Whom God says further on : "He shall call on Ps. cxxxii.
me, Thou art my father ; and I will make him my first- 11.
born."   And about Him he says again, "And he shall rule Ps.lxxxviii.
from the one sea to the other, and from the rivers even 26.
unto the ends of the world."   And once more, "All the Ps. lxxi.
Gentiles shall serve him, and all the tribes of the earth 8.
shall be blessed in him."   And moreover, the definite Ps. lxxi.
place of His prophesied birth is foretold by Micah, saying : 11 and 17.
"And thou, Bethlehem, House of Ephratha, art the least
that can be among the thousands of Judah.   Out of thee
shall come a leader, who shall feed my people Israel.   And (c)

Micah v.
2 ; Matt.
ii. 6.
his goings forth are from the beginning from the days of
eternity."

Now all agree that Jesus Christ was born in Bethlehem,[1]
and a cave [2] is shewn there by the inhabitants to those who
come from abroad to see it.   The place of His birth then
was foretold.   And the miracle of His birth Isaiah teaches
sometimes mysteriously, and sometimes more plainly : mysteriously, when he says :

"Lord, who hath believed our report?   And the arm
of the Lord to whom hath it been revealed ? we proclaimed him before as a child, as a root in a thirsty
soil."

(d)
Isa. liii. 1.

Instead of which Aquila interpreted thus : "And he
shall be proclaimed as a suckling before his face, and as
a root from an untrodden ground."   And Theodotion :
"And he shall go up as a suckling before him, and as a
root in a thirsty land."

For in this passage, the prophet having mentioned "the
Arm of the Lord," which was the Word of God, says :
"In his sight we have proclaimed (him) as a sucking
child, and one nurtured at the breast, and as a root from
untrodden ground."   The child that is "a suckling and
nurtured at the breast" exactly therefore shews forth the
birth of Christ, and "the thirsty and untrodden land " the
Virgin that bare Him, whom no man had known, from
whom albeit untrodden sprang up "the blessed root," and
"the sucking child that was nurtured by the breast."   But
this prophecy was darkly and obscurely given : the same
prophet explains his meaning more plainly, when he says :

"Behold a Virgin shall be with child, and shall bring
forth a son, and they shall call his name God with us,"
for Emmanuel signifies this.

(98)

Isa. vii. 14.

(b)

Such were the thoughts of Hebrews long ago about the
birth of Christ among men.   Do they, then, describe in

---

[1] Cf. I. i.

[2] ὀλιγοστὸς εἶ τοῦ εἶναι ; cf. Origen, contra Celsum, l. i. §51.   "The
cave is shewn where He was born, and the manger in which He was
swaddled ; and that which is widely spoken of in those places, even
among aliens from the faith, viz. that Jesus . . . was born in that
cave."   Earlier Apologists, e.g. Justin, do not mention the cave.
Helena, A.D. 326, "left a fruit of her piety to posterity" in two
churches which she built, "one at the cave of the nativity."   Eus., Vita
Const. cc. 42, 43 : cf. Dem. p. 1.

their prophecy some famous prince or tyrant, or some one
in any other class of those who have great power in earthly
things? One cannot say so, for no such man appeared.
But as He was in His life, so they prophesied that He
would be, in no way failing in truth. For Isaiah said:
"We proclaimed him before, as a child, as a root in thirsty Is. liii. 2.
soil." And then he proceeds saying:

"2. He hath no form or glory, and we saw him, and
he had no form or beauty, 3. And his form was dis-
honourable and slight even compared with the sons of (c)
men, a man in suffering, and knowing to bear sickness [1]
he was dishonoured, and not esteemed."

What remains for him to say? Surely, if they predicted
His tribe and race and manner of birth, and the miracle
of the Virgin, and His manner of life, it was impossible for
them to pass over in silence that which followed, namely
His Death: and what does Isaiah prophesy about it?

"3. A man" he says "in suffering, and knowing to
bear sickness,[1] he was dishonoured and not esteemed.
4. This man bears our sins, and is pained for our sake.
And we thought him to be in trouble, in suffering, and
in evil; 5. He was wounded for our sins, and bruised (d)
for our iniquities. The chastisement of our peace was
upon him, and by his stripe we are healed. 6. All we
as sheep have gone astray,[2] and the Lord delivered him
for our sins, and he because of his affliction opens not
his mouth. He was led as a sheep to the slaughter,
and as a lamb dumb before her shearers, so he opens
not his mouth.[3] 8. Who shall declare his generation?
for his life is taken from the earth."   Isa. liii. 3-
                                                                        8.
In this he shews that Christ, being apart from all sin,
will receive the sins of men on Himself. And therefore (99)
He will suffer the penalty of sinners, and will be pained
on their behalf; and not on His own. And if He shall
be wounded by the strokes of blasphemous words, this
also will be the result of our sins. For He is weakened
through our sins, so that we, when He had taken on Him
our faults and the wounds of our wickedness, might be

---

[1] E. omits: ὅτι ἀπέστραπται τό πρόσωπον αὐτοῦ.
[2] E. omits: ἄνθρωπος τῇ ὁδῷ αὐτοῦ ἐπλανήθη.
[3] E. omits: Ἐν τῇ ταπεινώσει ἡ κρίσις αὐτοῦ ἤρθη.

healed by His stripes. And this is the cause why the Sinless shall suffer among men : and the wonderful prophet, (b) in no way shrinking, clearly rebukes the Jews who plotted his death ; and complaining bitterly of this very thing he says : "For the transgressions of my people he was led to death." And then because total destruction overtook them immediately, and not a long time after their evil deed to Christ, when they were besieged by the Romans, he does not pass this over either, but adds : "And I will give the wicked for his tomb, and the rich for his death."

It would have sufficed for him to have concluded the prophecy at this point, if he had not seen that something (c) else would happen after the death of Christ. But as He after His death and entombment is to return and rise again almost at once, he adds this also concerning Him, saying next :

"The Lord also is pleased to purify him from his stroke—if ye can give an offering for sin, your soul shall see a life-long seed. And the Lord wills to take

Isa. liii. 10.   away from the travail of his soul, to shew him light."

He said above : "A man stricken, and knowing to bear weakness"; and now after his death and burial, he says : "The Lord wishes to cleanse him from his strokes." And (d) how will this be done? "If ye offer," he says, "for sin, your soul shall see a seed that prolongs its days." For it is not allowed to all to see the seed of Christ that prolongs its days, but to those only who confess and bring the offerings for sins to God. For the soul of these only shall see the seed of Christ prolonging its days, be it His eternal life after death, or the word sown by Him through the whole world, which will prolong its days and endure for ever.

And as he said above : "And we reckoned him to be in trouble," so, now, after His slaughter and death, he says : "And the Lord wills to take his life away from its (100) trouble, and to give it light." Since then the Lord, the Almighty God, willed to cleanse Him from this stroke, and to show Him light, if He willed He would most certainly do what He willed ; for there is nothing that He wills which is not brought to pass : but He willed to cleanse Him and to give Him light : therefore he accomplished it, He cleansed Him and gave Him light. And since He willed it, and being willing took away the travail of His soul, and shewed Him light, the prophet rightly proceeds with the words : "Therefore he shall inherit from many, and shall divide the spoil of the strong." Isa. liii. 12.

Here it remained for him to mention the heritage of (b) Christ, in agreement with the Second Psalm, in which the prophetic word foretells the plot that was hatched against Him, giving His name :

" 2. The kings of the earth stood up,
　　And the rulers were gathered together
　　Against the Lord and against his Christ." Ps. ii. 2.

And it adds next :

" 3. The Lord said to me, Thou art my son,
　　To-day I have begotten thee ;
　　Ask of me and I shall give thee the Gentiles for
　　　thine inheritance
　　And the bounds of the earth for thy possession."

It was to these Gentiles that the Prophet darkly referred, (c) saying : "He shall inherit from many, and shall divide the spoil of the strong."　For he rescued the subject souls Isa. liii. 12 from the opposing powers, which of old ruled over the Gentiles, and divided them as spoils among his disciples. Wherefore Isaiah says of them : "And they shall rejoice Isa. ix. 3. before thee, as they who divide the spoils."

And the Psalmist :

" 12. The Lord will give a word to the preachers with
　　　much power.

13. The king of the powers of the beloved, in the Ps. lxvii.
　　　beauty of his house divideth the spoils."　12.

He rightly, therefore, says this also of Christ : "Therefore (d) he shall have the inheritance of many, and divide the spoils of the strong."　And shortly after he tells us why, saying :

　　" Because his soul was delivered to death, and he
　　was reckoned among the transgressors, and he himself
　　bare the sins of many, and was delivered for their
　　iniquities."

For it was as a meet return for all this, because of His obedience and long-suffering, that the Father gave Him what we have seen, for He was obedient to the Father even unto death.　Wherefore it is prophesied that He should receive the inheritance of many, and should be reckoned with the transgressors not before but after His being delivered to death. For therefore He is said "to receive the inheritance of many, and to share the spoil of the strong." And I consider that it is beyond doubt that in these words the resurrection from the dead of the (101) subject of the prophecy is shewn. For how else can we regard Him as led as a sheep to the slaughter, and delivered to death for the sins of the Jewish people, numbered with transgressors, and delivered to burial, then cleansed by the Lord, and seeing light with Him, and receiving the inheritance of many, and dividing the spoils with his friends? David, too, prophesying in the Person of Christ says somewhere of His Resurrection after death:

(b)   " 10. Thou wilt not leave my soul in Hades,
          Neither wilt thou give thine Holy one to see
Ps. xvi. 10.   corruption."
And also:
      " 4. Lord, Thou hast brought my soul out of Hades,
          Thou hast kept my life from them that go down
Ps. xxx. 4.   into the pit."
And also:
      " 14. Thou that liftest me up from the gates of death.
Ps. ix. 14.   15. That I may tell all thy praises."
I consider that not even the most obtuse can look these things in the face [1] (and disregard them). And the conclusion of the prophecy of Isaiah, tells of the soul once sterile and empty of God, or perhaps of the Church of the (c) Gentiles, agreeably to the view I have taken. For since Christ has borne all for its sake, he rightly goes on after the predictions about them, to say:

      "Rejoice, thou barren that bearest not; break forth and cry, thou that travailest not; for more are the children of the desolate, than of her that hath a husband,[2] for the Lord has said, Enlarge the place of thy tent, and the skins of thy hangings [3] peg down, do not spare. Widen thy cords, and strengthen thy pins: spread out still more to the right and left, and
Is. liv. 1.   thy seed shall inherit the heathen."

---

[1] ἀντιβλέψαι. Cf. P.E. 289 B, from Orig., Tom. iii. in Gen. ἀντιβλέπειν ἡδονῇ = to *resist* pleasure.

[2] LXX: καὶ τῶν αὐλαίων σου.

[3] E. : καὶ τὰς δέρρεις τῶν αὐλαίων.

This is the good news the Word gives the Church (d) gathered from the Gentiles scattered throughout the world and stretching from sunrise to sunset, shewn forth very clearly when it says: "And thy seed shall inherit the Gentiles."

And now, though this part of my subject needs more elaboration, I will conclude it, as I have said sufficient for the present. You yourself will be able at your leisure to make selections relating to the subject, and this present work on the Proof of the Gospel will adduce and interpret individual details in their place. Meantime, for the present what has been said will suffice, on the predictions (and foreknowledge) of the prophets about our Saviour, and that it was they who proclaimed the good news that the good things of the future were coming for all men. (102) They foretold the coming of a prophet and the religion of a lawgiver like Moses, his race, his tribe, and the place he should come from, and they prophesied the time of his appearance, his birth, and death, and resurrection, as well as his rule over all the Gentiles, and all those things have been accomplished, and will continue to be accomplished in the sequence of events, since they find their completion in our Lord and Saviour alone.

But such arguments from the sacred oracles are only (b) intended for the faithful. Unbelievers in the prophetic writings I must meet with special arguments. So that I must now argue about Christ as about an ordinary man and one like other men,[1] in order that when He has been shewn to be far greater and more excellent in solitary pre-eminence than all the most lauded of all time, I may then take the opportunity to treat of His diviner nature, and shew from clear proofs, that the power in Him was not (c) of mere humanity. And after that I will deal with the theology of His Person, so far as I can envisage it.

Since then many unbelievers call Him a wizard and a deceiver, and use many other blasphemous terms, and cease not yet to do so, I will reply to them, drawing my

---

[1] Unbelievers in the prophecies must be approached by another method. To them E. must speak of Christ, ὡς περὶ ἀνδρὸς κοινοῦ καὶ τοῖς λοιποῖς παραπλησίου. The uniqueness of His Humanity will point the way to the revelation of His Divinity, as foretold by the prophets. Of what nature then was His power? Was it wizardry?

arguments, not from any source of my own, but from His own words and teaching.

CHAPTER 3

Addressed to those that suppose that the Christ of God was a Deceiver.

(d) THE questions I would ask them are these: whether any other deceiver, such as He is supposed to have been, is ever reported to have become as a teacher the cause of meekness, "sweet reasonableness," [1] purity, and every virtue in those that he deceived? Whether it is right to call by these names one that did not permit men to gaze on women with unbridled lust, whether He was a deceiver Who taught philosophy in its highest form in that He trained His disciples to share their goods with the needy, and set (103) industry and benevolence in the front rank? Whether He was a deceiver Who wakened [2] (men) from common, vulgar, and noisy company, and taught them to enjoy only the study of holy oracles?

He dissuaded from everything false, and exhorted men to honour truth before all, so that so far from swearing false oaths, they should abstain even from true ones. "For let your Yea be yea, and your Nay, nay." How could He be justly called a deceiver? And why need I say more, since it may be known from what I have already said what kind of ideal of conduct He has shed forth (b) on life, from which all lovers of truth would agree that He was no deceiver, but in truth something divine, and the author of a holy and divine philosophy, and not one of the common vulgar type?

He has been proved in the first book of this work to have been the only one to revive the life of the old Hebrew saints, long perished from amongst men, and to have spread it not among a paltry few but through the (c) whole world: from which it is possible to shew that men [3]

---

[1] ἐπιεικείας.   [2] Or "reassembled."

[3] Reading ἀνθρώπους αὐτοὺς καθ' (Paris ed.), and supplying, "are following the way of": "Plura mihi videnter emendationis egere" (Gaisford).

in crowds[1] through all the world (are following the way) of those holy men of Abraham's day, and that there are innumerable lovers of their godly manner of life from Barbarians as well as Greeks.

Such then is the more ethical side of His teaching. But let us also examine whether the word *deceiver* applies to Him in relation to His most central doctrines. Is it not a fact that He is recorded Himself to have been devoted to the One Almighty God, the Creator of Heaven and earth and the whole Universe, and to have led His disciples to Him, and that even now the words of His teaching lead up the (d) minds of every Greek and Barbarian to the Highest God, outsoaring all visible Nature? But surely He was not a deceiver in not allowing the real deceiver, fallen headlong[2] from the loftiest and the only true theology, to worship many gods? Remember that this was no novel doctrine or one peculiar to Him, but one dear to the Hebrew saints of long ago, as I have shewn in the *Preparation*, from whom lately the sons[3] of our modern philosophers have derived great benefit, expressing approval of their teaching. Yes, and the most erudite of the Greeks pride themselves, forsooth, on the fact that the oracles of their own gods mention the Hebrews in terms like these.[4]   (104)

" The Chaldeans alone possess wisdom, and the Hebrews,
    Who worship in holy wise, God their King, self-born."

Here the writer called them Chaldeans because of Abraham, who it is recorded was by race a Chaldean. If, then, in the ancient days the sons of the Hebrews, to whose (b) eminent wisdom even the oracles bear witness, directed men's worship only towards the One God, Creator of all things, why should we class Him as a deceiver and not as a

---

[1] $\dot{\epsilon}\pi\grave{\iota}$ $\sigma\pi\epsilon\acute{\iota}\rho\alpha s$: $\sigma\pi\epsilon\hat{\iota}\rho\alpha$, equivalent of Roman "manipulus" (Polyb. xi. 23. 1).   In Acts x. 1 a larger body, probably "a cohort."

[2] $\tau\rho\alpha\chi\eta\lambda\iota\sigma\theta\acute{\epsilon}\nu\tau\alpha$.   Cp. Heb. iv. 13.   The spirit of Heathenism was the true deceiver which had deluded an originally monotheistic world into polytheism.

[3] *i.e.* followers of Porphyry.

[4] Cf. *Sib. Or.* iii. 218 *sqq.* for an eulogy of the Jews : "There is on earth a city, Ur of the Chaldees, from which springs a race of upright men, ever given to wise counsel and good works." See Bate, *The Sibylline Oracles*, S.P.C.K., pp. 31–36, for an account of the Sibyl in early Christian literature.

wonderful teacher of religion Who, with invisible and inspired power, pressed forward and circulated among all men the very truths which in days of old were only known to the godly Hebrews, so that no longer as in ancient days some few men easily numbered hold true opinions about God, but many multitudes of barbarians who were once like (c) wild beasts, as well as learned Greeks, are taught simply by His power a like religion to that of the prophets and just men of old?

But let me now examine the third point—whether this is the reason why they call Him a deceiver, viz. that He has not ordained that God should be honoured with sacrifices of bulls or the slaughter of unreasoning beasts, or by blood, or fire, or by incense made of earthly things. That He thought these things low and earthly and quite unworthy of the immortal nature, and judged the most (d) acceptable and sweetest sacrifice to God to be the keeping of His own commandments. That He taught that men purified by them in body and soul, and adorned with a pure mind and holy doctrines would best reproduce the likeness of God, saying expressly : " Be ye perfect, as your Father is perfect."

Now if any Greek is the accuser, let him realize that his accusations would not please his own teachers, who, it may be, assisted by us, for they have come after us in time, I mean after the gifts to us of our Saviour's teaching, have expressed such sentiments as these in their writings— listen.

That we ought not to burn as Incense, or offer in Sacrifice, any of the Things of Earth to the Supreme God.

(105)   From Porphyry [1] *On Vegetarianism*
[II. 34.   Cf. *Praep. Evan.* IV. p. 149 B.]

To the supreme God, as a certain wise man has said, we must neither offer by fire, nor dedicate any of the things

---

[1] Porphyry (Malchus, *Vit. Plot.* vii. 107) "the soberest of the Neoplatonic philosophers" (Cheetham), succeeded Plotinus. He was born A.D. 232 at Batanea, probably of a Tyrian family, *Vit. Plot.* 8 ; Jerome, *Praef. in Gal.* ; Chrysost. *Hom. on 1 Cor.* vi. p. 58. He met Origen (Vincent Lerin. *Commonit.* i. 23) and afterwards ridiculed

known by sense. (For everything material is ·perforce impure to the immaterial.) Wherefore not even speech is germane to Him, whether of the speaking voice, or of the voice within when defiled by the passion of the soul. By (b) pure silence and pure thoughts of Him we will worship Him. United therefore with Him and made like Him, we must offer our own "self-discipline"[1] as a holy sacrifice to God. That worship is at once a hymn of praise and our salvation in the passionless state of the virtue of the soul. And in the contemplation of God this sacrifice is perfected.

From the *Theology* of Apollonius of Tyana[2] (*Praep. Ev.* p. 150).

In this way then, I think, one would best shew the the proper regard for the deity, and thereby beyond all other men secure His favour and good will, if to Him, Whom we called the First God, and Who is One and separate (c) from all others, and to Whom the rest must be acknowledged

---

his method (Eus., *H.E.* vi. 19). He was a pupil of Longinus at Athens (Eus., P.E. x. 3. 1). He joined Plotinus at Rome, and earlier in Eusebius' life lived in Sicily. He died about 305. His philosophy was intensely ethical, and emphasized personal access to God, in faith, truth, love, and hope. He was hostile to Christianity, though he reverenced Christ as a man, and wrote a work called *To the Christians.* His chief remaining works are *De Abstinentia, Lives of Plotinus and Pythagoras, Letters to Marcellus, Anebo* and *Sententiæ.* See also note p. 155.   [1] ἀγωγήν.

[2] Philostratus' Life of Apollonius. See *Praep. Evan.* p. 150, where G. quotes from Ritter and Preller "a brief summary of Suidas of the life of this notorious philosopher and imposter." He flourished in the reigns of Caius, Claudius, and Nero, and until the time of Nerva, in whose reign he died. After the example of Pythagoras he kept silence five years: then he sailed away to Egypt, afterwards to Babylon to visit the Magi, and thence to the Arabians: and from all those he collected the innumerable juggleries ascribed to him. He composed *Rites, or concerning Sacrifice, A Testament, Oracles, Epistles, Life of Pythagoras.* The life by Philostratus, written at the request of the wife of the Emperor Septimius Severus, is accessible in Phillimore's edition and in the Loeb Series. (See Dill, *Roman Society from Nero to Marcus Aurelius,* pp. 40, 399, 472, 518.) "As against unmodified Judaism the Christians could find support for some of their own positions in the appeal to religious reformers like Apollonius of Tyana; who condemning blood-offerings as he did on more radical grounds than themselves was yet put forward by the apologists of paganism as a half-divine personage."—T. WHITTAKER, *The Neo-Platonists,* p. 138.

inferior, he should sacrifice nothing at all, neither kindle
fire nor dedicate anything whatever that is an object of
sense—for He needs nothing even from beings that are
greater than we are ; nor is there any plant at all, which the
earth sends up, nor animal which it, or the air, sustains, to
which there is not some defilement attached—but should
ever employ towards Him only that better speech : I mean
(d) the speech which passes not through the lips, and should
ask good things from the noblest of beings by what is
noblest in ourselves, and this is the mind, which needs no
instrument.   According to this, therefore, we ought not to
offer sacrifice to the great God, that is over all.[1]

If then these are the conclusions of eminent Greek
philosophers and theologians, how could he be a deceiver
who delivers to his pupils not words only but acts, which
are far more important than words, to perform, by which
they may serve God according to right reason ?   The
manner and words of the recorded sacrifices of the
(106) ancient Hebrews have been already dealt with in the first
Book of the present work, and with that we will be satisfied.
And now, since besides what I have so far examined, we
know that Christ taught that the world was created,[2] and
that the heaven itself, the sun, moon, and stars, are the
work of God, and that we must not worship them but their
Maker, we must inquire if we are deceived, in accepting
this way of thinking from Him.
It was certainly the doctrine of the Hebrews, and the
(b) most famous philosophers agreed with them, in teaching
that the heaven itself, the sun, moon, and stars, indeed the
whole universe, came into being through the Maker of all
things.   And Christ also taught us to expect a consummation and transformation of the whole into something better,
in agreement with the Hebrew Scriptures.   And what of
that ?   Did not Plato [3] know the heaven itself, the sun,
moon, and other stars to be of a dissoluble and corruptible
nature, and if he did not say they would actually be dis-

---

[1] Gifford's translation.

[2] γενητὸs ὁ κόσμοs, cf. note by Gifford in P. E. 18 c. 3 on distinction
between ἀγένητοs (uncreated) and ἀγέννητοs (unbegotten).

[3] E. quotes *Phædo*, 96 A. (P.E. 26) on the research into the
natural laws of growth and decay ; cf. *Republ.* viii. 546.

solved, it was only because (he thought that) the One Who put them together did not will it?

And though He willed us to be part of such a natural (c) order, yet He taught us to think that we have a soul immortal and quite unlike the unreasoning brutes, bearing a resemblance to the powers of God; and He instructed every barbarian and common man to be assured, and to think that this is so. Has He not made those, who hold His views through the whole world wiser than the philosophers with their eyebrows raised,[1] who claim that in essence the human soul is identical with that of the flea, the worm, and the fly; yea, that the soul of their most philosophic brethren, so far as essence and nature go, differs not at all from the soul of a serpent, or a viper, or a bear, or a leopard, or a pig?

And if moreover He persisted in reminding men of a (d) divine judgment, and described the punishments and inevitable penalties of the wicked, and God's promises of eternal life to the good, the kingdom of heaven, and a blessed life with God, whom did He deceive?—nay, rather, whom did He not impel to follow virtue keenly, because of the prizes looked for by the holy, and whom did He not divert from all manner of sin through the punishment prepared for the wicked?

In His doctrinal teaching, we learn that below the Highest God there are Powers, by nature unembodied and spiritual, (107) possessing reason and every virtue, a choir around the Almighty, many of whom are sent by the will of the Father even unto men on missions of salvation. We are taught to recognize and honour them according to the measure of their worth, but to render the honour of worship to Almighty God alone.

In addition to this He has taught us to believe that there are enemies of our race flying in the air that surrounds the earth, and that there dwell with the wicked powers of dæmons, evil spirits and their rulers, whom we are taught (b) to flee from with all our strength, even if they usurp for themselves without limit God's Name and prerogatives.

---

[1] τας ὀφρῦς ἀνασπακότων, cf. P. E. 135 d of theosophical philosophers, 224 a from Oenomaus = to draw up the eyebrows, and so put on a grave important air. Ar. *Ach.* 1069, Dem. 442, 11, etc. (L. and S.) This satirical account echoes the irony of Plato.

And that they are to be shunned even more because of their warfare and enmity against God, according to the proofs I have given at great length in the *Praeparatio*.[1] Whatever teaching of this kind is found in the doctrine of our Saviour is exactly the same religious instruction as the godly men and prophets of the Hebrews gave.

If, then, these doctrines are holy, useful, philosophic and full of virtue, on what fair ground can the name of deceiver (c) be fastened on their teacher?

But the above inquiry has had to do with Christ as if He only possessed ordinary human nature, and has shewn forth His teaching as weighty and useful—let us proceed and examine its diviner side.

CHAPTER 4

Of the Diviner Works of Christ.

WE must now proceed to review the number and character of the marvellous works He performed while living among men : how He cleansed by His divine power those leprous (d) in body, how He drove dæmons out of men by His word of command, and how again He cured ungrudgingly those who were sick and labouring under all kinds of infirmity. As, for instance, one day He said to a paralytic, " Arise, take Matt iv. up thy bed, and walk," and he did what he was told. Or 10 ; Mark as again He bestowed on the blind the boon of seeing the ii. 11. light ; and once, too, a woman with an issue of blood, worn down for many long years by suffering, when she saw great crowds surrounding Him, which altogether prevented her approaching Him in order to kneel and beg from Him the cure of her suffering, taking it into her head that if she could (108) only touch the hem of His garment she would recover, she stole through, and taking hold of His garment, at the same moment took hold of the cure of her illness. She became whole that instant, and exhibited the greatest example of our Saviour's power. And another, a man [2] of courtly

---

[1] See chiefly, P.E., Books iv. v. and vi.
[2] Βασιλικὸς ἀνήρ.

rank, who had a sick son, besought Jesus, and at once John v. 8. received him safe and well.

Another, again, had a sick daughter, and he was a chief ruler of a Synagogue of the Jews, and He (restored her) though she was even now dead. Why need I tell how (b) a man four days dead was raised up by the power of Jesus ? Or how He took His way upon the sea, as upon the earth we tread, while His disciples were sailing ?—and how when they were overtaken by the storm He rebuked the sea, and the waves, and the winds, and they all were still at once, as fearing their Master's voice ?

When He filled to satisfaction five thousand men in addition to another great crowd of women and children, with loaves five in number, and had so much over that there was enough to (c) fill twelve baskets to take away, whom would He not astonish, and whom would He not impel to an inquiry of the true source of His unheard-of power ? But in order not to extend my present argument to too great length, to sum all up I will consider His Death, which was not the common death of all men. For He was not destroyed by disease, nor by the cord,[1] nor by fire, nor even on the trophy[2] of the Cross were His legs cut with steel like those of the others who were evil-doers ; neither, in a word, did He reach His end by suffering from any man any of the usual forms of violence which destroy life. But as if He were only handing His (d) life over willingly to those who plotted against His body, as soon as He was raised from the earth He gave a cry upon the tree, and commended His Spirit to His Father, saying these words : " Father, into thy hands I commend my spirit " ; thus uncompelled and of His own free will He departed from the body. And His body having then been taken by His friends, and laid in the fitting tomb,[3] on the third day He again took back again the body which He had willingly resigned before when He departed.

And He shewed Himself again in flesh and blood, the very self He was before, to His own disciples, after staying a brief while with whom, and completing a short time, He returned where He was before, beginning His way to the (109)

---

[1] Or " choked by a cord."

[2] τὸ τρόπαιον : the other reading is τὸν τρόπον which hardly yields sense.

[3] Or " buried in the fitting way."

heavens before their eyes.   And giving them instructions on
what was to be done, He proclaimed them teachers of the
highest religion to all the nations.   Such were the far-famed
wonders of (our Saviour's) power.   Such were the proofs of
His divinity. . And we ourselves have marvelled at them
with reverent reasoning, and received them after subjecting
them to the tests and inquiries of a critical judgment.   We
have inquired into and tested them not only by other plain
facts which make the whole subject clear, by which our Lord
is still wont to shew to those, whom He thinks worthy, some
slight evidences of His power,[1] but also by the more logical
(b) method which we are accustomed to use in arguing with
those who do not accept what we have said, and either completely disbelieve in it, and deny that such things were done
by Him at all, or hold that if they were done, they were
done by wizardry for the leading-astray of the spectators, as
deceivers often do.   And if I must be brief in dealing with
these opponents, at least I will be earnest, and refute them
in some way or other.

CHAPTER 5

*Against those that disbelieve the Account of Our Saviour's
Miracles given by His Disciples.*

(c) Now if they say that our Saviour worked no miracle at all,
nor any of the marvels to which His friends bore witness,
let us see if what they say will be credible, if they have
no rational explanation why the disciples and the Master
were associated.   For a teacher always promises some
special form of instruction, and pupils always, in pursuit
of that instruction, come and commit themselves to the
teacher.

---

[1] *i. e.* The Lord's miracles have been tested both by their agreement
with what the Christian recognizes as miraculous in a minor degree
still, and also by a logical method that should appeal to the unbeliever.
(There seems to be something corrupt in the text.)   For the continuance of miraculous powers in the third century, cf. Origen *c. Cels.* i.
13, also i. 9 (pp. 411, 405).

What cause then shall we assign to the union of the (d)
disciples with Christ and of Christ with them, what lay at
the root of their earnestness, and of what instruction did
they rank Him as Master?

Is not the answer clear? It was only and altogether the
instruction which they carried to other men, when they
had learned it from Him. And His precepts were those
of a philosopher's life, which He outlined when He said
to them: "Provide neither gold nor silver [1] in your girdles, Matt. x. 9.
nor a staff for the road," and similar words, that they
should commit themselves to all-governing Providence, and
take no care for their needs, and bade them to aim
higher than the Jews under Moses' commandments, to
whom he gave a law as to men prone to murder. "Do (110)
not kill," and likewise, "Thou shalt not commit adultery"
as to men who were lascivious and lecherous, and again,
"Thou shalt not steal," as to men of the type of slaves;
but our Saviour taught that they must regard such laws
as not applying to them, and aim above all at a soul free
from passion, cutting away from the depths of their minds
as from the roots the shoots of sin: they must try to (b)
master anger and every base lust, and more, they must
never ruffle the sublime calm of the soul with anger: they
must not look upon a woman with unbridled lust, and so
far from stealing they must lavish their own property on
the needy: they must not be proud of not defrauding one
another, but consider rather that they must bear no malice
against those who defrauded them. But why should I
collect everything that He taught and that they learned? (c)
He commanded them besides all this to hold so fast to
truth, that so far from swearing falsely they should not
need to swear at all, and to contrive to exhibit a life more
faithful than any oath, going so far only as Yea and Nay,
and using the words with truth.

I would ask, then, where would be the sense in suspecting
that hearers of such teaching, who were themselves masters
in such instruction, invented their account of their Master's
work? How is it possible to think that they were all in (d)
agreement to lie, being twelve in number especially chosen,
and seventy besides, whom He is said to have sent two

---

[1] W.H. add μηδὲ χαλκόν.

and two before His face into every place and country into which He Himself would come? But no argument can prove that so large a body of men were untrustworthy, who embraced a holy and godly life, regarded their own affairs as of no account, and instead of their dearest ones —I mean their wives, children, and all their family—chose a life of poverty, and carried to all men as from one mouth a consistent account of their Master. Such would be the right and obvious and true argument; let us (111) examine that which opposes it. Imagine the teacher and his disciples. Then admit the fanciful hypothesis that he teaches not the aforesaid things, but doctrines opposed to them, that is to say, to transgress, to be unholy, to be unjust, to be covetous and fraudulent, and anything else that is evil; that he recommends them to endeavour so to do without being found out, and to hide their disposition quite cleverly with a screen of holy teaching and a novel profession of godliness. Let the pupils pursue these, and more vicious ideals still, with the eagerness and (b) inventiveness of evil: let them exalt their teacher with lying words, and spare no falsity: let them record in fictitious narrative his miracles and works of wonder, so that they may gain admiration and felicitation for being the pupils of such a master. Come, tell me, if such an enterprise engineered by such men would hold together? (c) You know the saying, "The rogue is neither dear to rogue nor saint."[1] Whence came, among a crew of so many, a harmony of rogues? Whence their general and consistent evidence about everything, and their agreement even unto death? Who, in the first place, would give heed to a wizard giving such teaching and commands? Perhaps you will say that the rest were wizards no less than their guide. Yes—but surely they had all seen the end of their (d) teacher, and the death to which He came. Why then after seeing His miserable end did they stand their ground? Why did they construct a theology about Him when He was dead? Did they desire to share His fate? No one surely on any reasonable ground would choose such a punishment with his eyes open.

And if it be supposed that they honoured Him, while

---

[1] κακῷ κακὸν οὐ φίλον, οὐδὲ ἀγαθῷ.

He was still their comrade and companion, and as some might say their deceitful cozener, yet why was it that after His death they honoured Him far more than before? For while He was still with men they are said to have once deserted Him and denied Him, when the plot was engineered against Him, yet after He had departed from men, they chose willingly to die, rather than to depart from their good witness about Him.   Surely if they recog- (112) nized nothing that was good in their Master, in His life, or His teaching, or His actions—no praiseworthy deed, nothing in which He had benefited them, but only wicked-ness and the leading astray of men, they could not possibly have witnessed eagerly by their deaths to His glory and holiness, when it was open to them all to live on un-troubled, and to pass a life of safety by their own hearths with their dear ones.   How could deceitful and shifty men have thought it desirable to die for some one else, especially, if one may say so, for a man who they knew had been of no service to them, but their teacher in all evil?   For (b) while a reasonable and honourable man for the sake of some good object may with good reason sometimes undergo a glorious death, yet surely men of vicious nature, slaves to passion and pleasure, pursuing only the life of the moment and the satisfactions which belong to it, are not the people to undergo punishment even for friends and relations, far less for those who have been condemned for crime.   How then could His disciples, if He was really a deceiver and a wizard, recognized by them as such, with their own minds enthralled by still worse viciousness, (c) undergo at the hands of their fellow-countrymen every insult and every form of punishment on account of the witness they delivered about Him?—this is all quite foreign to the nature of scoundrels.

And once more consider this.   Granted that they were deceitful cozeners, you must add that they were uneducated, and quite common men, and Barbarians to boot, with no knowledge of any tongue but Syrian—how, then, did they go into all the world?   Where was the intellect to sketch out[1] so daring a scheme?   What was the power that

---

[1] ἐφαντάσθησαν, cf: P.E. 17 c, of learning God's greatness from His works : here it has the Aristotelian sense of something imagined.

enabled them to succeed in their adventure? For I will admit that if they confined their energies [1] to their own (d) country, men of no education might deceive and be deceived, and not allow a matter to rest.[2] But to preach to all the Name of Jesus, to teach about His marvellous deeds in country and town, that some of them should take possession of the Roman Empire, and the Queen of Cities itself, and others the Persian, others the Armenian, that others should go to the Parthian race, and yet others to the Scythian, that some already should have reached the very ends of the world, should have reached the land of the Indians, and some have crossed the Ocean and reached the Isles of Britain, all this I for my part will not admit (113) to be the work of mere men, far less of poor and ignorant men, certainly not of deceivers and wizards.[3]

I ask you how these pupils of a base and shifty master, who had seen His end, discussed with one another how they should invent a story about Him which would hang together? For they all with one voice bore witness that He cleansed lepers, drove out dæmons, raised the dead (b) to life, caused the blind to see, and worked many other

---

[1] Καλινδουμένοι; cf. ἐκαλινδοῦντο, P.E. 511, a, 1. Lit.: "rolling about," so in common idiom "busied." So Dem. 403, 9; Xen. *Cyr.* I. 4, 5; Isoc. 295 B.

[2] ἐφ' ἡσυχίας. Cf. Arist. *Vesp.* 1517.

[3] Cf. *H.E.* iii. 1, which gives the tradition that the apostles evangelized the whole world: Thomas receiving Parthia, Andrew Scythia, John Asia, Peter the Jews of the Dispersion in Pontus, Galatia, Bithynia, Cappadocia and Asia; Paul, preaching from Jerusalem to Illyricum, and ii. 16 makes Mark the apostle of Egypt, and v. 10 tells how Pantænus (*circa* 160) went to India, and found a Church that had been founded by Bartholomew.

Harnack regards all traditions of apostolic missions as legendary, except those of Paul, Peter, and "perhaps John of Ephesus," but accepts the Mission of Pantænus (*Expansion of Christianity*, I. pp. 439–441). For earlier statements of the diffusion of Christianity cf. Justin, *Trypho*, c. cxvii.; Tertullian *Apol.* xxxvii., *adv. Jud.* 7: "The haunts of the Britons inaccessible to the Romans subjugated to Christ." About A.D. 150 the Church of Edessa counted the king among its members (see F. C. Burkitt, *Early Christianity outside the Roman Empire*, p. 11, Cambridge, 1899) and Persia, Media, Parthia and Bactria were evangelized. Origen (185–254) visited the Arabian Churches more than once. In Africa, Egypt, Cyrene, and Carthage were evangelized before 200. In Gaul there were strong Churches, e. g. Lyons and Vienne. (G. P. Fisher, *History of the Church*, pp. 46, 47. London, 1892.)

cures on the sick—and to crown all they agreed in saying
that He had been seen alive after His death first by them.
If these events had not taken place in their time, and if
the tale had not yet been told, how could they have
witnessed to them unanimously, and guaranteed their
evidence by their death, unless at some time or other they
had met together, made a conspiracy with the same intent,
and come to an agreement with one another with regard to
their lies and inventions about what had never taken place?
What speech shall we suppose was made at their covenant?
Perhaps it was something like this:

"Dear friends, you and I are of all men the best- (c)
informed with regard to the character of him, the deceiver
and master of deceit of yesterday, whom we have all
seen undergo the extreme penalty, inasmuch as we were
initiated into his mysteries.[1] He appeared a holy man to
the people, and yet his aims were selfish beyond those
of the people, and he has done nothing great, or worth a
resurrection, if one leaves out of account the craft and
guile of his disposition, and the crooked teaching he
gave us and its vain deceit. In return for which, come,
let us join hands, and all together make a compact (d)
to carry to all men a tale of deceit in which we all
agree, and let us say that we have seen him bestow
sight on the blind, which none of us ever heard he
did, and giving hearing to the deaf, which none of us
ever heard tell of: (let us say) he cured lepers, and
raised the dead. To put it in a word, we must insist that
he really did and said what we never saw him do, or
heard him say. But since his last end was a notorious
and well-known death, as we cannot disguise the fact,
yet we can slip out even of this difficulty by determin- (114)
ation, if quite shamelessly we bear witness that he
joined us after his resurrection from the dead, and
shared our usual home and food. Let us all be impudent and determined, and let us see that our freak
lasts even to death. There is nothing ridiculous in
dying for nothing at all. And why should we dislike
for no good reason undergoing scourging and bodily

---

[1] οἷα μύσται τῶν ἀπορρήτων αὐτοῦ γεγενημένοι.

torture, and if need be to experience imprisonment,
dishonour, and insult for what is untrue? Let us now
(b)   make this our business. We will tell the same falsehoods, and invent stories that will benefit nobody,
neither ourselves, nor those we deceive, nor him who
is deified [1] by our lies. And we will extend our lies
not only to men of our own race, but go forth
to all men, and fill the whole world with our fabrica-
tions about him. And then let us lay down laws for
all the nations in direct opposition to the opinions they
have held for ages about their ancestral gods. Let us
bid the Romans first of all not to worship the gods
(c)   their forefathers recognized. Let us pass over into
Greece, and oppose the teaching of their wise men.
Let us not neglect the Egyptians, but declare war on
their gods, not going back to Moses' deeds against
them of old time for our weapons, but arraying against
them our Master's death, to scare them; [2] so we will
destroy the faith in the gods which from immemorial
time has gone forth to all men, not by words and
argument, but by the power of our Master Crucified.

Let us go to other foreign lands, and overturn all their
(d)   institutions. None of us must fail in zeal; for it is no
petty contest that we dare, and no common prizes lie
before us—but most likely the punishments inflicted
according to the laws of each land: bonds, of course,
torture, imprisonment, fire and sword, and wild beasts.
We must greet them all with enthusiasm, and meet evil
bravely, having our Master as our model. For what
(115)   could be finer than to make both gods and men our
enemies for no reason at all, and to have no enjoyment
of any kind, to have no profit of our dear ones, to make
no money, to have no hope of anything good at all, but
just to be deceived and to deceive without aim or object?
This is our prize, to go straight in the teeth of all the
nations, to war on the gods that have been acknowledged
by them all for ages, to say that our Master, who
(was crucified) [3] before our very eyes was God, and to
represent Him as God's Son, for Whom we are ready to

---

[1] ἐκθειαζόμενον ; cf. P.E. 41 a, 780 b.   [2] ὥσπέρ τι φόβητρον
[3] σταυρωθέντα supplied by Gaisford.

die, though we know we have learned from Him nothing either true or useful. Yes, that is the reason we must (b) honour Him the more—His utter uselessness to us—we must strain every nerve to glorify His name, undergo all insults and punishments, and welcome every form of death for the sake of a lie. Perhaps truth is the same thing as evil, and falsehood must then be the opposite of evil. So let us say that He raised the dead, cleansed lepers, drove out dæmons, and did many other marvellous works, knowing all the time that He did nothing of the kind, while we invent everything for ourselves, and deceive those we can. And suppose we convince nobody, at any rate we shall have the satisfaction of (c) drawing down upon ourselves, in return for our inventions, the retribution for our deceit."

Now is all this plausible? Does such an account have the ring of truth? Can any one persuade himself that poor and unlettered men could make up such stories, and form a conspiracy to invade the Roman Empire? Or that human nature, whose characteristic element is self-preservation, would ever be able for the sake of nothing at all to undergo a voluntary death? (or) that our Saviour's (d) disciples reached such a pitch of madness, that, though they had never seen Him work miracles, they with one consent invented many, and having heaped together a mass of lying words about Him were ready to suffer death to uphold them? What is that you suggest? That they never looked forward to or expected to suffer anything unpleasant because of their witness [1] to Jesus, and so they had no fear in going forth to preach about Him? What, you think it unlikely, that men who announced to Romans, Greeks, and Barbarians the total rout of their gods, would expect to undergo extreme sufferings on behalf of their (116) Master? At least the record about them is clear in shewing, that after the Master's death they were taken by plotters, who first imprisoned them, and afterwards released them, bidding them speak to none about the Name of Jesus. And discovering that after this they had publicly discussed the questions about Him before the multitude, they took them in charge and scourged them as a punishment

[1] ὑπ' αὐτοῦ (P.). Amended to ὑπέρ by Gaisford.

for their teaching. It was then Peter answered them,
Acts v. 29. and said: "It is right to obey God rather than men."
And after this Stephen was stoned to death for boldly
addressing the Jewish populace, and an extraordinary
(b) persecution arose against those who preached in Jesus'
Name.

Herod again later on, the King of the Jews, killed James
Acts xii.
1-3. the brother of John with the sword, and cast Peter into
prison, as is written in the Acts of the Apostles. And
yet, though they had suffered thus, the rest of the disciples
held tenaciously to Jesus, and were still more diligent in
preaching to all of Him and His miracles.

Afterwards James, the Lord's brother, whom of old the
people of Jerusalem called "the Just" for his extraordinary
(c) virtue, being asked by the chief priests, and teachers of
the Jews what he thought about Christ, and answering
that He was the Son of God, was also stoned by them.[1]
Peter was crucified head downwards at Rome,[2] Paul be-
headed,[3] and John exiled to an island. Yet though they
suffered thus, not one of the others gave up his intention,
(d) but they made their prayer to God that they themselves
might suffer a like fate for their religion, and continued
to bear witness to Jesus and His marvellous works with yet
more boldness.

And even supposing that they combined together to
invent falsehoods, it is surely wonderful that so large a
number of conspirators should continue to agree about
their inventions even to death, and that not one of them
in alarm at what happened to those who had been already
killed ever severed himself from the association, or preached
against the others, and brought to light their conspiracy;
nay, the very one who dared to betray his Master while
He lived, dying by his own hand, at once paid the penalty
for his treachery.

(117) And would it not be a most inexplicable thing that
shifty and unlettered men, unable to speak or understand
any other language but their own, should not only take it
into their heads to dare to go forth to the whole circle[4]
of the nations, but that having gone forth they should

---

[1] See Eus., *H.E.* ii. 23.   [2] *Ibid.* ii. 25.
[3] *Ibid.* iii. 23.   [4] περίοδος. Cf. P.E. 72 b.

succeed in their undertaking.   And note, what a remarkable thing it is that they all agreed in every point in their account of the acts of Jesus.   For if it is true that in all matters of dispute, either in legal tribunals or in ordinary (b) disagreements, the agreement is decisive (in the mouth Deut. xiv. of two or three witnesses every word is established),[1] 15; 2 Cor. surely the truth must be established in their case, there xiii. 1. being twelve apostles and seventy disciples, and a large number apart from them, who all shewed an extraordinary agreement, and gave witness to the deeds of Jesus, not without labour, and by bearing torture, all kinds of outrage and death, and were in all things borne witness to by God, Who even now empowers the Word they preached, and will do so for ever.

I have thus concluded the working out of what would (c) follow if for the sake of argument a ridiculous hypothesis were supposed.   This hypothesis was, to make suppositions contrary to the records, and to argue that Jesus was a teacher of impure words, injustice, covetousness, and all kinds of intemperance, that the disciples, profiting by such instruction from Him, surpassed all men in cupidity and wickedness.   It was, indeed, the height of absurdity, equivalent to saying that when Moses said in his laws: "Thou shalt not kill, Thou shalt not commit adultery, Thou shalt not steal, Thou shalt not bear false witness," he should be calumniated and accused falsely of speaking in irony and pretence, and of really desiring that (d) his hearers should kill and commit adultery, and do the opposite to what his laws commanded, and of merely putting on the appearance and disguise of a holy life for a pretence.   In this way, too, any one might slander the records of all the Greek philosophers, their strenuous life and sayings, with the calumny that their disposition and mode of life was contrary to their writings, and that their choice of a philosopher's life was but a hypocritical pretence.   And in this way, to speak generally, (118) one might slander all the records of the ancients, annul

---

[1] S. (Deut. xix. 15): ἐπὶ στόματος δύο μαρτύρων, καὶ ἐπὶ στόματος τριῶν μαρτύρων στήσεται πᾶν ῥῆμα.

W.H. (2 Cor. xiii. 1): ἐπὶ στόματος δύο μαρτύρων καὶ τριῶν στα-θήσεται πᾶν ῥῆμα.

E.: ἐπὶ στόματος δ'οὖν δύο καὶ τριῶν μαρτύρων συνίσταται πᾶν ῥῆμα.

their truth, and turn them upside down. But just as
no one who had any sense would not scruple to set down
one who acted thus as a madman, so also (should it be)
with regard to our Saviour's words and teaching, when
people try to pervert the truth, and suggest that He really
believed the opposite to what He taught. But my argument has been, of course, purely hypothetical, with the
object of shewing the inconsistency of the contrary, by
proving too much would follow from granting for the
moment an absurd supposition.

(b)   This line of argument, then, being refuted, let me recur
to the truth of the sacred writings, and consider the
character of the disciples of Jesus. From the men as
they stand, surely any sensible person would be inclined
to consider them worthy of all confidence ; they were
admittedly poor men without eloquence, they fell in love
with holy and philosophic instruction, they embraced and
persevered in a strenuous and a laborious life, with fasting
and abstinence from wine and meat, and much bodily
restriction besides, with prayers and intercessions to God,
(c) and, last but not least, excessive purity, and devotion both
of body and soul.

And who would not admire them, cut off by their divine
philosophy even from lawful nuptials, not dragged in the
train of sensual pleasure, not enslaved by the desire of
children and descendants, since they did not yearn for
mortal but immortal progeny? And who would not be
astonished at their indifference to money, certified by
their not turning from but welcoming a Master, Who forbade
the possession of gold and silver, Whose law did not even
allow the acquisition of a second coat? Why, any one only
hearing such a law might reject it as too heavy, but these
men are shewn to have carried out the words in fact.
For once, when a lame man was begging from Peter's
companions (it was a man in extreme need who begged
for food), Peter, not having anything to give him, confessed
that he had no belongings in silver or gold, and said :
(119) "Silver and gold have I none, but such as I have, give I
Acts iii. 6. unto thee : In the Name of Jesus Christ,[1] arise and walk."
When the Master gave them gloomy prophecies, if they

----

[1] W. H. add τοῦ Ναζωραίου.

gave heed to the things He said to them : " Ye shall have John xvi
tribulation," and again : " Ye shall weep and lament, 33.
but the world shall rejoice"—the strength and depth of John xvi.
their nature is surely plain, since they did not fear the 20.
discipline of the body, nor run after pleasures. And the
Master also, as One Who would not soothe them by deceit
Himself, was like them in renouncing His property, and
in His prophecy of the future, so open and so true, fixed in
their minds the choice of His way of life. These were (b)
the prophecies of what would happen to them for His
Name's sake—in which He bore witness, saying that they
should be brought before rulers, and come even unto
kings, and undergo all sorts of punishments, not for
any fault, nor on any reasonable charge, but solely for
this—His Name's sake. And we who see it now fulfilled
ought to be struck by the prediction ; for the confession of
the Name of Jesus ever inflames the minds of rulers. And (c)
though he who confesses Christ has done no evil, yet they
punish him with every contumely "for His Name's sake,"
as the worst of evil-doers, while if a man swears away the
Name, and denies that he is one of Christ's disciples, he
is let off scot-free, though he be convicted of many
crimes.[1] But why need I attempt to describe further the
character of our Saviour's disciples? Let what I have said
suffice to prove my contention. I will add a few words (d)
more, and then pass to another class of slanderers.

The Apostle Matthew, if you consider his former life,
did not leave a holy occupation, but came from those
occupied in tax-gathering and over-reaching one another. Luke v
None of the evangelists has made this clear, neither his 27 ; Mark
fellow-apostle John, nor Luke, nor Mark, but Matthew ii. 14.
himself,[2] who brands his own life, and becomes his own
accuser. Listen how he dwells emphatically on his own
name in the Gospel written by him,[3] when he speaks in
this way :

[1] Cf. Tertull., *Apol.* c. 2 : " Illud solum expectatur quod odio
publico necessarium est, confessio nominis, non examinatio criminis."
[2] W.H. : λεγόμενον. E. : ὀνόματι.
[3] That Matthew " wrote in Hebrew the Gospel that bears his
name " is stated by Eus., *H.E.* iii. 24. And the words of Papias that
" Matthew compiled the *Logia* in Hebrew, while they were interpreted
by each man according to his ability," are quoted, *H.E.* iii. 39. It is
agreed that E. was wrong in thinking our Matthew a translation of the

(120)   " 9. And as Jesus passed by from thence, he saw a
man, called Matthew, sitting at the place of toll, and
he saith unto him, Follow me.   And he arose, and followed him.   10. And it came to pass, as he sat at meat
in the house, behold, many publicans and sinners came
Matt. ix. 9.   and sat down with Jesus and his disciples."

And again further on, when he gives a list of the disciples,
he adds the name " Publican " to his own.   For he says :

(b)   " Of the twelve apostles the names are these : First,
Simon, called Peter, and Andrew his brother ; James
Matt. x.   the son of Zebedee, and John his brother ; Philip and
2–3.   Bartholomew ; Thomas, and Matthew the publican."

Thus Matthew, in excess of modesty, reveals the nature
of his own old life, and calls himself a publican, he does
not conceal his former mode of life, and in addition to this
he places himself second after his yoke-fellow.   For he is
paired with Thomas, Peter with Andrew, James with John,
and Philip with Bartholomew, and he puts Thomas before
himself, preferring his fellow-apostle to himself, while the
(c) other evangelists have done the reverse.   If you listen to
Luke, you will not hear him calling Matthew a publican,
nor subordinating him to Thomas, for he knows him to be
the greater, and puts him first and Thomas second.   Mark
has done the same.   Luke's words are as follows :

" And when it was day, he called his disciples unto
him, and chose twelve whom he also named apostles,
Simon whom he also called Peter, and Andrew his
Luke vi.   brother, James and John, and Philip and Bartholomew,
13   Matthew and Thomas."

(d) So Luke honoured Matthew, according to what they
delivered, who from the beginning were eye-witnesses and
ministers of the word.   And you would find John like
Matthew.   For in his epistles he never mentions his own

Hebrew *Logia*.   But there is no doubt a strong Matthæan element in
the non-Marcan, and even in some of the Marcan, constituents of our
Matthew.   See J. V. Bartlet (Hastings' *D.B.* vol. iii. p. 296 *sq.*), who
postulates Palestinian catechetical Matthæan Logia, earlier than the
matter used by Mark in its Petrine form, taking written form as the
main constituent in our Gospel, which was composed either before or
after A.D. 70, as the basis of them and the Marcan memoirs of Peter
(*ib.* p. 304).   If this be so, the argument of E. as to Matthew's modesty
would to a slight extent hold good.

name, or call himself the Elder, or Apostle, or Evangelist;
and in the Gospel, though he declares himself as the one
whom Jesus loved, he does not reveal himself by name.
Neither did Peter permit himself to write a Gospel through (121)
his excessive reverence.[1]　Mark, being his friend and companion, is said to have recorded the accounts of Peter
about the acts of Jesus, and when he comes to that part of
the story where Jesus asked whom men said that He was,
and what opinion His disciples had of Him, and Peter had
replied that they regarded Him as (the) Christ, he writes
that Jesus answered nothing, and said naught to him,
except that He charged them to say nothing to any one
about Him.

For Mark was not present when Jesus spoke those
words; and Peter did not think it right to bring forward
on his own testimony what was said to him and concerning him by Jesus.　But Matthew tells us what was
actually said to him, in these words:

"15. But whom say ye that I am?　16. And Simon (b)
Peter answered and said, Thou art the Christ, the Son
of the living God.　17. And Jesus answered and said
unto him, Blessed art thou, Simon bar-Jonah: for
flesh and blood have not revealed it unto thee, but my
Father which is in heaven.　18. And I also say unto
thee, That thou art Peter, and upon this rock I will
build my Church; and the gates of hell shall not prevail
against it.　19. And I will give unto thee the keys of
the Kingdom of Heaven: and whatsoever things[2] thou
shalt bind on earth shall be bound in heaven: and
whatsoever things thou shalt loose on earth shall be Matt. xvi.
loosed in heaven."　　　　　　　　　　　　　　　15.

Though all this was said to Peter by Jesus, Mark does not
record it, because, most likely, Peter did not include it in
his teaching—see what he says in answer to Jesus' question: (c)
"Peter answered and said, Thou art the Christ.　And Mark viii.
he straitly charged them that they should tell no man."　29.
About this event Peter for good reasons thought it best to
keep silence.　And so Mark also omitted it, though he
made known to all men Peter's denial, and how he wept

---

[1] εὐλάβεια: cf. Hebrews xii. 29, μετὰ εὐλαβείας καὶ δέους.
[2] W.H.: ὃ ἐάν and singular participles.　E.: ὅσα ἄν and pl.

about it bitterly. You will find Mark gives this account of him:

(d) "66. And as Peter was in the court,[1] there cometh one of the maids of the high priest; 67. and when she saw Peter warming himself, she looked upon him and said, And thou also wast with Jesus of Nazareth. 68. But he denied saying (I know not)[2] neither understand what thou sayest; and he went into the outside porch, and the cock crew. 69. And the maid saw him again, and began to say to them that stood by, This is one of them. 70. And he denied it again. And a little after, they that stood by said again to Peter, Surely thou art one of them: for thou art a Galilæan. 71. But he began to curse and to swear, saying, I know not this man of whom ye speak. 72. And the second time the cock crew."

Mark xiv. 66.

(122) Mark writes thus, and Peter through him bears witness about himself. For the whole of Mark's Gospel is said to be the record of Peter's teaching. Surely, then, men who refused (to record) what seemed to them to spread their good fame, and handed down in writing slanders against themselves to unforgetting ages, and accusations of sins, which no one in after years would ever have known of unless he had heard it from their own voice, by thus placarding themselves, may justly be considered to have (b) been void of all egoism and false speaking, and to have given plain and clear proof of their truth-loving disposition. And as for such people who think they invented and lied, and try to slander them as deceivers, ought they not to become a laughing-stock, being convicted as friends of envy and malice, and foes of truth itself, who take men that have exhibited in their own words good proof of their integrity, and their really straightforward and sincere char- (c) acter, and suggest that they are rascals and clever sophists, who invent what never took place, and ascribe gratuitously to their own Master what He never did?

I think then it has been well said: "One must put complete confidence in the disciples of Jesus, or none at all." And if we are to distrust these men, we must distrust

---

[1] E. changes order of words: Verses 67 and 69 read εἰς τὴν ἔξω πρόαυλιν, for ἔξω εἰς τὸ προαύλιον (68). W.H. add κάτω (66).

[2] Paris Text adds οὔτε οἶδα.

all writers, who at any time have compiled, either in Greece or other lands, lives and histories and records of men of their own times, celebrated for noble achievements,[1] or else we should be considering it reasonable to believe others, (d) and to disbelieve them only.[2]   And this would be clearly invidious.   What! Did these liars about their Master, who handed down in writing the deeds He never did, also falsify the account of His Passion? I mean His betrayal by one of His disciples, the accusation of the false witnesses, the insults and the blows on His face, the scourging of His back, and the crown of acanthus set .on His head in contumely, the soldier's purple coat thrown round Him like a cloak, and finally His bearing[3] the very trophy of the Cross, His being nailed to it, His hands and feet pierced, His being given vinegar to drink, struck on the cheek with a reed, and reviled by those who looked on. Were these things and everything like them in the Gospels, (123) also invented by the disciples, or must we disbelieve in the glorious and more dignified parts, and yet believe in these as in truth itself? And how can the opposite opinion be supported? For to say that the same men both speak the truth, and at the same time lie, is nothing else but predicating contraries about the same people at the same time.

What, then, is the disproof? That if it was their aim to deceive, and to adorn their Master with false words, they would never have written the above accounts, neither would they have revealed to posterity that He was pained and (b) troubled and disturbed in spirit, that they forsook Him and fled, or that Peter, the apostle and disciple who was chief of them all, denied Him thrice though untortured and

---

[1] It is certainly true that modern Criticism has judged the Gospels by canons that would be considered unduly rigorous in other fields of history. But the enormous importance of the issues has made this inevitable, and the Church has not shrunk from the minutest examination of her documents.   I do not know the author of the saying : "One must . . . . at all."

[2] The χλαμύς was the short military cloak. It is used by Plutarch (Peric 35, Lysander 13) for the "paludamentum," or general's cloak, and also for the royal cloak.   The χιτών was the soldier's frock worn under the outer garment. E. says the "frock" was used in mockery for a (royal) cloak.

[3] ἐπικομίζοντα usually "carry to " There seems no force here in the ἐπί.

unthreatened by rulers.   For surely if their aim was solely
to present the more dignified side of their Master they
would have had to deny the truth of such things, even when
stated by others.   And if their good faith is evident in
(c) their gloomier passages about Him, it is far more so in the
more glorious.   For they who had once adopted the policy
of lying would have the more shunned the painful side,
and either passed it over in silence, or denied it, for no
man in an after age would be able to prove that they had
omitted them.

Why, then, did they not lie, and say that Judas who
betrayed Him with a kiss, when he dared to give the sign
of treachery, was at once turned into a stone?[1] and that
the man who dared to strike Him had his right hand at
once dried up; and that the high priest Caiaphas, as he
conspired with the false witnesses against Him, lost the
(d) sight of his eyes?   And why did they not all tell the lie
that nothing disastrous happened to Him at all, but that
He vanished laughing at them from the court, and that
they who plotted against Him, the victims of an hallucination
divinely sent, thought they were proceeding against Him
still though He was no longer present?[2]   But what?   Would
it not have been more impressive, instead of making up
these inventions of His miraculous deeds, to have written
that He experienced nothing of the lot of human beings or
mortals, but that after having settled all things with power
(124) divine He returned to heaven with diviner glory?   For, of
course, those who believed their other accounts would have
believed this.

And surely they who have set no false stamp[3] on anything that is true in the incidents of shame and gloom,
ought to be regarded as above suspicion in other accounts
wherein they have attributed miracles to Him.   Their
evidence then may be considered sufficient about our
(b) Saviour.   And here it will not be inappropriate for me to
make use of the evidence of the Hebrew Josephus[4] as

---

[1] Possibly E. is condemning by implication some absurd tales in the
Apocryphal Gospels.

[2] As the Docetists taught.

[3] Παραχαράξαντες, cf. P.E. 495 a.   A word used both literally and
metaphorically of "marking with a false stamp," "falsifying."

[4] Josephus, *Ant.* XVIII. iii. 3.   The passage is also quoted, *H.E.* I.
11. 6, 7.   It is found in all MSS. of Josephus, none being earlier than

well, who in the eighteenth chapter of *The Archæology of the Jews*, in his record of the times of Pilate, mentions our Saviour in these words :

"And Jesus arises at that time, a wise man, if it is befitting to call him a man.   For he was a doer of no common works, a teacher of men who reverence truth. And he gathered many of the Jewish and many of the Greek race.   This was *Christus ;* and when Pilate con- (c) demned him to the Cross on the information of our rulers, his first followers did not cease to revere him.   For he appeared to them the third day alive again, the divine prophets having foretold this, and very many other things about him.   And from that time to this the tribe of the Christians has not failed."[1]

If, then, even the historian's evidence shews that He attracted to Himself not only the twelve Apostles, nor the seventy disciples, but had in addition many Jews and Greeks, He must evidently have had some extraordinary power beyond that of other men.   For how otherwise could (d) He have attracted many Jews and Greeks, except by wonderful miracles and unheard-of teaching?   And the evidence of the *Acts of the Apostles* goes to shew that there were many myriads of Jews who believed Him to be the Christ of God foretold by the prophets.   And history also assures us that there was a very important Christian Church in Jerusalem, composed of Jews, which existed until the siege of the city under Hadrian.[2]   The bishops, too, who stand first in the line of succession there are said to have been Jews, whose names are still remembered by

---

the eleventh century.   But it is not quoted by Origen (*contra Celsum*, i. 47, and the extant part of *Comm. in Matt.* Tom. x. 17), and his use of *Ant.* xx. 9, for Josephus' evidence to Christ seems to count against his knowledge of this passage.   W. E. Barnes' recent re-examination of the question makes out a strong case for its authenticity. (See H. St. J. Thackeray in Hastings' *D.B.* extra vol., p. 471, and, on the other side, W. E. Barnes, *The Testimony of Josephus to Christ*, 1920, S.P.C.K.)

[1] E. has ἐκεῖνον for τοῦτον.   σεβομένων for δεχομένων.   τοῦ Ἰουδαϊκοι for Ἰουδαίους.   τῶν παρ' ἡμῖν ἀρχόντων for τῶν πρώτων ἀνδρῶν παρ' ἡμῖν. ὅθεν εἰς ἔτι for εἰσ-έτι δε—and ἀπὸ τοῦδε τῶν χρ : οὐκ ἐπίλιπε for τῶν χρ : ἀπὸ τοῦδε ὠνομασμένον οὐκ ἐπέλιπε.

[2] A.D. 130.   Cf. *H.E.* iv. 6, "eighteenth year of Hadrian."   In his *Chronicon* Eusebius puts the rebellion in Hadrian's sixteenth year. Hadrian reigned from A.D. 117 to A.D. 138.

(125) the inhabitants.[1] So that thus the whole slander against His disciples is destroyed, when by their evidence, and apart also from their evidence, it has to be confessed that many myriads of Jews and Greeks were brought under His yoke by Jesus the Christ of God through the miracles that He performed.

Such being my answer to the first division of the unbelievers, now let us address ourselves to the second body.

(b) This consists of those, who while they admit that Jesus worked miracles, say that it was by a species of sorcery that deceived those who looked on, like a magician or enchanter. He impressed them with wonder.

CHAPTER 6

Against Those who think that the Christ of God was a Sorcerer.

OF course, such opponents must first of all be asked how they would reply to what has been already said. The question is about the possibility of a teacher of a noble and virtuous way of life, and of sane and reasonable doctrines, such as I have described, being a mere sorcerer in character. And supposing He was a magician and (c) enchanter, a charlatan and a sorcerer, how could He have become the source to all the nations of such teaching, as we ourselves see with our eyes, and hear even now with our ears? What sort of a person was He Who undertook to unite things which have never before been united? For a sorcerer being truly unholy and vile in his nature, dealing with things forbidden and unholy, always acts for the sake of base and sordid gain. Our Lord and Saviour Jesus, the Christ of God, was surely not open to such a charge. In (d) what sense could such a thing be said of One Who said to His disciples, according to their written record: "Provide neither gold nor silver in your girdles, nor a staff for the Matt. x. 10. road, nor shoes"? How could they have heeded His sayings, and thought fit to hand them down recorded in

[1] See Eus., *H.E.* iv. 5.

writing, if they had seen their Master bent on making
money, and Himself doing the opposite of what He taught
others? They would soon have ridiculed Him and His
words and left their discipleship in natural disgust, if they
had seen Him laying down such noble laws for them, and
Himself the Lawgiver in no way following His own words.
Once more, sorcerers and real charlatans devote themselves (126)
to the forbidden and the unholy in order to pursue vile
and unlawful pleasures, with the object of ruining women
by magic, and seducing them to their own desires. But
our Lord and Saviour is devoted to purity beyond the
power of words to say, for His disciples record that He
forbade them to look on a woman with unbridled lust,
saying :

> "It was said to them of old time, Thou shalt not
> commit adultery : but I say unto you, that every one
> that looketh on a woman to lust after her hath committed   Matt. v.
> adultery with her already in his heart."   27.

And on one occasion when they saw Him conversing with (b)
a woman of Samaria when it was the only possible way
to aid and save many, they wondered that He spoke with
the woman, thinking they saw something marvellous, such
as they had never before seen. And surely our Saviour's
words commend a serious and severe tone of behaviour :
while of His purity the great evidence is that teaching of
His, in which He taught men to attain purity by cutting
away from the depth of the heart the lustful desires :

> "There are some eunuchs who so were born,[1] and
> there are eunuchs who were made eunuchs of men,
> and there are eunuchs who have made themselves   Matt. xii.
> eunuchs for the kingdom of heaven's sake."   19.

The sorcerer again and the true charlatan courts notoriety (c)
and ostentation[2] in all his enterprises and actions, and
always makes a boast of knowing more and having more
than other people. But that our Lord and Saviour was
not thirsty for notoriety, or a braggart or ostentatious, is
shewn by His bidding those He cured to tell no one, and
not to reveal Him to the crowd, so that He might escape
notice, and also from His seeking periods of retirement in

---

[1] W.H. add : ἐκ κοιλίας μητρὸς.
[2] δοξοκοπῶν. Cf. δοξοκοπία, P.E. 167 a.

(d) the mountains, and shunning the vicious society of the crowd in cities. If then He neither devoted Himself to teaching for glory, nor money, nor pleasure, what ground of suspicion remains for considering Him a charlatan and a sorcerer? But once more think of this point. A sorcerer, when he shares the fruits of his wickedness with others, makes men resemble himself: how can he help making sorcerers and charlatans and enchanters in all ways like himself? But who has ever so far found the whole body of Christians from His teaching given to sorcery or enchant-

(127) ment? No one would suggest that, but rather that it has been concerned with philosophic words, as we have shewn. What, then, could you rightly call One Who was the source to others of a noble and pure life and of the highest holiness, but the prince of philosophers and the teacher of holy men? And I suppose so far as every master is better than his pupils, our Lord and Saviour must be considered, so far from being a charlatan and a sorcerer, but philosophic and truly holy

(b)   If, then, He was such, He could only have attempted His miracles by divine and unspeakable power and by the highest piety towards the Supreme God, Whom He is proved to have honoured and worshipped as His Father in the highest degree, from the accounts of Him. And the disciples, who were with Him from the beginning, with those who inherited their mode of life afterwards, are to such an incalculable extent removed from base and evil suspicion (of sorcery), that they will not allow their sick

(c) even to do what is exceedingly common with non-Christians, to make use of charms written on leaves or amulets, or to pay attention to those promising to soothe them with songs of enchantment, or to procure ease for their pains by burning incense made of roots and herbs, or anything else of the kind.[1]

---

[1] ἢ πετάλων ἐπιγραφαῖς καὶ περιάμμασι χρῆσθαι, ἢ τοῖς κατεπᾴδειν ἐπαγγελλομένοις προσέχειν τὸν νοῦν, ἢ ῥιζῶν καὶ βοτανῶν θυμιάμασι. Cf. Origen, c. Celsum, i. 402, for incantations. The πετάλων ἐπιγραφαί were mystic figures or words on metal disks, such as the shield of David, the Tetragrammaton, or the Acrostic AGLA, cf. Isa. iii. 23. The catacombs reveal the Christians using such tokens and medals far more than E. would allow in this passage. The περιάμματα or περίαπτα were charms or amulets used as φυλακτήρια against dæmons or the evil eye. For the use of incantations to expel spirits, cf. Origen, c. Celsum,

All these things at any rate are forbidden by Christian teaching, neither is it ever possible to see a Christian using an amulet, or incantations, or charms written on curious leaves, or other things which the crowd consider quite permissible. What argument, then, can rank the disciples of such a Master with the disciples of a sorcerer and charlatan?

And yet the one great proof of the worth of any one who (d) promises to effect anything is found in the circle of his pupils. In the arts and sciences it is so, men always claim him who was the source of their skill to be greater than themselves ; so medical students would witness to the excellence of their instructor in their own subject, geometricians will not regard any other as their master but a geometrician, and arithmeticians any but one skilled in arithmetic. In the same way, also, the best witnesses to a sorcerer are his pupils, who it may be presumed will themselves share in the character of their master. And yet through all these (128) years no disciple of Jesus has been proved a sorcerer, although rulers and kings from time to time have attempted by means of torture to extract the exactest information about our religion. No, in spite of all, none has admitted himself to be a sorcerer, though had he done so he might have gone free, and without any danger, only being compelled by them to offer sacrifice. And if not one of our own people has ever been convicted of sorcery, nor any of those ancient disciples of Jesus, it follows that their Master could not have been a sorcerer.

But that my argument may not be based solely on the (b) unwritten, hear the proofs also that I draw from the written record. The first disciples of Jesus in the Book of their own Acts, describe without doubt how the Gentiles thronging to their teaching (were so impressed),[1] that many of those

---

i. 6. Hippolytus, *Refutation of all Heresies*, IV. 28–42, gives a full account of the tricks of the magicians of the fourth century, cf. W. R. Inge, *The Philosophy of Plotinus*, i. 50 ; " We probably realize very inadequately the pernicious effects of astrology and magic in the last days of pagan antiquity. These superstitions were all-pervading . . . Christian apologists might well claim more credit than they have done for the Church, as the liberator of Europe from these two causes of human wretchedness."

[1] The lacuna is thus supplied by Gaisford (οὔτω διατίθεσθαι).

with a bad reputation for sorcery, changed their ways to such an extent that they had the courage to bring the forbidden books into the midst, and commit them to the fire in the sight of all.   Hear how the Scripture describes it :

(c)   "And many of those who used curious arts, brought their books, and burned them before all, and they reckoned the price of the books, and found it fifty thousand pieces of silver."

Acts xix. 19.

It shews what our Saviour's disciples were, it shews the extraordinary influence of their words when they addressed their audience, that they so touched the depths of their souls, caught hold of and pierced the individual conscience, that men no longer hid anything away in concealment, but brought their forbidden things to light, and (d) themselves completed the indictment of themselves and their own former wickedness.   It shews what their pupils were like, how pure and honourable in disposition, determined that nothing evil in them should lurk below the surface, and how boldly they prided themselves on their change from the worse to the better.   Yes, they who gave their magic books to the flames, and voted for their complete destruction, left no one in any doubt that they would never again have anything to do with sorcery, and from that day forth were pure from the slightest suspicion of it.

If, then, our Saviour's disciples are seen to have been like this, must not their Master have been so long before them ?

(129)   And if in the widest sense you wish to deduce from the character of His followers the character of their Head, you have to-day a myriad disciples of the teaching of Jesus, great numbers of whom have declared war against the natural pleasures of the body, and guard their minds from the stroke of every base passion, and when they grow old in temperance provide bright evidence of the nurture of His words.   And not men only live the life of wisdom in this wise for His sake, but innumerable myriads of women, too, throughout the world, like priestesses of the Supreme God, embracing the highest wisdom, enraptured with the love of (b) heavenly wisdom, have lost all joy of bodily progeny, and spending all their care on the soul, have devoted themselves entirely body and soul alike to the King of kings, the Supreme God, practising complete purity and virginity.

Of one shepherd,[1] we know, who left his own country for the sake of philosophy the sons of Greece are ever carrying the story hither and thither. This was their Democritus. (c) And Krates[2] is the second man who is a miracle among them, because, forsooth! he resigned his property to the citizens, and boasted that "Krates himself had freed himself." But the zealots of the teaching of Jesus are myriads in number, not one or two, who have sold their goods and given them to the poor and needy, a fact to which I can witness, as I am specially concerned in such matters, and can see the results of the discipleship of Jesus not only in their words, but in their works as well.

But why need I tell how many myriads of actual bar- (d) barians, and not Greeks only, learning from the teaching of Jesus to despise every form of polytheistic error, have borne witness to their knowledge of the one God as Saviour and Creator of the Universe? Whom long ago, Plato was the only philosopher who knew, but confessed that he dare not carry His Name to all, saying in so many words: "To discover the Father and Creator of the Universe is a hard matter, and when He is found it is impossible to tell *Timæus,* of Him to all."[3]   Yes, to him the discovery seemed a p. 28.

---

[1] μηλόβατον. See Menag. ap. Diog. Laërt. ii. 6. For the exile of Democritus, the Atomic philosopher of Abdera, 430–360 B.C., cf. Clem. Alex., *Strom.* i. 15. "About himself, too, where, pluming himself on his erudition, he says, 'I have roamed over the most ground of any man of my time, investigating the most remote parts. I have seen most skies and lands, and I have heard of learned men in great numbers. And in composition no one has surpassed me; in demonstration, not even those among the Egyptians, who are called ARPENODAPTAE, with all of whom I lived in exile eighty years.' For he went to Babylon, and Persia, and Egypt, to learn from the Magi and the priests" (trans. in Ante-Nicene Library). Cf. Ritter and Preller, p. 143. He combined an explicit theory of knowledge with scientific atomism; he distinguished primary and secondary qualities of matter, making the latter unreal, and thus was the originator of subjective idealism. He postulated a plurality of real beings in the conception of reality as a congeries of quantitative atoms, which was further developed by Epicurus. Thus, in a sense, Democritus is the father of modern mechanism, of the Leibnizian monadology, and also of Berkeleyanism. Cf. T. Whittaker, *The Neo-Platonists* (1901), pp. 10, 11.

[2] He was a Platonic philosopher, and head of the Academy at Athens, *circa* 315. Diog. Laërt. iv. 24; Ritter and Preller, p. 247. He is quoted by Clem. Alex., *Strom.* ii. 20.

[3] Πατέρα. Gaisford from Paris MS.

hard matter, for it is indeed the greatest thing of all, and it seemed to him impossible to speak of Him to all, because he did not possess so great a power of holiness as the (130) disciples of Jesus, to whom it has become easy by the co-operation of their Master to discover and to know the Father and Creator of all, and having discovered Him to bear forth that knowledge, to unveil it, to supply it, and to preach it to all men among all races of the world, with the result that even now at the present time owing to the instruction given by these men there are among all the nations of the earth many multitudes not only of men, but of women and children, slaves and country-folk, who are so far away from fulfilling Plato's dictum, that they know (b) the One God to be the Maker and Creator of the Universe, worship Him only, and base their whole theology on Christ. This, then, is the success of the new modern sorcerer ; such are the sorcerers who spring from Him Who is reckoned a charlatan ; and such are the disciples of Jesus, from whose character we may deduce that of their Master.

But once more, let us follow the argument in this direction : You say, my friend, that He was a sorcerer, and dub Him a clever enchanter and deceiver. Would you say, then, that He was the first and only discoverer of the (c) business, or that we must not, as would be done in similar cases, look for the original source of His work directly in His own teaching ? For if nobody taught Him, and He was Himself the first and only discoverer of the enterprise, if He had no benefit at all from the teaching of others, if he did not share in the feast [1] of the ancients, we ought surely to ascribe divinity to Him, as One Who (d) without books, or education, or teachers, self-taught, self-educated, is assumed to have discovered such a new world. We know that it is impossible to acquire the knowledge of a lower-class trade, or of the art of reasoning, or indeed of the elements of knowledge without the help of a guide or teacher, unless the learner transcends the powers of ordinary people. I am sure we have not yet had a teacher of literature who was self-taught, nor an orator who had not been to school, nor a physician "born and not made," nor a carpenter, nor any other kind of craftsman ; and these

---

[1] ἐρανισάμενος.   Cf. P.E. 358 d, 780 d, and 460 d.

things are relatively insignificant and human ; what does it mean, then, to suggest that the Teacher of true religion to men, Who worked such miracles in the period of His earthly life, and did the extraordinary prodigies which I have lately described, was born actually endowed with (131) such power, and had not to share the feast of the ancients, nor to take advantage of the instruction of modern teachers, who had done like things before Him ? What is it but to witness and confess that He was indeed divine, and that He altogether transcended humanity ?

And supposing you say that He had foregathered with masters of deceit, and was acquainted with the wisdom of the Egyptians, and the secret knowledge of their ancient teachers, and that collecting His equipment from them, He appeared in the character that His story exhibits.[1] (b) How is it, then, I reply, that no others have appeared greater than He, and no teachers antecedent to Him in time, either in Egypt, or anywhere else? Why has not their fame among all men preceded this accusation of Him, and why is not their glory even now celebrated in strains like ours? And what enchanter from the remotest age, either Greek or Barbarian, has ever been the Master of so many pupils, the prime mover of such laws and (c) teaching, as the power of our Saviour has shewn forth, or is recorded to have worked such cures, and bestowed such marvellous blessings, as our Saviour is reported to have done? Who has had friends and eye-witnesses of his deeds, ready to guarantee by the proof of fire and sword the truth of their witness, like the disciples of our Saviour, who have borne all insults, submitted to all forms of torture, and at last have sealed their witness about Him with their very blood?

Then, moreover, let him who supports the contention opposed to mine, inform me if any enchanter that ever existed has ever even taken it into his head to institute a new nation called after his own name ? To go beyond the (d) mere conception, and to succeed in effecting it, is surely beyond the power of humanity.

What sorcerer has ever thought of establishing laws against idolatry in direct opposition to the decrees of kings,

---

[1] Cf. Origen, c. Celsum, I. 38.

ancient legislators, poets, philosophers, and theologians, and of giving them power, and of promulgating them so that they should last on unconquered and invincible for long ages? But our Lord and Saviour did not conceive and not dare to attempt, neither did he attempt and not succeed.

(132)   With one word and voice He said to His disciples: "Go, and make disciples of all the nations in My Name, Matt.   teaching them to observe all things whatsoever I have xxviii. 19. commanded you," and He joined the effect to His Word; and in a little while every race of the Greeks and Barbarians was being brought into discipleship, and laws were spread among all nations opposed to the superstition of the ancients, laws inimical to dæmons, and to all the deceits of polytheism, laws that have made Scythians, Persians, and the other barbarians temperate, and revolutionized every lawless and uncivilized custom, laws that have overturned the immemorial habits of the Greeks themselves, (b) and heralded a new and real religion.[1] What similar daring has been shewn by the ancient sorcerers before the time of Jesus, or even after Him, which would make it plausible that He was assisted in His sorcery by others? And if the only answer to this is that no one has ever been like Him, for no one was the source of His virtue, surely it is time to confess that a strange and divine Being has sojourned in our humanity, by Whom alone, and for the first time in (c) man's history, things unrecorded before in human annals have been effected.

In such wise I will conclude this part of the subject. But I must again attack my opposer, and inquire if he has ever seen or heard of sorcerers and enchanters doing their sorcery without libations, incense, and the invocation and presence of dæmons. But no one surely could venture to cast this aspersion on our Saviour, or on His teaching, or on those even now imitating His life. It must be clear even to the blind that we who follow Jesus are totally opposed to such agencies, and would sooner dare to sacrifice our (d) soul to death than an offering to the dæmons, yea, would

---

[1] What Apologist would have written thus in fifty years' time? Did the State recognition of Christianity hinder a great moral triumph of the Church?

sooner depart from life than remain alive under the tyranny
of evil dæmons.　Who does not know how we love by the
mere Name of Jesus and the purest prayers to drive away
all the work of the dæmons?　The mere word of Jesus
and His teaching has made us all far stronger than this
invisible Power, and has trained us to be enemies and foes
of dæmons, not their friends or associates, and certainly
not their slaves and tributaries.　And how could He Who (133)
has led us on to this, Himself be the slave of the dæmons?
How could He sacrifice to evil spirits?　Or how could
He have invoked the dæmons to aid Him in His Miracles,
when even to-day every dæmon and unclean spirit shudders
at the Name of Jesus as at something that is likely to punish
and torment its own nature, and so departs and yields to
the power of His Name alone?　So was it of old in the
days when He sojourned in this life : they could n t bear
His Presence, but cried, one from one side and one from
another : "Come,[1] what have we to do with thee, Jesus, (b)
Son of God?　Art thou come to torment us before the Matt. viii.
time?"　　　　　　　　　　　　　　　　　　　　　　29.

And a man whose mind was wholly devoted to sorcery,
and in every way involved in the quest of the forbidden,
would surely be (would he not?) unholy in his ways ;
scandalous, base, atheistic, unjust, irreligious.　And if He
were such, from what source, or by what means, could He
teach others about religion, or temperance, or the knowledge of God, or about the tribunal and judgment of
Almighty God?　Would He not rather commend the (c)
opposites of these, and act according to His own wickedness, deny God and God's Providence, and God's Judgment, and revile teaching about virtue and the immortality
of the soul?　And if one could see such a character in our
Lord and Saviour, there would be no more to say.　But (d)
if instead we see Him calling on God the Father, the
Creator of all things, in every act and word, and training
His pupils to resemble Him, if He being pure Himself
teaches purity, if He is a maker and herald of justice,
truth, philanthropy, and every virtue, and the introducer
of the worship of God the King of kings, surely it follows
from this that He cannot be suspected of working His

---

[1] W. H. omit Ἔα.

miracles by sorcery, and that we must admit that they were the result of unspeakable and truly inspired power.

(134) But if you are so far gone in folly as not to pay any heed to temperate argument and logical consistency of thought, and are not impressed by probable proofs,[1] because you suspect me perhaps to be a special pleader—at least you will hear your own dæmons, the gods I mean who give the oracles, hear them bearing witness to our Saviour, not like you of His sorcery, but of His holiness, His wisdom, and His Ascension into Heaven. What could be a more persuasive testimony than that written by our enemy[2] in the third chapter of his book, *Concerning Philosophy from Oracles*, where he thus speaks in so many words.

CHAPTER 7

Oracles about Christ.

"WHAT I am about to say may seem surprising to some. It is that the gods have pronounced Christ to have been most holy and immortal, and they speak of Him reverently."

And lower down he adds:

"To those asking the question, 'Is Christ a God?' the oracle replied:

That the soul goes forth immortal after (its severance from) the body.[3]

Thou knowest, severed from wisdom it ever roams.

That soul is the soul of a man signal in holiness."[4]

---

[1] εἰκόσι τεκμηρίοις.

[2] Porphyry: see notes, pp. 120 and 155. "The Neoplatonists praised Christ while they disparaged Christianity" (Aug., *De Consensu Evang.* i. 15), *D.C.B.* iv. 442.

[3] ὅττι μὲν ἀθανάτη ψυχὴ μετὰ σῶμα προβαίνει. ἀθανάτη must be complementary, "becomes immortal." μετὰ σῶμα can only mean "after its union with the body is dissolved"; "after its bodily experience." It is not plain whether the first ψυχή = the human soul, or like the second = the soul of Christ.

[4] Traditional text, adopted by Migne, is γιγνώσκει σοφίη τετιμημένος, ἀλλά γε ψυχὴ ἀνέρος εὐσεβίη προφερεστάτη ἐστὶν ἐκείνου. Paris Codex

He certainly says here that He was most holy, and that His soul, which the Christians ignorantly worship, like the souls of others, was made immortal after death. And when asked, "Why did He suffer?" the oracle replied:

The body of the weak has ever been exposed to torments,

But the soul of holy men takes its place in heaven." [1]

And he adds after the oracle:

"Christy, then, was holy, and like the holy, went to the (d) heaven. Wherefore you will say no evil about Him, but pity the folly of men."

So says Porphyry [2] even now. Was He then a charlatan, my friend? Perhaps the friendly words of one of your kidney may put you out of countenance. For you have our Saviour Jesus, the Christ of God, admitted by your own teachers to be, not an enchanter or a sorcerer, but holy, wise, the justest of the just, and dwelling in the vaults of heaven. He, then, being such, could only have done

---

469 has γνώσκει σοφίῃ τετιμημένην ἐνάλατε ἀνέρος εὐσεβείῃ προφερεστάτου ἐστὶν ἐκείνη ψυχή. Augustine (*De Civ. Dei*, XIX. c. 23, 2) renders the passage, "nosti, a sapientia autem abscissa semper errat. Viri pietate praestantissimi est illa anima." Hence Gaisford supposes Augustine's text of Porphyry was probably: γιγνώσκεις, σοφίης τετμημένη αἰὲν ἀλᾶται. ἀνέρος εὐσεβίῃ προφερεστάτου ἐστὶν ἐκείνη ψυχή, and adopts it. He is followed by Dindorf. In favour of such a reading it must be said: (i) Porphyry's comment seems to imply that the oracle stated that Christ's soul became immortal after death; (ii) Augustine's translation must be the first guide to the true text; (iii) Porphyry's comment and Augustine's translation agree.

[1] Augustine seems to have had a reading, which is not so much a general statement, but one that directly refers to Christ.

[2] Porphyry was born of Christian parents (Soc., *H.E.* iii. 23), had known Origen (Vincent Lerin, *Commonit.* i. 23), whose allegorism he ridiculed after he had left the Church (Eus., *H.E.* vi. 19). He was well acquainted with Christianity, and shared its ethical standpoint (*Ad Marcellam*, 18, 24). In his book against the Christians he carefully and skilfully examined the Christian Scriptures, pointing out apparent contradictions. He contended that in spite of all Christ was worthy of all reverence; cf. Aug., *De Consensu Evang.* i. 15, and *De Civ. Dei*, XIX, 23; Harnack, *Expansion of Christianity*, vol. ii. p. 138; W. R. Inge, *The Philosophy of Plotinus*, vol. i. pp. 65, 66: "His polemic is thoroughly modern. He has not much quarrel with Christian ethics, nor (except in certain points) with the Christian philosophy of religion. . . . The real quarrel between Neoplatonism and Christianity in the third century lay in their different attitudes towards the old culture."

His miracles by a divine power, which also the holy writings bear witness that He had, saying that the Word of God and the highest Power of God dwelt in man's shape and form, nay, even in actual flesh and body therein, and performed all the functions of human nature.

(135)   And you yourself may realize the divine elements of this power, if you reflect on the nature and grandeur of a Being who could associate with Himself poor men of the lowly fisherman's class, and use them as agents in carrying through a work that transcends all reason.   For having conceived the intention, which no one ever before had done, of spreading His own laws and a new teaching among all nations, and of revealing Himself as the teacher of the religion of One Almighty God to all the races of men, He
(b) thought good to use the most rustic and common men as ministers of His own design, because maybe He had in mind to do the most unlikely things.   For how could men unable even to open their mouths be able to teach, even if they were appointed teachers to only one person, far less to a multitude of men?   How should they instruct the people, who were themselves without any education?

But this was surely the manifestation of the divine will and of the divine power working in them.   For when He called them, the first thing He said to them was : " Come,
Mark i. 17. follow me, and I will make you fishers of men."   And
(c) when He had thus acquired them as His followers, He breathed into them His divine power, He filled them with strength and bravery, and like a true Word of God and as God Himself, the doer of such great wonders, He made them hunters of rational and thinking souls, adding power to His words : " Come, follow me, and I will make you fishers of men," and sent them forth fitted already to be workers and teachers of holiness to all the nations, declaring
(d) them heralds of His own teaching.   And who would not be amazed and naturally inclined to disbelieve a thing so extraordinary, for none of those who have ever won fame among men—no king, no legislator, no philosopher, no Greek, no barbarian—are recorded to have ever conceived such a design, or dreamed of anything at all resembling it ? For each one of them has been satisfied, if he could establish his own system over his own land only, and if he were able to enforce desirable laws within the limits of his own race.

Whereas He, who conceived nothing human or mortal, see (136)
how truly He speaks with the voice of God, saying in these
very words to those disciples of His, the poorest of the Matt.
poor: "Go forth, and make disciples of all the nations." xxviii. 19.
"But how," the disciples might reasonably have answered
the Master, "can we do it? How, pray, can we preach to
Romans? How can we argue with Egyptians? We are
men bred up to use the Syrian tongue only, what language
shall we speak to Greeks? How shall we persuade Persians,
Armenians, Chaldæans, Scythians, Indians, and other bar- (b)
barous nations to give up their ancestral gods, and worship
the Creator of all? What sufficiency of speech have we to
trust to in attempting such work as this? And what hope
of success can we have if we dare to proclaim laws directly
opposed to the laws about their own gods that have been
established for ages among all nations? By what power
shall we ever survive our daring attempt?"

But while the disciples of Jesus were most likely either
saying thus, or thinking thus, the Master solved their
difficulties, by the addition of one phrase, saying they should (c)
triumph "In My NAME." For He did not bid them simply
and indefinitely make disciples of all nations, but with the
necessary addition of "In my Name." And the power of
His Name being so great, that the apostle says: "God has Phil. ii. 9.
given him a name which is above every name, that in the
name of Jesus every knee should bow, of things in heaven,
and things in earth, and things under the earth," He
shewed the virtue of the power in His Name concealed (d)
from the crowd when He said to His disciples: "Go, and
make disciples of all nations in my Name." He also most
accurately forecasts the future when He says: "For this
gospel must first be preached to all the world, for a witness Matt. xxiv.
to all nations." 14.

These words were said in a corner of the earth then, and
only those present heard it. How, I ask, did they credit
them, unless from other divine works that He had done
they had experienced the truth in His words? Not one
of them disobeyed His command: but in obedience to (137)
His Will according to their orders they began to make
disciples of every race of men, going from their own country
to all races, and in a short time it was possible to see His
words realized.

The Gospel, then, in a short time was preached in the whole world, for a witness to the heathen, and Barbarians and Greeks alike possessed the writings about Jesus in their ancestral script and language.[1] And yet who would not quite reasonably be at a loss to explain how the disciples of Jesus gave this teaching? Did they go into the (b) middle of the city, and stand there in the Agora, and call on the passers-by with a loud voice, and then address the populace? And what were the arguments in their address, which would have any chance of persuading such an audience? How could untrained speakers, quite deficient in education, give addresses at all?

Perhaps you suggest they did not speak in public, but in private to those they met. If so, with what arguments could they have persuaded their hearers?—for they had (c) a most difficult task, unless they were ready to deny the shameful death of Him they preached. And suppose they concealed it, and passing over the nature and number of His sufferings at the hands of the Jews, retailed simply the noble and the glorious incidents (I mean His miracles and mighty works, and His philosophic teaching), they had even so no light problem to solve in gaining easily the adherence of listeners, who spoke strange tongues, and then for the first time heard novelties talked of by men who brought with them nothing sufficient to authenticate

---

[1] There are three principal classes of ancient translations of N.T., the Latin, the Syriac, and the Egyptian :

(i) The Latin, (a) old Latin originating in Africa current early in the second century.

(b) European Latin current in N. Italy in fourth century.

(c) Other "Italian" texts. The basis of Jerome's Vulgate of A.D. 383.

(ii) The Syriac. (a) The Pĕshitta, a revision about A.D. 300 of (b) an earlier old Syriac.

(iii) The Egyptian. (a) The Memphitic or "Coptic." The greater part cannot be later than the second century (Westcott and Hort).

(b) The Thebaic, of about the same date.

(c) The Bashmuric, of which only 330 verses survive.

Besides these there are : (iv) The Æthiopic, of fourth or fifth century.

(v) The Armenian, early fifth century.

(vi) The Gothic of Ulfilas, circa A.D. 350.

(The New Testament in Greek, B. F. Westcott and F. J. A. Hort, vol. ii. pp. 78-86.)

what they said.   Yet such a Gospel would, perhaps, have (d)
seemed more plausible.

But in fact they preached, first, that God came on an
embassy in a man's body, and was actually the Word of
God by nature, and had wrought the wonders He did as
God.   And next—a tale opposed to this, that He had
undergone insult and contumely, and at last the Cross,
the most shameful punishment and the one reserved for
the most criminal of mankind ; who would not have had
ground for despising them as preaching an inconsistent
message?

And who could be so simple, as to believe them easily
when they said that they had seen Him after His death
risen to life from the dead, One Who was unable to
defend Himself when alive?   Who would have believed
common and uneducated men who told them they must (138)
despise their fathers' gods, condemn the folly of all who
lived in the ages past, and put their sole belief in them
and the commands of the Crucified—because He was
the only-beloved and only-begotten Son of the One
Supreme God?   I myself, when I frankly turn the account
over in my own mind, have to confess that I find in it
no power to persuade, no dignity, no credibility, not even
enough plausibility, to convince just one of the most simple. (b)
But when I turn my eyes away to the evidence of the
power of the Word, what multitudes it has won, and what
enormous churches have been founded by those unlettered
and mean disciples of Jesus, not in obscure and unknown
places, but in the most noble cities—I mean in Royal
Rome, in Alexandria, and Antioch, throughout the whole
of Egypt and Libya, Europe and Asia, and in villages and (c)
country places and among the nations—I am irresistibly
forced to retrace my steps, and search for their cause, and
to confess that they could only have succeeded in their
daring venture, by a power more divine, and more strong
than man's, and by the co-operation of Him Who said to
them : " Make disciples of all the nations in my Name." [1]

And when He said this He appended a promise, that
would ensure their courage and readiness to devote themselves to carrying out His commands.   For He said to

---

[1] With regard to Eusebius's text of Matt. xxviii. 19, ἐν τῷ ὀνόματί
μου may here be his paraphrase for the Trinitarian formula.

them : "And lo! I am with you all the days, even unto the end of the world." Moreover, He is said to have breathed into them a holy Spirit, yea to have given them divine and miraculous power—first saying : "Receive ye Holy Spirit," and then : "Heal the sick,[1] cleanse lepers, cast out demons; freely ye have received, freely give."

John xx. 22.

Matt. x. 8.

You yourself will recognize what power their word has had, for the *Book of the Acts* agrees with their having these powers, and gives consistent evidence, where these men are reported by their power of working miracles by the Name of Jesus to have astonished the spectators present.

(139)

They amazed the spectators first most probably by the miracles themselves ; they then found men bent on inquiring Who He was, Whose power and Name had caused the wonder ; then they taught them and found that their faith had preceded the teaching. For without persuasion by words, being first convinced by works, they were easily brought into the state that the words required. For some are said to have been about to offer sacrifices and libations to the disciples of Jesus, as if they had been gods. And the exhibition of their miracles so struck their minds, that they called one Hermes and the other Zeus. And, of course, whatever they told about Jesus to men in such a state, was naturally after that considered the truth, and thus their evidence for His Resurrection after death was not given by simple or unproven words, but came with the persuasion of the very working, since they could shew forth the works of One living still.[2]

Acts xiv. 12.

(b)

And if they preached that He was God, and the Son of God, being with the Father before He came to earth, to this truth they were equally open, and would certainly have thought anything opposed to it incredible and impossible, reckoning it impossible to think that what was done was the work of a human being, but ascribing it to God without any one telling them.

(c)

Here, then, in this and nothing else is the answer to our question, by what power the disciples of Jesus convinced

---

[1] W.H. add νεκροὺς ἐγείρετε.

[2] This is in harmony with Eusebius's fundamental evidential teaching. See Intr. p. xv.

their first hearers, and how they persuaded Greeks as well
as barbarians to think of Him as of the Word of God, and
how in the midst of cities, as well as in the country, they (d)
instituted places of instruction in the religion of the One
Supreme God.

And yet all must wonder, if they consider and reflect,
that it was not by mere human accident, that the greater
part of the nations of the world were never before under
the one empire of Rome, but only from the times of Jesus.
For His wonderful sojourn among men synchronized with
Rome's attainment of the acme of power, Augustus then
first being supreme ruler over most of the nations, in whose
time, Cleopatra being captured, the succession of the
Ptolemies was dissolved in Egypt. And from that day (140)
to this, the kingdom of Egypt has been destroyed, which
had lasted from immemorial time, and so to say from the
very beginnings of humanity.[1] Since that day the Jewish
people have become subject to the Romans, the Syrians
likewise, the Cappadocians and Macedonians, the Bithynians
and Greeks, and in a word all the other nations who are
under Roman rule. And no one could deny that the
synchronizing of this with the beginning of the teaching
about our Saviour is of God's arrangement, if he considered
the difficulty of the disciples taking their journey, had the (b)
nations been at variance one with another, and not mixing
together because of varieties of government. But when
these were abolished, they could accomplish their projects
quite fearlessly and safely, since the Supreme God had
smoothed the way[2] before them, and subdued the spirit
of the more superstitious citizens under the fear of a strong
central government.

For consider, how if there had been no force available
to hinder[3] those who in the power of polytheistic error
were contending with Christian education, that you would
have long ago seen civil revolutions, and extraordinarily
bitter persecutions and wars, if the superstitious had had (c)
the power to do as they willed with them.

Now this must have been the work of God Almighty,
this subordination of the enemies of His own Word to a

---

[1] ἀνθρωπείας. G. supplies γενέσεως.
[2] προεξευμαρίσαντος. Cf. *Laud. Const.* 16. 3.
[3] τὸ κῶλυον. Cf. 2 Thess. i. 7.

greater fear of a supreme ruler. For He wills it daily to
advance, and to spread among all men. And, moreover,
that it might not be thought to prosper through the leniency
of rulers, if some of them under the sway of evil designed
(d) to oppose the Word of Christ, He allowed them to do what
was in their hearts, both that his athletes might display
their holiness, and also that it might be made evident to
all that the triumph of the Word was not of the counsel
of men, but of the power of God. Who would not wonder
at what ordinarily happened in times like those? For the
athletes of holiness of old shone forth clear and glorious
to the eyes of all, and were thought worthy of the prizes
of God; while the enemies of holiness paid their meet
penalty, driven mad with divine scourges, afflicted with
(141) terrible and vile diseases in their whole body, so that at
last they were forced to confess their impiety against Christ.
And all the rest who were worthy of the Divine Name, and
gloried in their Christian profession, passing through a
short discipline of trial, exhibited the nobility and sincerity
of their hearts, received back again once more their own
liberty, while through them the word of salvation shone out
daily more brightly, and ruled even in the midst of foes.

And not only did they struggle against visible enemies,
(b) but against the invisible, such evil dæmons and their
rulers as haunt the nebulous air around the earth, whom
also Christ's true disciples by purity of life and prayer to
God and by His Divine Name drove off, giving proofs of
the miraculous signs, which of old were said to have been
done by Him, and also, to eyes that could see, of His
divine power still active.

And now that these preliminary topics are concluded,
in their right order, I must proceed to handle the more
mystical theology about Him, and consider Who He was
that performed miracles through the visible humanity[1]
(of Jesus).

---

[1] διὰ τοῦ φαινομένου ἀνδρός.   Lit. "by the man that appeared."

BOOK IV

CHAPTER 1

Of the Mystical Dispensation of Our Lord and Saviour Jesus, (144)
the Christ of God.

As I have treated at sufficient length the topics connected
with the Incarnation of our Saviour in the preceding Book, (b)
the third Book of the *Proof of the Gospel*, it is now the
place to approach more recondite doctrine, I mean the
more mystical theology of His Person.

Now common to all men is the doctrine of God, the
First and the Eternal, Alone, Unbegotten and Supreme
Cause of the Universe, Lord of lords, and King of kings.
But the doctrine of Christ is peculiar and common to
the Hebrews and ourselves, and, though following their (c)
own scriptures, they confess it equally with us, yet they fall
far asunder from us, in not recognizing His Divinity, nor
knowing the cause of His coming, nor grasping at what
period of time it was predicted that He should come.
For while they look forward to His Coming even now, we
preach that He has come once already, and believing the
predictions and teaching of the inspired prophets, pray
that we may behold His second Coming in divine glory.

The account of our Lord is of two kinds : the one may (d)
be called the later, brought but recently before mankind,
the other is older than all time and all eternity.

For since God, Who is alone good and the Source and
Spring of everything good, had willed to make many partakers of His own treasures, He purposed to create the
whole reasoning creation, (comprising) unembodied, intelligent and divine powers, angels and archangels, spirits
immaterial and in all ways pure, and souls of men as well
endued with undetermined liberty of Free-willed Choice

between right and wrong, and to give them whatever bodily
(145) organs they were to possess, suitable to the variety of their
lives, with countries and places natural to them all. (For
to those who had remained good He gave the best places,
and to those who did not He gave fit abodes, places of
discipline for their perverse inclinations.)

He, foreseeing the future in His foreknowledge, as God
must, and aware that as in a vast body all these things
about to be would need a head, thought that He ought
to subordinate them all to one Governor of the Whole
Creation, ruler and king of the Universe, as also the holy
oracles of the earliest Hebrew theologians and prophets
(b) mystically teach. From which it is to be learned, that
there is one principle of the Universe, nay more, one
even before the principle, and born before the first, and
of earlier being than the Monad,[1] and greater than every
Name, Who cannot be named, nor explained, nor sought
out, the good, the cause of all, the Creator, the Beneficent,
the Prescient, the Saving, Himself the One and Only God,
from Whom are all things, and for Whom are all things:
"For in him we live and move, and have our being."

Rom. xi.
36; Acts
xvii. 28.

And the fact that He wills it, is the sole cause of all
things that exist coming into being and continuing to be.
(c) For it comes of His will, and He wills it, because He
happens to be good by nature. For nothing else is
essential by nature to a good person except to will what
is good. And what He wills, He can effect. Wherefore,
having both the will and the power, He has ordained for
Himself, without let or hindrance, everything beautiful and
useful both in the visible and invisible world,[2] making His
own Will and Power as it were a kind of material and
substratum of the genesis and constitution of the Universe,
so that it is no longer reasonable to say that anything that
exists must have come from the non-existent, for that
(d) which came from the non-existent would not be anything.
For how could that which is non-existent cause something
else to exist? Everything that has ever existed or now
exists derives its being from the One, the only existent
and pre-existent Being, Who also said: "I am the existent,"
because, you will see, as the Only Being, and the Eternal

Heb. xi. 3.

Exod. iii.
14.

---

[1] See note, p. 173.
[2] Gaisford notes the echo of Plato, *Tim.* 29 E., in this passage.

Being, He is Himself the cause of existence to all those to whom He has imparted existence from Himself by His Will and His Power, and gives existence to all things, and their powers and forms, richly and ungrudgingly from Himself.

CHAPTER 2

That we hold that the Son of God was before the Whole Creation.

AND then He makes first of all existences next to Himself (146) His child,[1] the first-born Wisdom, altogether formed of Mind and Reason and Wisdom, or rather Mind itself, Reason itself, and Wisdom itself, and if it be right to conceive anything else among things that have come into being (b) that is Beauty itself, and Good itself, taking it from Himself, He lays it Himself as the first foundation of what is to come into being afterwards.   He is the perfect creation of a perfect Creator, the wise edifice of a wise Builder, the good Child of a good Father, and assuredly to them that afterwards should receive existence through Him, friend and guardian, saviour and physician, and helmsman holding the rudder-lines of the creation of the universe.   In agreement with which the oracles in theological phrase call Him, "God-begotten," [2] as alone bearing (c) in Himself the image of the Godhead, that cannot be explained in word, or conceived in thought, through which image (they say that) He is God, and that He is called so, because of this primary likeness, and also for this reason, too, that He was appointed by the Father His good Minister, in order that as if by one all-wise and living instrument, and rule of art and knowledge, the universe might be guided by Him, bodies and things without body, things living and things lifeless, the reasoning with the irrational, mortal with immortal, and whatever else coexists and is woven in with them, and as if by one force running (d) through the whole, all things might be harmonized together,

[1] γέννημα αὐτοῦ.   Θεὸν γεννητόν.

by one living active law and reason existing in all and extending through all things, in one all-wise bond—yea, by the very Word of God and His law, united and bound in one.

CHAPTER 3

That we rightly teach that there are not many sons of the Supreme God, but One only, God of God.

(147) AND as the Father is One, it follows that there must be
(b) one Son and not many sons, and that there can be only one perfect God begotten of God, and not several. For in multiplicity will arise otherness and difference and the introduction of the worse. And so it must be that the One God is the Father of one perfect and only-begotten Son, and not of more Gods or sons. Even so, light being of one essence, we are absolutely obliged to regard the perfect thing that is begotten of light to be one also. For what other thing would it be possible to conceive of as begotten of light, but the ray only, which proceeds from it, and fills and enlightens all things? Everything surely
(c) that is foreign to this would be darkness and not light. And analogously to this there can be nothing like unto, nor a true copy of, the Supreme Father, Who is unspeakable light, except as regards this one thing only, Whom we are able to call the Son. For He is the radiance of the eternal light, and the unblurred mirror of the activity of God, and the image of His goodness. Wherefore it was
Heb. i. 3. said: "Who being the brightness of his glory, and the express image of his person." Except that the radiance is inseparable from the light of sense, while the Son exists in Himself in His own essence apart from the Father. And the ray has its range of activity solely from the light, whereas
(d) the Son is something different from a channel of energy, having His Being in Himself. And, moreover, the ray is coexistent with the light, being a kind of complement thereof; (for there could be no light without a ray :) they exist together and simultaneously. But the Father precedes

the Son, and has preceded Him in existence, inasmuch as He alone is unbegotten. The One, perfect in Himself and first in order as Father, and the cause of the Son's existence, receives nothing towards the completeness of His Godhead from the Son : the Other, as a Son begotten of Him that caused His being, came second to Him, Whose Son He is, receiving from the Father both His Being, and the character of His Being. And, moreover, the ray does (148) not shine forth from the light by its deliberate choice, but because of something which is an inseparable accident of its essence : but the Son is the image of the Father by intention and deliberate choice. For God willed to beget a Son, and established a second light, in all things made like unto Himself. Since, then, the unbegotten and eternal light is one, how could there be any other image of it, except the ray, which itself is light, preserving in all respects its likeness to its prototype? And how could (b) there be an image of the One itself, unless it were the same as it in being one? So that a likeness is implied not only of the essence of the first, but also one of numerical quantity, for one perfect Being comes of the one eternal light, and the first and only-begotten Issue was not different or many, and it is this very Being to Which, after that Being which had no origin or beginning, we give the names of God, the Perfect, the Good : for the Son of a Father who is One must be also One. For we should (c) have to agree that from the one fragrance of any particular object that breathes it forth, the sweet odour shed forth on all is one and the same, not diverse and many. So it is right to suppose that from the first and only Good, Which is Almighty God, is supplied an odour divine and life-giving, perceptible by mind and understanding, which is one and not many. For what variation could there be from this complete likeness to the Father, except one that was a declension and an inferiority ; a supposition that we must not admit into our theology of the Son : for He is (d) a breath of the power of God, and a pure effluence of the glory of the Creator. For a fragrant breath is poured forth from any sweet-scented substance, say from myrrh or any of the flowers and odorous plants that spring from the earth, beyond the original substance into the surrounding atmosphere, and fills the air far and wide as it is shed forth, without any deprivation, or lessening, or scission, or division of the said substance. For it still remains in its own place, and preserves its own identity,[1] and though begetting this fragrant force it is no worse than it was before, while the sweet odour that is begotten, possessing its own character, imitates in the highest degree possible the nature (149) of that which produced it by its own [fragrance]. But these are all earthly images and touched with mortality, parts of this lower corrupt and earthly constitution, whereas the scope of the theology we are considering far transcends all illustrations, and is not connected with anything physical, but imagines with the acutest thought a Son Begotten, not at one time non-existent, and existent at another afterwards, but existent before eternal time, and pre-existent, and ever with the Father as His Son, and yet not Unbegotten, but (b) begotten from the Father Unbegotten, being the Onlybegotten, the Word, and God of God, Who teaches that He was not cast forth from the being of the Father by separation, or scission, or division, but unspeakably and unthinkably to us brought into being from all time, nay rather before all times, by the Father's transcendent and inconceivable Will and Power. "For who shall describe Isa. liii. 8; his generation?" he says, and "As no one knoweth the Matt. xi. Father save the Son, so no one knoweth the Son save 27. the Father that begat Him."

CHAPTER 4

That the Only-begotten Son of God must be considered necessarily Anterior to the Whole Universe.

But it seemed good to the Father, source of all goodness, that (His) One only-begotten and beloved Son should be the Head of the Creation of all things begotten, when He (d) was about to create One Universe, like a body one and vast consisting of many limbs and parts. . . .[2]

And that He should not govern it from above, as merely

---

[1] Τὴν ταυτότητα πρὸς ἑαυτό.   [2] Lacuna.

depending on the greater Headship of the Divinity of the Father (for the Head of Christ is the Father), but as leader of and antecedent to all things after Him, being verily all the while the lasting agent of His Father's commands,[1] and of the creation that was yet to be.

And therefore it is we say that He first before all things was made by the Father, as something one in form, the instrument of every existence and nature, alive and living, nay divine, lifegiving and all-wise, begetting good, Choregus of Light, Creator of the Heaven, Architect of the Universe, (150) Maker of Angels, Ruler of Spirits, Instrument of the Salvation of Souls, Source of Growth to bodies, all things foreseeing, guiding, healing, ruling, judging, proclaiming the religion of the Father.

CHAPTER 5

That we hold that there are Numberless Divine Created Powers but One Alone of the Son, whereby We describe Him as the Image of God the Father.

WHEREFORE we must recognize with awe throughout the whole of the sphere of creation generally one divine Power, and not suppose there to be many.　For the general creative (c) Power is One, and One is the Word, Creator of the Universe, in the beginning with God : Whom it truly behoves us Cf. John i not to ignore, but to worship and honour worthily, because 1. not only at the beginning of the Creation did all things exist through Him, but since then for ever and now as well, and without Him nothing was made.　For if there is life in things that exist, that life was what was begotten in Him. (For from Him and through Him is the life-power and the soul-power of all things.)　Be it rhythm, beauty, harmony, (d) order, blending of qualities, substance, quality, quantity, the one Word of the Universe holds all in union and order, and One Creative power of God is at the Head of all.　And as in our own bodies there are great and various differences in

[1] διαρκοῦσαν εἴς τε τὴν τοῦ πατρὸς ἐπικέλευσιν : διαρκ. either " sufficiently subservient " or " permanent."

the parts, but one creative power in the whole (for the nature of the head is not dependent on one power of God, that of the eyes on another, and that of ears and feet on other distinct powers), so also there is one general identical divine power governing the whole Universe, creative of the (151) heaven and the stars, the living things in earth and air and sea, the elements generally and individually, and all kinds of natural things in their genera and species. So there is not one force productive of fire, another of water, another again of earth and of air. But one and the same wisdom is crafts-man of the whole, I mean this very creative Word of God of our theology, Who is the Maker of the Universe. The friendship of the elements for one another bears witness to this, proving the constitution of the Universe to be kindred and related and as it were the work of one Architect by the (b) mixing of blended qualities. Earth, for instance, the heavy element, floats on water, and is not drawn down below by its natural solidity, but always remaining on the surface and not immersed, bears witness to the Word of God and the Will and Power of God. The union of wet with dry, again, without producing corruption, and without completely swamping everything, being hindered by the awful will of God, shews the power of the Word of God, Who is One and the same.

And what of fire? Although its nature is burning and (c) destructive, it lurks in logs, and is mingled in all living bodies ; it is combined elementarily with earth and air and water, and thus supplying by proportion and measure to all things what they need in so far as it can aid each sister element, and forgetting its own proper power, does it not seem another instance of subservience to the Word of God and His Power?

When you behold the regular succession of day and night, the waxing and waning of hours and seasons, the circles of the years and the cycles of time, the wheelings of the (d) stars, the courses of the sun and the changes of the moon, the sympathy and antipathy of all things, and the one Cosmos formed of all, would you think it right to say that Unreason, and Chance, and random forces were the cause of all, or rather the Word which is truly God's Word and God's Wisdom and God's Power, and would you not hymn Its praise as one and not many? Then, again, in a man one soul and one power of reason may be creative of many things, since one and the same faculty by concentration can be applied to agriculture, to ship-building, to steering and to house-building. And the one mind and reasoning faculty in a man can acquaint him with many different spheres of knowledge, for the same man will know geometry and astronomy, and will lecture on grammar and medicine, (152) and will excel in intellectual pursuits and handicraft as well. And yet no one has ever yet supposed that there are more souls than one in one body, or has thought it strange that man should have many faculties, through his interest in many studies.

And again, if one should find a shapeless piece of clay, and then softening it in his hands give it the shape of an animal, moulding with plastic art the head into one form, the hands and feet differently, the eyes again otherwise, and the cheeks as well, ears and mouth, nose, chest and shoulders, would you say, when many forms and limbs and parts have (b) been framed in the one body, that one must reckon there to have been the same number of makers, or rather praise the craftsman of the whole complete figure, who worked out the whole thing with one reasoning faculty and one power? Why, then, in the case of the Universe, which consists of a unity in many parts, must we suppose many creative powers, and name many gods, and not confess that that which is (c) truly " the power of God and the wisdom of God " in one 1 Cor. i. power and goodness supports and gives life to all things at 24. the same time, and gives to all from itself their various supplies? So also the light of the sun is one, and the same rays at one and the same time irradiate the air, enlighten the eyes, warm the touch, enrich the earth, cause plants to grow, are the foundation of time, the guide of the stars, the patrol of the heavens, the joy of the Cosmos, shew the clear power of God in the whole Universe, and fulfil all those effects with one pulse of their being.

Fire, again, by its nature purifies gold, and melts lead : wax it dissolves, clay it hardens, wood it dries, by one burning force accomplishing so many changes. And thus, too, the heavenly Word of God, the Creator of sun and (d) heaven and of the whole Cosmos, present in all things with effective power, and reaching through all things, showers light on sun and moon and stars from Its own eternal force,

and having first formed the heaven to be the meetest likeness of Its own greatness rules over it for ever, and fills the
powers of angels and spirits beyond the heaven and the
Cosmos, and the beings who have mind and reason, at once
(153) with life, and light, and wisdom, and all virtue, and every good
thing from Its own treasures, with one and the same creative
art.   And It never ceases to bestow their special being to
the elements, their mixings, combinations, forms, shapes
and fashions, and their many qualities, in the animal and
vegetable world, and in souls, and in bodies rational and
irrational, varying Its gifts now in one way now in another,
and supplying all things to all together at the same time,
and dowering all mankind with self-conscious mind able to
(b) contemplate Its wisdom, standing close by all and shewing
beyond all doubt that the one Cosmos is the work of the
one Cosmos-making Word.

Such, then, was the Son, sole-begotten of His will, Master
of fair crafts and Creator of all things, Whom the Highest
God, God and Father of the Creator Himself first before all
begat, setting in Him and through Him the creative propor-
tions[1] of things about to be, and casting in Him the seeds of
(c) the constitution and the government of the Universe.   Do
you not see with your eyes the whole Cosmos, which one
heaven encircles, and the myriad dances and circlings of the
stars around it?   One sun again, and not many suns, veils
the flashings of all things with excess of light.   So, then,
since the Father is one, the Son must be one also.   And if
one should find fault because there are not many, let such
an one see that he find not fault because He made not
more suns than one, or moons, or universes, or anything
else, like a maniac[2] attempting to turn what is right and
good in nature out of its course.

[1] λόγους.
[2] Cf. Tennyson, *In Memoriam* :
　　" This round of green, this orb of flame,
　　　Fantastic beauty, such as lurks
　　　In some wild poet, when he works
　　Without a conscience or an aim."

CHAPTER 6

*That from the First Constitution of the Universe the Christ of
God has been the Invisible Guardian of Godly Souls.*

THUS, then, as the one sun among things visible lights the (d)
whole Cosmos of sense, so also among the things of thought
the one perfect Word of God gives light to the immortal
and unembodied powers, the myriad existences of mind and
reason, like stars and founts of light.   And since it behoved (154)
that the law over all through the Universe, and the Word of
God in all and reaching through all, should be one, so that
in Him the likeness to the Father even in all respects might
be preserved, in virtue, in power, in essence, in the number
of the Monad and the Unit,[1] since the essence of things
about to be begotten would be of many forms and many
kinds, subject through weakness of nature to many changes
and variations, one at one time, another at another, and (b)
would fail of the highest power of the Father through the
exceeding greatness of His nature inexpressible and infinitely
vast to all, and fated for ever being itself but a begotten
thing to be unable to mingle with the unbegotten and
incomprehensible Godhead, or to look up and gaze upon the
unspeakable flashings pouring out from the eternal light, it
was above all necessary that the Father all-good and the
Saviour of the Universe, that the nature of things soon to
be might not in exile from His fellowship be deprived of
the greatest good, should interpose the divine, all-strong, (c)
and all-virtuous power of His only-begotten and first-born Cf. Col. i.
Son. For though He was in the most certain and the closest 15;
association with the Father, and equally with Him rejoiced Heb. i. 6.
in that which is unspeakable, yet He could descend with all
gentleness, and conform Himself in such ways as were
possible, to those who were far distant from His own height,
and through their weakness crave amelioration and aid

---

[1] ἡ μονάς; cf. 145 b, and Zeller, i. 391. Ritter and Preller: The
Pythagoreans made unity, or the One, an essential element of Deity,
and antecedent to all oppositions of principles. The Divine Unity
secondarily, as a member of the subsequent opposition, was called the
Monad. For ἐνάς "the unit," cf. Plato, *Philebus* 15 a, περὶ τούτων
τῶν ἐνάδων καὶ τοιούτων—cf. P.E. 749 a.

(d) from a secondary Being,[1] that they might behold the flashings of the sun falling quietly and gently on them, though
they are not able to delight in the fierce might of the sun
because of their bodily weakness.

Suppose, as the hypothesis of an argument, that the sun
all-glowing came down from heaven and lived among men,
it would be impossible for anything on earth to remain
undestroyed,[2] for everything alive and dead would be
destroyed together by the rushing stroke of light, swiftly
enough would he make blind the eyes of those that see,
being far more the source of harm and destruction than of
(155) usefulness to all, not that it is his nature so to be, but that
he would become such to those who would be unable from
their own weakness to support his surpassing glare.

Why, then, are you surprised to learn the like about
God (Whose work is the sun, and the whole heaven, and
the Cosmos)?[3] That it is impossible for any that exist
to have fellowship in His unspeakable and inexplicable
Power and Essence save for One alone, Whom the Father
Himself in His Foreknowledge of the Universe established
before all things, so that the nature of begotten things
might not altogether through their own lack of energy and
strength fall away, being severed from the Father's un-
(b) begotten and incomprehensible Essence, but might endure
and increase and be nourished, enjoying that mediated
supply,[4] which the Only-begotten Word of God ceases not
to provide to all, and passing everywhere and through all
provides for the salvation of all equally, whether they have
reason or not, whether they be mortal or immortal, of
heaven or of earth, both divine and invisible powers, and,
in a word, of all things whatsoever that shared in being
through His agency, and far more peculiarly still of those
who possess reason and thought, for which things' sake
(c) He does not at all despise the human race, but rather
honours and cares for it, for the sake of the kinship and
connection of their reason with Himself, inasmuch as it
was said in the holy oracles that they were formed after
His likeness. Yea, He, as being the Word of God, made

Gen. i.
26, 27.

---

[1] ἐκ τοῦ δευτέρου: i. e. "they needed a mediator."
[2] ἀδιάφθορον amended by Billius (Obs. Sacr. i. 28) from ἀδιάφορον.
[3] In Paris Codex, and Donatus' rendering. Rejected by Migne.
[4] τῆς μέσης χορηγίας.

His own image, all that is of thought and reason, the foundation of His own creation from the beginning, and set man, therefore, in a kingly and ruling relation to all living things on earth, and sent him forth free and with the power of undetermined choice between his good and evil inclinations. But man using his free-will badly, turning (d) from the right road, went wrong, caring neither for God nor Lord, nor distinguished between holy and unholy, with all manner of rude and dissolute actions, living the life of the irrational beasts.   Then surely the All-Good, the King of kings, the Supreme, God Almighty, that the men on earth might not be like brute beasts without rulers and guardians, set over them the holy angels to be their leaders and governors like herdsmen and shepherds, and set over all, and made the head of all His Only-begotten and First-born Word.   He gave Him for His own portion the angels (156) and archangels, and the divine powers, and the immaterial [1] and transcendent spirits, yea, verily, of things on earth as well the souls among men beloved by God, called by the names of the Hebrews, Jacob and Israel.

CHAPTER 7

That to the Hebrews alone of Old was the Knowledge of the (b)
*True God revealed, being known by the Manifestation of
the Christ.*

INTO this truth Moses, the first mystic theologian,[2] initiated the Hebrews of old, saying :
    " 7. Ask thy father, and he shall announce to thee, thine elders, and they shall tell thee.   8. When the Most High divided the nations, when he distributed the sons of Adam, he set the bounds of the nations according to (c) the number of the angels of God.   9. His people Israel became the portion of the Lord : Israel was the line of Deut. his inheritance."   xxxii. 7.

[1] ἄϋλα : cf. P. E. 106 c, 149 b.
[2] Or "saying in mystic language."

In these words surely he names first the Most High God, the Supreme God of the Universe, and then as Lord His Word, Whom we call Lord in the second degree after the God of the Universe. And their import is that all the nations and the sons of men, here called sons of Adam, were distributed among the invisible guardians of the nations, that is the angels, by the decision of the Most (d) High God, and His secret counsel unknown to us. Whereas to One beyond comparison with them, the Head and King of the Universe, I mean to Christ Himself, as being the Only-begotten Son, was handed over that part of humanity denominated Jacob and Israel, that is to say, the whole division which has vision and piety.

For the one engaged in the contest of the practice of virtue, even now struggling and contending in the gymnasium of holiness, was called in Hebrew nomenclature Jacob: while he that has won victory and the prize of God is called Israel, one like that actual famed forefather of the whole race of the Hebrews, and his true sons and their descen-(157) dants, and their forefathers, all prophets and men of God. Do not suppose, I beg you, that the multitude of the Jews are thus referred to, but only those of the distant past, who were made perfect in virtue and piety.

These, then, it was, whom the Word of God, the Head and Leader of all, called to the worship of the Father alone, Who is the Most High, far above all things that are seen, beyond the heaven and the whole begotten essence, calling them quietly and gently, and delivering to them the worship of God Most High alone, the Unbegotten and the Creator of the Universe.

CHAPTER 8

That the Other Nations, assigned to Certain Angels,
worshipped only the Stars of Heaven.

(c) BUT the angel-guardians and shepherds of the other races allowed them, inasmuch as they were not able with their mind to see the invisible, nor to ascend so high through their own weakness, to worship things seen in the heavens, the sun and moon and stars.   For these, indeed, being the most wonderful of the things of the phenomenal world, invited upwards the eyes of those who see, and as near as possible to heaven, being as it were in the precincts of the King's court, manifesting the glory[1] of Him that is the Source of all by the analogy of the vastness and beauty of created visible things.   "For his invisible things," as the divine Apostle says, "from the creation of the world are Rom. i. 20. clearly seen, being understood by the things that are made, (d) even his eternal power and Godhead."   And this again the great Moses mystically says.   For in exhorting the portion of the Lord to grasp with clear mind and pure soul that which is known to the mind only and unembodied, he prohibits all terror of the things seen in heaven, adding that "The Lord thy God has divided them for all the Deut. iv. nations."   And it is worth realizing why he says that they 19. were divided.   Since unseen by us they that bear the earthy and dæmonic nature are everywhere wanderers, flying through the air around the earth unknown and un- (158) distinguished by men, and the good spirits and powers and, indeed, the divine angels themselves are ever at variance with the worse, there was but one way for those who failed of the highest religion of the Almighty to prosper, namely to choose the best of things visible. in heaven.   For there was no slight danger, lest seeking after God, and busy with the unseen world, they should turn towards the opposing dæmonic powers amid the stress of things obscure and dark.   So all the most beautiful visible created things were (b) delivered to them who yearned for nothing better, since to some extent the vision of the unseen shone in them, reflected as in a mirror.

[1] θεωρία.

CHAPTER 9

Of the Hostile Power opposed to God, and of its Ruler,
and how the Whole Race of Mankind was in Subjection
thereto.

SUCH was their position. While those on the side of the
opposing rebel power were either dæmons, or vile spirits
immersed more or less in wickedness, with the cunning
ruler of them all the mighty dæmon, who first failed of
their reverence of the Divinity and fell from their own
portion, when envy of man's salvation drew them the
(d) contrary way, plotting with all sorts of evil devices against
all the nations, and even against the Lord's portion in their
jealousy of the good. It is this godless and unholy scheme
of the great Dæmon, which the prophetic spirit in Isaiah
reproves in this way, saying :

> " 13. I will act in strength, and in the wisdom of
> understanding I will take away the boundaries of the
> nations, and will diminish their strength, 14. and I will
> shake inhabited cities. And the whole inhabited world
> I will take in my hand as a nest, and I will take them
> even as eggs that have been left ; and none shall escape
> me or say me nay."

Isa. x. 13.

(159)

These are the words of God's antagonist, boasting in the
strength of his wickedness, as he threatens to steal and
obliterate the divisions of the nations delivered by the Most
High to the angels, and loudly cries that he will spoil the
earth, and shake the whole race of men, and change them
from their former good order. But hear the same prophecy
speak about him again, how he thought about himself and
(b) how he bragged :

> "How has Lucifer that rose at morn fallen from
> heaven : He is crushed to earth that sent to all the
> nations. But thou saidst in thy heart, 'I will go up
> to heaven, I will set my throne above the stars of
> heaven.[1] . . . I will ascend above the clouds, I will be

---

[1] E. omits καθιῶ ἐν ὄρει ὑψηλῷ, ἐπὶ τὰ ὄρη τὰ ὑψηλὰ τὰ πρὸς
Βορρᾶν.

like the Most High.'   But now thou shalt go down to
hell, and to the foundations of the earth."   Isa. xiv. 12.

Truly Scripture shews many things at once in this, the
madness of the said spirit, his fall from the better to the
worse, and the end of his fall.   And having uttered terrible (c)
threats against all mankind, he discovered that men could
be caught otherwise by his weapons,[1] since they possessed
in their power of free choice the ever-ready possibility of
falling into evil from their own thoughts.   Then he turned
the conditions of states from the better to the worse, and
drew away the souls of the multitude by the bait of pleasure
to every form of wickedness, and left no sort of device
untried, and with base myths of the gods and impure stories (d)
he tempted his victims with what they loved and with what
gave them pleasure, using the artful deceit of the dæmons.
And in this way he took the whole world and held it
captive, and obliterated the boundaries of the nations, as
he had threatened to do when he said : " I will remove the
boundaries of the nations, and I will diminish their strength,
and I will take the whole world in my hand as a nest."
And from that day forward he ruled all men with deceit,
and the evil dæmons were arrayed under their king in
every place and city and land.[2]   And thus the whole of
human life was enslaved by earthly powers and evil spirits
instead of the earlier ministers of God, and all gave themselves over in throngs and swiftly to the snares of pleasure ;
so that they soon overleapt the bounds even of nature, in
unnatural offences of one kind or another, and they not
only did things of which it is wrong even to think, but (160)
connected them with their conceptions of their own gods,
and worked their lust with all the more freedom as a thing
supposed to please the gods.   Hence soon, according to
the holy Apostle, they took no heed of the works of God
still bright in heaven.

[1] Dindorf reads with Viguier προβολίοις.   (προβολίον, a hunting
spear.)   MS. has προβουλίοις.   Gaisford refers to Viguier, *De Idiotismis*,
iii. 1, 7.
[2] The passage seems rhetorically to suggest that the Roman Empire
was the negation of the divine plan of nationalities.   But E. abundantly
recognizes elsewhere the providential preparation of the world for
Christ, and for the evangelization of men of all races, through the
existence of one central authority, and the cessation of wars in the Pax
Romana.   Cf. Tertullian, *Apology*, cc. xxx.–xxxvi.

"They became vain in their reasonings: and their senseless heart was darkened. 22. Professing themselves to be wise, they became fools. 23. And changed [1] the glory of the incorruptible God into an image made like to corruptible man, and of birds and four-footed beasts and creeping things."

(b)

Rom. i. 21.

And that in the earliest age those upon earth worshipped only the lights of heaven, and knew no image, nor were concerned with the error of the dæmons, there is satisfactory proof to be found in the evidence of those, who are strangers to my argument, which I drew upon in the first book of the *Preparatio* (which I wrote) before the present treatise ; (c) they clearly prove that the earliest men did not serve idols fashioned by hand from lifeless matter, nor even invisible dæmons, but only those beings, which are said in Holy Scripture to have been distributed among the nations. It is time for the Greeks themselves, therefore, whose statements I have arranged in the work mentioned, to agree that the superstition connected with idols was something more recent and novel, being introduced subsequently to the worship of the ancients, as well as the devotion to unseen spirits. All this was the work of the said antagonist of God, who plotted against all those on earth. And all (d) the tribe of unclean spirits co-operated with him. Yea, he surely, the prince of evil himself, worked this result, fulfilling in very deed, in the madness of strange pride, the threats he had uttered against all men, raising the godless cry, "I will be like the Most High," and with the aid of impure and evil dæmons offering oracles and cures and such like in response to human sorcery.

CHAPTER 10

That the Only-begotten Son of God made His Entry among Mankind of Necessity.

(161) THEY that were their guardian angels before were unable to defend in any way the subject nations now involved in

---

[1] W.H. : ἤλλαξαν.   E. : ἠλλάξαντο.

such a flood of evil. They took care of the rest of the created world. They guarded the other parts of the Cosmos, (b) and served according to their wont the will of God the Creator of all. But they did not realize the fall of mortal men through the undetermined human choice of evil. Wherefore a sickness great and hard to heal overcame all on the face of the earth, the nations being driven now one way now another by the evil spirits, and falling into a depthless abyss of evil. Yea, now some thought it good to feast on the bodies of their dearest, like wild beasts that devour the raw flesh of men, and to lie shamelessly with (c) mothers, sisters and daughters, to strangle their old men, and cast their bodies to the dogs and birds. Why should I recall the cruel and terrible human sacrifices of the "gods," I mean the evil dæmons, into which they maddened the human race? I have dealt sufficiently with them previously in the *Prolegomena* to the present treatise. But it was when evils of such magnitude had fallen on the (d) whole world from the wicked and vile spirits and their king, and none of the guardian angels was able to defend them from the evils, that He, God the Word, the Saviour of the Universe, by the good will of His Father's love to man, that the human race so dear to Him might not be seethed in the gulf of sin, sent forth at last some few and watery rays of His own light to shine through the prophet Moses and the godly men before and after him, providing a cure for the evil in man by the holy Law. It is exactly this that the Word says to the race of the Hebrews when giving the law by Moses:

"Ye shall not do according to the devices of Egypt, (162) in which ye dwelt,[1] and according to the devices of the land of Canaan, into which I bring you shall ye not do, and ye shall not walk in their ordinances, ye shall observe my judgments, and ye shall keep my ordinances.[2] Lev.
I am the Lord your God." xviii. 2.

Then, having forbidden all unlawful marriage, and all unseemly practice, and the union of women with women and men with men, he adds:

"Do not defile yourselves with any of these things; (b)

---

[1] S. : κατοικήσατε for παρῳκήσατε.
[2] S. adds : "to walk in them."

for in all these things the nations were defiled, which I will drive out before you. And the land was polluted, and I have recompensed (their) iniquity upon it, and the land is aggrieved with them that dwell upon it."

Lev. xviii. 24.

And again, he says:

"And when thou shalt have entered into the land which the Lord thy God gives thee, thou shalt by no means learn to do according to the abominations of those nations. There shall not be found in thee one who purges his son or his daughter in the fire, one who uses divination, and who deals in the omens, a sorcerer using incantations,[1] a divining spirit, an observer of auguries, a questioner of the dead. For every one that doeth these things is an abomination to the Lord thy God. For because of these abominations the Lord will destroy them from before thy face.[2] Thou shalt be perfect before the Lord thy God."

(c)

Deut. xviii. 9.

These and many other holy teachings and commands God the Word gave to them of old by Moses, as delivering the elementary truths at the entry of the life of holiness, by means of symbols, and worship of a shadowy and external character, in bodily circumcision, and other things of that kind, which were completed on the earth. But since as time went on none of the prophets who succeeded Moses had the power to cure the evils of life owing to excess of wickedness, and the activity of the dæmons daily waxed greater, so that even the Hebrew race was hurried along in the destruction of the godless, at last the Saviour and Physician of the Universe comes down Himself to men, bringing reinforcement to His angels for the salvation of men, since the Father had promised Him that He would give Him this boon, as He therefore teaches in the Psalms, when He says:

(d)

"7. The Lord said to me, Thou art my Son,
This day have I begotten thee,
8. Desire of me, and I shall give thee the heathen for thine inheritance,
And utmost parts of the earth for thy possession."

Ps ii. 7.
(163)

---

[1] S. has φαρμάκοις ἐπαείδων ἐπαοιδήν, "chanting an incantation with sorcery," for φάρμακος ἐπᾴδων.
[2] S.: "from thee."

And thus He no longer claimed as under His own authority
just and clear-sighted Israel, nor His own proper portion
only, but all the nations on the earth, which before were
allotted to many angels, and were involved in all sorts of
wickedness, and He came announcing to all the knowledge
and love of His Father, and promising the remission and
forgiveness of their former ignorance and sins, which He
also announced clearly when He said: "The strong have Matt. ix.
no need of a physician, but they that are sick: I came not 12.
to call the righteous, but sinners to repentance."   And (b)
He came, too, as overseer of His own angels, who were
first set over the nations: and they at once very distinctly
recognized their helper and Lord, and came gladly and
ministered to Him, as the Holy Scripture teaches, saying: Matt. iv.
"And angels came and ministered to him," and when, too, 11.
"a multitude of the heavenly host praising God said, 'Glory (c)
to God in the highest, and on earth peace, goodwill among Luke ii. 13.
men.'"   These, then, as being His own angels He thus
received, since they were in need of His help, but those
that of old had flown around the pursuits of men, the
malicious dæmons who both visibly and invisibly had
tyrannized over those on earth, and the tribes of wild and
merciless spirits, with their leader in all evil, that cunning
and baneful one [1] He put to flight and subdued with mighty
and divine power, as certain of them that recognized Him (d)
said: "What have we to do with thee, Son of God? Matt. viii.
Hast thou come to torment us before the time?"   29.

And these by His deeds and words He mightily
plagued, while He healed and cured the whole human
race with the gentle and kind medicines of His words, and
with the tonic of His teaching. He freed them from all
sorts of sicknesses and suffering of body as well as soul, He
set all that came to Him free from age-long superstition,
and the fears of polytheistic error, and from a low and
dissolute life. He converted and changed those who
listened to Him from lust to purity, from impiety to piety,
from injustice to justice, yea, verily from the power of the (164)
malicious dæmons to the divine acceptance of true holiness. In addition to all this He threw open the gates of

---

[1] ἀλαστόρα.   Originally "the Avenging Deity," as in Æsch., *Pers.*
354, *Agam.* 1501, 1508.   Then of any plague, as in Soph., *Trach.*
1092.

heavenly life and of His holy teaching to all the nations of the world, and so greatly condescended, as not only to (b) extend His saving hand to the sick and grievously afflicted, but also to save the half-dead from the very gates of death, and to loose from the bonds of death those who had been a long time dead and buried.   And for this reason especially there was need for Him to be active, even as far as the resting-places of the dead, that He might be Lord not only of the living but of the dead as well.

So long, then, as He is with the Father, and steers the Providence of the Universe with divine power, the Divine Word and Wisdom and Power oversees and protects the heaven itself and the earth likewise, and the things by (c) nature included in them, as well as the divine and unembodied essences beyond the heaven.   He is their Ruler and Head and King, and is already hymned as God and Lord in the sacred oracles, and He gives light to the unembodied and purely rational natures.   And He is called Sun of Righteousness, and the True Light, carrying out and co-operating in His Father's commands, wherefore He is also styled minister of the Father and Creator, but since He (d) alone in His ordained rank knows how to serve God, and stands midway between the unbegotten God and the things after Him begotten, and has received the care of the Universe, and is Priest to the Father on behalf of all who are obedient, and alone shews Himself favourable and merciful to all, He is called as well Eternal High Priest, and also the Anointed (Christ) of the Father, for so among the Hebrews they were called Christs, who long ago symbolically presented a copy of the first (Christ).   And when as Captain of the Angels He heads them, He is Isa. ix. 6. called : "The Angel of Great Counsel," and as Leader of the Armies of Heaven : "Captain of the Host of the Jos. v. 14. Lord." [1]

But now descending to our world, receiving our rational nature, for the sake of His own likeness to it by the goodwill of the Father, as He is like to rule over infants and as it were over the flocks, He is named Shepherd of the Sheep, while as promising to care for sick souls, He would rightly be called Saviour and Physician.   And this of (165) course is the meaning of the name "Jesus" in Hebrew.

[1] κατὰ τάξιν.

And since He needed a human organism, so that He could show Himself to men, and give true teaching of the knowledge of the Father and of holiness, He did not even refuse the way of the Incarnation ; but assuming our nature in a moment He came among men, shewing the great Miracle to all of God in Man.   So that He did not take command (b) imperceptibly and obscurely as a being without flesh or body, but seen by the very eyes of flesh, and allowing the eyes of men to see miracles even beyond the power of man, and moreover giving His teaching by tongue and articulate sound to the bodily ears, He manifested Himself—and truly it was a divine and miraculous thing, such as never before or since is recorded to have happened—the Saviour and the Benefactor, too, of all.   So, then, God the Word was called the Son of Man, and was named Jesus, because He made His approach to us to cure and to heal the souls of men.   And therefore in Hebrew the name Jesus is inter- (c) preted Saviour.   And He led the life which we lead, in no way forsaking the being that He had before, and ever in the Manhood retaining the Divinity.

Immediately, therefore, at the first moment of His descent among men, He mingles with God the divine glory of our human birth,[1] for while He is born like us, and arrayed like men with mortality, yet as One Who is not man, but God, He is born into the phenomenal world from an undefiled and unwedded maiden, and not of sexual union and corruption.

CHAPTER 11

That He passed through the Life of Men.   (d)

AND He lived His whole life through in the same manner, now revealing His nature as like our own, and now that of God the Word, doing great works and miracles as God,

[1] So Donatus: "cum Deo divinam commiscet nostri ortus admirabilitatem." We may interpret: "He associated humanity with God, so that it became gloriously divine."

(166) and announcing beforehand predictions of the future, and shewing clearly by His deeds God the Word Who was not seen by the multitude, and He made the end of His life, when He departed from men, in tune with and similar to its beginning.

CHAPTER 12

That the Laws of Loving-kindness called Him even to them that had been long dead.

(b) Now the laws of love summoned Him even as far as Death and the dead themselves, so that He might summon the souls of those who were long time dead.   And so because He cared for the salvation of all for ages past, and

Heb. ii. 14. that "He might bring to naught him that hath the power of death," as Scripture teaches, here again he underwent the dispensation in His mingled Natures: as Man, he left His Body to the usual burial, while as God He departed

Luke xxiii. 46. from it.   For He cried with a loud cry, and said to the Father: "I commend my spirit," and departed from the

(c) body free, in no wise waiting for death, who was lagging as it were in fear to come to Him; nay, rather, He pursued him from behind and drove him on, trodden under His feet and fleeing, and He burst the eternal gates of his dark realms, and made a road of return back again to life for the dead there bound with the bonds of death.   Thus, too, His own body was raised up, and many bodies of the sleeping saints arose, and came together with Him into the holy and

(d) real City of Heaven, as rightly is said by the holy words:

Isa. xxv. 8. "Death has prevailed and swallowed men up"; and again: "The Lord God has taken away every tear from every face."

And the Saviour of the Universe, our Lord, the Christ of God, called Victor, is represented in the prophetic predictions as reviling death, and releasing the souls that are bound there, by whom He raises the hymn of victory, and He says these words:

"From the hand of Hades I will save them, and from death I will ransom their souls.[1] O Death, where is thy victory?[2] O Death, where is thy sting? The sting of death is sin, and the strength of sin is the law."[3]

Hos. xiii. 14; 1 Cor. xv. 55.

Such was the dispensation that brought Him even unto (167) death, of which one that wishes to seek for the cause, can find not one reason but many. For firstly, the Word teaches by His death that He is Lord both of dead and living; and secondly, that He will wash away our sins, being slain, and becoming a curse for us; thirdly, that a victim of God and a great sacrifice for the whole world might be offered to Almighty God; fourthly, that thus He might work out (b) the destruction of the deceitful powers of the dæmons by unspeakable words; and fifthly also, that shewing the hope of life with God after death to His friends and disciples not by words only by deeds as well, and affording ocular proof of His message, He might make them of good courage and more eager to preach both to Greeks and Barbarians the holy polity which He had established. And so at once He (c) filled with His own divine power those very friends and followers, whom He had selected for Himself on account of their surpassing all, and had chosen as His apostles and disciples,[4] that they might teach all races of men His message of the knowledge of God, and lay down one way of religion for all the Greeks and Barbarians; a way which announced the defeat and rout of the dæmons, and the check of polytheistic error, and the true knowledge of the one Almighty God, and which promised forgiveness of sins (d) before committed, if men no longer continued therein, and one hope of salvation to all by the all-wise and all-good polity that He had instituted.

---

[1] LXX: αὐτούς.   [2] ἡ δίκη σου.

[3] "Eusebius prophetam in parte, et in parte apostolum sequitur."— *Gaisford.*

[4] θιασώτας: so for "disciple" in Lucian: *Fugit.* 4; *Themist.* 33 c.

CHAPTER 13

*That even when He was made Man, He remained in the
Nature that cannot suffer, or be harmed, or embodied.*

AND since this is so, there is no need to be disturbed
(168) in mind on hearing of the Birth, human Body, Sufferings
and Death of the immaterial and unembodied Word of
God. For just as the rays of the sun's light undergo no
suffering, though they fill all things, and touch dead and
unclean bodies, much less could the unembodied Power of
God suffer in its essence, or be harmed, or ever become
worse than itself, when it touches a body without being
really embodied.[1] For what of this? Did He not ever and
(b) everywhere reach through the matter of the elements and
of bodies themselves, as being the creative Word of God,
and imprint the words of His own wisdom upon them,
impressing life on the lifeless, form on that which is form-
less and shapeless by nature, stamping His own beauty
and unembodied ideas on the qualities of matter, moving
things by their own nature lifeless and immovable, earth,
air, fire, in a wise and harmonious motion, ordering all
things out of disorder, increasing and perfecting them,
(c) pervading all things with the divine power of reason,
extending through all places and touching all, but yet
receiving hurt from naught, nor defiled in His own nature.
And the same is true of His relation to men (as well as
nature). Of old He appeared to a few easily numbered,
only the prophets who are recorded and the just men,
now to one, now to another, but finally to us all, to the
(d) evil and unholy, to the Greeks as well as the Hebrews,
He has offered Himself as Benefactor and Saviour through
the surpassing goodness and love of the Father, Who is
all-good, distinctly announcing it thus: "They that are
whole have no need of a physician, but they that are sick:
I have not come to call the righteous, but sinners to
repentance." Yea, the Saviour of all cried unto all, saying:
"Come unto me, all ye that labour and are heavy laden,

Matt. ix.
12 ; Matt.
xi. 28.

---

[1] In such statements of the relation of the Logos to the human
body of Christ, Eusebius, if pressed, would be found to be teaching
Docetism.

and I will refresh you." He called and healed ungrudgingly through the human organism which He had assumed,
like a musician showing his skill by means of a lyre, and
exhibited Himself as an example of a life wholly wise,
virtuous, and good, unto the souls diseased in human
bodies, just as the most clever physicians heal men with (169)
remedies akin to and resembling them. For, now, He
taught them truths not shared by others, but laid down
as laws by Him or by the Father in far distant periods
of time for the ancient and pre-Mosaic Hebrew men of
God. And now He cared as kindly for their bodies as
for their souls, allowing them to see with eyes of physical
sight the things done by Him in the flesh, and giving His
teaching to their physical ears again with a tongue of flesh.
He fulfilled all things by the Humanity that He had taken, (b)
for those who only in that way were able to appreciate His
Divinity. In all this, then, for the advantage and profit
of us all the all-loving Word of God ministered to His
Father's Counsels, remaining Himself immaterial and unembodied, as He was before with the Father, not changing
His essence, not dissolved from His own nature, not bound
with the bonds of the flesh, not falling from divinity, and
neither losing the characteristic power of the Word, nor (c)
hindered from being in the other parts of the Universe,
while He passed His life where His earthly vessel was.
For it is the fact that during the time in which He lived
as a man, He continued to fill all things, and was with the
Father, and was in Him too, and had care of all things
collectively even then, of things in heaven and on earth,
not being like ourselves debarred from ubiquity, nor
hindered from divine action by His human nature. But
He shared His own gifts with man, and received nothing
from mortality in return. He supplied something of His (d)
divine power to mortals, not taking anything in return for
His association with mortals. He was, therefore, not defiled
by being born of a human body, being apart from body,
neither did He suffer in His essence from the mortal, being
untouched by suffering. As when a lyre is struck, or its
strings torn asunder, if so it chance, it is unlikely that he
who played it suffers, so we could not say truly that, when
some wise man is punished in his body, that the wisdom
in him, or the soul in his body, is struck or burned.

(170) Much less is it reasonable to say that the nature or power of the Word received any hurt from the sufferings of the body. For it was granted in our illustration of light that the rays of the sun sent down to earth from heaven are not defiled by touching all the mud and filth and garbage. We are not even debarred from saying that these things are illuminated by the rays of light. Whereas it is impossible to say that the sun is defiled or rendered muddy

(b) by contact with these materials. And these things could not be said to be foreign to one another. Whereas the immaterial and unembodied Word of God, having His life and reason and everything we have said in Himself, if He touch aught with divine and unembodied power, the thing touched must necessarily live and exist with the light of reason. Thus therefore, also, whatever body He touches, that body is made holy and illuminated at once, and all disease and weakness and all such things depart. Its emptiness is exchanged for the fullness of the Word. And

(c) this was why a dead body, though but a small part of it came in contact with the power of the Word, was raised up to life, and death fled from life, and darkness was dissolved by light, the corruptible put on incorruption, and the mortal immortality.

CHAPTER 14

That renewing Humanity He afforded to us all the Hope of Eternal Good.

(d) Now it was actually the case that the whole Humanity was absorbed by the Divinity, and moreover the Word of God was God as He had previously been man, and He deified humanity with Himself,[1] being the firstfruits of our

---

[1] συναποθεόω, to deify together. Cf. Greg. Nyss. For a full discussion of the doctrine of Deification, see W. R. Inge, *Christian Mysticism*, Appendix C, pp. 356–368. He quotes Clement, *Strom.* V. 10. 63, and Hippolytus, *Philos.* x. 34, "Thou hast become God," and notes that Harnack says: "After Theophilus, Irenæus, Hippolytus, and Origen, the idea of deification is found in all the Fathers of the ancient Church, and that in a primary position." The

hope, since He thought actual manhood worthy of eternal
life with Him, and of fellowship in the blessed Godhead,
and afforded to us all equally this mighty proof of an
immortality and kingdom with Him.

CHAPTER 15

What the Advent of Christ is meant to shew forth, and that (171)
   He is called God and Lord and High Priest of the God of
   the Universe by the Hebrew Prophets.

THIS then was the object of His coming to men, to bring back (b)
that which had of old wandered away from the knowledge
of the Father to its own way, and to crown that which was
thought worthy of being made in- His own image as a
relation and a friend with the joy of His own life, and to
show that the humanity was beloved by and belonged to
the Father, since for its sake the Word of God Himself
consented to become man.   And now to speak briefly,
the doctrine connected with our Lord and Saviour Jesus
Christ, in its wonderful dispensation, shall be supported from
the Hebrew prophecies, as presently their evidence will (c)
shew ; the new Scriptures shall prove the old, and the
Gospels set their seal on the prophetic evidence.

   But if this is so, it is now time to discuss His Name,
why He is called Jesus and Christ, and saluted beforehand
by name by so many prophecies.   And first, let us inquire
the meaning of the name Christ, before we begin a detailed
collection of the prophetic passages connected with the
present question.   I think it convenient to consider first
the name "Christ," and to distinguish the conception it (d)
conveys, so that we may be well acquainted with all the
questions usually associated with the subject.

---

words of Athanasius are the most famous statement of the doctrine :
" He became man that we might be deified."   Inge suggests that the
Fathers chiefly meant that man becomes "imperishable" (*Ibid.* 13).
See also Intr. to *Dionysius the Areopagite* in the present series of
translations.

Another writer,[1] you will remember, whose ideas spring from modern times and our own day, has said that Moses was the first of all lawgivers to appoint that those who were to act as priests to God must be anointed with prepared myrrh, since he thought that their bodies ought to smell sweet and have a good odour : for as everything ill-smelling is dear to vile and impure powers, so contrariwise the sweet-smelling is dear to the powers that love good.   And he therefore made the law as well that the priests should use every day in the Temple prepared incense, (172) that sweet smells might abound.   So that while the air was mingled with it, and dispersed evil smells, a kind of divine effluence might mingle with those who prayed.   And that for the same reason fragrant anointing oil was made by the perfumer's art, for all to use who were going to take the leading place in the State on public occasions, and that Moses first gave the name of "Christ" to those thus anointed.   And that this chrism was not only conferred on chief priests, but afterwards on prophets and kings, (b) who alone were allowed to be anointed with the sacred unguent.

This account seems, no doubt, very obvious, but it is far removed from the actual intention of the divine and sublime prophet.   For we may be sure that that wonderful man, and truly great Hierophant, knowing that the whole of earthy and material being was distinguished in its qualities alone, in no sense honoured one form above another, for he knew that all things were the product of one matter, never stable, having no firmness in its nature, which is (c) ever in flux, and hastening to its own destruction.   He, therefore, made no choice of bodies for their sweetness, nor preferred the pleasure of the senses for its own sake. For this would be the condition of a soul fallen to the ground and under the power of bodily pleasure.   There are, we know, many men effeminate in body, and in other ways vicious and lustful, who make use of superfluous unguents and a variety of things, but carry souls full of every horrible and offensive stench, while on the other hand the men of God, breathing out virtue, send forth a (d) fragrance that comes from purity, justice, and all holiness

---

[1] I am unable to identify this writer.

far better than the scents of earth, and hold the smell of material bodies of no account.

And the prophet, well understanding this, had none of these ideas that have been suggested about unguents or incense, but presented the images of greater and divine things, so far as he could, in an outward way to those who could learn the divine in that way only and no other. And that is exactly what the divine oracle is reported to have expressed, when it said : "See thou make (all) things accord- Exod. xxv. ing to the type shewn in the Mount."[1] Therefore, when com- 40. pleting the symbols of the other things, which it is usual to call types, it appointed the anointing with the unguent. (173) The account of it loftily and mysteriously expressed as it is, so far as I can explain it, had this meaning, that the only good and only truly sweet and noble, the cause of all life, and the gift bestowed on all in their being and their well-being, that this One Being was believed by the Hebrew reason to be the first cause of all, and Itself the highest and the All-Ruling and the All-Creating God.

It is thus the power of this Being, the all-strong, the all-good, the source of all beauty in the highest unbegotten Godhead, the Divine Spirit (which by the use of a proper and natural analogy)[2] it calls the (Oil of God), and there-fore it calls one who partakes of it Christ and Anointed. Do not think of oil as pity in this connection, nor as (b) sympathy for the unfortunate, but as that which the fruit of the tree affords, something unmixed with any damp matter, nourisher of light, healer of toilers, disperser of weariness, that which makes those who use it of a cheerful countenance, streaming with rays like light, making bright and shining the face of him who uses it, as holy Scripture says : "That he may rejoice my face with oil." Ps. ciii. 15

Therefore the prophetic word by this analogy referring to the highest power of God, the King of kings and Lord of (c) lords, calls Him the Christ and the Anointed, Who is the first and only one to be anointed with this oil in its fullness, and is the sharer of the Father's divine fragrance communi-cable to none other, and is God the Word sole-begotten of Him, and is declared to be God of God by His communion

---

[1] S. omits "all."

[2] Paris MS. and Donatus add οἰκείῳ καὶ προσφυεῖ συμβαλὸν παρα-δείγματι ἔλαιον Θεοῦ. Migne omits.

with the Unbegotten that begat Him, both the First and the Greater. Wherefore in the Psalms the oracle says thus to this same Being anointed of the Father :

(d) "7. Thy throne, O God, is for ever and ever :
A sceptre of righteousness is the sceptre of thy kingdom :
8. Thou hast loved righteousness, and hated injustice :[1]
Wherefore God, thy God,
Hath anointed thee with the oil of gladness above thy fellows."

Ps. xliv. 7.

But the nature of the oil of olive is one, whereas the nature of the unguent shews a union of many in one. And so the original and unbegotten power of Almighty God, insofar as it is conceived of as simple, uncompounded, and unmingled with any other essence, is metaphorically compared with the simple essence of the olive oil. But insofar as it is inclusive of many ideas in the same, *i. e.* the (174) creative or kingly, the conceptions of providence, judgment, and countless others, such power as inclusive of many good qualities is more suitably likened to the unguent, which the holy Scriptures teach us that the true and only High Priest of God uses. And Moses himself having first been thought worthy to view the divine (realities) in secret, and the mysteries concerning the first and only Anointed High Priest of God, which were celebrated before him in His Theophanies, is (b) ordered to establish figures and symbols on earth of what he had seen with his mind in visions, so that they who were worthy might have the symbols to occupy them, previously to the full vision of the truth.

And when afterwards he set apart from all men on earth one man who was fit to act as priest to God Himself, he from the first called him Christ, transferring the name from its spiritual meaning. and shewed that He was greater than (c) the rest of mankind by the sweet-smelling unction, clearly and emphatically proclaiming that the whole nature of the begotten, much more human nature, lacks the power of the Unbegotten, and craves the fragrance of the better. But it is allowed to no man to reach the Highest and the First ; this prize is given to the Only-begotten and the Firstborn

---

[1] S. : ἀνομίαν. E. : ἀδικίαν.

only.   For those after Him there is only one way of grasping good, through the mediation of a second principle.[1]   So
the symbol of Moses was of the Holy Spirit.   " And there   1 Cor. xii.
are diversities of gifts, but the same spirit " : of which Spirit 4.
he thought that prophets and kings before all others ought (d)
to be ambitious to partake, as being consecrated to God not
for themselves only, but for all the people.

But now let us inquire somewhat more exactly about the
symbols of Moses being symbols of the more divine (realities),
and about the possibility of those who were endued with the
Holy Spirit without the unction of earth being called Christs.

David in Ps. civ. when touching the stories of Abraham,
Isaac and Jacob, the very men who were his godly ancestors,
who lived before Moses' day, calls them Christs, for the
outpouring of the Holy Spirit, in which they shared, and
for that alone.   And when he tells how they were hospitably (175)
received by foreigners, and how they found God was their
Saviour when plots were laid against them, following Moses'
account, he names them prophets also and Christs, although
Moses had then not yet appeared among men, nor was his
law about the prepared unguent laid down.   Hear what the
Psalm says :

" 5. Remember the wonderful works, that he hath done, Ps. civ. 5.
       His wonders and the judgments of his mouth
  6. Ye seed of Abraham, his servants,
       Ye children of Jacob, his chosen,
  7. The Lord himself is your God,   (b)
       His wonders are in all the world.
  8. He remembered his covenant for ever
       The law which he gave to a thousand generations,
  9. Which he commanded to Abraham,
       And the oath which he sware unto Isaac,
 10. And established it to Jacob for a law,
       And to Israel for an everlasting covenant.
 11. Saying ' To you I will give the land of Canaan,
       The lot of your inheritance.'—[2]
 13. And they went from one nation to another,
       From one kingdom to another people.
 14. He suffered no man to do them wrong,
       And reproved kings for their sake :

---

[1] διὰ μόνης τῆς τοῦ δευτέρου μετουσίας.   [2] Verse 12 omitted.

15. ' Touch not my Christs,

(c)   And do my prophets no harm.' "

So David wrote.   And Moses informs us what kings He reproved, saying :

Gen. xii. 17.   "And God afflicted Pharaoh with great plagues [1] because of Sarra, Abraham's wife."

And again he writes about the King of Gerar :

Gen. xx. 3.   "And God came to Abimelech in a dream by night, and said, Behold thou diest for the woman thou hast taken ; for she is the wife of Abraham." [2]

Of whom he says further on :

(d)   " And now give back the woman to her husband, for
Gen. xx. 7.   he is a prophet, and will pray for you."

You see from these instances how David, or rather the Holy Spirit Who spoke through him, called the godly men of old and the prophets Christs, though they were not anointed with the earthly unguent.   For how could they have been, since it was in after years that Moses commanded the unction of the High Priest ?

Now listen to Isaiah prophesying in the clearest words thus about Christ, as one to be sent by God to men as their Redeemer and Saviour, and coming to preach forgiveness to those in bondage of spirit, and recovery of sight to the blind.   For here again the prophet teaches that the Christ has been anointed not with a prepared unguent, but with the spiritual and divine anointing of His Father's Divinity, con-
(176) ferred not by man but by the Father.   He says then in the person of Christ :

Isa. lxi. 1.   "The Spirit of the Lord is upon me, because he has anointed me.   He has sent me to preach glad tidings to the poor, to proclaim liberty to the captives, to heal the broken in heart,[3] and recovery of sight to the blind."

Let this point then be regarded as certain, that Isaiah, equally with David, prophesies that He that should come to mankind to preach liberty to the captives and recovery of sight to the blind would not be anointed with a prepared unguent, but with an anointing of the power of His Father
(b) Unbegotten and Perfect.   And according to the manner of

---

[1] S. adds "and evil."

[2] S. reads, "αὐτὴ δέ ἐστιν συνῳκηκυῖα ἀνδρὶ" ("and she is wedded to a husband)" for "αὕτη δὲ ἦν τοῦ Ἀβραάμ."

[3] LXX : These clauses are inverted.

prophecy the prophet speaks of the future as past, and as one predicting about himself.

So far, then, we have learned that they who are called "Christs" in the highest sense of the term are anointed by God, not by men, and with the Holy Spirit, not with a prepared unguent.

It is now time to see how the teaching of the Hebrews shews that the true Christ of God possesses a divine nature higher than humanity. Hear, therefore, David again, where he says that he knows an Eternal Priest of God, and calls (c) Him his own Lord, and confesses that He shares the throne of God Most High in the 109th Psalm, in which he says as follows—

"The Lord said unto my Lord, Sit thou on my right hand, | till I make thine enemies the footstool of thy feet. | 2. The Lord shall send the rod of power for thee out of Zion, | and thou shalt rule in the midst of thine enemies. | 3. With thee is dominion in the day of thy power, | in the brightness of thy saints. | I begat thee from my womb before the Morning Star. | 4. The Lord sware and will not repent, | Thou art a priest for ever, after the order of Melchizedek." | 　　　　Ps. cix. 1.

And note that David in this passage, being king of the (d) whole Hebrew race, and in addition to his kingdom adorned with the Holy Spirit, recognized that the Being of Whom he speaks Who was revealed to him in the spirit, was so great and surpassingly glorious, that he called Him his own Lord. For he said "The Lord said to my Lord." Yea: for he knows Him as eternal High Priest, and Priest of the Most High God, and throned beside Almighty God, and His Offspring. Now it was impossible for Jewish priests to be consecrated to the service of God without anointing, wherefore it was usual to call them Christs. The Christ, then, mentioned in the Psalm will also be a priest. For how (177) could He have been witnessed to as priest unless He had previously been anointed? And it is also said that He is made a priest for ever. Now this would transcend human nature. For it is not in man to last for ever,[1] since our race is mortal and frail. Therefore the Priest of God, spoken of in this passage, Who by the confirmation of an oath received a perpetual and limitless priesthood from God, was

---

[1] διαιωνίζειν.

(b) greater than man. " For the Lord sware," he said, " and will not repent, Thou art a priest after the order of Melchizedek." For as Moses relates that this Melchizedek was priest of the Most High God, not anointed with a prepared unguent, since he was priest of the Most High God long before the Institution of the Law, and far above

Heb. vii. 1. the famous Abraham in virtue—for he says, " And Melchizedek, King of Salem, Priest of the Most High God,

(c) blessed Abraham." " And without any contradiction," says the apostle, " the less is blessed by the greater." As therefore, Melchizedek, whoever he was, is introduced as one who acts as priest to the Most High God, without having been anointed with a prepared unguent, He that is prophesied of by David as of the order of Melchizedek, is also spoken of as a great Being surpassing everyone in nature, as being Priest of the supreme God, and sharing the throne of His unbegotten power, and as the Lord of the prophet ; and He is not simply "priest," but "eternal priest of the Father." And the divine apostle also says, examining the implications of these passages :

(d)   " 17. Wherein God, willing more abundantly to shew to the heirs of promise the immutability of his counsel, confirmed it by an oath : 18. That of two immutable

Heb. vi.   things, in which it was impossible for God to lie, we
17.   might have a strong consolation."

And again :

          " 21. For those priests were made without an oath : but this with an oath by him that said unto him : ' The

Heb. vii.   Lord sware and will not repent, Thou art a priest for
21.   ever after the order of Melchizedek.' "

And :

          " 23. They truly were many priests, because they were not suffered to continue by reason of death. 24. But this man because he continueth ever hath an unchangeable priesthood. 25. Wherefore he is able also to save them to the uttermost that come unto God by him, seeing he ever liveth to make intercession for them."

In this a divine Power is represented as being in existing things, and underlying things that are only grasped by the mind, Which according to the Hebrew oracles is Priest to the

(178) God of the Universe, and is established in the office of priest-

hood to the Most High, not by earthy and human unguent, but by holy and divine virtue and power.   The Object of the Psalmist's prophecy therefore is presented distinctly as an eternal Priest, and Son of the Most High God, as begotten by the Most High God, and sharing the throne of His Kingdom.   And the Christ foretold by Isaiah has been shewn not to have been begotten by man but by the Father, and to have been anointed by the Divine Spirit, and to (b) have been sent to deliver men from captivity.   This Being, then, it was that Moses had seen by the help of the Divine Spirit, when he established figures and symbols of Him, as suitable for men, anointing and hallowing the priest selected from among men with prepared unguents as yet, and not with the Holy Spirit, and calling him Christ and anointed, as a representation of the true.   And who could give better evidence of this than Moses himself?   In his own writings (c) he distinctly says that the God and Lord Who answered him bade him establish a more material worship on earth according to the spiritual and heavenly vision that had been shewn him, which should form an image of the spiritual and immaterial worship.   And so he is said to have sketched [1] a kind of copy of the order of the angels of heaven and the powers divine, since the oracle said to him, "Thou shalt make all things according to the pattern shewed thee in the Mount."   So then he introduces the High Priest, as he did all the other elements, and anointed him with earth- (d) born unguents, working out a Christ and a High Priest of shadow and symbol, a copy of the Heavenly Christ and High Priest.

Thus I think I have clearly proved that the essential Christ was not man, but Son of God, honoured with a seat on the right hand of His Father's Godhead, far greater not only than human and mortal nature, but greater also than every spiritual existence among things begotten.

But moreover, according to what was previously said, the same David in Ps. xliv., using as inscription the words "Concerning the beloved, and those to be changed," [2]

---

[1] σκιογραφῆσαι, cf. σκιαγραφία, P. E. 730 b, 780 c.

[2] τῶν ἀλλοιωθησομένων ; cf. P. E. 333 d, ταῖς θεοποιήτοις ἀλλοιώσεσι : of changes wrought on matter by the ideas ; and Gifford's note.

S. gives heading—εἰς τὸ τέλος, ὑπὲρ τῶν ἀλλοιωθησομένων.   τοῖς υἱοῖς Κόρε εἰς σύνεσιν. ᾠδὴ ὑπὲρ τοῦ ἀγαπητοῦ.

speaks of one and the same Being as God and King and
Christ, writing thus :

(179)   " 1. My heart has uttered a good matter : I declare my
Ps. xliv. 1.   works to the King: My tongue is the pen of a ready
                writer, 2. Thou art more beautiful than the sons of
                men."

To which he adds :

" 6. Thy throne, O God, is for ever and ever, a
sceptre of righteousness is the sceptre of thy kingdom :
7. Thou hast loved righteousness and hated iniquity,
wherefore God, even thy God, hath anointed thee with
the oil of gladness above thy fellows."

Now look a little more carefully, and see how in the
inscription of the Psalm he prefaces that the subject is " con-
(b) cerning the beloved," adding the words "for instruction"
to prepare the hearers for what he is about to say.   He
shews also the reason of the Incarnation of the Word,[1] with
the words :

Inscrip-   "For the end, for the changed, with a view to under-
tion.   standing, for the beloved."

And whom could you better regard as "those to be
changed," for whom the Psalm is spoken, than those who
are going to be changed from their former life and conversa-
tion, to be transformed and altered by Him Whom the
(c) prophecy concerns?   And this was the beloved of God, on
whose behalf the Psalm's preface advises us to have understanding with regard to the prophecy.   And if you were at
a loss about the Person of this Beloved One, with whom the
prophecy in the Psalm is concerned, the word that faces you
at the very beginning will inform you, which says : " My heart
hath produced a good word."   It may surely be said that
by this is meant the Word that was in the beginning with
God, Whom the great Evangelist John shewed forth as
(d) God, saying : "In the beginning was the Word, and the
John i. 1.   Word was with God, and the Word was God."   And the
words, "My heart hath produced a good word," if it be
spoken in the person of the Supreme God and Father, would
suggest the Only-begotten Word of God, as being the Son of
the Father, not by projection, nor by division, or scission, or

---

[1] τὸ αἴτιον τῆς οἰκονομίας τοῦ λόγου.   Conceivably might mean simply
"the reason of the arrangement of his matter."

diminution, or any conceivable mode of bodily birth ; for
such ideas are blasphemous, and very remote from the
ineffable generation.   And we must understand this according to our previous interpretation ; as when it was said that
He was born from the womb of God before the Morning
Star, and we understood it figuratively, so we must understand this similar statement only in a spiritual sense.   For
in the words " My heart has produced a good word," the (180)
Holy Spirit inspires this saying also as purely spiritual.
To which it seems right for me to add what I am accustomed
to quote in every question that is debated about His Godhead, that reverent saying : " Who shall declare his generation ? " even if the holy Scriptures are wont in our human and
earthly language to speak of His Birth, and use the word
" womb."

For such expressions are connected with mental imagery
alone, and are accordingly subject to the laws of metaphor.
And so the words, " My heart hast produced a good word," (b)
may be explained as referring to the constitution and
coming into being [1] of the primal Word, since it would not
be right to suppose any heart, save one that we can understand to be spiritual, to exist in the case of the Supreme
God.

One might also say that the Psalmist referred to " the
Word that was in the beginning with God," a Word rightly
named " good " as being the offspring of a Father All-Good.
And if we read a little further on in the Psalm we shall find
that the subject of the prophecy, this very " beloved of
God," is anointed, once more not as by Moses, nor as by any
human being, but by the Most High and Supreme God and (c)
Father Himself.   As he says further on, " Wherefore God,
even thy God, hath anointed thee with the oil of gladness
above thy fellows."   And by what name else could one
call Him that is here acknowledged to have been anointed
by the Supreme God Himself, but Christ ?   So we have
here in this passage two names of the subject of the
prophecy, Christ and the Beloved, the author of this anoint- (d)
ing being one and the same : and it shews the reason why

---

[1] οὐσίωσις : cf. P.E. 314 b, 541 a, τῆς τοῦ δευτέρου αἰτίου συστάσεως
τε καὶ οὐσιώσεως.   " It is literally the act which gives τὸ εἶναί τε καὶ τὴν
οὐσίαν." Cf. Phil. Jud. 332. M.—(*Gifford.*)

He is said to be anointed with the oil of gladness, which will be plain to you, when we proceed a little further, and still more if you take into account the whole intention of the passage.   For the Psalm addresses the subject of the prophecy, Christ the Beloved of God, in the words quoted a little before, in which it was said : " Thy throne, O God, is for ever and ever : a sceptre of righteousness is the sceptre of thy Kingdom.   Thou hast loved righteousness and hated injustice : therefore God, even thy God, hath anointed
(181) thee with the oil of gladness above thy fellows."   See, then, if these words are not addressed directly to God : He says, " For thou, ὁ Θεός," instead of ὦ Θεέ.   " Thy throne is for ever and ever, and a sceptre of righteousness is the sceptre of thy Kingdom."   And then, " Thou, O God, hast loved righteousness and hated injustice ; therefore God, even Thy God, hath anointed thee," and established Thee as Christ above all.   The Hebrew shews it even more clearly, which Aquila most accurately translating has rendered thus : " Thy throne, God, is for ever and still, a sceptre of right-
(b) eousness is the sceptre of thy Kingdom.   Thou hast loved justice and hated impiety : wherefore God, thy God, hath anointed thee with the oil of gladness apart from thy fellows." Instead therefore of " God, thy God " the actual Hebrew is, " O God, thy God."   So that the whole verse runs : " Thou hast, O God, loved justice and hated impiety : therefore in return, O God, the highest and greater God,[1] Who is also thy God "—so that the Anointer, being the Supreme God, is far above the Anointed, He being God in a different sense. And this would be clear to any one who knew Hebrew.
(c) For in the place of the first name, where Aquila has " Thy throne, O God," clearly replacing ὁ Θεός by Θεέ, the Hebrew has Elohim.   And also for " Therefore, O God, he has anointed thee " the Hebrew has Elohim, which Aquila shewed by the vocative ὦ Θεέ.

Instead of the nominative case of the noun, which would be " Therefore God, even thy God, hath anointed thee—" the Hebrew with extreme accuracy has Eloach, which is the
(d) vocative case of Elohim, meaning " O God," whereas the

---

[1] We have here one of the " Arian " passages in the *Demonstratio.* " Majorem et minorem Deitatem statuit.   Vide p. 191, ubi μείζονα Θεὸν τὸν πάτερα nominat." (Paris Edition.)

nominative Elohim means "God."   So that the interpretation which says "Therefore, O God, thy God hath anointed,"
is accurate.

And so the oracle in this passage is clearly addressing
God, and says that He has been anointed with the oil of
gladness beyond any of those who have ever borne the
same name as He.   Therefore in these words you have
it clearly stated that God was anointed and became the
Christ, not with prepared unguent nor at the hands of man,
but in a way different from other men.   And this is He Who
was the Beloved of the Father, and His Offspring, and the
eternal Priest, and the Being called the Sharer of the Father's
Throne.   And Who else could He be but the Firstborn
Word of God, He that in the beginning was God with God, (182)
reckoned as God through all the inspired Scriptures, as
my argument as it proceeds further will abundantly prove?

Now after this preliminary study of the coming into
being and the appellation of the Christ, it remains for us
to take up our previous subject, and consider in what
a number of prophetic predictions the Christ was foretold
by name.

CHAPTER 16

From Psalm ii.

*In which Scriptures the Christ is foretold by Name as plotted
against by Kings and Rulers, Nations and Peoples, being
begotten of God Himself, and called the Son of Man,
receiving the Inheritance of the Nations and of the Ends
of the Earth from His Father.*

[Passages quoted, Ps. ii. 1, 2, 7, 8]

IN these words the Holy Spirit very clearly addresses (d)
Christ, and calls Him the Son of God, as has been said
before, and at the same time indicates that there will be
a plot against Him, and foretells the calling of the Gentiles
as brought about through Him.   And all this the course
of events has shewn to be exactly fulfilled by the actual

facts in our Lord and Saviour Jesus Christ. For even now nations, rulers, peoples and kings have not yet ceased their combined attack on Him and His teaching. And if the Jews prefer to refer these predictions to some time yet to come, they ought to agree that their expected Christ will again be plotted against, according to the present (183) oracle: "The kings of the earth stood up, and the rulers were gathered together against the Lord and against his Christ." Which they would never grant, inasmuch as they expect the coming Christ to be a great Ruler, and an eternal King, and their Ransomer. But supposing their Christ should indeed come and suffer the same as He Who has already come, why ought we to believe or disbelieve in theirs rather than ours?

And if they cannot give an answer to this, but proceed (b) to refer the oracle to David or some one of the Jewish kings of his stock, even then we can shew, that neither David nor any other celebrated Hebrew is recorded to have been proclaimed as Son of God by the oracle, nor as begotten of God, as was the subject of the prophecy in the Psalm, nor to have ruled over nations, kings, rulers and people while involved in plots. Wherefore if none of them (c) is found so to have done, whereas all this agrees in actual fact in His case, both in His patience long ago, and in the attack made on Him to-day as the Christ of God by kings and rulers, nations and peoples, what hinders Him from being the subject of the prophecy in the words which said, "The kings of the earth stood up, and the rulers were gathered together against the Lord and against his Christ"?

And what follows in the Psalm would agree with Him alone, where it says: "The Lord said to me, Thou art my Son. To-day have I begotten thee. Desire of me, and I shall give thee the heathen for thine inheritance, and (d) the utmost parts of the earth for thy possession." For surely only in Him has this part of the prophecy received an indubitable fulfilment, since the voice of His disciples has gone forth into all the earth, and their words to the ends of the world. And the passage distinctly names Christ, saying as in His own person, that He is the Son of God, when it says: "The Lord said unto me, Thou art my Son. To-day I have begotten thee." With which you may compare the words in the Proverbs, also spoken in His own Person: "Before the mountains were established, Prov. viii. before all the hills he brings me forth." And also the 25. address by the Father to Him in Psalm cix.: "I begat (184) thee from my womb before the Morning Star." Under- Ps. cix. 3. stand then how the holy Scriptures prophesy that one and the same Being, Christ by name, Who is also Son of God, is to be plotted against by men, to receive the nations for His inheritance, and to rule over the ends of the earth, shewing His dispensation among men by two proofs : the one being the attacks upon Him, and the other the subjection of the nations to Him.

Psalm xix.

Christ named, receiving all His Requests from His Father.

" 5. The Lord fulfil all thy requests. | 6. Now I know (b) that the Lord has saved His Christ, | and will hear him from his holy heaven. | "

Since it is now my object to shew in how many places the Christ is mentioned by name in the prophecies, I naturally set before you those which plainly foretell the Christ. And all this Psalm voices a prayer as spoken by holy men to the Person of Christ. For since for our sakes (c) and on our behalf He received insult when He had become man, we are taught to join our prayers with His as He prays and supplicates the Father on our behalf, as one who repels attacks against us both visible and invisible. And so we speak to Him as such in the Psalm.

" 1. The Lord hear thee in the day of affliction | , the name of the God of Jacob shield thee. | 2. May he send thee help from his holy (place) | , and strengthen thee from Zion. | "

And then, since it is fitting for Him, as being our great High Priest, to offer the spiritual sacrifices of praise and (d) words to God on our behalf, and since as a priest He offered both Himself, and the Humanity which He assumed on earth as a whole burnt-offering for us, to God and the Father, we therefore say to Him :

" 4. May he remember all thy sacrifice, | and fatten thy burnt sacrifice. | "

And since all that He plans is saving **and** useful to the world, we rightly call on Him :

"5. The Lord give thee thy heart's desire,"

saying :

"And fulfil all thy mind."

And afterwards remembering His Resurrection from the dead, we say :

(185)   "6. We will exult in thy salvation."

For what else could the salvation of Christ be, but His Resurrection from the dead, by which also He raises all the fallen?   Next we say :

"8 *b*. And we will triumph in the name of our God : and the Lord fulfil all thy requests."

And to crown all we are taught to say :

"7. Now I know that the Lord has saved his Christ."

As if we had not known it before, we understand His Salvation in perceiving the power of His Resurrection.

Psalm xxvii.

Christ named as having the Father as His Lord and Shield.

(b)   "8. The Lord is the strength of his people, | and is the shield of salvation of his Christ."

The Psalm we are considering also is referred to Christ, including the prayer of Christ which He prayed at the time of His Passion, and therefore in the opening of the Psalm He says :

"1. To thee, O Lord, have I cried : My God, | be not silent before me, | [1] Lest I be like unto them that go down into the pit. | "

(c) And at the end He prophesies His Resurrection, saying :

"6. Blessed be the Lord, for He hath hearkened to the voice of my prayer. | 7. The Lord is my helper and my defender; | my heart hoped in him, and I was helped : | and my flesh has revived, | and I will gladly give him praise : | "

To which the divine and prophetic Spirit adds :

"8. The Lord is the strength of his people, and the shield | of his Christ."

Teaching us that all the wonders of Christ written in the

---

[1] S. repeats μή ποτε παρασιωπήσῃς ἐπ' ἐμοί.

holy Scriptures, done for man's salvation, whether teachings (d)
or writings, or the mysteries of His Resurrection now
referred to, were all done by the will and power of the
Father defending His own Christ as with a shield in all
His marvellous and saving words and works.

Psalm lxxxiv.

*Christ described by Name as God the Overseer,[1] and the One
Day of His Resurrection, and the One House of God, His
Church.*

"9. Behold, O God, our defender, | and look upon (186)
the face of thy Christ. | 10. For one day in thy courts
is better than a thousand. | I have chosen to abase
myself in the house of my God, rather than to dwell
in the tabernacles of sinners | ."
They who know the Christ of God to be the Word, the
Wisdom, the True Light and the Life, and then realize that
He became man, are struck by the miracle of His Will,
so that they exclaim :
"And we saw him, | and he had no form nor beauty. Isa. liii. 2.
3. But his form was ignoble, and inferior to that of
the sons of men. He was a man in suffering, and (b)
knowing the bearing of affliction, because he turned
away his face, he was dishonoured."
They rightly call on God to look upon the Face of the
Christ, dishonoured and insulted for our sake, and to be
merciful to us for His sake. "For He bore our sins, and
on our behalf is pained." Thus they beseech, altogether
desiring and expressing in their prayer the desire to see
the face of the glory of Christ, and to behold the day of
His light. And this was the day of His Resurrection from
the dead, which they say, as being the one and only truly
Holy Day and the Lord's Day,[2] is better than any number (c)
of days as we ordinarily understand them, and better than
the days set apart by the Mosaic Law for Feasts, New
Moons and Sabbaths, which the Apostle teaches are the
shadow of days and not days in reality. And this Lord's
Day of our Saviour is alone said to shew its light not in

---

[1] ἐπόπτης.

[2] The "one day" of the Psalm is referred to the Christian Sunday :
the κυριακὴ ἡμέρα : cf. Justin Martyr, *Apol.* lxvii.

every place but only in the courts of the Lord. And these must mean the Churches of Christ throughout the world, which are courts of the one House of God, in which he (d) who knows these things loves and chooses to be abased, prizing far more the time spent in them than that spent in the tabernacles of sinners. Unless we are to understand that everyone who chooses the synagogues of the Jews, which deny the Christ of God, or those of godless sectaries and other unbelieving heathen, professes them to be better than the Churches of Christ.

Psalm lxxxviii.

Christ named as made of None Account, and suffering shame-fully, and His People reviled by the Enemy in Exchange for Him.

(187)   " 39. But thou hast cast off and made of no account, | thou hast rejected thy Christ, | 40. and overthrown the covenant of thy servant. | Thou hast desecrated his sanctuary even to the ground. | "
And the context. To which he adds :
" 51. Remember, Lord, the reproach of thy servants, | which I have borne [1] in my bosom, even (the reproach) of many nations, | 52. wherewith thine enemies, O Lord, have reviled, | wherewith they have reviled those who suffer in exchange for thy Christ." [2]
Christ is here clearly mentioned by name, and the circumstances attending His Passion predicted. If I had time (b) I could shew by examining the whole Psalm that what is expressed can only apply to our Lord and Saviour, and no one else. But when Christ is named the second time here it refers to some one else thàn Him, in exchange for whom He is the one taken, and the Church is plainly meant, and indeed those who are called Christ's enemies have reviled it, and even now revile it. Yea, every one opposed to Christ's teaching is wont to revile us about the Sufferings of our Saviour, which He underwent for us, and especially about His Cross and Passion.

---

[1] S. has. οὖ ὑπέσχου. E. : εὖ ὑπέσχον.
[2] Τὸ ἀντάλλαγμα τοῦ χριστοῦ σου,

Psalm cxxxi.

Christ named as rising from the Seed of David, called the (c)
Horn of David, bringing to Shame the Jews His Enemies,
restoring the Sanctuary of the Father.

"11. The Lord sware to David the truth, and he
will never set him at naught,[1] | of the fruit of thy body
I will set upon thy seat."
And lower down,

"17. There will I lift up the horn of David, | I have
prepared a lantern for my Christ : | 18. As for his
enemies I will clothe them with shame, | but upon
himself shall blossom my holiness. | "

Now here the Lord swears about one of the seed of David, (d)
Whom He calls His seed and horn.   And again addressing
Christ by name, He says that He has prepared a lantern
for Him, which seems to refer to the prophetic word,
which shewed the coming of Christ before, Who alone,
like the light of the sun, has now risen on all men through
the whole world.   And David Himself was prepared as
a lantern for the Christ, taking the place of a lantern in
comparison with the perfect light of the sun.   And then
He says : "I will lift up the horn," shewing the place where
He means Christ to be born.   For when David is praying
that he may behold before in spirit the place of Christ's
birth, and saying :   (188)

"3. I will not go into the tabernacle of my house, |
I will not climb to the couch of my bed. | 4. I will not
give sleep to my eyes, nor slumber to my eyelids, | nor
rest to my temples, | 5. until I find a place for the
Lord, a tabernacle for the God of Jacob. | "

—the Holy Spirit reveals the place as Bethlehem.   Therefore he proceeds :

"6. Behold we heard of it in Ephratha | (that is,
Bethlehem), and we found it in the fields of the wood. |
7. We will go[2] into his tabernacle, | we will worship (b)
in the place, where his feet stood. | "

---

[1] S. : αὐτὴν.: E.: αὐτὸν.
[2] S. : εἰσελεύσομαι . . . προσκυνήσομεν. E. : εἰσελευσόμεθα—προσκυνήσομεν.

And suitably after this revelation He adds :
> "There will I lift up the horn of David, I have prepared a lantern for my Christ."

(c) Maybe also the Body assumed by Christ at Bethlehem may be meant, since the Divine Power inhabiting it through His body as through an earthen vessel,[1] like a lamp, shot forth to all men the rays of the Divine Light of the Word.

From Amos.

Christ announced by Name by God, and made known to All Men as liberating the Jewish Race.

[Passage quoted, Amos. iv. 12—v. 2.]

God now proclaiming the Christ by name the seventh time is said to "strengthen the thunder" and "to create the wind," the proclamation of the Gospel being called thunder from its being heard by all men, and similarly the spirit that Christ breathed on His apostles is meant ; and also the Saviour's sojourn among men has clearly fulfilled the prophecy in which God is said to make "morning" and "mist" together, morning for those that receive salvation, but for the Jews that disbelieve in Him the contrary. On (189) whom also Scripture foretells an extreme curse, adding a lamentation for the Jewish race, which actually overtook them immediately after their impiety against our Lord and Saviour Jesus Christ. For of a truth from that day to this the House of Israel has fallen, and the vision [2] once shewn by God and the rejection have been brought to pass, concerning the falling of their house in Jerusalem, and against their whole state, that it should not be possible for any one to lift them up, who will never more be lifted up.

(b) "There is," he says, "therefore no one to lift her up." For since they did not accept the Christ of God when He came, perforce He left them and turned to all the Gentiles, telling the cause of his turning, when He said with tears, as if almost apologizing :
> "Jerusalem, Jerusalem, which killeth the prophets, and stonest them which are sent unto her, how often [3]

---

[1] δι' ὀστρακίνου σκεύους.   Cf. 2 Cor. iv. 7.

[2] ὄρος in Migne from Paris text.   Gaisford and Dindorf read ὄρασις following Donatus' rendering, and the Oxford Codex.

[3] W.H. : ποσάκις.   E. : πολλάκις.   W.H. omit ἔρημος.

would I have gathered thy children together, even as
a bird gathereth her nestlings under her wings, and ye (c)
would not: behold, your house is left unto you Matt. xxiii.
desolate."   37,

From Habakkuk.

Christ is named as preserved by His Father and saving His
Own Christs.

"Thou wentest forth for the safety of thy people to
save thy Christs: Thou hast brought[1] death on the Hab. iii.
heads of transgressors."   13.

Aquila: "Thou wentest forth for the safety of thy people,
for the safety of thy people with thy Christ." As Aquila
renders by the singular instead of the plural, saying (d)
that the Supreme God has made salvation for the people
"with Christ," I have rightly set down the passage, which
clearly supports my position. But there would be according to the Septuagint version more persons who are called
Christs from Him and for the sake of Whom it is said:
"Touch not my Christs, and do my prophets no harm," Ps. cv. 15.
who believed on Him, and were thought worthy of the
holy anointing of regeneration in Christ, and who were
able to say with the holy apostle: "We are become Heb. iii.
partakers of Christ."   14.

From the Lamentations of Jeremiah.   (190)

Christ is named as plotted against by the Jews, and made
known to the Gentiles.

"20. The breath of our countenance, the Lord Christ
was taken in their destructions, of whom we said, In Lam. iv.
his shadow we shall live among the Gentiles."   20.

The inspired prophets of God, knowing the future by
the Holy Spirit, foretold that they themselves would live,
and that their words would work among the Gentiles as
the words of living men, but not in Israel. They said (b)
again that the Christ (Whom they named) as being He
from Whom the prophetic spirit was supplied to them,
would be taken in their snares. The snares of whom?
Plainly of the Jews who plotted against Him. And notice
here that the prophecy says that the Christ will be taken,

[1] LXX: βαλεῖς.

which would not correspond with the second Coming of Christ, which the prophecies predict will be glorious and bring in the Divine Kingdom. Wherefore it seems that (c) the Jews are wrong in taking the sayings about His second Appearance, as if they were about His first Coming, which the sense will in no way allow. Since it is impossible to regard Him as at one and the same time glorious and without glory, honoured and kingly, and then without form or beauty, but dishonoured more than the sons of men ; and again, as the Saviour and Redeemer of Israel, while plotted against by them, and led as a sheep to the (d) slaughter, delivered to death by their sins. The prophecies about the Christ should be divided, as our investigation of the facts shews, into two classes : the first which are the more human and gloomy will be agreed to have been fulfilled at His first Coming, the second the more glorious and divine even now await His second Coming for their fulfilment. And a clear proof of the former is the actual progress of the knowledge of God through Him in all nations, which many prophetic voices foretell in various strains, like the one before us, in which it is said : "Of whom we said, In his shadow we will live among the Gentiles."

(191)
From the 1st Book of Kings [1 Samuel].

Christ is named as exalted by the Lord and Father.

I Kings
ii. 10 =
1 Sam. ii.
10.

"The Lord has ascended to the heavens and has thundered : he will judge the extremities of the earth, and he gives strength to our kings, and will exalt the horn of his Christ."

The words mean the return of Christ (Who is named) or of God to heaven, and His Teaching heard like thunder by all, and Holy Scripture foretells His future Judgment (1) of all afterwards. And after this it is said that the Lord will give strength to our kings. And these would be the apostles of Christ, of Whom it is written in Ps. lxvii. : "The Lord will give a word to the preachers of the Gospel with much power." Here, also, he mentions Christ by name, humanly known as our Saviour, Whose horn he says shall be exalted, meaning His invisible Power and Kingdom. For it is usual for Scripture to call a kingdom a "horn."

It is found also in Ps. lxxxviii. : "And in my Name shall (c) his horn be exalted."

From the 1st Book of Kings [1 Samuel].

Christ is named as receiving a faithful House from His Father, that is the Church, and as a Faithful High Priest for All Time leading His Church.

"Behold, the days come when I will destroy thy 1 Sam. seed, and the seed of thy father's house. And thou ii. 31. shalt not have an old man in thy house for ever."

The oracle speaks these words to Eli, but adds these (d) others :

"And I will raise up to myself a faithful priest, who shall do all that is in my heart and in my soul; and I will build him a sure house, and he shall dwell before my Christ for ever" (v. 35).

The divine Word after threatening doom and rejection on those who do not worship in the right way, promises that He will raise up another priest of another tribe, who He also says will come before His Christ, or "will walk in the person of my anointed," as Aquila has translated it, or as Symmachus, "will continue before his Christ." And who could this be? Surely every one who is enrolled in holiness in the priesthood of the Christ of God, to Whom the Supreme God promises that He will build the House of (192) His Church, as a wise Architect and Builder, not meaning any house but the Church established in Christ's Name throughout the whole world, wherein every one who is consecrated priest of the Christ of God is said in the spiritual worship to offer things acceptable and well-pleasing to God : the sacrifices of the blood of bulls and goats offered in the old religion of types, being admitted by the prophecy of Isaiah to be hateful to God.   (b)

Such are the many instances of the prediction of the Christ by name; but, as in most cases, the Sufferings of Christ are conjoined to His Name, we must return to what was said before about His Divinity, which I have showed previously to be touched on in the 45th Psalm, entitled FOR THE BELOVED, where Scripture, after first describing Him as King, proceeds to say other things about the Divinity of Christ :

(c)

Ps. xlv. 6.

"Thy throne, O God, is for ever and ever : a sceptre of righteousness is the sceptre of thy kingdom : Thou hast loved righteousness, and hated injustice : therefore God, even thy God, hath anointed thee with the oil of gladness above thy fellows."

For, as I have already shewn, these words clearly imply that the God referred to is one and the same Being, Who loved righteousness and hated iniquity ; and that because of this He was anointed by another greater God, His Father,[1] with a better and more excellent unction than that foreshadowed (d) by the types, which is called "the oil of gladness." And what else could He be properly named but Christ, Who is anointed with this oil, not by man but by God Most High? The same Person, therefore, is shewn to be called God, as indeed I have already shewn in the proper places. And we should here again remember Isaiah, who said :

"The Spirit of the Lord is upon me, for whose sake he hath anointed me. He has sent me to preach the gospel to the poor, to heal the broken-hearted, to proclaim liberty to the captives, and sight to the blind."

And we have already shewn that the priests from among men, who in long distant times were consecrated to the (193) service of God, were anointed with a prepared unguent. But he that is spoken of in the prophecy is said to have been anointed with the Divine Spirit. And this passage in its entirety was referred to Jesus the only true Christ of God, Who one day took the prophecy in the Jewish synagogue, and after reading the selected portion, said that what He had read was fulfilled in Himself. For it is written, that having read it :

(b)

Luke iv.
20 *sq.*

"And closing the book, and giving it to the minister, he sat down. And the eyes of all them that were in the synagogue were fastened upon him, 21. And he began to say unto them, This day is this Scripture fulfilled in your ears."

With all this we should again compare the records of Moses, who when he established his own brother as High Priest, according to the pattern that had been shewn to him, agreeably to the oracle which said to him : "Thou

---

[1] An Arian phrase.

shalt make all things according to the pattern shewn to
thee in the Mount," plainly shews that he had perceived (c)
with the eyes of the mind and by the Divine Spirit the
great High Priest of the Universe, the true Christ of God,
Whose image he represented together with the rest of the
material and figurative worship, and honoured the person
named with the name of the real Christ.

And this has the support of the inspired apostle, who Heb. viii.
says when treating of the law of Moses: "Who serve under 5·
the example and shadow of heavenly things." And again: (d)
"For the law having a shadow of good things to come." Heb. x. 1.
And again: "16. Let no man, therefore, judge you in meat Col. ii. 17.
or in drink, or in respect of a holy day, or of the new
moon, or of the Sabbath days, 17. which are a shadow
of things to come." For if the enactments relating to
the difference[1] of foods, and the holy days and the
Sabbath, like shadowy things, preserved a copy of other
things, that were mystically true, you will say not without
reason that the High Priest also represented the symbol
of another High Priest, and that he was called Christ,
as the pattern of that other, the only real Christ: and so
far was he from being the real one, that the real Christ
hears from the Supreme God: "Sit thou on my right
hand, until I make thine enemies the footstool of thy feet."
And: "Be thou ruler in the midst of thine enemies."
And: "The Lord sware, and will not repent. Thou art a
priest for ever after the order of Melchizedek." By which (194)
He was revealed clearly as eternal Priest, existing as Offspring and Son of God before the Morning Star and before
the whole creation. And the Christ of Moses, like one
who has acted the character in a drama for a short time,
retires as one reckoned among mortals, and hands on the
reality to the only true and real. While the real Christ
needing not the Mosaic unction, nor prepared oil, nor
earthly material, yet has filled the world with His goodness
and His name, establishing the race of Christians, named (b)
after Him, among all nations. But Moses' Christ, not
that he was ever plainly so called among men, except
through the writings of Moses—he, I say, some time long

---

[1] ἀδιαφορίας. Billius, *Obs. Sac.* i. 28, replaces by διαφορᾶς, which
the sense requires.

after the Exodus from Egypt purified with certain lustrations and sacrifices of blood was anointed with prepared oil, Moses anointing him.   But the Christ, archetypal, and
(c) real from the beginning, and for infinite ages whole through the whole, and Himself ever like Himself in all ways, and changing not at all, was ever anointed by the Supreme God, with His unbegotten Divinity, both before His sojourn among men, and after it likewise, not by man or by any material substance existing among men.

And as we are examining His Name, the seal of all we have said may be found in the oracle of Solomon the wisest of the wise, where he says in the Song of Songs :
Cant. i. 2. "Thy name is as ointment poured forth."   Yea, he being supplied with divine wisdom, and thought worthy of more
(d) mystic revelations about Christ and His Church, and speaking of Him as Heavenly Bridegroom, and her as Bride, speaks as if to Him, and says, "Thy name, O Bridegroom, is ointment," and not simply ointment, but "ointment poured forth."   And what name could be more suggestive of ointment poured forth than the Name of Christ?   For there could be no Christ, and no Name of Christ, unless ointment had been poured forth.   And in what has gone before I have shewn of what nature the ointment was
(195) with which Christ was anointed.   So now that we have completed our examination of the Name Christ, let us proceed to consider the Name of Jesus.

CHAPTER 17

(b) *That the Name of Jesus was also honoured among the Ancient Friends of God.*

MOSES was also the first to use the Name Jesus, when he changed the name of his successor and altered it to Jesus. For it is written : "These are the names of the men whom Moses sent to spy out the land, and Moses called Nauses,
Num. xiii. the son of **Nave**, Jesus, and sent them."   And notice how
17.   the prophet, who was deeply versed in the significance of

names, and had gone to the roots of the philosophy of the changed names of the inspired men in his record, and the (c) reasons why their names were changed, introduces Abraham as receiving as a reward of virtue from God a complete change of name from that of his father, the meaning of which it is now the time to explain at length. And so, also, in naming Sara Sarra, and Isaac called before his birth " the laugh," and Jacob given as a reward of his struggle the name of Israel, and in exhibiting in many other cases connected with the power and significance of names super-human insight in his inspired wisdom and knowledge, (d) when no one of those before him had ever used the name Jesus, he first of all, impelled by the Holy Spirit, gives the name of Jesus to him whom he is about to constitute the successor of his rule over the people, changing the other name he had used before. He did not consider the name of his forefather given him when he was born sufficient (for his parents called him Nauses). But being the prophet of God he changed the name received by birth, and called the man Jesus at the bidding of the Holy Spirit ; that he might lead the whole people after his own death,[1] (with the knowledge that) when the law laid down by Moses some day should be changed and have an end, and should pass away like Moses himself, that no one else (196) but Jesus the Christ of God would lead that other polity, which would be better than the former. And so Moses, the most wonderful of all the prophets, understanding by the Holy Spirit both the names of our Saviour, Jesus Christ, honoured the choicest of all his rulers by bestowing them as kingly crowns, naming worthily the two leaders and rulers of the people the high priest and his own successor, (b) Christ and Jesus, calling Aaron Christ, and Nauses Jesus, as his successor after his death. In this manner, then, the writings of Moses himself are adorned with the names of our Saviour Jesus Christ.

There is a lacuna in the text.

From Exodus.

(c) *How Jesus, the Successor of Moses, called the Angel, and about to be the Leader of the People, is said to bear the Name of Christ.*

"20. And behold, I send my angel before thy face, that he may keep thee in the way, that he may bring thee into the land which I have prepared for thee. Take heed to thyself and hearken unto him and disobey him not; for he will not give way to thee, for my name is upon him."

Exod.xxiii. 20.

"With my Name, who teach you these things," says the Lord Himself, is he inscribed, who is to lead the people into (d) the land of promise. And if He was Jesus and none other, it is plain how He says that His name is set on Him. Nor is it strange that he calls him Angel, since it is said of John also, who was but a man: "Behold, I send my angel before thy face, who shall prepare thy way before thee."

From Zechariah.

(197) *That Jesus, the Son of Josedek the High Priest, was a Figure and Type of Our Saviour, Who turned to God the Slavery that of Old ruled the Souls of Men.*

[Passages quoted, Zech. iii. 1–6, 9; vi. 9–13.]

In this passage too the prophet-high-priest called Jesus presents, I think, a very clear picture and plain symbol of our Lord and Saviour Jesus Christ, being honoured by bearing His Name, and made the leader of the return of the people from the Babylonian captivity. Since, also, our Saviour Jesus Christ is said by the Prophet Isaiah to have been sent to preach liberty to the captives and recovery of sight to the blind, to comfort all that mourn,

Isa. lxi. 1.
(198)

and to give to all that mourn in Zion glory for dust, the ointment of gladness. You have, therefore, her two great High Priests, first the Christ in Moses, and second the Jesus of whom I am speaking, both bearing in themselves the signs of the truth concerning our Lord and Saviour Jesus Christ.

But Aaron, the "Christ" in Moses' writings, having freed the people from slavery in Egypt, and led them in

freedom and with all carefulness in their journey from
Egypt, seems to present a picture of the real Lord, Who has
redeemed us, who are of all nations, from Egyptian idolatry ;
while the Jesus in the prophet, the High Priest who was (b)
at the head of the return from Babylon to Jerusalem, also
presents a figure of Jesus our Saviour, Whom we have as a
great High Priest, that has passed through the heavens,
through Whom also we ourselves, redeemed as it were in
this present life from Babylon, that is from confusion and
slavery, are taught to hasten to the heavenly city, the true
Jerusalem.

Jesus too, since he bore in himself the image of the (c)
true, was naturally clad in filthy garments, and the devil is
said to stand at his right hand and to oppose him, since
also Jesus, truly our Saviour and Lord, descending into our
state of slavery took away our sins, and washed away the
stains of humanity, and underwent the shame of the Passion,
through His love for us.   Wherefore, Isaiah says :

"He bears our sins, and is pained for us, and we Isa. liii. 4.
thought him to be in labour, and smitten, and afflicted : (d)
He was wounded for our sins, and weakened for our
iniquities."

And John the Baptist also, seeing the Lord, said :
"Behold the Lamb of God, which taketh away the sins John i. 29.
of the world."   Paul also, writing in the same way about
Him, says : "Him that knew no sin made sin for us, that 2 Cor. v.
we might become the righteousness of God in Him," and 21.
"Christ has ransomed us from the curse of the law, being Gal. iii. 13.
made a curse for us."   All these things the inspired prophet
referred to when he said, "And Jesus was clad in filthy
garments."   But He put them from Him by His Ascen- (199)
sion into the heavens, and the return from our condition
of slavery to His own glory, and He is crowned with the
diadem of His Father's Divinity, and is girt with the
bright robe of His Father's light, and is glorified with
the divine Mitre,[1] and the other high priestly adornments.
Nor is it difficult to explain the part about the devil,
who even now is opposed to the teaching of Christ, and
to His Church established throughout the whole world,
and has ever been opposed to our Saviour, and marched

---

[1] κιδάρει.

(b) against Him before, when He came to save us from our slavery to himself. He tempted Him also the first time, and the second time again, when by the Passion he arranged a plot against Him. But in all battles He triumphed over the devil, and all the unseen enemies and foes led by him, and made us who were slaves His own people, and built of us, as of living stones, the house of God, and the state of holiness, so that He exactly agrees with the oracle, which says:

Zech. vi.
12, 13.
(c)

"Behold a man, whose name is the Branch. And he shall spring up from below, and shall build the house of the Lord. And he shall receive virtue, and shall sit and rule upon his throne."

Note, therefore, with care, in what manner in speaking mystically of the Jesus of days of old, who bears the image of the true, he says: "Behold a man, whose name is the Branch." And a little later, it is said to Jesus himself then present, as if concerning some one else who was the (d) Branch: "Hear, Jesus, the High Priest, thou and thy neighbour, for the men are diviners. Behold, I bring my servant the Branch."

If, then, the speech related to some one yet to come, who was more truly called the Branch than he that bore the name then, he must have been only an image of him that was yet to come, as he is not only called Jesus in figure, but the Branch as well, if this was said to him when present: "Behold a man, whose name is the Branch." He was, therefore, naturally because he was the image thought worthy of the name of the Saviour, as well as of the Branch: for the name of Jesus translated into Greek (200) means "Salvation of God." For in Hebrew "Isoua" is "salvation," and the son of Nave is called by the Hebrews Joshua, Joshua being "Salvation of Jah," that is, Salvation of God. It follows that wherever the Salvation of God is named in the Greek versions, you are to understand that nothing but Jesus is meant. Having now brought to this point what I had to say concerning the Name of our Saviour, I will take up the argument from another starting-point, and pass on to the more important prophetic proofs about Him.

BOOK V

INTRODUCTION

Two ways of considering our Saviour Jesus Christ have (202) been illustrated in the previous book of the *Proof of the Gospel:* the first takes us above nature and beyond it: on its road we defined Him to be the Only-begotten Son of (b) God, or the Word Who is of the essence of God, the secondary cause of the Universe, or a spiritual substance, and the firstborn nature of God all-perfect, His holy and perfect Power before things created, or the spiritual image of the Unbegotten nature. The second was akin and more familiar to ourselves; on its road we defined Christ as the Word of God, proclaiming in human nature the holiness of the Father, according as He appeared in human form long before to those with Abraham, that famous ruler of the men of God, and was predicted to (c) appear again among men by human birth, and with flesh like ours, and to suffer the extremest shame.

This being so, the argument will proceed in its natural order, if I proceed to display the prophetic evidence about Him, if, that is to say, we make our chief aim to discover what was essential in the promises made, and justify the Divinity ascribed to Him in the Gospels from the ancient prophetic evidence. And it will be necessary (d) first to discuss the nature of prophetic inspiration [1] among the Hebrews, from whom we learned beforehand what they proclaimed.

Greeks and Barbarians alike testify to the existence of oracles and oracular responses in all parts of the earth, and they say that they were revealed by the foresight of the Creator for the use and profit of men, so that there need be no essential difference between Hebrew prophecy (203)

---

[1] θεοληψία.

and the oracles of the other nations. For as the Supreme God gave oracles to the Hebrews through their prophets, and suggested what was to their advantage, so also He gave them to the other nations through their local oracles. For He was not only the God of the Jews, but of the rest of mankind as well ; and He cared not more for these than those, but His Providence was over all alike, just as He has given the sun ungrudgingly for all, and not for the Hebrews only, and the supply of needs according to the seasons, and a like bodily constitution for all, and one

(b) mode of birth, and one kind of rational soul. And, thus, they say he provided ungrudgingly for all men the science of foretelling the future, to some by prophets, to some by oracles, to some by the flight of birds, or by inspecting entrails, or by dreams, or omens contained in word or sound, or by some other sign.[1] For these they say were bestowed on all men by the Providence of God, so that the prophets of the Hebrews should not seem to have an advantage over the rest of the world.

(c) This, then, is their contention. Mine will meet it in this manner. If any argument could prove that the gods, or divine powers, or good dæmons really presided over the oracles named, or over the omens from birds, or any of those referred to, I should have to yield to what was stated, that the Supreme God had given these things as well as the Hebrew prophecy to those who used them, for their good. But if by complete demonstration, and by the

---

[1] διὰ προφητῶν ἀνδρῶν, τοῖς δὲ διὰ χρηστηρίων, τοῖς δὲ διὰ ὀρνίθων πτήσεως, ἢ διὰ θυτικῆς ἤ δι᾽ὀνειροπομπείας, ἢ δια κληδόνων, ἢ παλμῶν.— The Praeparatio, Books IV., V. and VI., is occupied with the worthlessness of the Greek oracles on the grounds here summarized. Jevons explains divination from the entrails of a sacrifice, or from the flight of birds as an attempt to discover the inward disposition of a deity, who habitually manifests himself in animal form. Oneiromancy is not illicit in the O.T. For an account of Artemidorus, who wrote exhaustively on dreams, circa A.D. 180, see Dill, Roman Society from Nero to Marcus Aurelius, pp. 467 sq. Divination, "διὰ κληδόνων" was the interpretation of a word accidentally said as an expression of the Divine Will. By divination, "διὰ παλμῶν" (sounds), omens taken from the rustling of the leaves from the Oracle of Dodona and such-like are meant.

[H.D.B., arts. : Divination, Dreams, Magic, Soothsaying. See Dill. op. cit. 443–483. C. Bigg, The Church's Task in the Roman Empire, 74–81.]

confessions of the Greeks themselves already given, that (d)
they were dæmons, and not good ones but the source of
all harm and vice, how can they be the prophets of God?
And my argument in *The Preparation for the Gospel* has
convicted them of worthlessness, from the human sacrifices
connected with their rites from ancient days in every place
and city and country, from their deceiving their questioners
through ignorance of the future, through the many falsehoods in which they have been convicted, sometimes
directly, sometimes through the ambiguity of the oracles
given, by which they have been proved over and over
again to have involved their suppliants in a host of evils.
And they have been before shewn to be a vile and unclean
crowd from their delight in the low and lustful odes sung
about them, the hymns, and recitals of myths, the improper (204)
and harmful stories, which they were convicted of having
stamped as the truth, though they knew that they told
against them.

And the final proof of their weak nature is shewn by
their extinction and ceasing to give responses as of old :
an extinction which can only be dated from the appearance
of our Saviour Jesus Christ. For from the time when the
word of Gospel teaching began to pervade all nations, from (b)
that time the oracles began to fail, and the deaths of
dæmons are recorded. All these reasons and many others
like them were used then in that part of *The Preparation of
the Gospel*, which is concerned in proving the wickedness
of the dæmons. And if they are so wicked, what possible
ground can there be for thinking that the oracles of the
dæmons are prophecies of the Supreme God, or for comparing their position with that of God's prophets ; of what sort (c)
were the predictions they gave to their questioners, those
even which seemed to have some foundation ? Were they
not about low and common men, boxers for instance,
and such people, whom they ordered to be honoured with
sacrifices ? What was their position about human sacrifice ?
For this question is the touchstone of the whole matter.
What evil thing could surpass in absurdity the idea that
the Gods, the very Saviours of men, and the good dæmons,
could command their suppliants and holy inquirers to
slaughter their dearest, as if they were mere animals, actually (d)
thirsting for human blood more than any wild beasts, and

could be convicted of being neither more nor less than drinkers of blood, cannibals, and friends of destruction. Or let him speak who will, if he has anything holy or worthy of the name of virtue to tell about them, any prophecies or predictions affecting mankind as a whole, any laws or enactments for the State, laying down general rules for human life, any philosophical doctrines and instruction provided by the gods for the lovers of philosophy.

But it would be impossible to say that any such advantage ever accrued to human life from the famous oracles. (205) For if this had been the case, men having their laws laid down for them by the gods would not have used different and irreconcileable systems of law. For if the gods existed and were good they must surely have inspired the same enactments: they must have inspired pure and most just legal systems: and where would have been the need of Solon or Draco or any of the other Greek or barbarian legislators, if the gods were present and gave all necessary commands through the oracles? And if it should be said (b) that they alone are meant, who established laws for each separate race of men, I should ask who that god was, and what was his character, who, for instance, ordered the Scythians to devour human beings, or laid down laws to others that they should lie with their mothers and daughters, or enacted as a good thing that they should throw their aged people to the dogs, or allowed men to marry their sisters and to defile one another. But why should I enumerate the lawless stories of Greeks and Barbarians, in order to prove that they were not gods, but (c) vicious and evil dæmons, these famous oracle-mongers of theirs, driving the thrice-wretched race of men to incredible depths of unnatural crime, whereas the famous Greek gods and oracles are not proved to have brought any advantage or profit whatever for their souls' health to those who sought their aid? And if it was open to them to use their own gods for teachers, why did the Greeks ever leave what did them good at home and make for foreign lands, as if they wanted to enjoy the merchandise of learning from some- (d) where else? [1]

---

[1] An interesting example of the ancient idea of "cujus (dei) regio, ejus religio." Cf. "Go, serve other gods."

And if it had been the gods or the good dæmons, who gave the answers, sometimes shewing their own power by foreknowledge or in some other unexpected way, sometimes teaching true wisdom by the infallible truth of their instruction, what could have prevented the sons of the philosophers being instructed by them, and why did various schools of philosophy [1] arise from the deep oppositions of those who procured conceptions of teaching, one from one source, one from another? And even if the multitude had given them no heed, yet surely religious and godly men would have procured infallible truth from the gift of the gods. Who, then, were they? Whoever (206) you say they were, those who take the other view will expose them as deceivers.

But it seems probable that the oracles were given by dæmons, and were genuine up to the point of discovering a thief, or the loss of property, and things of that kind, which it was not unlikely that beings who passed their time in the air should have knowledge of: but they were never responsible for a good and wise philosophic saying, or for a state, or for a law laid down by right reason; nay, more, (b) if I may speak quite frankly, one ought to consider them all instigators of evil; for when they listened either to the odes and hymns and recitals of men, or to the secret rites of the mysteries, retailing their own adulteries and unnatural crimes, their marriage of mothers and lawless union with sisters, and the many contests of the gods, enmities and wars of gods against gods, not one of them has ever, so far (c) as I know, been angry at what was said, as if it were only suitable for lustful, and not for pure, minds to think and say such things. And why need I enlarge, when from one most significant example I can crowd into one view their cruelty, inhumanity and real viciousness? I refer to the human sacrifices. Surely to delight not only in the slaughter of irrational beasts, but also in the destruction of men, overshot the highest limit of cruelty.

---

[1] The varieties of Greek philosophy in the early Empire were a frequent object of attack by the Apologists. In the XIVth Book of the *Praeparatio*, E. has dealt with the contradictions of Greek philosophers, showing how the systems opposed to Christianity were criticized by the best Greek thinkers themselves. In the XVth he attacked the Stoics, Peripatetics and all classes of materialists.

For, as I said in the *Preparation*, my evidence is drawn
(d) from the Greek philosophers and writers themselves, who
conclusively prove that the evil dæmons perverted the
human race by their involved intrigues, now by oracles,
now by omens from birds, or signs or sacrifices or things
of the kind.   Wherefore it is altogether to be denied that
the oracles came from the Supreme God.   And so it is not
allowable to class them with the Hebrew Prophets, whose
first Hierophant and divine teacher was Moses.   See, what
(207) a wealth of good he brought to human life.   First he produced a sacred writing of evangelical and true doctrines
about God the Maker and Creator of all things, and about
the secondary Cause of the rational and spiritual essences
after Him, and about the creation of the world and of man ;
and then he moved the obedient spirits of good men to
ambition, by outlining like figures of virtue the stories of
(b) the holy and godly Hebrews of long ago ; he began the
teaching of a legislation divine and suitable to the light
they then had, and introduced a godly worship, and revealed
predictions of all that was to take place in after years, as I
hope presently to shew.   Such was Moses.   And following
his steps the prophets who succeeded him foretold some
things incidentally to inquirers if anything was asked relating
to their daily life ; but their prophecy in its main purpose
(c) was concerned with great issues.[1]

For they did not reckon it worthy of their divine duty to
deal with those who sought oracles about daily matters or
that actual time, or about slight and trivial things, but the
illumination of the Holy Spirit in them including in its vast
scope the whole race of mankind, promised no prediction
about any particular man who was sick, nor about this
present life so open to accidents and sufferings, nor about
any one dead, nor, in a word, about ordinary and common
(d) things, which when present make the soul no better, and
when absent cause it no harm or loss.   And, as I said,
when their predictions referred to such things, it was not
in the line of their main meaning, but as accompanying a
greater conception.   And the causes which were at the root
of their prophetic inspiration involved a greater scheme
than the things instanced.

[1] ἐπὶ μεγάλοις.

If, then, one were to explore carefully the whole circuit of the writings of Moses and his successors, one would find it included exhortation and teaching of duty to the God of the Universe, Who is the Creator of all things, and the knowledge and divine teaching relating to the highest secondary Cause, and prohibition of all polytheistic error, (208) and then the memorial of the godly men of old days who began the said religion, and predictions and proclamations of those who would live in after days, as they themselves had lived, through the appearance and presence of God among men, I mean of the secondary Lord and God after the Supreme Father, Who Himself would become the Teacher of the same religion, and be revealed as Saviour (b) of the life of men, through Whom they foretold that the ideals of the ancient godly Hebrews would be handed on to all nations. This was the Gospel that Moses foretold, as well as the sons of the other prophets, who all spake as with one mouth. And this was the reason of the descent of the Holy Spirit to men, to teach men the knowledge of God, and the loftiest theology of the Father and the Son, to train them in every form of true religion, to give a record of those who lived well long ago, and those who afterwards fell away from the religion of their forefathers, and to exhibit the case against them at great length: and then (c) to prophesy the coming of the Saviour and Teacher of the whole race of mankind, and to herald the sharing of the religion of the ancient Hebrews by all nations.

These were the unanimous proclamations of the prophets of old days inscribed on tables[1] and in sacred books: yea, these very things, which we see even now after long ages in process of fulfilment; they all in the power of the Holy (d) Spirit with one voice foretold would come to all men a light of true religion, purity of mind and body, a complete purging of the heart, which having first gained themselves by discipline, they urged upon the obedient, prohibiting their converts from every lustful action, and teaching them not to imitate the lawless ways of polytheistic error, and to avoid with one consent all intercourse with dæmons, the popular human sacrifices of days gone by, and the base and secret tales about the gods. Against these they warned

---

[1] στήλαις.

them and counselled them to set their hearts only on God
(209) the Creator of all things, Who is as it were the Overseer
and Judge of all human doings, and to remember the future
Coming among men of the Christ of God, the Saviour of
the whole human race, established to be the Teacher of
the true religion to Greeks and Barbarians alike. This
was the vast difference between those who were possessed
by the Holy Spirit and those who pretended to prophesy
under the influence of dæmons.

Then, too, the evil dæmon, being akin to darkness,
(b) involved the soul in darkness and mist by its visitation,
and stretched out him who was under its power[1] like a
corpse, divorced from his natural faculties of reason, not
following his own words or actions, completely insensible
and demented, in accordance with which perhaps they may
have called such a condition "Manteia," as being a form
of "Mania,"[2] whereas the truly divine Spirit, Which is of
the nature of light, or rather light itself, brings at once a
new and bright daylight to every soul on whom It comes,
(c) revealing it as far more clear and thoughtful than ever it
was before, so that it is sober and wide awake, and above
all can understand and interpret prophecies. Wherefore
we seem rightly and truly to call such men prophets, because
the Holy Spirit gives them a sure knowledge and light
on the present, as well as a true and accurate knowledge of
the future. See, then, if it is not a far better and truer
argument, which says that the Holy Spirit visits souls
purified and prepared with rational and clear minds to
(d) receive the divine, than that of those who shut up the

---

[1] τὸν ὑπ' αὐτοῦ οἶα νεκρόν (Dindorf). Gaisford reads τοῦ ὑποφήτου
οἶα νεκρόν. This is a description of the well-known phenomena of the
hypnotic state of the spiritualistic medium or subject : cf. T. J. Hudson,
The Law of Psychic Phenomena (London, 1905), p. 47 : "All the facts
of hypnotism shew that the more quiescent the objective faculties
become, or, in other words, the more perfectly the functions of the
brain are suspended, the more exalted are the manifestations of the
subjective mind . . . the nearer the body approaches the condition of
death, the stronger become the demonstrations of the power of the
soul." Cf. J. Jastrow, *The Subconscious* (London, 1906), especially
c. iv. "The dissociated consciousness," and B. Sidis, *The Psychology
of Suggestion* (New York, 1903), p. 90: "Suggestibility varies as
the amount of disaggregation, and inversely as the unification of
consciousness."

[2] μαντεία and μανία. See also Plato, *Phædrus*, p. 244 c.

divine in lifeless matter and dusky caves, and in the impure souls of men and women; yea, and rest it on crows and hawks and other birds, on goats and other beasts, ay, even on the movements of water, the inspection of entrails, the blood of hateful and ugly monsters, and in the bodies of poisonous creeping things, like snakes and weasels, and such things, by the help of which these strange people understood that the Supreme God revealed a knowledge of (210) future events. But this was the way of men who had no conception of the nature of God, and no idea of the power of the Holy Spirit, Who does not delight in lurking in lifeless things, or irrational beasts, nor even in rational beings, except[1] . . . in such virtuous souls, as my argument just now described the Hebrew prophets as possessing, whom we reckon worthy of the Holy Spirit, because of their great contribution to the progress of humanity throughout the world.

And if sometimes the knowledge of contemporaneous (b) events, unimportant and of no moment, followed them like a shadow, and the foretelling of the unknown opportunely to inquirers, it was because they were obliged to give such help to their neighbours of old time, to prevent those who were hungry for predictions having an excuse for turning to the oracles of foreign races through a lack of prophets at home.

But I will close here my vindication of the divine power of the Hebrew Prophets. For it is right for us to obey (c) them, if they teach us, as men inspired and wise, not according to humanity but by the breath of the Holy Spirit, and to submit to the discipline of their doctrine, and holy and infallible theology, which no longer involves any suspicion, that they include any elements alien to virtue and truth.

So, then, it now remains for me to take up the thread of my argument from the beginning, and rest the theology of our Saviour Jesus Christ on the prophetic evidence.

The Gospel evidence gives this theology of Christ: "In (d) the beginning was the Word, and the Word was with God, and the Word was God. All things were made by him,

---

[1] εἰ μή ποτε ἄρα ἤ μόνων ψυχῶν καὶ ἐναρέτοις ψυχαῖς, οἵους ἡμῖν ἀρτίως ὁ λόγος ὑπέγραψε . . . (obviously corrupt).

John i. 1.   and without him was not anything made." It calls Him
also "Rational Light,"[1] and it calls Him Lord, as if He
were also God.   And the prophetic Paul, as a disciple and
apostle of Christ, agrees with this theology when he says
Col. i. 15.   this about Him : "Who is the image of the invisible God,
the firstborn of every creature, because in him were created
all things, things in heaven and things in earth,[2] whether
thrones or dominions, or principalities, or powers.   All
things were created by him and for him, and he is before
all things, and by him all things consist."

1 Cor.i.24.   He is also called "Power of God" and "Wisdom of
(211) God."[3]   It is our present task, therefore, to collect these
same expressions from the prophetic writings of the Hebrews,
so that by their agreement in each separate part the
demonstration of the truth may be established.   And we
must recognize that the sacred oracles include in the
Hebrew much that is obscure both in expression and in
meaning, and are capable of various interpretations in
(b) Greek because of their difficulty.   The Seventy Hebrews
in concert have translated them together, and I shall pay
the greatest attention to them, because it is the custom of
the Christian Church to use their work.[4]   But wherever
necessary, I shall call in the help of the editions of the
later translators, which the Jews are accustomed to use
to-day, so that my proof may have stronger support from
all sources.   With this introduction, it now remains for me
to treat of the inspired words.

<hr>

[1] νοερὸν φῶς.
[2] W.H. add, τὰ ὁρατὰ καὶ τὰ ἀόρατα.
[3] W.H. ἐν αὐτῷ.   E. δι' αὐτοῦ.
[4] The Septuagint version was the one commonly read in church, but
Eusebius claims that he corrects it with the versions of Aquila, Symmachus and Theodotion.   He, of course, had before him Origen's
Hexapla.

CHAPTER 1

That the Most Wise Solomon in the Proverbs knew of a First- (d)
born Power of God, which He calls the Wisdom and
Offspring of God : just as we glorify It.

Passage quoted, Prov. viii. 12–31.]   (212)

THE divine and perfect essence existing before things
begotten, the rational and Firstborn image of the Unbegotten nature, the true and Only-begotten Son of the
God of the Universe, being One with many names, and
One called God by many titles, is honoured in this passage
under the style and name of Wisdom, and we have learned
to call Him Word of God, Light, Life, Truth, and, to crown 1 Cor. i.
all, "Christ the power of God and the wisdom of God." 24.
Now, therefore, in the passage before us, He passes through
the words of the wise Solomon, speaking of Himself as the
living Wisdom of God and self-existent, saying : "I, Wisdom,
have dwelt with counsel and knowledge, and I have called
upon understanding," and that which follows. He also
adds, as who has undertaken the government and providence of the Universe : "By me kings reign, and princes
decree justice. By me princes become great." Then
saying that He will record the things of ages past, He goes
on to say : "The Lord created me as the beginning of
his ways for his works, he established me before time Prov. viii.
was." By which He teaches both that He Himself is 12.
begotten, and not the same as the Unbegotten, one called (213)
into being before all ages, set forth as a kind of foundation [1]
for all begotten things. And it is probable that the divine
apostle started from this when he said of Him : "Who is
the image of the invisible God, the firstborn of every
creature, for all things were created in him, of things in
heaven and things in earth." For He is called "Firstborn Col. i. 15.
of every creature," in accordance with the words : "The
Lord created me as the beginning of his road to his
works." And He would naturally be considered the image (b)
of God, as being That which was begotten of the nature
of the Unbegotten. And, therefore, the passage before

---

[1] θεμελίου τρόπον.

us agrees, when it says: "Before the mountains were established, and before all the hills, he begets me."

Hence we call Him Only-begotten Son, and the First-born Word of God, Who is the same as this Wisdom.   In what sense we say that He is the Begotten of God would require a special study, for we do not understand this un-speakable generation of His as involving a projection, a separation, a division, a diminution, a scission, or anything (c) at all which is involved in human generation.   For it is not lawful to compare His unspeakable and unnameable genera-tion and coming into being with these things in the world of begotten things, nor to liken Him to anything transitory and mortal, since it is impious to say that in the way in which animals are produced on earth, as an essence coming from an essence by change and division, divided and separated, the Son came forth out of the Father.   For the Divine is without parts, and indivisible, not to be cut, or (d) divided, or extended, or diminished, or contracted, It cannot become greater, or worse or better than Itself, nor has it within Itself anything different from Itself that it could send forth.   For everything that is in anything is either in it as (1) accident, as white is in a body, or (2) as a thing in something different from it, as a child is in the womb of its mother, or (3) as the part is in the whole, as the hand, foot and finger exist in the body, being parts of the whole body, and if either of them undergo any maiming or cutting or division, the whole of the body is rendered useless and mutilated, as a part of it has been cut off.   But surely it (214) would be very impious to employ a figure and comparison of this kind in the case of the Unbegotten nature of the God of the Universe, and of the generation of His Only-begotten and Firstborn (Son).

For the Son was certainly not Unbegotten for ages infinite and without beginning within the Father, as one thing within another that differs from itself, being a part of Him which afterwards was changed and cast out from Him; for such a being would be subject to change; and there would also be according to this two Unbegotten Beings, He that cast forth and He that was cast forth. And which condition would be the better? Would not that before the change which caused a division by the (b) sending forth? It is, then, impossible to conceive of the

Son coming from the Father as a part or a limb that had always previously been united to Him, afterwards separating and coming apart from the whole.   For these are unspeakable and quite impious ideas, proper enough to the relations of material bodies, but foreign to a nature without body or matter.   And, therefore, here again we had best say : Who shall declare His generation ?

It is equally perilous to take the opposite road, and say thus without qualification that the Son was begotten of things that were not, similarly to the other begotten beings ; for the generation of the Son differs from the Creation (c) through the Son.   But yet as Holy Scripture first says that He is the Firstborn of every creature, speaking in His Person, " The Lord created me as the beginning of his ways," and then says that He is the Begotten of the Father in the words : " Before all the hills he begets me " ; here we, too, may reasonably follow and confess that He is before all ages the Creative Word of God, One with the Father, (d) Only-begotten Son of the God of the Universe, and Minister and Fellow-worker with the Father, in the calling into being and constitution of the Universe.

For if there is anything in the nature of the Universe left unexplained and inconceivable for us, and we know that there are many, such things as are promised to the godly— which eye hath not seen, nor ear heard, neither hath entered into the heart of man—according to the holy apostle, much further beyond our conception, unexplained and unnamed, inconceivable and unimaginable must be that which concerned the generation of the Only-begotten of God, since we have nothing else to say or to think of Him, except, " Who shall declare his generation ? "   And if one, greatly (215) daring, were led to compare things in all ways inconceivable with visible and physical likenesses, one perchance might say that, like a fragrance or a ray of light, the Son underlay from infinite ages or rather before all ages the Father's Unbegotten Nature and ineffable Essence, and was one with Him, and was always united to the Father, as fragrance to an ointment and the ray to the light, but not (b) analogously in all senses to such likenesses, as was said before.   For lifeless bodies hold their accidents in qualities ; and the ray being of one origin with the nature of light, and being in essence the same as light, could not exist

outside that in which it is. Whereas the Word of God
has Its own essence and existence in Itself,[1] and is not
identical with the Father in being Unbegotten, but was
begotten of the Father as His Only-begotten Son before all
(c) ages ; while the fragrance being a kind of physical effluence
of that from which it comes, and not filling the air around
it by itself apart from its primary cause, is seen to be itself
also a physical thing. We will not, then, conceive thus about
the theory of our Saviour's coming-into-being. For neither
was He brought into being from the Unbegotten Being by
way of any event, or by division, nor was He eternally coexistent with the Father, since the One is Unbegotten and
the other Begotten, and one is Father and the other Son.
And all would agree that a father must exist before and
(d) precede his son. Thus also would the image of God be
a kind of living image of the living God, in a mode once
more that is beyond our words and reasoning, and existing
in Itself immaterially and unembodied, and unmixed with
anything opposite to Itself, but not such an image as we
connote by the term, which differs in its essential substance
and its species, but one which itself contains the whole of
its species,[2] and is like in its own essence to the Father, and
so is seen to be the liveliest fragrance of the Father, in a
mode once again beyond our words and reasoning. For
everything that is true about Him could not be spoken
in human words, and could not be reasoned with the
(216) reasoning of men according to strict logic. But the Scriptures give us such instruction as it is good for us to hear.
Has not the holy apostle described himself and those like
2 Cor. ii. him as "a fragrance of Christ," by their participation in the
15. Spirit of Christ ; and is not the heavenly Bridegroom in the
Cant. i. 2. Canticles addressed as "Ointment poured forth"? Wherefore all things visible and invisible, embodied and unembodied, rational and irrational participating in that outpouring of Him in due proportion are thought worthy of
His presence, and have their lot in the communion of the
(b) divine Word. Yes, the whole universe imparts a share of
His divine breath to those whose rational perception is not

---

[1] καθ' ἑαυτὸν οὐσίωται καὶ ὑφέστηκε.

[2] ἀλλ' οὐχ οἴα τις πάλιν ἡ παρ' ἡμῖν εἰκὼν, ἕτερον μὲν ἔχουσα τὸ κατ'
οὐσίαν ὑποκείμενον, ἕτερον δὲ τὸ εἶδος, ἀλλ' ὅλον αὐτὸ εἶδος ὤν. Cf.
P.E. 331 b, 325 a.

maimed,[1] so that bodies by nature earthy and corruptible give forth an immaterial and uncorrupted fragrance; for as the God of the Universe wells down from above, Who, being Father of the Only-begotten Word, Himself must be the first and chief and only true good, begetting good, so taking the second place the Son draws His supplies from the primary and original Essence, Who also is alone called the fragrance of His Father's Essence by us who use the Scripture that teaches us concerning Him, that He is "a breath of the power of God, and a pure effluence of the (c) glory of the Almighty,[2] and a radiance of the everlasting light, and an unsullied mirror of the action of God, and an image of his goodness."

Wisdom vii. 25.

But with regard to these questions, let men decide them as they will. It is enough for me to repeat again that true and blessed saying, and so conclude my quest, the saying which I have often repeated : "Who shall describe His generation?" For of a truth the generation of the Only- Isa. liii. 8. begotten of God is seen to be beyond the reach not only (d) of men, but of the powers that are beyond every being, as also our Lord and Saviour Himself says in mystic language this very thing to His own disciples. "No one knows the Father save the Son." To which he adds "and no one knows the Son save the Father." Since then the theology Matt. xi. both of the Father and of the Son is equally unknown to 27. all but Themselves, let us heed Wisdom speaking as it were in secrets in the passage of Solomon set before us : "Before the mountains were established, and the earth formed, and before all the hills he begets me." And also Prov. viii. He says that He was present with the Father when He 25. formed the Heaven. "For when he formed the heaven, (217) I was present with him." And He reveals the eternity Prov. viii. from endless ages of His presence with the Father, where 27. He adds: "I was by him in harmony, I was that in which he delighted, and I daily delighted in his presence." And we must either understand the abysses and founts of waters, the mountains and hills, and the other things which in this place are designated by common words, to refer to the constitution of the Universe, referring to the whole by

---

[1] πεπηρωμένοις, or "blinded." See J. A. Robinson's note in his Commentary on Ephesians, iv. 18.

[2] S. adds : διὰ τοῦτο οὐδὲν μεμιαμμένον εἰς αὐτὴν παρεμπίπτει.

(b) its part, or interpreting more metaphorically, we must transfer the meaning to spiritual essences and divine powers, all of whom the Firstborn Wisdom and the Only-begotten and First-begotten Word of the Father, Whom we call Christ, preceded; so the apostle teaches us, who says, "Christ the power of God and the wisdom of God." And He is called here probably by the Name of Wisdom, as He Who —— the all-wise and prudent plans of the only wise Father.[1] . . .

1 Cor. i. 24.

CHAPTER 2

[From Psalm xliv.]

(c) . . . And in the second place he honours Him with the kingly sceptre. In the third he witnesses to the perfection of His virtue. And then in addition he teaches that He, this same Person, was anointed as God and King by the Highest God, and so that He was Christ. For what else could one be called, who was anointed not by men, but by Almighty God Himself? Of Him therefore he says, "O God (addressing the anointed one), thou hast loved (d) righteousness and hated injustice; wherefore God, thy God, hath anointed thee." As if he were to say, "The Almighty God has anointed thee with the oil of gladness above thy fellows." So that this ointment mentioned was nothing common or earthy, nothing resembling that ordained by the Mosaic Law, fashioned of corruptible matter, with which it was the custom to anoint Hebrew priests and kings. Hence we call him properly both Christ and God, being the only one anointed with the immaterial and divine ointment of holy joy and gladness not by men nor by human agencies but by the Creator of the Universe Himself. (218) Wherefore He only has a just, an indefeasible, a good and peculiar right to the title of Christ beyond those who are called His fellows. And who could His "fellows" be but those who are able to say: "We are partakers of Christ,"

Ps. xliv. 7.

---

1 There is a long lacuna at the end of this chapter, noted in the Paris MS., " ἐλλείπει πολλά."

of whom it is said, "Touch not my Christs, and do my prophets no harm." So then as Christ by this is clearly revealed as Beloved, and as God, and as King, it is time to inquire, how so great a Being can be said to have enemies, and who they are, and for what cause He sharpened his (b) arrows and sword against them, so that He subjected many peoples to Himself not by array of soldiers, but by truth, gentleness and righteousness.

A careful inquirer would do well to refer this to our Lord and Saviour Jesus the Christ of God, and to turn back again to the record, relating to His Presence among men, by which He routed the hostile invisible powers of evil and corrupt dæmons and of wicked and impure spirits, and won very many peoples[1] for Himself out of all nations. Whom also it were fitting to call for this reason the true (c) Christ of God, as one not anointed with common oil like the priests of old days, for we have no record of anything of the kind about Him, but with a better divine unction, in reference to which Isaiah says: "The Spirit of the Lord God is upon me, because he hath anointed me." Where- Isa. lxi. 1. fore also this one Christ is more famous among all, through all the world, than all those who ever were anointed with material ointment among the Hebrews; and has filled the whole world with those who are called Christians after Him. Now in the preceding book I have dealt sufficiently (d) with the questions why we say He was anointed, what the unction was, and the mode of His anointing. Such grace was poured on His lips and on His teaching that in a short time it filled every place with the religion proclaimed by Him; so that now among all nations among those who receive His teaching, agreeably to the prophecy before us, He is clad with the glory of a king and of God, and is called Christ by all men.

And it is clear who are His enemies, not only those who were such of old, but those who are ever fighting against His word, whether they be men, or invisible powers, whom (219) everywhere He has cleared away with unseen and hidden power, and has made all sorts of people from all nations subject to Him.

And that which follows in the Psalm, "Myrrh, aloes and

---

[1] λαούς, λαός generally = "the sacred people."

cassia from his garments," and the other words besides, which speak as of a princess leaving her father's house, and being wedded to Him who has been foreshewn to be Christ and, King and God, and calling Him her Lord,

(b) might be referred to the Church of the nations, forsaking ancestral dæmonic error, and purified and brought into the communion of the divine Word, if time allowed them to have their true interpretation.

(c)

CHAPTER 3

(d) *That the same Prophet also plainly confesses Two Lords in Ps. cix.: the One, the First and Highest God; the Other, Whom He calls His Own Lord, and that He was begotten by God before the Foundation of the World, and He knows the Second God, and that He is the High Priest Eternal of the Father, shares the Throne of the God of the Universe, holding the same Faith as We about Christ.*

[Passage quoted, Ps. cix. 1–5.]

THE Lord upon thy right hand! The Psalmist here calls " Lord," our Lord and Saviour, the Word of God, " first-born of every creature," the Wisdom before the ages, the Beginning of the Ways of God, the Firstborn and Only-begotten Offspring of the Father, Him Who is honoured with the Name of Christ, teaching that He both shares the seat

(220) and is the Son of the Almighty God and Universal Lord, and the Eternal High-Priest of the Father. First, then, understand that here this Second Being, the Offspring of God, is addressed. And since prophecy is believed by us to be spoken by the Spirit of God, see if it is not the case that the Holy Spirit in the prophet names as His own Lord

(b) a Second Being after the Lord of the Universe, for he says, " The Lord said to my Lord, Sit thou on my right hand." The Hebrews named the First Person Lord, as being univer-sally the Lord of all, by the unspeakable Name expressed in the four letters. They did not call the Second Person Lord in a like sense, but only used the word as a special title. Naturally, then, our Lord and Saviour, Jesus Christ Himself, the Son of God, when He inquired of the Pharisees, "What think ye of Christ? Whose son is he?" on their saying, (c) "The son of David," asked, "How then can David in spirit call him Lord, saying, The Lord said to my Lord, Sit thou on my right hand"? practically interpreting the text as not only calling Him the Lord of David, but the Lord also of the Spirit in the prophet.[1] And if the prophetic Spirit, which we believe to be the Holy Spirit, confesses Him to be Lord, Who He teaches shares the Father's Throne, and not generally but as "His own Lord," how incomparably more certain is it that the rational powers, (d) who come after the Holy Spirit, must say the same, and the whole visible creation, embodied and unembodied, of which of course the only Sharer of the Father's Throne would be marked out as Lord, by Whose agency all things came into being, as the holy apostle says: "In him all things were Col. i. 16 created, of things in heaven, and things in earth, visible and invisible." For He alone would have the authority of likeness to the Father,[2] as being the only Person shewn to be throned with Him.

It is therefore plain that it would be wrong to allot to any among begotten beings the sitting at the right hand of the Almighty's rule and kingdom, except to Him alone Whom I have shewn in many ways, by what I have laid before you, to be God. Understand then, that the Highest and (221) Almighty Lord bestows on one and the same being the words, "Sit thou on my right hand," and also, "Before the morning-star I have begotten thee," and He delivers with an oath of confirmation the honour unshakeable and immutable of the continuous priesthood for ever and ever, "The Lord swore and will not repent, Thou art a priest for ever." And who could be supposed—leaving human beings out of account—even of those of the nature of

---

[1] This passage is one of the chief instances in which Donatus, the Latin translator, completely altered the sense of the Greek, in order to bring Eusebius into line with orthodoxy. Billius in a fiery note points out that "David in Spiritu" cannot imply that the Holy Spirit was calling His son Lord (quo nec falsius nec absurdius cogitari potest). To say that the Father is Lord of the Son, and the Son the Lord of the Spirit, Billius says, destroys all the value of Eusebius as an exponent of Trinitarian doctrine. For similar statements of the relations of the Person of the Trinity, see P.E. 325 a and Gifford's note.

[2] τῆς τοῦ Πατρὸς ὁμοιώσεως ἔχειν τὸ κῦρος.

angels, to have been begotten of God, and made a priest
for ever, but He alone Who also said in the former pro-
(b) phecy, "The Lord created me as the beginning of the way
for his works, before the ages he established me, in the
beginning before the mountains were established, before all
the hills he begets me." Give your careful attention to
understanding the relations of the present Psalm to the
words quoted in the previous passage; in this one the Most
High God establishes to share His own throne the Second
Lord, who is our Lord, saying, "Sit thou on my right
hand," while in the preceding one the Scripture said that
(c) His throne would remain for ever and ever, calling Him at
the same time God when it says, "Thy throne, O God, is
for ever and ever." Again, in the passage before us, it says,
"The Lord shall send the rod of thy power out of Sion,"
and in the other, "The sceptre of righteousness is the
sceptre of thy kingdom"; and once more this passage
says, "Sit thou on my right hand, until I make thine
enemies the footstool of thy feet, and thou shalt rule in
the midst of thine enemies," and the former one, "Thy
arrows are sharp, O mighty one,[1] in the heart of the
(d) king's enemies." So that what is said about His enemies in both is in agreement. Who, then, seeing with
his eyes in the midst of cities, villages and countries
throughout the world the Churches of our Saviour, the
peoples ruled by Him, and the vast multitudes of those
sanctified by Him encircled on all sides by enemies and
foes of the teaching of Christ, some visible among men,
some invisible and beyond the power of sight, would
not wonder at this oracle addressed to the person of
the subject of the prophecy, which says, "Rule in the
(222) midst of thine enemies"? And while in the previous passage we read, "Anointed with the oil of gladness above
thy fellows"—it being the Hebrew custom to anoint priests
—the passage before us now pronounces Him priest in
clearer terms, adding more teaching about Him, by which
we learn that He unlike all previous priests is the Eternal
Priest, an idea which cannot be associated with mere
(b) humanity. He says that He is made a priest after the order
of Melchizedek, in contradistinction to the ordinance of

---

[1] δυνατέ with Gaisford from Paris MS. Migne has δυνατά.

the Mosaic priesthood, held either by Aaron or any of his
descendants, none of whom were priests until they had
been anointed with a prepared ointment, and so became,
as by type and symbol, a kind of shadowy and symbolical
Christ.   He was one of course that because of his mortality
could not extend his priesthood long, and moreover was
only consecrated for Jewish people, not for the other
nations.   He did not enter on his priestly duty under an
oath of God, but was only honoured by the judgment of (c)
men, so that it was sometimes the case that something unworthy of God's service was found in them, as is recorded
of Eli.   And moreover besides all this, that ancient priest
of the Mosaic order could only be selected from the tribe of
Levi.   It was obligatory without exception that he should
be of the family descending from Aaron, and do service to
God in outward worship with the sacrifices and blood of
irrational animals.   But he that is named Melchizedek,
which in Greek is translated "king of righteousness," who (d)
was king of Salem, which would mean "king of peace," Heb. vii.
without father, without mother, without line of descent, not 3.
having, according to the account, "beginning of years, nor
end of life," had no characteristics shared by the Aaronic
priesthood.   For he was not chosen by men, he was not
anointed with prepared oil, he was not of the tribe of those
who had not yet been born ; and strangest of all, he was
not even circumcised in his flesh, and yet he blesses Abraham, as if he were far better than he ; he did not act as
priest to the Most High God with sacrifices and libations,
nor did he minister at the Temple in Jerusalem.   How (223)
could he? it did not yet exist.   And he was such of course
because there was going to be no similarity between our
Saviour Christ and Aaron, for He was neither to be designated priest after a period when He was not priest, nor was
He to become priest, but be it.   For we should notice
carefully in the words, "Thou art a priest for ever," He does
not say, "Thou shalt be what thou wert not before," any
more than, "Thou wert that before, which thou art not
now"—but by Him Who said, "I am that I am," it is said,
"Thou art, and remainest, a priest for ever."

Since, then, Christ neither entered on His priesthood in
time, nor sprang from the priestly tribe, nor was anointed (b)
with prepared and outward oil, nor will ever reach the

end of His priesthood, nor will be established only for the Jews but for all nations, for all these reasons He is rightly said to have forsaken the priesthood after Aaron's type, and to be a priest after the order of Melchizedek. And the fulfilment of the oracle is truly wondrous, to one who recognizes how our Saviour Jesus the Christ of God even now performs through His ministers even to-day (c) sacrifices after the manner of Melchizedek's. For just as he, who was priest of the Gentiles, is not represented as offering outward sacrifices, but as blessing Abraham only with wine and bread, in exactly the same way our Lord and Saviour Himself first, and then all His priests among all nations, perform the spiritual sacrifice according to the customs of the Church, and with wine and bread darkly express the mysteries of His Body and saving Blood. This (d) by the Holy Spirit Melchizedek foresaw, and used the figures of what was to come, as the Scripture of Moses witnesses, when it says :

"And Melchizedek, king of Salem, brought out bread and wine : and he was priest of the Most High God, and he blessed Abraham."

Gen. xiv. 18.

And thus it followed that only to Him with the addition of an oath :

Heb. vii. 21.

"The Lord God sware, and will not repent, Thou art a priest for ever after the order of Melchizedek."

Hear, too, what the apostle also says about this :

Heb. vi. 17.

" 17. Wherein God willing more abundantly to shew unto the heirs of the kingdom [1] the immutability of his counsel mediated it by an oath : 18. That by two (224) immutable things, in which it was impossible for God to lie, we might have a strong encouragement, who have fled for refuge to lay hold on the hope set before us."

And he adds :

Heb. vii. 23.

" 23. And they indeed have been made priests many in number, because that by death they were hindered from continuing. 24. But he, because he abideth, [2] hath an unchangeable priesthood. 25. Wherein he is able to save to the uttermost them that come unto (b) God by him, seeing he ever liveth to make intercession

---

[1] W.H.: ἐπαγγελίας. E.: βασιλείας.   [2] W.H. add εἰς τὸν αἰῶνα.

for them.   26. For such an high priest became us, who
is holy, guileless, undefiled, separated from sinners, and
made higher than the heavens."

And he adds:

"1. Now in the things which we are saying the Heb. v
chief point is this : We have such an high priest, who 1.
sat down on the right hand of[1] the Majesty in the
heavens, 2. a minister of the holy things, and of the
true tabernacle, which God has pitched, and not man."

So says the apostle.

The Psalm too, continuing, shews in veiled phrase even
the Passion of the Subject of the prophecy, saying : "He Ps. cxxiii.
shall drink of the brook in the way, therefore shall he 4.
lift up his head."   And another Psalm shews "the brook" (c)
to mean the time of temptations : "Our soul hath passed
through the brook, yea, our soul has passed through
the deep waters."   He drinks, then, in the brook, it
says, that cup, evidently, of which He darkly spoke at
the time of His Passion, when He said : "Father, if it be
possible, let this cup pass from me."   And also, "If it Matt. xxvi.
be not possible for it to pass from me, except I drink it, 42.
thy will be done."

It was, then, by drinking this cup that He lifted up His
head, as the apostle also says, for when he was "Obedient (d)
to the Father[2] unto death, even the death of the cross, Phil. ii. 8.
therefore," he says, "God hath highly exalted him," rais- Eph. i. 20.
ing Him from the dead, and setting Him at His right
hand,[3] far above all rule and authority and power and
dominion, and every name which is named, not only in
this world, but in that which is to come.   And He hath
put all things in subjection under his feet, according to
the promise made to Him, which He expresses through
the Psalmist, saying, "Sit thou on my right hand, until
I make thine enemies the footstool of thy feet.   Be thou
ruler in the midst of thine enemies."

It is plain to all that to-day the power of our Saviour
and the word of His teaching rule over all them that have
believed in Him, in the midst of His enemies and foes.

---

[1] W.H. add τοῦ θρόνου.   [2] W.H. omit τῷ πατρί.
[3] W.H. add ἐν τοῖς ἐπουρανίοις.

CHAPTER 4

(b) *That Isaiah also the Greatest of the Prophets clearly knew Him to be God in God, agreeing in His Words with Us Who glorify the Father in the Son, and the Son in the Father.*

[Passage quoted, Isa. xlv. 12–13.]

In these words God the Creator of the Universe first foretells by the prophet a King and Saviour who will come to build up a holy constitution, and ransom all men who (c) are enslaved by the errors of dæmons. And next in order the prophetic Spirit darkly tells of the subjection of the different nations, which shall be subject to the One of Whom he prophesies, and how they will worship Him as God, how they will pray in His name, because of the greater God dwelling in Him, that is to say the Most High Father and God of the Universe. And this is how it is expressed.

(d) "14. Thus saith the Lord: Egypt hath laboured for thee, and the merchandise of the Ethiopians, and the Sabeans, great in stature, shall pass over to thee, and shall be thy servants; and they shall follow thee bound in fetters,[1] and shall worship thee anew, and shall pray in thy name, because God is in thee, and there is no God but thee. 15. For thou art God, and we knew it not, God of Israel, Saviour.[2] 16. All that are opposed to Him shall be ashamed and confounded, and shall walk in shame."

Isa. xlv.
14-16.

This is the prophecy. And I do not think that any one, however deficient in judgment he may be, can fail to see how clearly and plainly the words evidently refer to God, Israel's Saviour, and another God in Him. "The just," he says, "shall worship thee, and make their prayers in thee. Because God is in thee, and there is no God but thee. For thou art God, and we knew it not, the God of Israel, the Saviour." And the words "we knew it not" spoken (226) in the person of those of old who did not know Him, only

---

[1] E. omits καὶ διαβήσονται πρὸς σέ. For νέοι, S. reads σοι.
S. omits σωτήρ, and reads ὁ Θεὸς τοῦ Ἰσραήλ.

occur in the Septuagint, for the Hebrew is different, and translated by Aquila, " God then is strong and hidden, God that saves Israel," and by Theodotion, " Therefore a strong secret God preserves Israel." It is remarkable how he calls Christ a hidden God, and gives the reason clearly, why he calls Him God alone among the ones begotten after the First and Unbegotten, viz. the dwelling of the Father in Him.

" For in him " according to the holy apostle " it pleased (b) that all the fullness of the godhead [1] should dwell." This Col. i. 19. the passage plainly expresses when it says " God is in thee, and there is no God but thee." Instead of, " But thee " Theodotion has " But him," translating : " There is no God but him," that is to say, " But the God that is in thee, by whom thou also art God."

According to Aquila it runs thus : " But a strong one is in thee, and there is none beside thee : God the strong and the one that hides himself preserving Israel." And Symmachus, " God is in thee alone, and there is no other and exists no other God, verily thou art a hidden God, (c) God preserving Israel," in which the words clearly shew the reason of the Christ of God being God. It is where he says, "God is in thee and therefore thou art a strong and hidden God." According to this, then, the true and only God must be One, and alone owning the Name [2] in full right. While the Second, by sharing in the being of the True God, is thought worthy to share His Name, not being God in Himself, nor existing apart from the Father Who gives Him Divinity, not called God apart from the Father, (d) but altogether being, living and existing as God, through the presence of the Father in Him, and one in being with the Father, and constituted God from Him and through Him,[3] and holding His being as well as His Divinity not from Himself but from the Father. Wherefore we are

---

[1] W. H. omit τῆs θεότητοs.

[2] The Greek is, ὁ μὲν ἀληθὴs καὶ μόνοs Θεὸs εἶs ἂν εἴη, μόνοs κυρίωs τυγχάνων τῆs προσηγορίαs, and Diodatus in order not to pass on the heresy, replaces κυρίωs by κύριοs, translating, qui hujus appellationis est Dominus ("who is Lord of this designation"). Pie, sed perperam, is the comment of the Paris editor.

[3] Diodatus in his translation omits " constituted God through Him," and "after the Father."

taught to honour Him as God after the Father, through the Father dwelling in Him, as we see these prophecies before us intend.

For as the image of a king would be honoured for the sake of him whose lineaments and likeness it bears (and though both the image and the king received honour, one person would be honoured, and not two ; for there would not be two kings, the first the true one, and the one represented by the image, but one in both forms, not only conceived of, but named and honoured), so I say the Only-begotten Son, being the only image of the Unseen (227) God, is rightly , called the image of the Unseen God, through bearing His likeness, and is constituted God by the Father Himself : thus He is, with regard to essence, and gives an image of the Father that grows from His nature and is not something added to Him, because of the actual source of His existence. Wherefore He is by nature both God and Only-begotten Son, not being made such by adoption like those who were without, who only acquire an accidental right to the Name of God. But He (b) is celebrated as Only-begotten Son by nature and as our God, but not as the first God,[1] but as the first Only-Begotten Son of God, and therefore God.

And the general cause also of His being God, would be the fact that He alone is Son of God by nature, and is called Only-begotten, and that He completely preserves the living and vivid spiritual image of the One God, being made in all things like the Father, and bearing the likeness of His actual Divinity. Thus therefore Him also, as being the only Son and the only image of God, endued with the powers of the Father's Unbegotten and eternal essence (c) according to the example of likeness, and fashioned to the extremest accuracy of likeness by the Father Himself, Who is the most skilled and the wisest delineator and maker of life conceivable, the holy Scriptures salute as God, as One worthy of receiving this Name of the Father with His other (names), but as one Who receives it, and does not

---

[1] οὐχ ὁ πρῶτος θεός. Donatus translates to avoid the Arian phrase, "non tamen a seipso deus." The Paris editor reminds us that Eusebius did not intend in this passage the orthodox theology of the Nicene Fathers, but regarded the Son as "minor et secundæ classis Deus."

possess it in His own right.[1] For the One gives, and the
Other receives ; so that strictly the First is to be reckoned
God, alone being God by nature, and not receiving (d)
(divinity) from another. And the Other is to be thought
of as secondary, and as holding a Divinity received from
the Father, as an image of God, the Divinity in both being
conceived of as one in type,[2] God in Himself being one
without beginning and unbegotten, but He is seen through
the Son as by a mirror and image. And this is exactly
the teaching of the prophetic oracle, which says that He
is only to be worshipped as God, because the Father dwells
in Him. For it says, "In thee shall they pray, because
God is in thee, and Thou thyself art God, the Saviour of
Israel, and therefore Thou art a strong and a hidden God.
Since God is in Thee, and there is none beside Him."   (228)

Instead of "Egypt laboured," the Hebrew has, and the
other translators render, "Labour of Egypt," so that the
passage runs : "The Labour of Egypt and the merchandise
of the Aethiopians shall worship Thee and be Thy slaves,
and the Sabeans," by which I understand to be meant
barbarous and obscure nations, in fact all those that long
ago were a prey to dæmonic superstition. For as the
Egyptians seemed to be the most superstitious of all
nations, and to have begun the errors of idolatry, it is (b)
natural that they should be represented as first coming
under the yoke of Christ, and should represent all the rest
of idolatry. And this was fulfilled in our Lord and Saviour,
by the worship and service rendered to Him in all nations
by many multitudes of nations throughout the world.

And I understand that the Ethiopians and Sabeans here
foretold as worshipping Christ are also meant in Ps. lxxi.,
where it is said : "The Ethiopians shall fall down before Ps. lxxi. 9.
him, and the kings of Arabia and Saba shall bring gifts,
and shall worship him." And it is plain from the context
that it is Christ Who it is there predicted will also be the (c)
Object of their worship.

---

[1] εἰληφότα δὲ, ἀλλ᾽ οὐκ ἰδιόκτητον αὐτὴν ἐσχηκότα.
[2] κατὰ τὸ παράδειγμα.

CHAPTER 5

Psalm xxxii.

How David equally with Us knows the Word of God, Who is of His Essence, to be by the Command of the Father Creator of All Things ; and how the Same Prophet witnesses that the Same Word of God was sent by the Father for the Saving of Men, and how He prophesies that in a Short Time the Whole World would be filled by His Teaching.

(d)

"By the word of the Lord the heavens were made firm, and all the power of them by the spirit of his mouth."

Ps. xxxii.

And in Ps. cvi. it is said :

"He sent his word and healed them, and saved them from their destruction."

Ps. cvi.

And again in Ps. cxlvii. :

Ps. cxlvii.

"He sendeth his oracle upon earth, his word runneth swiftly."

Now it is evident that with the Psalm before us which says, "By the word of the Lord the heavens were made firm,"

(229) the holy gospel exactly agrees when it says, "In the beginning was the Word, and the Word was with God, and the Word was God. The same was in the beginning with God. All things were made by him, and without him

John i. 1.

was not anything made." The Gospel rightly calls Him God : for this same being who is now regarded as God, has been called in our previous quotations, the Word, the Wisdom and the Offspring of God, and the Priest, the Christ, King, Lord, God, and the Image of God. And

(b) that He is other than the Father, and His Minister, so that He as the greater can bid Him to create, is added in the Psalm before us :

"8. Let all the earth fear the Lord, | and let all the dwellers on earth be moved by him. | 9. For he spake, and they were created, | he commanded and they were made. | "

For it is plain that a speaker must speak to some one else, and one who issues a command must issue it to another beside himself.   And clearly since our Saviour's Incarnation

many multitudes from all the earth, that is to say from all the (c)
nations of the earth, have ceased to fear dæmons as before,
and have feared the Lord Jesus, and all the inhabitants of
the world have been moved at the Name of Christ, agreeably
to the oracle which here says, " Let the earth fear the Lord :
By him shall be moved all the inhabitants of the world."
These, then, come from Ps. ii. and xxx.   And you would
find similar prophecies also in Ps. cxlviii., which teaches
that not only things in earth, but also things in heaven, the
whole creation in a word, came into being by the command
of God.   For it says :

" 1. Praise the Lord from the heavens, | praise him (d)
in the height ; | 2. Praise him all ye angels of his, | Ps. cxlviii.
praise him all his powers, | 3. Praise him sun and 1.
moon, | Praise him all ye stars and light,1 | . . . 5. For
he spake, and they were made, | he commanded, and
they were created."

For if He commanded, Who was great enough to receive
such a command, but the Word of God, who in many ways
has been proved to be God in this treatise, and naturally
called the Word of God, because the Almighty has set in
Him the words that make and create all things, delivering
to Him the task of governing all things and steering them
by reason and in order?   (230)

For of course no one should imagine that the Word of
God is like to articulate and spoken speech, which among
men consists of syllables, and is compounded of nouns and
verbs : for we know that our speech consists essentially of
sounds and syllables and their significations, and is produced
by the tongue and the organs 2 of the throat and mouth,
whereas that of the eternal and unembodied nature,
totally divorced from all our conditions, could not possibly
involve anything human : It uses the name of speech and (b)
nothing more.   Since we must not in the case of the God of
the Universe postulate a voice that depends on the movements of the air, nor words, nor syllables, nor tongue,
nor mouth, nor anything indeed that is human and mortal.3

---

1 E. omits ver. 4 and part of 5 in S. and A.V.

2 ἀρτηριῶν.

3 The Paris editor notes that Eusebius has in view the teaching of
Marcellus, the heretical Bishop of Ancyra, displaced by Basil A.D. 335,
against whom Eusebius wrote the *Ad Marcellum*.

For His must be a Word of the soul, and quite incapable of existence or being apart from the soul.   For human speech is in itself without essence and substance, and regarded generally is a self-movement and activity of thought.   But the Word of God is other than this : It has its own substance

(c) in Itself altogether divine and spiritual, It exists in Itself, It is active also in Itself, and being divorced from matter and body, and made like to the nature of the first Unbegotten and Only God, It carries in Itself the meaning of all begotten things, and the ideas of things visible, being Itself without body and invisible.   Wherefore the divine oracles call It Wisdom and the Word of God.

(d)   CHAPTER 6

That Isaiah, as well as David, acknowledges Two Lords, and the
(231)   *Second, as in David, is the Creator, as We also confess.*

[Passage quoted, Isa. xlviii. 12–15.]

(b) SEE now how He that says, " I am the first, and I am the last.   He that established the earth and the heaven," clearly confesses that He was sent by "the Lord, the Lord," calling the Father Lord twice, and you will have undeniable evidence of what we seek.   And He says that He is first among beings begotten in all reverence, since He allots Being, original, unbegotten, and beyond the first, to the Father.   For the customary meaning of first in the sense of " first of a greater number," superior in honour and order,

(c) would not be applicable to the Father.   For the Almighty God of course is not the first of created things, since the idea of Him does not admit of a beginning.   He must be beyond and above the first, as Himself generating and establishing the First, and the Divine Word alone is to be called the First of all begotten things.   So if we ask with reference to the words, " He spake and they were made, he commanded and they were created," to which of the begotten beings He gave the command to create, we see now clearly that it was given to Him, Who said, " My hand has laid the foundation of the earth, and my right hand has

made the heaven strong": Who also confesses that He was
sent by One greater than Himself, when He says: "Now (d)
the Lord, the Lord has sent me, and his Spirit." And it
must be the Word of God Who said also, "By the word of
the Lord were the heavens made firm," if we compare the
Psalm. And yet though the Word of God is Himself proclaimed divine by the word "Lord," He still calls One
Higher and Greater His Father and Lord, using with
beautiful reverence the word Lord twice in speaking of
Him, so as to differentiate His title. For He says here,
"The Lord, the Lord has sent me," as if the Almighty God
were in a special sense first and true Lord both of His Only- (232)
begotten Word and of all begotten things. after Him, in
relation to which the Word of God has received dominion
and power from the Father, as His true and Only-begotten
Son, and therefore Himself holds the title of Lord in a
secondary sense.

CHAPTER 7

From Genesis.

*That Moses, God's Greatest Servant, knows the Father and
God of the Universe to have been associated with Another in
the Creation of Man: And that We have learned already
that this Being was the Divine Word.*

"AND God said, Let us make man in our image, and Gen. i. 26.
likeness." And also: "And God said, It is not good for (c)
man to be alone, let us make a helper for him." And he Gen. ii. 18.
at once shews that the Being addressed is not an angel of
God, so that it may not be thought that this was said to
angels, with the words: "And God made man, in the Gen. i. 27.
image of God he made him."

CHAPTER 8

From the same.

That Moses clearly without Veil reveals God to be Two Lords.

(d) "THE sun arose on the earth, and Lot entered Segor, and
Gen. xix. the Lord rained upon Sodom brimstone and fire from the
23.   Lord."
It is clear here that the second "Lord" refers to him that
was sent by the greater Lord to punish the ungodly. Yet
if we unreservedly confess two Lords, we do not regard them
both as God in the same sense. We are taught in all
reverence to admit an order, that One is the Most High
Father and God and Lord, and God and Lord of the
Second : but that the Word of God is the Second Lord,
Lord of those below Him, and yet not equally with the
(233) greater. For the Word of God is not Lord of the Father,
nor God of the Father, but His Image, and Word, and
Wisdom, and Power, and Lord and God of those that come
after Him ; whereas the Father is Father and Lord and God
even of the Son. Wherefore a reverent theology in our
opinion rightly recurs to one Source of being and to one
God.

CHAPTER 9

From the same.

*That the Same Servant of God shews a Second Being called God
and Lord, and relates that He was seen in Human Shape
and Form and answered Them of Old Time.*

[Passages quoted, Gen. xii. 7 ; xvii. 1 ; xviii. 1, 17.]

AND again he adds to this, as if speaking of Another :
"For I knew that he will establish his children, and
his house after him, and they will keep the ways of the
Lord, to do righteousness and judgment, so that the

Lord will bring on Abraham what things he spake to Gen. xviii. him."   19.

The Lord Who answers, Who is recorded to have said this (234) to Abraham, is represented as clearly confessing another Lord to be his Father and the Maker of all things.   At least Abraham, who as a prophet has a clear conception of the speaker, prophetically continues with the words :

"Wilt thou destroy the righteous man with the Gen. xviii. wicked, and shall the righteous be as the wicked? If 23–25. there be fifty righteous in the city, wilt thou destroy them? Wilt thou not spare [all] the place, because of the fifty righteous?   Be it far from thee to fulfil this (b) word, and destroy the righteous with the wicked, and that the righteous should be as the wicked.   In no way let him, that judgeth all the earth, not do judgment." [1]

I hardly think that this could have been said suitably to angels or to any of God's ministering spirits.   For it could not be regarded as a minor duty to judge all the earth. And he is no angel who is named in the previous passage, but One greater than an angel, the God and Lord who was seen beside the before-mentioned oak with the two angels in human form.   Nor can it be thought that Almighty God Himself is meant.   For it is impious to suggest that the (c) Divine changes and puts on the shape and form of a man. And so it remains for us to own that it is the Word of God who in the preceding passage is regarded as divine : whence the place is even to-day honoured by those who live in the neighbourhood as a sacred place in honour of those who appeared to Abraham, and the terebinth [2] can still· be seen

---

[1] S. puts stop at " In no way " = " certainly not " ; and ends the verse as in A.V. with a question.

[2] " Was the tree an oak or a terebinth ?   The ancient testimonies are conflicting, but the balance of evidence is in favour of the terebinth." (J. G. Frazer, *Folklore in the O.T.* iii. 57.)   It is a terebinth in Josephus, *Bell. Jud.* iv. 9, 7 ; and in the *Itinerarium Burdigalense* (A.D. 333) ; *Itineraria Hierosolymitana*, P. Geyer, Vienna, 1898, p. 25. Eusebius (*Onomasticon*, s. v. ᾿Αρβώ, pp. 54, 56, ed. F. Carsow and G. Parthey) mentions an oak, a memorial, and a terebinth.   Jerome (*circa* A.D. 388, *Liber de situ et nom. loc. Heb.* s. v. " Arbo ") implies that the terebinth no longer existed.   (Migne, *Pat. Lat.* xxiii. 862.)

For Constantine's Church, and Sozomen's description of the Festival there (Sozomen, *H.E.* ii. 4), connected with ancient Tree-Worship, see Fraser, *loc. cit.*   The tree now shewn is a large oak, one and a half miles west cf Hebron.

there. For they who were entertained by Abraham, as represented in the picture,[1] sit one on each side, and he in the midst surpasses them in honour. This would be our Lord and Saviour, Whom though men knew Him not they (d) worshipped, confirming the Holy Scriptures. He then thus in person from that time sowed the seeds of holiness among men, putting on a human form and shape, and revealed to the godly ancestor Abraham Who He was, and shewed him the mind of His Father.

CHAPTER 10

(235)   From the same.

That the same Prophet shews more clearly in the Matter of Jacob the said Person to be Lord, Whom also He calls God, and an Angel of God Most High, in addressing Him.

[Passage quoted, Gen. xxviii. 10–19.]

(b) THIS Being who here answers him at such length, you will find, if you read on, to be Lord and God, and the Angel of God, from the words Jacob himself says to his wives :

Gen. xxxi.   "And the angel of the Lord said to me in sleep,
11.   Jacob. And I said, Here am I."

And also :

(236)   "I have seen, he says, all that Laban doeth to thee. I am the God, that was seen of thee in the place where thou anointedst the pillar for me, and offeredst prayer to me."

Therefore He that said before, I am the Lord God of Abraham thy Father, and the God of Isaac, to whom godly

---

[1] ἐπὶ γραφῆς ἀνακείμενοι, that is, a picture.—For condemnation of painting see Tertullian, *adv. Hermog.* c. i. ; *de Idolatr.* c. 5. Clement Alex., *Protrept.* c. 4 ; Origen, *c. Celsum*, iv. 31. Pure symbolism only slowly gave way to historical subjects, which were limited to a conventional cycle, typifying church doctrines. Abraham and the Angels were not in this cycle, but they formed one of the twenty-one scriptural frescoes painted in the latter half of the fourth century for the Ambrosian Basilica at Milan. See *D.C.A.*, art. "Fresco," by Venables. E. does not seem here to suggest that a picture was an unusual ornament of shrines connected with sacred events.

Jacob raises the pillar, was indeed God and Lord: for we must believe that which He Himself says. Not of course the Almighty, but the Second to Him, Who ministers for His Father among men, and brings His Word. Wherefore Jacob here calls Him an Angel: "The Angel of God said to me, speaking in my sleep, 'I am the God who was seen (b) by thee in this place.'" So the same Being is clearly called the Angel of the Lord, and God and Lord in this place. And by Isaiah the Prophet he is called "Angel of Great Counsel," as well as God and Ruler and Potentate, where His Incarnation is prophesied in the words:

"For unto us a child is born, and to us a son is given, Isa. ix. 6. on whose shoulder shall be the rule, and his name shall be called the Angel of Great Counsel,[1] Prince of Peace, the Mighty God, the Potentate, the Father of the Age to Come."

(c)

CHAPTER 11 (d)

That Jacob also beholds the Before-named as Both God and Lord, and also as an Angel in Human Form in Common with Abraham, in the Course of the History that so tells.

[Passage quoted, Gen. xxxii. 22–31.]

It was said to Moses, No one shall see My face and live. (237) But here Jacob saw God not indefinitely but face to face. (b) And being preserved, not only in body but in soul, he was thought worthy of the name of Israel, which is a name borne by souls, if the name Israel is rightly interpreted "Seeing God." Yet he did not see the Almighty God. For He is invisible, and unalterable, and the Highest of all Being could not possibly change into man.

But he saw Another, Whose name it was not yet the time to reveal to curious Jacob.[2] And if we were to suppose that (c) he saw an angel, or that one of the divine spirits in heaven whose duty it is to bring oracles to the holy, we should

---

[1] The following titles do not occur in LXX.
[2] πολυπραγμονοῦντι τῷ Ἰακώβ.

clearly be wrong; firstly, because He is called Lord and
God, for certainly Holy Scripture calls him God in distinct
terms, and names Him Lord, honouring Him with the
name signified by the Tetragram, which the Hebrews only
apply to the unspeakable and secret name of God: and
secondly, because when Scripture desires to speak of angels,
it clearly distinguishes them as such, as when the God and
(d) Lord Who replies to Abraham no longer thinks the sinners
of Sodom worthy of His presence, and Holy Scripture says :

Gen. xxxii.
2.

"And the Lord departed, and ceased speaking with
Abraham. And the two angels departed to Sodom at
evening."

And to Jacob :

Gen.xxxii.
1.

"There came two angels of God : and he saw them,
and said, It is the camp of God. And he called the
name of that place, Encampments."

Here, then, the godly man clearly distinguished the nature
of the visions, since he now called the name of the place
Encampments, from his seeing the encampments of the
angels. Whereas when he communes with God, he calls
the name of the place, Sight of God, adding, "For I have
seen God face to face."

And when an angel appears to Moses, Holy Scripture also
(238) makes it plain, saying : "The angel of the Lord appeared

Exod. iii.
2.

to him in a flame of fire in a bush." But when it refers to
the actual being who replies, it calls him God and Lord,
and no longer an angel. It is equally clear in its distinction
between the angel and the Lord in the account of what
happened at the Red Sea, where it says :

Exod. xiv.
19.

"And the angel of the Lord that went before the
children of Israel, removed and went behind them ; and
the pillar of the cloud also removed from before them."

And as in the former passage the Lord is introduced as
(b) answering the men of the old time in human form, so also
is He here by the cloud. For it is said afterwards :

"And it came to pass in the morning-watch, that the
Lord looked upon the camp of the Egyptians in a pillar
of fire and cloud. And God answered Moses in the
pillar of the cloud through the whole of the wanderings
in the wilderness."

So Scripture is quite exact when the nature of an
(c) angel is meant, for it calls him neither God nor Lord,

but simply Angel. But when it knows that He that appears was Lord and God, it clearly uses those terms. And that by Lord and God they do not mean the First Cause, the passages of Holy Scripture clearly shew which call Him the Angel of God, Who had previously been called Lord and God in the part concerning Jacob. It only remains for Him then to be God and Lord among beings, after the Almighty God of the Universe. And He would thus be the Word of God before the ages, greater than all angels, but less than the First Cause.

CHAPTER 12　　　　　(d)

That again in the Story of Jacob the Story supposes a Secondary God.

[Passage quoted, Gen. xxxv. 1–3.]

HERE the very God of the Universe, the only Unbegotten (239) and Most High (not seen, for He answers Jacob invisibly, and moving him by His unspeakable power), speaks clearly of Another than Himself. God then said to him, "Make an altar to the God that appeared to thee." I have already shewn Who this was that was described before as appearing to him, and proved that it was the Word of God.

CHAPTER 13

From Exodus.

That the Almighty God, being He that answered Moses by an Angel, teaches that He was seen by the Fathers, not by means of an Angel, but by His Son.

[Passages quoted, Exod. iii. 1, 2, 4, 5, 14 ; vi. 2–4.]

IN the case of the Prophets, Isaiah, say, or Jeremiah, or those like them, a man was seen, and God prophesied

through him that was seen, as by an instrument; and now
the Person of Christ, now that of the Holy Spirit, and now
that of Almighty God, answered through the prophet. So
we must suppose the Most High and Almighty God now
prophesies the things before us to Moses who is under
(240) instruction [1] by the angel that appeared to him. The
intention of which must have been of this nature : "To
you, O prophet, as one being instructed and not fit for
aught but angelic visions, hitherto I have willed to send my
angel; and I make my Name clear to thee alone, teaching
thee that I am what I am, and that my Name is the Lord ;
but I not only showed this to thy fathers, but I gave them a
greater gift, I appeared to them." I have already shewn
Who it was that appeared to the fathers, when I shewed that
(b) the angel of God was called God and Lord. It will naturally
be asked how He that is beyond the universe, Himself the
only Almighty God, appeared to the fathers. And the
answer will be found if we realize the accuracy of Holy
Scripture. For the Septuagint rendering, "I was seen of
Abraham, Isaac, and Jacob, being their God." Aquila says,
"And I was seen by Abraham, Isaac, and Jacob as a
sufficient God," clearly shewing that the Almighty God
Himself, Who is One, was not seen in His own Person ;
(c) and that He did not give answers to the fathers, as He did
to Moses by an angel, or a fire, or a bush, but "as a
sufficient God": so that the Father was seen by the fathers
through the Son, according to His saying in the Gospels,
"He that hath seen me, hath seen the Father." For the
knowledge of the Father was revealed in Him and by Him.
But in cases when He appeared to save men, He was seen
in the human form of the Son, giving an earnest before the
time [2] to the godly of that salvation which should come
(d) through Him to all men ; whereas when He was going to be
the avenger and chastiser of the wicked Egyptians, He
appeared no longer as a sufficient God, but as an angel
ministering punishment, and in form of fire and flame,
ready at once to devour them like wild and thorny under-
growth. So they say that the bush darkly refers to the

---

[1] εἰσαγομένῳ = a catechumen.
[2] προαρραβωνιζόμενος. The verb, ἀρραβωνιζέσθαι is used by Eusebius
in *Vit. Const.* I. 3, for "to hire." Cf. 2 Cor. i. 22, v. 5, and Eph. i.
14, for ἀρραβών.

wild, savage, and cruel character of the Egyptians, and the fire to the avenging power of the chastisement that overtook them.

(241)

CHAPTER 14   (b)

That God the Word appeared in the Form of a Cloud to Moses and All the People, as in Human Form to the Patriarchs.

[Passages quoted, Exod. xix. 9 ; xxxiii. 9 ; Num. xii. 5.]

The people then beheld the pillar of cloud, and it spoke (c) to Moses.   But who was the speaker?   Obviously the pillar of cloud, which before appeared to the fathers in a human form.   And I have already shewn that this was not the Almighty God, but another Being Whom we name, as the Word of God, the Christ Who was seen for the sake of the multitude of Moses and the people in a pillar of cloud, because it was not possible for them to see Him like their (d) fathers in human shape.   For, surely, it was reserved for the Perfect to be able to see beforehand His future In- carnate appearance among men, and since it was im- possible then for the whole people to bear it, He was seen now in fire in order to inspire fear and wonder, and now in a cloud, as it were in a shadowy and veiled form ruling them, as He was also seen by Moses for their sake.

CHAPTER 15   (242)

That it was not an Angel, who gave Answers to Moses, but Some One More Excellent than an Angel.

[Passages quoted, Exod. xxiii. 20, 21 ; xxxii. 34 ; xxxiii. 1.]

It will be plain to all that these could not be the words of a mere angel of God.   But of what God could they (c) be, but of the One seen by the forefathers, whom Jacob

clearly called the Angel of God? And He we know was
the Word of God, being called both the Servant of God,
and God Himself and Lord.

CHAPTER 16

(d) *That the same Lord teaches of another Lord, namely, His Son.*

(243)   [Passage quoted, Exod. xx. 2, 5, 7.]

From the Decalogue.

HERE, too, the Lord Himself teaches in the passage before
us about another Lord. For He says: "I am the Lord
thy God," and adds: "Thou shalt not take the name of
the Lord thy God." The second Lord is here mystically
instructing His Servant about the Father, that is to say,
the God of the Universe. And you could find many other
similar instances occurring in Holy Scripture, in which
God gave answers as if about another God, and the Lord
Himself as if about another Lord.

CHAPTER 17

*That this Lord again Who gave Answers to Moses, knowing
another Lord Greater than Himself as Father, called Him
the True God.*

(d)   [Passages quoted, Exod. xxxiii. 17–18; xxxiv. 5–8.]

NOTICE, then, here how the Lord that descended in the
cloud, and stood by Moses in the name of the Lord, called
Another beside Himself, Who is twice called Lord, in a
common form of reduplication, as one reckoned as God
to be His own Master and Master of all others, and His
Own Father, and that here it is not Moses, as might be
supposed, but the Lord Himself Who calls another Lord
His Father; for He speaks first, and say to Moses: "I

will pass before thee in my glory, and will call upon the
name of the Lord." And when He has so said, Scripture
goes on in narrative form : "And the Lord descended in (244)
a cloud, and stood beside him there, and called on the
name of the Lord."

Thus the Lord Himself in fulfilment of His promise
descends and passes before the face of Moses. And the
Lord Himself calls and says : "O Lord, the God of pity
and mercy," and that which follows, clearly teaching His
servant Who He was, and teaching mystically the knowledge of a Lord greater than Himself. And Moses implies
this, when in his prayer for the people he records the (b)
words of the Lord before us, that the Lord spoke them,
and not he himself, when he says :

> "And now let the hand of the Lord be exalted, as
> thou saidst, The Lord is long-suffering and very pitiful
> and true, taking away sins and injustice, and iniquity,
> and will not clear the guilty with purification, avenging
> the sins of fathers upon their children to the third and Exod.
> fourth generation." xxxiv. 5.

Notice the way in which the Lord Himself addressing
the Father in these words as "long-suffering and of tender
mercy," calls Him also "true," agreeing with the words : John xvii.
"That they may know thee the only true God," spoken 3.
in the Gospels by the same Being, our Saviour. Yea, (c)
with exceeding reverence He calls the Father the only true
God, given meet honour to the Unbegotten Nature, of which
Holy Scripture teaches us He is Himself the Image and
the Offspring.

CHAPTER 18

From Numbers.

*That Holy Scripture teaches that God was seen by Israel,
darkly meaning the Word of God.*

IN the Book of Numbers Moses prays, saying : "Since (d)
thou art the Lord of this people that art seen of them Num. xiv.
face to face." 14.

For which Aquila substitutes : " Since thou art the Lord in the hearts of this people, which sees thee, O Lord, face to face."   And Symmachus : "Since thou art, O Lord."

Exod. xxiv. 9.

And it is said in Exodus : "And Moses, and Aaron, and Nadab, and Abihu, and seventy of the elders of Israel went up, and saw the place where the God of Israel stood." Instead of which Aquila says : "And they saw the God of Israel." (245) And Symmachus : "And they saw in a vision the God of Israel."

John i. 18.

From the text : "No man has seen God at any time," perhaps it might be thought that the above quotation contradicts the Saviour's words, as implying that the invisible is visible.   But if they be understood, like our former quotations, of the Word of God, Who was seen by the fathers "in many ways and in sundry manners," no contradiction is involved.

Heb. i. 1.

(b)   The God of Israel here seen is shewn to be the same Being Who was seen by Israel, when a man wrestled with Him, Who first changed his name from Jacob to Israel, saying : "Thou hast power with God," and when, also, Jacob appreciating His divine power called the place of

(c) the struggle the Sight of God, saying : "I have seen God face to face, and my life is preserved."   I showed in the proper place that this was no other than the Word of God.

CHAPTER 19

(246)   From Joshua, the son of Nave.

That God the Word, Who answereth Moses, appeared also to the Forefathers of Old Time, and to Joshua, Moses' Successor, in Human Form.

[Passage quoted, Josh. v. 13–15.]

THE same words, you will remember, were said by the same Lord to Moses at the beginning of the vision of the Bush, for Scripture says :

" 4. And when the Lord saw that he drew nigh to see,
He called him from the midst of the Bush, saying,
Moses, Moses, come not near here;[1] loose thy shoes
from off thy feet, for the place whereon thou standest (b)
is holy ground."   Exod.iii.4.
So, then, the command that was given shews that the God
Who answered on both occasions was one and the same.
Though here He prophesies through the Chief and Captain
of His power, and to Moses by the vision of the angel.
And of the heavenly armies, celestial powers and invisible
spirits, holy angels and archangels ministering to God the
King of kings and the Lord of lords (as Daniel says :
" Thousand thousands ministered to him, and ten thousand (c)
times ten thousand stood before him "), what other could Dan. vii.
be highest of all but the Word of God, His Firstborn 10.
Wisdom, His Divine Offspring?   Rightly, then, He is here
called Chief Captain of the Power of the Lord, as also
elsewhere " Angel of Great Counsel," " Throned with the
Father," " Eternal and Great High Priest."   And it has
been proved that the same Being is both Lord and God,
and Christ anointed by the Father with the oil of gladness.

Thus, appearing to Abraham by the oak in human form, (d)
He reveals Himself in a calm and peaceful guise, foreshow-
ing by it His future Coming to save mankind ; He appeared
to Jacob, as to an athlete and a champion destined to
wrestle with enemies, in the form of a man, and to Moses
and the people in the form of cloud and fire, and led them,
shewing Himself terrible and shadowy.

And as Joshua, the successor of Moses, was about to
fight against the former possessors of Palestine his enemies,
foreign and most ungodly races, He rightly appears to him
with a sword drawn and pointed against the enemy, shewing
by the vision that He Himself is about to attack the ungodly with an unseen sword and with divine power, the
fellow-soldier and the fellow-combatant of His people.
Wherefore He gives Himself the name of Chief and (247)
Captain of the Lord to suit the occasion.

---

[1] S. adds ὁ δὲ εἶπεν, Τί ἐστιν ;

CHAPTER 20

How the Creator of the Universe, the Word of God, answered
Job, and is said to have appeared to Him, just as He
(b)   *did to the Fathers.*

[Passages quoted, Job xxxviii. 1, 4, 7, 8, 14–17 ;
xlii. 4–6.]

IT is easy to distinguish that the words before us are the
Words of the Lord the Creator, not only from what has
previously been considered but from the impression they
make on you.   And, moreover, that the passages : " Hast
thou gone to the source of the sea, and trodden in the
footprints of the deep?" and : "Do the gates of death
open to thee for fear, and did the fortress of hell quake
when they saw thee?" prophesy our Saviour's descent
into Hades I will prove in the proper place, only now
remarking that it is more reasonable to refer this passage
to God the Word than to the God of the Universe.

(248)   Job certainly afterwards bears witness that he has seen
with his own eyes, as the fathers did the Lord Who spoke
to him through the whirlwind and the clouds, saying :
     " Hear me, Lord, that I also may speak : and I will
     ask thee, and teach thou me.   I have heard of thee
     by the report of the ear, but now mine eye seeth thee ;
     wherefore I have humiliated myself and have melted,
     and I reckon myself dust and ashes."

But how could a soul clothed in flesh and mortal eyes
(b) behold the Most High God, the Being beyond the Universe,
the Unchangeable and Unbegotten Essence, unless we
could say that here also God the Word proved to be Lord
in varying instances shews Himself as passing from His
own proper majesty?   This we may learn to be so from
the oracles themselves, in which the Lord again narrating
the story of the devil, under the name of the Dragon, to
Job, insisted, Do not you fear because he is prepared for
me?   For what Lord ought we to think that the Dragon
(c) was prepared, but our Saviour the Divine Word?   He it
was that destroyed the Prince of this world, who of old
besieged the human race, loosing the pains of death, as

He Himself also shews, saying: "Didst thou come to the spring of the sea, and troddest thou the traces of the depth? Did the doors of death open to thee in fear, and the warders of hell seeing thee tremble?" and He naturally gave this answer to Job after the great trial and contest through which He had gone, teaching him that though he has struggled more than his share, a greater and sterner (d) battle and contest is reserved for the Lord Himself against the time of His Coming to earth to die.

CHAPTER 21

From Psalm xc.

That this Psalm knows Two Lords.

[Passage quoted, Ps. xc. 9–13.]

THESE are the words that the devil uses in the Temptation (249) of our Saviour. Notice, then, how the Psalm says to the Lord Himself: "For thou, O Lord my hope, hast made the Most High thy refuge." For Thou Thyself, he says, my hope, O Lord, hast made thy refuge One greater than Thyself, God Himself the Most Highest over all and Thine own Father; wherefore evils shall not come upon Thee, (b) and no scourge shall come nigh Thy dwelling. And although wicked men attempt to scourge Thee, when Thou shalt become man, and to put Thee to death, yet for all that the scourge of God shall not come nigh Thy dwelling, that is Thy body, which Thou shalt wear for our sakes having become man. In the same way you will refer to Him all the remainder of the Psalm, which I will consider also in its fit place.

CHAPTER 22

(c)   From Hosea.

About the Word of God and about the Father, as about a Lord.

[Passage quoted, Hos. xi. 9.]

(d) IN these words God the Word says when He has become man to those who confess Him to be a holy man, but not God : " I am God and not a holy man among you." And, then, having called Himself God, He shews the Almighty Lord and God, His Father, adding : " I will go behind the Lord." And the words : " I will not enter into the city," are of one who refuses to take part in the common and vulgar life of men, from which also He dissuades his own disciples : " Go not on a road of the Gentiles, and enter not Matt. x. 5. into a city of the Samaritans."

CHAPTER 23

(250)   From Amos.

(b) *Of Our Saviour as of a Lord, and of His Father as of God, and of the Destruction of the Jewish People.*

[Passage quoted, Amos iv. 11.]

AND here the Lord Himself says that some God has caused the destruction of Sodom, since He Himself must plainly be a different Being from the One of Whom He speaks. Therefore two Lords stands out in the destruction (c) of Sodom and Gomorrah, when the Lord rained the fire of the Lord on them. You also, he says, will suffer a destruction such as Sodom underwent for its unnatural wickedness, and even so did not turn to Me. Scripture generally regards the future as past, so that we must understand the past to be meant in spite of the tense. The future " I will overthrow" must be understood for the past " I overthrew," and " ye will not turn," for " ye did turn."

This is levelled at the Jewish race, and only received its fulfilment in their case, after their plot against our Saviour. (d) Their ancient holy place, at any rate, and their Temple are to this day as much destroyed as Sodom.   Yet though they have suffered in accordance with the prediction, they have not hitherto turned to Christ, on Whose account they have suffered so much.   And so the prophecy before us is justly inspired to say : " And neither so have ye returned to me, saith the Lord."

CHAPTER 24   (251)

From Obadiah.

Of the Two Lords, Father and Son, and of the Call   (b)
of the Gentiles.

[Passage quoted, Obad. 1.]

THE Lord God has heard a report from the Lord.   And this report was about the call of the Gentiles.

CHAPTER 25

From Zechariah.

That God the Word being Lord confesses that He was sent (c)
by a Greater Lord.

[Passage quoted, Zech. ii. 8.]

IF, then, the Lord that sent (Him) is Lord Almighty, and He that says He was sent is so also, surely there are Two ; And He that was sent as Almighty Lord of the nations says clearly, " He sent me."

CHAPTER 26

(d)   *The same, and concerning the Call of the Gentiles.*

[Passage quoted, Zech. ii. 10, 11.]

AND this prophecy is like the former one, telling of the coming of the Christ to men, and the call of the Gentiles to salvation through Him.

(252)   "For I the Lord myself will come," He says, "and at My coming no longer Israel of old, nor one single nation of the earth alone, but many nations shall take refuge in the greater and high Lord, the God of Me Myself and of the Universe, to Whom fleeing the nations shall reap the great harvest of being called and actually becoming the people of God, and of dwelling in the midst of her that is called the daughter of Zion."

(b) So it is common in Holy Scripture to call the Church of God on earth, as being as it were a daughter of the heavenly Zion.   And this good news is told in the oracle which says : "Rejoice and be glad, O daughter of Zion, because I come, and I will dwell in the midst of thee."   For we believe that God the Word dwells in the midst of the Church.   As indeed He promised when He said, "Lo, I am with you all the days, until the end of the world"—and, "Where two or three are gathered together in my name, there am I in the midst of them."   And when, He says :

Matt. xxviii.20.

Matt. xviii. 20.   (c)

"I the Lord Myself, do come and dwell in the midst of you ; thou shalt receive a greater knowledge of God, for I the Lord will refer the cause of My being sent to men to My Father who sent Me.   Thou shalt know that the Lord Almighty has sent Me unto you."

And then in such words as these the Lord Himself speaks about another Lord and God, "And I will strengthen them in the Lord their God, and in my name shall they boast, saith the Lord."   Who then are those who boast in the

(d) Lord ?

CHAPTER 27

*How again the Lord narrates concerning another
Lord, and this is clearly His Father.*   (253)

[Passage quoted, Zech. iii. 1.]

AND here again the Lord says that another Lord will
rebuke the devil. The Lord that is speaking with Him is
not himself the rebuker, but tells of another Lord. Wherein
I consider there is clear proof of the existence of two Lords,
the Father and God of the Universe, and One after the
Father, Who has received the lordship and dominion of all
things begotten.

CHAPTER 28   (b)

From Malachi.

*That the Almighty God calls the Angel of the Covenant
Christ, and the same Being Lord.*

[Passage quoted, Mal. iii. 1–2.]

THIS, too, is like the former prophecies. For the Lord God (c)
Himself, the Almighty, says that a Lord will come in His
own temple, speaking of another : And He surely means
God the Word. And after this also He names Him "the
Angel of the Covenant" of Whom, too, Almighty God teaches
that He will Him send forth before His face, saying,
" Behold, I send forth my angel before my face." And this
same Being, Whom He has called " My angel," He calls
Lord directly after, and adds, "The Lord shall suddenly
come, and the Angel of the Covenant." Thus having (d)
referred to one and the same Being, He proceeds, " Behold
he comes, and who will abide the day of his coming?"
meaning His Second and Glorious Coming. And the Lord
who makes this prophecy is God, the Sovereign of the
Universe.

(254)

CHAPTER 29

*That the God of the Universe names Christ the
Sun of Righteousness.*

[Passage quoted, Mal. iv. 2.]

He that has often been named Lord, and God, and Angel,
and Chief Captain, Christ and Priest, and Word and Wisdom
(b) of God, and Image, this same Being is now called Sun of
Righteousness. And we see that the Father that begat Him
proclaims that He will rise not on all, but only on those that
fear His Name, giving them the light of the Sun of Righteousness as a reward for their fear. He, then, must be God the
John viii. Word, Who said, "I am the Light of the world"; for He
12 and i. 9. was "the light that lighteth every man coming into the
world." He of course, and not the sun of nature, perceptible to all alike whether they have reason or not, He
(c) that is divine and spiritual, and the cause of all virtue and
justice, God says in this passage, will rise only on those that
fear Him, hiding Himself from the unworthy. Concerning
which He says somewhere else, " And the sun shall set upon
Mic. iii. 5 the prophets that deceive my people."
and 6.

CHAPTER 30

From Jeremiah.

(d)   *That God the Word, being Lord, prays to His Father,
prophesying the Conversion of the Gentiles.*

[Passage quoted, Jer. xvi. 19–21.]

(255) The Lord prays to another Lord, clearly His Father and
the God of the Universe, and says in the opening of His
prayer, "O Lord, thou art my strength," and that which
follows. And He clearly prophesies the conversion of the
Gentiles from idolatrous error to godly religion. And this
prophecy, moreover, has been shewn most clearly to have
been fulfilled after the Coming of our Saviour Jesus Christ
to men.

But now that we have, by thirty prophetic quotations in all, learned that our Lord and Saviour the Word of God is (b) God, a Second God after the Most High and Supreme, we will pass to another topic in connection with the theology of His Person, and prove from the holy books of the Hebrews that it was necessary for this same God to come to men.

The
Proof
of the
Gospel

EUSEBIUS

Edited and translated by
W. J. Ferrar

VOLUME II

EUSEBIUS: SON OF PAMPHILUS

THE PROOF OF THE GOSPEL

BOOK VI

In my fifth book of the *Proof of the Gospel* the doctrine of (257)
the Father and the Son has been clearly defined in the
confession of one Almighty God, and in the proof of a
Second Being coming after Him as Head of all begotten
things, Whom the Holy Scriptures named of old the Firstborn Wisdom of God, the Only-begotten Son, God of God, (b)
the Angel of Great Counsel, the Leader of the Host of
Heaven, the Minister of the Father, yea, even Lord of the
Universe, Word of God and Power of God, and if now
the witness of the prophets should shew that they foretold
that God intended to come to men, it will be abundantly
evident to whom we must apply this prediction, especially
as, according to what I have said already, the Word of God,
under the Name of Lord and God, appeared to human eyes,
to the pious men of Abraham's day, made in the form and (c)
likeness of man.

So let us now examine any such predictions of the Hebrew
oracles, that now the Lord, now God, would descend to
men and again ascend in their sight, and the causes of His
descent: and you will note that some prophecies are veiled
and some clearly expressed. I hold that the secret prophecies
were delivered in a disguised form because of the Jews, as (d)
the predictions concerning them were unfavourable; because
they would most probably have destroyed the writing, if it
had plainly foretold their final ruin; just as history shows
that they attacked the prophets, because they rebuked them.
But the prophecies that are clear include beyond all doubt

I

the call of the Gentiles, and announce the promises of the
reward of holiness not only to the Jewish race, but to all
men throughout the world.   As this is so, we must now
hear the divine oracles.

CHAPTER 1

(258)   *Of the Sojourn of the Word of God with Men.*

From Psalm xvii.

*The Shewing forth of the Coming of God to Men, and
the Consequent Call of the Gentiles.*

[Passage quoted, Ps. xvii. 9–11.]

I CONSIDER that we have here an express prophecy of God's
Descent from heaven.   For after telling many divine truths
he adds the above.   In saying "He bowed the heavens and
came down," he notes that humiliation of the Divine Glory,
which the divine apostle expressed, when he said :

(c)   "Who being in the form of God, did not consider it
Phil. ii. 6,   a prize to be equal with God, but emptied himself, and
7.   took the form of a servant."

And by the words, "He rode upon Cherubim and flew," I
believe he presents darkly the return to Divine Glory, which
He made surrounded by troops of angelic and divine powers.
And this also seems to be intended by, "He flew upon the
wings of the wind."   And by, "making darkness his secret-
place, and darkness under his feet," is signified the hidden
and secret dispensation, under which He accomplished all
this.   What shall we understand by "round about him
was his tabernacle" but His Holy Catholic Church, either
(d) the earthly, or the heavenly?   And afterwards at the end of
the same Psalm, there is a prophecy of the rejection of the
former people coincident with the call of the Gentiles :

"43. Save me from the gainsayings of the people,
thou wilt make me the head of the Gentiles.   A people
whom I have not known shall serve me.

"44. At the hearing of the ear they obeyed me : the
strange children lied to me.

"45. The strange children waxed old : and grew lame from their paths."
I will examine in the proper place what meaning is to be attributed to this.

CHAPTER 2   (259)

Psalm xlvi.

The Ascent of God Who had First descended, and the Calling of all the Gentiles thereafter, to know the One and Only God.

[Passage quoted, Ps. xlvi. 1–9.]

WHAT can the Ascension of the Lord God here mentioned imply, but a Descent previous to His Ascension, after which the calling of all the Gentiles is again prophesied, and good news of joy and gladness announced to all nations in their future knowledge of God, when the Lord Himself, He that is the one Most High God and King of all the earth, is said to subdue the peoples under us. And who are meant by "us"? Surely those who give the prophecy : which will (d) be clearly seen to be fulfilled, when all the nations that believe in Christ are subdued to the teaching of the prophets.

Or they might be spoken in the person of our Saviour's apostles, who also could say, " He has chosen out an inheritance for us." And what else could be understood by "his inheritance," but the calling of all nations, which the Christ of God shewed forth Himself, when He said : " The Lord said unto me, Thou art my Son : to-day have I Ps. ii. 7. begotten thee . . . Desire of me and I shall give the heathen for thine inheritance, and the bounds of the earth for thy possession ? " This inheritance, then, that was given Him by the Father He subordinated to His apostles and (260) prophets, by subduing those that believed on Him to their words agreeably to the above prophecies.

And the Word of God, of Whom I have discoursed so much, after accomplishing all things in His appearance among men, "ascended with a shout." This is interpreted by the apostle, who says : " That he ascended, what is it but Eph. iv. 9.

that he also descended first to the lower parts of the earth?
He that descended is the same as He Who ascended far above
all heavens." And he says that He ascended with a shout,
because of the companies of angels proclaiming His
(b) Divinity [1] as He went up, who also said : "Open your gates,
ye rulers, and be ye lift up, ye everlasting doors, and the
King of glory shall come in."

Ps. xxiii.
7.

And you would not err in identifying the sound of the
trumpet with the preaching of the Gospel heard in all the
world. For as the trumpet is the loudest of all musical
instruments, it seems a fit symbol to shew forth that the
teaching given to all men about Christ is proclaimed in
stronger and louder tones than any other teaching has ever
been, by which as by a trumpet for the hearing of all men
(c) the Holy Spirit shouts and cries what follows in this Psalm,
"Sing to the Lord, sing, sing to our King, sing, That God
is King" not only of the Jewish race in the future, he says,
but " of all the earth, sing with understanding."

No more the dæmons of old, he says, no more the earth-
bound and weak spirits,[2] but God Himself rules over all
the nations, God Himself, Who sits upon His holy seat.

(d) I have already in the preceding book treated of the throne
of God the Word, on which the Father bade Him sit,
"Sit thou on my right hand, till I make thine enemies the
footstool of thy feet." And we can still more clearly refer
the words, "The princes of the peoples were gathered
together with the God of Abraham," to the Gentile rulers of
the Christian Church coming into the inheritance of God's
pious prophets of old, who, waxing strong by the power of
the Saviour, have been lifted up, no man being able to cast
them down or humble them because of the right hand of
God that raises them and gives them power. But of this
(261) I will give fuller treatment when I have leisure.

---

[1] διὰ τὴν εἰς αὐτὸν θεολογίαν τῶν δορυφορούντων αὐτὸν ἀνιόντα
ἀγγέλων.
[2] ἀπατηλὰ πνεύματα. Cf. P.E. 7 a, 132 c, 242 c.

CHAPTER 3

From Psalm xlix.

How it is said that God will come clearly to Men, and will call all Races of Men to Himself.

[Passage quoted, Ps. xlix. 1–14.]

HERE the divine prediction clearly prophesies that God will come manifestly, meaning none other but the Word of God. And it shews the reason of His coming, again emphasizing the calling of all nations of the world. For it says, " He (d) has called the earth from the rising of the sun to the setting " ; and it teaches that the rejection of the outward worship according to the Mosaic Law will follow hard after His Manifestation and the calling of the Gentiles, a worship which actually ceased after the manifestation of the Word of God to all men. For from that day to this all men throughout all the world have been called, and all the nations of the east and west. And the Jewish worship has ceased (262) and been abolished, all men being called to worship according to the new Covenant of the preaching of the Gospel, and not according to the Law of Moses. We might also apply these prophecies to our Saviour's second and glorious Coming.

CHAPTER 4

From Psalm lxxxiii.

That God is said to be about to be seen on Earth through the Manifestation of the Christ to Men.

[Passage quoted, Ps. lxxxiii. 7.]

AFTER saying that the God of gods shall be seen, he prays (c) that His Manifestation may take place quickly, teaching in what manner He will be seen in the words, " Look on the face of thy Christ," as if he said more clearly, " Manifest thyself to us in the person of Christ." For since " He that John xiv hath seen me hath seen the Father that sent me," He naturally 9. promises that the God of God who dwells in Christ will manifest Himself in the Person of Christ.

CHAPTER 5

From Psalm xcv.

The Coming of Christ on Earth, and His Kingdom over the Gentiles, and the New Song which shall be given, not to Israel but to the Gentiles.

[Passage quoted, Ps. xcv. 1–13.]

(b) HERE again the Coming of the Lord to men is foretold, and that a new song shall be sung at His Coming, by which is meant the new Covenant, by the whole earth, not by the Jewish race ; and that the good news will be no longer for Israel, but for all the nations, since it says that the Lord Who is to come will be their King. But who could this be but God the Word, Who, intending to judge the world in righteousness and the human race in truth, reckons all men in the world equally worthy of His call, and of the salvation of God consequent thereon ?

(c)

CHAPTER 6

From Psalm xcvii.

The New Song, the Knowledge of the Heathen of the Lord's Righteousness and His Own Coming as Judge of the Universe.

[Passage quoted, Ps. xcvii. 1–8.]

IT is prophesied here that the Coming of the Lord will be the cause of great benefits to the nations, which have been proved to have actually accrued to them, through the manifestation of our Saviour. For of a truth from then and not before the new song of the new Covenant has been sung among all men, and His wonders have been known
(264) and heard by all men through the written gospels. Yea, and salvation also, by the Resurrection of the Lord from the dead, has been revealed to all nations, and the true righteousness, by which it has been clearly proved, that God is not the God of the Jews only, but of the Gentiles. "Since there is one God," in the words of the holy apostle,

"who will judge the circumcision from their faith, and the Rom. iii. uncircumcision through faith."[1]   And the words, "for he 30. cometh to judge the earth," might refer also to His second Coming."

CHAPTER 7

From Psalm cvii.

The Word of God sent forth for the Healing and Salvation of Souls Long Time afflicted with Evil.

[Passages quoted, Ps. cvii. 15–19, 32–36.]

THIS clearly gives the good news of the Descent of God the Word from heaven, Who is named, and of the result of His Coming.   For it says, "He sent his Word and healed them."   And we say distinctly that the Word of God was He that was sent as the Saviour of all men, Whom we are taught by the Holy Scriptures to reckon divine.   And it (265) darkly suggests that He came down even unto death for the sake of those who had died before Him, and in revealing the redemption of those to be saved by Him it shews the reason of His Coming.   For He saved without aid from any one those that had gone before Him even to the gates of death, healed them and rescued them from their destruction.   And this He did simply by breaking what are called the gates of death, and crushing the bars of iron.   And (b) then the prophecy proceeds to predict the state of desolation of those who rejected Him when He came.   For it says, "He turned rivers into a wilderness, and rivers of waters into thirst, a fruitful land into saltness for the wickedness of them that dwell therein": which you will understand if you behold Jerusalem of old, the famous city of the Jewish race, her glory and her fruitfulness, despoiled now of her holy citizens and pious men.   For (c) after the coming of Christ she became as the prophet truly says without fruit or water, and quite deserted, "saltness for the wickedness of them that dwell therein."

---

[1] καὶ ἀκροβυστίαν διὰ πίστεως : those words have dropped out of the Paris Edition.   Migne rejects.

To this is added quite in the prophetic manner a veiled prediction of the change of the long-time desert and thirsty land, referring either to the individual soul, or to the turning of the Gentile Church to holiness, and of its fertility in divine words. This is clearly predicted in a veiled way, when it says, "He made the desert into pools of water," and that which follows. But to understand this one must have wisdom from God; according to the monition at the end of the Psalm, which says, "Who is wise, and he will

(d) keep this?" and that which follows.

CHAPTER 8

From Psalms cxvii. and cxviii.

The Calling of the Gentiles, God Manifested, and Blessed is He that cometh in the Name of the Lord.

[Passages quoted, Pss. cxvii. 1 and cxviii. 25.]

(266) HOLY Scripture records that this prophecy was fulfilled when our Lord and Saviour Christ entered Jerusalem, and a great multitude of men and children went before Him
(b) crying with joy, "Hosanna to the Son of David, Blessed be he that cometh in the name of the Lord, Hosanna in the highest." For instead of, "O Lord, save us," as expressed
Matt. xxi. in the Psalm, they cried out the Hebrew "Hosanna," which
9. is translated by "save." And the words, "Blessed is he that cometh in the name of the Lord," explain the words that follow, "The Lord is God and hath appeared to us." It was, then, one and the same Lord God that appeared to them, that is to say the Word of God, as He Who is therefore blessed, because He came among men in the name of
(c) the Lord His Father that sent Him. It was therefore in reproof of the Jews that disbelieved in Him, that He said: "I came in the name of my Father, and ye received me not.
John v. 43. But if one come in his own name, him will ye receive." So the Holy Spirit suitably addresses the opening verses of the Psalm not to the Jewish people, but to all the nations.

CHAPTER 9

From Psalm cxliii.

The Descent of the Lord from Heaven for Men's Salvation, (d)
*and the New Song sung thereafter, which is the Song
of the New Covenant.*

[Passages quoted, Ps. cxliii. 3, 5, 9.]

I CONSIDER this to be connected with my present subject. (267)
For in his wonder at the knowledge of God the Word
coming to men, the Psalmist is astonished above measure
at the love by which He descends from His Divinity, and
lessens His natural Majesty, and reckons the human race
worthy of bearing Him.   So here he prays, saying, "Lord,
bow the heavens and descend."   While in the Seventeenth
Psalm it is written, "And he bowed the heavens, and
descended, and it was dark under his feet.   And he rode
upon Cherubim, and flew, he flew upon the wings of the
winds," wherein there is a prophecy of His Ascension (b)
from earth to heaven.   And when there is a fit opportunity
I will shew that we must understand the Descent and
Ascension of God the Word not as of one moving locally,
but in the metaphorical sense which Scripture intends in
the use of such conventional terms.[1]

But we should also note here the new Covenant, into
which the Coming of Christ was about to invite men.   And
the new Covenant is that which succeeds the old and is
given to all nations.   And so the oracle before us says,
"O God, I will sing a new song to thee."   The words, (c)
"Touch the mountains and they shall smoke," I think are
a veiled prophecy of the burning and abolition of all forms
of idolatry, which had its chief seats among the ancients
in mountains, it being a common charge against the Jews
themselves, that they worshipped idols on every high
mountain in imitation of foreign nations.

---

[1] Interesting in view of modern controversies.

CHAPTER 10

(d)
From Psalm cxlvii.

The Word of God sent on Earth, and in a Short Time running through All Nations.

[Passage quoted, Ps. cxlvii. 12, 15.]

"HE that sendeth his word on earth, until his word runs swiftly." He that sends is evidently distinct from Him that (268) is sent. You have then, here, both the Sender, the Almighty God, and also the Word that was sent, Who having many names is called by the holy oracles now Wisdom, now Word, now God, and also Lord. And as you know how in a very short time the word of His teaching has filled the whole world, I am sure you will wonder at the fulfilment of the prophecy, "Till his word runs swiftly."

CHAPTER 11

From the Second Book of Kings [= 2 Samuel].

(c) *The Lord descending from Heaven, Leader of the Nations that before knew Him not, and about to cast off the Jewish Nation.*

[Passages quoted, 2 Sam. xxii. 1, 10–12, 44–46.]

(d) THE God that bowed the heavens and came down, Who mounted upon the man whom He had chosen, called here Cherubim by Scripture, flew up with Him making His Ascension with the divine spirits as His bodyguard, and these are called the wings of the winds. And it suggests that this was done darkly and in obscurity [1] by some secret and hidden words, when it says, "And he made darkness his secret place." What follows agrees with the Incarnation of Christ and shews the opposition of the Jewish people to Him, and the obedience of the Gentiles to His teaching.

---

[1] ἐν παραβύστῳ = " pushed aside or in a corner," a term borrowed from a minor Athenian Law Court (Lys. ap. Poll. 8, 121 ; Pausan. 1, 28, 8). Cf. Dem. 715, 20 ; Arist. Top. 8, 1, 17.

You will find similar sayings in the Seventeenth Psalm, about which I have already given my views.[1]

CHAPTER 12   (269)

From the Third Book of Kings [= First Book of Kings].

*God descending from Heaven, and dwelling with
Men on Earth.*

[Passage quoted, 1 Kings viii. 26, 27.]

THIS is also found in the same words in Chronicles. God (b) then promised David He would raise up a king from His body, and would be His father, so that the offspring of the seed of David should be called the Son of God, and should have His throne in an eternal kingdom. This was prophe- (c) sied to David by Nathan in the Second Book of Kings as follows :

"And it shall come to pass when thy days shall have been fulfilled, and thou shalt sleep with thy fathers, that I will raise up thy seed after thee, who shall come from thy body, and I will prepare his kingdom. He shall build a house to my name, and I will establish his throne for ever. I will be to him a father, and he shall 2 Sam. vii. be to me a son." 12.

The same is also said in Chronicles. And in the 88th Psalm it is written :

"27. He shall call on me, Thou art my Father, | my God and the helper of my salvation. | 28. And I will (d) will make him my firstborn, | high among the kings of the earth. | 29. I will keep my mercy for him for ever, | and my covenant shall stand fast with him, | 30. and I Ps. will make his seed last for ever and ever, | and his lxxxviii. throne as the days of heaven." | 27.

And again :

"4. I have sworn | to David my servant, | 5. I will prepare thy seed for ever, | and I will build thy throne from generation to generation." |

----

[1] See ii. 2.

And once more :

"36. I have sworn once by my holiness that I will
not lie to David. | 37. His seed shall remain for ever, |
and his throne is as the sun before me, | 38. and as
the moon that is established for ever." |

(270) And Psalm 131, too, when it records this, refers the matter
to Christ.   Hear what it says :

"1. Remember, Lord, David and all his gentleness ; |
2. how he sware to the Lord and vowed a vow unto the
God of Jacob." |

Ps. cxxxi.
1.

To which he adds afterwards :

"11. The Lord sware the truth to David, and he will
not abolish him.[1] | Of the fruit of thy body will I set
upon thy seat." |

And a little lower down he names more definitely Him that
is to arise of the fruit of David's body, as follows :

(b)   "17. There will I raise up the horn of David, | I have
prepared a lantern for my Christ. | 18. His enemies I
will clothe with shame ; | but on him shall his glory
flower." |

And so Solomon being unique in wisdom, understanding
this oracle given to his father, and perceiving it to be no
slight thing, but something beyond human nature, and
more suitable to God than to himself, son of David though
he was, and knowing who was meant by God by the Firstborn, and who was clearly foretold as the Son of God, was
overjoyed at the message, and prayed that the words of the
prophecy might be confirmed, and that He that was foretold might come, calling Him Firstborn and Son of God.

(c) So he says, " And now, O God of Israel, let thy word be
confirmed which thou spakest to thy servant David my
father : Shall God truly dwell with men on earth, if the
heaven and the heaven of heavens will not suffice thee ? "

[1] S.: αὐτήν.   E.: αὐτὸν.

CHAPTER 13

From Micah.

Concerning the Descent from Heaven to Men, and concerning the Fall of the Jewish Nation at His Coming, and the Incorporation of All the Other Nations.

[Passage quoted, Micah i. 2–5.]   (271)

HERE, too, in this passage the Descent of the Lord coming forth from His place is proclaimed plainly. This must mean (b) the Word of God, Whom I have proved in the previous books to be alone God and Lord after the Supreme and Almighty God. His place you would rightly understand to be the kingdom of heaven, and the glorious throne of His Divinity, of which the prophet sang in praise of God, saying, "Thy throne, O God, is for ever and ever," on which the Father bade Him sit as being His Only-begotten Son, saying, "Sit thou on my right hand." For I have already shewn (c) that these words can only be referred to our Saviour, God the Word. So, then, the prophecy before us says that He comes forth from His place, and will descend upon the high-places of the earth. How are we to understand this? Shall we take it literally of the hills and mountains of Israel, which are the subjects of so many prophecies, Jerusalem itself and Mount Sion, in which our Lord and Saviour spent so much time? If so, their destruction and ruin at (d) the descent of Christ would be prophesied. And it is the fact that after the Saviour's coming and the treatment He received all the hills mentioned were besieged, and utterly desolated. But the rulers of the Jewish people as well, and their kingdom that existed previously, their sacrificial system and the seats of their teachers, here called Mountains metaphorically, are said to be shaken by the Descent of the Lord from heaven. And who could deny that this was fulfilled after the time of our Saviour Jesus Christ, when he sees all these things not only shaken, but abolished? And the valleys even now melting are the Jewish synagogues established in all cities instead of Jerusalem and Mount (272) Sion, which are full of lamentation and wailing, and melting as wax at the fire with grief and extreme sorrow for the desolation of their homes and their long and lasting slavery. And the coming of the Word of God regarded in another light took place not in chasms and valleys, nor in lowly and earth-bound thoughts, but in exalted souls. And so the Lord Himself is said in a wider metaphor to be about to (b) descend on the high-places of earth. Then the mountains shaken under Him will be those very heights whither He "was led by the spirit to be tempted of the devil," "when the devil leadeth him to an exceeding high mountain, and he was with the wild beasts." Or the mountains again might represent in metaphor the idolatry practised formerly on mountains, and the principalities and powers working there invisibly, which our Saviour's teaching was to shake and (c) overthrow in no small degree. For His inspired word and His miraculous and wondrous strength have insensibly destroyed the powers which from far ages have attacked mankind. In like manner also the hills melting like wax from the presence of the fire would be the infernal and earth-bound dæmons, against whom He sent forth fire to consume their lust, saying, "I came to cast fire upon the earth, and what will I if it be already kindled?" Burned by which fire, and unable to bear the torture of its unseen flame, they withdrew from the bodies of men, and acknow- (d) ledged that which controlled them and drove them out, crying, "Let us alone, what have we to do with thee, Son of God? Hast thou come to torment us before the time? We know thee who thou art, the Holy One of God." And these He chiefly chastised, and destroyed their princes, because not content with the corruption of the other nations, whereby they had cast them all into the errors of polytheism, they had also plotted against God's ancient people, those of the Circumcision, and had endeavoured to seduce even them from their God to all manner of impiety. And this was the chief reason why the Lord descended from heaven. Wherefore He says next, "For the iniquity of Jacob is all this done, and for the transgression of my people Israel." And then He gives an additional reason for the Descent of (273) the Word, recounting the impiety of the Jews, and the destruction falling upon them, and heralding the calling of all nations throughout the world. For these things' sake the Word of God came down from heaven to earth. Hear this passage:

Marginal notes:

Matt. iv. 8 with Mark i. 13 b.

Luke xii. 49.

Matt. viii. 29. Mark i. 24.

Micah i. 5.

"5. For the impiety of the House of Jacob is all this
done, and for the transgression of the House of Israel.
What is the impiety of the House of Jacob? Is it not
Samaria? And what is the sin of Judah? Is it not
Jerusalem? 6. And I will make Samaria a lodge of
the field, and a plantation of a vineyard, and I will draw (b)
down to chaos the stones thereof, and will hide the
foundations thereof."

And He adds :

"12. Evil hath descended from the Lord on the gates Micah i.
of Jerusalem, the noise of chariots and horsemen."　　12.

And again :

"15. O glory of the daughter of Jerusalem, shave
and cut off thy choice children. Enlarge thy widow-
hood, as an eagle, when thy captives are led from Micah i.
thee."　　　　　　　　　　　　　　　　　　　　15.

And moreover :

"Sion shall be ploughed as a field, and Jerusalem
shall be as a granary, and the mount of the house as Micah iii.
a grove of the wood."　　　　　　　　　　　　　　12.

Sion and Jerusalem and the so-called " mount of the house " (c)
are what were represented before in, " And the mountains
shall be shaken from beneath him, and, the valleys shall be
melted as wax before the fire for the iniquity of Jacob."
For the mountains and the dwellers thereon were besieged
for the iniquity they had wrought against Him soon and not
long after Mount Sion was burned and left utterly desolate,
and the Mount of the House of God became as a grove of
the wood.

If our own observation has any value, we have seen in
our own time Sion once so famous ploughed with yokes of
oxen by the Romans and utterly devastated, and Jerusalem, (d)
as the oracle says, deserted like a lodge.[1] And this has
come to pass precisely because of their impieties, for the

---

[1] Cf. 406 c : Σιὼν ὄρος . . . διὰ Ῥωμαίων ἀνδρῶν κατ' οὐδὲν τῆς λοιπῆς
διαφέρουσα χώρας γεωργεῖται, ὡς καὶ ἡμᾶς αὐτοὺς ὀφθαλμοῖς παραλαβεῖν
βουσὶν ἀρούμενον καὶ κατασπειρόμενον τὸν τόπον.—Epiphanius (de Mens.
et Pond. xiv. ; Migne, P.G. xliii. col. 259) in the fourth century states
that Hadrian found the Temple trodden under foot, with a few houses
standing, the Cœnaculum, and seven synagogues " that stood alone in
Sion like cottages." There is no reason to suppose that Eusebius'
valuable witness that part of the Temple area was under cultivation in
his day is incorrect or merely rhetorical.

sake of which the Heavenly Word has come forth from
His own place.

And I have already said that the Word of God came
down from heaven and descended on the high places of the
earth for other reasons, both that the mountains which of
old lifted themselves up and exalted themselves against the
(274) knowledge of God might be shaken beneath Him (that is
to say the opposing powers, which before His coming enslaved the Hebrew race as well as the rest of mankind in
the practice of impiety and idolatry), and also that the
evil dæmons called valleys (through their living in gloomy
(b) chasms, and in the recesses of the body) might melt as wax
before the fire and flee away from men by the power of the
divine Word.   And there was another additional reason
by no means fortuitous for the descent of the Lord from
heaven, which this prophecy recognizes, namely that all the
nations on earth, the dæmons being banished and the ruling
spirits shaken, recovering from the cruel and ceaseless
tyranny which had long afflicted them, might attain the
knowledge of Almighty God.   And the voice of the same
prophet proclaims the same things further on as follows,
uniting them in the same manner under one head :

"And in the last days the Mount of the Lord shall
(c)   be glorious, prepared [1] upon the tops of the mountains,
and it shall be exalted above the hills, and peoples shall
haste unto it, and many nations shall come and say,
Come, let us go up to the Mount of the Lord, and the
house of the God of Jacob, and they will shew us his
way, and we will walk in his paths.[2]   For out of Sion
shall come forth a law, and the word of the Lord from
Isa. ii. 2.   Jerusalem, and he will judge in the midst of the nations."

One can learn at one's leisure in what sense such prophecies of the Call of the Gentiles are to be understood, and
that they were only fulfilled after the coming of our Saviour.
And the opening of the prophecy is in full agreement with
(d) the truth that the Lord descended not only for the salvation
of the Jewish race, but for that of all nations, in proclaiming to all peoples and all the inhabitants of the earth, saying,
"Hear all peoples, and let the earth attend, and all that are

---

[1] LXX : καὶ ὁ οἶκος τοῦ Θεοῦ ἐπ᾽ ἄκρου τῶν ὀρέων, καὶ ὑψωθήσεται.
E. : ἕτοιμον ἐπὶ τὰς κορυφὰς τῶν ὀρέων, καὶ μετεωοισθήσεται.
[2] LXX : ἐν αὐτῇ, for ἐν ταῖς τρίβοις αὐτοῦ.

therein." And it darkly foretold the witness of the Passion of our Lord, adding, "And the Lord our God shall be for a witness."

And after this the same prophet, having prepared the way by telling of what related to the fact of the Descent of God the Word from heaven, and foretold what should be the causes of His coming, proceeds to relate His birth among men, and to name the place where He should be born, in (275) the following words :

> " 2. And thou, Bethlehem, house of Ephratha, art the least to be among the thousands of Judah, out of thee shall come forth for me a leader,[1] to be for a ruler in Israel, and his goings-forth are from the beginning from the days of eternity."

Micah v 2.

Note with care how he says that the goings-forth of Him that shall appear at Bethlehem are from above and from eternity, by which he shews the pre-existence and essential origin of Him that is to come forth from Bethlehem. Now if (b) any person can apply the oracle to any one but Jesus, let him shew who it is ; but if it is impossible to find any one but our Lord Jesus Christ, Who is the only Person after the date of this prophecy Who came forth thence and attained to fame, what should hinder us from acknowledging the truth of the prophecy, which directs its prediction on Him only? For He alone of all men is known to have come forth from the before-named Bethlehem after the date of the prophecy, putting on a human shape, and what had been (c) foretold was fulfilled at His coming. For at once and not after a long time the woes that were foretold fell on the Jewish nation, and blessings in accordance with the prophecies on the nations as well, and He Himself, our Lord and Saviour Who came from Bethlehem, was shewn to be the ruler of the spiritual Israel, such being the name of all people of vision and piety. Note too that it is said that the goings-forth of His Divine Pre-existence are from the beginning and from the days of eternity, which would not agree with mere humanity. (d)

Then the word of the prophet, a little further on, suggests again the curtailing and abolition of the ancient ritual of the Law, speaking in the person of the people :

---

[1] LXX omits ἡγούμενος.

"6. Wherewithal shall I reach the Lord, and lay hold of my God most high? Shall I reach him by whole burnt-offerings, by calves a year old?[1] 7. Should I give my firstborn for my ungodliness, the fruit of my body for the sin of my soul?"

Micah vi. 6.

And he makes this answer to them in the person of God:

"8. Has it not been told thee, O man, what is good? And what does the Lord require of thee, but to do judgment, and to love mercy, and to be ready to walk after thy God?"[2]

(276) You have then in this prophecy of the Descent of the Lord among men from heaven, many other things foretold at the same time, the rejection of the Jews, the judgment on their impiety, the destruction of their royal city, the abolition of the worship practised by them of old according to the Law of Moses; and on the other hand, promises of good for the nations, the knowledge of God, a new ideal of holiness, a new law and teaching coming forth from the land of the Jews. I leave you to see, how wonderful a fulfilment, how wonderful a completion, the prophecy has reached after the

(b) Coming of our Saviour Jesus Christ.

CHAPTER 14

From Habakkuk.

(c) *That it was prophesied that the Word of God that cometh will come and will not tarry.*

[Passage quoted, Hab. ii. 2.]

AND here it is clearly foretold that the subject of the prophecy who is coming will come. Who could this be but he (d) who is referred to above in the words, "Blessed is he that cometh in the name of the Lord, the Lord God also has shone upon us"? With which also Zechariah agrees, when he says: "Behold a man, the Dawn[3] is his name, and

Hab. ix. 26.
Zech. vi. 12.

---

[1] E. omits Εἰ προσδέξεται κυρίος ἐν χιλιάσι κριῶν; ἢ ἐν μυριάσι χιμάρων πιόνων;
[2] LXX: μετὰ κυρίου Θεοῦ σου. E.; ὀπίσω.
[3] ἀνατολή.

he shall rise from below." The same prophet, too, noting Zech. xiv.
the time adds, "At eventide it shall be light. If he delays, 7.
wait for him." Instead of which Aquila reads, "If he tarry
expect him, for he that cometh will come, and will not
tarry." And the Epistle to the Hebrews has this in mind
when it says:

> "Cast not away then your confidence, which has
> great recompense of reward. For ye have need of
> patience, that, doing the will of God, ye may receive
> the promise. For yet a little while, and he that cometh (277)
> will come, and will not tarry. And the just shall live Heb. x.
> by my faith.[1] And if he draw back, my soul hath no 35.
> pleasure in him."

And note how clearly the Epistle arranges what was
obscure in the prophetic writing, because of the inversion
of the clauses.[2] For the prophecy says," He that cometh
will come and will not tarry, and adds, "If he draw back,
my soul hath no pleasure in him," and this addition would
seem to refer to him that cometh and doth not tarry, which (b)
is absurd. For how could it be said of him that God
takes no pleasure in him?[3] But the placing side by side of
the divided clauses by a change in the arrangement of
them preserves the sense. For after, "Yet a little while and
he that cometh will come and shall not tarry," it adds next,
"The just shall live by my faith.[4] Then what was first in
the prophecy it places second in, "And if he draw back my
soul taketh no pleasure in him." For as Scripture has
already once foretold through the prophecy, that the light (c)
promised to all nations by Christ's Coming "shall rise late
and in the evening, and shall not deceive" (for so Aquila
interprets instead of "come to nothing,") it next exhorts to
patience, because the coming of the subject of the prophecy
is to be late and in the evening, in the words, "If he tarry (d)
await him, or if he delay expect him, for he that cometh

---

[1] W. H.: ὁ δὲ δίκαιός [μου] ἐκ πίστεως ζήσεται. E.: ὁ δὲ δίκαιος ἐκ
πίστεώς μου ζήσεται.

[2] διὰ τὸ καθ᾽ ὑπερβατόν — The figure Hyperbaton, i. e. a trans-
position of words or clauses. Quintil. Inst. 8, 6, 65, etc. ὑπερβατικός,
of Thucydides. Marcellin. Vit. Thucy. 50. σύνθεσις ὑπερβατή. Arist.
Rhet. Al. 26, 1 and 3. Cf. Plato, Prot. 343 e.

[3] ἀλλ᾽ ἡ τῆς διαστολῆς παράθεσις ἐναλλάξασα τὴν τοῦ λόγου σύνπαξιν
τὴν διάνοιαν ἐσώσατο.

[4] ἐκ πίστεώς μου.

will come and will not tarry," and encourages the hearer to trust the prediction, saying, that he that trusts it, shewn by his very faith to be just, shall live the life according to God, as on the other hand he that does not trust, drawing back through lack of boldness, and putting no faith in the words, "My soul hath no pleasure in him." So, then, if we follow this course and place the first clause last, and the last first, we shall preserve the sense of the passage, putting, "The just shall live by my faith," after, "For he that cometh will come and will not tarry," by transposing the clauses, and (278) adding to this, "If he draw back my soul taketh no pleasure in him." And Aquila agrees with this interpretation saying, "If he delay, expect him, for he that cometh will come, and will not tarry. Lo, if he be sluggish,[1] my soul is not true in him, and the just shall live by his faith."

CHAPTER 15

From the same.

That the Hearing about the Descent of the Lord from Heaven is Terrible, and His Works Wonderful, and at His Coming the Whole Earth shall be filled with His Praise, when the Word of His New Covenant shall pervade all Men.

[Passage quoted, Hab. iii. 2–5.]

(d) LISTENING to himself, or rather to the divine prophetic spirit within him, which said of the subject of the prophecy, "He that cometh will come, and will not tarry, and the just shall live by my faith," and believing as a just man in the oracle, the holy prophet says in the passage before us, "O Lord, I have heard thy report, and I was afraid," and the words that follow in which he clearly announces that God will come to men.

And who could this be who was known of old, and was to be known afterwards when the time drew near, and (279) was to be shewn forth at the date predicted, but that same Being before shewn to be the second Lord of the Universe, who agreeably to the prophecy at the end of the ages has

---

[1] νωχελευομένου. Cf. νωχελής. P.E. 114 a. Eur., Or. 800. The verb seems only to be used here.

been proclaimed for all to hear? It was surely His works that are written in the Holy Gospels, and it was clearly His Birth from the Virgin Tabernacle whence he sprang, and how "being in the form of God, he thought it not a thing to be grasped at to be equal with God, but emptied himself, taking the form of a slave," and it was the miracles He Phil. ii. 6. performed among men, and the insults offered to Him by the Jewish race that the prophet anticipated with the eyes (b) of his soul; and learning of the Holy Spirit his Teacher what would accrue to minds purified from sin, he confessed that he was astonished and afraid at what he heard, and said, "Lord, I have heard thy report, and I was afraid, I understood thy works, and was astonished."

Our Lord and Saviour, too, the Word of God Himself, "was known between two lives." The word ζωῶν is plural and accented with circumflex on the last syllable as the plural of the singular noun ζωή (life). It is not ζώων [1] (c) *accented acute on the penultimate* from ζῶον (a living creature), but [2] *with circumflex on the last syllable* (ζωῶν) from nominative plural ζωαί (lives). He says, therefore, He was known between two *lives*. One life is that according to God, the other that according to man; the one mortal, the other eternal. And the Lord having experienced both, is rightly said to have been made known between two lives in the LXX translation. Aquila translates differently: "In the nearing of the years, cause it to live." What does "it" mean here but "thy work"? And Theodotion says: "In (d) the midst of the years, cause him to live," and Symmachus renders: "Within the years, revive him." They all by the use of ζώωσον (cause to live) shew clearly that the word in the original does not refer to irrational or rational animals. And so following the rendering of the Septuagint, "He was made known between two lives," and not the commentators who have preceded me, I understand that the two lives of the Subject of the prophecy are referred to, the Divine and the Human.[3]

---

[1] παροξύτονος: Jo. Alex. τῶν παραγγ, p. 16. For the adverb: Ath. 409 A. For παροξυτονέω, Eust. 1600, 18. The older grammarians always have παροξύνω, as Ath. 320 C.

[2] περισπώμενος, Ath. 400 A. Gramm.

[3] Hab. iii. 2 has ἐν μέσῳ δύο ζῴων γνωσθήσῃ (Swete), in opposition to E.'s ζῴων. See S. R. Driver, Minor Prophets, *Century*

To this the prophet adds : "When my soul is troubled thou wilt in wrath remember mercy," teaching that when he foresaw the time of the Passion of the Subject of the (280) prophecy he was troubled in spirit. Yet at that very time, he says, in which I was troubled in spirit, though at no other time such anger ever threatened men for the impiety dared against their Lord, the Lord of Love Himself in place of wrath remembered mercy, as the Son of the good Father. For His Passion became to all the world the ground of God's salvation and mercy.

To this is added : "God will come from Thæman." (b) And Thæman translated into Greek is "consummation," so that it means simply, "God will come at the consummation." For at the consummation of the age and in these last days the kindness of the God of the Universe has been made evident to us through our Saviour.

But perhaps he foretells also His Second Coming in glory, in which case a fresh beginning is made at "God will come from Thæman," as shewing that at the consummation of the age He will come from the southern part of the heaven. For Thæman is translated "south." Wherefore Theodotion (c) translates thus : "God will come from the south." And you will understand the sentence that follows if you compare with it these words in Zechariah :

"8. I saw the night, and behold a man sitting on a bay horse, and he stood in the midst of the shady Zech. i. 8.   mountains."

I believe this rider on the bay horse who stands in the midst of the shady mountains to be the same person mentioned in the prophecy before us, which says that the Holy One will come from a thick and shady mountain.

Bible, p. 86 (ver. 2) : "LXX for most of the last clause and for this have the curious and in part double and even treble rendering, 'In the midst of two animals [a misreading or confusion of the Heb. words rendered rightly, "In the midst of years revive it"] thou shalt be known, when the years draw nigh thou shalt be recognized, when the time approaches thou shalt be declared.'" Driver says this is the origin of the pictures of the Infant Jesus between an ass and an ox, suggested also by Isa. i. 3. He quotes A. West (*Contemporary Review*, Dec. 1903, pp. 873 *sq.*, who states that this interpretation of the LXX of Hab. iii. 2 b is first found in *The Gospel of Pseudo-Matthew* at the end of the fifth century.

In each passage shady mountains are mentioned, and I
believe they refer to the Paradise of God, which He planted (d)
eastward in Eden, or perhaps to the Heavenly Jerusalem.
For "there are mountains around it, and the Lord is in Ps. cxxv.
the midst of his people."   And these mountains are said 2.
to be shady, because they are full of divine powers and
holy spirits, as of trees planted there and far-spreading.
But in Zechariah clearly the vision was of a man riding on
a bay horse, by which the Incarnation of our Saviour was
meant, and the flesh in which He rode : while here "God
a Holy One" is named.   For to mark that it was from
God that He made His approach to men, and that He
arrived from diviner regions, it is said, "God came from
Thæman, and the Holy One from a thick and shady
mountain."   And then it adds : "His glory covered the
heavens, and the earth is full of his praise, and his ray (281)
shall be as light."   In which both the glory of His Heavenly
Kingdom is shewn, and also the increase of the praise of
the teaching about Him that will be spread through all the
earth.   And the expression, "horns in his hands," shews
the symbols of His rule, wherewith He drives away the
invisible and opposing powers by pushing and butting them.
And agreeing with this he adds : "He made the love of
his power strong"; and the greatest sign of His strong (b)
affection and love to men was "that his Word should go
before his face," meaning the Gospel of Salvation, which
should come forth and scour the plains, so that soon all
the world should be filled with the salvation offered by Him
to all men according to the prophecy which said, " Before
his face shall his Word go forth, and shall go out into the
plains."   His Word will bring a further and more exact (c)
fulfilment to this prophecy and its context at His Second
Coming, which it is not now the place to expound.

CHAPTER 16

From Zechariah.

*That the Almighty Lord states that He is sent by Another
Almighty Lord for the Destruction of the Wicked.*

[Passage quoted, Zech. ii. 8.]

IN these words the Almighty Lord Himself says that He
has been sent, and teaches who it was that sent Him,
saying, "And ye shall know that the Almighty Lord has
sent me." Here, then, you have clearly two Persons using
one Name, the Almighty Lord that sent, and Him that is
(282) sent having the same Name as the Sender. And whom else
could you suppose Him that is sent to be, but Him that
we have so often called God the Word, Who states that He
is sent by the Father, and says clearly, "After his glory
he has sent me," shewing that though pre-existing in the
glory of the Father He was sent afterwards unto the nations
that spoiled you? For the Word of God was sent unto the
nations, who before were hostile to the people of God, and
subjected them to Himself, making a spoil of them by His
(b) disciples, who belonged to the Jewish nation, which the
Gentiles had long spoiled enslaving it to their own idolatry.
This, then, He says that the nations will suffer, as He
ordained. For as they perverted the people of God from
their ancestral religion, and made them a spoil for their
own dæmons, so some day shall they be made spoils from
their fathers' idolatry to them who of old have served them,
and be brought under the yoke of the Jewish religion.
And the Lord says that this will be done by Himself, as
(c) He will be sent by His Father to accomplish it. It might
also be said that certain invisible spiritual powers are meant
by the nations which spoiled and enslaved the souls of men,
which the Word of God here says He loves as the apple of
His eye. And the proof of His great love to the human
race is that He did not draw back, though He was the
(d) Word of God and in the glory of the Father, but agreed to
live with men and govern them.

CHAPTER 17

From the same.

How the Lord foretells that He will come from Heaven and dwell among Men, and that the Nations will flee to Him, and He states that He was sent by Another Almighty Lord stronger than Himself.

[Passage quoted, Zech. ii. 10.]

As it is now my object to unfold from the prophets the (283) second cause of our Lord's living our life on earth, the prophecy before us appears to state it so clearly that it hardly needs any elaboration.   You will notice that He (b) gives the cause of His coming, where He says, "And many nations shall flee unto the Lord in that day, and they shall be to me for a people."   And the Word announces this to the daughter of Sion, calling the Church of God by this name, through her seeming to be the daughter of the heavenly Jerusalem, she that is the mother of the Saints, according to the holy apostle.   Or the Church of God (c) might be called the daughter of Sion for another reason as one separated from the former congregation of the Jews by the apostles and evangelists, who also were the children of a mother divorced for her own impiety, and a widow because she had driven away her Husband, Who rebuked her by the prophets and said, "Hast thou not called me Jer. iii. 4. as a husband, and father, and leader of thy virginity?" And accusing their mother's ways also to them that were born of her He says: "Where is the bill of thy mother's divorcement, by which I rejected her?"[1]   And again: Isa. l. 1. "Judge the cause of your mother, judge it, because she (d) is not my wife, and I am not her husband."   Hos. ii. 2.

So, then, this prophecy rightly announces the presence of the Lord to those who had rejected their mother (calling them) the daughter of the Lord.   And it is the Church of the Gentiles that is reckoned by the apostles of our Saviour to have taken the place of her that before was daughter.

[1] S.: τὸ ἥμισυ αὐτοῦ πρὸς ἀνατολὰς καὶ θάλασσαν.

CHAPTER 18

From the same.

(284)   *Of the Coming of the Lord, and of the Events of His Passion.*

[Passage quoted, Zech. xiv. 1–10.]

AFTER the first siege of Jerusalem, and its total destruction and desolation by the Babylonians, and after the Return of the Jews from their enemies' land to their own, which came to pass in the time of Cyrus king of Persia, when (285) Jerusalem has just been restored, and the Temple and its Altar renewed by Darius the Persian, the present prophecy foretells a second siege of Jerusalem which is to take place afterwards, which it suffered from the Romans, after its inhabitants had carried through their outrage on our Saviour Jesus Christ. Thus the coming of our Saviour and the events connected therewith are very clearly shewn in this passage—I mean what was done at the time of His Passion, and the siege that came on the Hebrew race directly after, the taking of Jerusalem, the call of the Gentiles also, and the knowledge attained by all nations of (b) the one and only God. But the inspired prophet pathetically bewails the woes of the Jews as those of his own people, and begins his prophecy with a cry against them. He means by "days of the Lord," here as well as in other places, the time of our Lord's presence among men. And he clearly shews how the Lord Himself, as being the true (c) Light, will become some day the maker of His own days, and will shine on all men in the world, all the nations receiving Him and the rays of His light, when all nations are enlightened, according to the words, "I have set Thee for a light to the Gentiles, for a covenant of my race," and the Jewish nation through their unbelief will fall into great trouble.

For such is the meaning of "Behold the days of the Lord come, and thy spoils shall be divided within thee, and I will gather all the Gentiles to Jerusalem to war. And the city shall be taken, the houses plundered, and (d) the women ravished, and half of the city shall go into Isa. xlii. 6. captivity."

And after the siege of Jerusalem, and the captivity of the Jews which succeeds it, he next adds a prophecy of good things for all: "And the Lord shall be King over all the earth." And again: "There shall be one Lord, and his name one, encircling all the earth and the wilderness."

But who would not be surprised at the fulfilment of a prophecy which revealed that the Jewish people would undergo these sufferings in the days of the Lord? For as soon as Jesus our Lord and Saviour had come and the Jews had outraged Him, everything that had been predicted was fulfilled against them without exception 500 years after (286) the prediction: from the time of Pontius Pilate to the sieges under Nero, Titus and Vespasian they were never free from all kinds of successive calamities, as you may gather from the history of Flavius Josephus. It is probable that half the city at that time perished in the siege, as the prophecy says. And not long after, in the reign of Hadrian, there was another Jewish revolution, and the remaining half of the city was again besieged and driven out, so that from that day to this the whole place has not been trodden by (b) them.

Now if any one supposes that this was fulfilled in the time of Antiochus Epiphanes, let him inquire if the rest of the prophecy can be referred to the times of Antiochus—I mean the captivity undergone by the people, the standing of the Lord's feet on the Mount of Olives, and whether the Lord became King of all the earth in that day, and whether the name of the Lord encircled the whole earth and the desert during the reign of Antiochus. And how can the (c) fulfilment of the remainder of the prophecy in the days of Antiochus be asserted? But, according to my interpretation,[1] they are fulfilled both literally and also in another sense. For after the coming of our Saviour Jesus Christ, their city, Jerusalem itself, and the whole system and institutions of the Mosaic worship were destroyed; and at once they underwent captivity in mind as well as body, in (d) refusing to accept the Saviour and Ransomer of the souls Isa. lxi. 1; of men, Him Who came to preach release to those enslaved Luke iv. by evil dæmons, and giving of sight to those blind in mind. 18. And while they suffered through their unbelief, those of

---

[1] καθ' ἡμᾶς.

them who recognized their Ransomer became His own disciples, apostles and evangelists, and many others of the Jews believed on Him, of whom the apostle says, "So also now there is a remnant according to the election of grace." And "If the Lord of Sabaoth had not left unto us a seed we should have been as Sodom, and we should have been like unto Gomorra." They were preserved safe from the metaphorical siege, and also from the siege literally understood. For the apostles and disciples of our Saviour, and all the Jews that believed on Him, being far from the land of Judæa, and scattered among the other nations, were enabled at that time to escape the ruin of the inhabitants of Jerusalem. And the prophecy anticipated and foretold this where it said, "And the remnant of my people shall not be utterly destroyed." To which it adds afterwards, "And the Lord shall go forth, and shall fight for those nations, as a day of his battle in the day of war." For which nations will the Lord fight, but for those that shall besiege Jerusalem? The passage shews that the Lord Himself will fight for the besiegers, being among them and drawn up with them, like their general and commander warring against Jerusalem. For it does not say that the Lord will fight against the nations. With whom and against whom, then, will He fight? Surely against Jerusalem and her inhabitants, concerning whom it is spoken.

And the words, "And his feet shall stand in that day on the Mount of Olives, which is before Jerusalem to the eastward," what else can they mean than that the Lord God, that is to say the Word of God Himself, will stand, and stand firm, upon His Church, which is here metaphorically called the Mount of Olives? For as "My Beloved had a vineyard," and "There was a vineyard of the Lord of Sabaoth," are used in a figurative sense of "the house of Israel and the plant of Judah His beloved vine," so also we may say in the same sense that the Church of the Gentiles has become an olive-garden to the Master, which of old He planted with wild olives, and grafted them on the apostolic roots of the good olive after cutting away the old branches, as the apostle teaches. And the Lord planted it for Himself, saying as much in the prophecy: "The Lord hath called thy name a beautiful and shady olive." For when the first vineyard should have brought forth

Rom. xi.
5.

(287)

(b)

(c)

Isa. v. 1.

(d)

Rom. xi.
24.

Jer. xi. 16.

grapes it brought forth thorns, and not justice but a cry,
God rightly withdrew from it as unfruitful, its mound and
its wall, and gave it to its enemies, "to rob and to tread
down," according to the prophecy of Isaiah, but established Isa. v. 4.
another field for Himself, here named "the olive-garden," (28S)
as that which had obtained God's mercy, and been planted
by Christ with ever-flourishing plants, that is with souls
that are holy and nourish the light, which can say, "I am
like a fruitful olive-tree in the house of God." Ps. lii. 8.

And this Mount of Olives is said to be over against
Jerusalem, because it was established by God after the fall
of Jerusalem, instead of the old earthly Jerusalem and its
worship. For as Scripture said above with reference to (b)
Jerusalem : "The city shall be taken, and the nations that
are her enemies and foes shall be gathered together against
her, and her spoils shall be divided," it could not say that
the feet of the Lord should stand upon Jerusalem. How
could that be, once it were destroyed? But it says that
they will stand with them that depart from it to the mount
opposite the city called the Mount of Olives. And this,
too, the prophet Ezekiel anticipates by the Holy Spirit and
foretells. For he says :

> " 22. And the Cherubim lifted [1] their wings, and the
> wheels beside them, 23. and the glory of the God of
> Israel was on them above them, and he stood on the Ezek. xi.
> mount which was opposite to the city." 22

Which it is possible for us to see literally fulfilled in another
way even to-day, since believers in Christ all congregate
from all parts of the world, not as of old time because of
the glory of Jerusalem, nor that they may worship in the
ancient Temple at Jerusalem, but they rest there that they
may learn both about the city being taken and devastated (d)
as the prophets foretold, and that they may worship at the
Mount of Olives opposite to the city, whither the glory of
the Lord migrated when it left the former city.[2] There

---

[1] LXX : ἐξῆραν.   E. : ἐξήγειρε.

[2] E. refers to the stream of pilgrims to the Holy Places, also pp. 81 c,
97 c, 275 a, 340 d.   Calvary and the Holy Sepulchre had been covered
with a mound of earth from Hadrian's destruction of Jerusalem,
A.D. 135, to Constantine; in *Vita Const.* iii. 26, he attributed this to
a desire to hide the truth.   Alexander, A.D. 212 (*H.E.* vi. 11 : εὐχῆς
καὶ τῶν τόπων ἱστορίας ἕνεκεν), and Origen (*Comm. in Ev. S. Joann.*,

stood in truth according to the common and received account the feet of our Lord and Saviour, Himself the Word of God, through that tabernacle of humanity He had borne up the Mount of Olives to the cave that is shewn there ; there He prayed and delivered to His disciples on the summit of the Mount of Olives the mysteries of His end, and thence He made His Ascension into heaven, (289) as Luke tells us in the Acts of the Apostles, saying that while the apostles were with Him on the Mount of Olives :

Acts i. 9.   "While they beheld he was taken up, and a cloud received him out of their sight.   And as they gazed steadfastly into heaven while he went up, behold two men stood by them in white apparel, who also said, Ye men of Galilee, why stand ye gazing into heaven ? This same Jesus that is taken up from you into heaven shall so come in like manner as ye have seen him go into heaven."

To which he adds : "Then they returned from the mount called the Mount of Olives, which is opposite [1] to Jerusalem." The Mount of Olives is therefore literally opposite (b) to Jerusalem and to the east of it, but also the Holy Church of God, and the mount upon which it is founded, Matt. v. of which the Saviour teaches : "A city set on a hill cannot 14. be hid," raised up in place of Jerusalem that is fallen never to rise again, and thought worthy of the feet of the Lord, is figuratively not only opposite to Jerusalem, but east of it as well, receiving the rays of the divine light, and become

---

tom. vi.; § 24), A.D. 230, are the earliest recorded pilgrims.   Cf. Jerome, de Viris illust. 54, of Firmilian, circa 240.   Next, A.D. 328, we have the pilgrimage of Helena, mother of Constantine (Eus., Vit. Const. iii. 42), and A.D. 333 that of the pilgrim from Bordeaux (Itineraria Hierosolymitana, P. Geyer, Vienna, 1898).   Paula, the friend of Jerome, systematically visited all the sacred places with Eustochium towards the end of the fourth century (Jerome, Ep. 108 ; Ep. 46 : inter. Epp. Jerome ad Marcellam).   We have also the pilgrimage of Etheria in the fourth century.   From the fifth century onwards recorded pilgrimages are frequent.   Cf. Pallad., Hist. Laus. 118, for Melania's hospitality to pilgrims from A.D. 370 to 410, when she died.   And for depreciation of the value of pilgrimages, Gregory of Nyssa, A.D. 370, De euntibus Hierosolyma, pp. 6–13, ed. Molinaci. Jerome, Ep. xlix. (A.D. 393).

1 W.H.: ἐγγὺς Ἱερουσαλήμ.   E.: κατέναντι Ἱερουσαλήμ.

much before Jerusalem, and near to the Sun of Righteousness Himself, of Whom it is said : " And on them that fear (c)
me shall the sun of righteousness arise." Mal. iv. 2.

And if it says next : "That the Mount of Olives shall
be divided, half of it to the east and towards the sea,
a very great chasm, and half of it shall lean towards the
north, and half of it towards the south," it possibly
shews the expansion [1] of the Church throughout the
whole inhabited world, for it has filled the east, and the (d)
western and eastern nations ; it stretches to the western
sea, and the isles therein ; yea, it has reached to
west and south, and to north and north-east. On all
sides and everywhere the Church figuratively called the
Olive of the Lord is planted. And it is possible that by
its division is figuratively meant the schisms and heresies
and moral declensions in everyday life that have taken
place in the Church of Christ, and are even now taking
place ; for it says, the mountain shall be divided, half of
it towards the east and the sea, a very great chasm, and
half of it shall lean towards the north, and half of it
towards the south, as being divided into four parts, two (290)
of which are worthier and better, and two the reverse.
And note in this passage how the part to the east and the
part to the south may refer to two sections of those who
have made progress in the things of God,[2] the first those
who are perfected in knowledge and reason and the other
graces of the Holy Spirit ; and the second, those who live
a good life but pass their time in ways self-chosen.[3] And
the other two parts separated from the first, one to the
sea and one towards the north, both signify tendency to
evil. For "from the face of the north," he says, "shall be (b)
burned the evil of all the inhabitants of the earth," while Jer. i. 14.
the Dragon is said to have his home in the sea. So that, Is. xxvii. 1.
probably, two kinds of character in those that fall away
from the Church, the morally sinful, and the one who
slips away from healthy and orthodox knowledge, are here

---

[1] ἐξάπλωσις : cf. the verb. P.E. 130 b and 519 b.

[2] τῶν τῆς κατὰ Θεὸν προκοπῆς ἐπειλημμένων.

[3] τῶν δὲ διὰ βίου κατορθούντων, ἐν ἐκλογαῖς γε μὴν διατριβόντων.
Diodatus renders : "Sed tamen in suis seligendis rationibus detinentur."
Any translation seems forced, for " ἐκλογαῖς " means simply "selections,"
or "elections." Possibly the text is corrupt.

figuratively represented by the prophecy as divisions in the Mount of Olives.[1]

To this he adds afterwards: "And the valley of my mountains shall be closed up, and the cleft of my mountains shall be joined unto Asael, and shall be closed up as it was blocked up in the days of the earthquake in the days (c) of Ozias king of Judah."

What can God's "valley of mountains" mean here, but the outward Jewish worship according to the Mosaic Law practised for long ages before in Jerusalem, which the present prophecy foretells is to be cut off, as if it were closed up, saying: "And the valley of my mountains shall (d) be closed up, and the cleft of mountains shall be joined unto Asael, and shall be closed up"? Instead of which Symmachus translated: "And the valley of my mountains shall be closed up, and also the cleft of mountains shall approach that which is beside it, and shall be closed up," shewing the cause of the closing up of the valley. And what was this, but that it came near and approached what was beside it? And this mount of the Lord was the before-named Mount of Olives, which is called Asael in the Septuagint. And this word means in Hebrew "Work of God."

And so, he says, the ancient valley coming near to the mountains, and to the Christian Church, and to the work of God, will be closed up and shut off, as it was closed up before the earthquake in the days of Ozias king of Judah. (291) Though I have set myself to the task of inquiring, and gone through the Holy Scripture to discover if the valley mentioned here was "closed up before the earthquake" in the days of Ozias, I have found nothing in the Books of 'Kings, for there was no physical earthquake in his time, nor is anything recorded in those books such as is here told about the valley.

But Ozias is described as at first having been righteous, and then it is related that he was lifted up in mind, and dared to offer sacrifice to God Himself, and that his face (b) became leprous in consequence. This is what the Book

---

[1] For the Tehom-Myth, cf. Amos ix. 3, Isa. xxx. 7, xxvii. 1, li. 9, 10; Ps. lxxiv. 12–15. Cheyne, *Traditions and Beliefs of Ancient Israel*, pp. 1–154; Oesterley, *Evolution of Messianic Idea*, c. v.

of Kings establishes.   But Josephus carefully studied the 2 Chron.
additional comments of the expounders[1] as well, and a xxvi. 19.
Hebrew of the Hebrews as he was, hear *his* description of
the events of those times.   He tells how :

> "Though the priests urged Ozias to go out of the
> Temple and not to break the law of God, he angrily
> threatened them with death, unless they held their
> peace.   And meanwhile an earthquake shook the earth, (c)
> and a bright light shone through a breach in the
> Temple, and struck the king's face, so that at once
> it became leprous.   And before the city at the place
> called Eroga, the western half of the Mount was split
> asunder, and rolling four stadia stopped at the eastern
> mountain, so as to block up the royal approach and
> gardens.   [Jos., *Ant.* ix. 10, 4.]

This I take from the work of Josephus on Jewish Antiquities.   And I found in the beginning of the Prophet (d)
Amos the statement that he began to prophesy "in the
days of Ozias, king of Judah, two years before the earthquake."   *What* earthquake he does not clearly say.   But Amos i. 1.
I think the same prophet further on suggests this earthquake, when he says : "I saw the Lord standing on the
altar.   And He said, Strike the altar, and the doors shall
be shaken, and strike the heads of all, and the remnant Amos ix.
I will slay with the sword."   1.

Here I understand a prediction of the earthquake, and
of the destruction of the ancient solemnities of the Jewish
race, and of the worship practised by them in Jerusalem,
the ruin that should overtake them after the coming of our
Saviour, when, since they rejected the Christ of God, the
true High Priest, leprosy infected their souls, as in the days (292)
of Ozias, when the Lord Himself standing on the altar
gave leave to him that struck, saying : "Strike the altar."
For He shewed this in effect,[2] when He said : "Your house

---

[1] τὰς ἔξωθεν ᾿Ιουδαϊκὰς δευτερώσεις ἀπηκριβωκώς ; cf. Schürer, *Jewish
People*, I. i. 119 ; Gifford, P. E., Note on 574 a.   The Deuterotists were
the expounders of the Mishna, the traditional interpretation of the law,
and their interpretations were the Gemara.   G. quotes Margoliouth,
Expositor, Sept. 1900: δευτέρωσις in Epiphanius, Jerome, etc., is a
mistranslation of Mishna, which means "Oral tradition." . . . The
correct translation is ἄγραφος παράδοσις.

[2] δυνάμει.

is left unto you desolate." Concurrently, too, with His
(b) Passion "The veil of the Temple was rent from the top
to the bottom," as Josephus records as happening also in
the time of Ozias. Then, first the courts were shaken,
when the earth was shaken at the time of His Passion, and
not long after, they underwent their final ruin, the striker
received authority and struck upon the heads of all.

And so we see how at this time the valley of the
mountains of God was closed up, as was done in the
days of Ozias. Actually and literally in the siege by
the Romans, in the course of which I believe such things
happened, and figuratively, also, when the outward and
lower worship of the Mosaic Law was prevented any longer
from activity by the earthquake which according to his
prophecy came upon the Jewish race, and by the other
(c) causes recorded.

After this the prophecy recurring to the Coming of the
Lord announces it more clearly, saying : " And the Lord
my God shall come, and all His holy ones with Him,"
referring either to His apostles and disciples as holy ones,
or certain invisible powers and ministering spirits, of whom
it was said : "And angels came and ministered to him."
And then of the Coming of the Lord, he says : " It shall
be day, and it shall not be light, and cold and frost shall
(d) be for one day." Instead of which Symmachus translated :

"And in that day there shall be no light, but frost
and cold shall be for one day, which is known to the
Lord, not day nor night, but at eventide it shall be
light."

See how clearly this description of the day of our Saviour's
Passion, a day in which "there shall be no light," was
fulfilled, since "from the sixth hour to the ninth hour
there was darkness over all the earth." And also the
"frost and cold," since according to Luke :

"They led Jesus to the palace of the high priest.
And Peter followed afar off. And while they kindled
a fire in the midst of the hall, he sat down, according
to Mark, with the others to warm himself. And John,
too, especially mentions the cold, saying, The servants
and the ministers stood, having made a fire of coals,
for it was cold, and they warmed themselves."

And this day, he says, was known to the Lord, and was not

Matt.
xxvii. 51.

Matt. iv.
11.

Matt.
xxvii. 45.

Luke xxii.
54.

Mark xiv.
54.

(293)

John xviii.
18.

night.   It was not day, because, as has been said already,
"there shall be no light"; which was fulfilled, when "from
the sixth hour there was darkness over all the earth until
the ninth hour."   Nor was it night, because "at eventide it (b)
shall be light" was added, which also was fulfilled when
the day regained its natural light after the ninth hour.
And this was fulfilled figuratively as well, generally in the
Jewish race, darkness, cold, and frost coming on them
after their outrage on the Christ, their understanding being
darkened, so that the light of the Gospel should not shine
in their hearts, and their love to God waxing cold, and
then at eventide the light of the knowledge of the Christ
arose, so that they who sat of old in darkness and the
shadow of death saw a great light, in the words of the (c)
prophet Isaiah.

And in that day it says: "Living water shall come forth
out of Jerusalem."   This is that spiritual, sweet, life-giving
and saving drink of the teaching of Christ, of which He
speaks in the Gospel according to John, when instructing
the Samaritan woman :

"If thou knewest[1] who it is that saith to thee,
Give me to drink, thou wouldst have asked of him, John iv.
and he would have given thee living water."   10.

This was the living water, then, that came forth from
Jerusalem?   For it was thence that its Gospel went forth,
and its heralds filled the world, which is meant by the (d)
words : "The living water shall go forth to the first sea
and the last sea," by which is meant the bounds of the
whole world, that toward the Eastern Ocean being called
"the first sea," that toward the West being meant by
"the last sea," which, indeed, the living water of saving
Gospel teaching has filled.[2]   Of which He also taught,
when He said : "Whosoever shall drink of the water, which John iv.
I shall give him, shall never thirst."   And again He says : 14.
"Rivers of living water shall flow out of his belly, springing John vii.
38.

[1] W.II.: εἰ ᾔδεις τὴν δωρεὰν τοῦ Θεοῦ, καὶ τίς ἐστιν ὁ λέγων
σοι. . . .

[2] Zech. xiv. 8., A.V., "former sea and hinder sea." R.V., "eastern
sea and western."   E. by his comment shews he is using besides 𝕲.
some version nearer to the Hebrew.   In Zechariah the Persian Gulf
and the Mediterranean would be meant.   It is a question whether E.
means anything more definite than the utmost bounds of the earth.

John vii.
37.

(294)

Micah iv.
2 b.

(b)

(c)

up into everlasting life." And again: "If any thirst, let him come unto me and drink."

Then after the refreshing saving spiritual blood has fallen on every race of mankind from Jerusalem, which is more clearly described in another place in the words: "A law shall go forth from Sion, and the Word of the Lord from Jerusalem, and it shall judge in the midst of the nations," it says: "The Lord shall be King." He shall not be King in Jerusalem, nor of the Jewish race; but, over all the earth in that day. And this agrees with what I have quoted from the Psalms, where it was said: "The Lord reigneth over the nations," and also: "Tell it among the nations, the Lord reigneth." The prophecy is that this will be fulfilled in the days of the Lord. For the whole prophecy opens with: "Behold, the days of the Lord come, and these things shall come to pass." And what is meant by "these things," but the siege of Jerusalem, and the passing of the Lord to the Mount of Olives, according to the words, "The Lord shall come," and the events of the day of His Passion, and the living water, flowing in all the world, and to crown all, the Kingdom of the Lord ruling over all the nations, and His One Name, filling all the earth—in short, what I have briefly shown to be fulfilled?

It is also quite clear that the name "Christian," derived from the name of the Christ of God, has filled the whole world. This, too, the prophecy foretells, when it says: "And his name shall be one, encircling all the earth, and the wilderness." And you can test each expression at leisure for yourself, and carry the interpretation still further.

CHAPTER 19

From Baruch.

It is prophesied that the God of the Prophets, having laid down the Complete Way of Knowledge by the Mosaic Law to the Jews, will some Day afterwards be seen on Earth, and mingle among Men.

[Passage quoted, Baruch iii. 29–37.]

I NEED add nothing to these inspired words, which so (295) clearly support my argument.   (c)

CHAPTER 20

From Isaiah.

It is prophesied that the Christ will come into Egypt, and What Things will come to pass at His Coming.   (d)

[Passage quoted, Isa. xix. 1–4 and the context.]

HERE the prophecy before us states that the Second after (296) the God and Lord of the Universe, I mean the Word of God, will come into Egypt, and will come not imperceptibly nor invisibly, nor without any bodily vesture, but riding on a light cloud, or better "on light thickness": for such is said to be the meaning of the Hebrew word.   Let the sons of the Hebrews tell us, then, on what occasion after Isaiah's time the Lord visited Egypt, and what Lord he was.   For the Supreme God is one: let them say how He is said to ride on [1] "light thickness," and to alight locally on any part of the earth.   And let them interpret "light thickness," and (b) explain why the Lord is said not to visit Egypt without it. And also when the words of the prophecy are recorded to have been fulfilled, the shaking of the idols of Egypt made by hand, I mean, and the warring of Egyptians with Egyptians through the Coming of the Lord.   And their gods, that is to say the dæmons, that were so mighty of old, when did they have power no more, and refrain from answering their (c)

---

[1] ἐπὶ πάχους ἐλαφροῦ.

inquirers through fear of the Lord? And into the hands of
what cruel lord, let them say, and of what kings was Egypt
delivered after the coming of the Lord that was foretold,
and why when the Lord came they were delivered to evil
rulers? And let him, who likes, interpret the rest of the
prophecy in the same way. But I contend that it can only
be understood consistently, of the appearing of our Saviour
Jesus Christ to men. For He, being Word of God and
(d) Power of God, fulfilled the aforesaid prediction both literally
and metaphorically, visiting the land of the Egyptians on a
light cloud. The name, "light cloud," is allegorically given
to the visitation He made by means of the Body, which He
took of the Virgin and the Holy Spirit, as the Hebrew
original and Aquila clearly suggests, when he says, "Behold
the Lord rides on light thickness, and comes to Egypt,"
naming the body that came from the Holy Spirit, "light
thickness." And surely this part of the prophecy was
literally fulfilled, when the Angel of the Lord appeared in a
dream to Joseph and said: "Arise, and take the young
child and his mother, and flee into Egypt, and stay there
(297) until I tell thee." For then, the Lord God the Word,
uniting with the child's growth, and present in the Flesh that
had been furnished Him of the Holy Virgin, visited the
land of the Egyptians. (His flesh was "thick" as representing bodily substance, "light" again through its being
better than ours, and it is called "a light cloud" because it
was not formed of the sensuous passions of corruption, but
of the Holy Spirit.) But the cause of His journey thither is
as follows. When it is remembered that the first origin of
idolatrous error was in Egypt, and the Egyptians seemed to
(b) be the most superstitious of men, and bitter enemies of the
people of God, and as far removed from the prophets as
possible, we can see why the Power of God came to them
first of all. And therefore the word of Gospel teaching has
waxed stronger among the Egyptians than among any other
men.[1] Hence this prophecy foretells that the Lord will

---

[1] There is an interesting passage in Chrys., *Hom. in Matt. viii.* on
the pre-eminent place of Egypt in the Church. It is probably truer of
his day than of that of Eusebius. "The vast increase of information
about the condition of Egypt under the Empire which the last fifty
years has witnessed, has served only to confirm the familiar words
of Gibbon," writes F. C. Burkitt, quoting the passage, beginning,

sojourn among them.   But it does not say that the Egyptians
will come to the land of the Jews, nor worship him at
Jerusalem, nor become Jewish proselytes there according
to the enactments of Moses, nor sacrifice at the altar in
Jerusalem.   It says naught of this, but that the Lord will (c)
Himself visit the Egyptians, and will think these men worthy
of His Presence, and will be the occasion of great blessings
to them.   For His sojourn would accomplish those very
things, which we see to have been actually fulfilled after the
appearance of our Saviour Jesus Christ.   Let us see what
these were.   The evil and noxious dæmons who infested
Egypt before, inhabiting images [1] for long ages, and enslaving (d)
the souls of the Egyptians with all manner of deceitful
superstition, when they became aware of a strange divine
power sojourning among them, were all at once disturbed
and tossed to and fro, and their heart and power of thought
was minished within them, yielding to and conquered by the
invisible power that drave on them and consumed them
with its sacred word as with fire.   Yea, the dæmons suffered
thus invisibly when our Saviour Jesus Christ sojourned in
Egypt in flesh and blood ; and, again, when afterwards His

"The progress of Christianity was for a long time confined within the
limits of a single city, which was itself a foreign colony," and ending,
"As soon, indeed, as Christianity ascended the throne . . . the cities
of Egypt were filled with bishops, and the deserts of Thebais swarmed
with hermits."—(*Early Christianity*, p. 10, and Bury's *Gibbon*, ii. 60.)
Yet the position of Alexandria and the prestige of its School must have
made Egyptian Christianity count for much in the world of culture.

For the special cult of dæmons in Egypt cf. Origen. *c. Cels.* viii. 58 :
"Let any one inquire of the Egyptians, and he will find that everything,
even to the most insignificant, is committed to the care of a certain
dæmon," note their guardianship over the thirty-six parts of the body,
and their names, Chnoumen, Chnachoumen, Cnat, etc.

In *the Gospel of Pseudo-Matthew*, which uses early sources, the
355 Egyptian idols bow down and break when Mary and Jesus enter
the Egyptian Temple.   These are, of course, the habitations of dæmons
(c. xxii., xxiii.)   There were probably other legends about dæmons
connected with the Flight into Egypt.

Cf. the extract from the London magical papyrus, No. 46, 145 ff.,
written in the fourth century, A.D. quoted by A. Deissmann, *Light from
the Ancient East*, p. 139 : "I am the headless dæmon, having eyes in
my feet, the strong one, the deathless fire . . . " and the *The Lausiac
History of Palladius*, W. K. L. Clarke, especially, "Macarius of
Alexandria," pp. 78–80.

[1] ξοάνοις : Cf. P.E. 12 a.

(298) Gospel was preached openly to the Egyptians as well as to the other nations, for His unseen power was with His Apostles imperceptibly working with them, co-operating, announcing by their tongues His holy teaching, exhorting men to worship only the one and true God, and rescuing the victims from the dæmons that of old had been deceived by them.   Hence, soon among the. Egyptians as among

(b) other nations, revolution and civil war arose, between those who gave up polytheistic error and turned to the Word of Christ, and those who warred with them, urged on by their own dæmons, so that brothers were parted one from the other, and the dearest fought together because of the Gospel of Christ, for the oracle says, " And Egyptians shall rise against Egyptians, and a man shall fight with his brother, and a

(c) man with his neighbour."   And our Saviour Himself confirms the prophet's prediction, saying in the Gospels :

"Brother shall deliver brother to death, and father child, and children shall rise up against their parents

Matt. x.   and slay them."
21.

And again :

"Think not that I came to give peace on earth.   I say not so unto you, but division.   For there shall be from this time five in one house divided, three against two and two against three : For the father shall be divided from his son, and the son from his father, the mother against her daughter, and the daughter against

Luke xi.   her mother, the mother-in-law against the bride, and the
51 ; Matt.   bride against her mother-in-law."
x. 34.

(d) How do those words differ from the prophet's cry concerning the coming of the Lord to Egypt : " Egyptians shall rise against Egyptians, and man shall war against his brother " ? [1]

And the law of the new Covenant of Christ was raised against the law of polytheistic superstition, when the law of idolatrous nations warred against the teaching of Christ, and the city and polity of the Church of Christ took the

---

[1] The impression conveyed is that there had been religious wars in Egypt between Christian and non-Christian, apart altogether from Imperial persecution.   Egypt was certainly in an unsettled state during the third century.   The destruction of the Temple of Jahveh at Elephantine at the instigation of the priests of Chnut, seven hundred years before (S. R. Driver, *Schweich Lectures*, p. 30), no doubt shews the spirit in which the changeless Egyptian religion met the advance of all foreign faiths.

place of the polities of the heathen nations.   And this explains "city against city, and law against law."   It is the fact also that all the Egyptian idolaters, and the spirit of idolatry working in them, are even now conscious of their confusion, and though they make many plans against the teaching of Christ, to quench it, and abolish it from among (299) men, yet they are ever scattered by God, as it is said in the prophecy, "And the spirit of the Egyptians shall be disturbed within them, and I will scatter their counsel."

And they who make many inquiries and ask endless questions against us of the oracles and diviners of their gods, and of the dæmons that haunt the idols, and the familiar spirits who were of old so powerful among them, get no more profit of them.   For Scripture says :

> "And they will inquire of their gods, and their idols, (b) and the familiar spirits."

But when they flee, it says, to them that falsely appear to be gods, they will receive no help, for then will God chiefly deliver them to cruel kings and rulers, when under the influence of their dæmons, and in their power, they arouse persecutions against the Churches of Christ.   And, please, notice the fact, that until the appearance of our Saviour Jesus Christ all Egypt had its own kings, as a separate (c) and responsible state, and the Egyptians were autonomous and free, and their dynasty was great and famous through long ages, and it was after that date, when Augustus, in whose time our Lord was born, being the first Roman to subjugate Egypt, captured Cleopatra the last of the Ptolemies, that they came under the Roman power, laws, and enactments, losing their former autonomy and freedom.   So that here also the prophecy is true, regarding first the governors (d) and rulers sent out to those places, and the other officials in their several positions, saying, "And I will deliver Egypt into the hand of cruel rulers," and also in what follows regarding the general conduct of the government.

Instead of which Aquila says, "And a mighty king shall reign over them."   And Symmachus, "And a strong king shall reign over them."   Thus the kingdom of Rome seems to be meant, which has bound with bridle and bond not only the Egyptians, the most superstitious of men, but all other men as well, so that they dare no longer to blaspheme against the Church of our Saviour Jesus Christ.   And after (300) this the prophecy proceeds to darker and disguised sayings, which require longer and more profound allegorical interpretation, which in the proper place shall receive their proper exposition at leisure when with God's help I treat of the promises.

CHAPTER 21

From the same.

A Promise of Good Things to the Church of the Gentiles, that before was deserted, and to Sick Souls the Manifest Presence of God, and Marvellous Saving Acts.

(c)

[Passage quoted, Isa. xxxv. 1–7.]

HERE also the Coming of God for salvation, bringing many blessings, is precisely foretold. The prophet says that there will be a cure for the deaf, sight for the blind, yea, even healing for the lame and tongue-tied, and this was only fulfilled at the Coming of our Saviour Jesus Christ, by Whom the eyes of the blind were opened, and the deaf regained their hearing; why need I say, how many palsied and deaf and lame also received physical cure by the hands of His (301) disciples? And how many others, afflicted with various diseases and maladies, received of Him healing and salvation, according to the inspired prediction of prophecy, and according to the unimpeachable testimony of the Holy Gospels? And the prophecy here disguises under the name of " desert " the Church of the Gentiles, which for long years deserted of God is being evangelized by those of whom we are speaking,[1] and it says that besides other blessings the glory of Libanus will be given to the desert. Now it is customary to call (b) Jerusalem Lebanon allegorically, as I will show, when I have time, by proofs from Holy Scripture. This prophecy before us, therefore, teaches that by God's presence with men the glory of Libanus will be given to that which is called " desert," that is to say, the Church of the Gentiles. And for, " And the honour of Carmel," Aquila says, " the

---

[1] διὰ τῶν ἐν χερσίν.

beauty of Carmel, and of Sharon, they shall see the glory of (c)
the Lord." Symmachus, "The grace of Carmel and of
the plain, those shall see the glory of the Lord." And
Theodotion, "The beauty of Carmel and of Sharon, they
shall see the glory of the Lord." In which I think the
prophet means, figuratively, not that Jerusalem, nor Judæa,
but the land of the Gentiles will be counted worthy of divine
knowledge. For Carmel, and that which is called Sharon
were places that belonged to foreign races. That would be
the literal meaning; but figuratively, even to-day, they that
were before so blinded in soul, as to bow down to wood and
stone and other lifeless substances, earth-bound dæmons,[1] (d)
and evil spirits instead of the God of the Universe, and they
that were deaf in the ears of their mind, and lame, and
palsied in all their life, are even now being released from all
these and many other sufferings and weaknesses by the
teaching of our Saviour Jesus Christ, receiving far better
healing and benefit than that of the body, and shewing forth
clearly the divine and superhuman power of the presence of
the Word of God among men.

CHAPTER 22

From the same.

How the First and Everlasting Word of God, the Creator of (302)
the Universe, confesses that He is even now sent by the (b)
Lord His Father.

[Passage quoted, Isa. xlviii. 12 and 16.]

YOU have here the Lord sent and the Lord sending, that is
to say the Father and God of the Universe, entitled Lord
twice as was usual.

---

[1] δαίμονάς τε περιγείους. Cf. P.E. 181 a : οἱ δὲ περίγειοί τινες ὄντες καὶ
καταχθόνιοι, etc.

CHAPTER 23

From the same.

How the Lord rebukes the Jewish People, because They will not receive Him when He comes, nor hear His Call, and what He will suffer at Their Hands.

[Passages quoted, Isa. l. 1, 2 a, b.]

HERE the Lord Himself recording plainly His Coming among
(303) men rebukes the Jewish people, because they will not receive
Him when He comes, nor hear Him when He calls. And
He teaches, as if by way of apology, that this is the cause of
their own rejection. "For when I came," He says, "I was
not among you as a man : I called, and there was none that
heard : therefore," He says, "ye were sold for your sins, inasmuch as ye were of yourselves divorced from my call, not
that I had given you a bill of divorcement." This is clearly
(b) addressed to the Jews, and at the same time reveals their
outrages on Him at His Passion, when it says : "I gave my
back to scourges, and my cheeks to blows," and that
which follows. But these words shall be properly interpreted
at leisure.

CHAPTER 24

From the same.

How the Same Lord that spake in the Prophets will come Among Men and be seen by Their Eyes, and be known to the Gentiles.

[Passage quoted, Isa. lii. 5–10.]

THE prophecy of Christ's Passion immediately succeeds
this in one and the same passage,[1] which I shall expound
at leisure. One and the same Lord, who said in the previous
(304) quotation to the Jewish people, "You were sold for your
sins, and for your iniquities I sent away your mother, because
I came, and there was no man : I called and there was none

---

[1] εἰρμόν. Cf. P.E. 252 a.

to hear," says in the passage before us to the Jews again:
"Because of you my name is blasphemed among the
Gentiles."

Then, as though having another people besides them, he
adds, "Therefore my people shall know my name," and
teaches that not another, but the same Lord that spoke in
the prophets, will sojourn some day in our life, saying, "I am
he that speak; I will come." And the words, "As a season (b)
upon the mountains, as the feet of one preaching a message
of peace, as one preaching good things, I will make thy
salvation known, saying, Sion, thy God reigneth," the other
translators make it clearer. For Aquila says: "How beautiful upon the mountains are the feet of Him that preacheth
the gospel, who publisheth peace, who preacheth the gospel
of good things, publishing salvation, saying to Sion, Thy
God reigneth."

And Symmachus says, "How lovely on the mountains
are the feet of him that preacheth the gospel, making peace
known, publishing good things, making salvation known,
saying to Sion, Thy God reigneth": and instead of "The (c)
voice of thy guards is lifted, and they shall rejoice with the
voice together, because they shall see eye to eye." Symmachus translates thus: "The voice of thy guards; they
have raised their voice. Together will they praise: For
they will see openly." By "guards" would here be meant
the holy apostles of our Saviour, who also saw openly Him
that was foretold, and raised their voice preaching to all the
world. Sion and Jerusalem that here have the good news (d)
told them the apostle knew to be heavenly, when he said,
"But Jerusalem that is above is free, that is the mother of Gal. iv.
us," and, "Ye have come to Mount Sion, and the city of the 26.
living God, heavenly Jerusalem, and to an innumerable Heb. xii.
company of angels." [1] Sion might also mean the Church 22.
established by Christ in every part of the world, and Jerusalem the holy constitution which, once established of old
time among the ancient Jews alone, was driven into the
wilderness by their impiety, and then again was restored far
better than before through the coming of our Saviour.
Therefore the prophecy says, "Let the waste places of (305)

---

[1] W. H. : καὶ μυριάσιν ἀγγέλων, πανηγύρει καὶ ἐκκλησίᾳ—(ἀγγέλων
πανηγύρει in margin). E. : μυριάσιν ἀγγέλων πανηγύρει.

Jerusalem break forth into joy together, for the Lord has pitied her, and saved Jerusalem."

Nor would you be wrong in calling Sion the soul of every holy and godly man, so far as it is lifted above this life, having its city in heaven, seeing the things beyond the world. For it means "a watch-tower."[1] And in so far as

(b) such a man remains calm and free from passion, you could call him Jerusalem—for Jerusalem means "Vision of Peace."

After this the call of the Gentiles to the worship of God is very clearly shown in the words, "And the Lord God will reveal His holy arm before all nations; and the high places of the earth shall see the salvation of our God." And consider that the arm of the Lord is nothing else but the Word and Wisdom, and the Lord Himself, Who is the Christ of God.

It is easy to shew this from many instances. In the Exodus you have Israel saved by the arm of God from

(c) slavery to the Egyptians. While the prophecy before us says that that same arm of the Lord, which of old appeared to save His people will be revealed to all nations, as if it formerly were hidden from them. And "the salvation, which" he says "all the high places of the earth shall see," and which he mentioned before when he said, "I will make my salvation known," know that it is the Hebrew for the name of Jesus.

CHAPTER 25

(d)   From the same.

How, again, the Coming of God the Word and the Gathering of All Nations is foretold.

[Passage quoted, Isa. lxvi. 18, 19.]

HERE also the Coming of the Lord to men is exactly foretold. And as it said, "He will come as fire," our Saviour rightly says, "I came to cast fire on the earth, and what will I, if it be already kindled?" You may say His "chariots"

Luke xii. 49.

(b) are His attendant divine powers, and the holy angels chosen

---

[1] A thought in harmony with the highest mysticism.

to minister to Him, of whom it is said, "and angels came and ministered to Him," and His holy apostles and disciples, borne up by whom, the Word of God with divine invisible power ran through all the world.   One might also literally in another way connect fire and chariots with His coming, through the siege that attacked Jerusalem after our Saviour's Advent, for the Temple was burned with fire not long after, (c) and was reduced to extreme desolation, and the city was encircled by the chariots and camps of the enemy, after which too the promises to the Gentiles were fulfilled in harmony with the prophecy.   Who would not wonder hearing the Lord say by the prophet, "I come to bring together all nations and tongues," and then seeing through- out the whole inhabited world the congregations welded (d) together in the Name of Christ through the Coming and the Call of our Saviour Jesus Christ, with the tongues of all nations in varying dialects calling on one God and Lord? To crown all, who beholding all them that believe in Christ using as a seal the sign of salvation,[1] would not rightly be astounded hearing the Lord saying in days of old, "And they shall come and see my glory, and I will leave my sign upon them"?

We see in part, indeed, now with our own eyes the fulfil- ment of the holy oracles as to the first Epiphany of our Saviour to man.   May it be seen completely as well in His second glorious Advent, when all nations shall see His glory, and when He comes in the heavens with power and great glory.

To that day the remainder of the prophecy must be (307) referred, as I shall show in my own argument.

As I have in this Book collected so many passages con- cerning the prophecies of the coming of God, my next task should be to connect with them an account of what was foretold as to the nature of His entry [2] into human life.

---

[1] Cf. p. 450 d.   The sign of the Cross in Baptism was an essential part of the ceremony by Cyprian's day : "By whatever lips the sacred words are uttered, it is the authoritative use of the sign of the Cross which works the effect in all the sacraments" (*De Pass. Christi*, cf. St. Augustine, *Hom. cxviii. in S. Joan.* xi. 24).   At Baptism it was used over the water (Aug., *Hom.* xxvii.) ; in the exorcism and im- position of hands (Aug., *Conf.* I. cap. 11) and at the unction (Tertul., *De Resur.* cap. 8.).

[2] παρόδου.

BOOK VII

WE have learned in the preceding Book from the words of the prophets that God would come to men and would live among men on earth, and that the two chief signs of His presence would be the calling of the nations of the world to receive the true knowledge of God, and the ruin and desolation of the Jews through their unbelief in Him ; and we have investigated how the prophecies were fulfilled. (309) We will now attempt in this Seventh Book of *The Proof of the Gospel* to treat in due order of the way in which He says that He is to make His entrance into humanity. So then our present object is to see what kind of prophecies were made of God's coming among men, where it was predicted He should be born, and from what race it was proclaimed that He should come.

CHAPTER 1

(b)
From Isaiah.

The Manner of the Lord's Stay among Men.

A prediction of the Jews' unbelief in Christ, and the sign (c) that was given them by the Lord. It was this : A Virgin giving birth to God, at Whose Birth the complete destruction of the Jewish race was foretold, the subjection of their land to foreign enemies, and the flourishing of that, which before was desert, under divine cultivation. Thus the Church of the Gentiles was shewn forth. As the great Evangelist St. John, teaching of our Lord and Saviour as the very Word of God full of supernatural power, begins his holy Gospel, by setting side by side His Divinity and His

---

[1] Donatus does not translate the first eight lines Πρόρρησις . . . τὸν τρόπον). They are supplied in the Paris Edition.

Humanity in His presence among men, saying, "In the beginning was the Word, and the Word was with God, and (d) the Word was God. He was in the beginning with God. All things were made by him," and adding after this, "and John i. 1– the Word became flesh, and tabernacled among us"; so 3a, 14a. in the same strain the inspired prophet, about to proclaim God born of a Virgin, tells first the vision of His Divine glory, when he thus describes the Being of God:

"1. I saw the Lord sitting upon a throne high and exalted. And the house was full of his glory. 2. And Seraphim stood round about him: each one had six wings: with two he covered his face, and with two he covered his feet, and with two he did fly. 3. And they (310) cried one to another and said, Holy, Holy, Holy, the Isa. vi. 1– Lord of Sabaoth, the whole earth is full of his glory." 3.
And he adds also:

"8. And I heard the voice of the Lord saying, Whom shall I send, and who will go to this people? And I said, Behold, Here am I. Send me. 9. And he said, Go and say to this people, Ye shall hear indeed, but shall not understand; and ye shall see indeed, but not perceive. 10. For this people's heart has become gross, and their ears are dull of hearing, and their eyes have they closed; lest they should see with their eyes, and hear with their ears, and understand with their (b) heart, and be converted, and I should heal them. 11. And I said, How long, O Lord? And He said, Until the cities be deserted, by reason of their being unin- Isa. vi. 8– habited, and the houses by reason of there being no 11. man."

What Lord may we say the prophet saw but Him Whom we have proved to have been seen and known by the fathers with Abraham in previous days? He, we have already learned, was both God and Lord, and Angel and Captain of the Lord's power as well. So then in approaching the account of (c) His Coming to men the prophecy before us tells first of His divine kingdom, in which it says that the prophet saw Him Ps. xliv. sitting on a throne high and exalted. This is that throne 6. which is mentioned in the Psalm of the Beloved, "Thy throne, O God, is for ever and ever," on which the Most High Creator of the Universe, His God and Father, bade his Only-begotten sit, saying, "Sit thou on my right hand, until I

Ps. cix. 1. make thine enemies thy footstool." John the Evangelist
(d) supports my interpretation of this passage, when he quotes
the words of Isaiah, where it is said, "For this people's
heart is become gross, and their ears are dull of hearing,
and their eyes have they closed," referring them to Christ,
John xii. saying, "This said Isaiah, when he saw his glory, and bare
41. witness [1] of him." The prophet then seeing our Saviour
sitting on His Father's throne in the divine and glorious
kingdom, and moved by the Holy Spirit, and being about
to describe next His coming among men and His Birth of a
Virgin, foretells that His knowledge and praise would be
(311) over all the earth, by introducing the song of the Seraphim
round His throne : Holy, Holy, Holy, Lord of Sabaoth, the
whole earth is full of his glory. And who are the Seraphim
around the Christ of God ? Perhaps the choirs of angels
and divine powers, perhaps the prophets and apostles. For
the translation of Seraphim is "Rule of His Mouth."
The prophets and apostles would bear this name, because
from their mouth were the firstfruits of the preaching of
(b) salvation. So also the powers of the Holy Spirit are called
"Wings," as hiding the beginning and the end of the
knowledge of God, as being secret and inconceivable in
nature, but they reveal the central parts of his dispensation,
since these alone are knowable by men ; that which is
beyond and that which comes after them is left unsaid.
And the divine and heavenly powers are signified by the
Seraphim, according to another rendering of the word, as
(c) "fires." As it is said, "He maketh his angels spirits and
Ps. civ. 5. his ministers a flame of fire." These cry and shout one to
another according to their power, shewing forth the holiness
of the Being acclaimed as God, and, strangest of all, they
do not acclaim His Godhead because heaven and the things
of heaven alone are full of His glory, but because all the
earth also shares in His power by His Coming from heaven
to men as prophesied, in the prediction which follows,
(d) announcing His Birth of a Virgin and His glory spread
through all the earth.

Lord of Sabaoth is translated "Lord of Powers." And He
is the Captain of the Powers of the Lord, Whom also the
divine powers salute as Lord of Sabaoth in the 23rd Psalm,

---

[1] W.H.: ἐλάλησε.   E.: ἐμαρτύρησε.

foretelling His return from earth to heaven : " Lift up your
gates, ye princes, and be lifted up, ye everlasting doors, and
the King of glory shall come in.   Who is the King of Ps. xxiii.
glory ? The Lord of Powers, He is the King of glory."

In the Hebrew He is here again called Lord of Sabaoth. (312)
And since He is the King of glory, and by His sojourn
here the whole earth would be filled with His glory, both
in the psalm and in the prophecy the fulfilment is rightly
placed in the present : in the prophecy in the words, "The
whole earth is full of his glory," in the psalm at the beginning where it says, "The earth is the Lord's and the
fullness thereof, the world and all that dwell therein."
After this prophecy, the prophet next proceeds to bear
witness, that though the whole earth shall be full of His (b)
glory, yet the Jewish race shall not participate, where he
says, "And the Lord said (that is to say, the Lord of
Sabaoth in the vision), Whom shall I send, and who will go
to this people ? And I said, Behold, here am I. Send
me. And He said, Go and say to this people, Ye shall
hear, and shall not understand. And ye shall see and not
perceive : For this people's heart is become gross, and their
ears are dull of hearing, and their eyes have they closed,
lest they should hear with their ears, and see with their eyes, (c)
and understand with their heart, and be converted, and I
should heal them." Here he expressly foretells the opposition of the Jews to Him, and how they will see Him, and
not understand Who He is ; how they will hear Him, speaking and teaching them, but will be quite unable to grasp
Who it is that speaks with them, or the new teaching He
offers them. And John the Evangelist witnesses to the
fulfilment of these words referring to Our Saviour, where
he says, "Though he had done so many signs before them,
yet they believed not on Him, that Isaiah the prophet's (d)
words might be fulfilled, which he spake, Lord, who hath John xii.
believed our report, and to whom hath the arm of the Lord 37.
been revealed ?

"Therefore they were not able to believe, because again
Isaiah said, He hath blinded their eyes, and hardened their
heart, so that they should not see with their eyes, and
understand with their heart, and be converted, and I should
heal them. These things said Isaiah, when he saw His
glory, and bare witness of Him." Thus the Evangelist

most certainly referred the Theophany in Isaiah to Christ, and to the Jews who did not receive the Lord that was seen by (313) the prophet according to the prediction about Him. To the prophet, then, who had seen the Lord of Sabaoth the oracle says that he is to tell the Jewish race, that they shall see Him at some future time, but shall not understand Who He is, and shall hear Him speak and teach among them, but shall not know Him, because of the hardening of their hearts. Then Isaiah, after the prophecy here quoted, describes in the course of his record the enemy's attack on Ahaz, who at that time held the kingdom of the Jewish people, and declares that the destruction of their visible (b) enemies [1] will be at no distant date. And he shews that the defeat of their spiritual and unseen foes will be as complete, those dæmons and unseen powers, of whom I treated at the beginning of this work, for having involved not only the Jewish race but the whole of mankind in every form of evil, and especially in godless idolatry; and that could only be achieved by the sojourn of the Word of God among men as prophesied, and His receiving His earthly tabernacle (c) from a pure Virgin. Why this was necessary, it is now the time to explain.

Concerning the Sojourn of Our Saviour.

Rom. v.   Since the apostle said, "By man death entered into the
12.   world," it was surely essential that the victory over death
(d) should be [2] achieved by man as well, and the body of death be shewn to be the body of life, and the reign of sin that before ruled in the mortal body be destroyed, so that it should no longer serve sin but righteousness. And since long ago man fell through the sins of the flesh, the standard of victory over his enemies was rightly upraised again by one that was sinless and undefiled of all evil. And who were these enemies, but they who of old had overcome the human race by the pleasures of the flesh? And moreover men required that the Word of God coming to dwell with

---

[1] αἰσθητῶν πολεμίων.

[2] βραβευθῆναι: "to be judged, or decided on as by a βραβεύς, or arbitrator.' So the passage literally runs: "it was necessary that the victory over death be decided as complete through the agency of the same humanity." (διὰ τοῦ αὐτοῦ ἀνθρώπου.) Cf. note, vol. ii. p. 228.

them, and to give holy teaching to their earthly ears, and to
shew the power of God clearly to their eyes by signs and (314)
wonders, should accomplish His work through our natural
equipment,[1] for it is only possible for men to see bodily
things with their eyes, and to hear that which is spoken by
the tongue.   It was then in order that we might receive the
knowledge of spiritual and unembodied things by our
bodily senses that God the Word employed a [2] speech that
was akin and familiar to us, and shewed forth all the
salvation given through Him to those who themselves could (b)
hear and see His divine words and works.   And this He
did, not being like ourselves bound down by the limitations
of the body, nor experiencing aught below or above His
Divinity, nor hampered as a human soul is by the body so
as to be unable to act as God, or to be omnipresent as the
Word of God, and to fill all things and to extend through
all: but He incurred no stain or corruption or pollution
from the body He had taken, because, as the Word of God,
He remained by nature without body, or substance, or flesh,
and went through the whole dispensation of His Incarnation
with divine power and in ways unknown to us, sharing (c)
what belonged to Him, but not receiving what belonged to
others.   What, then, was there to fear in the dispensation of
the Incarnation, since the undefiled was incapable of defilement, and the pure of being soiled by the flesh, and the
passionless Word of God of corruption by the proper
nature of the body, any more than the rays of the sun are
harmed by touching corpses and all sorts of bodily things?
Nay, on the contrary, the corruptible was transformed by
the divine Word, and was made holy and immortal, even (d)
as He willed: yea, and so it ministered to the divine
purpose and works of the Spirit.   And all this was done by
a loving God and by the Word of God for the curing and
salvation of all men, in accordance with the words of the
prophets who had foretold from ancient days His wondrous
Birth of a Virgin.   And quite necessarily the prophet prefaces Christ's Birth of a Virgin by an exhortation to attention,
crying aloud to his hearers, " If ye will not believe, neither (315)
shall ye understand."

And then he adds the following words :

1 διὰ τοῦ συνήθους ἡμῖν ὀργάνου.
2 λόγον—omitted in Paris MS.

"10. And the Lord added to speak unto Ahaz saying,
11. Ask for thyself a sign from the Lord thy God in the
depth or in the height.   12. And Ahaz said, I will not
ask, neither will I tempt God.   13. And he said, Hear
now, house of David; is it a small thing to you to strive
with man, and how do ye strive with the Lord?   14.
(b)   Therefore the Lord shall give you a sign: Behold a
virgin shall conceive, and bear a son, and thou shalt
call his name Emmanuel: 15. Butter and honey shall
he eat, before he knows to choose the good and refuse
the evil.   16. Wherefore before the child know good or
evil, he does not obey wickedness, that he should choose
Isa. vii. 9–   the good.   And the earth shall be forsaken, on account
15.   of that which thou fearest, of her two kings."
Such is the prophecy.   But the opening of the prophecy
(c) is worthy of our study, which bears witness to those that
read it, "If ye do not believe, neither will ye understand."
And it is above all necessary to note that the words shew
that its readers need not only intellect but faith, and not
only faith but intellect.   Hence the Jews who do not
believe in Christ, though they are even now hearers of these
words, have not even yet understood Him of Whom the
prophecy was given, so that in their case the prediction has
its primary fulfilment.   For though they hear daily with
their ears the prophecies about Christ, they hear them not
(d) with the ears of their mind.   And the sole cause of their
ignorance is unbelief, as the prophecy truly reveals of them
and to them.   For it says, "If ye will not believe, neither
shall ye understand."
And if they say that she who conceived is called not a
virgin but a young woman [1] in Scripture (for so it is said it
is explained among them) what worthy sign of the promise
of God, we answer, would this be, if like all women after
union with a man a young woman were naturally to conceive?   And how could he that were born of her be God?
And not simply God, but "God with us"?   For that is the
meaning of Emmanuel, which name it says the child is to
be called.   "For behold a virgin," it says, "shall conceive
(316) and bear a son, and thou shalt call his name Emmanuel,
which is interpreted God with us."   Where would be

---

[1] μὴ παρθένον, νεᾶνιν δέ—so Celsus (Origen c. Cels. i. 35).

God's struggle, where His labour and difficulty, if a woman were to bring forth in the accustomed manner?

For in our versions translated by the Seventy, men of Hebrew race, experts in the accuracy of their knowledge of their national language, we find: "Is it a small thing for you to contend with man? And how will ye contend with God also? Therefore the Lord himself will give you a sign: Behold, a virgin shall conceive and bear a son, who (b) shall be called God with us." (For as I said this is the meaning of Emmanuel.) And in the versions of the Jews according to the transcript of Aquila [1] [Aquila was a prose-lyte, and not a Jew by birth] we have a rendering to the same effect, "Hear then, house of David; is it a small thing with you to weary men that ye would weary my God also? Therefore He will give you this sign: Behold, a young woman shall conceive and bear a son, and thou shalt call His name Emmanuel." In Symmachus it stands thus— [Symmachus is said to have been an Ebionite.[2] There was a sect of the Jews so designated said to have believed in Christ, to which Symmachus belonged, and his rendering is as follows]—"Hear, house of David, is it not enough for you to weary men, that ye weary my God?" Therefore the Lord Himself will give you this sign: "Behold a young woman conceives and bears a son, and thou shalt call his name Emmanuel." For since the hardness of the Jewish (d) character and their disinclination for holiness caused sweat and toil, and no common labour and struggle to the prophets of old time, therefore he says, "Is it not enough for you to weary the prophets of God, and to contend with men: but now will ye even weary my God, and contend even with my God also?" Such is Theodotion's translation. Thus the prophet calls the God, Who is like to be wearied

---

[1] See note, vol. i. p. 66.

[2] E. says the same (*H. E.* vi. 17). He gives an account of the Ebionites (*H. E.* iii. 27), describing their low view of Christ, their observance of the Law, their rejection of St. Paul's Epistles, and the Gospels, using only the Gospel of the Hebrews. Ebionitism was the generic name for judaizing Christians in the second century. The more rigid would have no fellowship with Gentile Christians, and regarded Jesus as a human prophet: they were the successors of the judaizers of St. Paul's day. The less rigid, the Nazareans, descended from the more moderate Jewish Christians, and continued their ancient rites after the fall of Judaism. —(G. P. Fisher, *History of the Church*, p. 75.)

and challenged to contend, his own God, and not the God of those whom he addresses, which he could hardly do if he referred to the Supreme God of the Jews, among whom it had been handed down from their Fathers that they must (317) preserve the worship of God the Creator of all things. And what could the contest and labour or the toil of this God in the prophecy refer to but His entry by human birth, as I and the Septuagint interpret it, of a virgin, or even according to the current Jewish rendering, of a young woman? For you will find in Moses [1] the phrase "young woman" used of one who is undoubtedly a virgin, at least he uses the word of one who has been violated by one person after her betrothal to another.

(b)   But also Emmanuel, the child of the Virgin, is to be endowed with more than human power, He is to choose the good before He knows evil, and to refuse evil in choosing the good : and this not in manhood but in childhood. Therefore it runs, "Before the child knows good or evil, he shall refuse evil in choosing the good," which shews that He is completely immune from evil. And He (c) bears a greater than any human name, God with us. And this is why the sign connected with Him is said to have depth, and also height : depth, by reason of His descent to humanity, and His presence here even unto death : height, by reason of the restitution of His divine glory from the depth, or because of the divine nature of His pre-existence. Emmanuel can only be He Who has already

---

[1] See Deut. xxii. 19 *sq.* : καὶ ζημιώσουσιν αὐτὸν ἑκατὸν σίκλους καὶ δώσουσιν τῷ πατρὶ τῆς νεάνιδος, ὅτι ἐξήνεγκεν ὄνομα πονηρὸν παρθένον ἐπὶ Ἰσραελεῖτιν.

Trypho referred the prophecy of Isa. vii. 14 to Hezekiah, arguing that the Hebrew word translated Virgin, merely means "young woman." Justin uses the argument from Deut. xxii. 19 here used by E. and asserts that a natural birth would be in no sense "a sign," while a Virgin Birth is (*Trypho*, 84; cf. Tert. *adv. Jud.* 9. *adv. Marc*, iii. 13). Origen speaks in the same way against Celsus (*c. Cels.*, i. 35). In each case the chapter of Isaiah is introduced by the Apologist, not the Sceptic.

Matthew's account of the Birth of Christ is evidently the common Church doctrine early in the second century, for Ignatius writes : "And hidden from the prince of this world were the virginity of Mary, and her child-bearing, and likewise also the death of the Lord, three mysteries to be cried aloud—the which were wrought in the silence of God" (Ignatius, *Eph.* xix.). The topic by E.'s day was stereotyped,

been proved to be God the Lord, Who was seen by Abraham in human shape.   And if the Jews refer the prophecy to Hezekiah, son of Ahaz, saying that his birth was thus pre- (d) dicted to his father, we answer that Hezekiah was not God with us, nor was any sign shewn forth in him of a divine nature.   Nor was there any divine struggle or labour attendant on his birth.   Hezekiah, moreover, can be shewn to be excluded by the date of the prophecy.   For this prophecy was given about future events when his father Ahaz was actually king, whereas Hezekiah is known to have been born before Ahaz came to the throne.   And if the prophecy we are considering has no reference to him, it is still further from referring to any other Jew who lived after its date, except to the birth of the true Emmanuel, that is, (318) God born with us, and to the sojourn among men of our Saviour the Word of God.   For the land of the Jews was left desolate by the loss of its two kings, as the oracle said would come to pass as follows : " The land shall be deserted from the face of two kings " ; and this actually and literally took place.   For in the time of King Ahaz and Isaiah son of Amos at the date of this prophecy, the king of Syria in Damascus, and the king of Israel in Samaria, not the king (b) who ruled at Jerusalem, but the king of the multitude of Jews who revolted from the law of God, made a compact one with another, and besieged them that were under the sove- reignty of David's successors.   The prophecy foretells the destruction of both these kings, both the Jew and the one of foreign race, who had combined together against the Lord's people, and says that they will swiftly be severed and give up the war : and that their kingdom and succession (c) will be completely destroyed and extinguished after the birth of Him who is foretold as " God with us."

Now recognize at what date the kingdoms of Damascus and Judæa both ceased to exist, and at what period the land of the Jews was left without a king, as well as the land of the Damascenes, once so powerful, formerly the great over- lord of all Syria.   For the probability is that at the time of their destruction Emmanuel would be born, and He that was foretold would come.   If we to-day could see the king- (d) doms referred to still in existence, it would be vain to inquire further, we could only extend our hopes into the future ; but if their destruction is actually evident, so that

our time sees no kingdom either of Damascus or of Judæa,
it is clear that the prophecy has been fulfilled which said,
" And the land shall be deserted from the face of two
kings, whom thou fearest, from their face,"—kings being
used for " kingdoms." For Symmachus says, " The land
shall be left, from which you suffer ill, by the face of her
(319) two kings." And Aquila, " The land shall be left, which
thou disdainest,[1] from the face of her two kings." And
Theodotion translates thus, " The land shall be left, which
thou hatest, from the face of her two kings." Do you see
how it is prophesied that the land shall be left kingless ?
What land, but that of Damascus, and that of Israel ? For
the kings to whom the prophecy refers ruled these lands. It
was their lands that Ahaz despised or hated, wearied and
suffering under their attacks. When then did they fall ?
For if this part of the prophecy was fulfilled, the foregoing
part must have also taken place, and this was, that a Virgin
should bear " God with us."

(b)   Now if we inquire of history it is abundantly clear that
2 Cor. xi. the line of kings of Damascus was uninterrupted up to
32.   the date of the appearance of our Saviour Jesus Christ.
The holy apostle mentions Aretas, King of Damascus,[2]
and the kingship of the Jews continued untouched even
until then, though it was irregular : for Herod and his
successors in the time of our Saviour did not inherit the
throne as being of David's line.

(c)   And it was after His Appearing, and the preaching of the
Gospel of the Virgin's Son to all mankind, that the land was
" left of the face of two kings." For from that date by the
rule of the Roman Emperor over all nations, all local
dominion in city and state ceased, and the prophecy before
us in common with the others was fulfilled.

----

[1] σικχαλνεις.

[2] Cf.: 2 Cor. xi. 32 ; Acts. ix. 23. The statement of St. Paul is
important for N. T. chronology. Aretas was the hereditary chief of
the Nabatæan Arabs, with whom Rome was fighting up to the end of
the reign of Tiberius. So that Damascus could not have been ceded
to him till A.D. 34 by Caligula. The incident took place after St. Paul's
return from Arabia. Syrian coins before 33–34 and after 62–63 bear
the heads of the Emperors Tiberius and Nero. This Aretas (Hari-
thath IV.) began to rule at the end of Herod the Great's reign
(Jos., Ant. xvi. 9, 4), and he probably ruled from 9 B.C. to A.D. 40
(D.A.C., vol. i., arts. Aretas, Dates, Damascus ; Exp. New Test.
[J. H. Bernard], iii. 108).

Such was the literal fulfilment.   But the prophecy also shews figuratively the stability, the calmness and peace of every soul, who receives the God that was born, Emmanuel Himself.   For now that the one Christ, and the Word (d) proclaimed by Him, rule as kings over the souls of men, the old enemies have been put to flight, the two forms of sin, the one that leads men into idolatry and into a diversity of varied beliefs, the other that tempts them to moral ruin. Of these I say the earthly kings of old above-named were symbols.   Of these the king of Damascus was the picture of the Gentile errors with regard to idols.   And the other, of those who had rebelled from Jerusalem, that is to say from the worship of God according to the Law.

That we should understand the passage figuratively can (320) also be seen from what follows, where it is prophesied that in the time of Emmanuel certain flies and bees will attack the Jews, some from Egypt, some from Assyria, and that a man will shave their head and feet and beard, and that a man will nourish a heifer and two sheep, and other things destined to happen at one and the same time, which it is impossible to understand literally, but only figuratively.   (b)

This, then, is so. And the proof that the Scripture before us foretold the manner of the Birth of our Saviour Jesus Christ, is supported by the Evangelist, who wrote :

"18. The birth of Jesus Christ was on this wise. When his mother Mary was espoused to Joseph, before they came together, she was found with child of the Holy Ghost.   19. And Joseph her husband being a just man, and not willing to make her a public example, was minded to put her away secretly.   20. And while he thus intended, behold the Angel of the Lord appeared to him saying, Joseph, Son of David, fear not to take unto thee Mary thy wife ; for that which is conceived in her is of the Holy Ghost.   21. And she shall bear a son, and thou shalt call his name Jesus.   For he shall save his people from their sins.   22. And all this was done that the word of the Lord spoken by the prophet might be fulfilled, saying, Behold, a virgin shall conceive, and bear a son, and thou shalt call[1] his name Emmanuel, which is being interpreted, God with us."   Matt. i 18-23.

---

[1] W. H.: καλέσουσιν.   E.: καλέσεις.

(d)   And thus according to our teaching the reality of the divine foreknowledge is confirmed by the course of events, otherwise the truth of the prophecy could not have been shewn. Let us now consider the important things which it is said in the next part of the prophecy will happen in that day, that is to say at the time of Christ's appearing.

(321)   [Passage quoted, Isa. vii. 18–25.]

Such are the events included by this prophecy in its prediction of the day of Emmanuel. I will now go through the revelations they give us, epitomizing[1] their meaning. "The Lord," it says, "will hiss for flies in that day, which shall rule over part of the river of Egypt, and for the bee which is in the land of the Assyrians."

(c)   The souls of the men who before worshipped idols, or the impure and horrid powers, I think, are called flies, and flies of Egypt, as delighting in sacrifices and the blood of idols. And the bee is an animal armed with a sting, that knows how to rule and to obey and to fight, and can defend itself and wound its enemies. These two then combining together, the one from the land of the Rulers (which is the meaning of "Assyrians") the other from the land of the idolaters, will be bidden, it says, as by the hissing of the

(d) Lord God of the Universe, to rule the whole of Judæa, because of their unbelief in Christ, in the day of Emmanuel. And it means by this that a foreign military power will occupy Jerusalem and Judæa. This too our Saviour fore-

Luke xxi. told more definitely, when He said, "And Jerusalem shall
24.   be trodden by the Gentiles." This was fulfilled not long after our Saviour spoke, when the Romans took the city, and settled strangers there, and established them on its site.

It is also said that the same Lord will shave with the razor of the Assyrian king, that is to say with the discipline of the Prince of this world,[2] the head and the feet and the beard of what can only mean the Jewish race. That is to

(322) say He will take away their order and beauty by the might of some universal Empire. He disguises the Romans in this way. For I believe that under the name of Assyrians he means the rule of races, that gain Empire at each period

---

[1] ἐπιτέμνω. Cf. P. E. 272 d.
[2] τοῦ ἄρχοντος τοῦ αἰῶνος τούτου, the Johannine phrase. Cf. John xii. 31, xiv. 30, xvi. 11.

of history, because Assyrians in Hebrew means Rulers.
And the Romans are now such Rulers.

And in truth the God of the Universe has taken away all
the glory of the Jews, which was as their hair, and all their
manhood, signified by their beard and the hairs of their
feet, by means of the Roman razor, that is to say their state- (b)
craft and military power. And it was only after the Birth
of our Saviour, Emmanuel Himself, that God took away all
their glory through the Roman rule.

Aquila translates, " By the kingdom of Assyria," for " of the
king of Assyria," Theodotion and Symmachus, " By the
king of the Assyrians," making it clear that there is no
threat to shave the head of the king of Assyria, but that by
means of his razor and by means of the king of Assyria the
things prophesied will fall on the Jewish nation. And the event (c)
justified the prophecy. And one could note carefully at leisure
many other sayings in the prophecies apparently directed
against the Assyrians, which are quite inapplicable to them,
since they refer to the rule of the dominant nation at some
particular period. We have thus already seen the Persians
called Assyrians by the Hebrews ; and so we may conclude
that the prophecy here refers to the Roman Empire. For (d)
we see them as Rulers under the Rule of God in the period
after our Saviour's coming. Yet no one must understand
me to say that every reference to the Assyrians in Holy
Scripture refers to the Romans ; that would be foolish and
absurd. But I will shew in the proper place that there are
certain prophecies concerned with the witness to Christ,
which are to be understood of the Romans under the name
of Assyrians, since the meaning of the word always implies
the dominant Power of an epoch.

For my part, and I have thoroughly reasoned out the
grounds of my opinion, I am persuaded that the only (323)
reason why the prophetic writings abstain from naming
the Romans is that the teaching of our Saviour Jesus Christ
was going to shine throughout the Roman Empire on all
mankind, and that the books of the prophets would be
popular in Rome itself, and among all the nations under
Roman rule. It was therefore to prevent any offence being
taken by the rulers of the Empire from a too clear reference
to them, that the prophecy was cloaked in riddles, in many (b)
other contexts, notably in the visions of Daniel, just as in

the prophecy we are considering, in which it calls them Assyrians, meaning Rulers.

It is then with their razor that it prophesies that after the birth of Emmanuel the whole order of the Jews will be abolished.

And also on that day, I mean the day of Emmanuel, or of Christ's Appearing, "A man, it says, will rear a heifer,
(c) and two sheep. And it shall come to pass from the abundance of milk, he that is left on the land shall eat butter and honey." By this he suggests the hunger and extreme penury of the Jews, not enjoying their natural food of corn, neither ploughing, sowing, nor reaping, possessing no flocks of sheep nor herds of cattle, but only possessing two sheep and a heifer to provide them with milk. Or perhaps he means figuratively, that those Jews
(d) left in the land, the choir of apostles and evangelists of
Rom. xi. 5. our Lord and Saviour Jesus Christ, each one of whom was a remnant according to the election of grace, and therefore called "he that is left" in the land, will rear a heifer and two sheep, three orders in each church, one of rulers, two of subordinates, since the Church of Christ's people is divided into two divisions, the faithful, and those not yet admitted to the laver of regeneration, to whom the holy
1 Cor. iii. apostle says, "I have fed you with milk, not with strong
2. meat"; while he aptly calls those who are in a state of greater perfection a heifer, because they are the offspring of the more perfect bulls, like the apostle himself, who says
(324) of his own labour and that of his fellow-workers, "Does
1 Cor. ix. God take care for oxen, or is this said altogether for our
9. sakes?" Thus the whole order of the leaders of the Church is called a heifer, for they are occupied in ploughing and sowing the souls of men, being the offspring of the ways and teaching of the apostles, who are said so to abound in virtue, that they provide of their fruitfulness fruitful and spiritual milk in elementary teaching, and nourish many besides themselves.

(b)   And it predicts also of those that shall be left in the land, that something else will happen in that day, that is to say at the time of Emmanuel's presence. What is it? Every place, it says, of the people of the Circumcision, where there were 1000 vines for 1000 shekels, shall be dry and thorny. For with arrow and bow they shall come there

(obviously the enemy) and the land shall be dry and
thorny.

And note that everything the prophecy predicts will fall on
the Jewish race in the day of Emmanuel, I mean at the time (c)
when the spiritual light of our Saviour's gifts shines on all
men.   He says that unclean and hostile powers which
worked of old among the Gentiles, in Egypt and the land
of the Assyrians, when the Lord hisses, and as it were
urges them on and encourages them, will come upon their
land, because they deserved the visitation.   And it says
that these powers will rest in valleys, and in caves of the
rocks, in caverns, and in all their clefts, both figuratively
understood of their souls, their bodily senses, their reason, (d)
and their divided minds, and directly in a literal sense
of the whole country.   Who would not wonder, when he
sees how enemies have taken possession of every part of
Judæa, and how foreigners and idolaters rest in all their
cities and country?   And the prophecy says that He
will not only treat them thus, but will shave their head,
the hairs of their feet and their beard, that is to say the
whole order that of old was theirs, with the razor of the
king of the Assyrians, as I have interpreted him.

At the same day and at the same time he threatens
that he will plunge them into an extreme poverty of godly
riches, so that they are devoid of rational bread, and of (325)
solid spiritual food, and are all content to be nourished
with the milk of infants, and with elementary teaching.
And to crown all, their vines will be dry.   For when, as
the same prophet says, their farmer and master expected Isa. v. 4.
them to bring forth a bunch of grapes, and they brought
forth thorns, and not justice, but a cry, it is said that he
will take away his mound and destroy the wall, and turn
the vineyard into a dry place, and will deliver it to enemies, (b)
who, he says, will come there with arrow and bow, receiving
their authority from God, Who delivers it to them not
unjustly, but most justly, because all their land is become
dry and thorny.   Therefore, then, since they have made
themselves dry and thorny, men will come, he says, with
arrow and bow, with authority against them.   Wonder not
if this is expressed in dark and riddling figures.   For I
have already attributed the cause of such economy of (c)
Scripture to the desire to hide the final destruction of the

Jewish race, so that they might preserve the Scriptures for our benefit and use.   For if the prophets had openly predicted destruction for them, and prosperity for the Gentiles, none of the Jews would have loved them, but they would have destroyed their writings as hostile and opposed to them, and it would have been impossible for us Gentiles to have made use of the prophetic evidence

(d) about our Saviour and ourselves.   But yet when all this shall have happened to the Jewish race in Emmanuel's day, according to my interpretation of the prophecy, a scanty remnant of them is said to be left, of which the apostle says: "There was a remnant according to the election of grace."   This it is surely, which shall rear a red heifer and two sheep, and from the abundance of their milk feed on butter and honey.   And I have shewed according to my second interpretation that this describes the whole apostolic choir of the disciples of our Saviour Jesus Christ.   But as those who are left behind are thus described in the prophecy, so also when the whole land of the Jewish nation and their vineyard has been transformed into sand and thorns, and therefore delivered to the enemy, it is prophesied in direct opposition to this that every arable

(326) mountain shall be ploughed.   And I think that the Church of our Saviour Jesus Christ is thus suggested, of which He

Matt. v. also says: "A city set on a hill cannot be hid."   For
14. I think that the exalted, high, and lofty constitution of the Church is here called a mountain.   It is, then, this arable mountain that it says shall be ploughed, so that no fear may attack it, and that it shall be so far changed from its former desolation, aridity, and thorns, as to be fit for "a pasture for sheep, and a place for cattle to tread."

(b)   And we can remember, that the Church of Christ which of old was dry and thorny, has undergone by His grace such a transformation, that it grows such a crop of the grass and fodder of spiritual harvest, that the sheeplike and simpler souls can delight in it, and that those who have reached a more perfect development, here called bulls, can plough and till it, as I shewed that the holy apostle taught, when he said:

1 Cor. ix.   "Doth God take care for oxen, or doth he say it
9.   altogether for your sakes?   For your sakes was it

written, that he that plougheth should plough in hope, (c)
and he that harroweth in hope to share therein."
Thus the land that was before desert and dry has been
transformed after the coming of Christ, so that it is fit
for those, whom I understand as the bulls, to cultivate
suitably.

And notice how the Virgin Birth is prophesied under the
same figure, by which at the same time the prophecy says
that the land that of old bore fruit worth a thousand shekels
will be dry and thorny, and all the land because it is so dry
and thorny will be delivered to those that attack it with (d)
arrow and bow; while to every mountain the opposite will
happen. They will be transformed from their previous dry
and thorny state into a pasture of flocks and a place for
cattle to tread, and no fear shall enter there. Whereby
I think our Saviour's Virgin Birth is clearly meant, and
all that happened after it both to the whole Jewish com-
munity and to the other nations. The prophecy plainly
foretells the change of each of these divisions to the
opposite of what they were before, the .change of the
Jewish nations from better to worse, and the change of
the Gentile Church from its old desolation to a divine fruitfulness, both of which are to be brought to pass according
to the prophecy at the same time, that of the appearance of (327)
Emmanuel, and are shewn to have actually been fulfilled
after our Saviour's birth, and at no other time, both by the
events in Jewish history which have been clearly told, and
by the existence of the Gentile Church.

For if after the coming of our Saviour Jesus Christ
Himself the kingdoms of Damascus and Judæa had not
come to an end, and if we could not see with our own
eyes their lands released from them, and given over to
foreign idolaters to inhabit; and, moreover, if the old (b)
stately beauty [1] of their very Temple had not become sand
and thorns, and if no impure idolaters had come as their
enemies to attack them with bow and arrow, urged on by
the Lord Himself from abroad, and stayed in their country
making every place and every city their own; and on the
other side, if by the teaching of our Saviour no nations
brought to believe in Him had changed from the sands

---

[1] σεμνοτάτη ὥρα.

and thorns of their ancient barrenness and brought forth
(c) a holy and godly spiritual harvest ; and again, if they who
saw Christ with their eyes had not rejected Him, if they who
heard Him speak had not turned a deaf ear to Him, and
if the rest of the prophecy could not be proved to have
been most exactly fulfilled from the days of Jesus our
Saviour—then He would not be the subject of the prophecy.
But if the fulfilment of the prophecies is, as the saying is,
clear to a blind man, as only brought to pass from the
(d) period of His coming, why need we any longer be in doubt
about the Virgin Birth, or refuse by wise reasoning to base
our belief in that which was the beginning of this matter,
on the evidence of what we can even now see? And
what do we even now see, but the Jews' disbelief in Him, so
clearly fulfilling the oracle, which said : " Hearing ye shall
hear and not understand, and seeing ye shall see and not
Isa. vi. 9. perceive, for the heart of this people is waxed hard," and
the siege of Jerusalem, and the total desolation of their
ancient Temple, and the settling of foreign races on their
land, enslaving them with stings, that is to say with harsh
(328) enactments—for this is meant by the figures of the flies
and bees—and above all the transformation of the heathen
world from its former desolation into the field of God.
Who would not be struck with astonishment at these
spectacles? And who would not agree that the prediction
is truly inspired, when he heard that these words were
consigned to books and taken care of by our ancestors
a thousand years ago, and only brought to a fulfilment
(b) after our Saviour's coming? If, then, the prediction was
wonderful, and the result of the prediction yet more
wonderful, and beyond all reason, why should we disbelieve that the actual entrance of Him that was foretold
was allotted a miraculous and superhuman kind of birth,
especially as the clear evidence of the other miracles, as
marvellous (as the Birth itself) in their sequence from that
Birth compels us to accept the evidence of the other
wonders connected with Him.[1]

---

[1] Reading comma at οὖσα, with Migne. The sentence gives the
core of the argument for the Virgin Birth : The subsequent miracles,
the Life and Risen Life of Christ, authenticate the record for the
original miraculous entry of the Word into the conditions of human
life.

But following this, after, For a pasture of flocks, and a place for cattle to tread, a second prediction is attached, to the foregoing : " And the Lord said to me, Take a book (c) for thyself," which we will consider, when I have quoted it.

From the same.   (d)

Concerning a New Writing, that is to say the New Covenant;
a Prophetess is said to conceive of the Holy Spirit and
bear a Son, Who, conquering Foes and Enemies, shall be
rejected by the Jews, and will be a Saviour to the Gentiles.
And what the Nation of the Jews will suffer after their
Disbelief in Him, is shewn at the Same Time.

[Passage quoted, Isa. viii. .1–4.]

This prophecy is connected with the preceding.   For she that was there called a Virgin, and was said to bear God with us, is here called a Prophetess.   And if it be asked whence she should conceive being unmarried, the prophecy (b) now gives teaching on this point, for it says : " And I went in to the prophetess ; and she conceived and bare a son." This must be understood of the Holy Spirit, under Whose Divine influence the prophet spoke.   The Holy Spirit then Himself confesses that He went in to the prophetess : and this is clearly fulfilled in the birth of our Saviour Jesus Christ, when :

"The angel Gabriel was sent by God to a city of Galilee, named Nazareth, to a virgin betrothed to a man, whose name was Joseph, of the house and lineage of David.   And he said to her, Hail, thou that art highly favoured, the Lord is with thee, blessed art thou Luke i. among women."   26–28.

And again :   (c)

"Fear not, for thou hast found favour with God. And, behold, thou shalt conceive in thy womb, and bear a son, and shall call his name Jesus.   And Mary said, How shall this be, seeing I know not a man?" He answered, "The Holy Spirit shall come upon thee, and the power of the Highest shall overshadow thee. Wherefore the holy thing that is born shall be called Luke i. 30, Son of God."   31, 34, 35.

(d) And in the preceding prophecy, coincident with the birth
of Emmanuel, before the Child knows good or evil, it is
said that the land is forsaken by the two kings that
are attacking it, namely the kings of Samaria and
Damascus; while in this prophecy it says that before the
Child calls on His father or mother, He shall take the
power of Damascus and the spoils of Samaria, whose kings
He previously prophesied would be destroyed at the birth
of Emmanuel.

I have already pointed out that actually in the time
of Ahaz two kings made a covenant and attacked those
ruled by David's successors; the one, ruler of the idolatrous
Gentiles of Damascus; the other, king of the Jewish
people in the city of Palestine called Samaria, which we
(330) call Sebaste.   Concerning whom God said to Ahaz:
" Fear not, let thy heart not be sick, for these two smoking
firebrands."   And he foretells that the destruction of these
men will be immediate, and proceeds to prophesy that on
the birth of God with us, both their kingdoms will be
utterly extinguished and destroyed. And we know from
history that until the coming of our Saviour Jesus Christ
(b) the kingdoms of Judæa and Damascus continued, but that
after His appearance to all men, they ceased in accordance
with the prophecy, for the Roman Empire absorbed them
concurrently with the preaching of our Saviour.

And after this literal prediction the prophecy passes to
a figurative and generally more spiritual form of revelation,
and it understands two ranks of invisible enemies and
hostile dæmons, warring in different ways against humanity,
one active always and everywhere in promoting idolatry
and false beliefs among mankind, the other occasioning the
(c) corruption of morals.   And taking the type of idolatrous
error in the king of Damascus, and of the decline of the
pure and healthy life in the king of Samaria, it says that
the earth, meaning thereby the men who inhabit it, will
only be released from their power, when God appears on
earth as Emmanuel. When He has shone forth and ruled
over the soul of man, none of the old tyrants will be left.
Thus, then, you will understand that here it refers to the
(d) same beings, when it says: " He will take the power of
Damascus and the spoils of Samaria," for our Saviour
Jesus Christ's power conquers completely all our unseen

enemies, who for long ages besieged all men with their
aforesaid godless and harmful activities.   And in the literal
sense as well you may see the power of Damascus destroyed concurrently with the Birth and appearance of our
Saviour, and the spoils of Samaria taken, that is to say
their kingdoms, which continued up to the time stated,
but in the fulfilment of the divine prediction have ceased
from then till now.   (331)

Some say, interpreting otherwise, that the Magi, who
came from the East to worship Christ, the young Child,
are meant by the "power of Damascus": and you might
say more universally that all who have rejected godless,
polytheistic idolatry, and obeyed the word of Christ,
especially if they be furnished with this world's reason and
wisdom, are those meant by the "power of Damascus."
And by the "spoils of Samaria" you will in this case
understand our Saviour's Jewish apostles and disciples, (b)
whom as it were He took as His spoils from the hostile
Jews who attacked Him, and armed for the conflict with
the king of the Assyrians, by whom again the Prince of
this world is figuratively meant.   But as Aquila has translated more clearly: "The adversary of the king of the
Assyrians" by "In the face of the king of the Assyrians,"
it is worth considering whether here the Roman Empire
is not meant, if the translation given a little before of
"Assyrians" as "rulers or ruled" be correct.   As then (c)
here, also, the king of the Assyrians is connected with the
appearing of our Saviour, it is probable that here also the
Roman Empire is intended, through their being directed
by God to subject the nations to themselves.   It is therefore prophesied that the child that is born will take the
power of Damascus, and the spoils of Samaria, and will
deliver them against the face of the Assyrians, and before
the eyes of those ruled by God, and that He will do this
at the time of His Birth, directing the fate of humanity
with secret divine power, while physically still a babe.   (d)

The prophet commands all this to be delivered in a new
and great book in the writing of a man, by which is meant
the new Covenant.   And he adds as witnesses of his sayings
a priest and a prophet: his word thus teaching us, of the
necessity of using in Christian evidences the witness of the
sacrificial system in the law, and of the prophets who

succeeded it; and he desires, for other reasons, that there should be eye-witnesses of the Child's birth, that we might be able to understand what is prophesied of Him. For it was said above: "For if ye will not believe, neither will ye understand," and (he writes) that the one should have (332) "the Light of God" (this is the meaning of Uriah), and that the other being "the Son of Blessing" should bear the "memory of God in himself" (this is the meaning of Zachariah son of Barachiah).

Such is my exposition of the passages, and if any of the Jews does not agree with me, let him point out to me who at any time was born in this nation as Emmanuel, and how the prophet came in to the prophetess, and who she was, and how she conceived immediately, and who was the child that was born of the prophetess, whom the Lord (b) Himself named: "Take the spoil speedily, keenly rob," and why the child was so called. They must shew, too, that the child, before he called on his father and mother, took the power of Damascus, and the spoils of Samaria against the king of the Assyrians. For we, understanding these sayings both literally and figuratively, hold that they were fulfilled in our Saviour's Birth, shewing that you must deal with the prophecies first in their literal and (c) obvious sense, and next allegorically. Immediately after the aforesaid words another prophecy follows in disguised language.

[Passage quoted, Isa. viii. 5–8.]

It is clear that the only way to preserve the sense of this passage is to explain it figuratively. Thus it means by the water of Siloam that goes softly, the Gospel teaching of the word of salvation. For Siloam means "sent." And this would be God the Word, sent by the Father, of Whom Moses also says, A ruler shall not fail from Juda, nor a prince from his loins, until he come for whom it is stored Gen. xlix. up, and he is the expectation of nations. For instead for 10. whom it is stored up, the Hebrew has "Siloam," the word (333) of prophecy using the same word Siloam there and here, which means "the one that is sent,"[1]

And Raashim again was king of the idolatrous Gentiles in Damascus, as was also the son of Romelias of the Jews

---

[1] See note, vol. i, p. 21.

in Samaria who deserted the Jewish worship of their ancestors.   And so God threatens that on those who will not
accept Siloam, that is to say Emmanuel, who is sent to
them, and the Son born of the prophetess, and His pleasant
and fruitful Word, but reject it, though it flows softly and (b)
gently, and choose for their own selves the prince of idolatrous Gentiles or the leaders of the apostasy of God's
people, He will bring the strong and full flood of the river,
which the word of the prophecy interprets for us to be the
king of the Assyrians : meaning here again either figuratively the Prince of this world, or the power of Rome
actually dominant, to which they were delivered who rejected the said water of Siloam that went softly, and (c)
embraced beliefs utterly hostile to good teaching.   At once
surely and without delay on those who rejected the Gospel
of our Saviour, and refused the water of Siloam that went
softly, the Roman army came under God's direction through
all their valleys, trod down all their walls, took away from
Judæa every man who could raise his head, or was able to
do anything at all, and so great was their camp that it filled
the whole breadth of Judæa.   (d)

So the prophecy was literally fulfilled against them.   Learn
why it was if you desire to know.   Because Emmanuel, God
with us, the Child of the Virgin, was not with them,
for if they had had Him, they would not have suffered thus.
Wherefore the prophet next cries to the Gentiles, saying,
"Emmanuel, God with us : know ye nations and yield."
And this I have interpreted, so as to shew that most prophecies can be explained either literally or figuratively.   Hence
we must proceed to consider the remainder of the prophecy
before us in both ways.   And if the Jews say that even now (334)
we are to expect the fulfilment in the future, expecting
these things to be accomplished actually and literally by the
Christ they look for, let us ask them, how he that is to
come will take the power of Damascus and the spoils of
Samaria against the king of the Assyrians, inasmuch as
Samaria at the present time is destroyed, and no longer
exists, and the power that bore the name of Damascus is
abolished, and so is the Assyrian Empire, which the Medes (b)
and Persians destroyed and superseded between them?
And as none of these people hold empire, how is it possible
to look for their destruction in the future?

Neither is it possible to claim that they were fulfilled at any other time in the distant past. No Hebrew sprung from the union of a prophetess with the prophet Isaiah ever (c) took the spoils of Samaria and the power of Damascus warring against the king of Assyria, as the literal sense would imply. So that everything compels us to agree that the fulfilment has only been in the way I have described, and at no other time than that of the appearance of Jesus our Saviour, in Whose day I have proved that the things aforesaid were fulfilled.

And there was therefore written according to the prophecy on His appearing a new book, the word of the new Covenant containing the birth of the Son of the prophetess, (d) Who also has literally by secret and divine power delivered the kingly power of both Damascus and Samaria and their spoils as explained by me into the hands of the Roman Empire : and figuratively of course as well, He has drawn up His Jewish disciples, claiming them as it were for His spoils, girding them with arms of spiritual strength, against the face of the said king of the Assyrians, and made them into heavy-armed soldiers, as His own soldiers. But those who refused the fruitful and life-giving water of His own teaching, which goes softly, and preferred what is hostile and opposed to God, He has handed over to the king of (335) the Assyrians, by whom they are even now enslaved. For verily He has gone up all their valleys, and all their walls, and taken away from Judæa every ruler and king, denominated "head," and every one capable of doing anything, with the result that from that time to this they have possessed no head, no able man of God, as were their ancient saints, whether eminent for prophecy, or even for righteousness and godliness.

And it is evident that their whole country is even now (b) subject to their enemies, and that this was all completed when Emmanuel came. Thus, then, the Hebrew Scriptures contain the double message that Emmanuel would be rejected by the Jews and cause their great miseries, and that He would be accepted by us Gentiles and prove Himself our source of salvation and of the knowledge of God. Wherefore the next saying is, "God is with us : know ye Gentiles and yield." How truly do we yield, we Gentiles that believe on Him, vanquished by the truth and power of Him

Who is God with us, and conquered we obey Him every- (c)
where alike, even though we dwell in the very ends of the
earth, according to the prophecy which says, "Obey even
at the ends of the earth." Yet though we obey Him and
hear His call, the prophecy as it proceeds must refer to
those nations that do not yet believe, saying, "Ye that were
strong be vanquished. For if ye again be strong, ye shall
again be vanquished, and whatever word ye take, shall not
remain among you, for God is with us. Thus saith the
Lord to them that disbelieve with strong hand." (d)

In which words the prophecy says clearly to them that
are restive under and rebel against Christ's teaching and
put no trust in His strong hand, that they will have no
strength if they attempt to war with the God with us, and
that whatever counsel they take against Him shall not abide
with them, because Emmanuel is with us, and it is easy for
us who see the threats directed against us and the attacks
of rulers in these days, to realize the truth of the conclusion, and that they can never carry out their threats because
God is with us. (336)

From the same.

That the Son to be Born of the Virgin prophesied of, or
Prophetess, is Called God, Angel of Great Counsel, and by
Other Strange Names, and that His Birth is the Occasion
of the Light of Holiness to the Gentiles.

[Passage quoted, Isa. ix. 1–7.[1]]

This is the third prophecy of the Child, making known the
same thing in different ways. As our present object is to
exhibit the manner of God's coming to men, note the
number of ways in which He is shewn forth. First, He was
set before us under the name of Emmanuel, God born of a
Virgin; secondly, as the Child of the prophetess and the
Holy Spirit, being none other than the before-named;
thirdly, in the present passage, being one and the same as
in the former, wherein His Name is said to be, according to
the Septuagint, Angel of Great Counsel, and as some of

---

[1] Verse 6. E. adds after Μεγάλης βουλῆς ἄγγελος (LXX): θαυμαστὸς
σύμβουλος, Θεὸς ἰσχυρὸς, ἐξουσιαστὴς, ἄρχων εἰρήνης, πατὴρ τοῦ μέλ-
λοντος αἰῶνος.

the copies[1] have, "Wonderful Counsellor, Mighty God,
(337) Potentate, Prince of Peace, Father of the World to Come."
In the Hebrew, as Aquila says :

"For unto us a child is born, to us a son is given,
and a measure was upon his shoulders. And his name
was called Wonderful Counsellor, Mighty, Powerful,
Father, even Prince of Peace, and of his peace there
is no end."

And as Symmachus :

"For a youth is given to us, a son is given us ; and
his instructions shall be upon his shoulders, and his
name shall be called Miraculous, Counselling, Strong,
Powerful, Eternal Father, Prince of Peace, and of his
(b) peace there is no end."

In the Septuagint it is not simply Angel, but that he
should be born as Angel of Great Counsel, and Wonderful
Counsellor, and Mighty God, and Potentate, and Prince of
Peace, and Father of the World to Come, and it was there
prophesied that He should be a Child. He is referred to
that was previously called differently the Word of God, and
God and Lord, and also named the Angel of His Father,
and the Captain of the Lord's Host. But who can this be
who, in Aquila's version and those even now current among
(c) the Hebrews, is "begotten among men, and become a child,
Wonderful and Strong, Counsellor, Powerful, and Father,
yea even Prince of peace, Whose peace, he says, will never
end?" or in that of Symmachus, "Miraculous, Counselling,
Strong, Powerful, Eternal Father, Prince of peace, and that
endless and infinite"; or in Theodotion's "Counselling
wonderfully, Strong, Powerful, Father, Prince of peace, for
increasing instruction, of Whose peace there is no end."

And that which follows I leave you to consider by yourself,
only remarking that this Being Who is called Eternal Father,
(d) and Prince of Endless Peace, and Angel of Great Counsel is
prophesied of as being begotten and becoming a child, and
on His birth among men wills that they shall be burnt with
fire who grudge the salvation He wins for the Gentiles, be
they evil dæmons, or be they wicked men, of whom He
says, "That every garment and raiment wrought by guile,
they will repay with interest." And who can these be, but

---

[1] ἀντίγραφα.

those of whom it was elsewhere spoken in the person of our
Saviour, " They parted my garments among them, and upon Ps. xxii.
my vesture did they cast lots "? And they who are partakers 18.
of their sin, who will also desire, when they shall see their
own judgment at some future time, that they had been
burnt with fire before they sinned, before the Angel of Great (338)
Counsel had been sinned against by them?

Now consider yourself whether it does not overstep the
limits of human nature that His peace should be said to be
endless, and that He should be called Eternal Father ; and
also that He should be called not simply Angel, but Angel
of Great Counsel, and Mighty God, and the other names in
the list. And it says too that the kingdom of David will (b)
be restored by Him, which you will understand thus :
there were many promises given to David, in which it was
said :

> " And I will set his hand in the sea, and his right
> hand in the rivers : he shall call upon me, Thou art my
> father, my God, and the helper of my salvation, And I
> will make him my firstborn, high above the kings of the
> earth. For ever I will keep my mercy for him, and my
> covenant shall stand firm with him, and I will make his (c)
> seed for ever and ever, and his throne as the days of Ps. lxxxix
> heaven." 25.

And again :

> " Once have I sworn by my holiness, I will not fail
> David, his seed shall remain for ever, and his throne is
> as the sun before me, and as the moon established for Ps. lxxxix.
> ever." 35.

God promised all this to David in the Psalms, but through
the sins of his successors the opposite actually happened—
for the kings of David's seed lasted until Jeremiah, and (d)
ceased on the siege of the holy city by the Babylonians, so
that from that date neither the throne of David nor his
seed ruled the Jewish nation. And the Holy Spirit thus
foretells the failure of the promises made to David in the
same passage of the Psalm :

> " But thou hast rejected, and made of no account,
> thou hast cast down thy Christ : Thou hast destroyed
> the covenant of thy servant, and cast his glory to the
> ground, thou hast broken down all his strongholds."

And a few verses later :

"Thou hast broken down his throne to the ground, thou hast lessened the days of his time, thou hast proved dishonour upon him " ;

a course of events which has been begun and carried to its conclusion from the Babylonian captivity of the Jews up to (339) the Roman Empire and Tiberius.   For no one of the seed of David appears to have sat on the throne of the Hebrews in the intervening period up to the coming of Christ.   But when our Lord and Saviour Jesus Christ, Who was of David's seed, was proclaimed King of all the world, that very throne of David, as though renewed from its degradation and fall, was restored in the divine kingdom of our (b) Saviour, and will last for ever ; and even now, like the sun in God's Presence, is lighting the whole world with the rays of His teaching, according to the witness of the Psalm and the prophecy before us, which says concerning the Child that should be born, on the throne of David (that is to say, the eternal and lasting throne promised to David), He should sit in His kingdom, to guide it, and uphold it in (c) justice and judgment from now even for ever.   The Angel Gabriel should be a sufficient teacher that this was fulfilled, when he said in his sacred words to the Virgin :

"Fear not, Mary, for thou hast found favour with God ; and behold thou shalt conceive in thy womb, and bear a son, and thou shalt call his name Jesus.   He shall be great, and shall be called Son of the Highest, and the Lord God shall give unto him the throne of his father David, and he shall reign over the house of Luke i. 30.   Jacob for ever, and of his kingdom there shall be no end."

(d)   And the prophet expecting this birth of Christ in the aforesaid Psalm, and regarding its postponement and delay as if it were the cause of the fall of David's throne, cries in disgust, " But thou hast refused, and made of no account, and cast off thy Christ."·   And he prays as though doubting the Divine Being, that the promise may be somehow swiftly fulfilled : "Where is thine ancient pity, Lord, which thou swarest unto David in thy truth ? " which same things his prophecy most clearly says will be fulfilled at the birth of the Angel of Great Counsel.   "Wherefore they will wish," he says, " to have been burnt with fire, those before-named

for unto us a child is born, and to us a son is given, the
Angel of Great Counsel." To us, that is, who in Galilee of
the Gentiles have believed on Him, to whom He has
brought light and joy, and the new and fresh drink of the
mystery of the new Covenant : according to the prophecy
which says :

> "First drink this, drink quickly—land of Zabulon, (340)
> and land of Nephthalim, and the rest who dwell by the
> coast, across Jordan, Galilee of the Gentiles : O people
> that sat in darkness, behold a great light, and to them
> that sat in darkness and the shadow of death a light is
> risen."

These are they who from the Gentiles believed in the
Christ of God, and the disciples and apostles of our Saviour,
whom He called from the land of Zabulon and Nephthalim,
and chose for the preachers of His Gospel. To them therefore who believed, the Angel of Great Counsel is given as a
son to bring them salvation, but to them who disbelieved (b)
fire and burning.

He says that the ground of this whole dispensation is the
zeal of the Lord, " The zeal of the Lord of Sabaoth will do
this." What is the character of this zeal ? Is it not that
recorded by Moses, where he says :

> "They have provoked me to jealousy, but not accord-
> ing to God. They have angered me with their idols.
> And I will provoke them to jealousy by a nation which Deut.
> is not. By a foolish nation I will anger them "? xxxii. 21.

But as I have by God's help solved the problems of the (c)
sojourn on earth of Him that was prophesied, and also the
character of His coming from prophetic evidence, it is now
the time to investigate the place where He should be born,
His race, and the Hebrew tribe from which it was predicted
He should come. These, then, shall be our next subjects.

CHAPTER 2

From Micah.

(341) *Of the Place of the Birth of the God fore-announced, and how
He will come forth from Bethlehem, a Town of Palestine,
being from Eternity, as Governor of the Race of the Holy,
and how it is foretold that the Lord will feed them that
have believed in Him unto the Ends of the Earth.*

[Passage quoted, Micah v. 2–6.]

EMMANUEL, which is interpreted God with us, has been
clearly shewn in the passages quoted to have been born of
(b) the Virgin, and the Angel of Great Counsel to have become
a child. But the place of His Birth had also to be pointed
out. It was therefore prophesied that a ruler would come
forth from Bethlehem, whose goings forth were from
eternity. And this could not be referred to a human
being, but only to the nature of Emmanuel and the Angel
of Great Counsel.

For eternal existence can be assumed only of God. A
person who exists from eternity, then, is predicted as about
to come forth from Bethlehem, a Jewish town not far from
(c) Jerusalem. And we find that the only famous man who
was born there was David, and then later our Lord and
Saviour, Jesus the Christ of God, and besides them no
other. But David, who came before the date of the
prophecy, was dead many years before the prediction : nor
were his goings forth from the days of eternity. It only
remains that the words were fulfilled in Him that was born
afterwards from Bethlehem, the true Emmanuel, God the
Word going forth before the whole creation, and called
(d) "God with us," especially as His Birth at Bethlehem
undoubtedly shewed God's Presence, by the wonders connected with it : for St. Luke writes its record thus :

[Passage quoted, Luke ii. 1–18.[1]]

So Luke writes. And Matthew tells the story of our
Saviour's birth as follows : [Matt. ii. 1–12.[2]]

---

[1] Variations from W.H. Verse 2 : E. add ἤ. Verse 5, E.: Μαριὰμ
τῇ μεμνηστευμένῃ αὐτῷ [γυναῖκι] (Gaisford). Verse 12 : Add τὸ.
Verse 13 : E. οὐρανίου. W.H. [οὐρανίου]. Verse 14 : E. εὐδοκία.
W.H. [εὐδοκίας]. Margin εὐδοκία.

[2] Variation. Verse 6 : W.H., "καὶ σύ, Βηθλεὲμ γῆ 'Ιούδα." E.: "καὶ
σύ Βηθλεὲμ οἶκος τοῦ 'Εφραθά."

I have quoted these passages in full to shew that what happened at Bethlehem at the Birth of our Saviour furnishes adequate evidence that He was the Person meant by the prophecy.   And to this day the inhabitants of the place, who have received the tradition from their fathers, confirm the truth of the story by shewing to those who visit Bethlehem because of its history the cave in which the (c) Virgin bare and laid her infant,[1] as the prophecy says :

> "Therefore he shall give them until the time of her that brings forth : She shall bring forth, and the rest of their brethren shall turn to them."

And by " her that brings forth " he means accordingly her that in the former prophecies was called a Virgin, and the prophetess who was delivered of Emmanuel and the Angel of Great Counsel.   For until her day and that of Him she bare the old conditions of the nation were unaltered, the prescription being laid down until the time of " her that (d) brings forth," that is, until the miraculous Birth of Him that was born of the Virgin ; but after His day their kingdom was taken away, and the remnant of their brethren, those, that is to say, who believed in the Christ of God, became apostles and disciples and evangelists of our Saviour, whom, when they turn to Him, the Lord Himself is said to feed, not as before by angels or men that served him, but by Himself personally, so that thus they might be glorified to the ends of the earth.   For they were glorified when "their voice went into all the earth, and their words to the end of the world."   It is clear what a great flock of spiritual human sheep has been won for the Lord throughout the whole world by the apostles : and this flock the Lord Himself is (344) said personally to look after and feed with His strength, being both Shepherd and Lord of the flock, so that the sheep are protected by the strong hand and mighty arm of their Master and Shepherd, from danger of attack from wild and savage beasts.

Such is the character of the events at Bethlehem, and of the Coming of the God that was fore-announced.   But the account of the Coming from Heaven to men of the Lord and (b)

---

[1] " Alone of all the existing local traditions of Palestine, this one indisputably reaches beyond the time of Constantine." (Stanley, *Sinai and Palestine*, p. 440.) Cf. Justin, *Trypho.* 78 ; Origen, *c. Cels.* i. 51.   See Stanley's note, from Thilo's *Codex Apocryphus*, pp. 382, 383.

Shepherd Himself I have already quoted from the prophecy
we have before us, in which it is said :

"Hear all peoples, and let the earth attend, and all
that are therein, and the Lord shall be a witness to you,
the Lord from his holy house.   Wherefore behold the
Lord, the Lord comes forth from his place, and shall
descend,"

(and that which follows); to which he adds, "For the sin of
Jacob is all this done, and for the transgression of the house
of Israel."   But it is clear, from what the same prophet goes
on to say, that it was not only because of the sin of the
Jews, that the Lord came down, but also for the salvation
and calling of all nations.   For he proceeds to say :

"And the mountain of the Lord shall be visible to
the end of the days, and many peoples shall haste to it,
and many nations shall come and say, Come, let us go
up to the Mount of the Lord."

And therefore, after the proclamation that the Eternal
shall come forth from Bethlehem, he says that he will no
more rule only over Israel, but over all men together even
unto the ends of the earth ; for he says :

"And he shall stand and see, and shall feed his flock
with the strength of the Lord, and they shall live in the
glory of the name of the Lord God : wherefore now
they shall be glorified even unto the ends of the earth,
and this shall be peace."

Who shall have this peace, but the earth, in which the
flocks of the Lord shall be glorified?   And it is plain to
all that this was fulfilled after the coming of our Saviour
Jesus Christ.

For before Him there was great variety of government,
all nations being under tyrannical or democratic constitutions, as for instance, Egypt was ruled by its own king,
and so were the Arabs, the Idumæans, the Phœnicians, the
Syrians and the other nations ; there were risings of nations
against nations and cities against cities, there were countless sieges and enslavements carried through in every place
and country, until the Lord and Saviour came, and concurrently with His coming, the first Roman Emperor,
Augustus, conquered the nations, variety of government
was almost completely ended, and peace was spread through
all the world, according to the prophecy before us which

Micah i.
2 *sq.*

(c)

(d)

(345)

(b)

expressly says of Christ's disciples : "Wherefore they shall
be glorified to the ends of the earth, and this shall be
peace."

And the oracle in the Psalms, which says about Christ, Ps. lxxii.
"There shall rise in his days justice and peace," is in agree- 7.
ment with this.   And I think that is why He is called
"Prince of Peace" in the prophecy that I quoted before
this.   And I would ask you to notice that the prophet we
are considering says at the outset that the Lord will come
from heaven, and that the subject of the prophecy will
only pasture his flock *after* His birth at Bethlehem.   And (c)
the Evangelist, whose words I have cited, furnishes the
evidence that this was the case with regard to our Lord
and Saviour.

The Christ is called the governor and shepherd of Israel,
in accord with the custom of Holy Scripture to give the
name of the true Israel figuratively to all who see God
and live according to His Will: just as contrariwise it
calls the Jews, when they sin, by names that suit their
ways, Canaanites, and seed of Canaan not Judah, Rulers
of Sodom, and people of Gomorrah.   Though, of course, (d)
also, all our Saviour's life was literally passed with the
Jewish race, and He was the Leader of many gathered out
of Israel, as many of the Jews as knew Him and believed
in Him.

Such, then, was the fulfilment of the prophecy quoted.
But one must start fresh in considering that which succeeds
it, which runs thus :

> "When the Assyrian shall attack your land, and
> come against your country, there shall be raised up
> against him seven shepherds, and eight 'bites'[1] of
> men,"

with that which follows, whose meaning we are not now
called upon to unfold.

Now it might be said that after the expedition of the
Assyrians into Judæa, when they overcame the Jews, the
number of rebellions against them is shewn by the seven
shepherds and the eight "bites": and that historians of (346)
Assyria would know this, and at the end of their rule the
one foretold was born at Bethlehem, after the seven
shepherds and the eight "bites" had happened to the

---

[1] δήγματα.

Assyrians in the period after their expedition against
Judæa.   But we must not now devote more time to what
would entail a long inquiry.

From Psalm cxxxi.

*To David, inquiring where should be the Birthplace of the
Predicted God, Ephratha, which is Bethlehem, is made
known by the Holy Spirit.*

(c)   [Passages quoted, Ps. cxxxi. 1–7, 10, 11, 17.]

This prophecy agrees with the preceding in stating that
the God about Whom the prophecy is made will come forth
from Bethlehem.   And it is about this place that David
first prays God to teach him, since he does not know it,
(347) and then after his prayer he is taught.   For when he has
received the oracle addressed to him in the Psalm which
said : "Of the fruit of thy body I will set upon thy seat,"
and, "There will I raise up a horn for David, I have prepared a lantern for my Christ," he rightly falls down before
God, and there fallen to the earth worships, and with yet
greater intensity of prayer swears that he will not enter
the tabernacle of his house, nor allow his eyes to sleep, nor
his eyelids to slumber, nor ascend the couch of his bed,
(b) but will lie on the ground worshipping and adoring, until
he finds a place for the Lord, and a tabernacle for the
God of Jacob—that is, until he learns by the Lord's
revelation to him the birthplace of the Christ.

So having prayed and desired to learn it, not long after
he beholds by the Holy Spirit what will be in the future ;
for God has promised to His people that he will hear them
even while they speak.   So his prayer being heard he
(c) is favoured with an oracle which cries "Bethlehem," that
being the place of the Lord, and the tabernacle of the
God of Jacob.   And so when the Holy Spirit prophesied
that this was within him, he, listening to his inner voice,
adds : "Lo, we heard of it in Ephratha."   And Ephratha
is the same as Bethlehem, as is clear from Genesis, where it
Gen. xxxv. is said of Rachel, "And they buried her in the Hippodrome
19. of Ephratha,"[1] and this is Bethlehem.   And the previous
prophecy ran : "And thou, Bethlehem, house of Ephratha."

---

[1] S. reads : ἐν τῇ ὁδῷ Ἐφράθα—for ἐν τῷ ἱπποδρόμῳ.

"Behold," he says, "we have heard it ! "--evidently mean- (d)
ing the birth of Christ and the entering of the God of
Jacob into His tabernacle. For what else could the
tabernacle of the God of Jacob be but the Body of Christ,
which was born at Bethlehem, in which, as in a tabernacle, the divinity of the Only-begotten dwelt? And the
habitation is not said to be simply of God, but is qualified
as of the God of Jacob, that we may know that it is the
God that dwells therein, Who was seen by Jacob in human
form and shape, wherefore he was deemed worthy of the
name, Seer of God, for such is the translation of his name.
And I have established in the early part of this work that
He that was seen by Jacob was none other than the Word
of God. Bethlehem was therefore revealed to David when
he prayed and desired to know the place and the habitation
of the Lord and God of Jacob, wherefore he said : " Behold,
we heard it at Ephratha," and added : "Let us worship at (348)
the place where his feet stood." Therefore in these words
the Lord God of Jacob Himself foretold that His own
place and habitation would be in Ephratha, which is
Bethlehem, agreeing with the prophecy of Micah, which
said : "And thou, Bethlehem, house of Ephratha, out of
thee shall come a governor, and his goings forth are from
eternity," which, when we lately examined, we found could
only apply to our Lord and Saviour Jesus Christ, Who
was born at Bethlehem according to the predictions. For (b)
it is certain that no one else can be shewn to have come
forth from there with glory after the date of the prophecy :
there was no king, or prophet, or any other Hebrew
saint who can be shewn to have been of David's seed,
and also born at Bethlehem, except our Lord and
Saviour, the Christ of God. We must, therefore, own that
He, and no one else, is the subject of this prophecy, and (c)
for the additional reason that further on the same Psalm
proves it, calling Him Christ by name, where it says :
"For the sake of David thy servant, turn not away the
face of thy Christ." And again : "There will I raise up
a horn for David, I have prepared a lantern for my Christ,
his enemies I will clothe with shame, but upon him my
holiness shall flower." Where else does he say : " I will
raise up a horn for David," but in Bethlehem—Ephratha ? (d)
For it was there the horn of David, the Christ according

to the flesh, arose like a great light, and there the God of the Universe prepared the lantern of the Christ. And the human tabernacle was the lantern as it were of his spiritual light, through which, like an earthen vessel, as if through a lantern, He poured forth the rays of His own light on all who were oppressed by ignorance of God and thick darkness.

Yes, indeed, I think that it was clearly revealed here that the God of Jacob, from the beginning the Eternal, would dwell among men, and that He would be born nowhere else but in the place at Bethlehem, near Jerusalem, in the spot that is even now pointed out, for there no one is witnessed to by all the inhabitants as having been (349) born there in accordance with the Gospel story, no one remarkable or famous among all men, except Jesus Christ. And Bethlehem is translated, "House of Bread," bearing the name of Him Who came forth from it, our Saviour, the true Word of God, and nourisher of spiritual souls, which He Himself shews by saying: "I am the Bread that came down from heaven." And since it was David's mother-town as well, the Son of David according to the (b) flesh rightly made His entrance from it according to the predictions of the prophets, so that the reason is clear why He chose Bethlehem for His mother-town.

But He is said to have been brought up at Nazara, and also to have been called a Nazarene. We know that Lev. xxi. the Hebrew word "Naziraion" occurs in Leviticus in con-12. nection with the ointment which they used for unction. And the ruler there was a kind of image of the great and (c) true High Priest, the Christ of God, being a shadowy type of Christ. So there it is said about the High Priest according to the Septuagint: "And he shall not defile him that is sanctified to his God, because the holy oil of his God hath anointed him": where the Hebrew has *nazer* for oil. And Aquila reads: "Because the separation, the oil of God's unction, is on him"; and Symmachus·: "Because the pure oil of his God's anointing is on him"; and Theodotion: "Because the oil nazer anointed by his God is upon him." So that *nazer* according to the Septuagint is "holy," according to Aquila "separation," according to Symmachus "pure," and the name Nazarene will therefore mean either holy, or separate, or pure. But the ancient

priests, who were anointed with prepared oil, which Moses (d)
called *Nazer*, were called for that reason Nazarenes ; while
our Lord and Saviour having naturally holiness, purity, and
separation from sin, needed no human unguent, yet received the name of Nazarene among men, not because He
was a Nazarene in the sense of being anointed with the oil
called *Nazer*, but because He naturally had the qualities it
symbolized, and also because He was called Nazarene from
Nazara, where He was brought up by His parents according
to the flesh and passed His childhood.   And so it is said (350)
in Matthew :

> "Being warned of God in a dream [Joseph is re-
> ferred to] he departed into the regions of Galilee, and   Matt. ii.
> came and lived in a city called Nazara,[1] that the say-   22.
> ing of the prophets might be fulfilled, He shall be
> called a Nazarene."

For it was altogether necessary that He Who was a Nazarene
naturally and truly, that is holy, and pure and separate
from men, should be called by the name.   But since, needing no human unction, He did not receive the name from
the oil *nazer*, He acquired it from the place named (b)
Nazara.

This proof being thus complete, let us now investigate
from what race, and from which Hebrew tribe, it was foretold that the Saviour of our souls, the Christ of God, should
come.   And I will first quote the Gospel passages about it,
and then add the prophets' evidence to theirs, like seals
that agree together.[2]   Matthew thus gives the genealogy of
Christ according to the flesh :

---

[1] W.H.: Νηζαρέτ ; E.: Ναζαρά.   E. accepts the interpretation of
Matt. ii. 23, "that he should be called Ναζωραῖος," which makes it
refer directly to Isa. xi. 1, and assumes a connection between
Ναζωραῖος and Nazarene.   Jerome, commenting on Isa. xi. 1, ob-
jected to the interpretation, since the ζ is not represented by the צ of
the Hebrew.   Thatcher, *H.D.B.* ii. 496, supposes with Weiss that the
pl. προφητῶν precludes any reference to a single prophecy, and that
Matthew alludes generally to prophecies that the Messiah would be
despised.   This is Jerome's view in his commentary on Matt. i. 23.   In
W.H. Ναζαρηνός occurs, Mark i. 24 ; x. 47 ; xiv. 67 ; xvi. 6 ; and
Luke iv. 34 ; and only Luke xxiv. 19. (A.D., etc.), Ναζωραῖος.   It is
thus probable that Ναζαρηνός was the only form used in the original
Synoptic source.

[2] Cf. T. R. Glover, *The Conflict of Religions in the Early Roman
Empire*, p. 182 *sq.* : "We may discover two great canons in the opera-

"The book of the generation of Jesus Christ, the son of David, the son of Abraham. Abraham begat Isaac, and Isaac begat Jacob, and Jacob begat Juda," and that which follows.

Matt. i. 1.

And the apostle agrees with this, when he says:

Rom. i.1b.

"Separated to the gospel of God, which he had before promised by his prophets in the holy scriptures concerning his son, who was born of the seed of David according to the flesh."

These words would agree with the corresponding predictions.

CHAPTER 3

(d)   From the Second Book of Chronicles.

From what Race and from what Hebrew Tribe it was foretold that the Christ should come.

(351)   [Passages quoted, 1 Chron. xvii. 11–13 ; Ps. lxxxviii. 26 ; verses 4, 35, 29 ; and cxxxi. 11.]

THERE is no doubt that Solomon was the son of David (c) and his successor in the kingdom. And he first built the Temple of God at Jerusalem, and perhaps the Jews understand him to be the subject of the prophecy. But we may fairly ask them whether the oracle applies to Solomon,

Ps. lxxxviii. 29 ; Ps. cxxxi. 11.

which says, "And I will set up his throne for ever," and also where God sware with the affirmation of an oath by his holy one, "The throne of him that is foretold, shall be as the sun, and the days of heaven." For if the years of the (d) reign of Solomon are reckoned, they will be found to be forty and no more. Even if the reigns of all his successors be added up, they do not altogether come to 500 years. And even if we suppose that their line continued down to the final attack on the Jewish nation by the Romans, how can they fulfil a prophecy which says, " Thy throne shall

---

tions of the Apologists. In the first place, they seek to shew that all things prophesied of the Messiah were fulfilled in Jesus of Nazareth ; and secondly, that everything which befell Jesus was prophesied of the Messiah."

Luke xxiv. 27 is the root of the apologetic system, which Lactantius (*circa* 300) practically attributes in its completeness to our Lord (*de mort. persec.* 2).

remain for ever, and be as the sun and the days of heaven "?
And the words, " I will be to him a father, and he shall be
to me a son," how can they refer to Solomon, for his history
tells us much about him that is foreign and opposed to the
adoption of God ?   Nay, hear the indictment against him :

> " And Solomon loved women,[1] and took many strange
> wives, even the daughter of Pharaoh, Moabites, Am-
> monites, and Idumæans, Syrians and Chatteans, and
> Amorites, from the nations of whom the Lord said to the
> children of Israel, that they should not go in to them."

1 Kings
xi. 1.
(352)

And in addition to this :

> " And his heart was not right with the Lord his God,
> as was the heart of David his father ; and Solomon
> went after Astarte, the abomination of the Sidonians,
> and after their king, the idol of the sons of Ammon.
> And Solomon did evil before the Lord."

1 Kings
xi. 4.

And again further on he adds :

> " And the Lord raised Satan [2] against Solomon, Ader
> the Idumæan."

(b)

Now who would venture to call God his father, who lay
under such grievous charges, and to call himself the
firstborn son of the God of the Universe ?   Or how could
these sayings apply first to David, and then to his seed ?
But they do not even apply to David, if you reflect.
Therefore we require some one else, here revealed, to arise
from the seed of David.   But there was no other born
of him, as is recorded, save only our Lord and Saviour
Jesus the Christ of God, Who alone of the kings of David's
line is called through the whole world the Son of David
according to His earthly birth, and Whose Kingdom continues and will continue, lasting for endless time.   It is
attacked by many, but always by its divine superhuman power
proves itself inspired and invincible as the prophecy foretold.

(c)

(d)

And if you hear God swear by His holy one, hear Him
swear as Father by the Word of God, existing before all
ages, His Holy and Only-begotten Son, of Whose divinity the
passages I have quoted have spoken in many ways, by
Whom His God and Father swears as by His dearly beloved,
that He would glorify Him that was of the seed of David
for ever.

---

[1] S. adds " And he had 700 queens and 300 concubines."
[2] σάταν : A.V. " An adversary."

And this came to pass when the Word became flesh, and took and made divine Him that was of David's seed. Wherefore he calls him Son, saying, "I will be to him a father, and he shall be to me a son." And again, "And I will make him my firstborn." From this it is then clearly (353) explained that the firstborn Son of God will be of the seed of David, so that the Son of David is one and the same as the Son of God, and the Son of God one and the same as the Son of David. And thus it was prophesied that the Firstborn of the whole creation, Himself the Son of God, was to become Son of man.

The Scripture of the Gospel sets its seal on this oracle, where it says that the Angel Gabriel, standing by the holy Virgin, spake thus concerning our Saviour :

" He shall be great, and shall be called the Son of the Highest, and the Lord God shall give to him the throne of his father David, and he shall rule over the house Luke i. 32.   of Jacob for ever ; and of his kingdom there shall be no end."

(b) And after a little, Zacharias the father of John, prophesies thus concerning Christ in the same gospel :

" Blessed be the Lord God of Israel, for he hath visited and wrought redemption for his people, and hath raised a horn of salvation for us in the house of David Luke i. 68.   his son, as he spake by the mouth of his holy prophets from ages past."

The fact that our Lord and Saviour Jesus the Christ of God, (c) and none other, has received the throne promised for ever to David, has then been adequately proved by the prophecies quoted, and by the words of Gabriel and Zachariah, in which He is regarded as of the seed of David according to the flesh.

But the reason why the holy evangelists give the genealogy of Joseph, although our Saviour was not His son, but the son of the Holy Ghost and the holy Virgin, and how the mother of our Lord herself is proved to be of the race and (d) seed of David, I have treated fully in the First Book of my *Questions and Answers concerning the genealogy of our Saviour*,[1] and must refer those interested to that book, as the present subject is now occupying me.

---

[1] ἐν τῷ πρώτῳ τῶν εἰς τὴν γενεαλογίαν τοῦ Σωτῆρος ἡμῶν ζητημάτων καὶ λύσεων. The work *On the Discrepancies of the Gospel* consisted

From Psalm lxxii.

Of Solomon and of His Seed that is to come.

[Passages quoted, Ps. lxxii., 1, 5-8, 16 *b*.]

As this Psalm is addressed to Solomon, the first verse of (354) the Psalm must be referred to him, and all the rest to the son of Solomon, not Rehoboam, who was king of Israel after him, but Him that was of his seed according to the flesh, the Christ of God : for all who are acquainted with the Holy Scriptures will agree that it is impossible to connect (c) what is said in this Psalm with him or his successors, because of what they reveal about him.   Nay, how is it possible to apply to Solomon, or his son Rehoboam, the burden [1] of the whole Psalm ?—for instance, " He shall rule from sea to sea, and from the river to the ends of the earth."   And " He shall remain as long as the sun, and before the moon for ever," and other similar statements. Yet the words at the beginning of the Psalm are at once seen to apply to Solomon, which say, " O God, thou wilt give judgment to the king."   And the addition, " And thy justice to the king's son," to the Son of Solomon, not his (d) firstborn who succeeded him in the kingdom (for he only ruled the Jewish nation seventeen years, being a wicked king), nor any of the successors of Rehoboam, but only to one of the seed of David, who could thus be called the son both of David and Solomon.   And this is our Lord and Saviour Jesus Christ.   For His Kingdom and its throne will stand as long as the sun.   And He alone of men, as the Word of God, existed before the moon and the creation of (355) the world, and He alone came down like dew from heaven on all the earth : and it was said in our quotation a little above, that He had risen on all men and that His justice would remain even until the consummation of life, which is called the removal of the moon.   And our Saviour's power is supreme from the eastern sea to the west, beginning its

---

of two parts, addressed to Stephanus and Marinus respectively.   Mai published an epitome and also unabridged portions from Vatican MS.   The first portion was in two books [Op. iv. 879 *sq*., 953 *sq*.]. It is also mentioned by Nicephorus Callistus.   (See *D.C.B.* ii. 338.)

[1] τὰ ἐμφερόμενα.

(b) activity at the river, which is either the Sacrament of Baptism, or from Jordan, where He first appeared to benefit mankind. Yea, from that time His kingdom has spread and extended through the whole world. And Jerusalem being meant by Libanus, as is made clear by many prophecies, because of its ancient altar and temple, and the offerings thereon to the honour of God like Libanus, the Church of the Gentiles the fruit of Christ is said to be

(c) about to be exalted above Libanus. And if the studious consider this Psalm in its literal sense at leisure, they will find that its contents only apply to our Lord, and not to Solomon of old, or any of his successors on the throne of Judæa, who reigned but a few years, and only over the Jewish land.

(d)   From Isaiah.

Of Jesse, and the Seed to be born of Him.

[Passage quoted, Isa. xi. 1–10.]

(356)   This Jesse was David's father. As, then, in the preceding prophecies it was foretold that one should come forth of the fruit and seed of David, and also of the seed of Solomon, in the same way here it is prophesied that one will come forth of the seed of Jesse, that is to say of David, many years after the death of both David and Solomon. And this

(b) passage decides the quibble [1] of the Jews already noticed with regard to Solomon. For Isaiah writes this prophecy about some one other than him many years after the death of Solomon, who should arise from the stem of Jesse, and the seed of David. And I do not think it can be doubted that the words apply only to our Saviour, the Christ of God, considering the promise in the prediction, which says, "And

(c) there shall be a root of Jesse, and he that riseth to rule the nations, in him shall the nations trust," and the way in which our Saviour fulfils them.

For He alone, after His Resurrection from the dead, intended here I think by the word "Arise," ruled not only the Jews but all nations, so that the prophecy does not lack fulfilment, as it is quite clear that the words, "In Him

---

[1] ἀμφιβολίαν, cf. P.E. 34 d, 133 a.

shall the Gentiles trust," are fulfilled in Him, as well as the other prophecies.

And the references to the animals and wild beasts becoming tame and laying aside their fierce and untameable nature through His sojourn here will be allegorically understood of men's rough and wild ways and fierce characters being changed by Christ's teaching from irrational savagery. They must certainly be allegorically understood, especially (d) if one understands the root of Jesse mentioned by the prophet, and the rod, figuratively, and expounds in an intelligible way, "Justice shall be the girdle of his loins, and truth the girdle of his reins." For if one can only interpret this allegorically it follows that one must treat the passages that refer to the animals necessarily in a figurative way as well.

From Jeremiah.   (357)

A Righteous Rising from the Seed of David upspringing, and the same a King of Men, and a New Name to be given to those ruled by Him, and the Forgiveness of their Former Sins.

[Passages quoted, Jer. xxiii. 6–8, xxx. 8, 9.] [1]

Jeremiah prophesies thus long after the death of David and even the time of Solomon concerning a king who is to arise from the seed of David, whom he first calls "the rising," not simply but with the adjective "just," as though he were to shine forth from the sun of righteousness, of whom I treated in my evidences about the Second Cause, where I shewed that the pre-existent Word of God besides (d) many other names was called Sun of Righteousness, quoting the prophecy which said, "To them that fear my name shall the sun of righteousness arise." Therefore the prophecy in the present passage is that God will raise up "a righteous rising" to David, in the sense of a sun of righteousness. And he calls the same Being an understanding king, and one who does judgment and justice on the earth. He gives him too the same name as David, who died very long before. For you must note carefully how at the beginning

---

[1] Verses 7 and 8 are missing in LXX. They occur in the Hebrew Jer. xxx. 8 *sq.* ; ἐν τοῖς προφήταις is the heading of the following section not connected with Ἰωσεδέκ.

he says, "And I will raise up to David a righteous rising,"
(358) and adds at the end, "And I will raise up David to be his
king." Whose, but David's?—for it was to him that he said
He would raise up a righteous rising.

And Zechariah prophesying of the same Being likewise

Zech. vi.
12.
Zech. iii. .
8.

calls Him "a rising," saying, "Behold I will raise up my
servant, the rising," and also, "Behold a man whose name
is 'The Rising,' and beneath him springs righteousness."

But no one, it is certain, arose after the time of Jeremiah among the Jews who could be called "a righteous
rising" and "an understanding king doing judgment and
righteousness on the earth." For if it be suggested that
Jesus son of Josedec is meant, it must be answered that the
(b) prophecy is inapplicable to him. For he was neither of
David's seed nor did he reign as king. How could this
apply to him, "And I will raise up David to be his king,"
when he was of the tribe of Levi, and of high-priestly rank,
and of another tribe than David, and is never recorded to
have been king? We conclude that, as no other can be
discovered, we must agree that the subject of this prophecy
(c) can only be our Lord and Saviour, called in other places
"the light of the world," and "the light of the nations."
He therefore must be the subject of this prophecy, and the
prediction is absolutely true. For He alone of David's
seed and figuratively named after his ancestor, for David
means "strong-handed," preached judgment and justice by
His teaching to all men on earth, and alone of all that ever
lived is king not of one land only, but of the whole world,
and alone has caused righteousness to arise over all the
world, according to what is said of Him in the Psalm:
"Righteousness shall arise in his days, and abundance of
peace."

And Judah and Israel were to be saved in His days, that
(d) is to say all the Jews who through Him reached holiness,
His apostles, disciples and evangelists, or perhaps all who
represent the Jew mystically understood and the true Israel
which sees God spiritually.

"For he is not a Jew," the apostle says, "that is one
outwardly, nor circumcision the outward circumcision in
the flesh, but he is a Jew which is one in secret, and
Rom. ii.
28.
circumcision is of the heart in the spirit not the letter,
whose praise is not of men, but of God."

It is these, then, the secret Jew and the true Israel, that he says are through Christ's calling to be named by a new name, neither Jew nor Israel, but one quite different from these. For He says that the Lord will call them by the (359) name of Josedekeim, which means, "The Lord's just ones."

And I ask you to consider whether this name Josedekeim, by which the disciples of Jesus are called by God, be not formed from Joshua; they would thus be named by men from the name of Christ which is Greek (*i. e.* Christians), and by the prophets, from Jesus, in the Hebrew tongue, because they are saved by Him, Josedekeim. So it is said, " And this is the name by which the Lord shall call them, (b) Josedekeim among the prophets." So, then, we see that the people that are to become through the subject of the prophecy the spiritual Jews and the true Israel, will be called Josedekeim from Joshua, and they will be called by this name, he says, not by men, but by God, and by His prophets. For you must note carefully the passage that says, " And this is the name which the Lord shall call them, Josedekeim by his prophets." And its translation in Greek is, as I said, " God's just ones." And God promises that (c) He will break from those who are thus to be saved the old heavy yoke of bitter dæmons. and shatter the bonds of the sins by which they were held of old, so that they will no more serve strange gods, but bear fruit and please Him only. Compare with this the oracle in the Second Psalm concerning the Coming of Christ and the calling of the Gentiles, which says : " Let us break their bonds asunder, and cast off their yoke from us." To which, I think, this we are considering is akin when it says :

" In that day, saith the Lord, I will break the yoke from off their necks, and shatter their bonds, and they (d) shall not serve other gods, but shall serve the Lord their God."

But in proof that it was predicted that the Christ of God should be born of the fruit of David's body, and of the seed of Solomon, as actually was the case, since the Holy Scriptures call Him David as well as by many other names, I have given sufficient confirmation.

And it should raise no question, that He is said to come from the tribe of Judah, for that was the tribe to which David belonged.

But I will give the oracle of Moses that states this, though it is already proved sufficiently. It runs thus :

(360)

From Genesis.

How from the Tribe of Judah shall be born the Christ of God, and shall be established as the Expectation of Nations.

[Passage quoted, Gen. xlix. 8–10.]

The whole Hebrew race consisted of twelve tribes, one of which had Judah for its ancestor and head, to whom the above words were addressed, telling him that the Christ should spring from him. And if you compare with this

(c) prophecy the other prophecies I have quoted, you will find all through them that the same Being is proclaimed by a sign common to all. For one said of Him that springs from the root of Jesse, " And there shall be one arising to rule the nations, on him shall the nations trust." Another said of the son of Solomon, " He shall rule from sea to sea, and from the river to the ends of the world, and in him all

Isa. xi. 10. nations shall be blessed." And the one before us similarly says, " Until he come for whom it is laid up, and he shall

Ps. lxxii. 8. be the expectation of nations."

(d) If, then, the predictions about the nations are in accord, and the previous ones have been proved to refer to our Saviour, nothing prevents us referring this one to Him as well, if these prophecies are agreed to be in harmony, especially with regard to the fact that the kings and rulers of the Jewish nation continued in the same line of succession until the period of Christ's appearing, but failed directly He appeared, and by the prediction of Jacob the expectation of the nations demanded a satisfaction.

Christ therefore is foretold here also, as destined to come from the tribe of Judah, and since He has been shewn to

(361) have been born of David, Solomon, and the root of Jesse, it is evident He came from the same tribe as they. For David was son of Jesse, and Solomon of David, both of the tribe of Judah. Our Lord and Saviour must therefore spring from it, as the wonderful evangelist Matthew states

---

[1] S. reads τὰ ἀποκείμενα αὐτῷ for ᾧ ἀπόκειται.

in his geneaology, " The Book of the generation of Jesus Christ, son of David, son of Abraham.   Abraham begat Isaac, Isaac begat Jacob, Jacob begat Judah."

And now that I have adequately proved these points, it is time to consider the period of the fulfilment of the prophecies.

BOOK VIII

INTRODUCTION

I HAVE proved by how many prophecies the coming of the Word of God to men was foretold, and that it was announced by the Hebrew prophets whence He should (b) come, and where and how He should be seen by men on earth, and that He was actually the Person, the eternal pre-existent Son of God, Whom we have learned to recognize by the other names of God and Lord and Chief Captain, and Angel of Great Counsel and High Priest. And I begin at this point, in continuance of the preceding proof, to give the evidence with reference to the period of His Appearing drawn again from prophetic predictions.

(363) The Holy Scriptures foretell that there will be unmistakable signs of the Coming of Christ. Now there were among the Hebrews three outstanding offices of dignity,[1] which made the nation famous, firstly the kingship, secondly that of prophet, and lastly the high priesthood. The prophecies said that the abolition and complete destruction of all these three together would be the sign of the (b) presence of the Christ. And that the proofs that the times had come, would lie in the ceasing of the Mosaic worship, the desolation of Jerusalem and its Temple, and the subjection of the whole Jewish race to its enemies. They suggest other signs of the same times as well, an abundance of peace, the overturning in nation and city of immemorial local and national forms of government,[2] the

---

[1] ἐπιφανῶν ἀξιωμάτων.

[2] τοπαρχίας καὶ πολυαρχίας: for πολυαρχία, cf. P.E. 10 a, d, 178 b; also τοπάρχης, ibid. 10 b, 60 d, 179 a. For the argument cf. Melito's *Apology* (*H.E.* IV. 26. 7), and G's. quotation from Ranke's *History of the Popes*, i.: "The earth was suddenly left void of independent nations."

conquest of polytheistic and dæmonic idolatry, the knowledge of the religion of God the one Supreme Creator.
The holy oracles foretold that all these changes, which had (c)
not been made in the days of the prophets of old, would
take place at the coming of the Christ, which I will presently shew to have been fulfilled as never before in
accordance with the predictions. I have already, you will
remember, accounted for the Christ coming in these last
times and not long ago, but I will here shortly repeat
myself. In the old days the souls of men were tyrannized
over by squalid folly and sin, and a strange godlessness ruled (d)
over all human life, so that men were like wild and un-
tamed beasts. They knew nothing of cities, or constitutions, or laws, nor anything honourable or progressive; they
set no store on arts and sciences, they had no conception
of virtue and philosophy, they lived in lonely deserts, in
mountains, caves, and villages; they preyed on their neighbours like robbers, and gained their livelihood mostly by
tyrannizing over those weaker than themselves. But
though they did not know the Supreme God, nor the path
of true religion, yet inspired by conceptions of natural
religion they agreed in self-taught principles about the (364)
existence of a divine power, regarded it as and called it
God, and considered the name one of salvation and benefi-
cence, but they were not yet able to realize anything beyond
a Being transcending the world of visible nature. Wherefore
some of them—

25. "worshipped and served the creature rather than
the creator; 21. and they became vain in their imagi-
nations, and their foolish heart was darkened; 23. and
they changed the glory of the incorruptible God into an
image made like unto corruptible man, and to birds Rom.i. 21,
and four-footed beasts and creeping things." [1] 23, 25.

And so they made images of their kings and tyrants long
dead, and paid them divine honours, and by imputing
divinity to them sanctified their wicked and lustful deeds
as works of the gods.[2]

[1] W.H.: Ver. 22: Φάσκοντες εἶναι σοφοὶ ἐμωράνθησαν, καὶ ἤλλαξαν. . . .
E. : ὡς ἐναλλάξαι. . . .
[2] Cf. Athenagoras, c. xxviii. The theory first advanced by
Euemerus (316 B.C.), which E. examines, *Praep. Ev.* ii. 55. "In a
kind of philosophical romance Euemerus declared that he had sailed

How could the wise and good word of Christ, instilling the
(c) quintessence of wisdom, be in harmony with men in that
condition, and involved in such depths of evil? So that
holy and all-seeing Justice, pruning them like a wild and
dangerous wood, now afflicted them by floods, now by fire,[1]
now delivered them to wars, butchery and sieges at one
another's hands, urged on as they were to war against
(d) each other by those very dæmons whom they regarded as
their gods, with the result that human life in those days
admitted no neighbourly intercourse, mutual association
or union. Those were few, as might be expected in such
days, and easily numbered, who, as the Hebrew oracles
tell us, were found to be godly; with such, Justice met
by the use of oracles and theophanies, she took them by
the hand and cared for them with the elementary but
helpful Mosaic legislation.

But when at last by the legislation laid down for them,
and by the later teaching of the prophets poured out like
a sweet smell upon all men, the character of the people
became civilized, and constitutions and legal systems were
(365) established among most nations, and the name of virtue
and philosophy became popularly honoured, as if their
old savagery had ceased and their wild and cruel life were
transferred to something gentler: then at length, at the
fitting time, the perfect and heavenly teacher of perfect
and heavenly thoughts and teaching, the leader to the
(b) true knowledge of God, God the Word, revealed Himself,
at the time announced for His Incarnation, preaching the
Gospel of the Father's love, the same for all nations,
whether Greeks or Barbarians, to every race of men,
moving all to a common salvation in God, promising the
truth and light of true religion, the kingdom of Heaven,
and eternal life to all.

Such, then, is my account of the reasons why the Christ
(c) of God shone forth on all men now and not long ago.

---

to some No-man's land, Pandræa, where he found the verity about
mythical times engraved on pillars of bronze. This truth he published
in the *Sacra Historia*, where he rationalized the fables, averring that
the gods had been men, and that the myths were exaggerated and
distorted records of facts. There was an element of truth in his
romantic hypothesis."—A. Lang, *Myth, Ritual and Religion*, i. 15.

[1] πυρπολήσεσι. Cf. the verb πυρπολέω, P.E. 368 a.

We will now, retracing our steps, examine in detail the signs portending His Coming, first noting what is said in the Gospels about the date of His Birth.   Matthew then records the date of His appearance in the flesh, thus : "When Jesus was born in Bethlehem of Judæa, in the days of Herod the king"; and a little later, he says : "Hearing Matt. ii. 1 that Archelaus reigned over Judæa, instead of Herod his father."   And Luke shewed the date of His teaching and (d) manifestation, saying :

"In the fifteenth year of the reign of Tiberius Cæsar, Luke iii. 1. Pontius Pilate being governor [1] of Judæa, Herod tetrarch of Galilee, and his brother, Philip, tetrarch of Ituræa and the land of Trachonitis; and Lysanias tetrarch of Abilene, Annas and Caiaphas being High Priests."

With these we shall do well to compare the prophecy of Jacob given by Moses to this effect.

CHAPTER 1   (366)

Of the Time of His Appearance among Men.   How at the Time when the Hebrews fail of their Kingdom, the Expectation of the Gentiles shall approach, which also came to pass at Our Saviour's Appearing.

From Genesis.

1. "Jacob called his sons and said, Come together (b) and hear what shall befall you at the end of the days.   Come together and hear, ye sons of Jacob, Gen. xlix. hear your father."   1.

Then, after rebuking his elder sons, one for one thing, one for another, as being unworthy because of their sins (c) of the prophecy about to be given, he prophesies thus to his fourth son, as having shewn himself a better man than his brothers :

8. "Judah, thy brethren shall praise the, | thy hands shall be on the back of thy enemies, | the sons of thy father shall bow down to thee. | 9. Judah is a lion's

---

[1] W. II. : ἡγεμονεύοντος.   E. : ἐπιτροπεύοντος.

whelp, | Thou hast sprung up, my son, from a slip. |
Lying down thou didst sleep as a lion and a whelp. |
(d)   Who shall arouse thee? | 10. A ruler shall not fail
from Judah, | nor a governor from his loins, | until the
things laid up for him come, | and he is the expectation
of the nations."

First, consider what is meant by " the things laid up for
him," and see if they be not the prophecies about the
calling of the Gentiles, that God gave to those with
Abraham. For it is written, that God said to Abraham :

"And thou shalt be blessed, and I will bless them
that bless thee, and curse them that curse thee : and
Gen. xii.2.   in thee shall all the families of the earth be blessed."
And again :

"Abraham," he says, "shall become a great and
Gen. xviii.   mighty nation, and in him shall all the nations of the
18.   earth be blessed."
Similar oracles were spoken to Isaac in this wise :

(367)   "And I will multiply thy seed as the stars of heaven,[1]
Gen. xxvi.   and in thy seed shall all nations of the world be
4.   blessed."
And also to Jacob this is said :

Gen.   "I am the Lord God of Abraham thy father, and
xxviii. 13.   the God of Isaac, fear not."
And then :

"And in thee shall all the families of the earth be
Gen. xxxv.   blessed."
11.   And at another time God said to him :

"I am thy God, increase and multiply : nations and
assemblies of nations shall come out of thee, and kings
shall come out of thy loins."
Jacob, who knew the predictions of God concerning the
calling of the nations, having twelve sons,[2] called them
(b) all together to his deathbed, to discover in the line of
which son God's predictions would be fulfilled. And, then,
having laid rebukes on the three first for their wrong-
doings, he tells them also that the fulfilment of the
prophecies will not come about through them because
of their wicked deeds. But coming to the fourth, who was

---

[1] S. adds: "And I will give to thy seed all this land."
[2] δεκάδυο.

Judah, he at once prophesies to him that the oracle, which says, "kings shall come from thy loins," will be fulfilled in his descendants. For it was plain that the kingly family was established in the tribe of Judah: and (c) he shews at the same time at what period the prophecies of God and the promises to the Gentiles will fall due, and he teaches that one will come forth from him who will cause all nations and tribes to be admitted to the blessings of Abraham. All these things, then, were "the things laid up for him," that is to say, the ancient prophecies concerning the nations, and the words, "kings shall come (d) out of thee," whereby his tribe has precedence of those of his brethren, as royal and pre-eminent.

Directly the whole nation was organized in the time of Moses God gave his tribe the chief rank among the tribes. For it is written:

"And the Lord spake to Moses and Aaron, saying, Numb Let the children of Israel encamp fronting one another, ii. 1. every man keeping his own rank, according to their standards, according to the houses of their families before the Lord, around the tabernacle of witness; and they that encamp first towards the east, shall be the order of the camp of Judah with their host."[1]

And later in the part that refers to the renewing of the sanctuary:

"The Lord said to Moses, One prince each day shall offer their gifts. And he that offered the first day Numb. was Naason, son of Aminadab, prince of the tribe of vii. 11. Judah."

And in the Book of Joshua, son of Nave, when the land (368) of promise was divided by lot among the other tribes, the Josh. xv. tribe of Judah took its own portion of the land without casting lots,[2] and first of all. And, moreover, "After the Judg. i. 1. death of Joshua the children of Israel inquired of the Lord, saying, Who shall go up for us against the Canaanite, leading our fighting against him? And the Lord said, Judah shall go up. Behold, I have given the land into his hands." These words, then, make it clear that God (b)

---

[1] S. reads: παρεμβαλέτωσαν οἱ υἱοὶ Ἰσραήλ · ἐνάντιοι κύκλῳ τῆς σκηνῆς: "Let the children of Israel encamp: let them face each other around the tent."

[2] Gr.: ἀκληρωτί.

ordained the tribe of Judah to be the head of all Israel, and the account goes on: "And Judah went up, and the Lord delivered the Canaanite and Perizzite into his hand." And also: "And the children of Judah fought against Jerusalem and took it, and the sons of Judah came down from fighting against the Canaanite." And again: "And Judah went up with Symeon, his brother." And then: "And the Lord was with Judah, and gave him the Mount as his portion." And after this: "And the sons of Joseph went up, they also who were in Bethel, and Judah with

(c) them." And in the Book of Judges, when different men at different times were at the head of the people, though individually the Judges were of different tribes, yet speaking generally the tribe of Judah was head of the whole people, and much more so in the times of David and his successors, who belonged to the tribe of Judah, and continued to rule until the Babylonian Captivity, after which the leader of those who returned from Babylon to their own land was Zerubbabel, the son of Salathiel, of the tribe of Judah, who also built the Temple. Hence, too, the Book of Chronicles, when giving the genealogies of the twelve tribes of Israel,

(d) begins with Judah. And you will see it follows from this that, in the days that succeeded, the same tribe had the headship, although different individuals had temporary leadership, whose tribes it is impossible to decide with accuracy, because there is no sacred book handed down to give the history of the period from then to the time of our Saviour. But it is true to say that the tribe of Judah continued so long as the free and autonomous constitution of the whole nation lasted under its own leaders and kings. And this was the case from the beginning until the time of Augustus,

(369) when, after our Saviour's appearance among men, the whole nation became subject to Rome. And then instead of their ancestral and constitutional rulers they were ruled first by Herod, a foreigner, and next by the Emperor Augustus. And so long as there had not yet failed a prince from Judah, nor a leader from his loins, the dates of the prophecies are given from the reigns of the kings. Thus Isaiah prophesies in the reigns of Uzziah, Jotham, Ahaz and Hezekiah, kings of Judah. As did Hosea. Amos, in the days of Uzziah, king of Judah, and in the days of

(b) Jeroboam, son of Joash, king of Israel; and Zephaniah

in the days of Josiah, son of Amos, king of Judah.   And
Jeremiah too.   But when a prince failed from Judah, and
a governor from his loins, when the expectation of the
Gentiles foretold in Christ was just about to shine on
human life, there were no longer any rulers styled kings in
Judah or governors in Israel.   And since they had failed
at the appointed time in accordance with prophecy,
Augustus first, and then Tiberius, was called king of the
Jewish nation, in common with the other nations, and under (c)
them were procurators and tetrarchs of Judæa, and Herod
of course, who, as I have already said, was not a Jew by
birth, and received his authority over the Jews from
Rome.

After these observations, we will now attempt a consideration of the prophecy : "Judah, thy brethren shall
praise thee."   Jacob had twelve sons, the fourth being
Judah, who as I have said already, was the one and only
head of the Hebrew tribes.   But it will be evident, that (d)
the words addressed to him by his father did not refer
to him as an individual man, if we consider the words
of Holy Scripture, and especially the speech of Jacob to
his sons :

"And Jacob called his sons to him, Come together
and I will tell you what shall come to pass in the last
days.   Gather together and hear, ye sons of Jacob, hear
Israel your father."

For he clearly promises here to predict what will happen
to them a long time afterwards, or, in his own words, in
the last days.   And for other reasons what Jacob said could
not apply to the first individual who bore the name of
Judah.   His brethren did not praise him : for what great
deed of his could they have done so?   It would have been
more applicable, if it had been addressed to Joseph, for (370)
we know that Judah himself with his other brethren bowed
down to him, except of course that this happened before
the prophecy ; but afterwards there is no record of anything
of the kind connected with Joseph, or Judah.   And the
words, "Thou didst fall and sleep as a lion and a lion's
whelp," seem to call for a wider interpretation than one
concerning Judah.   The words that follow, too : "There
shall not fail a prince from Judah, nor a governor from his
loins, until that come which is laid up for him, and he is

(b) the expectation of nations," seem to me to give in a disguised form the time of the coming of the subject of the prophecy. For the one event, he says, will not take place, until the other does. The kings and rulers of the Jewish nation, that is, will not cease before the expectation of the nations shall come, and that which is laid up for the subject of the prophecy. Theodotion agrees with this rendering of the Septuagint, but Aquila thus translates:

> "The sceptre shall not be removed from Judah, and he who knoweth exactly from between his feet, until also there come to him a congregation of people."

(c) And this saying, "There shall not fail a prince from Judah," cannot be referred to Judah as an individual man any more than, "Judah, thy brethren shall praise thee." For there were rulers and governors of the Jewish nation at many times who were not descended from him. Moses, for instance, its first ruler, was not of the tribe of Judah but of Levi. Joshua was of the tribe of Ephraim; after whom their ruler was Deborah, of the tribe of Ephraim, and Barak

(d) of the tribe of Naphthali, then Gedeon of Manasseh, then Gedeon's son, and after him Thola of the same tribe, then Esebon of Bethlehem, and then Ailon of Zabulon, Labdon of Ephraim, and Samson of Dan; then there being no regular ruler, Eli the priest, of the tribe of Levi, was their leader. All these Judges judged Israel, not in the line of succession from Judah, but one from one tribe and one from another. And they were followed by the first king, Saul, of the tribe of Benjamin. How, then, can the words, "there shall not fail a prince from Judah, nor a governor

(371) from his loins," be referred, as one would suppose they should be, to rulers and governors of the tribe of Judah, when from the time of Jacob's death, for nearly a thousand years, they do not appear to have been drawn from the tribe of Judah only, but some from one tribe, some from another, up to the time of David? And if it be true that David and his successors sprung from the tribe of Judah ruled the Jewish nation, after so many others, yet we must remember that they did not continue to rule the

(b) whole people for the whole of those five hundred years, but only three tribes, and not the whole of them, for during their reigns other kings governed the larger part of the nation— that is to say, the whole of the other nine tribes. For after

the death of Solomon, since the whole nation was divided
from Judah, the successors of David, as I said, did not rule
the whole Jewish nation up to the time of the Babylonian
Captivity.   And in their times the heads of Samaria, which
was the name of the State held by the nine tribes, were
not drawn from Judah, but now from one tribe, now from (c)
another, the first being Jeroboam, of the tribe of Ephraim,
and those immediately after him, so that in the period
between David and the Babylonian Captivity, kings of the
line of Judah never ruled the whole nation.

There is no need to add that after the return from
Babylon for more than five hundred years again until the
birth of Christ the Jewish constitution was aristocratic,[1]
the high priests, for the time being, acting as heads of the
State, none of whom came from the tribe of Judah.   So from
all these reasons it is proved that there is no reference here
to Judah the original individual, to his descendants, nor in
the oracle that said : "A prince shall not fail from Judah, (d)
nor a governor from his loins," but that the only consistent
interpretation of the passage is the one I have already
given, that we must understand it of the tribe as a whole.
The tribe most certainly was leader of the whole nation
from the very beginning, from Moses' own time.   And in
accordance with such headship, as being designed by God
from the outset, the country is even now called Judæa
after the tribe, and the whole race are known as Jews.
We must, therefore, understand it to mean what would be
expressed more clearly, if it were said that the tribe of Judah
would never lose its headship of the whole nation.   So
Symmachus says: "The power shall not be taken away (372)
from Judah," shewing of course the authority and the royal
position of what was afterwards to be the tribe of Judah.
From it neither "the sceptre," as Aquila says, this being the
symbol of royal rule, nor "the power," according to Symmachus, shall be taken away, the prophecy affirms, "until
he come," it says, "for whom it is laid up, and he shall
be the expectation of the nations."   What expectation was
this, but that of which Abraham and those after him had
received the prophecies?   First, is it not very striking that (b)
though there were twelve Hebrew tribes, the race even now

---

[1] πολιτείᾳ χρώμενοι ἀριστοκρατικῇ.

has its name from none but Judah? It can only be explained by the prophetic oracle, which attached the royal position to the tribe of Judah. And it is for this same reason that their fatherland is called Judæa. For why was not the nation called after the eldest of the twelve, I mean (c) Reuben, according to the divine law of primogeniture? Why not from Levi, who was greater than Judah in order of birth, and also in receiving the priesthood? Why not, even more, was the race and the country not called after Joseph, from his acquiring rule not only over the whole of Egypt, but over his own relations, and because his descendants, long years after, were to rule as many as nine tribes of the nation, on whose account it was far more probable that the whole race and the country would have been named after their ancestor? And who would not agree (d) that they might reasonably have been called from Benjamin, since their famous mother-city and the all-holy Temple of of God was in the portion of his tribe?[1] But yet, in spite of all, the name of the Lord and of the whole nation was drawn from none of them but Judah, as the prophecy foretold. I have, therefore, referred the words, "A prince shall not fail from Judah," to the tribe, and only in that sense is the prediction true. For from the time of Moses there has not failed a continued line of rulers of part of the nation,[2] drawn as I said from different tribes, but the tribe of Judah has all along stood forth as the head of the whole (373) nation. An illustration will make what I have said clear. Just as the procurators and governors appointed in the Roman Empire over nations, their præfects and military chiefs,[3] and their highest kings, are not all drawn from

---

[1] Cf. A. S. Peake : Hastings's *D.B.* ii. 793, art. "Judah": "One of David's greatest and most far-sighted acts was the selection of Jerusalem, as his capital and the home of the Ark. Jerusalem did not actually lie in Judah, except possibly to a small extent, but it was on the border; and the possession of it, with the ark and temple, guaranteed the survival of the Southern Kingdom, after the loss of the Northern tribes."

[2] μερικοὶ μὲν αὐτῶν ἄρχοντες . . . καθόλου δέ.

[3] οἱ μὲν κατ' ἔθνος ἐπίτροποί τε καὶ ἡγούμενοι, ἔπαρχοί τε καὶ στρατοπεδάρχοι· ἐπίτροπος—governor or viceroy (Herod. 3. 27, 5. 30). ἐπ : Καισάρος, Plut. 2. 813. ἡγούμενοι—generally for chiefs, Soph. *Phil.* 386. ἔπαρχος translates the Roman "praefectus" (Polyb. 11. 27. 2; Plut. *Otho.* 3), ἔπαρχος τῆς αὐλῆς = praefectus praetorio (Plut. *Galb.* 2., cf. 8. 13). στρατοπεδάρχης is "a military com-

Rome nor from the seed of Remus and Romulus, but
from many different races, and yet all their kings and the
rulers and governors below them are all called Romans,
and their power is named Roman, and the rule of them
all generally has this appellation, in the same way we (b)
should think of the Hebrew state, where you have the
name of the tribe of Judah applied generally to the whole
nation, though there be kings and governors of divisions
from different tribes, but all honoured with the name of
Judah.   We understand then that the prophet's words :
"Judah, thy brethren shall praise thee," were to be applied
to the whole tribe.   For he knew that being marked out
for precedence it would be honoured more than the other
tribes, and since it was best in warfare, and the sole leader
of the whole nation in operations against the enemy, he
rightly continues : "Thy hands shall be on the back of thy (c)
enemies."   Then for its ruling and royal position he calls it,
"a lion's whelp."   And as ancestor and prophet, glorying
in the reputation of the tribe, he adds : "From a seed, my
son, thou hast ascended"; while the words : "Falling
down thou hast slept as a lion, and as a lion's whelp," shew
its character of terror and bravery, its utter fearlessness of
external attack, and contempt of its foes.   He being such, (d)
or rather, his tribe being such, who, he says, shall arouse
it?   He suggests that the Person who is to remove the
tribe in question from its throne, and move it from its
royal position, will be some one great, wonderful, unusual,
and hard to imagine.   Then he tells us who it is to be,
telling us that it is He Who is the Expectation of nations,
of Whom it is predicted that He will only appear among
men, when the ruler fails, and the governor is changed,
and the tribe of Judah is removed from its position of
power.   Who is this, but our Lord and Saviour Jesus
Christ?—at Whose birth, as the prophecy before us pre- (374)
dicted, the rulers and governors set over their nation from
the Jews themselves would fail, the tribe of Judah lose the
dominant and royal position that it had held over the
nation for so long, and be subject to the Romans, their
rulers from that day to this, who overcame the Jewish (b)

---

mander" = Lat. "tribunus legionis," Dion. H. 10. 36 ; Luc., *Hist.
Conscr.* 22.

nation together with the rest of the world, and under
whom Herod, a man of alien birth apart from their race,
was appointed king by Augustus and the Roman Senate.[1]
For Herod was son of Antipater, and Antipater belonged
to Ascalon, and was son of some [2] temple-server at the
Temple of Apollo, who married a woman named Kuprine,
of Arab race, and begat Herod. He, you will remember, being sprung from this family, got rid of and slew
Hyrcanus, the last of the line of ruling high-priests, with
(c) whom the government of the Jews by native rulers came
to an end, Herod being, as I say, the first foreigner to
be called the King of the Jews.   In his time Jesus Christ
was born, and at one and the same time the position of
the tribe of Judah was taken away, the authority of the
kingdom of the Jews destroyed, and the prophecy preceding this fulfilled : "There shall not fail a prince from
Judah, nor a governor from his loins, until there come the
things laid up for him," who, he says, will not only be the
expectation of the Jews, but of the Gentiles.   As, therefore,
the expectation of the call of the Gentiles, prophesied long
(d) before to Abraham, was "laid up," until the rulers and
governors of the Jewish race should have ceased, and their
independent government should have been changed to
submission to Rome, and to the Gentile Herod, the
Evangelist Luke, noting the date of the cessation of Jewish
rulers, tells us that the teaching of Christ began in the
fifteenth year of the reign of Tiberius Cæsar, when Pontius
Pilate was governor of Judæa ; and Matthew says the same

---

[1] τῆς 'Ρωμαίων συγκλήτου βουλῆς.   That is, the Senate.   Cf.
Polyb. 20. 12. 3, etc.
[2] ἐκ τῶν ἱεροδούλων : cf. H.E. I. vii. 11, where Eusebius quotes the
story of Julius Africanus, that Idumæans carried away from Ashkelon
Antipater's father, who was the son of a temple-server, and thus
Antipater was brought up in Idumæa ; Nicolaus of Damascus
(Jos. Ant. xiv. 1, 3), said he was of the Jewish stock that came back
from Babylon.   Justin (Dial. c. 52) makes him a Philistine.   His son
Antipater married a Nabatæan Arab, named Cypros, and attached
himself to the party of Hyrcanus as against his brother Aristobulus.
On the taking of Jerusalem by Pompey (63 B.C.), Hyrcanus was made
high priest, and Herod Antipater was made governor of Galilee (47) ; and
after the attempt of Antigonus in which Hyrcanus was mutilated (40),
Herod was given the title of king by Antony and Octavius.   After the
battle of Actium (31), he joined the party of Augustus and was
confined to his kingdom.

in a disguised form. For having described the birth of
our Lord and Saviour, he adds: "And when Jesus was
born in Bethlehem of Judæa, in the days of Herod the
king, behold wise men came from the East to Jerusalem,
saying, Where is that which is born king of the Jews?"
wherein he shews clearly enough both that they were under (375)
foreign rule, and also the calling of the foreign nations
from the East by God. For foreigners ruled over the
Jews, and foreigners coming from the East recognized and
worshipped the Christ of God, Who had been prophesied
of old. The prophecy of Jacob is thus seen clearly to have
been fulfilled, being brought to pass at the end of the
national existence of the Jews, even as he predicted to his
sons, saying: "Come together, that I may announce to
you, what shall happen to you at the end of the days." (b)
For we must understand by the end of the days the end
of the national existence of the Jews. What, then,
did he say they must look for? The cessation of the
rule of Judah, the destruction of their whole race, the
failing and ceasing of their governors, and the abolition
of the dominant kingly position of the tribe of Judah, and
the rule and kingdom of Christ, not over Israel but over
all nations, according to the words, "This is the expectation
of the nations."

And who would not agree that all this has been definitely (c)
fulfilled in the coming of our Saviour, when they who
of old before Christ's birth, with their native rulers and
governors and wise hearers of the holy oracles, prided
themselves in their own kings, high priests and prophets,
and when the tribe of Judah, being the royal tribe, the
conqueror of their enemies, the leader and ruler of the
whole nation, with its men of old renown has from that
day to this lain under the heel of Rome? For the Christ
of God was definitely manifested, and from that day the
said expectation of the Gentiles is preached to all nations. (d)
Or who can deny, that concurrently with the appearance
of our Saviour Jesus the solemnities of the Jews, their
city with its Temple and the worship performed therein,
have come to an end, together with their native rulers
and governors, and that from that time the hope and
expectation of the nations through all the world has
been made known, since the things laid up in the Lord

have come. What are these things, but those set forth by
Judah?—

> "Thy brethren shall praise thee, thy hands shall be on
> the back of thine enemies, lion of the tribe of Judah.
> O my son, thou hast ascended from a seed, falling thou
> hast slept as a lion and as a lion's whelp: who shall
> awake thee?"

(376) But the words, "The things laid up for him," have another
sense; let us now consider them, only premising that the
Holy Scriptures are accustomed to give the Christ different
names. Sometimes they call Him Jacob:

> "Jacob, my son, I will help thee; Israel, my chosen,
> my soul hath received him, he shall bring judgment
> unto the nations,"

Isa. xlii. 1.

and that which follows. To which is added, "Till he place
judgment on the earth, and in his name shall the Gentiles
(b) hope." Sometimes they name Him Solomon or David:
Solomon as in the 71st Psalm, inscribed to Solomon, whose
contents evidently refer to Christ. For the words, "He
Ps. lxxi. 8. shall rule from sea to sea, and from the river to the world's
end, and all the nations shall serve him," and the contents
of the Psalm that follow, can only apply to the Christ.
Christ, again, is called David in the 88th Psalm, for expressions therein are only applicable to Him, and not to David,
for instance:

Ps.
lxxxviii.
26.

> "He shall call me, Thou art my father, and I will
> make him my firstborn, high above the kings of the
> earth. I will keep my mercy for him for ever."

(c) And again:

> "His seed shall remain for ever, and his throne
> is as the sun before me, and as the moon fixed in
> the heaven."

So, then, besides the many other names given to Christ by
the Holy Scriptures, it is possible that He may be called
Judah also in the passage before us, especially as He sprang
from the tribe of Judah. For the apostle certifies the fact
(d) that our Lord and Saviour sprang from the tribe of Judah.
For Him, then, were "the things laid up for Judah"
figuratively intended in the prophecy. And what were
they? First, the praise of His brethren; second, to lay
his hands on the back of His enemies; third, to be worshipped by the sons of His Father. And they came to pass,

for His performance of miracles and wondrous prodigies
aroused wonder, and He was praised and worshipped by
His own disciples and apostles, whom He shrank not from
calling brethren, saying by the Psalm, "I will declare thy
name to my brethren, in the midst of the Church I will Ps. xxi. 22.
praise thee," and also when He bids the women with Mary
announce the news to thém as His brethren, for He says,
"Make known to my brethren that I ascend to my Father, (377)
and your Father, and to my God, and your God."[1] Thus Matt.
then, His brethren at first praised Him only as a remarkable xxviii. 10,
man because of His miracles, believing Him most likely to and John
be one of the prophets; but when meanwhile they saw His xx. 17.
wonderful miracles, and how He destroyed the enemy and
the avenger, and death the prince of this world, together
with the other unseen hostile powers, thenceforth they (b)
believed Him to be God and worshipped Him.   And the
hands of our Saviour were upon the back of His enemies,
when He directed all His deeds and powers and miracles
to the destruction of the dæmons and evil spirits.   Yea,
when too He spread out His hands on the Cross, even then
His hands were on the back of His enemies, since they fled
and turned their backs on Him, and even more, when
yielding up His spirit to the Father, disembodied and (c)
stripped of that flesh,[2] which He had assumed, He went to
the place of His enemies, having life in Himself, to loose
death, and the powers arrayed against Him, which perhaps
at first conceived that He was an ordinary man and like all
men, and so encircled Him and attacked Him as they
would any one else, but when they knew that He was
superhuman and divine, they turned their backs and
fled from Him, so that He laid His hands on them,
and drave them on with His divine and sharpened arrows,
as is here said, "Thy hands shall be on the backs of thy
enemies."[3]

---

[1] W.H.: Matt. xxviii. 10, ἀπαγγείλατε τοῖς ἀδελφοῖς μου ἵνα ἀπέλ-
θωσιν. . . . John xx 17, πορεύου δὲ πρὸς τοὺς ἀδελφούς μου καὶ εἰπὲ
αὐτοῖς. Ἀναβαίνω πρὸς τὸν πατέρα μου. . . .

E.: Ἀπαγγέιλατε τοῖς ἀδελφοῖς μου ὅτι ἀνέρχομαι πρὸς τὸν πατέρα
μου. . . .

[2] γυμνὸς οὗ ἀνειλήφει σώματος.

[3] *He went to the place of His enemies.* Cf. the longer passage,
501 b—503 d, expounding Ps. xxi. 19–21, with references to Isa. xiv. 9
and Job. The incidents and scenery are plainly the traditional ones of

And if to-day many enemies of our Saviour attempt from
(d) time to time to war against His Church, these too He routs
with invisible hand and divine power,[1] even as it is said of
them, " His hands shall be on the back of his enemies."
And since also He has received the trophies of victory over
His enemies, the words, " The sons of thy father shall
worship thee," are also fulfilled : that is to say, all the angels
of heaven, and the ministering spirits, and the divine powers,
and on earth the apostles and evangelists, and after
them those of all nations who through -Him are enrolled
under the one and only true God and Father, have learned
that Christ is God the Word, and have consented to worship
(378) Him as God.

But as it was necessary for the mysteries of both His
Birth and Death to be included in the prophecy concerning
Him, Jacob rightly proceeds to add to what has gone
before :

"Judah is a lion's whelp. From a seed, my son,
thou hast ascended, falling down thou hast slept as a
lion and a lion's whelp : who shall arouse thee?"

He calls Him then a lion's whelp because of His being
born of the royal tribe. For He was of the seed of
(b) David according to the flesh. "From a shoot thou hast
grown, my son," he says, because He was born of the seed
and root of Jacob who foretold it, being primarily God the
Word, and becoming secondarily the Son of man, through
the dispensation He undertook for us. And the words,
"Falling down thou didst sleep as a lion and a whelp," are
significant of His Death, because Scripture is accustomed,

"The Harrowing of Hell" accepted at the time : e. g. the shattering
of the gates and release of the prisoners, the fear of the janitors, the
humble prayer of Hades, the beasts of Tartarus, Christ's driving of the
Prince of this world and the evil powers before Him. These belong
to the cycle of, even if they are not directly derived from, the source
of the Apocryphal *Gospel of Nicodemus* (allied with Pilate literature of
fourth or fifth century, going back "possibly to the second century."
Moffatt, *D.A.C.*, i. 504) ; and from that of Bartholomew, the fragments
of which perhaps come from an original written "vers le IVme siècle."
Wilmart and Tisserant, quoted *D.A.C.*, i. 504. If these passages shew
the influence of the Apocryphal Gospels, the reverse is the case with
regard to the miracles of the Infancy, the accounts of which are
implicitly condemned, p. 426 d.

[1] Evidently written after the cessation of the persecution.

as is shewn in many other places, from the conviction of
their kinship to call death a sleep. And "Who shall awake
him?" is a wonderful reference to His Resurrection from
the dead. For he who said, "Who will awake him?" (c)
knew quite well that He would be awaked. And it is
remarkable that he should add, "Who then shall do this
and raise him up?" so as to impel us to ask who it was that
raised up our Lord Who died on our behalf. For Who else
was it, but the God of the Universe, His Father, to Whom
the Saviour's Resurrection is solely to be attributed, according to the Scripture which says, "Whom the Father raised 1 Thess.
from the dead"? i. 10.

Instead of, "Judah is a lion's whelp, from a shoot, my (d)
son, thou hast ascended, falling down thou hast slept,"
Aquila says more plainly, "Judah is a lion's cub, from
destruction, my son, hast thou ascended, bending thou hast
laid down." And Symmachus says, "Judah is a lion's
whelp, from capture, my son, hast thou ascended, having
knelt thou hast been established." By which the Resurrection of the dead is clearly meant, and the escape of our
Saviour from Hades, as from a trap for wild beasts. The
kneeling and the being established instead of falling, signify
death by the kneeling, and not being dragged away like the
souls of other men by "being established." All this then
was laid up before for Christ. But while this remained
unfulfilled, the Jewish nation lasted, and their rulers and
governors and they who were wise interpreters of the sacred
oracles about the Christ stood out among them ; but when (379)
that which had been laid up for Judah had come, and
He appeared on earth of Whom it was foretold that He
should spring from the seed and shoot of the prophet
himself, after falling down and sleeping, or "kneeling,"
according to Symmachus, He was established and raised
up, laying His hands on the back of His unseen spiritual
enemies ; and His brothers and disciples first praising Him
and wondering, afterwards were convinced that He was
God, and worshipped Him as God ; then were fulfilled the
things laid up for Him, for because of this the answer was
given, "Until there come the things laid up for him." For (b)
from that day to this, the things laid up for Him being
come, the rulers and governors of the Jewish nation have
ceased, the rulers of the Gentiles have been placed at their

head, and the nations on the other·hand knowing the
Christ of God have made Him their Saviour and Hope.

After all this there follows :

" Binding his foal to the vine, and the foal [1] of the ass
to the branch, he shall wash his robe in wine, and his
garment in the blood of the grape.   His eyes shall be
cheering from wine,[2] and his teeth white as milk."

Here I should understand by the foal, the choir of apostles
and disciples of our Saviour, and by the vine to which the
foal is bound, His divine and invisible power, as He Himself
taught when He said, "I am the true vine, and my Father
is the husbandman."   And the branch of the said vine is
the teaching of the Word of God, by which He bound the
foal of the ass—that is to say, the new people of the Gentiles,
the offspring of His Apostles.   And you may say that this
was literally fulfilled, when, according to Matthew, the Lord
said to His disciples :

"Go into the village over against you, and straightway
ye shall find an ass tied, and a colt with her ; loose
them and bring them to me."

And there is real food for wonder if one studies the
account in the prediction of the prophet, that he should
have foreseen by the Holy Spirit, that the subject of his
prophecy would not come riding on chariots and horses
like some distinguished man, but on an ass and a foal, like
a poor common man of the people.   And this raised another
prophet's wonder, who said :

" Rejoice greatly, daughter of Zion, behold thy King
cometh unto thee meek, sitting upon an ass, and a colt
the foal of an ass." [3]

And the words, " He will wash his garments in wine, and
in the blood of the grape his girdle," will shew you surely
how as in a secret way He suggests His mystic Passion,
in which He washed His garment and vesture with the
washing wherewith He is revealed to wash away the old
stains of them that believe in Him.   For with the wine
which was indeed the symbol of His blood, He cleanses
them that are baptized into His death, and believe on His

(c)
Gen. xlix.
11.

John xv. 1.

(d)

Matt. xxi.
2.

(380)

Zech. ix. 9.

---

[1] S. has ὑποζύγιον for πῶλον.

[2] S. has ὑπὲρ οἶνον for ἀπὸ οἴνου.

[3] E. omits after Σιών, κήρυσσε θυγάτηρ Ἱερουσαλήμ, and after ἔρχεται
σοι, δίκαιος καὶ σώζων, αὐτὸς. . . .

blood, of their old sins, washing them away and purifying (b)
their old garments and vesture, so that they, ransomed by
the precious blood of the divine spiritual grapes, and with
the wine from this vine, "put off the old man with his
deeds, and put on the new man which is renewed into know- Col. iii. 9,
ledge in the image of Him that created him."   10.

The words, "His eyes are cheerful from wine, and his
teeth white as milk," again I think secretly reveal the (c)
mysteries of the new Covenant of our Saviour.   "His eyes
are cheerful from wine," seems to me to shew the gladness
of the mystic wine which He gave to His disciples, when He
said, "Take, drink ; this is my blood that is shed for you
for the remission of sins : this do in remembrance of me."
And, "His teeth are white as milk," shew the brightness [1] and
purity of the sacramental food.   For again, He gave Himself (d)
the symbols of His divine dispensation to His disciples,
when He bade them make the likeness [2] of His own Body.
For since He no more was to take pleasure in bloody
sacrifices, or those ordained by Moses in the slaughter of
animals of various kinds, and was to give them bread to use
as [3] the symbol of His Body, He taught the purity and
brightness of such food by saying, "And his teeth are white
as milk."   This also another prophet has recorded, where Ps. xl. 6.
he says, "Sacrifice and offering hast thou not required, but
a body hast thou prepared for me."

But these matters should be examined at leisure, for they
require deeper criticism and longer interpretation.   For the
present I must refuse to enter on that great task, in order
that I may incorporate in this work the evidence that the
time of the Saviour's Coming from above was known to the (381)
ancient prophets, and clearly handed down in writing.

---

[1] τὸ λαμπρὸν καὶ καθαρὸν τῆς μυστηριώδους τροφῆς.
[2] τὴν εἰκόνα τοῦ ἰδίου σώματος.   See Introduction, p. xxxii.
[3] συμβόλῳ τοῦ ἰδίου σώματος.

CHAPTER 2

From Daniel.

How after the Period of Seven Times Seventy Years, or 490 Years, the Christ having appeared to Men, the Jewish Prophets and their surpassing Temple Worship will be dissolved, and They Themselves will be taken by Mutual Sieges as by a Flood, and their Holy Temple undergo its Final Desolation.

[Passage quoted, Dan. ix. 20–27.]
(Given in full on account of wide divergence from S.)

(c) " 20. AND while I yet spake and prayed and confessed my sins and the sins of my people Israel, and casting my misery before the holy Mount of my God, 21. and while I yet spake in prayer, behold the man Gabriel, whom I had seen [1] at the beginning came flying, and he touched me about the time of the evening sacrifice. 22. And he instructed me and spake with me, saying, O (d) Daniel, 23. I am now come forth to impart to thee understanding.[2] At the beginning of thy supplication the word came forth, and I am come to tell thee, for thou art a man greatly beloved : therefore consider the matter, understand the vision, for thou art a man greatly beloved. 24. Seventy weeks have been decided on for thy people, and for the holy city,[3] for sin to be ended, and to seal up transgressions, and to blot out iniquities, and to make atonement for iniquities, and to bring in everlasting righteousness, and to seal the vision and the prophecy, and to anoint the Most Holy.   25. And

---

[1] E. omits ἐν τῇ ὁράσει.   [2] S. no stop.

[3] S. reads : ἐπὶ τὴν πόλιν καὶ ἀπαλεῖψαι τὰς ἀδικίας, καὶ διανοηθῆναι τὸ ὅραμα καὶ δοθῆναι δικαιοσύνην αἰώνιον καὶ συντελεσθῆναι τὰ ὁράματα καὶ προφήτην, καὶ εὐφρᾶναι ἅγιον ἁγίων. 25. Καὶ γνώσῃ καὶ διανοηθήσῃ καὶ εὐφρανθήσῃ καὶ εὑρήσεις προστάγματα ἀποκριθῆναι, καὶ οἰκοδομήσεις Ἰερουσαλὴμ πόλιν Κυρίῳ. 26. Καὶ μετὰ ἑπτὰ καὶ ἑβδομήκοντα καὶ ἑξήκοντα δύο ἀποσταθήσεται χρῖσμα καὶ οὐκ ἔσται, καὶ βασιλεία ἐθνῶν φθερεῖ τὴν πόλιν, καὶ τὸ ἅγιον μετὰ τοῦ χριστοῦ, καὶ ἥξει ἡ συντέλεια αὐτοῦ μετ᾽ ὀργῆς καὶ καιροῦ συντελείας· ἀπο πολέμου πολεμηθήσεται. 27. Καὶ δυναστεύσει ἡ διαθήκη εἰς πολλούς· καὶ πάλιν ἐπιστρέψει, καὶ ἀνοικοδομηθήσεται εἰς πλάτος καὶ μῆκος καὶ κατὰ συντέλειαν καιρῶν, καὶ μετ᾽ ἑπτὰ καὶ ἑβδομήκοντα καιροὺς καὶ ξβ᾽ ἐτῶν ἑῶς καιροῦ συντελείας πολέμου, καὶ ἀφαιρηθήσεται ἡ ἐρήμωσις ἐν τῷ

thou shalt know and understand, that from the going
forth of the command for the answer and for the building
of Jerusalem until Christ the Prince shall be seven (382)
weeks, and sixty-two weeks ; and then it shall return,
and the street shall be built, and the wall, and the times
shall be exhausted.   26. And after the sixty-two weeks,
the Anointing shall be destroyed, and there is no judgment in him, and he shall destroy the city and the
sanctuary together with the coming prince ; they shall
be cut off in a flood, and, to the end of the war which
is rapidly completed,[1] in desolations.   27. And one
week shall establish the covenant with many : and in
the midst of the week my sacrifice and drink-offering
shall be taken away : and on the temple shall be an (b)
abomination òf desolations : and at the end of time
shall an end be put to the desolation.

When the captivity of the Jewish people at Babylon was
near its end, the Archangel Gabriel, one of the holy ministers
of God, appeared to Daniel as he prayed, and told him that
the restoration of Jerusalem was to follow without the
slightest delay, and he defines the period after the restoration by numbering the years, and foretells that after the
predetermined time it will again be destroyed, and that
after the second capture and siege it will no longer have (c)
God for its guardian, but will remain desolate, with the
worship of the Mosaic Law taken away from it, and another
new Covenant with humanity introduced in its place.   This
was what the Angel Gabriel revealed to the prophet as by
secret oracles.   So then he says to Daniel :
    "I am now come forth to impart to thee under-
standing, at the beginning of thy supplication the word
came forth, and I am come to tell thee, for thou art a
man greatly beloved.   Consider the matter, understand
the vision " ;   (d)
clearly urging him to a deeper consideration and understanding of the meaning of his words.   He calls it then a
vision from its involving deeper consideration, and more

κατισχῦσαι τὴν διαθήκην ἐπὶ πολλὰς ἑβδομάδας· καὶ ἐν τῷ τελει . . .
ἐρημώσιν.
    [1] E. omits τάξει.

than common understanding: wherefore we, too, if we call
on Him who gives understanding, and pray that the eyes of
our understanding may be enlightened, should trust confidently in the vision of this passage:

"Seven times seventy weeks," he says, "have been
decided on for this people and for thy holy city, for sin
to be ended, and to seal up transgression, and to blot
out iniquities, and to make atonement for iniquities, and
to bring in everlasting righteousness, and to seal the
vision and the people, and to anoint the most holy."

(383) It is quite clear that seven times seventy weeks reckoned
in years amounts to 490. That was therefore the period
determined for Daniel's people, which limited the total
length of the Jewish nation's existence. And he no longer
calls them here "God's people," but Daniel's, saying, "thy
people." Just as when they sinned and worshipped idols in
the wilderness, God called them no more His people, but
Moses', saying, "Go, descend, for thy people has sinned."

(b) In the same way here too he explains why the definite limit
of time is determined for them. It was that they might
know they were no longer worthy to be called the people of
God. And he adds, "And for thy holy city": where we
hear again the unusual "thy," for he says, "for thy people,
and for thy holy city," as much as to say, "the city you think
to be holy." The original Hebrew and the other translators

(c) agree in the addition of "thy" both to the people and the
city. For Aquila has, "On thy people, and on thy sacred
city"; and Symmachus, "Against thy people, and thy holy
city": wherefore in accurate codices of the Septuagint
"thy" is added with an asterisk. For since Daniel had
often called the people "the people of God" in the words
of his prayer, and the place of the city "the holy place of

(d) God," the One who answers in contrast says that neither
people nor city are God's, but "thine," who hast prayed

Dan. ix.   and spoken thus of the people and the place and the city.
16-20.   Daniel's words run thus: "16. Let thy anger be turned
away, even thy anger from Jerusalem thy city, thy holy
mountain." And, "Thy people is a source of ridicule to all
that are round about them." And again, "17. Shew thy face
upon the desolation of thy sanctuary." And once more,
"18. Behold the ruin[1] of thy city, which is called by thy

---

[1] S. adds ἡμῶν καί.

name," followed by, " 19. That thy name may be named
upon thy city, and upon thy people." After this prayer
he adds: " 20. And while I was yet speaking and praying,
behold Gabriel, whom I saw in my vision, came flying,
and touched me, and said what is written above."   (384)

The prophet then clearly called the city not a city pure
and simple but "God's city," and the sanctuary, " God's
sanctuary," and the people "God's people," from his
feeling for the people. But Gabriel does not describe them
in this way; on the contrary, he says, "for thy people," and
" for thy holy city," shewing in so many words that city,
people, and sanctuary were unworthy to be called God's.

So, then, he first defines the length of time determined (b)
for the people, and then for the city. And it is seen to be
the period from the restoration of Jerusalem, which was in
the reign of Darius, King of Persia, until the reign of
Augustus, Emperor of Rome, and of Herod the foreign
King of the Jews, in whose times our Saviour's Birth is
recorded, as the prophecy goes on to shew. And he adds
next:

" For sin to be ended, and to seal up transgressions,
and to blot out iniquities, and to make atonement for (c)
iniquities, and to bring in everlasting righteousness, and
to seal the vision and the prophet, and to anoint the
most holy."

Instead of, " For sin to be ended, and to seal up transgressions," Aquila translated, "For ending disobedience,
and for completing transgression." I think that our Saviour's
words to the Jews, "Ye have filled up the measure of your Matt.
fathers," are parallel to this. For the transgression of xxiii. 32
the Jewish nation culminated in the plot they dared to
make against Him, and what Aquila calls their " disobedience" to God reached its end. For many times of
old the long-suffering of God had borne with. their transgressions before the Saviour came, as is shewn by the
prophet's words: but just as in the case of the ancient (d)
foreign inhabitants of the land of promise it was said to
Abraham, "The sins of the Amorites are not yet fulfilled," Gen. xv.
and if they were not yet fulfilled they could not yet be 16.
driven from their native land, but when they were fulfilled,
they were then destroyed by Joshua, the successor of Moses:
so also you will understand in the case of the before-

mentioned people. For while their sins were not fulfilled, the patience and long-suffering of God bore with them, calling them many times to repentance by the prophets. (385) But when, as our Saviour said, they had filled up the measure of their fathers, then the whole collected weight worked their destruction at one time, as our Lord taught again when He said :

"All the blood poured forth [1] from the foundation of the world, from the blood of righteous Abel to the blood of Zacharias, shall come upon this generation."

Matt. xxiii. 35.

For presuming last of all to lay their hands on the Son of God they completed their disobedience and completed their sins, according to Aquila's translation, or according to the Septuagint, "Their sin was bound and sealed." But since He came not only for the falling but for the rising again of many in Israel, as is said of Him, " Behold, he is set for the fall and rising again of many in Israel," Daniel rightly proceeds to add, " And for the blotting out of transgressions and for making atonement for iniquities." For since it was impossible for the blood of bulls and of goats to take away sins, and the whole race of mankind needed a living and true offering, of which the Mosaically designed propitiation was a type, and our Lord and Saviour was this Lamb of God, as it was said of Him, "Behold the Lamb of God, which taketh away the sin of the world ; and again, "He is the propitiation for our sins, and not for ours only, but for those of the whole world " ; He brings redemption also, according to Paul's words, "Who is become wisdom to us from God, and righteousness and sanctification and redemption "—he naturally teaches that His coming is at once the fulfilment and the completion of the sin of those who have sinned against Him, at the same time as it is the blotting out and purification of sins, and the propitiation for the transgressions of them that believe in Him.

Luke ii. 34.

(c)

Heb. x. 4.

John ii. 36.

1 John ii. 2.

(d)

1 Cor. i. 30.

And Aquila to the words, "For the fulfilling of their disobedience and the completion of their sin," added, " For the propitiation of their transgression," clearly suggesting that He would be the propitiation for all transgressions of old time done in ignorance. Next to this comes, " For the bringing in of everlasting righteousness." The Word of

---

[1] W. H.: ἐκχυννόμενον ἐπὶ τῆς γῆς.   E,: ἐκχυθέν.

God is in truth Himself eternal Righteousness, Who is
made unto us by God Wisdom, and Righteousness, and
Sanctification, and Redemption, in the words of the Apostle.
But further by His own Presence also He shared Righteousness with all men, shewing by His works that God is not
only the God of the Jews, but also of the Gentiles : for (386)
there is one God, Who will judge the Circumcision from Rom. ii.
their faith, and the Uncircumcision by faith.   Wherefore 29.
Peter wondering at those with Cornelius being thought
worthy of receiving the Holy Spirit says, "Of a truth I
perceive that God is no respecter of persons, but in every
nation he that feareth him, and worketh righteousness is
accepted with him."   And Paul also says that the Gospel Acts x. 34.
is of righteousness, saying, "For it is the power of God
unto salvation to every one that believeth, to the Jew first Rom. i. 16.
and also to the Gentile.   For the righteousness of God
is revealed in it."   And it is said of Christ in the Psalms : (b)
"In His days shall arise righteousness, and abundance of Ps. xxii.
peace."   And His coming shewed clearly the righteousness 7.
of God, who reckoned the whole of mankind worthy of the
calling of God.   Such was not the Mosaic dispensation,
which was given to the Jews only : wherefore having
appeared for a time it has passed away.   But the righteous- (c)
ness proclaimed by our Saviour is fitly called eternal
righteousness, as Gabriel said, "And to bring in eternal
righteousness."

Instead of "Seal the vision and the prophet," Aquila
gives, I think, a more suitable rendering, viz. "And for
fulfilling vision and prophet."   For our Lord Jesus Christ
did not come as it were to seal up the visions of the
prophets, for He rather opened and explained those that
were of old obscure and sealed, tearing away so to say
the seals impressed on them, and taught His disciples the
meaning of the Holy Scriptures. Hence He says, "Behold, (d)
the lion of the tribe of Judah hath prevailed, and he has
opened the seals that were set on the book," in John's Rev. v. 5.
Apocalypse. What are these seals but the obscurities of
the prophets?   Isaiah knew them well and definitely says
too : "And these words shall be as the words of the sealed Isa. xxix.
book."   The Christ of God did not come then to shut up 11.
the vision and the prophet, but rather to open them and
bring them to the light. Hence I prefer Aquila's rendering,

"For fulfilling the vision and the prophet." And it agrees also with our Saviour's words, "I have not come to destroy the law or the prophets, I have not come to destroy but to fulfil." "For the end of the law is Christ," and all the prophecies concerning Him we know remained unfulfilled and uncompleted, until He came and brought fulfilment to the prophecies about Himself. It is possible, too, for the version of the Septuagint, "To seal up the vision and the prophet," to bear this meaning : "For the Law and the prophets continued until John," and from his day the ancient inspiration of the Jewish race has ceased, and its predictions of the Christ, and they who in the Holy (b) Scriptures saw genuine visions have come to an end, as if divine grace were shut up and bound with seals : and so it is the case that from that day there has been no activity of prophet or seer among them ; this has altogether ceased from the time named till our own day.

He proceeds, "And to anoint the Most Holy" ; and this also is plain for the same reason, that until the time of our Saviour the Most Holy, the High Priests were anointed (c) following the ritual performed according to the Mosaic Law, but from that date they have ceased to be, as the prophecy foretells. So too the words of Jacob to Judah foretold the cessation of the princes and rulers of the Jewish nation, as I have already stated. Now since the prophets' and priests' primacy of the people was very much later than that of the kings, the oracle in the prophecy first quoted foretells the destruction of the princes and governors of the Jewish nation, while the one we are considering predicts (d) the cessation of the prophets and priests as well, who were of old their chief ornament, which the Coming of our Saviour actually fulfilled. And as Aquila translates, "For the anointing the most consecrated," it might be thought that the ancient Jewish High Priest was meant, since many of the inferior priests were called "holy," but only the High Priest "Most Holy." And this idea at first sight is tempting. For up to the times of our Saviour the High Priests in continuous line at the same time ruled the people, (388) as they continuously performed the service of God according to the ritual ordained by Moses ; but from our Saviour's times their order was first thrown into confusion, and shortly afterwards altogether abolished. But as I find

nowhere in the Holy Scriptures the High Priest called
"Most Holy," I am of opinion that in this passage only the
Only-begotten Word of God is meant, who is properly and
truly worthy of that name.   For if men excel and reach
all attainable virtue they should be content to be called
"holy," sharing and participating in the character of Him Lev.xix.2.
Who said, "Be ye holy, for I the Lord am Holy."   But (b)
what human being could rightly be called "Most Holy," 1 Pet. i.
except the one Beloved Son of the Father, called Holy of 16.
holies as also King of kings and Lord of lords?   For to
Him only, as excelling whoever of Moses' ordaining that
were anointed with earthly and manufactured oil, was it
said, "Thou hast loved righteousness, and hated iniquity, Heb. i. 9.
therefore God, even thy God, hath anointed Thee with the (c)
oil of gladness beyond thy fellows."

Being anointed wherewith, He says in His own Person
in Isaiah: "The Spirit of the Lord is upon me, because
he hath anointed me."   Since, then, it is evident that our Isa. lxi. 1.
Saviour was anointed uniquely beyond all that ever were
with the excellent spiritual, or rather divine unction, He is
rightly called "Holy of holies," as one might say, "High
Priest of high priests," and "Sanctified of the sanctified"
according to the oracle of Gabriel.   (d)

And all these things were fulfilled when the seventy weeks
were completed at the date of our Saviour's Coming.   So
when the aforesaid Angel had given this summary prediction
to the prophet, he again returns to the subject of the
seventy weeks, explaining accurately and in detail at what
point the weeks must begin to be counted, and what will
happen at the time said.   He therefore says: "And thou
shalt know and understand, that from the going forth of
the command for the answer and for the building of Jerusalem shall be seven weeks and sixty-two weeks, and then
it shall return, and the street and wall shall be built." (389)
And with regard to this I think it right not to leave unknown the studies of a predecessor on this subject, but to
quote from them as suitable to my readers.   For it is a
good saying that "the goods of friends are common." [1]
And as it is right to use what others have expressed well
in a right spirit, and not to deprive fathers of their children,

---

[1] Cf. Plato, *Republic*, 543 A.

or the first begetters of their own offspring, I will quote his exact words. This extract from Africanus[1] is to be found in the Fifth Book of his *Chronography*, and it runs as follows :

(b)   " The section thus expressed gives much strange information. But here I will make the necessary examination of the times and the matters connected with them. It is clear, then, that the coming of the Christ is foretold as to occur after seventy weeks. For in the time of our Saviour, or after His time, sins are done away and transgressions ended. And by this remission iniquities are blotted out
(c) by a propitiation together with unrighteousness, eternal righteousness is published beyond that of the law, visions and prophecies (last) until John, and the Holy of holies is anointed. For these things existed in expectation only before our Saviour's Coming. And the angel explains we must count the numbers, that is to say the seventy weeks, which are 490 years, from the going forth of the word of answer and from the building of Jerusalem. This took place in the twentieth year of Artaxerxes, King of Persia. For Nehemiah his cup-bearer made the request,
(d) and received the answer that Jerusalem should be rebuilt, and the order went forth to carry it out. For till that date the city lay desolate. For when Cyrus after the seventieth year of the Captivity spontaneously allowed every one who wished to return, those with Joshua the High Priest and Zerubbabel went back, and those afterwards with Ezra, and were at first prevented from building the Temple, and the wall of the City, as no order had been given for it ; and so

---

[1] Julius Africanus lived at the beginning of the third century at Emmaus in Palestine. He went on an embassy to Rome A.D. 221 about its restoration (Euseb., *Chron.* ap. Jerome, *De Vir. Illust.* 63). He visited Alexandria (Euseb., *H.E.* vi. 31), Mount Ararat and Celæne (Routh, *Rel. Sac.* ii. 243). His *Chronography* is the basis of the *Chronicon* of Eusebius. Its fragments are collected by Routh. It ran from the Creation to Olymp. 250, 1, A.D. 221. Its endeavour was "to establish a synchronism between sacred and profane history" in the interests of apologetics. Two letters of Africanus—one to Origen, one to a certain Aristides—exist, and some writings are wrongly ascribed to him (see Fabric., *Bibl. Gr.* iv. 240, Ed. Harles). "His Κεστόι has the distinction of being the only known work of early Christian literature which is not directly religious" (Gwatkin, *Early Church History*, ii. 196).

there was a delay until Nehemiah and the reign of Artaxerxes
and the one hundred and fifteenth year of the Persian
Empire.　And this was 185 years from the taking of Jerusalem.　It was then that King Artaxerxes gave the order (390)
for it to be built.　And Nehemiah was sent to take charge
of the work, and the street and wall were built, as it had
been prophesied.　And from that date to the coming of
Christ is seventy weeks.　For if we begin to count from
any other point but this, not only the dates will not agree,
but many absurdities arise.　If, for instance, we begin
counting the seventy weeks from Cyrus and the first Mission,
the period will be too long by more than a century, if from (b)
the day the angel prophesied to Daniel still longer, and
longer still if we start from the beginning of the Captivity.
For we find the length of the Persian Empire to be 230
years, and of the Macedonian 300, and from then to the
sixteenth year of Tiberius Cæsar 60 years.　And from
Artaxerxes to the time of Christ seventy weeks are com- (c)
pleted according to Jewish reckoning.　For from Nehemiah,
who was sent by Artaxerxes to rebuild Jerusalem, in the
one hundred and fifteenth year of the Persian Empire, and
in the twentieth year of Artaxerxes, and in the fourth year
of the eighty-third Olympiad up to that date, which was
the second year of the two hundred and second Olympiad,
and the sixteenth year of the reign of Tiberius Cæsar, there
are 475 years, or 490 according to Hebrew reckoning.　For
they reckon years by the course of the moon, I ought to (d)
tell you, counting 354 days, while the course of the sun is
$365\frac{1}{4}$ days, twelve lunar revolutions being exceeded by one
solar by $11\frac{1}{4}$ days.　Therefore the Greeks and the Jews add
three intercalary months to every eighth year.　For eight
times $11\frac{1}{4}$ days makes three months.　So then 465 years, in
eight-year cycles, makes fifty-nine years and three months.
Since adding the three intercalary months every eighth year,
we have a few days short of fifteen years.　And these added (391)
to the 475 years complete the seventy weeks."

This, then, is from Africanus.　And if I may make an
apposite comment myself on the passage, I would say that
the prophecy does not make the division of the seventy weeks
without an object or haphazard.　For having divided them
into the first seven, and another sixty-two, it adds the

last one after a quantity of intermediate matter, and thus
(b) determines the number of seventy weeks. And so it says,
" And thou shalt know and understand from the going out of
the word of answering and of building Jerusalem until Christ
the governor there are seven weeks and sixty-two weeks.'
Then having interposed other matter, it adds the last saying
" And He shall make a covenant with many one week."
I do not think that any one who regards these as the words
of God, can suppose that these statements have no object,
or are scattered without the divine intention. I thought it was
right first to draw attention to this, and then to give a more
(c) elaborate solution of the problem to my readers. And if I
must reveal what is in my mind,[1] I would say that according
to another meaning or interpretation, he that is called in the
preceding extract "Christ the governor" (viz. "From the
going forth of the word of answering and the building of
Jerusalem until Christ the governor"), is none other than
the roll of the high priests who governed the people after
(d) the prophecy and the Return from Babylon, whom Scripture
commonly calls Christs. For I have shewn that they were
the only governors of the nation, beginning with Joshua, son
of Josedec, the Great Priest, after the return from Babylon,
and up to the date of the Coming of our Saviour Jesus
Christ. For I think that the fact that the intermediate
period of their primacy, during which they governed, is
meant, is shewn by the words, " From the going forth of the
answering and the building of Jerusalem, until Christ the
governor, is seven weeks and sixty-two weeks." And
the weeks of years make 483 years added together from the
reign of Cyrus up to the Roman Empire, when Pompeius
(392) the Roman general attacked Jerusalem and took the city by
siege, and the whole city became subject to Rome, so
that thenceforward it paid taxes, and obeyed the Roman
enactments.

At this period, then, is concluded the 483 years, when
they came to an end who held, according to the Mosaic
Law, the primacy of the nation, and the priesthood, whom
I understand the Holy Scriptures to call here "Christ the
governor." And if it be necessary to publish a roll of the
succession of the high priests[2] who held office during this
(b) intermediate period, I have no objection so to do in con-

---

[1] τὸ ἐπείσιον.   [2] Lit. "list of the high priests."

firmation of my statements. First, then, after Daniel's
prophecy, in the reign of Cyrus, King of Persia, after the
Return from Babylon, came Joshua son of Josedec, called
the Great Priest, with Zerubbabel from captivity, and laid
the foundations of the Temple, but since he was hindered
in the work by the neighbours, the first seven weeks of years
named by the prophet came to an end, during which the
building of the Temple remained unfinished. This is why (c)
the divine word separates the first seven from the remaining
weeks, saying *seven weeks*, and then after an interval
adding, *and sixty-two weeks*. For from Cyrus to the completion of the building of the Temple are seven weeks of
years. Hence the Jews attacking our Saviour said, "Forty
and six years was this Temple in building, and wilt thou John ii. 20.
raise it up in three days?" These men, you say, said that
the Temple was built in forty-six years. So they reckoned (d)
from the reign of Cyrus first, who first permitted those of
the Jews who wished to go up to their own land, to the
sixth year of King Darius, in whose reign the Temple was
finally completed. But Josephus, a Jewish author, says that
three more years were spent in completing the surrounding
outside buildings, so that it seems probable that the seven
first weeks were divided in the prophet's words into nine
years and forty years, and that the remaining sixty-two were
counted from the reign of Darius, in whose time Joshua,
son of Josedec, and Zerubbabel, son of Salathiel, who were
still alive, were both at the head of the rebuilding of the (393)
Temple, when Haggai and Zechariah were prophets, after
whom Ezra and Nehemiah, who also came up from Babylon,
built the wall of the city, when Joiachim was high priest.
He was son of Joshua, son of Josedec, and Eliashib succeeded him in the high-priesthood, then Joiada, after him
Jonathan, and after him Jaddua. The books of Ezra record
them, saying, "And Jeshua begat Joiakim, Joiakim begat (b)
Eliashib, and Eliashib begat Joiada, and Joiada begat Nehemiah
Jonathan, and Jonathan begat Jaddua." xii. 10.

In the time of this Jaddua, Alexander of Macedon conquered Alexandria, and, as Josephus relates,[1] came to
Jerusalem and worshipped God. And Alexander died at
the beginning of the 114th Olympiad, 236 years after

---

[1] Jos., *Ant.* XI. 5. 8.

(c) Cyrus, who began to rule over the Persians in the first
year of the fifty-fifth Olympiad.

Now after the death of Alexander of Macedon, and after
the said High Priest, Onias ruled the nation, also enjoying
the high-priestly office : in whose day Seleucus conquered
Babylon and put on the crown of Asia, twelve years after
Alexander's death, and the whole period from him to Cyrus
is 248 years. From that point the Book of Maccabees
begins to count the years of the Hellenic Empire. And
after Onias, the High Priest Eleazar ruled the Jews, in whose
time the Seventy translated the Holy Scriptures and de-
(d) posited them in the Library of Alexandria.[1] And after him
a second Onias, followed by Simon, in whose day flourished
Jesus, son of Sirach, who wrote the excellent book called
Wisdom.   After him a third Onias ruled, in whose time
Antiochus besieged the Jews and compelled them to hellenize. After whom Judas, called the Maccabee, was at
the head of the State, and cleansed the land of the unholy,
being succeeded by his brother Jonathan.   And then

Macc. i.   Simon, to whose death the First Book of Maccabees
16, 14.   reckons 177 years from the beginning of the Syrian rule,
and ends its history at that date. , So that the period from
(394) the first year of Cyrus and the Persian Empire up to the
end of the record of the Maccabees and the death of
Simon is 425 years.   And then Jonathan held the high-
priesthood, according to Josephus, for twenty-nine years.[2]
After him Aristobulus ruled for a year, who was the first to
assume the royal diadem[3] besides the high-priesthood after

---

[1] Cf. *H.E.* v. 8, where E. quotes from Irenæus the legend exaggerated from the simpler account of the *Letter of Aristeas*. The latter
purports to be the work of a courtier of Ptolemy Philadelphus (285–
247 B.C.), but is placed by Schürer 200 B.C. and by Wendland 96–93
B.C. It relates the request by Ptolemy that Eleazar should send Jewish
scholars to Alexandria to translate the O.T. into Greek, and their completion of the task. Wendland suggests that the preservation of this
letter goes back to the Library of Cæsarea, as it was perhaps included in
some Bible MSS. issued by Eusebius and Pamphilus. In the *Chronicle*
of Eusebius, the MSS. give dates varying between the years 1734 and
1737 of Abraham for the translation. The translation probably arose
out of the needs of the Dispersion in Egypt, and was perhaps connected
with propagandism : the prologue to the Book of Sirach is the first
document which speaks of it, where its object is said to be useful—
τοῖς ἐκτός (*H.D.B.* art. "Septuagint," Nestle).

[2] "Thirty years."—Jos., *Ant.* XX. 10. 3.

[3] Jos., *Ant.* XIII. 11. 1.

the return from Babylon.   Alexander succeeded him, as
both king and high priest, and was at the head of the State
for twenty-seven years.   To whose date is comprised in all, (b)
from the first year of the reign of Cyrus and from the
return of the Jews from Babylon, 482 years, in which period
the high priests ruled, who I believe are called in the prophecy "Christs and governors."   After whom, when the last
of them the High Priest Alexander died, the State of the
Jews was left without king or leader, so that the kingdom
came to a woman.[1]   And when her two sons, Aristobulus
and Hyrcanus, were quarrelling with each other, Pompey, the (c)
Roman general, attacked Jerusalem, and took the city by
siege, defiled its holy places, and even entered the Holiest
of all.   And this came to pass in the first year of the 179th
Olympiad, 495 years after the empire of Cyrus, who began
to rule in the fifty-fifth Olympiad.   And Pompey, then,
having taken Jerusalem by force, sent the before-named
Aristobulus a prisoner to Rome, bestowing the High-
Priesthood on his brother Hyrcanus, and the whole nation
was from that date subject to Rome.   Then after this, Herod, (d)
the son of Antipater, destroyed Hyrcanus, and was entrusted
with the Jewish kingdom by the Roman senate, being the
first ruler of a foreign stock, and he destroyed the order of
the Mosaic High-Priesthood.   For the divine Law ordained
that the most high high-priest[2] should hold office for life ;
but Herod preferred to the office men who were not of the
priestly tribe nor otherwise suitable, who were alien and
strange to the priestly line of succession, and he gave the
position not even to them for life, but only for a short and
limited time, sometimes to one, sometimes to another ; so (395)
that the first seven weeks must be reckoned from Cyrus to
Darius, and the remaining sixty-two from Darius to Pompey
the Roman general.

    And if you reckon the period of the seven and sixty-two
weeks in another way a third time, they will comprise 483
years, up to Augustus and Herod, the first king of foreign (b)
stock, in whose reign the Birth of our Saviour Jesus Christ
is recorded to have occurred, if you begin to reckon from
Darius and the completion of the Temple.   For the prophet

---

[1] Alexandra, widow of Alexander Jannæus, "a woman of masculine
understanding and energy of character."—Milman's *History of the
Jews*, Book X.   [2] τὸν ἀνωτάτω ἀρχιερέα.

Zechariah shews that the seventy years of the Desolation of Jerusalem were completed in the second year of Darius, when he says: "On the twenty-fourth day of the eleventh (c) month (this is the Sabbath),[1] in the second year of Darius, Zech. i. 1. the word of the Lord came to Zechariah son of Barachiah." And then he adds, "And the Angel of the Lord answered, Zech. i. 12. and said, O Almighty Lord, how long wilt thou not pity Jerusalem, and the cities of Judah, which thou hast despised these seventy years past?"

This, then, was the very time that Daniel, inspired by the divine spirit, marked when he said, "I Daniel understood in the books the number of the years, what was the word of the Lord to Jeremiah the prophet, for the fulfilment of the desolation of Jerusalem seventy years, and I turned my face to the Lord my God, to present my prayer and Dan. ix. 2. petition." Then after his prayer the Angel prophesied to (d) him of the seventy weeks, and told him at what point to begin to reckon the time, saying, "And thou shalt know and understand from the going forth of the word of answering and from the building of Jerusalem until Christ the governor." The first answer allowing Jerusalem to be rebuilt was of course that of Cyrus, but it did not take effect, because the neighbours interfered. But when Darius gave his order afterwards, and the building of the Temple was also completed in his reign, from that date began to be fulfilled the prophecy of Daniel, which said, "From the going forth of the word of answering and from the building (396) of Jerusalem," and that which said, "I Daniel understood in the books the number of the years, which was the word of the Lord to Jeremiah the prophet, for the fulfilment of the desolation of Jerusalem seventy years." The completion of the period of seventy years is therefore shewn to have been reached in the second year of Darius, so that we must anyway reckon the seventy weeks from the sixty-sixth Olympiad, and from the second year of Darius, in which the building was completed. And if you reckon the suc- (b) ceeding period from that date up to King Herod and the Roman Emperor Augustus, in whose times our Saviour was born on earth, you will find it amounts to 483 years, which are the seven and sixty-two weeks of the prophecy of Daniel.

---

[1] S. : ὁ μὴ Σαβάτ. E. : αὐτός ἐστι Σαβάτ, (αὐτός going with μήν).

From the sixty-sixth Olympiad to the 186th Olympiad there are 121 Olympiads, or 484 years, an Olympiad consisting of four years, during which time Augustus the Roman Emperor, in the fifteenth year of his reign, gained the king- (c) dom of Egypt and of the whole world, under whom Herod was the first foreigner to ascend the Jewish throne, and our Lord and Saviour Jesus Christ was born, the time of His birth synchronizing with the fulfilment of the seven and sixty-two weeks of Daniel's prophecy.

And afterwards comes the one remaining week, separated from them and divided by a long interval,[1] during which occurred all the other events that are predicted in between, all of which being foretold in the middle of the oracle were fulfilled; they run in the following way: " After the seven [2] (d) and sixty-two weeks the Unction shall be cast out, and there is no judgment in it.   And he will destroy the city and the Holy Place with the leader that cometh, and they shall be Dan. ix. cut off as by a flood, and until the end of the completion of 26. the war by destructions."

And this was evidently fulfilled in the time of Augustus and Herod, at whose day I say the seven weeks foretold were summed up. The regular and orderly Unction of the High Priest continued uninterrupted until the time of Herod and Augustus, and the ancient line of the High-Priesthood was ended with Alexander, the Father of Hyrcanus; and Herod, after murdering Hyrcanus, is said to (397) have conferred the office no longer on members of the ancestral line, but on obscure and unknown men. This the oracle foresaw and predicted, when it said, " And after the seven and sixty-two weeks, the Unction shall be cast out, and judgment shall not be in it."   And this is made clear by the other translators : for Aquila says, " And after the seven weeks and the sixty-two, he that is anointed shall be cast out, and there is no place for him."   And Symmachus, " And after the weeks the seven and sixty-two the Christ shall be cut off, and shall not belong to him : " which (b) seems strong confirmation of my interpretation of " Christ the Governor."

It says then that Christ shall be cast out after the completion of the said weeks.   Who can this be but the

---

[1] μακρὰν ἀπεσχοινισμένης.   [2] LXX omits ἕπτα καά.

governor and ruler of the high-priestly line? He remained
therefore until the weeks were fulfilled ; and when they
came to an end, the ruler of the nation in the line of suc-
(c) cession was cut off as the prophecy foretold. And this
was Hyrcanus, whom Herod murdered, and seized the
kingdom on which he had no special claim,[1] and he was
its first king of alien stock. And moreover Hyrcanus was
not only personally cut off as the last anointed successor of
the ancient high-priests, but the line as well which descended
from those ancient high-priests was itself cut off, and the
Legal Unction was no longer used according to judgment,
but in a confused and disorderly way not according to the
Mosaic enactments. And these events happened concurrently and fulfilled the prediction, "The Unction shall
(d) be cast out, and there is no judgment in it." Josephus,
himself a Hebrew, is sufficient evidence of this, giving the
history of those times in the Eighteenth Book of the
Archæology of the Jews :[2]

"Herod was then made king by the Romans, but did
no longer appoint High-Priests out of the family of
Asamonæus, and these were called Maccabeans, but
made certain men to be so that were of no eminent
families, but only of the Hebrew race, excepting that
he gave that dignity to Aristobulus; for he made this
Aristobulus, the son of Hyrcanus, high priest, and took
his sister Mariamne to wife, aiming at winning the goodwill of the people through their memory of Hyrcanus.
Yet did he afterwards, out of his fear lest they should
(398)   all bend their inclinations to Aristobulus, put him to
death in Jericho, and that by contriving to have him
suffocated while swimming, as I have already related.
But after this man he never entrusted the High Priesthood to the descendants of Hyrcanus. Archelaus also
acted like his father Herod in the appointment of the
High-Priests, as did also the Romans, who took the
government over the Jews into their hands afterwards."[3]

---

[1] μηδὲν αὐτῷ διαφέρουσαν.

[2] The reference is to Jos., *Ant. Jud.* XX. (not XVIII.) cap. viii. (x.),
for the reading of E. μόνον ἐξ Ἑβραίων ὄντας the text of J. gives μόνον ἐξ
ἱέρεων. Theodoret *in Dan.* c. 9, p. 662 D =1246 gives the same reading
as E.

[3] Jos., *Ant. Jud.* XX. 10. 5.

And again in another place he says of them: (b)
"But when Herod came to be king he rebuilt this
tower, which was very conveniently situated, in a
magnificent manner, and called it Antonia, and he took
the high-priestly vestments, which he found lying there,
and kept them, believing that while he had them the
people would not revolt against him.   And Herod's
example was followed by Archelaus his son, who was
made king after him, after whom the Romans when
they entered on the government took possession of the
high-priestly vestments, and had them laid up in a stone
chamber under a seal." [1]

I think it must be clear to all that this was the fulfilment (c)
of the oracle, which said, "And after the seven and sixty-
two weeks the Unction shall be cast out, and there is no
judgment in it."

And you may see better the meaning of the words, "And
there is no judgment in it," if you consider the haphazard
appointments of the high-priests after Herod's time and in
the time of our Saviour.   For whereas by the divine Law (d)
it was ordained that a high-priest should hold office all his
life and be succeeded by his legitimate son, in the period
in question, when the Unction had been cast out as the
prophecy foretold, Herod first, and after him the Romans,
appointed what high-priests they liked haphazard or not
according to the Law, bestowing the dignity on common
and unknown men, selling and peddling the office, giving
it now to one now to another for a year.   And the Evangelist St. Luke seems to imply this, where he says, "In the
fifteenth year of the reign of Tiberius Cæsar, Pontius Pilate
being governor of Judæa, and Herod, Philip and Lysanias
being tetrarchs, Annas and Caiaphas being high-priests." Luke iii. 1.
For how could they both be high-priest at the same time
unless the rules of the high-priesthood were disregarded?
In witness whereof Josephus writes: (399)
"Valerius [2] Gratus the Roman General, after closing
the high-priesthood of Ananus, appointed Ismael the
son of Pheba, and removing him shortly afterwards
appointed Eleazar son of Ananus the high-priest.   A
year later he removed him, and gave the office to

---

[1] Jos., *Ant. Jud.* XVIII. 4. 3.   [2] See Eus., *H.E.* I. 10.

Simon son of Cathimus. He did not remain high priest more than a year, when Josephus, son of Caiaphas, took his place."[1]

(b) I was obliged to give this quotation because of the words "The Unction shall be cast out, and there is no judgment in it," which seem to me proved by it beyond any doubt.

After this the prophecy says, "And the city, and the holy place, he will destroy, with the governor that cometh." Here again I understand the rulers of foreign stock who succeeded him to be meant. For as above he named the High-Priests, Christs and Governors, saying, "Until Christ the Governor," in the same way after their time and after their abolition there was no other ruler to come but the

(c) same Herod of foreign stock, and the others ruled the nation in order after them, in whose company and by whose aid, using them as his agents, that hateful bane of good men is said to have destroyed the city and the Holy Place. And indeed he destroyed of a truth the whole nation, now upsetting the established order of the priesthood, now perverting the whole people, and encouraging the city (which

(d) stands metaphorically for its people) in impiety. And Aquila agrees with my interpretation of the passage, translating thus, "And the people of the governor that cometh will destroy the city and the holy place." Meaning that the city and the Holy Place are not only to be ruined by the leader to come, whom I have identified in my interpretation, but also by his people. And you would not be far wrong in saying, too, that the Roman general and his army are meant by the words before us, where I think the camps of the Roman rulers are meant, who governed the nation from that time, and who destroyed the city of Jerusalem itself, and its ancient venerable Temple. For they were cut off by them as by a flood, and were at once involved in destruction until the war was concluded, so that the prophecy was fulfilled and they suffered utter desolation

(400) after their plot against our Saviour, which was followed by their extreme sufferings during the siege. You will find an accurate account of it in the history of Josephus.

But after the prophecy of the events that happened to the Jewish nation in the intermediate period between the

[1] Jos., *Ant. Jud.* XVIII. 2. 2.

seven and sixty-two weeks, there follows the prophecy of the new Covenant announced by our Saviour. So when all the intermediate matter between the seven and the sixty-two weeks is finished, there is added, " And he will confirm (b) a Covenant with many one week," [1] and in half the week the sacrifice and the libation shall be taken away, and on the Holy Place shall come the abomination of desolation, and until the fullness of time fullness shall be given to the desolation. Let us consider how this was fulfilled.

Now the whole period of our Saviour's Teaching and working of Miracles is said to have been three-and-a-half years, which is half a week. John the Evangelist, in his Gospel, makes this clear to the attentive. One week of years therefore would be represented by the whole period of His association with the Apostles, both the time before His Passion, and the time after His Resurrection. For it is written that before His Passion He shewed Himself for the space of three-and-a-half years to His disciples and also to those who were not His disciples : while by teaching and miracles He revealed the powers of His Godhead to all equally whether Greeks or Jews. But after His Resurrection [2] He was most likely with His disciples a period equal

---

[1] The parenthetic nominative for duration of time is found in Eccles. ii. 16, Josh. i. 11 and in N.T., Matt. xv. 32, Mark viii. 2, and Luke ix. 28. It is common in the late Greek of the Papyri. It is a decay of language, not a Hebraism. See Moulton, *Grammar of N.T. Greek*, vol. i. 69, 70 ; Radermacher, 117 and 178 *sq*. Here ἑβδομὰς μία occurs only in Theodotion, and in margin of one cursive of G.

[2] The Greek is τὸν ἴσον, ὡς εἰκὸς, τῶν ἐτῶν χρόνον τοῖς ἑαυτοῦ μαθηταῖς καὶ ἀποστόλοις συνῆν, δι' ἡμερῶν τεσσαράκοντα ὀπτανόμενος αὐτοῖς— which must mean literally that the period between the Resurrection and Ascension was three-and-a-half years, equal to that of the Ministry, making up with it "a week of years." A. J. Maclean (*D.A.C.* i. 98) so takes it, classing it with " the Valentinian idea that the interval was eighteen months, or that of certain Ophite sects that it was eleven or twelve years." But we must remember that on page 108 d, Eusebius has described the same period in the words " after staying a brief while, and completing a short time." The "forty days of Acts i. 3 were not always taken exactly, previous to the fixing of the Feast of the Ascension in the fourth century ; *e.g.* Barnabas makes the Ascension take place on a Sunday (*Ep.* § 15), apparently the day of the Resurrection, while the Canons of Edessa commemorate the Ascension on Whitsunday ; but such instances merely shew that Acts i. 3 means "*about* forty days," and are very different to the suggestion of Eusebius. The only way to make Eusebius balance with Acts i. 3 is either (i) to suppose he implied that in the three-and-a-half years there were

to the years, being seen of them forty days,[1] and eating
with them, and speaking of the things pertaining to the
Kingdom of God, as the Acts of the Apostles tells us.   So
that this would be the prophet's week of years, during which
He "confirmed a covenant with many," confirming that is to
say the new Covenant of the Gospel Preaching.   And who
were the many to whom He confirmed it, but His own disciples and Apostles, and such of the Hebrews who believed
in Him?   And moreover, half through this week, during
which He confirmed the said Covenant with many, the
(401) sacrifice and libation was taken away, and the abomination
of desolation began, for in the middle of this week after the
three-and-a-half days of His Teaching, at the time when He
suffered, the Veil of the Temple was torn asunder from the
top to the bottom, so that in effect from that time sacrifice
and libation were taken away, and the abomination of desolation stood in the holy place, inasmuch as the Being had
left them desolate, Who had been from time immemorial till
(b) that day the guardian and protector of the place.   For it is
fitting to believe that up to the Saviour's Passion there was
some Divine Power guarding the Temple and the Holy of
Holies.   For He could not have attended with the multitude at the Temple to keep the Feasts according to the
laws, if He had not known that it still remained a place
worthy of God.   Therefore there were in the Temple also
some that prophesied up to that time, as Anna the Pro-
(c) phetess, daughter of Phanuel, and Simeon, who took Him
into his arms when He was an infant, whose prophecies are
handed down in Scripture.   Nor could our Lord have said
Matt. viii. to the leper, "Go, shew thyself to the priest, and offer the
4. gift which Moses commanded for a testimony unto thee,"
if He had not considered it right for the legal observances
to be carried out there as in a holy place worthy of God.
Matt. xxi. Nor would He have thrust out those who bought and
13. sold, saying, "Take these things hence, and make not

---

only forty days of intercourse between Christ and the disciples, or (ii),
that the ἴσον is not *numerical* here, but that Eusebius means that the
period of forty days in power, importance and blessing was equivalent
to the period of the Ministry.   It should be remembered that the suggestion is introduced by ὡς εἰκός, and the support of Acts i. 3 directly
invoked.

[1] συναλιζόμενος, Acts i. 4—συναυλιζόμενος, Migne.

my Father's House a house of merchandise," if He had John ii. 16.
not thought that the Temple was still to be reckoned sacred. (d)
But it was when the hour of their extreme wickedness drew
near, that He explained all when He said, "Behold your Matt. xxiii.
house is left unto you desolate," which also was fulfilled, 38.
when at his Passion the Veil of the Temple was wholly
rent in twain, and from that moment the sacrifice and
libation well pleasing to God according to the ordinance
of the Law was in effect taken away, and when it was removed, the abomination of desolation, as the prophecy
before us says, appeared in its place.   And if it be said
that the worship of the Sanctuary appeared to continue for
a time, yet it was not pleasing to God, being offered without
judgment and not according to the Law.   For as before of (402)
old when the Unction was abolished, and the lawful line of
High Priests ceased after the death of Hyrcanus, they who
held the office afterwards seemed to perform disordered and
illegal rites, since they were breaking the fitting Laws, of
whom the prophecy said, "The Unction shall be cast out,
and there is no judgment in it," referring to its illegality and
lack of judgment; so here you will rightly say it has happened to the offering and libation, which were rightly and (b)
lawfully offered before our Saviour's Passion, while the
Power still guarded the Holy Places, but which were taken
away directly after the perfect and supreme Sacrifice which
He offered, when He offered Himself for our sins, being
the Lamb of God, that taketh away the sin of the world,
which sacrifice having been delivered to all men in the new
Sacraments of the new Covenant, the Sacrifices of the old
are taken away.   For concurrently with the fulfilment of
the oracle which says, "And he shall confirm a covenant (c)
with many one week," all that is connected with the old
Covenant is abolished.   And when was the new Covenant
confirmed, but when our Lord and Saviour, about to con-
summate the great Mystery of His delivery to death, on the
night in which He was betrayed, delivered to His disciples
the symbols of the unspeakable words of the new Covenant
referring to Him?   For concurrently with this celebration, (d)
the old Covenant of Moses was abolished, which was shewn
by the veil of the Temple being rent at the very time.
Sacrifice and libation being from that time abolished
and ceasing in effect and truth, any sacrifices that were

afterwards thought to be offered there were celebrated in a
profane place by profane and unhallowed men.   Hear the
witness of Josephus about this :

"On the day of Pentecost, the priests going by night
into the Temple, as was their custom, for the services,
said that they were first conscious of a quaking and a
sound, and afterwards of a sudden voice which said, Let
us depart hence."

And he records this to have taken place after the Passion
of our Saviour.[1]   And the same writer says elsewhere :

(403)   "Pilate the Governor" (meaning the Pilate of our
Saviour's time) "brought the images of Cæsar into the
Temple by night, which was unlawful, and caused
a great outburst of tumult and disorder among the
Jews."[2]

Which Philo[3] confirms, saying :

"Pilate laid up in the Temple by night the imperial
emblems, and from that time the Jews were involved
in rebellion and mutual troubles."

And from that time a succession of all kinds of troubles
afflicted the whole nation and their city until the last war
against them, and the final siege, in which destruction
(b) rushed on them like a flood with all kinds of misery of
famine, plague and sword, and all who had conspired
against the Saviour in their youth were cut off; then, too,
the abomination of desolation stood in the Temple, and it
has remained there even till to-day, while they have daily
reached deeper depths of desolation.   And perhaps this
will be so until the end of the world, according to the limit
set by the prophet when he said, "And unto the consummation of time a fulfilment shall be given to the desolation."

(c) These words our Lord and Saviour Jesus Christ sealed,
when He said, "When ye shall see the abomination of
desolation spoken of by Daniel the Prophet, standing in
Matt. xxiv. the Holy Place, then ye shall know that her desolation
15 ; Luke draws near."[4]
xxi. 20.
        And if the Jews are hard to persuade of this, they must
be convicted not only of a shameless opposition to truth

---

[1] Jos., *B.J.* VI. 5, 3.
[2] Jos., *Ant.* XVIII. 3, and *B.J.* II. 9. 2.
[3] Philo Jud., cf. *leg. ad caium* 38, pp. 589, 590.
[4] The first part is Matt. xxiv. 15 : from τότε γινώσκετε from Luke
xxi. 20.

and clear evidence, but also of misrepresenting, so far as they can, the predictions as falsehoods, if it is to be thought that in the seventy weeks of years some of them include all the time, while they prophesy of what is to happen in the intermediate period, while others, though we are now nearly a thousand years from the date of the prophecy, admit no (d) sign of the fulfilment of what was written, although their Unction has been abolished, as the divine prediction foretold, and their sanctuary, and the former inhabitants destroyed and utterly brought to naught in the flood of the completed war, and strangest thing of all even now to be seen, I mean, the abomination of desolation still standing in the one holy place, concerning which our Lord and Saviour said what I have quoted.

As this is before our eyes even now, it is extraordinary (404) that the Jews are not only so daring as to refuse to see what is clear, but so blind and dark in their minds as well as not to be able to see the clear and evident fulfilment of the Holy Scriptures.   But they are in the state now that Isaiah prophesied they should come to, and his words are fulfilled :

"Hearing ye shall hear, and shall not understand, and seeing ye shall see and not perceive. For the heart of this people is waxed gross, and their ears are dull of hearing, and their eyes they have closed, lest at (b) any time they should see with their eyes, and hear with their ears, and understand with their heart, and should be converted, and I should heal them."   Isa. vi. 9.

But since it was said of old of the nations that believe in Christ, "To whom it has not been announced concerning Him, they shall see, and they who have not heard, shall understand," I also by His grace and that of the Father that Isa. lii. 15. sent Him have given as full an interpretation as I could of this passage, and have quoted also the critical conclusions of Africanus, my predecessor, as germane and accurate, and therefore to be made use of as satisfactory.   (c)

CHAPTER 3

From Micah.

The Prophet foretells what will be the Signs of the Coming of the Lord to Men, the Complete Destruction of the Sacred Customs of the Jews, the Knowledge of the God that was announced by the Prophets, the Deepest Peace of All Nations.

(405)   [Passages quoted, Micah i. 2–4; iii. 9–12; iv. 1–4.]

(d) I HAVE already considered this prophecy among the passages. And I have pointed out that only from the date of our Saviour Jesus Christ's Coming among men have the objects of Jewish reverence, the hill called Zion and Jerusalem, the buildings there, that is to say, the Temple, the Holy of Holies, the Altar, and whatever else was there dedicated to the glory of God, been utterly removed or shaken, in fulfilment of the Word which said:

"Behold the Lord, the Lord comes forth from his place, and he shall descend on the high places of the earth, and the mountains shall be shaken under him."

And when those kings are shaken, the souls of the Jews, called "valleys," because of the contrast of their wretchedness with their former exaltation, bewailing the passing of (406) the aforesaid glory, will melt like wax before the fire, and be as water rushing down a chasm, through the multitude of those that fall from bad to worse. And all this it says will come to pass because of the sin of the house of Jacob, and the transgression of the house of Israel. And it goes on to describe this sin and transgression, "They that defile judgment and pervert all that is right, who build Sion with blood and Jerusalem with unrighteousness." With blood! Yes, this was the cause of their final misery, for that they pronounced the impious curse upon themselves, saying, (b) "His blood be on us and on our children." Therefore, it says this, "Zion shall be plowed as a field, and Jerusalem shall be as a storehouse of fruit," a prophecy which was only actually fulfilled after the impious treatment of our Saviour. For from that time to this utter desolation has possessed the land; their once famous Mount Sion, instead

Matt.
xxvii. 25.

---

[1] E. omits γῆν.

of being, as once it was, the centre of study and education based on the divine prophecies, which the children of the (c) Hebrews of old, their godly prophets, priests and national teachers loved to interpret, is a Roman farm like the rest of the country, yea, with my own eyes I have seen the bulls plowing there, and the sacred site sown with seed. And Jerusalem itself is become but a storehouse of its fruit of old days now destroyed, or better, as the Hebrew has it, a stone-quarry.

So Aquila says, "Therefore for your sake the land of Zion shall be ploughed, and Jerusalem shall be a quarry of (d) stone," for being inhabited by men of foreign race it is even now like a quarry, all the inhabitants of the city choosing stores from its ruins as they will for private as well as public buildings. And it is sad for the eyes to see stones from the Temple itself, and from its ancient sanctuary and holy place, used for the building of idol temples, and of theatres for the populace.[1] These things are open for the eyes to see, and it should be clear as well that it is hence that the new law and word of the new Covenant of our Saviour Jesus Christ goes forth. For countless companies (407) of people, races of all kinds deserting their fathers' gods and their old superstitions, call on the Supreme God. And thus it is reckoned the deepest peace, there being no diversity of government or national rule, that nation should not take up sword against nation, and that they should not learn war any more, but that each farmer should rest under his vine and under his fig tree, according to the prophecy, and that none should make him afraid.   (b)

As this state of things was never achieved at any other time but during the Roman Empire, from our Saviour's birth till now, I consider the proof irrefutable that the prophet refers to the time of our Saviour's coming among men.

[1] Πανδήμων θεαμάτων.

CHAPTER 4

From Zechariah.

Signs of the Time of the Coming of the Word of God to Men, the Call of the Gentiles, and Final Destruction of Jerusalem.

[Passages quoted, Zech. ii. 10, 11 ; ix. 9, 10.]

AFTER this prediction of our Saviour's Coming, the prophecy now goes on, after interposing other matter, to speak of the final desolation of Jerusalem, partly under figurative and disguised forms, and partly quite clearly. Figuratively, for example, when it says :

(408)   " 1. Open thy doors, Libanus, and let the fire devour thy cedars ; let the pine howl, because the cedar has fallen : for the mighty men have been greatly afflicted. 2. Howl, ye oaks of the land of Bashan, for the thickly planted forest has been torn down. 3. The voice of shepherds mourning, for their greatness is brought low : The voice of roaring lions, for the pride of Jordan is brought low."

Zech. xi. 11.

This is figurative. But the same prophet goes on to give a clear interpretation of it.

(b)   " 2. Behold, I will make Jerusalem as shaking doorposts to all the nations round about, and in Judæa there shall be a siege against Jerusalem. 3. And it shall be in that day, I will make Jerusalem a stone trodden under foot by all nations ; every one that tramples on it shall utterly mock it, and all the nations of the earth shall be gathered unto her."

Zech. xii. 2.

And shortly after he adds :

(c)   " 10*b*. And they shall look on me, whom they pierced,[1] because they have mocked me, and shall make lamentation for him as for a beloved, and grief as for a firstborn son. 11. In that day the lamentation of Jerusalem shall be increased, as the mourning for Roon cut down in the plain. 12. And the land shall mourn according to families. The family of the house of David by itself, and its women by themselves ; the family of the house of Nathan by itself, and its women by themselves ; the

---

[1] S. omits εἰς ὅν ἐξεκέντησαν, supported by G.

family of the house of Levi by itself, and its women by
themselves; the family of the house of Simeon by itself,
and its women by themselves. 14. All the families
that are left, each family by itself and their wives by Zech. xii.
themselves."   10.
And again, after other matter, he announces yet more (d)
clearly the siege of Jerusalem, saying:
    " 1. Behold the days of the Lord come, and thy spoils
shall be divided in thee. 2. And I will bring up all
nations unto Jerusalem unto war, and the city shall be
taken, and its houses plundered, and its women defiled,
and half of the city shall go into captivity, and the
remnant of my people shall not be cast out of the city.
3. And the Lord shall come forth, and shall fight with
those nations, as when he fought in the day of war.
4. And his feet shall stand in that day on the Mount of Zech. xiv.
Olives, which is before Jerusalem."   1.
Then, after an interval, he says:
    "And there shall be one Lord, and his name one, Zech. xiv.
encircling the earth and the wilderness."   9.
And again after other matter, concluding the book of His (409)
prophecy, He prophesies the calling of the Gentiles:
    "And it shall come to pass that whosoever shall be
left of all the nations that came against Jerusalem shall
even come up every year to worship the King the
Lord Almighty, and to keep the Feast of Tabernacles.
17. And it shall come to pass that whosoever of all the
families of the earth shall not come up to Jerusalem to
worship the King, the Lord Almighty, even these shall
be added to the others. 18. And if the family of Egypt (b)
shall not go up nor come thither, then upon them shall
come the fall, with which the Lord shall strike all nations,
as many as go not up to keep the Feast of Tabernacles.
19. This is the transgression of Egypt, and the transgression of all the nations, as many as go not up to keep Zech. xiv.
the Feast of Tabernacles."   16-19.
    So prophesied Zechariah after the Return from Babylon,
in the reign of Darius, King of Persia, when Jerusalem was
but just arisen from the desolation which it suffered under
the Babylonians. And the whole period from Darius the (c)
Persian, in whose time Zechariah prophesied, even to
Augustus, Emperor of Rome, amounts to the seven and

sixty-two weeks of years in Daniel, which are equivalent to
483 years, as I have shewn in my recent investigations.
And neither in the time of the Macedonians from Alexander
onwards, not even if you include the reign of Augustus, was
(d) anything similar to the words of the prophet fulfilled.   For
when in those days did the Lord, Whom the prophet speaks
of as divine, come among men, and many nations know
Him, and confess Him to the only God, and take refuge in
Him, and be to Him a people?   Or when in the times of
the Macedonians or Persians did the king who was foretold
come, sitting upon an ass and a young colt?   When did He
come and utterly destroy the royal array of the Jewish nation,
here called Ephraim, and of Jerusalem itself, called chariots
and horses, and conquer the army of the Jews?   For this is
what the oracle revealed, saying :

> " Behold thy king cometh to thee, righteous and a
> saviour, himself meek, and sitting upon an ass and a
> young colt, and he shall utterly destroy the warlike bow."

(410) For so it was prophesied concerning the destruction of the
royal glory of the Jewish nation, at the same time, as, on the
other hand, the prophecy of peace for the Gentiles was
repeated in agreement with those previously quoted, namely,
" And abundance of peace shall be from the Gentiles."
In place of which Aquila and the other translators render,
" And he shall speak peace to the Gentiles," which stands
specially and literally fulfilled from the reign of Augustus,
since from that date varieties of government ceased, and
(b) peace enwrapped most of the nations of the world.   And
before the Roman days under Persians or Macedonians
what King of the Jews was there, who "ruled from sea to
sea, and from the rivers to the ends of the earth?"   And so
the other translators have shewn.

Therefore Aquila says :

> " And he shall speak peace to the Gentiles, and his
> power shall be from sea to to sea, and from the river to
> the ends of the world."

With this agrees the passage in the 101st Psalm concerning
the Christ that is to be born of the seed of Solomon :

> " In his days righteousness shall arise, and abundance
> of peace, so long as the moon endureth, and he shall
(c) > rule from sea to sea, and from the river to the ends of
> the world."

For these words about the son of Solomon are as exalted as those in the prophet. When, then, this took place and in what way, and in what period, let him that can, inform me. And when did Jerusalem after its siege by the Babylonians undergo a second burning, and have its Temple thrown to the ground?

And the figure used by the prophet is also exceedingly (d) strange when he says, "O Libanus, open thy gates, and let fire devour thy cedars." For he calls the Temple here, as was not unusual, by the name of Libanus (it is so called in other prophecies). To this the Jews themselves now assent, since Isaiah, too, has a similar prophecy to the one before us, namely:

"Behold, the Lord of Sabaoth shall disturb the noble with might, and the lofty shall be crushed in their pride.[1] And Libanus shall fall with its lofty ones, and there shall come forth a rod from the stem of Jesse, and a flower shall spring up from his roots, and the spirit of the Lord shall rest upon him."

To which he adds:

"And there shall be a root of Jesse, and he that shall (411) rise to rule the Gentiles, in him shall the Gentiles trust." Isa. x. 33.

Here, too, the destruction of Libanus and the call of the Gentiles is connected with the birth of Christ, of the seed of Jesse and David. And Ezekiel actually calls Jerusalem Libanus when he says, "The great eagle, with great wings,[2] that hath the dominion, cometh to Libanus, and tore Ezek. xvii. off the tender boughs of the cedar." And he goes on to 3. explain this himself, as happening when Nebuchadnezzar shall come to Jerusalem and take her rulers, and that which follows. But Ezekiel's prophecy is about the first siege, and (b) Zechariah's about the second. When, then, after the time of Ezek. xvii. Zechariah in the time of the Macedonian Empire was the 12. Temple burnt? There was no such time. For after its burning by the Babylonians, it was not burned again till in the time of Titus and Vespasian, the Roman Emperors, it was utterly destroyed by fire, and it is in relation to this that the prophet summons the ancient rulers of the nation in a figure to mourn and weep, when he says: "Let the (c)

---

[1] E. omits καὶ οἱ ὑψηλοὶ τῇ ὕβρει ταπεινωθήσονται, καὶ 'πεσοῦνται ὑψηλοὶ μαχαίρᾳ. (S.)

[2] E. omits ὁ μακρὸς τῇ ἐκτάσει, πλήρης ὀνύχων. (S.)

pine weep because the cedar is fallen, because the great
ones are in great misery.   Let the oaks of Bashan weep,
because the wood that is planted is torn down : a voice of
shepherds that lament, because their greatness is in misery."
Then truly Jerusalem was as a portico shaken by all nations
around it, and there was a force encircling Judæa, and their
venerated Temple and its Holy Place is even to-day a stone
trodden under the feet of all nations, and all that mock are
mocked according to the prophecy.

(d)   Yea, in return for their insults to the Lord who thus
prophesied, there has not failed for them lamentation,
mourning and wailing.   And it was only after our Saviour
came, and even until our own time, that all the families of
the Jewish nation have suffered pain worthy of wailing and
lamentation because God's hand has struck them, delivering
their mother-city over to strange nations, laying their Temple
low, and driving them from their country, to serve their
enemies in a hostile land ; wherefore even now every house
and every soul is a prey to lamentation.   And so the
prophecy says, "And family shall mourn by family, the
(412) family of the house of David by itself, and their wives by
themselves, and all that follows this."

And which were the days after the age of Zechariah,
when the spoils of Jerusalem were divided, and all nations
were gathered against them in battle, and the city was
taken, their houses looted, their women defiled, and they
themselves led into captivity, while the Lord was at the
same time aiding the nations warring against Jerusalem
and drawn up against them?   Or when did His feet stand
(b) on the Mount of Olives?   Or when was the Lord King of
all the earth, when was there one Lord over all men, when
did His Name encircle the whole earth and the wilderness?
It is impossible to argue that this was fulfilled previously
to the period of the Romans, in whose time the Jewish
Temple was burnt for the second time after its destruction
by the Babylonians, and their city from then till now has
been inhabited by foreign nations.

And it was when our Lord Jesus, the Christ of God, had
(c) visited the olive-grove' over against Jerusalem, since the
words of the prophecy were fulfilled which said, "His feet
shall stand upon the Mount of Olives opposite to Jerusalem," that is, the life of holiness having been established

throughout all the world, that all the nations, according to the prophecy, kept the Feast of Tabernacles together in every place to the God of the prophets, and the Egyptians from that time recognizing God erected tents in every town and country place, which mean the local Christian Churches. For the power of our Saviour Jesus Christ has pegged them (d) far better than Moses' tents through the whole world, so that every race of men and all the Gentiles may keep their Feast of Tabernacles to Almighty God.

When, then, we see what was of old foretold for the nations fulfilled in our own day, and when the lamentation and wailing that was predicted for the Jews, and the burning of the Temple and its utter desolation, can also be seen even now to have occurred according to the prediction, surely we must also agree that the King who was prophesied, (413) the Christ of God, has come, since the signs of His coming have been shewn in each instance I have treated to have been clearly fulfilled.

CHAPTER 5

From Isaiah.

The Signs of the Times of the Lord's Coming, and the Egyptians' Acknowledgment of the God of the Prophets.

[Passages quoted, Isa. xix. 1–3 ; xix. 19–21.]

THIS is a passage that I have already partly expounded. Now if the Egyptians are not seen in our own time deserting their ancestral gods and calling upon the God of the prophets ; if throughout Egypt in every locality, town and country there are not altars erected to the God that was formerly acknowledged only by the Hebrews ; if the idols of (414) Egypt have not been shaken, for that the power of the dæmons that hung about them is gone, and the ancient superstition driven from the soul of the Egyptians ; and once more, if there is not intestine war arisen through all the households of Egypt, between them that receive the Lord and worship the God of the prophets and reject their

immemorial polytheistic error, and them that oppose the
(b) converts of the Lord in their adherence to the evil of their
fathers ; if they do not even now in their efforts to question
their own gods and the idols and them that speak out of
the ground and the diviners by familiar spirits,[1] make a vain
and useless appeal to them because the dæmons are no
longer able to work in them as they did of old—if all these
things are not seen to have been actually fulfilled, why
(c) then, you may consider that the prophetic oracle is unfulfilled, and that the Lord that was prophesied has not yet
visited our human life.

But if, on the other hand, we can see the people of
Egypt far more patently in actual fact than in mere description, some of them acknowledging the God of the prophets,
and for His sake renouncing their ancestral gods, some of
them raising political dissension against the converts, some
of them even now calling upon their gods and images and
them that speak from the ground, who no longer can effect
aught, and some throughout all Egypt raising an altar to
the Lord of the prophets for each local Church, calling no
(d) longer in their troubles and persecutions on beasts or
reptiles as their gods, nor on wild animals and unreasoning
brutes as their fathers did, but on the Supreme God, retaining Him only and the fear of Him in their minds, praying
to Him, and not to the dæmons, and promising what men
should promise God—how can we deny that the prophecies
of long ago have at last been fulfilled?[2]   And these foretold that the Lord would come to Egypt not in an unembodied state, but in a light cloud, or better "in light
thickness," for such is the meaning of the Hebrew, shewing
figuratively His Incarnate state.   Therefore the prophecy

---

[1] Cf. Isa. viii. 19, τοὺς ἐγγαστριμύθους καὶ τοὺς ἀπὸ τῆς γῆς φωνοῦντας
τοὺς κενολογοῦντας οἳ ἐκ τῆς κοιλίας φωνοῦσιν (Sept.).   See W. Robertson Smith, "On the forms of Divination and Magic enumerated in
Deut. xviii. 10, 11," *Journal of Philology*, xiv. (1885), pp. 127 *sq.* ;
J. G. Frazer, *Folklore in the O.T.*, "The Witch of Endor,' ii. 524.
In necromancy the wizard either made the voice appear to come from
the ground or from his own inside.   "The witch told Saul that the
ghost of Samuel rose out of the earth, and through the exertion of her
vocal talent she may have caused to issue apparently from the ground
a hollow and squeaky voice which the King mistook for the accents of
the deceased seer."   For necromancy in third century, see Hippolytus,
Refutatio omnium heresium, liv. 35, p. 102 (Göttingen, 1859).
[2] τὰ πρὸ τῶν ἀποτελεσμάτων εἰς ἔργον ἤδη κεχωρηκέναι.

goes on to call Him a man that is a Saviour, saying, "And (415) the Lord shall send to them a man that is a Saviour." Here again the Hebrew is, "And He shall send to them a Saviour, who shall save them." As the proof is now so clear from this, I consider that there is no question of the time at which the prophecies foretold the Lord's Coming.

I have here only briefly collected the evidence for the time of the Advent of our Lord. If the other Scriptures were searched at leisure much more could be discovered. But as I am well satisfied with what I have brought before (b) you, I will now address myself to the other prophecies. And our next task will be to collect from inspired prophecy the predictions about the earthly dispensation of the Incarnation.[1]

[1] τὰ οἰκονομηθέντα ἐν ἀνθρώποις.

BOOK IX

It remains for me now to redeem my promise to go on to expound the dispensation connected with the Incarnation of the very Word of God. My previous labours in the eight books already completed have been concerned (417) with Him. I have now devoted myself to tracing the Theology of His Person, now to considering His Descent to us from heaven, now His Character, His Name, and the time of His Advent. As the treatment of these subjects is complete, it is now time to consider the matters connected with His Coming, and to shew how these also were predicted among the Hebrews. And the fulfilment of the predictions shall be confirmed by the witness of (b) the Holy Evangelists, and their historical account of the actual events.

Let us then begin, as the proof about His Birth, tribe, and family is complete, by considering the star which appeared at His Birth, which was new and a stranger among the usual lights of heaven. For this, too, was proclaimed by Moses long before in times far distant in the following words.

CHAPTER 1

Of the Things that happened at the Incarnation, and of the Star that appeared at Our Saviour's Birth.

Moses, in the Book of Numbers, says of the star that appeared at the Birth ·of our Saviour, as follows.

[Passage quoted, Num. xxiv. 15–19.]

We are told that Balaam's successors moved by this (for the prediction was preserved most likely among them), when they noticed in the heavens a strange star besides the usual ones, fixed above the head, so to say, and

vertically above Judæa, hastened to arrive at Palestine, to (418)
inquire about the King announced by the star's appearance.[1]
Matthew the Evangelist witnesses to this as follows :

    1. "And when Jesus was born in Bethlehem of
Judæa, in the days of Herod the king, behold, wise
men from the east came to Jerusalem saying, 2. Where
is he that is born King of the Jews? for we have seen
his star in the east and are come to worship him."
And when they had been sent on their way they
reached Bethlehem.[2]

    9. "And, behold, again, the (same[3]) star, which
they saw before in the east, went before them, until
it came and stood over where the young child was.
10. And when they saw the star, they rejoiced with (b)
exceeding great joy, and going into the house they
saw the child with Mary his mother, and fell down   Matt. ii.
and worshipped him."   1-2, and
                                                      9-11.
This is the account in the Holy Gospel. But the word
of the prophecy says that striking events will be heralded
by the rising of the star and the birth of our Saviour Jesus
Christ, viz., the crushing of the leaders of Moab, and the
raid on the sons of Seth, and the inheriting by the Jewish
nation of its other enemies, these being Edom and Esau.
What could be thus figuratively described by the leaders (c)
of Moab, but the destruction of the invisible rulers, I mean
the dæmons whom the Moabites had of old considered
gods? But others were not mentioned, because of Israel's
idolatry in the wilderness, when "the people were initiated
into the rites of Belphegor."[4] (This dæmon was honoured Ps. cvi. 28.
as a god by Balak, King of Moab.)

As, therefore, Israel was conquered on this occasion by
the invisible powers of Moab, I mean by those regarded
as gods by the Moabites (for they committed idolatry and
worshipped idols, as Scripture says, and were initiated into
the cult of Belphegor, a Moabitish dæmon, and committed

---

[1] κατὰ κορυφῆς, ὥς ἄν εἴποι τις, καὶ κατὰ κάθετον τῆς Ἰουδαίας
ἐστηριγμένον—for κάθετον, cf. P.E. 291 a, 847 b, of the vertical position
of each planet at the birth of one whose horoscope was cast.
   [2] ὅτε καὶ παραπεμφθέντες εἰς Βηθλεέμ summarizes verses (3–8).
   [3] E. adds αὐτός.
   [4] βεελφέγωρ (Baal-Peor), (Deut. iv. 3 ; Numb. xxv. 5), the local
deity of Mount Peor, cf. Driver on Deut. iv. 3.

adultery with the women of Moab), Balaam in his prophecy
appositely paints the picture of a complete reversal and
change in days to come : "A star shall rise out of Jacob,
and a man shall spring from Israel, and he shall crush the
leaders of Moab." As if he had said, more plainly, that
the dæmons of Moab who once triumphed over Israel
would suffer a crushing defeat on the birth of the subject
(419) of the prophecy, and that when these were crushed, the
sons of Seth, Edom and Esau, and the other nations, by
whom, I think, are meant those that had long been the
slaves of dæmonic error, would be converted from their
superstition to the service of Him that was foretold. For
it says : "And Edom shall be an inheritance, and Esau
his enemy shall be an inheritance." So it says that those
who were once enemies of God and of Israel will become
the inheritance of Him that was prophesied. For He it
was to Whom it was said by God and His Father : "Desire
of me, and I will give thee the heathen for thine inherit-
Ps. ii. 8. ance." And while they enter into the inheritance of the
(b) saints, the reverse is prophesied for Israel—for it says :
"Israel hath wrought in strength." And it wrought in
strength the worst sin of all ; wherefore He will be aroused
by them, and will drive them out. Who is this but the
Word of God that was foretold, Who also "destroyed him
that was saved from the city"? And I think that this
refers figuratively to Jerusalem, in which all that were
saved perished, or perhaps to the whole constitution of
the Jewish nation. I need not describe at greater length
(c) how this was fulfilled, how, when our Saviour shone forth
on mankind, the nations that before were idolaters were
converted and became His portion, at the same time that
the Jewish nation and their mother-city underwent unexampled sufferings. Thus, I will conclude what I have
to say of the agreement of prophetic prediction with
Gospel fulfilment. Let us now learn the reason why
the star appeared. Now Moses says, that all the stars
Gen. i. were set in the firmament by God "for signs and for
14b. seasons." But this was a strange and unusual star, not
(d) one of the many known stars, but being new and fresh by
its appearance here it portended a new luminary that
should shine on all the Universe, the Christ of God, a
great and a new Star, whose likeness the star that appeared

to the wise men symbolically shewed.   For since in all
the holy and inspired Scriptures the leading object of the
meaning is to give mystic and divine instruction, while
preserving as well the obvious meaning in its own sphere
of historical facts, so the prediction before us was properly
and literally fulfilled in the matter of the star that was
prophesied to appear at our Saviour's Birth.[1]

In the case of other remarkable and famous men we (420)
know that strange stars have appeared, what some call
comets, or *meteors*, or *tails of fire*,[2] or similar phenomena that
are seen in connection with great unusual events.   But
what event could be greater or more important for the
whole Universe than the spiritual light coming to all (b)
men through the Saviour's Advent, bringing to human
souls the gift of holiness and true knowledge of God?
Wherefore the herald star gave the great sign, telling in
symbol that the Christ of God would shine as a great new
light on all the world.

And the prophecy foretells a man as well as a star, for
it says: "A star shall rise out of Jacob, and a man shall
spring from Israel," naming first the heavenly light, the
Word of God, and next the Humanity.   And He is called,
as I have shewn in my former books, in other places by
the varying names of Rising, Light, and Sun of Righteous- (c)
ness.   And here, by applying to Him the verb from
"Rising," "a star shall rise out of Jacob," it shews His
Diviner aspect, as "giving light to every man that cometh
into the world"; while it shews the Humanity, by the John i. 9.
suffering that comes to Him, where it foretells that He
will fall to rise again, in words like what Isaiah says of
Him: "And there shall be a root of Jesse, and he that
shall rise to rule the Gentiles; in Him shall the Gentiles

---

[1] A clear statement of the views of the mystical school on the
interpretation of prophetic Scripture—the literal historical event
happened, and the meaning enshrined in it was also fulfilled.

[2] κομητῶν, ἢ δοκίδων, ἢ πωγωνιῶν—for δοκίδος for meteor, cf. δοκός.
δοκίας, δοκίτης.   Diog. Laert. 5, 81.   For πωγωνίον, cf. Luc. *Paras.* 50.
We have πώγων πυρός or φλογός.   Æsch. *Ag.* 306; Eur. *Phrix.* 18.
πωγωνίας is the usual word (Arist. *Meteor*, 1. 7. 4; Plut. 2. 893 C.;
Diog. Laert. 7. 152, etc.).   For this superstition, cf. Shakespeare,
Julius Cæsar, Act II. sc. ii.—

"When beggars die, there are no comets seen;
    The heavens themselves blaze forth the death of princes."

trust." And we see how true it is that the light of our
(d) Saviour, which rose from Jacob, that is from the Jews, has
shone on all nations but Jacob, from whence it came
forth.

And while this can be found in many prophecies, which
say as it were to Christ Himself: "Behold, I have set
thee for a light to the Gentiles, for a covenant of thy
race," it is especially obvious in the words of Balaam,
when he says: "A man shall come from his seed, and
shall rule many nations." Whose seed but Israel's, as the
context shews? And thus our Saviour, the Word, as the
prophecy foretold, ruling over the nations threw down
the invisible noxious powers which had governed them so
long, the spirits of evil, and the band of dæmons, called
figuratively here the princes of Moab, Seth, Edom, and
(421) Esau.

The words: "I will point to him, but not now, I bless
him but he draws not near," which are obscure in the
Septuagint, are more clearly rendered by Aquila: "I shall
see him, but not now; I expect him, but he is not near."
And Symmachus more plainly still says: "I see him but
not near." Balaam would speak thus of things revealed
to him that would be accomplished a very long time after
(b) his own days. And so at the conclusion of two thousand
years after his prediction they were fulfilled in our Saviour's
Coming among men.

CHAPTER 2

From Isaiah.

*How the Lord resting in the Sacred Body which He took
from the Virgin will come to Egypt, is both Literally
and Figuratively foretold, and that all the Superstition
of the Heathen will be destroyed at His Advent.*

[Passage quoted, Isa. xix. 1.]

I SUPPOSE that the reason why it is foretold that the Lord
(d) would come to Egypt is this: The Egyptians are said to
have been the first to practise the errors of polytheism

and the dæmons, and to have introduced superstition to
the rest of mankind, and to have been concerned more
than others with the activities and meddling of the
dæmons.   And Holy Scripture witnesses that they were
the enemies of God's people from the very beginning, for
it is written that their ancient king confessed that he did
not know the Lord, when he said : " I do not know the
Lord, and I will not let Israel go."   So, then, it is because Exod. v. 2.
Scripture wishes to shew the great marvel of the divine
power of Christ that it foretells His going to Egypt, in (422)
predicting that the Egyptians will undergo an extraordinary conversion, when it goes on to say : " And the
Egyptians shall know the Lord, who before knew Him not,
and shall pray to the Lord," and so on.   Above in the
previous chapter Edom and Esau are called the inheritance
of the subject of the prophecy, these names being used
for strangers to Israel.   Here it is predicted of Egypt and
its people that they will not acknowledge idols any more, (b)
but the Lord revealed by the Jewish prophets.   Now if
we cannot see this actually fulfilled before our eyes, we
must not say that the Lord's coming to Egypt has taken
place ; but if beyond all need of argument the truth is
shewn by facts, and reveals clearly to the most unobservant
the Egyptians rescued from hereditary superstition, and
followers of the God of the prophets who foretold that this
would take place, serving Him only, and greeting every (c)
form of death for their duty to Him, to what else can
we attribute it, but to the Lord coming to Egypt, as the
prophecy before us predicted?

It is, of course, possible that the prophecy from another
point of view teaches in a figurative and disguised way
about the earthly universe, into which it prophesies that the
Lord will come on a light cloud, a figure of the Humanity
that He took of the Virgin and the Holy Spirit.   And that
the idols of Egypt to be shaken, are the idols of (all)
nations, while the vanquished Egyptians are all those (d)
who were of old distracted by idolatry.   This may be so,
yet when our Lord in bodily form was carried into Egypt,
when Joseph arose in obedience to the oracle, and took
Mary and the young Child, and went into Egypt, it is
probable that the evil dæmons who dwelt there of old were
greatly moved by His unspeakable power and might ; and

most of all when, through His teaching, so many of Egypt's inhabitants afterwards rejected the errors of the dæmons, and even now profess to know the God of the Universe alone.

(423)   That which immediately follows I will interpret when I have more leisure, for it is figuratively expressed, and would need considerable labour.

CHAPTER 3

From Numbers.

It is foretold that Christ would come into Egypt, and would return from thence again.

[Passage quoted, Num. xxiv. 3–9.]

THE oracle in the previously-quoted prophecy, in saying (d) that the Lord would come into Egypt, foretold the journey of our Lord Jesus Christ, when He went into Egypt with His parents. Here we have the prophecy of His return from Egypt in its natural order, when He came back with His parents into the land of Israel, in the words: "God led him out of Egypt." For our Lord and Saviour Jesus, the Christ of God, was the only one of the seed of Israel and of the Jewish race, Who has ruled over many nations, so that it is indisputable that He is the fulfilment of the prophecy which says, literally, "that a man will come from (424) the Jewish race, and rule over many nations." If He be not, let him who will suggest some other famous man among the Hebrews, who has ruled over many nations. But this he cannot do, for such a man never existed. But with regard to our Saviour, truth itself will shout and cry aloud, even if we say nothing, shewing plainly that His Divine Power through the human body He took of the seed of Israel according to the flesh has ruled, yea, and even now will rule many nations.

He it was, then, and none other, Whom the prophecy foretold, in Whose time the kingdom of Gog should be exalted concurrently with the growth of Christ's power.

(b) It is said that by this figure the Hebrews disguised the

Roman Empire, which grew concurrently with the teaching of Christ.   And the Prophet Ezekiel also mentions Gog, naming him Ruler of Ros, Mosoeh, and Thobel, probably disguising the city of Rome under the name of Ros, because empire and power are signified in Hebrew by that word; by Mosoeh, he meant Mysia and the adjacent nations, which are now subject to Rome; and by Thobel Josephus means Iberia,[1] saying that the Thobelian Iberians sprang from Thobel.   He says that Gog, the ruler of all of them, will be exalted at the coming of the Christ prophesied, Whom God led out of Egypt, when, as Matthew records, Herod laid a plot against Him when He was a Child, and Joseph informed by God took the young Child and His mother, and afterwards returned into the land of Israel.

Ezek. xxxviii. 3. (c)

Matt. ii. 13. (d)

And Christ possessed "the glory of an Unicorn," because in Him was pleased "to dwell all the fullness of the Godhead," in the words of the Holy Apostle.   And, therefore, as accounting the God of the Universe and His Father to be His Horn, He was called "Unicorn" also in other Scriptures.

Col. ii. 9.

And He, the Word of God, defeated with shafts of mind and spirit His enemy and opponent the devil, and all the invisible and evil powers around Him with greater invincible might, and even now rules over many nations whose gross fleshly instincts He fines down[2] and makes them fit to tread the narrow way of eternal life.

(425)

And moreover He too, the Man who came from Israel, Who ruleth many nations, having lain down, "rested as a lion," he says, plainly indicating the dispensation He had accepted, according to which like a kingly and terrible wild beast He rested, for none were able to remove His rule and His Kingdom, and all who blessed the Christ, glorifying the greatness of their teaching by word and deed, received in return the blessing of God, increasing and multiplying daily, according to the divine commandment, "Increase and multiply and replenish the earth," which in them is fulfilled more truly and divinely.   While in contrast to them, they who since their original plot against Him

Gen. i. 28. (b)

---

[1] Iberia, the country near the Caucasus, now Georgia. See Jos., *Ant. Jud.* I. 6.

[2] ὧν τὰ πάχη καὶ τὸ φρόνημα τῆς σαρκὸς λεπτύνων.

even until now curse Him in their synagogues, have drawn down the curse of God on their heads from that day to this. Wherefore they do not cease to behold the utter desolation and destruction of their kingdom and of their Temple of old so venerable. And it is worth comparing with this prophecy that of Jacob to Judah, which I have already shewn to be most clearly applicable to our Saviour, and to recognize

(c) the agreement of the two. For as we have here, "A man shall come forth from his seed," *i. e.* Jacob's, so we had there, "From a slip, my son, thou hast ascended," said by Jacob to the subject of the prophecy.

As we read too in this prophecy, "And he shall rule many nations," in the other we have similarly, "And he

(d) shall be the expectation of nations." Again this one says, "He shall eat the Gentiles his enemies, and with his darts he shall shoot his enemies," just as the other, "Thy hands shall be on the back of thine enemies"; while, "The whelp of the lion of Judah," and, "Falling down thou didst couch as a lion, and as a young lion who shall arouse thee?" in the other prophecy are, I think, identical with the words in the one before us, "Lying down he couched as a lion, and as a lion's whelp, who shall raise him up?" I have set these passages side by side, so that the proof concerning

Matt. xviii. our Saviour may rest on a firmer foundation, established on
16. the agreement "of the mouth of two witnesses."

All therefore that I have deduced from the prediction

(426) of Jacob would apply to that of Balaam, because of the similarity of their sayings. And if it was then established by a lengthy demonstration that the former were fulfilled in our Saviour, it follows that this is also true of the latter.

CHAPTER 4

From Hosea.

Again concerns the Words, Out of Egypt have I Called My Son, and King Herod, and the Destruction of the Kingdom of the Jews.

[Passages quoted, Hos. x. 14 ; xi. 1.]

FOLLOWING the Hebrew slavishly, Aquila translates, "Out (c) of Egypt have I called my son." But I have noted the exact words, because Matthew quoted the prophecy, when he recorded that Jesus was carried into Egypt, and returned thence to the land of Israel. And if any one objects to the idea of our Saviour's going into Egypt, let him know that He went for good reasons. For neither was it fitting for (d) Him to restrain Herod from his self-chosen wickedness, nor that our Saviour while still an infant should begin to shew His Divine Power by working miracles before the time, which would have been the case, if He had punished Herod miraculously for plotting against Him, and had not submitted to go down to Egypt with His parents.[1] For it was surely the note of a better dispensation that He should wait till the fitting time to begin the miracles of His Divinity, Whose whole life is known to have been gentle and patient, ready to do good deeds and acts of kindly service, and not to defend Himself from them that would not hear Him, even when "He was led as a Lamb to the slaughter, and as a sheep before her shearers was dumb." Where then is the (427) improbability that one like Him when a child should give way before Herod's wickedness, Who we know when a man yielded and submitted to evil men, hid Himself and shrank from the glory of His miraculous works? For He used to bid those He had healed tell no one.

And if any prefer to apply the prophecy to the people, regarding it as spoken concerning the people of Israel, let him consider the sequence of the argument, which implies that this will take place after the saying addressed as to Jerusalem itself, "And destruction shall be raised up in thy (b)

---

[1] An implicit condemnation of the miracles of the Infancy recorded in the Apocryphal Gospels—*e.g.* the παιδικά, or *Gospel of Thomas*, and the *Protevangelium Jacobi*.

people, and all thy strong places shall depart." And those
things, it says, which such and such a king suffered in a war
in which he was involved, when they dashed the mother to
the ground on her children, the like will I do unto you
because of your wickedness. He must mean by "you"
them that are called Israelites, who also were cast away
with their king, by whom he implies Herod. "And you
have suffered all this," it says, "because Israel is a child,
(c) and I loved him, and out of Egypt have I called my son."
But how can he praise and blame the same people at the
same time? The real meaning supplies the explanation.
The Christ is called "Israel," in other prophecies, as He
is in this. Since then, it says, being obedient to Me, He
took the form of a servant, and became My beloved Son,
fulfilling all My will, therefore I called Him back as My
(d) true and beloved Son from the Egypt whither He descended
when He became man, meaning by Egypt this earthly
sphere, or possibly Egypt itself. But you, to whom the
prophecy is spoken, shall suffer ruin and destruction, together
with your king. Such is the prophecy. And we can see
that from our Saviour's time by the siege of Jerusalem the
independence and national power of the Jewish race that
existed up till then was destroyed and utterly cast away.
This is the third prophecy concerning Egypt, and His
sojourn there.

But if any one say that it does not apply to our Saviour,
yet let him not deny that the words quoted by Matthew
were taken by him from the witness of Moses, which I have
lately expounded,[1] when explaining the words, "God led
(428) him out of Egypt," and as the evangelist himself never says
that the oracle was quoted from the prophecy of Hosea, he
can seek for it and find it laid up in any place, whence it is
probable that the evangelist quoted it.

ἀλλά γε τῆς τοῦ Ματθαίου παραθεσέως ἀπὸ τῆς παρὰ Μωσεῖ
μαρτυρίας αὐτῷ παρειλημμένα. Gaisford notes that there is a corruption
in the text. But the sense seems clear.

CHAPTER 5

From Isaiah.

Of the Preaching of John in the Wilderness.

[Passage quoted, Isa. xl. 3.]

THIS prophecy too was necessarily to be fulfilled in the (c)
times of our Saviour. And according to the Evangelist
Luke, in the fifteenth year of Tiberius Cæsar, when Pontius
Pilate was governor of Judæa, and those numbered with
him, the Word of God came to John, the son of Zachariah,
in the wilderness, "And he went into all the country around
Jordan, preaching the baptism of repentance for the remission of sins." To this the evangelist adds the witness, saying, Luke iii. 1.
"As it is written in the books of the words of Isaiah the
prophet, 'The Voice of One crying in the wilderness,
Prepare the way of the Lord,'" and that which follows.
What then did John's voice shout in its preaching in the (d)
wilderness, but an invitation to the crowds that came out to
be baptized by him, as to reptiles of the wilderness, akin to
his "generation of vipers, who hath warned you to flee
from the wrath to come?" And he changed too the crooked Matt. iii. 7.
souls into straight, and the rough roads into smooth by
saying to them, "Bring forth therefore fruits meet for
repentance." And this was fulfilled when John had prepared them to behold the glory of the Lord, and what
is called "the salvation of our God," which is the Christ,
as he bore witness, saying :

"I indeed baptize you with water, but there cometh (429)
one after me that is mightier than I, whose shoes I am
not worthy to bear : He shall baptize you with the Holy
Ghost and with fire."

Who also seeing Jesus coming cried :

"Behold, the Lamb of God, which taketh away the John i. 29.
sin of the world : This is he of whom I spake, a man
cometh after me, who was before me."

And Symeon also bare witness that the same Jesus was
"the salvation of God," who took Him in his arms when
He was still an infant, and said :

"Now thou art letting thy servant, O Lord, depart in Luke ii.
peace, according to thy word : For mine eyes have seen 29.

(b)   thy salvation, which thou hast prepared before the face of all people, a light to lighten the Gentiles."

With which the prophet agrees, saying, "And all flesh shall see the salvation of God." For "all flesh" stands for "all the nations." And I need not say this was fulfilled, and that all nations knew the Christ of God. Such was the literal fulfilment of the prophecy.

(c)   But why did John go forth to preach in the wilderness, and not in cities, or in Jerusalem itself? It might be answered that he did so in fulfilment of the prophecy. But a critical questioner will at once inquire, what this prophecy meant to teach when it spoke of the wilderness and the things to do with it. And I should reply to him that it is a symbol of the destruction of Jerusalem, and the Altar there, and of the Mosaic worship, because the forgiveness of sins was no longer extended to them by the legal sacri-

(d)   fices, but by the cleansing and washing delivered to her that was before thirsty and deserted; I mean the Gentile Church, in which also the prophetic voice bids to prepare the way of the Lord, foretelling that the souls which are lying deep in sin as in a valley will be raised up, and that the old heights of Jerusalem, and of her rulers and kings, called "mountains and hills," shall be laid low, which being completed, he says, "All flesh shall see the salvation of God," meaning every soul united with a body, both Greek and Barbarian, of every nation without exception, and this is seen to have been fulfilled according to the prophecy.

(430)   Now let me ask myself what it was in John that struck the multitude with fear, so that they marvelled at him and put trust in his baptism of repentance, and all from every side left their homes, and flowed in one stream into the wilderness, having regard to the fact that the records give no account of anything he did; for we are not told that he raised the dead, or worked other miracles.

What then was it that struck the multitude? Surely it was his manner of life so strange and different to that of the people; for he came forth from the desert clad in a strange

(b)   garment, refusing all social human intercourse, he went not into village or city or the human haunts of men, he did not even share their common food; for it is written that from childhood he was in the deserts, until the day of his shewing

forth, to Israel, yes, and his raiment was made of camels' Luke i. 80.
hair,[1] and his food locusts and wild honey.   Matt. iii. 4.

How, then, should they not have been naturally alarmed,
when they saw a man, with the hair of a Nazarite of God, (c)
and a divine face, suddenly appearing from the lonely
wilderness clothed in a strange kind of dress, and after
preaching to them going back again into the wilderness,
without eating or drinking or mingling with the people, and
must they not have suspected that he was more than human?
For how could a man not need food?   And so they understood him to be an angel, the very angel foretold by the
prophet, in the words, " Behold, I send my angel before (d)
thy face, who shall prepare thy way before thee," a Mark i. 2.
passage of Scripture which is quoted by the Evangelist
Mark.   And the Saviour also bears witness in the words,
" John came neither eating nor drinking,[2] and you say, He Luke vii.
hath a devil."   For it was just as natural that unbelievers, 33.
with minds hardened and shut against the truth, should thus
blaspheme John because of his living as he did, as that
those who were in accord with his noble character should
reckon him an angel.   Such, then, I understand to be the
reasons why John was a marvel to those who saw him ; and
therefore they hastened from all sides to the cleansing of
the soul, of which he preached.

Josephus, too, records his story in the Eighteenth Book (431)
of the *Jewish Archæology*, writing as follows :

" Now, some of the Jews thought that the destruction
of Herod's army[3] came from God, and that very justly
as a punishment of what he did against John, that was
called the Baptist; for Herod slew him, who was a good
man, and commanded the Jews to exercise righteousness
towards one another, and piety towards God, and so to
come to baptism.   For so the washing would be accept- (b)
able to Him."[4]

---

[1] W.H.: ἀπὸ τριχῶν καμήλου, καὶ ζώνην δερματίνην περὶ τὴν ὀσφὺν
αὐτοῦ.   E.: ἐκ τριχῶν καμήλων πεποιημένον.
[2] W.H. add οἶνον.   [3] Cf.: Euseb., *H.E.* I. 11.
[4] Jos., *Ant.* XVIII. 5. 2.

CHAPTER 6

From the same.

*Still concerning the Wilderness, and the River called
Jordan, by which John baptized.*

[Passage quoted, Isa. xxxv. 3–6.]

THIS, too, was fulfilled, was clearly fulfilled, by our Saviour's
miraculous works after John's preaching. Notice therefore
how He bears good tidings to the desert, not generally, or to
any desert, but to one particular desert by the bank of
Jordan. This was because John lived there and baptized
there, as Scripture says :

"John was in the desert baptizing, and there went
out unto him all the land of Judæa, and all they of
Jerusalem, and were baptized of him in Jordan."

I think the desert here is a symbol of that which of old was
void of all God's good things, I mean the Church of the
(432) Gentiles, and the river by the desert that cleanses all that
are bathed therein is a figure of some cleansing spiritual
power, of which the Scriptures speak, saying, "The move-
Ps. xlvi. 4. ments of the river make glad the city of God."   And this
means the ever-flowing stream of the Holy Spirit welling
from above and watering the city of God, which is the
(b) name for life according to God.   This river of God, then,
has reached even unto the desert, that is the Gentile
Church, and even now supplies it with the living water that
it bears.

Moreover, it is said in this prophecy that the glory of
Lebanon and the honour of Carmel shall be given to this
wilderness. What is the glory of Lebanon, but the worship
performed through the sacrifices of the Mosaic Law, which
Jer. vi. 20; God refused in the prophecy which says, "Why do you
Isa. i. 11. bring me Libanus from Saba?   And of what service to me
is the multitude of your sacrifices?"   He has transferred
(c) the glory of Jerusalem to the desert of Jordan, since, from
the times of John, the ritual of holiness began to be performed not at Jerusalem but in the desert. In like manner,
too, the honour of the Law and of its more external ordinances, was transferred to the wilderness of Jordan for the
same reason, viz. that they who need the healing of their

souls no longer hastened to Jerusalem but to that which
was called the wilderness, because there the forgiveness of (d)
sins was preached. And I think our Saviour's own Presence
at the Baptism is meant by, "And my people shall see the
glory of the Lord, and the majesty of God." For then it
was that the glory of our Saviour was seen, when :

"Being baptized he went up from the water, and the
heavens were opened to him, and he saw the Spirit of
God descending as a dove, and staying upon him."[1]

When also there was heard "A voice from heaven, saying, Matt. iii.
This is my beloved son, in whom I am well-pleased." Yea, 16.
and every one that rightly approaches the Sacrament of
Baptism, and accepts the teaching of Christ's Divinity, shall
see His glory, and shall say with Paul, "Even we have 2 Cor. v.
known Christ after the flesh, yet now we know him not." 16.

CHAPTER 7

From Psalm xc.   (433)

Of the Temptation of Our Lord After His Baptism.
[Passage quoted, Ps. xc. 1–13.]

Our Lord and Saviour Jesus the Christ, so far as He is (d)
regarded as Man, is said "to dwell under the succour of the
Most High, and to rest under the shelter of his God and
Father." We know that, by making His Father His only
refuge in the time of His Temptation by the devil, He was
saved from the nets of the powers opposed to Him, here
called "hunters," when, like an ordinary human being, He
was driven into the wilderness to be tempted of the devil,
and was in the wilderness forty days and forty nights tempted
of Satan, and was, as the evangelist tells us, "with the
wild beasts."[2] These were the same, as those this Psalm
mentions, when it says to Him that dwells under the

---

[1] W.H. have εὐθὺς ἀνέβη· καὶ ἰδοὺ ἠνεῴχθησαν, omit αὐτῷ and
article with πνεῦμα· and ἐρχόμενον for μένον (E.).

[2] Matt. iv. 1. W.H. : τότε ὁ Ἰησοῦς ἀνήχθη εἰς τὴν ἔρημον ὑπὸ τοῦ
πνεύματος, πειρασθῆναι ὑπὸ τοῦ διαβόλου.
The latter part in E. is from Mark i. 13.

protection of the Most High, "Thou shalt go upon the asp and the basilisk, and shalt trample on the lion and dragon."

(434) And it not only says that He shall be saved from them, but from "the troubling word" also.   What can this mean, but the words which according to the Holy Gospel were directed against Him by the tempter?

It is worth our consideration why our Saviour, being what He was, should undergo temptation.   He came to expel from man every disease and sickness, and the spirits that hampered him, and the unclean dæmons which had ruled all men on earth from immemorial time by means of polytheistic superstition.   He did not attack them secretly as one who hides himself, but He marched against their leaders who

(b) surrounded Him and were before invisible, in the Humanity that He had assumed, He charged into the midst of the devil and his array of dæmons, trod upon asp and basilisk, trampled on lion and dragon, and destroyed the thousands and ten thousands of enemies that had ruled so long,[1] some fighting on His right hand, some on His

Eph. vi. 12.

(c)

left, rulers and powers, and those too who are called "World-rulers of this darkness," and spiritual powers of evil; He proved thus, that they were quite powerless, and finally frightened away,[2] far from Him, with the word of His mouth the devil himself, their instigator to evil.   He went through and trampled on every power opposed to Him, He offered Himself as a target to those who wished to attack and tempt Him, and as none were able to resist Him, He won salvation for mankind.   Wherefore, when the

(d)

Matt. viii. 29.

dæmons saw Him, they recognized Him, because of the aforesaid sojourn in the wilderness, and said to Him, "What have we to do with thee, Jesus, Son of God?"   Let this suffice on this matter.   What follows in the Psalm is an address to the Christ, beginning at—

"With his shoulders he [that is the highest] shall overshadow thee, and under his wings shalt thou hope, and his truth shall surround thee with a shield."

And whereas His Temptation lasted forty days, and as many nights, it is said of those that attacked Him by night, "Thou shalt not fear the terror by night"; and of those

---

[1] πολὺ πρότερον is separated from ἀρχοντικῶν, so Diodatus renders.
[2] ἀποσοβήσας. Cf. Γ.Ε. 451 a, of bells on nets above the Temple to "frighten away" the birds.

that warred against Him by day, "From the arrow that
flieth by day." And also of the foe of night, "From the
thing that walketh in darkness," and of those of daytime,
"From the attack and the demon of mid-day." Then, as in (435)
the Temptation, the evil powers encircled Him, some on
His right side, and some on His left; the right being the
stronger side, it is naturally said to Him, "A thousand shall
fall at Thy side, and ten thousand at thy right hand, but they
shall not come near Thee." "At thy side" is used for
"on thy left hand," in order, perhaps, not to utter the
word "left," because nothing ill omened or left-handed was
found in Him. And since a myriad and a thousand are (b)
said to fall at His side and on His right hand, the next
sentence comes naturally, "Yea, with thine eyes shalt thou
behold, and see the reward of sinners." And this shall take
place, it says, "About thee, the Christ of God," for, "Thou
Thyself O Lord, who art my hope, hast made the Highest
thy refuge." Here, too, you will observe how the prophet,
in saying to the Lord Himself, "Thou, Lord, art my hope,
thou hast made the Highest Thy refuge," discriminates
carefully between One who is Lord in a special sense, and
His Father, God Most High. And, therefore, as Christ (c)
has made His Father, God Most High, His refuge, it is said
to Him:

> "Evil shall not attack thee, and no scourge shall
> approach thy dwelling, for he shall charge his angels
> concerning thee, to keep thee in all thy ways: They
> shall bear thee in their hands, lest at any time thou dash
> thy foot against a stone."

And note, carefully, how in, "For thou, Lord, art my hope,
Thou hast made the Highest thy refuge," the equivalent for
"Lord" in Hebrew is the Tetragram, which the sons of the
Hebrews say must not be spoken and reserve for God
alone; but I have previously shewn that it is also used for (d)
the Godhead of the Word in many places of Scripture, as
in this Psalm which says, as speaking to the person of the
Lord Himself, "For Thou, Lord, art my hope, thou hast
set the Most High for thy refuge"; as much as to say:

> "For thou thyself, O Lord, who art the hope of me
> that utter this prophecy, knowest a greater than thyself,
> God Most High, and thou hast made Him thy refuge."

So in the opening of the Psalm it was said of Him:

(436)   "He that dwelleth under the protection of the Most
High, shall abide under the shadow of the Almighty.
He shall say to the Lord, Thou art my helper and my
refuge, my God, my Succour, and I will trust on him."
"Since then, thou, O Lord, hast made the Most High
thy refuge."
the Psalmist therefore says :

"He shall save thee from the snares of the hunters,
and from the troubling word and with his shoulders he
shall overshadow thee.   Therefore, having such fatherly
succour from the Highest, Thou shalt not fear the terror
by night, nor any of the evils that are mentioned before,
(b)   or added after.   For thou, O Lord, hast made the
highest thy refuge, therefore evil shall not attack thee,
and no scourge shall come nigh thy dwelling."

You will find the activities of the dæmons, also called
scourges, in the Gospels, which the Psalmist says are incapable of daring to approach Christ's dwelling, that is His
Body.   How could they, when He could drive them out of
men by a mere word?   Of this dwelling, David also once
sware an oath to the Lord, and prayed to the God of Jacob,
saying :
(c)   "I will not climb up into my bed, I will not suffer
mine eyes to sleep, or my eyelids to slumber, nor the
temples of my head to take any rest, until I find out a
place for the Lord, an habitation for the God of Jacob."
And it was on account of this tabernacle that it was said :

"Thou shalt not fear any terror by night, and He
shall save thee from the snares of the hunters, and from
the troubling word, and evils shall not attack thee, and
a scourge shall not come nigh thy dwelling."
And other things that regard Him more from the side of
His Humanity, such as :

"He shall charge his angels concerning thee, and in
their hands they shall bear thee, lest at any time thou
dash thy foot against a stone."
For such words would not apply to God, but only to the
tabernacle, which He assumed for our sake, when the Word
became flesh and tabernacled amongst us.   Here I think it
will be well to quote the words of the other translators, to
put what I have said on an exact foundation.   Of whom,
Aquila said :

"For thou, Lord, my hope, hast set thy dwelling (437)
very high.   Evils shall not affect thee, and no touch
shall come near to thy shelter : for he gave command to
his angels to guard thee in all thy ways."
And Symmachus has :
"Thou, Lord, art my security, thou hast set thy dwelling
very high.   Evil shall have no power over thee, and no
touch shall draw near thy tent.   For he gave charge to
his angels concerning thee to keep thee in all thy ways."
The Lord, then, is here addressed about some one greater
than Himself, Who
"has charged his angels concerning thee, to keep thee
in all thy ways.   In their hands they shall bear thee
(*i.e.*, The Lord) lest at any time thou, O Lord, dash
thy foot against a stone."   Matt. iv. 5.
And the devil used these words in his Temptation of our (b)
Saviour, when he took Him into the holy city, and set Him
upon the wing of the Temple and said to Him :
"If thou be the Son of God, cast thyself down
hence,[1] for it is written, he shall give his angels charge
over thee, and in their hands they shall bear thee up,
lest at any time thou dash thy foot against a stone."
To whom the Lord answered and said :
"It is written,[2] Thou shalt not tempt the Lord thy
God."
Then, though the evangelist tells that, during the Temptation, He was with the wild beasts, we are not told what they
were, but the prophecy in the Psalm tells us more clearly
in a disguised way the kinds of beasts, viz. : "Thou shalt (c)
step on the asp and the basilisk, and shalt trample on the
lion and dragon."   It is thus said that he will trample on
the kingliest [3] of the wild beasts of the spirit, the lion and
dragon, as well as the asp and the basilisk, that is to say, the
devil himself, and the ruling evil powers that follow him.
And He bestows the power on His disciples and apostles
who possess goodness like His own of walking upon serpents
and scorpions, not allowing them to be tempted above that (d)
they are able ; for it was for Him alone to destroy the most
evil powers, and the chief of them all, the prince of this
world, by His Divine Power.

---

[1] W.H. omits ἐντεῦθεν.   [2] W.H. add πάλιν.
[3] τὰ ἀρχικώτατα τῶν νοητῶν θηρίων.

CHAPTER 8

From Isaiah.

Of Galilee of the Gentiles, where our Saviour worked most of His Miracles, and of the Call of His Apostles.

(438)   [Passage quoted, Isa. ix. 1–6.]

(c) THIS also was fulfilled in our Lord and Saviour Jesus Christ besides all the other prophecies, when according to the wondrous Evangelist—

(439)   [Passage quoted, Matt. iv. 12–25.]

I have quoted this passage in its entirety, because the (b) prophecy promised that there would be a great light in Galilee, or in the land of Zabulon and Nephthalim, which are the same as Galilee. Now why did He pass most of His life in Galilee of the Gentiles? Surely that He might make a beginning of the calling of the Gentiles, for He called His disciples from thence. Wherefore, shortly after, in the same Gospel you will find that Matthew was called from Galilee, and in another Gospel, Levi also. And Philip, according to John, came from Bethsaida, the city of Andrew (c) and Peter, which was in Galilee. The marriage too, in the same Gospel, was in Cana of Galilee, when the Lord miraculously transformed the water into wine. "There he made a beginning of signs, when also he manifested his John ii. 11. glory, and his disciples believed on him." Consider whether this first miracle of our Saviour that took place in Cana of Galilee, of the transformation of the water into wine, is not foretold in the beginning of this prophecy, where it says : "Drink this first. Act quickly, land of Zabulon and (d) Nephthalim, Galilee of the Gentiles." And if this miracle were a sign of the mystic wine, that wine of the faith of the new Covenant that is transformed from bodily joy to a joy of mind and spirit, consider whether this too was not suggested in what follows about Galilee, in the prophecy that the inhabitants of Zabulon and Nephthalim would be the first to come into the presence of Christ, to partake of the draught of Gospel preaching. It says, too, that the spring of their joy will be the shining of a great light, for them who before His Coming sat continually in darkness and the shadow of

death.　But that when the light of salvation has sprung up,
they will rejoice as men rejoice in harvest, and as they who (440)
divide the spoils.　And this was actually fulfilled, when our
Lord and Saviour, calling His Apostles from Galilee, shewed
forth to them His miracles and His teaching.　The prophecy
says that they will rejoice before Him, "as men rejoice in
harvest."　In what harvest, I ask, but that of which He
spake in His teaching, "Lift up your eyes and behold the John iv.
lands, that they are already white unto harvest"?　By this 35.
He meant the gathering in of the Gentiles: of whom it is
also said, "They shall rejoice, as they who divide the spoils." (b)
Therefore the disciples and evangelists of our Saviour,
dividing between them the lands of the nations, and all the
earth under heaven, despoiled the countless princes of this
world, who were before rulers of the nations.　And we
should also recognize that He says there will be another
reason for their joy, viz.: their relief from the external yoke Acts xv.
of the law, that of old was laid on them, which neither they 10.
nor their fathers were able to bear.　And not only was this (c)
yoke removed from them, but the rod of the exactors which
before pressed on their neck.　He shews who the exactors
are in another passage, where He says: "My people, your
factors take your corn, and the exactors rule over you." Isa. iii. 12.
But these men of Zabulon and Nephthalim will rejoice having
seen the great light for these reasons, and they who exacted
of them of old will be required to repay even to the last Matt. v.
farthing, and repaying every garment and vestment they will 26.
be burned with fire in the day of retribution.　And all this, (d)
He says, they will suffer, because "Unto us a child is born,
a son is given to us, the Angel of Great Counsel."　Who are
meant by "us," but we who have believed in Him, and all
Galilee of the Gentiles, on whom the great light is sprung
up?　And what is this light but the Child that was born,
and the Son that was given us by God, Who is named the
Angel of Great Counsel, and the Prince of Peace, the
Potentate, the Mighty God, and the Father of the world to
come?　But I have already shewn[1] in its right place that
these words can only be referred to our Lord and Saviour.

[1] See 164 a, 236 b.

CHAPTER 9

From Psalm lxvii.

Of the Calling of the Apostles.

(441)   [Passage quoted, Ps. lxvii. 24–27.]

I THINK that here none but the Apostles can be meant by the rulers of Nephthali. For thence our Lord and Saviour called them according to the quotation from Matthew. The Scripture is prophesying the Coming of the Word of God to men, and His Incarnate sojourn here,

(c) when it says, "Thy goings, O God, have been seen," and that which follows. And the prophets of old were like heralds of His Epiphany, and arrived before Him with proclamation and chant, with music of psaltery and choir and all kinds of spiritual instruments, in the midst of damsels playing on timbrels. For the inspired prophets going in every way into the midst of the Jewish synagogues, heralded the coming of the Christ, and by the Holy Spirit

(d) addressed the Apostles of our Saviour saying, "Praise the Lord God in the congregations from the fountains of Israel." And the "fountains of Israel" must be the words delivered to Israel. "For they first trusted the oracles of

Rom. iii. 2. God," whence it will be necessary for us to draw and water the churches of Christ. By "maidens playing on timbrels" he suggested the souls that lived of old by the more external Law of Moses, calling them "maidens" because of their youth and imperfectly developed minds, and "timbrel-players" because of their devotion to external worship.

(442)   ## CHAPTER 10

From Isaiah.

Of the Reading from the Prophecy by Our Lord in the Jewish Synagogue.

[Passage quoted, Isa. lxi. 1.]

Now this prediction our Lord Himself claims to be fulfilled in Himself, when He came to Nazareth, where He was brought up :

" He entered, as his custom was on the Sabbath day,
into the synagogue, and stood up to read. And there was
delivered unto him the book of the prophet Esaias.
And when he had opened the book he found the place
where it was written, The Spirit of the Lord is upon (c)
me, because he hath anointed me, to preach the
gospel to the poor: he hath sent me to proclaim deliverance to the captives, and giving of sight to the blind, to
set at liberty them that are bruised, to proclaim the
acceptable year of the Lord. And he closed the book,
and he gave it again to the minister, and sat down.
And the eyes of all them that were in the synagogue
were fastened upon him. And he began to say unto Luke iv.
them, This day is this Scripture fulfilled in your ears."　16-21.
Our Lord and Saviour is clearly shewn in this passage to (d)
have been anointed with another and a better unction than
the priests of old days, who were externally anointed, not
with oil manufactured, nor by men, as were those others,
but with the Divine Spirit of His God and Father, whereby
as sharing in His unbegotten Godhead He is called God
and Lord by the Holy Scriptures.

And in harmony with the prophecy before us He is
introduced by Matthew preaching the Gospel to the poor
when—

" Seeing the multitudes he went up into a mountain,
and when he had sat down, his disciples came unto
him, and he opened his mouth and taught them,
saying, Blessed are the poor in spirit, for theirs is the
kingdom of heaven."　　　　　　　　　　　　　　Matt. v. 1.
And it is recorded that He gave sight to many that were (443)
blind, not only enlightening them that were deprived of
bodily vision, but also causing them that were before blind
in soul to receive spiritual vision and the knowledge of
God. And, moreover, He preached freedom and release
from their bonds to the prisoners bound and constrained
by the unseen dæmonic powers, and hampered by the
chains of sin, if they, too, would believe His preaching,
and run to Him as their Ransom and Saviour, and trust
His promises.

The remainder of this oracle I will expound in its place (b)
in the section concerning the promises.[1]

---

[1] A section in one of the lost books.

CHAPTER 11

From Deuteronomy.

(c)   *Of the Lawgiving according to the Gospel of Christ.*

[Passage quoted, Deut. xviii. 15–19.]

IT must be noticed that no prophet like Moses has ever arisen among the Hebrews, who was a lawgiver and a teacher of religion to men, except our Saviour, the Christ of God.   Therefore at the end of Deuteronomy it is said:
Deut.   "There has not arisen a prophet in Israel like unto Moses,"
xxxiv. 10.   though, of course, many prophets succeeded him, but none were like him.   And the promise of God recognizes the whole future, that one only, and not many, should arise and be like him.   And it implies that he will be a lawgiver and a teacher of religion to men, such as none but our Lord and Saviour Jesus Christ has been proved to be, being lawgiver and prophet of the God of the Universe
(444) His Father at the same time.

But Moses was leader of but one nation, and his legisla-tion has been proved to be only applicable to that one nation ; whereas the Christ of God, receiving the promise from His Father, "Desire of me, and I will give thee the
Ps. ii. 8.   nations for thine inheritance," as being established by His
(b) Father the Giver of the new law of holiness not to the Jews only, but to the whole human race, in calling all nations set before them a legislation that they could obey and that suited them.[1]   Thus by a diviner power than that of Moses He ordained through all the world His holy laws by His evangelists, legislating with more than human authority, saying, "Ye have heard that it was said to them of old time, Thou shalt not kill : but I say unto you that
Matt.v.21. ye must not be angry without a cause," and that which follows this saying, as it is preserved in His written teach-ing, with regard to which the Evangelist says, "They were
Matt. vii. astonished at his teaching, for he taught them as one
29.   having authority, and not as their scribes."

As I have treated of the manner of our Saviour's teaching and legislation in the beginning of this work, when I

---

[1] ἁρμόδιον νομοθεσίαν. Cf. P.E. 332 c.

explained what Christianity is,[1] I will now refer my readers
to that exposition. But it is worthy of notice why the
Lord promises that a prophet shall arise. For when He
had commanded Moses to sanctify the whole people for
three days, that they might see and hear His Divine Appearing, and they were too weak for the favour of God : where- (d)
fore when they were at the beginning of the vision they
refused and said to Moses : "Speak thou to us, and let not
God speak to us, that we die not," and the Lord, as was Exod. xx.
meet, was pleased by their caution, and says, "They have 19.
rightly spoken all that they have spoken. A prophet will I Deut. v.
raise up to them from the midst of their brethren, like unto 27 ; Deut.
thee." Then it was that He gave the reason of His own xviii. 17.
future Coming to men like a prophet. It was man's weakness, and his refusal of the greater vision of the greater.
You see, too, the reason why the prophet that was foretold
should become Incarnate. And so it was natural for the (445)
Jews, who expected Him, to inquire of John the Baptist,
and say, "Art thou the prophet? and he said, No." And John i. 21.
John spoke the truth, he did not deny that he was a
prophet, for he was, but he denied that he was the prophet
meant by Moses, because he taught that he was sent before
that prophet.

And since the Word predicted that the prophet would
be raised up for them of the Circumcision, our Lord and
Saviour, being Himself the One foretold, rightly said :   (b)

"I am not come but to the lost sheep of the house
of Israel." "And He commanded His apostles saying,
Go not into the road of the Gentiles, and into any city Matt. xv.
of the Samaritans enter ye not, but rather go to the lost 24 ; Matt.
sheep of the house of Israel " ;   x 5, 6.
shewing clearly that He was primarily sent to them as the
prophecy required. But when they would not receive His
grace, He reproves them elsewhere, saying, "For I came,
and there was no man, I called and there was none that
heard." And He says to them, "The kingdom of God Isa. l. 2.
shall be taken away from you, and shall be given to a (c)
nation bearing the fruits of it." And He bids His own Matt. xxi.
disciples after their rejection, "Go ye and make disciples 43 ; Matt.
of all nations in my name." So, then, we that are the xxviii. 19.

---

[1] τὸν Χριστιανισμὸν ὅ τι ποτέ ἐστιν. See Book I. c. 2.

Gentiles know and receive the prophet that was foretold,
(d) and sent by His Father, as being Lawgiver to all men of
the religion of the God of the Universe, through His saving
Gospel teaching, that other prediction being fulfilled at the
same time which says, " Set, Lord, a Lawgiver over them,
Ps. ix. 20. let the Gentiles know themselves to be men," while the
Jewish nation, not receiving Him that was foretold, has paid
the fit penalty according to the divine prediction which
said, " And the man who will not hear all things whatsoever
the prophet shall speak in My Name, I will exact vengeance
on him." Surely He has avenged on that people all the
blood poured out on the earth, from the blood of Abel to
the blood of Zechariah, yea, even to crown all tó the Christ
Himself, Whose blood they called down not only on themselves but on their children, and even now they pay the
penalty of their presumptuous sin.

(446)

CHAPTER 12

From Job.

Of Christ walking on the Sea.

[Passage quoted, Job ix. 7.]

(b) THESE words also can only apply to our Lord and Saviour,
as the Creator of the Universe, God's Word. For He is
the only One ever said to have walked on the sea, which
He did when Incarnate, having taken the body and form
of man, when He—

" 22. constrained his disciples to get into a ship,
and to go before him unto the other side, while he
sent the multitudes away. 23. And when he had sent
the multitudes away, he went up into a mountain apart
to pray : and when the evening was come he was there
alone. 24. But the ship was now in the midst of the
(c) sea.[1] . . . 26. And when the disciples saw him walking
on the sea they were troubled, saying, It is a spirit ;

---

[1] Verse 24 begins, τὸ δὲ πλοῖον ἤδη ⌜σταδίους πολλοὺς ἀπὸ τῆς γῆς
ἀπεῖχεν (W.H.). E. has τὸ δὲ πλοῖον ἤδη ἦν ἐν μέσῳ τῆς θαλάσσης,
and omits verse 25.

and they cried out for fear.   27. But straightway he
spake unto them saying, Be of good cheer: It is I; be   Matt. xiv.
not afraid."   22–27.

Now it would not appear to agree with orthodox theology
to understand the oracle as referring to God Most High
and the Father of the Universe. For what reverence or
propriety is there in talking of the God of the Universe
walking on the sea? How could He be thought to walk (d)
on the sea Who includes all things, and fills heaven and
earth, and says, "The heaven is my throne and the earth   Ps. lxvi. 1.
my footstool?" And "I fill heaven and earth, saith the
Lord?" But our Lord and Saviour "emptied himself   Jer. xxiii.
and took the form of a slave, and being found in fashion   24.
as a man," offering a proof to His disciples of His Divine   Phil. ii 7.
Power which eluded the multitude, is described as having
walked on the waves of the sea, and to have rebuked the
storm and the winds, when they who saw Him were
astonished and said, "What manner of man is this, that   Matt. viii.
even the winds and the sea obey him?" And this was a   27.
symbol of something greater, that other spiritual sea, in
which a dragon is said to have been made to be mocked
by the angels of God,[1] on which also our Lord and Saviour
walked and is said to have crushed the head of the dragon   (447)
therein and of the other subject dragons, according to the
words, "Thou hast bruised the heads of the dragons in the   Ps. lxxiv.
water, and thou hast bruised the heads of the dragon": 13.
clearly of another spiritual sea of which He says again in
the Psalms, "I went into the depths of the sea." And   Ps. lxix. 2.
recounting to Job the things concerning himself:

"Hast thou gone to the spring of the sea, and hast
thou walked in the steps of the depth? The gates of (b)
death did they open to thee in fear, and did the porters   Job
of Hades fear when they saw thee?"   xxxviii.16.

Thus when He walked on the sea in our human life, and
rebuked the winds and the waves, He performed a natural
symbolism of something unspeakable.

---

[1] For the dragon legend, cf. note, ii. 32.

CHAPTER 13

From Isaiah.

Of the Miracles He Performed.

[Passage quoted, Isa. xxxv. 3.]

Now we have this prophecy fulfilled in the Gospels, partly, when they brought to our Lord and Saviour a paralytic lying on a bed, whom He made whole with a word; and partly, when many that were blind and possessed with (d) dæmons, yea, labouring under various diseases and weaknesses, were released from their sufferings by His saving power. Nor should we forget how even now throughout the whole world multitudes bound by all forms of evil, full of ignorance of Almighty God in their souls, are healed and cured miraculously and beyond all argument by the medicine of His teaching. Except that now we call Him God as we should, as One Who can work thus, as I have already shewn in the evidence of His Divinity. Yea, surely (448) it is right now to acknowledge Him to be God, since He has given proof of power divine and truly inspired.

For it was specifically God's work to give strength to the paralysed, to give life[1] to the dead, to supply health to the sick, to open the eyes of the blind, to restore the lame, and to make the tongue-tied speak plain, all of which things were done by our Saviour Jesus Christ, because He was God, and they have been witnessed to by many throughout (b) all the world that preach Him—whose evidence unvarnished and veritable is confirmed by trial of torture, and by persistence even unto death, which they have shewn forth before kings and rulers and all nations, witnessing to the truth of what they preach. And I think that the spirit of prophecy addresses to these apostles and evangelists the words that begin with, "Lift up the hands that hang down, and the palsied knees." For when they had grown weary (c) in their hands and powers of action,[2] in their feet and walking with the long circuit of Mosaic observance, He awaked them to the life of the Gospel, and said, "Be strong, ye hands that hang down, and feeble knees," to

---

[1] ζωογονεῖν.   Cf. P E. 20 b, d.
[2] πρακτικὰς δυνάμεις.

prepare them, that is to say, for the Gospel race. And be
strong, too, to encourage others, and to urge them to cling
to the salvation of the Gospel, ye that before were low in
spirit, and let not any fear take you of them that oppose (d)
the Gospel preaching, but against them be strong and of a
good courage.

For it is God and the Word of God, not one like Moses or
the prophets, that was not only the Worker of the Miracles,
but is also the Cause of your own strength.[1]   And the
strongest confirmation of the Divine Power of the Saviour
here foretold, by which He really used to cure the lame,
the blind, the lepers and the palsied with a word according
to that which is written concerning Him, is the power even
now energizing through the whole world from His Godhead,
by which is shewn to them that can see what He was while
on earth, since after so many years His proclamation of the
Word of God is seen to last on invincible and true, over- (449)
coming all that have attempted from the beginning until
now to withstand His teaching; He attracts to Himself
great multitudes from all the world, and releases them that
come to Him from all kinds of evil and diseases and
troubles of the spirit; He summons to His holy school
all races, Greek and Barbarian ; He leads countless hosts
to the knowledge of the one true God, and to a healthy and (b)
pure life, as befits those who promise to worship Almighty
God.   And He our God, since He is the Word of God, it
says, "Gives judgment and will give, He will come and
save us."   For, according to the Psalm which says, "Give
the King thy judgment, O God," and, according to the Ps. lxxi. 1.
Gospel teaching, in which it is said, "The Father judgeth (c)
no man, but hath committed all judgment unto the Son," John v. 2.
having received the authority to judge from the Father,
judging in righteousness, He repays justly to the Jewish
people the fit penalty for their presumptuous treatment of
Him and His prophets, and ever saves in justice as well
those who come to Him, whose spiritual ears and eyes He
has opened.   Wherefore the divine word calls the time of
His Appearance the time of retribution, saying elsewhere,
"Call on the acceptable year of the Lord, and the day of (d)
retribution."   This was the time of retribution in which all Isa. lxi. 2.

---

[1] This is Eusebius' ultimate defence, the last trench of his ἀπόδειξις.

the blood poured out from the blood of Abel to the blood of Zechariah, yea, even to the precious Blood of Jesus, was required of the generation of them that had sinned against Him, so that from that time they underwent utter destruction and their final siege.   And the judgment declared against them wrought this retribution ; wherefore the prophecy says, " Behold our God exacts judgment, and will repay." And the judgment on them that shall be saved by Him is foretold next in the words, "He will come and save us ; then the eyes of the blind shall be opened, and the ears of the deaf hear," and that which follows.   And another prophecy also promises that the Christ will bring this saving (450) judgment, saying :

> " Behold my Son, I will succour him, my chosen, my Spirit hath accepted him, he shall bear judgment to the nations."

Isa. xli. 1.

Wherefore it is also said concerning the Word of the new covenant :

> " For out of Zion shall come forth a law, and the word of the Lord from Jerusalem, and he shall judge in the midst of the nations."

Micah iv. 2.

For there is little doubt that He effects the calling of them that turn to Him with divine justice and ineffable counsels.   And, moreover, as teaching us of the divine judgment, and instructing us always to act as under judgment,[1] He is said "to bear judgment to the nations."

CHAPTER 14

From the same.

Of the Signs and Wonders which He worked.

[Passage quoted, Isa. viii. 16–20 a.]

IN the Epistle to the Hebrews, the apostle, quoting the (d) above passage, " Behold, I and the children which God has given me," expounds it of the Christ, saying, " Forasmuch then as the children are partakers of flesh and blood,

---

[1] κεκριμένως πράττειν.

he also himself took part of the same, that through death
he might destroy him that had the power of death."   Heb. ii. 14.

And here the prophet calls God's children the Apostles,
through whom he teaches that the Lord of Sabaoth, Who
dwells in Mount Zion, will do signs and wonders in the
house of Jacob, and that they will be manifest if sealed, as
is our custom, with the seal of Christ on their foreheads,
and taught no more to learn the Law of Moses, since it
stands no longer, and since that which is called the house
of Jacob is deserted by God.

This is rendered obscurely in the Septuagint :

"Then they shall be manifest who seal up the law, so (451)
as not to learn.   And he will say, I await God, who
turns his face away from the house of Jacob, and I will
trust in him."

Symmachus translates more clearly, thus :

"Bind the testimony, seal the law in my ordinances.
And I will expect the Lord that hides his face from the
house of Jacob, and I will await him."

And Aquila also translates in this way :

"Bind up the witness, seal the law in my teachings.
And I will expect God that hideth his face from the
house of Jacob, and I will await him."

This, then, the apostles of our Saviour are taught to do. (b)
And He proceeds to say to them :

"Behold, I and the children, which God has given
me.   And they shall be for signs and wonders in Israel
from the Lord of Sabaoth who dwells in Mount Sion."

And the Lord of Sabaoth, the Word of God dwelling in the
Humanity He has taken, and sojourning in Mount Zion,
working signs and wonders, commands both His disciples
and all those that believe on Him, sprung from all those who
before were idolaters, to fear idolatrous error no longer : (c)
therefore if idolaters of the Gentiles would sap their foundations and induce[1] them to inquire of pythons and the
dæmon oracles, as if they were equal to the prophetic
inspiration of inspired and godly men, they ought to answer
and say, "Wherefore do they inquire of the dead concerning
the living?   For he has given a law for succour," and the

---

[1] Παρασαλεύοιεν, cf. Philo 2. 69 and, perhaps, P.E. 380 d . . .
τὰ ἤθη. (where Gifford reads σαλεῦσαι), a quotation from Philo.

rest of the passage.   For they that have once taken the law
and the commandments of salvation for succour and help
(d) in their individual life have little need to trouble themselves
about the prophecy that springs from dæmonic deceit.

CHAPTER 15

From the same.

Concerning Christ's Reticence about His Miracles.

(452)   [Passage quoted, Isa. xlii. 1–7.]

THE Evangelist alludes to this passage, when the Pharisees
went out and took counsel against our Saviour to put Him
(c) to death, when He healed the sick on the Sabbath day.
Matt. xii.   But Jesus, knowing, as He says, this conspiracy against Him,
14.   departed thence, and great multitudes followed Him, and
He healed them all, and He straitly charged[1] them that
they should not make Him known.   And He adds to this
the words, "All this was done" (that is to say His departure, and His yielding to those that plotted, and His effort to
escape notice in the miracles that He did, and His pledging
those that were healed not to make Him known), in order
that what was said by the prophet might be fulfilled, when
He said :

"Behold, my son, in whom I am well pleased, my
beloved in whom my soul delighteth ; I will put my
spirit upon him, and he shall bear forth judgment to the
Gentiles ; he shall not strive nor cry, neither shall his
(d)   voice be heard in the streets.   A bruised reed shall he
not break, and smoking flax shall he not quench, until
he bring forth judgment to victory, and on his name
shall the Gentiles trust."

Notice carefully how Matthew, when he says, "Behold my
son, in whom I am well pleased, my beloved in whom my
soul delighteth," mentions neither Jacob nor Israel.   He
does not say, "Jacob my son and Israel my beloved,"
but simply "Behold, my son and my beloved."   Hence the

---

[1] W. H. : ἐπετίμησεν.   E. : ἐπέπληξεν.

names of Jacob and Israel are obelized [1] in the Septuagint,
as if the prophecy were not in the Hebrew. And it is
silently omitted by the other translators, as it is not found in
the Hebrew. And thus it is not inserted by the Evangelist, (453)
who was a Hebrew, and followed the Hebrew text in his
quotation. Therefore the prophecy does not apply either
actually or figuratively to the Jews, but only to the Christ of
God, to Whom the clear evidence and the results bear witness.
For He alone prophesied the future judgment to the Gentiles, quietly sojourning in human life, and setting judgment
on the earth. And not only did He not break the bruised (b)
reed, but so to say bound it up, setting up and strengthening the weak and the bruised in heart. And just as He
did not neglect the sick and corrupt, who needed His
medicine, nor bruise the repentant with hard judgment,
so He did not quench them that continued in evil, and
were smoking under the fire of passion,[2] by preventing their
following their own choice, nor did He punish any of (c)
them before the time, reserving the time of their due
chastisement for the general Judgment : therefore it is said,
" And the smoking flax He shall not quench."

The words, " And in his name shall the Gentiles trust,"
have also been exactly fulfilled. For the nations of Christians trust only in the Name of our Saviour Jesus Christ,
and are marked with His Name as that of the Father of
the religion with which they are associated. For it was
foretold that He should be given for a Light to none but
the Gentiles. And by Him in accordance with the prediction, the eyes of the blind—those that had long been
impaired in understanding, and not only of these but of (d)
those who had lost their very bodies,[3] and those who before
were involved, bound and chained in sin, in darkness and
ignorance of true religion, by Him freed from their sins—
were accounted worthy of the light of knowledge and of
the freedom of God. And if you at your leisure test the
rest of the passage, as I have so far done, you will find
each one of its predictions fulfilled in our Lord and Saviour,
and in Him alone.

---

[1] ὠβέλισται.   [2] ὑπὸ τῶν παθῶν τυφομένους.
[3] τῶν αὐτὸ τὸ σῶμα ἠφανισμένων, which seems to mean "the
dead."

CHAPTER 16

(454)

From the same.

Of the Disbelief of the Jewish People in Him.

[Passages quoted, Isa. vi. 1 ; 8–10.]

THIS, too, is fulfilled in our Saviour, according to John, when he says :

(c)

" 37. But though he had done so many miracles before them, yet they believed not on him : 38. That the saying of Esaias the prophet might be fulfilled, which he spake, Lord, who hath believed our report? and to whom hath the arm of the Lord been revealed?" 39. Therefore they could not believe, because that Esaias said again, 40. He hath blinded their eyes, and hardened their heart ; that they should not see with their eyes, nor understand with their heart, and be con-

John xii. 37–41.

verted, and I should heal them. 41. These things said Esaias, when he saw his glory, and spake of him."

Or according to Matthew :

(d)

" 10. And the disciples came and said to him, Why speaketh thou unto them in parables? 11. He answered and said unto them, Because it is given unto you to know the mysteries of the kingdom of heaven, but to them it is not given . . . 13. Therefore speak I unto them in parables, because they seeing see not, and hearing they hear not, neither do they understand . . .

Matt. xiii. 10–5.

15. lest they should be converted, and I should heal them."[1]

Then was fulfilled in them the prophecy of Isaiah which said, "Go and say to this people, Hearing ye shall hear, and not understand," and that which follows. Notice how S. John proceeds saying, "These things said Esaias, when he saw his glory, and spake of him." As the prophet had seen the Christ and the glory of Christ in the vision in

(455) which he said, "I saw the Lord of Sabaoth sitting upon a throne, high and lifted up," and that which follows. And who would not be struck by the prophecy, seeing so clearly

---

[1] E. omits verse 12. He softens ἵνα μὴ βλέπωσι—ἀκούωσι (W.H.) to ὅτι—οὐ βλέπουσιν—ἀκούουσιν, and adds from the end of the prophecy (verse 15) μήποτε ἐπιστρέψωσι καὶ ἰάσωμαι αὐτούς, giving no reference to Isaiah.

even now the unbelief of the Jews? Even so of old, when
they saw Him Incarnate and working miracles among them,
they did not behold Him with the eyes of their soul and
with understanding vision, nor had they any vision of
spiritual inspiration, so as to understand what power it
was that worked so wondrously and so prodigally among
them. Yes, they who were counted worthy to receive with (b)
their eyes the words of eternal life, and listened to the
voice of divine wisdom, did not hear with the ears of their
understanding, and so made themselves an evident fulfilment of the prophecy. And even until now, though the
power of Christ, by which every race of mankind, divorced
from its ancestral superstition, is being led to the Christian
religion, is so obvious to them, yet they do not regard it
with their understanding, nor consider that what neither
Moses nor his successors among the prophets achieved has
been brought to pass by these alone, namely, to give up
idolatry and pay no heed to polytheistic error, which has (c)
been accomplished among all nations by the power of our
Saviour. And so when they read the witness of the prophets
concerning Him, they hear with their ears and do not understand, and the prophecy before us is literally even now
fulfilled against them.

CHAPTER 17

From Zechariah.

*How it is foretold that He should ride into Jerusalem
on a Colt.*

[Passage quoted, Zech. ix. 9, 10]

As Zechariah prophesied thus after the Return from
Babylon towards the conclusion of prophecy, there is no
record of a Jewish king, such as the prophecy predicts, (456)
except our Lord and Saviour Jesus Christ, in Whom this
prediction was fulfilled, when He literally said to His
disciples:

"Go ye into the village over against you, and ye
shall find an ass tied and a colt with her; loose them

(b)

Matt. xxi.
2.

and bring them unto me. And if any man say, What
do ye? ye shall say to him, The Lord hath need of them.
And they went and did as he commanded them."

Such, then, was the prophecy and such the fulfilment.
But what was His riding on an ass meant to shew forth
but the lowly and humble manner which marked His first
Coming? For the second Coming shall be glorious, that of
which Daniel speaks unfolding and revealing his vision :

(c)

"9. I saw until the thrones were set, and the Ancient
of Days did sit. Thousand thousands ministered to
him, and ten thousand times ten thousand stood before
him. 13. And, behold, one as a son of man coming
with the clouds of heaven. And he came even to the
Ancient of Days, 14. and there was given to him rule
and honour and a kingdom, and all peoples, tribes, and
tongues serve him. His power is an everlasting power,
which shall not pass away, and his kingdom shall not be

Dan. vii. 9.

destroyed." [1]

(d)

But the first Coming of His Incarnation and humiliation
has this great symbol and sign among others, the prophecy
that He should be called meek and gentle, and that He
should come sitting upon an ass. For this is a proof of
His sharing our humanity. Whereas the glory of His
second divine Coming is shewn by His being borne on the
clouds of heaven, and His eternal rule over all nations.
And it is reasonable to quote them both to the Jews, and
to ask them to explain how they can save the credit of the
prophecies, if they confine them to a reference to a single
Coming of Christ : for if they both refer to Christ, as they
agree, they are bound to tell us when we ask them, how it
is possible for the same person at the same coming to be
(457) borne upon the clouds of heaven, and also to ride on an
ass and a young colt : for these two things are very different.
And if you collect the many similar prophecies concerning
Christ, and compare their differences side by side, you will
decide that some of them refer to His first Coming, being
fulfilled at His first Epiphany, while others apply to His
second Coming in glory.

For He utterly destroyed by His Divine Power the chariots
and horses and weapons of war at His first Coming from

---

[1] E. omits 9 b, 10 a (καὶ τὸ ἔνδυμα . . . αὐτοῦ), 10 c, 11, 12, 13 a
(κριτήριον . . . νυκτός), and also καὶ προσήχθη αὐτῷ (S.).

the material Jerusalem and the people of Ephraim : where- (b)
fore from that day to this their kingdom has never existed,
nor their ancient powerful military array or warlike power.
And all the Jewish people are here well called Ephraim, not
Israel or Judah, so as not to bring into dishonour names of
more dignity.   And you will find that other prophets call
the whole people Ephraim, when charging and accusing
them of great crimes, as here.   For after the return from (c)
Babylon, when the former division of the people had ceased,
who are more likely to be meant by Ephraim than the
actual inhabitants of Jerusalem ?   And it was their warlike
and military power, that had lasted until Roman times, that
our Saviour's Coming destroyed with divine secret power,
as the prophecy foretold.

The oracle also calls here on the Church of the Gentiles,
not simply to rejoice, but to rejoice greatly, in its message
of good news, because of the coming of the Word of God (d)
to her ; and it calls her the daughter of the heavenly Zion
and of the former congregation, because all we that are
Gentiles, who believe in Christ, are the offspring and children of Christ and His Apostles, as they whose mother is
the Jewish synagogue : and that which follows was also
fulfilled at our Saviour's Coming.   For unexampled peace
has filled all nations from the time of His coming : no
longer do states war with states as before, nor nations contend with nations, nor is human life as of old in a state of
constant disturbance ; Athenians do not attack Lacedæ- (458)
monians, Syrians Phœnicians, Arabians the inhabitants of
Palestine, nor the Egyptians their neighbours.   All have
been united from that time by God's help, and it is true
that there has been "abundance of peace" among the
nations from that day to this, according to the prophecy.
Jesus alone, and the word of Gospel teaching preached by
Him, have ruled men from sea to sea, from the east to the
setting sun, and from the rivers[1] to the bounds of the earth, (b)
as the prophecy foretold.

Aquila's rendering of this is as follows :

"He shall speak peace among the nations, and his
power shall be from sea to sea, and from the rivers to
the ends of the earth."

---

[1] *I.e.* from Mesopotamia to the far west.

Compare with this what occurs in the Psalm, inscribed "To Solomon, of the King's Son," that is to say, of Him that will spring from Solomon's seed, of Whom the Psalm says, "And he shall rule from sea to sea, and from the rivers to the ends of the world." And the same Psalm refers to the peace here described, when it says, "In his days righteousness shall arise, and abundance of peace." Isaiah, too, agrees with this when he says, "And they shall beat their swords into ploughshares, and their lances into pruning-hooks; nation shall not take up sword against nation, and they shall not learn war any more." You will find Micah in agreement with this, and many other prophets. And if you note, as I said, the dates, you will be able to appreciate that from the time of Augustus, and of the Epiphany of our Saviour that shone forth in his day, during the period of the Roman Empire the old dissensions and varieties of national government have ceased, and thus from that date the peace of the prophecy began. Just as it then began, a day will come when the prophecy will be fulfilled in all its fullness, when, as the apostle says, "the fullness of the Gentiles shall come in."

Ps. lxxi.

(c)

Ps. lxxi. 8.

(d)

Is. ii. 4.

Rom. xi. 25.

(459)

CHAPTER 18

From Psalm cxvii.

Of the Cry, Hosanna to the Son of David.

[Passage quoted, Ps. cxvii. 22–27.]

WHEN our Saviour Jesus Christ entered Jerusalem, riding on an ass according to the previous prophecy, He fulfilled the prediction of Zechariah, for as the Holy Evangelist tells us, the crowds that went before and followed Him cried, saying, "Hosanna to the Son of David, Blessed is he that cometh in the name of the Lord, Hosanna in the highest." And when He entered Jerusalem, "All the city was moved, saying, Who is this? And the multitudes said, This is the prophet Jesus, from Nazareth of Galilee." As, therefore, Hosanna is said in the Psalm we are considering, which is translated "Save us now," and the Hebrew has "Lord, save

Matt. xxi. 9.

(c)

us," and the words, " Blessed is he that cometh in the name of the Lord," are taken from the same Psalm, and these words can only refer to the Christ of God, we naturally apply the rest of the prediction to Him. For He is blessed, (d) Who is named by another prophet, "He that cometh," in Hab. the passage, " Yet a little while, and he that cometh will ii. 3; Heb. come, and will not tarry," Who also came in the Name of x. 37. the Lord God His Father. And He is the Lord God that appeared for us. For He insists that He has come in the Name of His Father when He says to the Jews, " I have come in my Father's Name, and ye receive me not. If another come in his own name, him ye will receive." He, John v. 43. then, that appeared for us, the Lord God, the Blessed, He that cometh in the Name of the Lord, was also the stone, (460) which they who of old built up the people on the foundation of the Mosaic teaching, set at naught, and which, set at naught by them, is become the head of the corner of the Church of the Gentiles, which the oracle says is wonderful, not to all that look on it, but only to the eyes of prophets, when it says, " And it is wonderful in our eyes."

And it calls His Epiphany also " the day which the Lord hath made," for He was the true Light, and the Sun of Righteousness, and the Day of God, in which we may also (b) say, " This is the day which the Lord hath made, we will rejoice and be glad in it."

Now that this part is thus concluded, I will proceed to consider the prophecies concerning the Passion.

BOOK X

INTRODUCTION

HAVING considered the passages that predict the Coming among men of the God that was foretold, we are now called to expound those that refer to His departure from this life, and to study what the prophets said would (462) happen to Him from the earliest days of prophecy. And I will begin by expounding those which have to do with the men that plotted His Death, which will occupy no small part of the present Book.

But before beginning my argument let me repeat what I have often said about the dispensation of Christ, that we must strictly distinguish what belongs to His Divinity from what belongs to His Humanity. As Divine we recognize Him as the Word of God, the Power of God, the Wisdom of God, the Angel of Great Counsel, and the Great Eternal High Priest, offering sacrifice for the existence and preservation of all, and propitiating the Father. (b) And as Human we know Him as the Lamb of God that taketh away the sin of the world, and as a sheep led to the slaughter. And this was the human body, which as a high priest He took like a lamb or sheep from the flock of humanity, and offering the firstfruits of the human (c) race,[1] sacrificed them to the Father. By it He entered into human nature, which could only thus perceive the Word of God, and His spiritual unembodied power, being able with eyes of flesh to see nothing higher than flesh and physical things. So that everything that follows, which may seem to lower His glory, must be taken as conceived of the Lamb of God that takes away the sin of the world, and of His human body.

---

[1] τὴν ἀπαρχὴν . . . καλλιερησάμενος. Cf. P.E. 157 c.

For He was the Lamb that takes away sin, according
to John the Baptist, when he said: "Behold the Lamb
of God, that taketh away the sin of the world," and He John i. 29.
was the Lamb led to the slaughter in the oracle of Isaiah,
which said: "He was led as a sheep to the slaughter, and
as a lamb before her shearers is dumb." And of Him as Isa. liii. 7.
of a lamb was it said: "For the sins of my people he was (d)
led to death." For it was necessary that the Lamb of Isa. liii. 8.
God, taken by the great High-Priest on behalf of the other
kindred lambs, for all the flock of mankind, should be
offered as a sacrifice to God: "For since by man came
death, by man came also the resurrection of the dead," 1 Cor. xv.
says the apostle; "and as by the offence of one, judgment 21; Rom.
came upon all men to condemnation: even so by the v. 18.
righteousness of one the free gift came upon all men unto
justification of life." Hence, also, He taught His disciples (463)
that He was life and light and truth, and the other conceptions of His Divinity, whereas to them that were not
initiated into the secrets of His nature, He said: "Why do John viii.
ye seek to kill me, a man that has told you the truth?" 40.

As then in what has gone before I have dealt with what
specially concerns His Divinity,[1] so now in like manner
I will shew the human sufferings of the Lamb of God,
since what occurred before His Passion lies between the
two, partaking both of the nature of His Divinity and His
Humanity. With this necessary proviso, let us now con- (b)
sider the oracles which concern the traitor Judas, and his
fellow-conspirators against Christ, and the events at the
time of His Passion.

CHAPTER 1

From Psalm xl.

*Of Judas the Traitor, and His Fellow-Conspirators
against Christ.*

[Passage quoted, Ps. xl. 1–12.] (464)

As it has been supposed by some that the Book of Psalms
merely consists of hymns to God and sacred songs, and

---

[1] τὰ τῆς θεολογίας ἰδιώματα.

that we shall look in vain in it for predictions and prophecies of the future, let us realize distinctly that it contains many prophecies, far too many to be quoted now, and it must suffice for proof of what I say to make use of (b) two Psalms ascribed to Asaph, written in the time of David.

I Chron.   For Asaph was one of the Temple Musicians [1] then, as
xvi. 4.   is stated in the Book of Chronicles, and was inspired by the Divine Spirit to speak the Psalms inscribed with his name. And what do these Psalms include? Predictions of the siege of Jerusalem, the royal city of the Jewish race, which took place nearly five hundred years after the prediction. For we read in the 73rd Psalm, inscribed " A Psalm of understanding for Asaph ": [2]

"Wherefore hast thou rejected us, O God, for ever? | Wherefore is thy wrath kindled against the (c)   sheep of thy pasture? | 2. Remember thy congregation, which thou hast possessed of old, | and hast ransomed as the rod of thy inheritance; | this Mount Zion wherein thou hast dwelt. | 3. Lift up thine hands against their pride unto the end: | what things hath the enemy done evilly in thy sanctuaries, | 4. and they that hate thee have boasted in the midst of thy Feast: | 5. they have set up their banners for signs,[3] ignorantly as it were in the entrance above. | They cut down its doors at once [4] with axes as in (d)   a wood of trees, | they have broken it down with hatchet and stone-cutter. | 7. They have burnt thy sanctuary to the ground with fire, | and have pro-

Ps. lxxiii.   faned even with the ground the dwelling-place of thy
1–8.   name."

This is in Psalm lxxiii.; and Psalm lxxviii. of Asaph contains this:

"O God, the Gentiles have entered into thine inheritance, and defiled thy holy temple; they have made Jerusalem a store-house of fruits, they have given the dead bodies of thy servants to be meat for the birds Ps. lxxviii.   of the air, the flesh of thy saints to the beasts of the
1, 2.   fields."

---

[1] τῶν ἱεροψαλτῶν.
[2] συνέσεως τῷ 'Ασάφ.
[3] S. omits ἔθεντο τὰ σημεῖα αὐτῶν σημεῖα, καὶ οὐκ ἔγνωσαν.
[4] S. puts ἐπὶ τὸ αὐτό with the following clause.

The first of these passages, I mean the one from Psalm lxxiii., was spoken in David's reign before the building of (465) Solomon's Temple, and it was only fulfilled the first time by the siege by the Babylonians, and the second time in the Roman war against the Jews.   For what was predicted and proclaimed in the said Psalms by Asaph was brought to pass in the destruction of the first and second Temples. And the second passage, from Psalm lxxviii., was fulfilled in the time of Antiochus, called Epiphanes, who being King of Syria entered Jerusalem, polluted the Temple, destroyed (b) the Altar, and in his endeavour to compel the Jews to hellenize, slew countless men and women who were martyrs for their law and their father's religion, and he inflicted all sorts of punishments on them.   It was therefore to that time, and to Antiochus' successors who emulated his deeds, that Asaph's prophecies in Psalm lxxviii. refer.   And the Book of those called Maccabees confirms what I say, which has this passage :

"And to Jakeimon and Bacchides there came a (c) deputation of scribes asking for justice."   And it proceeds to say : "And he sware to them saying, We will not bring evil on yourselves and your friends.   And they believed him.   And he took of them sixty men and slew them in one day, according to the word of Asaph, which he wrote, They gave the dead bodies of thy servants to be meat for the birds of the air, and the flesh of thy saints to the beasts of the land, their (d) blood have they poured out like water on every side of 1 Macc. Jerusalem, and there was no man to bury them."   vii. 12.

If these events were thus predicted and fulfilled, it is not surprising that in the same way the oracle quoted from Psalm xl. should announce what would happen in connection with the plot on our Saviour, though not all men should understand, that He being the Word of God, Wisdom, Life, and the True Light, and possessing all the wealth of the good, for our sakes became poor, taking our flesh, and being made like in kind to mortal man and beggars,[1] taking on Him the form of a slave and a poor man, and most of all when He fulfilled the Psalmist's prophecy.   He that understands these sayings to refer to

---

[1] πτωχοῖς.

Himself, naturally is blessed at the beginning of the Psalm, as receiving the written promise.

(466)   So it proceeds in the rest to speak in the person of a poor man and a beggar, that is to say of our Saviour Who for our sakes became poor: "I said, Lord, have mercy on me." And John, the Evangelist, is an independent witness that the words of this Psalm are spoken in the Person of our Saviour.   For he records, that:

"Jesus once took a towel and girded himself, and washed the feet of his disciples and said, I know whom I have chosen.   But that the Scripture may be fulfilled,
John xiii.   He that eateth with me, the same hath lifted his heel
4-18.   against me." [1]

For He made it clear there that the Scripture referred
(b) to was the Psalm before us, in which it is said: "For the man of my peace, in whom I trusted, he that ate of my bread hath raised his heel against me." He it is, then, Who says at the beginning: "I said, Lord, have pity on me, heal my soul, for I have sinned against thee," and speaks through the whole Psalm.   Symmachus gives a clearer rendering of these words, as follows:

"When I said, O Lord, have pity on me, heal my soul, even if I have sinned against thee, my enemies have spoken evil against me, when shall he die and
(c)   his name perish?   And when he comes to gaze on me his heart speaks vanity, it gathers unrighteousness on itself: and when he goes out he tells it.   All they that hate me have whispered against me with one consent, conceiving evil concerning me.   An unrighteous word is poured out within them, and when he fall may he never rise up.   Yea, even the man who was at peace with me, in whom I trusted, who did eat of my bread, has magnified himself against me accordingly.   But thou, O Lord, pity me, and raise
(d)   me, that I may reward them.   By this I shall know that thou wishest it, if my enemy does not revile me. Thou hast defended me because of my innocence, and shall set me before thee for ever."

---

[1] E. summarizes John xiii. 4–17 (W.H. καὶ λαβὼν λέντιον διέζωσεν ἑαυτόν. E. περιεζώσατο) to verse 18, where he adheres to the text, except οὓς for τινας, and μετ' ἐμοῦ for μου.

And Aquila is in exact agreement [1] with Symmachus. With regard first to the words which are apparently said in the Person of our Saviour : " Heal my soul, for I have sinned against thee," you will notice in Symmachus they are not so rendered, but thus : " Heal my soul, even if I have sinned against thee." And He speaks thus, since He shares our sins. So it is said : " And the Lord hath laid on him our iniquities, and he bears our sins." Thus the Lamb of God, that taketh away the sins of the world, (467) became a curse on our behalf :

" Whom, though he knew no sin, God made sin for our sake, giving him as redemption for all, that we might become the righteousness of God in him." 2 Cor. v. 21.

But since being in the likeness of sinful flesh He condemned sin in the flesh, the words quoted are rightly used. And in that He made our sins His own [2] from His love and benevolence towards us, He says these words, adding further on in the same Psalm : " Thou hast pro- (b) tected me because of my innocence," clearly shewing the impeccability of the Lamb of God. And how can He make our sins His own, and be said to bear our iniquities, except by our being regarded as His body, according to the apostle, who says : " Now ye are the body of Christ, 1 Cor. xii. and severally members? " And by the rule that " if one 27. member suffer all the members suffer with it," so when the many members suffer and sin, He too by the laws of (c) sympathy (since the Word of God was pleased to take the form of a slave and to be knit into the common tabernacle of us all) takes into Himself the labours of the suffering members, and makes our sicknesses His, and suffers all our woes and labours by the laws of love. And the Lamb of God not only did this, but was chastised on our behalf, (d) and suffered a penalty He did not owe, but which we owed because of the multitude of our sins ; and so He became the cause of the forgiveness of our sins, because He received death for us, and transferred to Himself the scourging, the insults, and the dishonour, which were due to us, and drew down on Himself the apportioned curse, being made a curse for us. And what is that but the price of our

---

[1] ἰσοδυναμεῖ. Cf. Polyb. 2. 56. 2.
[2] ἐξοικειούμενος τὰς ἡμετέρας ἁμαρτίας—as in P.E. 2 c, 37 c, etc.

souls?[1]   And so the oracle says in our person : "By
his stripes we were healed," and "The Lord delivered him
for our sins," with the result that uniting Himself to us
and us to Himself, and appropriating our sufferings, He
can say, "I said, Lord, have mercy on me, heal my soul,
(468) for I have sinned against thee," and can cry that they
who plot against Him, not men only but invisible dæmons
as well, when they see the surpassing power of His Holy
Name and title, by means of which He filled the world full
of Christians a little after, think that they will be able to
extinguish it, if they plot His death.   This is what is
proved by His saying : "My enemies have spoken evil of
me, saying, When shall he die and his name perish?"

And since they attacked Him with the words of guile,
attempting to entangle[2] Him, as Holy Writ bears witness,
(b) telling us how different charges and accusations were
engineered against Him at different times, He therefore
adds : "And if he come to see me, his heart speaks vanity,
he heaps unrighteousness on himself ; he has gone out, and
spoken the same against me."   After this, too, He clearly
reveals the vile traitor himself, who, after making a covenant
with the rulers of the Jews to betray his master, no more
(c) went as he used to the school of His holy teaching, nor
went as to His teacher, nor like the others passed His time
with the Saviour, but awaited and hunted for an opportunity
to lay hands on Him.   For this is what he is accused
of doing by the Holy Evangelists, of whom Matthew
says :

"Then one of the twelve, called Judas Iscariot, went
unto the chief priests, and said unto them, What will
ye give me, and I will deliver him unto you?   And
they covenanted with him for thirty pieces of silver.
And from that time he sought an opportunity to betray
him to them."

Matt. xxvi.
14.

(d) And Mark says :

"And Judas Iscariot, one of the twelve, went unto
the chief priests, to betray him unto them.   And when
they heard it they were glad, and promised to give him
money : and he sought how he might conveniently
betray him."

Mark xiv.
10.

---

[1] ἀντίψυχον.   [2] παγιδεύσωσιν.

And Luke writes thus:

"And Satan entered into Judas that was called
Iscariot, being of the number of the twelve, and he
departed and spake with the chief priests and scribes,
and the captains [1] of the Temple, that he might betray
him unto them, and they were glad, and covenanted to
give him money.[2]　And he sought opportunity to betray Luke xxii.
him unto them apart from the multitude."　　　　　3.

So the prophecy before us prophesies the same things,
when it says:

"And if he came to see me his heart spake vanity,
he gathered iniquity on himself.　He went out, and
spake the same.　Against me all my enemies
whispered";

where Symmachus renders:

"Coming in to spy on me, his heart spake vanity,
he heaped unrighteousness upon it: and when he went
out he spake against me.　All they that hate me (469)
whispered with one voice against me."

Yes, for he alone went into his master as a friend and a
disciple, to spy and search out, while he hid his plot in his
own heart.　And when he went out, he spake against Him (b)
at once with many of the same mind, betraying the Saviour
to His enemies, and secretly made a pact with the rulers of
the Jews, about other things, but of course about money as
well, for which he promised to betray Him, and about which
he whispered with them.　Wherefore it says:

"He went out and spake at once.　All my enemies
whispered against me, against me they imagined evils.
They determined an evil plan against me."

Perhaps the covenant for the money is meant by the
"unjust word" of the prophecy, or perhaps the impious (c)
and unjust intentions they had against Him, supposing that
He would be extinguished and destroyed after death, and
would no longer be reckoned among the living.　For such
is the meaning of: "When he sleepeth he shall surely never
rise up again," which Symmachus has expressed more
clearly: "And falling he will not arise"; where Aquila
says: "And whosoever sleep, he shall not rise again."　So

---

[1] W.H. have στρατηγοῖς τὸ πῶς αὐτοῖς παραδῷ—for στρατ. τοῦ ἱεροῦ
ἵνα αὐτὸν παραδῷ.

[2] W.H. add καὶ ἐξωμολόγησεν.

(d) far it has spoken generally about all those who conspired against Him at the time of His Passion ; but it goes on now to speak of the traitor particularly, as of one of His disciples : "For the man of my peace also, in whom I trusted, who ate of my bread, hath lifted up his heel against me." Instead of which Symmachus again renders : "And a man, who was at peace with me, in whom I had confidence, who ate of my bread with me, hath magnified himself against me." For of a truth it is the lowest and most accursed [1] of men who after sharing a master's table, and the nurture of his instruction, goes wrong and treats his benefactor in the opposite way to which he has been treated himself.

And since the enemies in their plotting said : "When shall he die, and his name perish?" and thought that if he lay down he would never rise up again, therefore (470) our Lord and Saviour praying for the reverse of this, and assured of an unhindered resurrection by His Father, says :

"Lord, have mercy upon me, and raise me up, and I will reward them. In this I know that thou hast favoured me, because my enemy shall not triumph over me."

And it is quite clear how after His resurrection from the dead immediate judgment, that did not tarry, fell on the conspirators, so that death who was the enemy of His return to life was made ashamed, and they that mocked (b) Him said, "O death, where is thy sting? O death, where is 1 Cor. xv. thy victory?" And those who have read the history of the 55. times after our Saviour's resurrection, in Josephus, will remember what troubles fell on the Jews and their rulers, involved in which they received the right reward for what they did to Him. All this, then, that fell upon them was the fulfilment of the prophecy : but our Saviour's Resurrection from the dead proved to all that in Him the Father was well pleased, as He tells us when He says :

(c)   "Have mercy upon me, and raise me up, and I will reward them. By this I know thou hast favoured me, because my enemy doth not triumph over me."

And notice how in pouring forth this prayer to His God and Father, with what confidence He witnesses boldly to

----

[1] ἐναγέστατος.

His own sinlessness, although He had said before, "Heal
my soul, for I have sinned against thee." But I have (d)
already shewn that the words, " I have sinned against thee,"
are not to be taken literally, and Symmachus interprets them
more clearly when he says, "Heal my soul, even if I have
sinned against thee," as could well be said of our sins, which
our Lord and Saviour took upon Himself. Whereas the
words, "Thou hast protected me for my innocence," exhibit
the absolute integrity of His nature, to which He traces in
His teaching the stability and sureness of His life and His
preservation after His Resurrection, when He adds, "Thou
hast established me before thee for ever ": or, "And thou
wilt establish me before thee for ever," according to
Symmachus.

CHAPTER 2

From Psalm liv.   (471)

*Also of Judas, and of them that with Him
conspired against Christ.*

[Passages quoted, Ps. liv. 2–5, 10–14.]

" 2. HEAR my prayer, O God, | and do not despise
my supplication. | 3. Attend to me and hearken to
me : | I was grieved in my meditation, and troubled |
4. by the voice of the enemy, and by the affliction of
the sinner. | For they brought iniquity against me, and (b)
in wrath reviled me. | -5. My heart was troubled within
me, and the fear of death fell upon me. | Fear and
trembling came upon me, and darkness covered me."
And that which follows, to which he adds :

" 10. Destroy, O Lord, and divide their tongues, | for
I have seen iniquity and strife in the city. | 11. Day and
night it shall go round it upon its walls, | and iniquity
and sorrow 12. and unrighteousness are in the midst
of it, | and usury and craft have not left its streets. (c)
13. For if an enemy had reproached me, I would have
borne it : | And if he that hated me had magnified
himself against me, I would have hid myself from him : |
14. but it was even thou, O man like-minded, my

guide, and my friend, | who in companionship with me
sweetened my food: | we walked in the house of God
in unity."

(d) The words:

"If an enemy had reproached me, I could have borne
it, and if he that hated me had magnified himself against
me, I would have hid myself from him : but it was even
thou, O man like-minded, my guide and my friend, who
in companionship with me sweetened my food,"

resemble—"For the man of my peace, in whom I trusted,
he that ate of my bread, hath lifted up his heel against me,"
said of Judas in the previous prophecy. As then there he
was shewn to be a man of peace, when he was the Saviour's
disciple and numbered among the apostles, so here he is
called like-minded, His guide and His friend. And as there
it was said of him, "He that eateth with me hath lifted up
his heel against me," so also here it is said to the same
person, "Who in companionship with me sweetened my
food." Yea, for he was privileged to be one of them that
partook of the secret companionship and spiritual food that
(472) our Saviour gave His disciples. For to the crowds and multitudes without He spoke in parables, but only to His disciples,
of whom Judas was reckoned one, did He unfold all things.
So it is said, "He that ate my bread hath lifted up his heel
against me," and, "who in companionship sweetened my
bread." This Aquila interprets more clearly, "We together
(b) supped sweetly on mysteries," and Symmachus, "We joined
together in sweet companionship." And instead of, "Thou,
O man like-minded, my guide and friend," Symmachus
renders, "Thou, O man of like disposition, my guide and
my friend." Now if he was privileged to stand so high
among the friends of our Saviour, His words about him are
natural, "If an enemy had reviled me, I would have borne
it," and that which follows.

Then after this prophecy about Judas, He proceeds to
foretell His own preservation and escape from death, in the
words:

"I cried unto God, and the Lord saved me. At
evening and morning and at noon I will tell and
proclaim, and he shall hear my voice, and shall ransom
my soul in peace."

(c) Thus in prayer He speaks of the time before His death

during which Judas hatched his treachery against Him.
And it was then that our Lord and Saviour, as one who
mourned for the destruction and ruin of His friend, and
still more for the casting away of the whole Jewish race, as
if in sympathy with friends gone mad who were very dear to
Him, calls all His union with them and instruction of them
wasted, in that it has profited them nothing, saying :

> "I was grieved with my wasted efforts, and I was
> moved by the voice of the enemy, and by the affliction
> of the sinner. For they fell," He says, " into iniquity,
> and reviled me in anger."

This may either be referred to the Jewish rulers, who (d)
attempted to catch Him with enmity and conspiracy, or
it may have been spoken of the invisible powers that fought
against Him from without, and inspired the plot that was
carried through by men.   And this I think agrees with His
words in the Gospels at the time of the Passion, when He
says to His disciples : " My soul is exceeding sorrowful, Matt. xxvi
even unto death : tarry ye here, and watch with me."   And 38.
again, " Now is my soul troubled."   The words of the John xii.
Psalm are similar to those, where it said : " My heart is 27.
moved within me, and the fear of death is fallen upon (473)
me : Fear and trembling have come upon me, and darkness hath covered me," in which He reveals the attacks
of the opposing powers upon Him.   As then in the
prophets a certain " spirit of adultery " is named, e.g. " They
were deceived by a spirit of adultery " and " the spirit of Hos. iii. 12.
error in the wilderness," so also the spirit of death would Jer. vi. 11.
cause fear, just as the spirit of strength would be the source
of power and divine bravery.   So we should call it " the (b)
spirit of fear and trembling," and, indeed, " the spirit of fear
and confusion " as well, which usually comes on nearly all
that die as martyrs for their religion, and much more would
be laid on Him that underwent death for all.   But whether
it was the spirit of fear and of death, or of fear and trembling,
or any other like power that fell upon Him, at any rate it
did not break Him down, for He, like a noble athlete, threw (c)
far from Him the fear of death by His assurance of life, for
He is the Life.   And so He drove far off the spirit of fear
and trembling which attacked Him by the power of the
spirit of bravery, might, and strength.   For according to
Isaiah, "There rested on Him (together with the other

Isa. xi. 2. spirits), the spirit of counsel and strength." So, too, He puts to flight the spirit of darkness by the power of His own John i. 5 ; light. For, "The light shineth in darkness, and the dark-
Ps. xxi. 12. ness comprehended it not." You will find similar passages
(d) in Psalm xxi., where again, in His person, it is said, "Many oxen have come about me : fat bulls hemmed me in. They gaped upon me with their mouths, as a ramping and roaring lion." And also, "Many dogs have encircled me, the council of the wicked-doers has surrounded me." And once more :

"Save my soul from the sword, and my only-begotten from the power of the dog. Save me from the lion's mouth, and my humility from the horns of the unicorns."
Here He clearly calls the evil powers bulls and calves, lions, dogs and unicorns, who hemmed Him in and surrounded
(474) Him at the time of His Passion, but were not able to do aught against Him. And this follows, only if these parts of the Psalm refer to our Lord and Saviour : but if they do not refer to Him, but to some one else, you must yourself reduce the passage to harmony.[1] And immediately after the prediction of the conspiracy against Him, He continues also about the mother-city of the Jews, Jerusalem, and says, "I saw iniquity and strife in the city," and that which
(b) follows, the meaning of which there is no time now to expound.

CHAPTER 3

From Psalm cviii.

Still of Judas, and of the Apostle elected in His Room, and of the Jewish Nation.

[Passage quoted, Ps. cviii. 1–8.]

AND the Apostle Peter is a sufficient[2] witness that this prophecy refers to the traitor Judas, when, after the Saviour's Ascension, all the apostles being gathered together with many of the brethren, he stood up in the midst, and said :

---

[1] ἐπιστήσεις καὶ αὐτὸς ὡς ἂν ἐξομαλισθέντα τὰ κατὰ τὸν τόπον.
[2] ἐχέγγυος μάρτυς.

"Men and brethren, this Scripture must needs have
been fulfilled, which the Holy Ghost spake before by
the mouth of David concerning Judas, which was guide
to them that took Jesus. For he was numbered with
us, and had obtained part of this ministry. Now this
man purchased a field with the reward of iniquity ; and
falling headlong, he burst asunder in the midst, and all
his bowels gushed out.   And it was known unto all the (475)
dwellers at Jerusalem, insomuch as that field is called in
their proper [1] tongue Aceldama, that is to say, The field
of blood.   For it is written in the Book of Psalms, Let
his habitation be desolate, and let no man dwell therein : Acts i 16-
and his bishopric let another take."   20.

Peter, then, in saying thus, suggested that another must be
chosen in place of Judas, to fill up the deficient number of
the twelve apostles, so that the prophecy might be fulfilled.
And when the lot had been cast, it fell upon Matthias, and
he was numbered with the twelve apostles. Since this was (b)
thus fulfilled, it follows that the person who speaks in this
Psalm can only be our Saviour, Who thought good to
anticipate by the record of the Holy Spirit the very prayer
that was sent up by Him to the Father at the time of
His Passion, foretelling what would happen to Him in the
future.

He says, then, "O God, pass not over my praise in
silence," praying that the instruction delivered by Him to
His disciples and the praise of the new Covenant might not
be lost in silence, but might live to the end of time.   "The (c)
mouth of the sinner and the mouth of the crafty " would
have special application to Judas, who went to the Chief
Priests and said to them :

"What will ye give me, and I will deliver him unto
you ? And they covenanted with him for thirty pieces
of silver. And from that time he sought opportunity
to betray him unto them."

And after making this covenant against Him, he was one of
those that sat down with Him at the Feast of the Passover,[2]
when our Saviour—

"sat down with the twelve, and as they were eating, (d)
said unto them, Verily, verily, I say unto you, that one

---

[1] W. II. omit ἰδίᾳ.   [2] ἐν τῷ τοῦ Πάσχα συμποσίῳ.

Matt. xxvi.
21. of you shall betray me.   And being very sorry they began
to say unto him, Lord, is it I?"

Among whom was Judas, who opened that mouth of his,
full of deceit and irony, and answered, "Is it I, Rabbi?" a
crafty mouth indeed, with which he gave the signal to the
Matt. xxvi. conspirators against our Saviour, saying, "Whomsoever I
48. shall kiss, that same is he."   And he fulfilled his words by
acts, when he went to Jesus, and said to Him, "Hail, Rabbi,
and kissed him."   And Jesus said to him, "Friend, wherefore art thou come?" and "Judas, betrayest thou the son
(476) of man with a kiss?"   So then in anticipation, he says by
the Psalm :

> "The mouth of the crafty is opened upon me.   They
> have spoken against me with crafty tongue, and have
> encircled me with words of hatred, and have fought
> against me without a cause."

Here He has in mind not only Judas, but the other conspirators against Him.   For the Gospel relates, that even
while the Saviour was still speaking to His disciples—

Matt. xxvi.
47.

(b)

Matt. xxvi.
55.

> "behold, Judas, one of the twelve, came, and with him
> a great multitude with swords and staves from the chief
> priests and elders of the people!   To whom the Lord
> said, Are ye come out as against a thief with swords and
> staves to take me?   I sat daily with you teaching in the
> Temple, and ye laid no hold on me.   But this is all
> come to pass, that the scriptures of the prophets might
> be fulfilled."

And He says also in the Psalms : "Instead of loving me,
they spake evil of me, but I continued to pray."   This,
too, was fulfilled, when, as our Saviour prayed with the
eleven apostles in the place called Gethsemane, and departed
(c) from them a little way, and knelt down to His Father, and
prayed a second and a third time, Judas with the Rulers of
the Jews matured his conspiracy, collecting and leading the
multitude of them that were prepared to take Him with
swords and staves.

And they did evil to Him instead of good, and gave Him
hate in return for His love, when they were ill-disposed
(d) towards the Saviour, and Benefactor and Teacher, Who had
given them such healing and treatment by His words and
teaching and all sorts of benefits.   In return for which,

since they did evil to Him instead of good, and gave Him
hatred for love, He rightly adds :

"Set a sinner over him, and let Satan stand at his
right hand. When he is judged let him go forth condemned, and let his prayer be turned into sin; let his
days be few, and another take his office."

And the holy apostle, applying this Scripture to the traitor,
shewed clearly by anticipation what would be the end of
these things. Now you yourself can see, how a sinful ruler
and head was given to the Jewish race, after their presumptuous deeds against the Saviour, and how they were
forced to serve strangers and idolators instead of their
ancient godly rulers. Who would not be struck by the (477)
fulfilment of the prediction? For the oracle says, " Let his
days be few," and there is no doubt that the whole period
after their plot against our Saviour was short, during which
they appeared to abide, after which they underwent the
siege and were utterly destroyed, and then another took
office, namely the people founded by Christ.

And you will understand the rest of the Psalm in a similar (b)
sense. The words that follow, spoken as of certain children
of Judas, "Let his children be orphans," and the like, may
be referred primarily to Judas, and secondarily to all who
like him betray the word of salvation. And you may understand in a similar way, his wife, and the sins of his father,
and of the Jewish Synagogue, which is called his mother.
For I think that this is meant by "let not the sin of his
mother be done away." But just as in the preceding (c)
prophecy, our Lord and Saviour was called a beggar and a
poor man, as I have pointed out in expounding, "Blessed
is the man that considereth the poor and needy," so in the
present Psalm He is called by these names.

May such and such judgments fall on Judas, He says, and
those who have like desires to his. What those judgments
are He adds in these words :

"Because he remembered not to do mercy, and persecuted the poor and the beggar and the stricken in
spirit even unto death. He loved cursing and it shall
come to him ; he wished not blessing, and it shall be far
off from him."

And a little lower down He again calls Himself a poor man (d)
and a beggar, and says :

"And thou, Lord most high, have mercy on me, for thy name's sake, for good is thy mercy. Save me, for I am poor and a beggar."

And he adds after an interval:

"My knees were weak through fasting, and my flesh was changed for lack of oil, and I become a jest to them. They saw me, and shaked their heads at me."

(478) And all this was fulfilled, when "The passers-by reviled him, wagging their heads and saying, He saved others, himself he cannot save." And since, even now, the Jews draw down the curse of their fathers upon themselves, and are wont with blasphemy and impious words to anathematize our Lord and Saviour and all that believe on Him, He goes on to say:

Matt. xxvii. 40.

"They shall curse, but thou wilt bless. May they that arise against me be ashamed, but thy servant shall rejoice. Let them who speak evil of me be clothed with shame, and be clothed in confusion as with a cloak. But I will confess the Lord with my mouth, and amid many will I praise him, for he stood by the right hand of the poor, to save my soul from the persecutors."

(b)

And it is quite clear, even now, to what evils they that invoke curses in their synagogues have grown accustomed, never at all being able to recover from those same times, while He offers to His Father in the midst of many nations the praise of His new Covenant, having the Father working with Him, Who sits at His own right hand. "Wherefore," He says, "in the midst of many will I praise him, for he stood at the right hand of the poor." And He assures of His own preservation after death in the words: "To save my soul from the persecutors." For after He had said above, "He persecuted the poor man and the beggar and him that was stricken in heart even unto death," and had shewed forth His own death outlining the prophecy, He said figuratively, "For he stood at the right hand of the poor, to save his soul from the persecutors."

(c)

CHAPTER 4

From Zechariah.

Still of Judas, and of the Money in Return for which He betrayed the Lord, and of the casting away of the Jewish Race, both Rulers and Ruled.

[Passage quoted, Zech. xi. 7 *b*–14.]   (479)

THIS was fulfilled when, according to Luke :

> " Judas went away, and spoke with the chief priests (c)
> and scribes and captains of the Temple, that he might
> betray him unto them. And they were glad, and Luke xxii.
> covenanted to give him money ; "   4.

or, according to Mark when, " he went to the chief
priests to betray him ; and they were glad and promised Mark xiv.
to give him money." In each case it is simply money 10.
that is named. But in Matthew the amount is
recorded, and it agrees with the quotation from Zechariah.
For Matthew says :

> " Then went one of the twelve, called Judas Iscariot, (d)
> to the chief priests, and said to them, What will ye give
> me, and I will deliver him unto you ? and they weighed Matt. xxvi.
> unto him thirty staters."   14.

And this agrees with, " And they weighed my price thirty
pieces of silver," spoken by the Lord in the prophecy.

And there is added to this, " And the Lord said to me,
Drop them into the furnace, and see if it is good metal, as
I was tested by them." For which Aquila renders : " And
the Lord said to me, Drop them into the furnace, cast
them to the potter : very great is the price, at which I was
valued by them."

And notice how the Lord Himself confesses that a sum of (480)
thirty pieces of silver was given for Him. The meaning of
His words implies something like this : I the Lord from the
very first day ceased not to give to you Jews proofs of My
kindness, and in countless ways I did you good, not only
through the earliest prophets, but also by My presence in
moral teaching and spiritual education, in signs and wonders,
and other miracles, and in cures and attentions : now you (b)
that were privileged to receive such benefits, give My price
or refuse it, demanding of them, it would seem, the fruits of
holiness, and the proof of their faith in Him. But they, as

the preceding quotation tells, instead of loving Me spoke
evil of Me, and laid evil on Me instead of good, and hatred
instead of My love, weighing out thirty pieces of silver, as if
they valued at that price Him that was sold.   But since
the fire shall try every man's work of what sort it is, He

1 Cor. iii.
13. rightly bids them cast it into the furnace, adding, "As I
was tested by them."   Perhaps the House of God is here
(c) called a Furnace.   For the Lord says, according to the
Septuagint, "Cast them into the Furnace," and adds, "And
they cast them into the Furnace, the House of God";
while according to Aquila the Lord says, "Cast it, that is
the money, to the potter," and adds, "And I cast it in
the House of the Lord to the potter."   According to
Symmachus, the Lord says, "Cast it into the furnace,"
(d) and adds, "I cast it into the House of the Lord, into the
Furnace."   And was not this fulfilled when Judas—

"3. that betrayed the Lord, seeing that he was condemned, repented and returned the money[1] to the chief
priests and elders, saying, I have sinned in that I have
betrayed the innocent blood? 4. And they said to him,
What is that to us? see thou to that.   5. And he cast
down the money in the Temple and went and hanged
himself.   6. And the chief priests took the money and
said, It is not lawful to put them in the treasury, for it is
(481) the price of blood.   7. And they took counsel, and
bought with them the potters' field to bury strangers in :
8. Wherefore that field is called the field of blood unto
this day.   9. Then was fulfilled that which was spoken
by Jeremiah the prophet saying, And they took the thirty
pieces of silver, the price of him that was valued, whom
Matt.
xxvii. 3. they of the children of Israel did value, 10. and gave
them for the potter's field, as the Lord appointed me."

But as this passage is not found in the prophecy of
Jeremiah, you must consider whether it is to be supposed
that they have been removed through any evil intention, or
whether there has been an error in copying,[2] through the

---

[1] W.H.: τὰ τριάκοντα ἀργύρια.

[2] κατά τινα ῥᾳδιουργίαν ἤ καὶ σφάλμα γραφικὸν γεγονέναι.   The
prophetic reference to Jeremiah is of course a mistake.   It should be to
Zechariah xi. 13.   A. B. Bruce attributes it to there being similar texts
in Jeremiah (e.g. xviii. 2, 3, xxxii. 6–15) running in the Evangelist's
mind (Exp. N.T. i. 323).

mistake of some careless transcriber of the Holy Gospels, who
wrote Jeremiah instead of Zechariah, where he ought to
have copied, " Then was fulfilled that which was written by
Zechariah the prophet," and instead of, "And they cast them
into the house of the Lord, into the furnace," wrote in error,
" And they bought with them the field of the potter."   For
the prophecy explicitly states that the money was cast into
the Temple of the Lord, so does the Gospel : for, " Judas," it (c)
says, " cast the money into the Temple, and departed."
And perhaps it was through this money that the Temple was
rendered profane, and the words, " Behold, your house is
left unto you desolate," were fulfilled.   And you may well
ask whether the House of God was called a Furnace, because
it is there that the souls of men are fashioned as in a
crucible by the fire of divine teaching, or convicted of
impurity, as if they were fired and tried in a furnace.
Hence Aquila says, " I cast the money in the house of the (d)
Lord to the potter," clearly teaching that the Divine Word
dwells like a potter in the House of the Lord, and moulds
and renews the souls of them that enter.

But if the price of Him that was valued, there cast down
rendered the House profane, it is natural for Him to
proceed to say, " And I cast the second rod, the Rope, to
break the covenant between Judah and Israel."

For from that day the multitude of the nation was cut
away from God's ancient providential guardianship.   And I
suppose the second rod to mean the whole Jewish nation.
It is therefore called a Rope in the words, "The one I
called Beauty, and the other I called a Rope."   And he (482)
proceeds to speak clearly of the second : "And I cast away
the second rod, the Rope, to break my covenant between
Judah and Israel."   For they were the Rope and the second
rod.   But the first rod, called Beauty, was Jerusalem itself,
and the Mosaic Worship, and the whole of the old covenant.   This is shewn by the prophecy, saying, "And I will
take my rod of beauty, and I will cast it away, to break my
covenant."   You see that it says that the first rod was the (b)
Covenant, and the second rod the Rope, but He threatens
to cast them both away, first saying, " And I will take for
myself two rods, the one I called Beauty, and the other I
called a Rope " ; or with Symmachus, " The one I called (c)
glory, and the other I called a Rope."   For thus he rightly

styled the glory and beauty of the whole nation the divine
Law, and the Covenant, which it included.   For the solemnities of Jerusalem, and the high-priestly ritual, and all the
ancient observances of the divine Law and old Covenant,
were a fair glory to them that lived under their order.   And
the multitude of the nation is called a Rope by Moses,
(d) when he says: "The portion of the Lord is His people
Jacob, and Israel is the Rope of His inheritance."

But here it is prophesied that there will be a complete
change of the two rods at the time named, so that the ancient
Covenant that was therein of old, and its ancient beauty
being destroyed, and the Rope and the whole nation broken
through, when they had valued for thirty pieces of silver
Him that was valued, they should bear the fit dishonour for
their impiety.   It therefore says, "And I will take my rod
of Beauty, and cast it away, and break my covenant."   And
also, "And I cast away the second rod, the Rope."

(483)   And when the prophecy goes on to say, "And I will take
away three shepherds in one month," I think that it refers
to the three divisions of the ancient leaders of the people of
God—the King, the Prophet, and the High-Priest—for by
those three shepherds all the affairs of the ancients were
managed.   But since those three offices were destroyed
together in our Saviour's time—(for their king reigned not in
accordance with the Law, being a foreigner and not a
member of the Jewish race ; their high-priest was appointed
to his office by the Romans, and did not attain his rank by
the order of succession of the tribe, nor according to lawful
(b) custom ; and their prophets that had ceased until John
arose were no longer active among them, but they had
instead a wicked false prophet who led the people astray)—
He rightly threatens that He will take away at one time the
three offices of grace,[1] that had of old adorned the whole
nation with wondrous glory, and says, "And I will take
away three shepherds in one month, and my heart shall be
sorrowful for them."   For which Aquila renders, "And my
soul was torn asunder for them," Symmachus, "And my
soul perished for them," and Theodotion, "And my soul
(c) perished about them."   And he gives the reason of the
perishing of his soul, saying, "For their souls were hardened

---

[1] χαρίσματα.

to me." Instead of this Aquila has, "For their soul was strong[1] in me"; and Symmachus, "And their soul reached its height[2] in me." And a similar expression to the words, "Their souls are hardened to me," of the Septuagint, is found in Jeremiah as spoken by the Lord, namely :

"I have left my home, I have forsaken my inheritance, I have given my beloved soul into the hand of its enemies. My inheritance has become to me as a lion in a forest, it has opened on me its voice. Is not my (d) beloved now to me as a hyæna's cave?"

Jer. xii 7

And then He naturally goes on to say :

"I will not shepherd you, that which is dying may die, that which is failing may fail, and let the remnant eat each one the flesh of his neighbour."

And after this He says, "I will take my rod of beauty and cast it away." For which Aquila renders : "And I took my rod, the Glory, and cut it off," meaning the Mosaic Worship. Thus the first rod mentioned in the beginning of the passage is said to be the first to be broken and cast away. But when the price of Him that was valued and the (484) money paid for Him to the traitor was cast into the House of the Lord as into a furnace, then we see what is prophesied will happen to the second rod, that is to say to the whole nation in the words, "And I cast away the second rod, the Rope, to break my covenant between Judah and Israel."

And as the oracle intended clearly their destruction by this, it naturally goes on to say that they shall no longer recognize the power of things prophesied, but the Canaanites will, when He says, "And the Canaanites shall know, my (b) sheep kept for me, because it is the Word of the Lord." Who are meant by the Canaanites but ourselves, who once were foreigners, and sheep kept for Christ from all the old heathen and sinful nations? We that have been converted by His grace, and understanding the things prophesied, have received the true knowledge of the word of the Lord ; yea, we Canaanites know and understand what was meant ; but they that boasted of Israel, and gloried in being of the (c) seed of Abraham, neither knew nor understood.

---

[1] ἐπέρκασεν.   [2] ἤκμασεν.

CHAPTER 5

From Jeremiah.

Still of Judas, Who is named.

[Passage quoted, Jer. xvii. 1–4.] [1]

THOUGH this passage is not found in the Septuagint, yet it is in the Hebrew and in the editions of the other translators, and is quoted with asterisks in the more accurate copies of the Septuagint. I have necessarily quoted it, (485) because it gives the name of the traitor Judas, and teaches that the sin he committed can never be wiped out. For this I think is implied by the words, " The sin of Judas is written with a pen of iron, and with the point of a diamond." It could refer also to the whole Jewish nation, as a threat of the utter destruction that would overtake them in the immediate train of their indelible iniquity, an interpretation I have no time now to expound word by word.

(b)   And now that I have prepared the way by giving so many examples of prophecies concerning him that was to betray our Lord and Saviour, and those that conspired against Him in other ways,[2] let us examine what was foretold in connection with His actual Passion.

CHAPTER 6

From Amos.

Of the Eclipse of the Sun at the Time of Our Saviour's Passion, and of the Total Destruction of the Jewish Nation.

[Passage quoted, Amos viii. 7–12.]

THIS prophecy foretells the pride, insolence and rebellion of the Jews against our Saviour, and says that the Lord (486) sware against the presumption of Jacob, that their insolence

[1] See also 54 b.
[2] τῶν τε ἄλλως ἐπιβεβουλευκότων αὐτῷ.   It would be simpler to read ἀλλῶν.

against Him should never be forgotten, and that their land and its inhabitants should undergo suffering and mourning, and that no more as before should they be punished a little while and then restored, but that this judgment should last for ever.   For He says, " Complete destruction shall come upon them," meaning that wrath in the time of the Roman Empire would attack them, that a river should rise on them as on men who before were lifted up.

And then after this anger of God against them, their state, He says, will again " Come down like the river of (b) Egypt."

By which I think is meant, that the ancient glories of the Jews once so lofty, so prized by God, and as it were exalted on high, will become like the state of the heathen nations, which flow and pass by like a river, and will go from height to depth.   And He next tells what will happen at the time of the saving Passion, " In that day," He says, saith the Lord, " the sun shall set at midday, and the light shall be (c) darkened on the earth at daytime," and this was plainly fulfilled, when our Lord was lifted up, according to the Gospel :

" And there was darkness over all the earth from the sixth hour even to the ninth hour, and about the ninth hour Jesus cried with a loud voice, Eli, Eli, lama Matt. sabachthani." [1]   xxvii. 46.

This prophecy was thus fulfilled, and it goes on to say :

" And I will turn your feasts into mourning, and all your song into lamentation.   And I will bring sackcloth (d) on all loins, and baldness on every head : And I will make him as grief for a dear one, and them with him as a day of pain.   Behold, the days come, saith the Lord, that I will send famine upon the earth, not a famine of bread, nor a thirst for water, but a famine of hearing the word of the Lord," etc.

And all this prophecy of what would result from their insolence against the Christ has been clearly proved to have taken place after their plot against our Saviour.   For it was not before it, but afterwards from that day to this that God turned their feasts into mourning, despoiled them of their famous mother-city, and destroyed the holy Temple (487)

---

[1] W.H. : Ἐλωί, Ἐλωί, λεμὰ σαβαχθανεί ; E. : Ἠλί, Ἠλί, λαμᾶ σαβαχθανί.

therein when Titus and Vespasian were Emperors of Rome, so that they could no longer go up to keep their feasts and sacred meetings. I need not say that a famine of hearing the Word of the Lord has overtaken them all, in return for their rejection of the Word of God ; since with one voice they refused Him, so He refuses them.

CHAPTER 7

(b)   From Zechariah.

Still concerning the Eclipse of the Sun, and of the Time of the Saving Passion.

[Passage quoted, Zech. xiv. 5–9.]

THIS was fulfilled by the coming of our Saviour, accompanied either by His holy apostles and disciples, or by His holy ones, the divine powers and unembodied spirits, His (d) angels and ministers, of whom the holy gospel says,
Matt. iv. "Angels came and ministered unto him." In that day (for
11. this is the usual name given in Holy Scripture to the time of His sojourn on earth) the prophecy before us was fulfilled as well as the other predictions, when at the time of His Passion,. "From the sixth hour unto the ninth hour there was darkness over all the earth." Therefore the prophecy says, "In that day there shall be no light." And also, "It shall not be day nor night : but towards evening it shall be light." Where we have, I think, an exact description of the time, when, our Lord being lifted up, though it was day,
(488) night filled the atmosphere from the sixth to the ninth hour. And afterwards the darkness cleared, and it was bright daylight, until night fell as usual. So the word of the prophecy implies, "And that day is known to the Lord, and it shall be neither day nor night : and towards evening it shall be light." For it was not day because of the midday darkness ; nor was it night because of the returning day, which is shewn by the words, "Towards evening it shall be light."
(b) And the mention of the wintry season is astonishing indeed in the words of the prophecy, which say, "There shall be frost and cold" ; for this is supported by the evidence of

the Gospel, which tells how Peter following Jesus warmed himself in the Hall of Caiaphas with the others, where a fire was kindled.   John actually mentions the cold, saying, "The servants and attendants stood round, having made a John xviii. fire of coals, for it was cold, and they warmed themselves." 18. The prophecy was thus literally fulfilled.   And figuratively, as well in regard to the whole Jewish nation the reality of which those things were symbols was also fulfilled—when the light of salvation shone on them, and they chose darkness rather (c) than light, and the light departed from them, and unspeakable night overwhelmed them, and the eyes of their mind were darkened, so that the rays of the Gospel should not shine in their hearts, and when too their love to God waxed cold.   And in them too the rest of the prophecy was fulfilled, when on the day of our Saviour's coming living water came forth from Jerusalem, and the fruitful living word of Gospel Teaching went forth to all nations, beginning from (d) Jerusalem, yea, from Jerusalem itself, and was spread over all the earth, even to the utmost bounds of the world.   The Lord and Saviour Himself speaks of this water to the Samaritan woman :

> "If thou knewest who it is that asketh thee for
> drink, thou wouldst have asked of him, and he would John iv.
> have given thee living water."   10.

And He goes on to teach what advantage would accrue to all that taste of the living spiritual spring, saying that they that drink thereof, denying the many evil dæmons who ruled them of old, will confess their one Lord and King, and that the Lord, that once was known only to the Hebrews, will become King of all nations that believe in (489) Him from all the earth, and that His Name will be one, encircling all the earth and the wilderness.   And who is not struck at seeing this fulfilled?   For the Christian name, derived from the Name of Christ (and Christ was indeed the Lord) has encircled every place and city and land, and the very nations that dwell in the wilderness and at the ends of the earth, as the prophecy foretold.

CHAPTER 8

From Psalm xxi.

*Of What was done at Our Saviour's Passion.   At the End
concerning His being succoured in the Morning.*

(490)   [Passage quoted, Ps. xxi. 2–32.]

THE words, " My God, give ear to me, why hast thou
forsaken me?" spoken at the opening of the Psalm, are
recorded by Matthew to have been said by our Saviour at
the time of the Passion :

> " And at the sixth hour, there was darkness over all
> the earth until the ninth hour, and at the ninth hour
> Jesus called with a loud voice, Eloim, Eloim,[1] lama
> sabachthani, that is to say, being interpreted, My God,
> my God, why hast thou forsaken me?"

Matt.
xxvii. 46.

And the Hebrew words are taken from this prophecy.
So, then, the beginning of the Psalm includes the words
" Eli, Eli, lama sabachthani " in the same syllables, which
(491) Aquila has thus translated : " My strong one, my strong one,
why hast thou left me?"   And everyone will agree that this
is equivalent to our Saviour's words at the time of His
Passion.   You may therefore be quite convinced that the
Psalm refers to Him and no one else, for its contents
harmonize with none other but Him.   The other predictions are exactly fulfilled in Him ; and especially the words,
" They parted my garments among them, and upon my
vesture did they cast lots."   It also foretells literally the
(b) driving in of the nails, when His hands and feet were nailed
to the Cross, saying " They pierced my hands and my feet,
they numbered all my bones."   And the other predictions
apply to Him alone, as my argument will shew.   But if any
one would apply them to some other person, whether king,
prophet, or other godly man among the Jews, let him prove
if he can how what is written is in harmony with him.   For
who of those who were ever born of women [2] has attained
such heights of virtue and power, as to embrace the know-
(c) ledge of God with unchanging reason, with unruffled soul,
and with sober mind, and to fasten all his trust on God, so

---

[1] Here : Ἐλωείμ, Ἐλωείμ.   W.H.: Ἐλωί, Ἐλωί,
[2] Τῶν πώποτε κυοφορουμένων.

as to say, "Thou art He that took me out of my mother's womb, my hope from my mother's breasts. I was cast on thee from my mother, from my mother's womb Thou art my God." And who that has ever been so cared for by God, has also become "a reproach of men" and "the out-cast of the people"? By what bulls and calves can we (d) suppose such a man to have been surrounded? And in what suffering was he "poured out like water"? How were "all his bones loosened"? How was "he brought into the dust of death," and being brought into the dust of death how does he say those words still and live and speak? Who are "the dogs" that surround him, that are other than the beforenamed "bulls and calves"? What gathering of evil men pierced his feet as well as his hands, stripped him of his raiment, divided some of it among themselves, and cast lots for the remainder? What was the sword, the dog, and the lion? Who are they that surrounded him that are called Unicorns? And how after (492 a struggle with such numbers, after being brought into the dust of death, can he promise to proclaim His Father's name, not to all, but only to his brethren?

Who are the brethren, and what church is it of which this sufferer says, "In the midst of the Church I will hymn thee," adding, not the one Jewish nation but, "All the earth shall understand, and turn to the Lord, and all the kindreds of the nations shall worship before him"? It is for you yourself to test every expression in the Psalm, and see if it is possible to apply them to any chance (b) character. You will find them only applicable to our Saviour, Who is most true and most to be trusted, and Who applied the words of the Psalm to Himself, as the Evangelists bear witness : Matthew in the quotations I have given, and Mark in his own record, where he says :

"And at the sixth hour there was darkness over all the earth until the ninth hour. And at the ninth hour (c) Jesus cried with a loud voice saying, Eli, Eli,[1] lama sabachthani, which·is to say, being interpreted, My God, my God, why hast thou forsaken me? And certain of Mark xv. them that heard [2] said, He calleth for Elias." 35·

Let us now proceed to investigate, in what way the

[1] W.H. : Ἐλωί, Ἐλωί.   E. : Ἠλεί, Ἠλεί.
[2] W.H. : Τινες τῶν ⌐παρεστηκότων⌐ ἀκούσαντες, margin ἑστηκότων.

expressions of the Psalm must be referred to Him. And first
we will deal with the inscription which says, "To the end,"
or according to Aquila, "To the Conqueror," or according [1]
(d) to Symmachus, "Ode of Victory concerning the Succour."
I have an idea, based on the words of the Evangelists,
"There was darkness from the sixth hour unto the ninth
hour," that our Saviour's Passion was concluded about the
ninth hour, when with a loud voice He spake the words
quoted a little before, and that we should consider that His
Passion was past at eventide on the approach of night.
Then His Resurrection from the dead, which was the Succour of the Father Who succoured Him, and drew Him to
Himself, from the land of death, and received Him, must
have taken place at dawn, as we learn from the Evangelists.
For Luke says, "On the first day of the week at the break
of dawn they came [that is the women], to the sepulchre,
(493) bearing the spices which they had prepared, and certain
Luke xxiv. others with them.[2]   And they found the stone rolled away
1.   from the sepulchre.   And going in they did not find the
Body, because our Saviour was already risen from the
dead." [3]   Mark also tells the same story, saying :
     " And very early in the morning, on the first day of
the week they went to the sepulchre, at the rising of
the sun, and said to one another, Who shall roll us
Mark xvi.   away the stone from the door of the Sepulchre? for it
2.   was very great."
(b) They went, and found it rolled away.   And He was
already risen.   There is the same witness in John : "On
the first day of the week cometh Mary Magdalene to the
sepulchre, while it was still dark, and seeth the stone taken
John xx. 1. away from the sepulchre."   And Matthew too, although he
had said, "late on the Sabbath," adds, "As it began to
Matt.   dawn on the first day of the week, came Mary Magdalene,
xxviii. 1. and the other Mary to see the sepulchre, and behold
there was a great earthquake.   For the Angel of the Lord
(c) descended from heaven and came and rolled away the stone
from the door of the sepulchre."   I have necessarily given

---

[1] ἐπινίκιος ὑπὲρ τῆς ἀντιλήψεως.
[2] W.H. omit καί τινες σὺν αὐταῖς.
[3] W.H. : εἰσελθοῦσαι δέ οὐχ εὗρον τὸ σῶμα [τοῦ Κυρίου Ἰησοῦ]
(διὰ τὸ ἤδη . . . ἐγεγέρθαι—the comment is wrongly included in
the quotation from the Gospel).

these quotations to shew the meaning of the "succour at dawn" predicted in the Psalm. For since it tells of our Saviour's Passion, and since the dispensation concerning Him was in no way hindered by the Passion, and the end of the Passion was His Resurrection from the dead and "the succour at dawn," the oracle crowns its description with the final miracle, as if the whole account and the sufferings before the end were incidental to the Resurrection from the dead, and the succour at dawn. For our Lord and Saviour said, (d) "My God, my God, give ear to me, why hast thou forsaken me?" And then added, "I am a worm and no man, a reproach of men, and the outcast of the people"; and in addition to this, "Many oxen have encircled me, fat bulls have hemmed me in"; and gave a clear prediction of His Death in the verse, "Thou hast brought me into the dust of death, for many dogs have surrounded me, the council of the wicked has hemmed me in, they pierced my hands and my feet;" and He gave still further details of His Passion in the words, "They parted my garments among them, and upon my vesture did they cast lots." And having given those and similar predictions He did not cease there, but added : "Ye that fear the Lord praise (494) him, for he hath not despised, nor been angered at the prayer of the poor, nor turned his face from him, but when I cried unto him he heard me." How could He claim to have been heard, unless He had had a complete answer to the prayers which He had just uttered, when He said, "Thou hast brought me into the dust of death. Save my soul from the sword, and my only-begotten from the power of the dog"? Nay, having prayed thus, and asked that He might be rescued and saved from these enemies, He adds, "He hath not despised, nor been angry at the prayer of the poor, nor turned away his face from him : but when I cried unto him, he heard me." He evidently means His Return to life after death, which came to pass through the Succour at dawn, which the Psalm goes on to shew, saying, "But thou, O Lord, do not remove thy help, come to my succour." And it is this succour that is referred to by the Inscription of the Psalm.

So much about the Inscription of the Psalm. Let us now (c) sound the deeper studies of the Hebrews on the words, "Eli, Eli, lama sabachthani," which were said by our

Saviour in the hour of His Passion in the actual Hebrew words, and which are enshrined in the Psalm. Now Elōeim is a name for God. And you will find it throughout nearly all the Scriptures : and even now in the Septuagint He is called properly by the Hebrew name. Though of course the Hebrews had other expressions for the divine Name—such as Saddai, Jao, El,[1] and the like.

(d)   This Psalm then uses "Eli, Eli, Eli, lama sabachthani," as our Lord Himself does, and not Eloeim. And so Aquila, aware of the distinct meaning of God's Hebrew name of Eloeim, did not, like the other translators, think good to render them "My God, my God"—but "My strong one, my strong one," or more accurately, "My strength, my strength." So that taking this sense the Lamb of God our Saviour, when he said, "Eli, Eli," to His Father, meant, "My strong one, my strong one, why hast thou forsaken me?" And maybe He was crucified, because His Strong One had left Him, as the apostle says, "For he was crucified in weakness, but he liveth by the power of God," implying that He would not have been crucified, unless His Strong One had left Him. And surely it befits the Lamb of God, Who was led as a sheep to the slaughter, and as a lamb before its shearers is dumb, to attribute His own powers to God, and to reckon He had nothing of His own except His Father : wherefore He calls His Father His Strength, just as in Psalm xviii. He gives Him the names

(b) of Strength and Refuge, saying :

"I will love thee, O Lord, my strength. The Lord is my foundation, and my refuge, and saviour. My God, my helper, and I will trust in him ; my protector, the horn also of my refuge, and my succour.

His Strong One forsook Him then, because He wished Him to go unto death, even "the death of the cross," and to be set forth as the ransom and sacrifice for the whole world, and to be the purification of the life of them that

(c) believe in Him. And He, since he understood at once His Father's Divine counsel, and because He discerned better than any other why He was forsaken by the Father, humbled Himself even more, and embraced death for us with all willingness, and "became a curse for us," holy and all-

Margin notes:
(495)
2 Cor. xiii. 4.

Ps. xviii. 1.

Phil. ii. 8.

Gal. iii. 13.

---

[1] Τὸ Σαδδαὶ, καὶ τὸ Ἰαὼ, καὶ τὸ ῾ΗΛ.

blessed though He was, and "He that knew no sin, became (d)
sin, that we might become the righteousness of God in 2 Cor.
Him." Yea more—to wash away our sins He was crucified, v. 21.
suffering what we who were sinful should have suffered, as
our sacrifice and ransom, so that we may well say with the
prophet, He bears our sins, and is pained for us, and he
was wounded for our sins, and bruised for our iniquities, so
that by His stripes we might be healed, for the Lord hath Isa. liii. 4.
given Him for our sins.   So, as delivered up by the Father,
as bruised, as bearing our sins, He was led as a sheep to the
slaughter.   With this the apostle agrees when he says, "Who Rom. vii.
spared not his own Son, but delivered him for us all." And 32.
it is to impel us to ask why the Father forsook Him, that
He says, "Why hast thou forsaken me?" The answer is, (496)
to ransom the whole human race, buying them with His
precious Blood from their former slavery to their invisible
tyrants, the unclean dæmons, and the rulers and spirits of
evil.

And the Father forsook Him for another reason, namely,
that the love of Christ Himself for men might be set forth.
For no one had power over His life, but He gave it willingly
for men, as He teaches us Himself in the words, "No one
taketh my life from me : I have power to lay it down, and (b)
I have power to take it again."   John x. 18

After this He says, "Far from my salvation are the words
of my sins." Instead of which Aquila translates, "Far from
my salvation are the words of my complaint"; and Symmachus, "The words of my lamentations are removed from
my salvation." And in yet a fifth [1] translation it is rendered,
"Far from my salvation are the words of my requests." It (c)
is to be especially remarked that in neither of these translations does the expression "of my sins" appear, as it sometimes happens that similar alterations are made in a text
by the error of a copyist.   And we must accept the version
given by the majority of the translators, unless we can
understand Him to mean that the sins are ours, but that
He has made them His own.

He next says, "My God, I will cry by day, and thou (d)
wilt not hear, and by night, and it shall not be folly for

---

[1] καθ' ἑτέραν δὲ φερομένην πέμπτην. We have had G., Aquila
and Symmachus. Is this last Theodotion's? Or has Theodotion's
dropped out of the text, and is the last really a "fifth" rendering?

me." Instead of which Symmachus has, "My God, I will call by day, and thou wilt not hear, and by night, and there is no silence." He is surely shewing His surprise here that the Father does not hear Him, He regards it as something strange and unusual. But that Father reserved His hearing till the fit time that He should be heard. That time was the hour of dawn, of the Resurrection from the dead, when to Him it could be more justly said than to any, "In a time accepted I heard thee, and in a day of

2 Cor. vi. salvation I succoured thee. Behold, now is the accepted
2 time; behold, now is the day of salvation." This, of course, could be said in another sense by our Saviour, as one always accustomed to be heard by the Father, as if He said, to put it more clearly: "Is it possible, O Father, that I, Thine only and beloved Son, should not be heard, when

(497) I cry and call to my Father?" For this is the very point He dwells on in John's Gospel at the raising of Lazarus, when He says, "Take away the stone from the sepulchre," and "raised his eyes to heaven and said, Father, I thank thee that thou hast heard me. And I knew that thou

John xi. hearest me always." If, then, He heareth Him always, it
39. is not in doubt but in absolute assurance that He will be heard, as if it were impossible for Him not to be heard, that He speaks in the form of a question the words: "My

(b) God, shall I cry in the day, and thou not hear?" And we must put a note of interrogation after "hear," and understand that the answer to the question is a negative.[1]

And He shews that this is right a little further on in the Psalm, when He says:

"He hath not despised, nor been angry at the prayer of the poor, nor turned his face from him, but when he cried unto him he heard him."

For how could He say negatively, "My God, I will cry by day, and thou wilt not hear," except in the sense I

(c) have suggested? And I think He implies this sense when He says, "My God, shall I cry by day, and wilt thou not hear? and by night, and it is not folly for me." "For I do not cry 'Thou wilt not hear,' He says, 'in folly': for I know that I say this inspired by the conviction that it is Thy nature to help and to hear not only me, but all Thy

---

[1] ὑποστιζόντων ἡμῶν ἐν τῷ "οὐκ εἰσακούσῃ" καὶ τὸ ἐναντίον ὑπονοούντων τῷ πύσματι.

saints.   For Thou ever 'dwellest in Thy saints' continually, and art 'the praise' of every godly man that is called 'Israel.'   For Thy sake to every one that worships Thee no (d) common praise accrues; in Thee our fathers hoped, and by their trust were saved from the evils that attacked them, 'Unto Thee they cried, and were saved.'   Since, then, all Thy saints have had this blessing of Thee, to cry unto Thee and be heard and not be ashamed, how much more readily and specially wilt Thou hear Thy beloved Son that cries? And, if I ask as one who wonders, 'Shall I cry and Thou wilt not hear?' yet shall not My words be regarded as folly. For I know that I utter My prayer, not as one that glories or as one that boasts, but as one of lowly mind.   For being gentle and lowly in heart, My words are humble and spoken in humility like My own gentleness, even as I call Myself a worm.   For what could be more lowly than a worm? Hence I call Myself 'no man,' since I have descended from (498) My own majesty to such lowliness, that I seem to be no more than a worm, so that I may undergo even death and the destruction of My body.   For how else can worms be generated but from the destruction of bodies, and I going to such destruction recognize Myself rightly as a worm and no man.   So, too, have I become a reproach of men and the outcast of the people, and I should have become neither unless I had reached the state of a worm at the time of My Passion.   For it was then that they who saw Me hanging (b) on the Cross mocked Me, and spake with their lips, and shook their heads saying, 'He trusted in God, let Him deliver him, let Him save him if He desires him.' "

This was the clear prophecy of the Psalmist of what was (c) to come to pass a long time after him, and it was fulfilled when, according to Matthew—

"Two thieves being crucified with him, one on the right of the Saviour and one on the left, the passers-by reviled him, wagging their heads and saying, Woe,[1] Thou that destroyest the temple and buildest it in three days, save thyself; if thou art the Son of God, come down from the cross.   Likewise the chief priests mocking him with the elders and scribes said, he saved others, himself he cannot save.   If he be the King of

---

[1] W.H. omit.

Israel, let him now come down from the cross, and we will believe him. If he trusted in God, let him deliver him now if he will have him, for he said, I am the Son of God."

Matt. xxvii. 39.

(d) And according to Luke :

"The people stood beholding, and the rulers with them [1] mocked him saying, He saved others, let him save himself if he is the Christ, the Son of God, the chosen."

Luke xxiii. 35.

And according to Mark :

"And they that passed by reviled him, wagging their heads, and saying, Ah, thou that destroyest the temple and buildest it in three days, save thyself and come down from the cross. Likewise the chief priests, mocking between themselves with the scribes, said, He saved others, himself he cannot save. Let Christ the King of Israel descend now from the cross, that we may see and believe in him."

(499) Mark xv. 29.

Where is the discrepancy between this and the prophecies in the Psalm,

"I am a worm and no man, a reproach of men and the outcast of the people. All they that saw me reviled me, they spoke with their lips, they shook their heads, saying, he trusted in the Lord, let him deliver him, let him save him if he desires him "?

Wonder not if this was said of and fulfilled by the Passion of our Saviour, for even now He is a reproach among all men who have not yet received faith in Him ! For what is more shameful or worse than any reproach than to be (b) crucified? Yea, He is an outcast of the people of the Jews, for even to-day that whole race loves to mock Him, to set Him at naught, and to spit on Him : wherefore the apostle rightly says :

"We preach Christ crucified, to the Jews a stumbling-block, and to the Gentiles foolishness."

1 Cor. i. 23.

And that which follows in the Psalm you will find even now said of Him by the multitude.[2] Such, then, was His prayer concerning the affliction that overtook Him. And since He knew that His original union with our flesh, and (c) His birth of a woman that was a Virgin was no worse

---

[1] W.H. omit σὺν αὐτοῖς.   [2] παρὰ τοῖς πολλοῖς.

experience than the suffering of death, while He speaks
of His death He also mentions His birth, saying to the
Father :

> "Thou art he that took me out of my mother's
> womb : Thou wast my hope even from my mother's
> breasts.   On thee was I cast from my mother : from
> my mother's womb thou art my God."

Thus He naturally remembers this to comfort Him in
His present affliction.

"For just as Thou wert My Succour," He says, "when I
took the body of man, when Thou, my God and Father, like
a midwife didst draw the body that had been prepared for
Me by the Holy Spirit from My travailing mother, putting (d)
forth Thy power, to prevent any attempt or plan of hostile
powers, envious of My entry into humanity.   And since at
the very Conception Thou didst overshadow that which was
in the womb, so that the rulers of this world might not be
aware of the Conception of the Holy Virgin by the Holy
Spirit; which mighty mystery thy Archangel Gabriel did
reveal to Mary, saying : 'The Holy Spirit shall come upon (500)
thee, and the power of the Highest shall overshadow thee.' Luke i. 35
Just as the power of the Highest overshadowed Me when
I was conceived, and took Me out of My mother's womb
when I was born, so it is now My sure consolation, that
Thou wilt much more save Me from death.   And in this
hope I put My trust in Thee, My God, My Lord, My Father :
I put My trust not as now first beginning My hope in Thee,
for I trusted Thee even when I drew My infant food from
My mother's breasts, and was thought to be like human
babes powerless and without reason.   Such I was not,
though I had a human body : it was not like in power or (b)
substance to other bodies, I was free and unfettered,[1] as
Thy Lamb, O God, though at that age nourished with milk,[2]
I mean from My mother's breasts.   And no one will think
this impossible, if he remembers that even before I was
cast on Thee from My mother, and from the womb of My
mother Thou art My God.   For while still carried in the
treasury of her that brought Me forth I saw Thee, My God, (c)
as one who continued separate and untroubled [3] though in

---

[1] ἄνετος καὶ ἀπόλυτος.   [2] γαλουχούμενος.
[3] ἀσύγχυτος καὶ ἀθόλωτος.

such close contact with things of flesh, yea, as one who had no body yet and was free of all bonds.   And so was I cast on Thee from My mother, on Thee, My God, from My mother's breasts, so that My power was felt while I was still borne in the womb of the Holy Virgin by My forerunner John, while he was yet in the womb of Elizabeth, so that, stirred by My divinity, he leapt for joy, and was filled with

(d) the Holy Spirit.

"Bearing such memories in My mind, and ever setting My God and Father before My eyes, it is not strange that in this present hour of supreme suffering I should do the same, when in My obedience to Thee, My Father, of My own will and consent I became a worm and no man, a reproach of men and the outcast of the people.   And now when all who gaze on My body nailed to the Cross think they see a sight of ill omen and mock Me, pouring such a flood of reviling and satire [1] upon Me, shewing that they not only think evil of Me and harbour it in their minds, but speak it without fear and say it openly : for 'They spoke with their lips, and shook their heads, saying, He

(501) trusted in the Lord, let Him deliver him.'

"So now when such troubles hem Me in, I call upon Thee, My Father, who drew Me out of My mother's womb, on Whom I was cast from My mother, in Whom I trusted from her breasts, made known to Me and acknowledged as My God even from My mother's womb, and I beseech Thee not to depart from Me, for affliction is near.   For there comes, He says, yea, is all but come and at the door, afflicting Me and pressing upon Me the last cloud of all, the cloud of My surpassing trouble.   I do not mean this

(b) trouble which now enfolds Me, nor the Cross, nor the jeers of men, nor the mockery, nor anything at all that I under-went before the Cross, scourging, insults, nor all My vile treatment from the sons of men ; but I look to the dissolu-tion of the body in death itself, and the descent into Hades next thereto,[2] and the onset of the hostile powers opposed to God.   And I therefore say, 'Trouble is near, and there is no helper.'"

It is surely the very climax of affliction to have no helper.

---

[1] διασυρμόν.
[2] For note on *The Harrowing of Hell*, see vol. ii. p. 111.

For Christ went thither for the salvation of the souls in (c)
Hades that had so long awaited His arrival, He went down
to shatter the gates of brass, and to break the iron bonds,
and to let them go free that before were prisoners in Hades.
Which was indeed done, when many bodies of the saints
that slept arose and entered with Him into the true Holy
City of God.   But the opposing powers, added to mere
human evil, attacked Him, grieving and afflicting Him
sorely, though in His excess of goodness He lamented even
over them.   (d)

But observe how all this is said, as in the person of Him
that was carried in a mother's womb, and born of a mother,
Whom we called the Lamb of God.   For the words about
the Passion apply to Him, just as did those about the
Incarnate Birth.   For that which is born must die, and
that which dies can only travel the road to death which
starts from birth.

This, then, our Lord and Saviour unfolds, not as being
in nature without flesh and body, nor in so far as He is
regarded as the Word of God and Divine, but in so far as
He was able to say in His prayer to His Father :

> "Thou didst draw me out of my mother's womb, (502)
> thou wast my hope from my mother's breasts.   I was
> cast on thee from my mother, thou art my God from
> my mother's womb."

He then in His Passion prays such a prayer to His Father,
and says :

"Many hostile forces will surround Me, unclean dæmons,
and spirits of wickedness, and above all the prince of this
world himself the vilest of them all, who because of their
wickedness may well be called after evil beasts, be it savage (b)
bulls, or calves, or lions, or dogs.   And as I essay to withstand them all, but to do them no good, because from the
intense evil of their nature [1] they are incapable of receiving
good from Me, with none of them for My helper or fellow-
worker in My contest on behalf of the souls in Hades, am
I not right in saying, 'Trouble is near, and there is no
helper'?"

Of course it was not to be expected that any of the evil

---

[1] δι' ἄκραν κακίας ἕξιν.

and hostile powers would have worked with Him, or aided
(c) Him in His mission of good.   But surely the bitterest
element in the cup of pain that was His, was that none of
the good and favouring angels, and none of the divine
powers, dared to venture to the halls of Death and help
Him in succouring the souls there.   For in Him alone was
there courage,[1] since to Him only were the gates of death
opened, Him only the janitors of Hades saw and feared, and
He that has the power of death, descending from His royal
throne, as recognizing Him only for His Lord, spoke gently
(d) to Him with prayer and supplication, as Job relates.   Yet
He, seeing the impious realm of the tyrant so strong that
no heavenly being dared to accompany Him to that bourne,
or to help Him in saving the souls there, cries naturally,
"Trouble is near, and there is no helper," since the only
Being from heaven who could have helped Him had forsaken Him, so that the glory and independence of His own
choice and of His own victory might be proclaimed to all.
And since the only Being that could help Him was not then
His helper, it is natural that His first words should be, "Eli,
Eli, lama sabachthani?" that is, "My God, My God, why
(503) hast thou forsaken me?"   For when He was conceived,
and when He was brought forth by the Holy Virgin His
Father's power was with Him, when the Holy Spirit came
upon the maiden, and the Power of the Highest overshadowed her, and the Father Himself, as the oracle shews,
drew forth Him that was begotten from her womb.   But
when in the hour of His Passion He entered on His struggle
with Death, the Helper was no longer with Him.   Yea, I
(b) believe His own witness of this.   For the words, "Eli, Eli,
lama sabachthani?" which He spoke on the Cross, and
which were prophetically foretold in the Psalm, what else
do they mean but that [2] like a great athlete He was matched

---

[1] μόνῳ γὰρ αὐτῷ τοῦτ' ἀτρεμὲς ἦν.

[2] ὡς μέγας ἀθλητὴς τοῖς τοσούτοις ἀντιπάλοις προβλημένος ἦν,
ἀγωνοθετοῦντος καὶ βραβεύοντος τοῖς γινομένοις τοῦ ἐπὶ πᾶσι Θεοῦ. Full
of words from the race-course.   The ἀγωνοθέτης (Herod. 6. 17) was
the president of the games, but often (Xen. An. 3. 1. 21; Æschin.
79. 30) equivalent to the βράβευς, umpire or judge.   Cf. Clement of
Alexandria, 839, where God is, as here, the President of the games, the
Son of God the Giver of the prizes, and angels and saints the spectators
of man's spiritual conflict.—(Quoted, Gwatkin, *Early Church History*,
ii. 176.   Cf. note, vol. ii. p. 52.)

against all these adversaries, while Almighty God ordered the contest and gave the decision? Thus He summons His Father as the overseer of what is being done, and as the adviser, like a clever Anointer, to come to Him, especially as He has no other helper, but only Him that governs (c) the contest. And so He says in prayer, "Be not thou far from me, for trouble is near, and there is no helper."

And when with divine eyes He saw His body being suspended on the tree, the unembodied and invisible powers without in the air hovering[1] around Him like voracious birds and wild beasts, and knew that almost at once His body would be a corpse, and felt the powers and rulers of the air surging around Him on every side, the spirit which now worketh in the children of disobedience, and the (d) dæmons flying over the earth wherever men inhabit, and perhaps also the wild and dreadful beasts of Tartarus, of which Isaiah said, addressing Lucifer that had fallen from heaven: "Hades beneath was disturbed to meet thee, all the giants rose before thee." When, then, He saw all those Isa. xiv. 9. without surrounding His crucified body, and preparing to attack Him, He describes their array when He says: "Many oxen have surrounded me, fat bulls hem me in. They have (504) opened their mouths against Me, as a lion voracious and roaring." For most likely they thought that the soul which dwelt in the body of Jesus was human and like other human souls; and opened their mouths as if to devour it like the other human souls. So He says, "They opened their mouths on me, like a lion voracious and roaring." And next He adds, "I am poured out like water." This may be said to have been fulfilled outwardly and historically, when one of the soldiers, according to the Evangelist John, (b) "pierced the side" of the Lamb of God "with a spear, and John xix forthwith came there out blood and water." But He rather 34. seems to refer to the dying of His entire spiritual being when He says:

"I am poured out like water, and all my bones are loosened, my heart in the midst of my body is like melting wax. My strength is dried up like a potsherd, and my tongue has cleaved to my throat."

For this is surely a description of a dead body. So, too,

---

[1] ἰλυσπωμένας. Cf. P.E. 112 d, 181 b.

(c) He adds, "And thou hast brought me to the dust of death."

And then, starting again from what was now past, to comfort Himself for what was yet to happen, He describes what He went through when they plotted against Him. "Many dogs surrounded me, the council of the wicked hemmed me in," meaning probably both the soldiers and the Jews who rose against Him.

(d)   "27. Then the soldiers of the governor[1] took Jesus into the common hall and gathered unto him the whole band of soldiers. 28. And they stripped him, and put on him a scarlet robe. 29. And when they had platted a crown of thorns, they put it upon his head, and a reed in his right hand: and they bowed the knee before him, saying, Hail, King[2] of the Jews! 30. And they spit upon him, and took the reed and smote him on

(505)   the head. 31. And after that they had mocked him,

Matt.   they took the robe off from him, and put his own

xxvii. 27.   raiment on him, and led him away to crucify him."

This is almost an exact fulfilment of "Many dogs surrounded me, the council of the wicked hemmed me in"; moreover, "They pierced my hands and my feet, they numbered all my bones," and also, "They came staring and looking upon me," and "They parted my garments among them, and upon my vesture did they cast lots," were all fulfilled, when they fastened His hands and feet to the Cross with nails, and when they took His garments and divided them among them. For John's record is:

(b)   "23. Then the soldiers, when they had crucified Jesus, took his garments, and made four parts, to every soldier a part: and also his coat.[3] Now the coat was without seam woven from the top throughout. 24. They said therefore among themselves, Let us not rend it, but cast lots whose it shall be; that the Scripture might be fulfilled, which saith: They parted my garments among

John xix.   them, and for my vesture did they cast lots. These

23.   things therefore the soldiers did."

---

[1] W.H. : τοῦ Πιλάτου.   [2] W.H. : βασιλεῦ. E. : ὁ βασιλεύς.
[3] W.H. καὶ τὸν χιτῶνα, ἦν δὲ ὁ χιτὼν ἄραφος . . . εἶπαν οὖν.
E. : τὸν χιτῶνα δὲ, ὅτι ἄρραφος ἦν . . . εἶπον πρὸς ἀλλήλους μὴ
σχίσομεν αὐτόν.

And Matthew witnesses to what was done as follows :

"And they crucified him, and parted his garments,
casting lots : that it might be fulfilled which was spoken
by the prophet, They parted my garments among them, (c)
and upon my vesture did they cast lots. And sitting Matt.
down they watched him." xxvii. 35.

The dogs that surrounded Him and the council of the
wicked were the rulers of the Jews, the Scribes and High
Priests, and the Pharisees, who spurred on the whole
multitude to demand His blood against themselves and
against their own children. Isaiah clearly calls them dogs,
when he says : " Ye are all foolish dogs, unable to bark." Isa. lvi. 10.
For when it was their duty, even if they could not acquire
the character of shepherds, to protect like good sheep-
dogs their Master's spiritual flock and the sheep of the (d)
house of Israel, and to warn by barking, and to fawn upon
their Master and recognize Him, and to guard the flock
entrusted to them with all vigilance, and to bark if necessary [1] at enemies outside the fold, they preferred like
senseless dogs, yes, like mad dogs, to drive the sheep wild
by barking, so that the words aptly describe them, which
say : " Many dogs have surrounded me, the council of the
wicked have hemmed me in." And all who even now (506)
conduct themselves like them in reviling and barking at
the Christ of God in the same way may be reckoned their
kin ; yea, they who like those impious soldiers crucify the
Son of God, and put Him to shame, have a character
very like theirs. Yea, all who to-day insult [2] the Body
of Christ, that is the Church, and attempt to destroy the
hands and feet and very bones, are of their number, if
it be true that :

"We are one body in Christ, and all members one (b)
of another, and the head must not say to the feet, 1 Cor. xii.
I have no need of you, nor the eyes to the hands." 21.
Thus in times of persecution, it may be aptly said of those
who work against the members of Christ on the side of
their enemies : " They pierced my hands and my feet,
they numbered all my bones." Then, too, they divide
His garments among them, and cast lots upon His vesture,
when each individual tears and destroys the glory of His

---

[1] ἐπιστημονικῶς ὑλακτεῖν.　　　[2] λωβώμενοι.

Word, I mean the words of the   oly Scriptures, now this way, now that, and when they take up opinions about (c) Him from misleading schools of thought such as godless heretics [1] invent.

To crown all this He addresses the following prayer to His God and Lord and Father: "But thou, O Lord, take not far off thy help." Left for a little while alone for the shewing forth of the contest, and stripped to contend with Death without a helper, well aware that His only succour from His Father will be by the Resurrection from the dead, He naturally now prays to escape from the (d) array of His adversaries. So He says: "Thou, O Lord, remove not far thy help, afford me succour. For my succour will come from thy help," and it is perhaps in reference to His succour that the whole Psalm is entitled "Concerning the succour at dawn."

"Have regard then to My succour, extending to Me as soon as dawn comes the succour of the Resurrection from the dead, which I know that I shall receive, if thou remove it not from Me. Save My soul from the sword, My Only-begotten from the power of the dog. Thou wilt save Me from the mouth of the lion, and (507)   my lowliness from the horns of the unicorns."

By which I understand Him to mean the powers of the under-world, which it is not in my power to distinguish and divide into classes, shewing which was the sword that threatened our Saviour's life, or which one like a dog of death stretched forth its death-fraught paw, to capture it. For He says: "Save my soul from the sword, my Only-begotten from the power of the dog." And another evil (b) power reckoned as one of the wild beasts there, called a lion, opening wide its vast and yawning mouth of death, essays to devour His soul with the others of them that go down to Hades, just as long before mighty Death devoured them, being none other than the lion that opened his mouth before our Saviour, from which He prayed to His Father to deliver Him, saying: "Save me from the lion's mouth."

And there were other evil and impious powers working (c) against the Unicorn of God, and attempting to seduce Him

---

[1] αἱρεσιώταις.

from His purpose, from whom too the Unicorn of God,
our Lord having His Father as His only horn, prays that
His lowliness may be saved, saying: "And my lowliness
from the horns of the unicorn." What lowliness, but that
wherewith, being in the form of God, He humbled Himself
and emptied Himself, being obedient unto death, even the
death of the Cross. Yea, so low descending, and coming
even to this, I mean even to the sword in Hades, and to (d)
the hand of Him that is called its dog. (Whence, perhaps,
the Greeks hearing of some such dog of death,[1] painted it
with three heads): and coming to the throat of the said
lion, and subjecting His lowliness to the attacks of the
impious Unicorns, and thus having completed the whole
dispensation of His self-emptying and humiliation, and
prayed that now at last He may receive help and the
succour of His Father, He adds: "Thou, O Lord, remove
not thy help far off, attend to my succour." And though
He says this, His Father is not too far off to hear Him,
He is not removed far off, He is not separated by the (508)
smallest space, but is actually saying to Him: "While Isa. lviii.
thou speakest, I will say, I am here."   9.

And He, well aware of this, and receiving succour from
His Father, as He had prayed, begins from that point to
chant the Hymn of Triumph, making the Psalm, "Concerning the succour at dawn," in which He says: "I will
recite thy name with my brethren, in the midst of the
Church I will hymn thee." First, of course, to the disciples
and apostles, whom He calls His brethren, He promises
to announce the good news of joy and gladness in Him. (b)
And in accordance with this, Matthew teaches, saying;

"And, behold, Jesus met them, that is to say, those
with Mary Magdalene, saying, All Hail. And they
came to him and clasped his feet, and worshipped
him. Then Jesus saith to them, Fear not, go tell my (c)
brethren, that they must go before me into Galilee. Matt.
And there shall they see me."   xxviii. 9.

And John, too, after the Resurrection from the dead,
introduces Jesus saying to Mary:

"Touch me not, for I am not yet ascended to my
Father. Go to my brethren and say to them, I ascend

---

[1] Cerberus.

John xx.
17.
to my Father and your Father, and to my God and
your God."

Thus He says that He will tell the Name of His Father first
to the apostles, whom He calls His brethren. And after
them, with swift progress, He promises that He will teach
the Hymn of His Father to the Church founded in His
(d) Name throughout all the world. It is just as if some
supreme teacher of philosophy should give a course of
instruction in the midst of his pupils for them to hear and
and understand,[1] that He in the midst of the Church
says: "I will hymn thy praise," that the Church, learning
and hearing His words, might in fit manner sing back the
praises, no longer of the dæmons, but of the One Almighty
God, by Him that preached Him. He promises so to do,
and from that very point earnestly bids the Church, and
His brethren to hymn the Father's praise. Wherefore He
says: "Ye that fear the Lord praise him, glorify him all
ye seed of Jacob." And: "Let all the seed of Jacob fear
him, for he hath not despised, nor been angered at the
(509) prayer of the poor, nor turned away his face from him,
but when he cried unto him he heard him." · And thus
he clearly shewed His release from the evils that were
named before. For if God heard Him when He cried to
Him, when He prayed for His life to be delivered from the
sword, and His Only-begotten from the dog, and His lowliness from the mouth of the lion, and the horns of the
unicorn, it follows that we must understand Him to be
released from them, when He says: "For God was not
(b) angered by his prayer, and turned not his face from him,
but when he called unto him, he heard him." And so it
came to pass that being rescued from His woes, and
escaping from death, He sojourned with His disciples and
brethren, and sang His Father's praise "in the midst of the
Church." And notice how He calls Himself "poor," in
harmony with the prophecies already quoted, in which He
was called poor and a beggar.

And when He has thus shewn His Resurrection, He
(c) again returns to His Father, and says: "From thee is
my praise in the great Church," remembering the great
Church of all nations established throughout all the

---

[1] προσυπακοῦσαι.

world, in which the Saviour's praise is for ever sung, by
the will and co-operation of His Father. So He says:
" From thee is my praise in the great Church." For of a
truth it is great, this Church, gathered of every race of
mankind, and above all comparison in gravity and nobility
of life, and majesty of belief, while the Jewish nation, and (d)
the synagogue of the Circumcision, is so attenuated in the
poverty of its teaching, and life, and thought, and conceptions of God.

Then He adds: " I will pay my vows in the sight of all
that fear him," meaning by " all that fear him," the aforesaid great Church, to which He said: " Ye that fear the
Lord, praise him." And what vows does He mean that
He will pay, but those which He promised? And what
did He promise, but those, of which He said: " I will tell
thy Name to my brethren. In the midst of the Church
I will praise thee?" And He proceeds: " The poor shall (510)
eat and be satisfied, and they that seek the Lord shall
praise him—their heart shall live for ever. All the ends
of the earth shall remember and shall turn to the Lord,
and all the kindreds of the nations shall worship before
him. For the Kingdom is the Lord's, and he rules over
the nations."

In these words He very aptly proclaims the glorious
works after His Resurrection, which are fulfilled in the
calling of men from all nations, and by the election of men
from the ends of the earth, the results of which being
visible to all eyes afford evidence of the truth of the words of (b)
the Psalm. And we, too, are the poor, whom like beggars
in the things of God, the word of salvation nourishes with
spiritual bread, the life-giving food of the soul, and affords
eternal life. So the Psalm says: " The poor shall eat and
be satisfied, and they that seek the Lord shall praise him,
their heart shall live for ever." And the peroration of the (c)
whole prophecy crowning all—" The generation that
cometh shall be announced to the Lord, and they shall
announce his righteousness to a people that shall be born,
whom the Lord has made "—specifically foretells the Church
of the Gentiles, and the generation established on the
earth, through our Saviour Jesus Christ. For what could
this people be which, it is here said, will be born for God after
these things, which did not exist of old, and did not appear

(d) among men, but will be hereafter? What was the generation, which was not then, but which it is said will come, but the Church established by our Saviour in all the world, and the new people [1] from the Gentiles, of which the Holy Spirit wonderfully spake by Isaiah, saying, "Who hath heard such things, and who hath seen them thus? The earth was in travail for one day, and a nation was born at once." [2]

In this exposition I have but touched the fringe of the subject, but I must now pass on in haste to other topics, since time presses. But whoever cares for the Saviour's John v. 39. bidding, "Search the Scriptures, in which ye think to have eternal life, and those are they that witness of me," let him plunge his mind in each word of the Psalm, and hunt for the exact sense of the truth expressed. [3]

A FRAGMENT OF THE FIFTEENTH BOOK

Given by A. Majus in the New Collection of Ancient Writers. Rome, 1825, tom. 1, par. 2, p. 173, in the Commentary on Daniel ii. 31.

I THOUGHT it incumbent on me to quote what is said by the famous Eusebius Pamphilus, of Cæsarea, in the Fifteenth Book of *The Proof of the Gospel;* for in expounding the whole vision he says as follows:—" I believe this in no way differs from the vision of the prophet: for the prophet saw a great sea, just as the King saw a vast image: the prophet again saw four beasts, which he interpreted to mean four kingdoms, just as the King from the gold, silver, brass, and iron, figuratively described four kingdoms: and, once more, as the prophet saw a division of the ten horns of the last beast, and three horns destroyed by one, so the King saw part of the extremities of the image to be iron and part clay. And, moreover, as the prophet, after the vision of the four kings, saw the Son of Man receive universal rule, power and empire, so the King seemed to

---

[1] ὁ νέος . . . λαός: cf. Harnack, *Mission and Expansion of Christianity*, I. pp. 300 *sq.*

[2] Isa. lxvi. 8.

[3] The last five lines are supplied by Fabricius from another MS.

see a stone destroy the whole of the image, and become a great mountain that filled the sea. And the explanation is easy, for it was natural that the King, deceived as he was by the outward appearances of life, and admiring the beauty of the visible like colours in a picture, to liken the life of all men to a great image, whereas the prophet was rather led to compare the vast and mighty surge of life to a great sea. So the King, who admired the substances of gold, silver, brass, and iron, which are costly among men, likened the dominant empires that succeed one another in the human world to substances, while the prophet described the same empires under the forms of wild beasts, according to the ideals of their rule. Then again the King, who probably was conceited, and prided himself on the empire of his ancestors, the mutability of human things is revealed, and the end of earthly kingdoms, to purify him of his pride, and to make him realize the instability of human things, or at least the final universal Kingdom of God. For after the first, or the Assyrian Empire, signified by the gold, was to come the Persian, shewn forth by the silver; and thirdly, the Macedonian, portrayed by the brass; and after that, the fourth, that of the Romans, would follow, more powerful than its predecessors, and therefore likened to iron. For it is said of it, 'And the fourth kingdom shall be stronger than iron': just as iron crushes and subdues everything, so did Rome crush and subdue. And after these four, the Kingdom of God was presented as a stone that destroyed the whole image. And the prophet agrees with this in not seeing the final triumph of the Kingdom of the God of the Universe before he has described the course of the four world-powers under the similitude of the four beasts. I consider, therefore, the visions both of the King and the prophets, that there should be four empires only, and no more, to be proved by the subjection of the Jewish nation to them from the time when the prophet wrote."

INDEX OF QUOTATIONS FROM HOLY SCRIPTURE

INDEX OF OTHER QUOTATIONS

INDEX OF GREEK WORDS

GENERAL INDEX

(References to Scriptural characters are not included as a rule.)